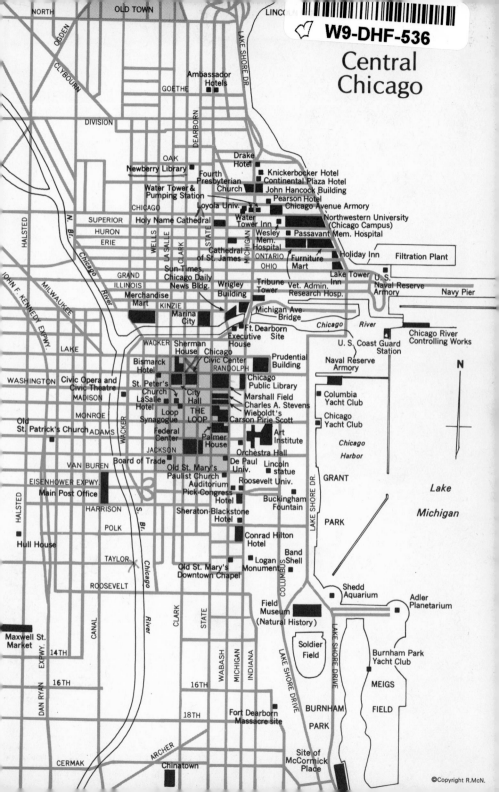

Central Chicago

NORTH
OLD TOWN
LINCOLN
OGDEN
CLYBOURN
DIVISION
GOETHE
Ambassador Hotels
Drake Hotel
OAK
Newberry Library
Fourth Presbyterian Church
Knickerbocker Hotel
Continental Plaza Hotel
John Hancock Building
Water Tower & Pumping Station
Pearson Hotel
Chicago Avenue Armory
CHICAGO
Loyola Univ.
Water Tower Inn
Northwestern University (Chicago Campus)
HALSTED
N. BR.
SUPERIOR
Holy Name Cathedral
Wesley Mem. Hospital
Passavant Mem. Hospital
HURON
ERIE
WELLS
LA SALLE
CLARK
STATE
MICHIGAN
Cathedral of St. James
ONTARIO
Furniture Mart
Holiday Inn
Filtration Plant
Chicago River
OHIO
Lake Tower Inn
U.S. Naval Reserve Armory
GRAND
Sun-Times, Chicago Daily News Bldg.
Wrigley Building
Tribune Tower
Vet. Admin. Research Hosp.
Navy Pier
ILLINOIS
Merchandise Mart
Milwaukee
KINZIE
Marina City
Michigan Ave. Bridge
Chicago River
JOHN F. KENNEDY EXPWY.
LAKE
WACKER
Sherman House
Chicago Civic Center
Ft. Dearborn Site
Executive House
U.S. Coast Guard Station
Chicago River Controlling Works
Bismarck Hotel
RANDOLPH
Prudential Building
Naval Reserve Armory
N
WASHINGTON
Civic Opera and Civic Theatre
St. Peter's Church
City Hall
Chicago Public Library
Columbia Yacht Club
MADISON
LaSalle Hotel
Marshall Field
Charles A. Stevens
Chicago Yacht Club
MONROE
Loop Synagogue
THE LOOP
Wieboldt's
Carson Pirie Scott
Old St. Patrick's Church
ADAMS
WACKER
Federal Center
Palmer House
Art Institute
Chicago Harbor
JACKSON
Orchestra Hall
Board of Trade
Old St. Mary's
De Paul Univ.
Lincoln statue
GRANT
Lake Michigan
VAN BUREN
Paulist Church
Roosevelt Univ.
EISENHOWER EXPWY.
Main Post Office
Auditorium
Pick-Congress Hotel
Buckingham Fountain
PARK
HALSTED
HARRISON
Sheraton-Blackstone Hotel
POLK
Conrad Hilton Hotel
Band Shell
Hull House
TAYLOR
Logan Monuments
COLUMBUS
Old St. Mary's Downtown Chapel
Shedd Aquarium
Adler Planetarium
ROOSEVELT
Field Museum (Natural History)
CANAL
CLARK
STATE
WABASH
MICHIGAN
INDIANA
Chicago River
LAKE SHORE DR.
Maxwell St. Market
14TH
Soldier Field
Burnham Park Yacht Club
DAN RYAN EXPWY.
16TH
16TH
MEIGS FIELD
18TH
Fort Dearborn Massacre site
BURNHAM PARK
LAKE SHORE DRIVE
ARCHER
CERMAK
Chinatown
Site of McCormick Place

©Copyright R.McN.

TOO LATE FOR PRESS

CHANGES IN WATERING PLACES

Sage's, 1 North LaSalle, page 11, is no longer owned by Gene Sage. The mad public parties attributed to Sage's on LaSalle now take place only at **Sage's East** (page 7).

Mr. T's, page 11, no longer has Sam Bari as its one great attraction.

Mother's Lounge (it replaced The Spirit of '76, page 12) is a body shop with a rock band for dancing and a noise level that makes your skin throb. $1 admission on weekends. The free Sunday lunch somehow costs $1.05.

RESTAURANT CHANGES

Atlantic Hotel, page 20. Under new management. Alas, almost nothing is as described.

Hartford Plaza French Room, page 30. Opened again with maitre d' Pierre Schmidt back at his post.

La Chaumiere, page 30, has changed ownership and name. It's now **La Cheminée.**

La Brasserie de Strasbourg, page 31, has also changed ownership and name. New name is **Le Pub.** Le Pub offers good booze; sangrias, mimosas and the like; and the kind of menu that's long been needed in this city—four pages of cabaret items, all a la carte. Hours: 11 AM to early the next day on weeknights, 5 PM to the same on weekends. The dance band starts after dusk. No cover; no minimum.

22 East, page 44, is now a private club.

Al Farber's Chateau le Boeuf, page 47, now offers the same menu as his Steak Room in the same premises.

Pete's Est! Est!! Est!!! page 47. New name is **House of Bertini.** New phone MI 4-1397. New owner John Rossi has vastly upgraded decor and menu and improved the quality of the steaks considerably. Norma and all the rest of the familiar waitresses are still around, too.

Gennaro's Tavern, page 52. Call to see if open for lunch—it's been dinner only of late due to a shortage of help. On the plus side, most of the homemade pastas can now be ordered for your freezer. Phone your order one day ahead. CH 3-1035.

Grecian Islands, formerly Deligiannis Bros., Inc., page 58, sports a big new dining room where most of the grocery store was. The little *tavernaki* is still there, however.

Cafe Azteca, page 61, is now **Azteca II,** located at 215 West North Avenue. It also has new ideas about menus—now a la carte only—and hours—now 5 PM to 2 AM.

Miyako, page 64. Now located at 3242 North Clark. Phone 549-1085.

Mickelberry's Log Cabin, page 67, was destroyed by fire. The old landmark of the South Side will not reopen.

Friends report that **Burger King** drive-ins, page 67, aren't what they used to be, but that the Big Mac hamburgers offered at any **MacDonald's** drive-in are big enough to get you through to the next day.

Woodlawn Club, page 70. Closed.

Pussycat, page 78. It's now the **Flower Pot.**

WHERE THE ACTION IS

Nightclub entertainers and jazzmen drift. **Terry Collier** is no longer at the Earl of Old Town (page 80); **Buddy Guy** hasn't been at Teresa's for some time (page 86); **Little Brother Montgomery** isn't playing at McPartlan's (page 83) right now. **June Ives Rapp** has left the Grapevine (page 75) for the Downstairs Lounge at the Sheraton-Chicago.

Game Theatre, page 76. Closed.

Second City, pages 75-6, now offers free improvisations on Monday nights. Admission other weeknights is $2.95; weekends, $3.95. Booze only policy is now in effect.

Your Father's Mustache, page 80. Closed.

Scotch Mist, page 82, is now **Magoons.** A beer and body shop with rock dance bands nightly (9:30 PM-3:30 AM). No minimum; no cover. Free booze for stag girls on ladies night.

Mother Blues, page 87. Closed. Currently, the only place in Old Town to hear traditional folk music is the **Quiet Knight,** next door.

Chances R, page 91, the place that started Old Town swinging, now at 860 North Wabash. Its Harper Court spot, 5225 South Harper, is still going strong.

Paul Bunyan of Old Town, page 92. So many customer complaints about it recently, it can no longer be recommended. One place you might enjoy instead is **Little Pleasures,** 1438 North Wells—a continental cafe with a wholly informal Old Town atmosphere and the nicest hippies you'll ever meet serving the sandwiches, sodas, and sundaes (Vala handmade ice cream) that are a specialty here.

On the premises weekdays from noon to 7 PM, crystal ball occult reader Robert Hilton, one of the best in the country. $5 declouds the ball.

SHOWCASE CITY

Frank Lloyd Wright's Unitarian-Universalist Church, page 126. Open for tours Tuesday, Thursday, Saturday, 1 PM to 5 PM. Admission, $1.

ART AND PERFORMING ARTS

Dell Gallery, page 163, and **Silverman Gallery,** page 167. Closed.

Try the new **October Gallery,** 200 East Walton, DE 7-1988. A graphics gallery so small you're advised to visit it by appointment in order to avoid group squeeze. October specializes in Matisse, Calder, Miro et al plus upcomers like Ku, Fu-Sheng. Co-owner Brooks McCormick, Jr. is happy to open the gallery on weekends.

Goodman Theatre, page 179, will become this city's only fully professional resident (repertory) theatre in fall, 1969. Producing directors will be John Reich and Douglas Seale. Opening play is the Midwest premiere of Rolf Hochhuth's **Soldiers** with Douglas Campbell as Churchill. Single tickets: weekdays $3.90-$4.40; weekends $4.40-$4.90; matinees $3.25-$3.75.

Goodman Studio Theatre will offer 10 productions acted by advanced students in the School of Drama.

Goodman Children's Theatre, page 315, switches to Saturday performances at 10:30 AM and 2:30 PM and Sunday matinees at 2:30 PM. Tickets: 75¢ to $1.75. Performances by advanced students under professional direction.

Academy Playhouse, page 179. Productions will be staged this summer in the new Drake Theatre, Barat College, Lake Forest (page 183).

Hull House Theatres, pages 180-81. Only two of the Hull House theatres are open currently—the Jane Addams Center and the Playwrights Center.

Pheasant Run Playhouse, pages 182-3, has a new Chicago (no-toll) phone number: 261-7943.

SHOPPING CHANGES

Model Mother Maternities, page 226. Closed.

Design Group, pages 268-9. Both locations closed.

City of Florence, page 229, is closed. For a superior substitute, **Danielo,** 142 East Ontario, MO 4-5633. Mr. Danielo has marvelous Italian imports in junior and misses sizes—day dresses, sportswear, a few offbeat hostess gowns. Winter clothes start at $35; summer stuff at $20. Nobody ever believes the prices, but they're true. His Italian cottons are the kind you're expected to machine wash.

Harry Gold Shoe Co., page 233. No longer bargains—just cheap shoes.

Man at Ease, page 233. Wells Street shop closed. Find the new shop at 105 East Ontario, phone: WH 3-1811, and another at 2630 North Clark, phone IR 2-5080. Late hours at the latter—to 10 PM nightly; Sunday 1 PM to 5 PM.

Crate & Barrel, page 261. Find a thriving branch shop in Plaza del Lago, Wilmette.

Caravan, page 269. Owner Harvey Caplin has moved some of the primitive art into his new **Harvey Caplin Gallery of Primitive Art** at 155 East Ontario. The gallery, the only one of its kind in Chicago, specializes in ethnographic African, Oceanic, Pre-Columbian, Ecuadorian, and Colonial art. Price range for collectors at all levels: $20 to $1,000.

HELP!

Red Carpet Car Wash, page 297. One-price car wash policy now—$2.50 any day of the week. New hours: 8 AM to 5 PM Monday through Saturday, to 2 PM Sunday.

Art Furniture, page 303. Now at 3516 North Clark. New phone GR 2-6804.

Totoh Company, page 304. Mechanic Paul Emerling has departed the firm.

NEIGHBORHOOD CITY

The "Annual Guide to Gourmet Shopping" in *Chicago* magazine, pages 360-61, is discontinued.

ANNUAL EVENTS

Goodwill Industries Antique Sales, pages 415, 431, have been converted from semi-annual events to something better: Monday and Friday sales each week at the Auxiliary Plum Tree Shop at Goodwill headquarters, 120 South Ashland. Hours: 10 AM to 3 PM. Items for sale are so often of exceptional value that dealers and crafty bargain hunters pounce as soon as the doors open.

HOTELS

New **Holiday Inn** just west of the Loop at 1 South Halsted Street (off the Kennedy Expy between Madison and Monroe streets). Phone TA 9-5000. The neighborhood isn't one to brag about—yet—but the Inn is shining new. Single rooms $14.50 to $24. Doubles $17.50 to $24.

Continental Plaza, page 456, allows small pets but not children under twelve.

CHICAGO
an extraordinary g

CHICAGO
an extraordinary guide

by Jory Graham

RAND McNALLY & COMPANY
Chicago • New York • San Francisco

Jacket illustrations: the Picasso sculpture, by Tony Linck, for United States Steel Corporation; the author, by John Groen.

Chicago Picasso © 1967 Public Building Commission of Chicago

Book designed by Elizabeth Riedel
Cartography by Don Pitcher

Other Books by Jory Graham
Katie's Zoo
Children on a Farm
I'm Driving My Analyst Crazy

PUBLISHER'S FOREWORD

Jory Graham is a well-traveled native Chicagoan. She proposed this book to us in 1965 and spent the next two years rediscovering and reevaluating her city. By car, by public transportation and on foot, she explored every part of Chicago and its environs, covering all but the Indiana sections of the 4,653 square miles that are metropolitan Chicago.

In the process, she took one of the most searching looks at Chicago that has ever been taken. She visited stores and shops anonymously to learn how strangers were treated. She went to restaurants and nightclubs in the same way. She took children on expeditions to watch their reactions. She went into neighborhoods where English is a weak second language, spoken infrequently; in the slums of the ghetto she spent days talking with black citizens at all levels.

She discussed the city with visitors from the United States and from overseas and with all kinds of Chicagoans whose experience might be helpful to a visitor: reporters, critics, columnists, historians, architects, museum directors, cops on the beat, sportswriters, bureaucrats, politicians, members of the Establishment, librarians, art gallery owners, antique dealers, restaurateurs. She accepted nothing at face value and made sure that facts were facts, not civic wishfulness or business propaganda.

The result is a genuinely extraordinary book about Chicago. It is authoritative. It is discriminating. It recommends the best, even when the best is not the best known. And it is complete. It shares with you an insider's detailed knowledge of the city and its citizens.

It is, in fact, the first truly comprehensive, knowledgeable guide to present-day Chicago, a guide to be consulted as a source, browsed through for enjoyment and followed with confidence and pleasure.

Rand McNally & Company

ACKNOWLEDGMENTS

All kinds of remarkable people helped with this book and made it better for their help. I'm indebted to:

Howard Alan

Robert Anson

V. Gilbert Beers

Karen Blaje

Betty and Ray Brennan

the late Richard McPherron Cabeen

Grant Dean

John D. Entenza

Kenneth Ehrlich

Katharine M. Fansler

Jane Fox

Sandra Hanzel

Beverly and Alvin L. Krieg

Jack M. Levin

Kathryn Hoover McAuley

Brooks McCormick, Jr.

Ludwig Mies van der Rohe

Martha and Richard H. Needham

Gail Parks

Suzanne and Brace Pattou

James W. Poling

Dave Potter

Herbert Reis

the late David Porter Sackett

Franz Schulze

Joseph Randall Shapiro

David C. Sharpe

the late Kurt Shery

Honore Singer

Susan Sinykin

Frank P. Stengel

Johanna and James Ward

Kendall White

Thomas Willis

Pamela Zekman

Six persons helped in extraordinary ways and deserve more thanks than I can adequately express. They are:

my parents, Rose-Frances and Ralph A. Reis

Jayne and James A. FitzSimmons

Robert Eck

Allen Van Cranebrock

And for their earlier books on Chicago which provided invaluable background and authentication, my thanks to Robert Cromie, author of *The Great Chicago Fire,* Emmett Dedmon, author of *Fabulous Chicago,* and Herman Kogan and Lloyd Wendt, coauthors of *Chicago, a Pictorial History.*

CONTENTS

CONTENTS

THE WAY IT IS...

Even when Chicago was a raw, jerry-built, lawless, amoral, cholera-ridden town, Chicagoans had greedy faith in it and didn't want to go back to wherever they'd come from or push on farther west. They were convinced of its future then; they're equally optimistic now, though their city has acquired all the digestive problems of big American cities: Hopelessly snarled traffic, high cost of living, a shortage of adequate middle and low income housing, organized crime, clogged courtrooms, corrupt officials, the ghettos of the underprivileged, racial strife, air pollution, and the pollution of its one great natural asset, Lake Michigan.

The typical Chicagoan ignores all these. He has an irrational love for his city and a pride in it he can't explain. He may occasionally grump about conditions and he's likely to be irritable during a siege of violent weather, but his bitching is not a symptom of chronic dissatisfaction; merely his annual midwinter catharsis. The day the sun shines again, so does he, and his Chicago looks better than ever. It's a great town, a great place to live—though if you ask him, he can't tell you why.

The unabated building and business boom of the past fifteen years has something to do with his conviction that things are happening, that the city is going places. Even a Negro or Puerto Rican cab driver, a citizen with something less than the average white Chicagoan's reason to have confidence in his future here, can be infected with the notion that his personal destiny is somehow linked to the one-hundred-story John Hancock building or the two serrated towers of Marina City. The Chicagoan's confusion of bigness with greatness is wholly American, but the degree to which he equates them is unmatched anywhere north of Texas.

So now he is proud of the massive Picasso sculpture in the Plaza of the Civic Center, though he screamed like a stuck pig for weeks after the unveiling because he couldn't understand it and was convinced he'd been had. Only when it became a number one tourist attraction did he change his mind. He still doesn't understand it as sculpture, but he's been assured that Picasso is big.

In the past, many of the things Chicagoans were proudest of were such strange choices that they mystified everyone else. Initially, it was the town's knee-deep mud and total lawlessness. At the turn-of-the-century it was the Everleigh Club, the nation's most famous bordello. During Prohibition it was Al Capone and the St. Valentine's Day Massacre. The citizenry worshipped the former and turned the site of the latter into a shrine, thus demonstrating how well it had learned the lesson taught by Big Bill Thompson, the corrupt two-term Prohibition mayor whose slogan was, "Be a Booster! Don't be a Knocker! Throw away your hammer and get a horn." The town hasn't really outgrown any of that: Its newspapers still keep front page count of the city's gangland murders, and the day the count broke the one thousand mark, the war in Vietnam was displaced by the more important local news.

A New Yorker once observed that Chicagoans see the crime syndicate in everything. Indeed they do. The Chicago Crime Commission even releases lists of Syndicate-controlled businesses, the newspapers publish them, the citizens read them—and the businesses continue to thrive. Most Chicagoans also know of a considerable number of not-yet publicly announced Syndicate-owned restaurants and nightclubs, which they patronize without a qualm, figuring that if the city officially won't or can't take action then there's no reason to stay away. They also rationalize that so long as a Syndicate spot gives fair value for the money, it's foolish to turn one's back on the place.

One of the biggest marvels of Chicago is its Democratic political machine, an antique but high-powered juggernaut that over the generations has almost completely atrophied the Chicagoan's sense of civic responsibility. Chicago is no more corrupt than New York or Los Angeles; the difference is that in Chicago indignant citizens are at a premium.

Cabbies break traffic regulations every time it's expedient to do so. Real estate operators manipulate zoning ordinances to suit their needs. Everyone ignores the posted ordinances against litter in the lakefront parks and beaches, and the aftermath of the Sunday crowds has to be seen to be believed. Conversely, there's no enforceable ordinance requiring property owners to keep their sidewalks clear of snow so most of them don't—not even those in charge of the city-owned-and-operated garages and parking lots. As columnist Mike Royko of the *Chicago Daily News* says, the city's unofficial slogan—"I Will"—really means "I Will if I don't get caught."

Yet, despite the city's outward air of cynicism, Chicagoans are not jaded. They don't snarl, they aren't deliberately rude, they do not take advantage of strangers. In fact, they will astonish you with their genuine friendliness. You do not have to be expensive-looking to get a response from them; and though the city itself is expensive, that's the result of heavy unionization, not pretentiousness. The atmosphere in most public places is comfortable; you can be yourself in Chicago, and it will never look down its nose at you. You can go anywhere and as long as you've got the price of admission, you're as welcome as anyone else. You can strike up a conversation with anyone and it's all right. You can even ask the man on the street where the nearest bookie is, and if he knows, he'll tell you. Chicagoans are not selfish; and they don't hide favorite places or the best aspects of their city from you. They're willing to share, eager to have you like and approve of their museums, symphony, universities, parks, zoos, lakefront and the architectural drama of their regenerated central business district. And the truth is, the visitor finds himself echoing Chicago sentiments—it is a great city, though he, too, cannot say why.

JORY GRAHAM

Note: At press date, all the information in this book was accurate and up to date. Obviously, there is no guarantee that admission prices, hours of admission, exhibits, merchandise, menus, hotel rates, ownership of places, or anything else will remain constant. Like Chicago itself, all are subject to change. Not subject to change, Chicago's street numbering system. Use the locator map, page 285, for quick reference to all major streets within the city limits. Directions to all places listed in this book are from the intersection of State and Madison streets downtown where the city's North-South, East-West street numbering system begins. When mileage is given it is also from the State and Madison intersection.

PART I: The Roaring City

THE BEST WATERING PLACES

1

Drinking With Formality
. . . With a View From Great Heights
. . . With Various Kinds of Atmosphere
Late Hour Drinking
Character Bars
In Places If You're Not Out Because of Age

CHAPTER 1

THE BEST WATERING PLACES

From its earliest days as the provisioning hole for pioneers heading west, Chicago has equated liquor with other staples; it runs like a *leitmotif* through all of Chicago's history.* By the mid-1870's saloons were so numerous in the downtown area that they were literally cheek by jowl and back to back in alleys as well as on streets. In all of them the standard drink was whiskey straight. WCTU national headquarters in Evanston, the attached suburb immediately north of the city, had no more influence on Chicago's affection for booze than did the 18th Amendment. During Prohibition, there were 7,000 speakeasies—only 642 less than the number of licensed drinking spots in 1968.

Yet, despite Chicago's deep thirst, few Chicagoans use the watering places as gathering places at the cocktail hour. Instead, they invite you to their homes or they meet in their clubs or at restaurants for dinner (in which case they order cocktails on the premises), but they almost never arrange to meet first in a public drinking place. This explains why you will look in vain for a hotel bar where you can drink among Chicagoans rather than other visitors or conventioneers.

Chicago is a good city in which to quench your thirst, and the range of places where you can is well above average. Easterners or anyone else who in ordering rye mean a blend are advised to order by brand here. If you don't, the bartender will either say he doesn't have rye or he'll pour rye whiskey—which you don't want. This is simply a case of regional semantics. Rye in Chicago always means rye whiskey.

---

* Like almost 6¼ million cases of distilled spirits as this year's motif.

DRINKING WITH FORMALITY

Prince of Wales, Ambassador East Hotel, Goethe and North State, SU 7-7200

A large room that achieves intimacy despite its size. It is also handsome and expensive-looking—like the customers. High tea may be ordered here, though the hour is apparently up for grabs. When asked, shortly before this book went to press, what time it was served, the captain said he guessed you could order it from about noon on. Which brings you right back to regional semantics; *high,* in Chicago, is a word more often used in tandem with drinking than with tea of any kind.

The **Pump Room Bar** in the same hotel is on a dais running the width of the famous dining room and offers a panorama of the lunch or dinner hour goings-on. Dancing is permitted from the bar, but you have to work to get to the dance floor since it's at the far end of the room through an obstacle course of diners, captains, serving carts, blackamoor-costumed coffee boys, and waiters.

Maxim's L'Imperiale, Astor Tower Hotel, 1300 North Astor, WH 3-1111

It's plush and offers fondue with drinks. It's open from noon on, but ungraciously turns into a private discotheque at 9:30 PM on Wednesday and Thursday and at 10:30 PM on Friday and Saturday.

Coq D'Or, Drake Hotel, 140 East Walton (Michigan), SU 7-2200

A gentlemen's pub for gentlemen and their ladies. Women alone are not permitted at the bar proper but are bowed by the captains to comfortable banquettes. Coq D'Or's gin-and-tonic is the best in the city. Also available: light lunches at noon and a small supper menu from 8 PM to midnight.

English Room Bar, Pearson Hotel, 190 East Pearson, SU 7-8200

A small bar at one end of the English Room offers enough space between drinkers and diners to permit full conversation. After the dinner hour, the entire room becomes a comfortable place to drink. A college and postcollege crowd tends to fill the room on weekends, but it's executive-level the rest of the week.

Cafe Bonaparte Bar, Sheraton-Blackstone Hotel, South Michigan and East Balbo, HA 7-4300

An intimate little bar, especially on a Saturday afternoon. At night, dancing from the bar permitted.

Jacques Restaurant Bar, 900 North Michigan, WH 4-4795

A chic little 1920's bar, once a private club, all black leather and chrome. The room is evocative of the era, including F. Scott Fitzgerald types at the bar.

5

... WITH A VIEW FROM GREAT HEIGHTS

LaTour Bar, 400 East Randolph (Outer Drive East Apts.), 527-1114

Far less formal than the above spots, the cocktail lounge in this lakefront apartment building offers a stunning view of the city, boat harbors and the lake. Weekdays 11:30 AM to 2 AM; Sunday 4 PM to 1 AM.

Consort Bar, Continental Plaza Hotel, 909 North Michigan, WH 3-7200

A sophisticated bar that's also one of the most comfortable in town. The east end of the premises looks directly into several floors of the John Hancock Building and will provide a nice nosey view of a number of the offices after the tenants move in. The west end offers an oblique view of Michigan Avenue and of the band and the dance floor in the Consort Room proper.

Pinnacle Bar, Holiday Inn, 644 North Lake Shore Drive, WH 3-9200

On a clear evening it offers one of the most spectacular lakefront views of Chicago to be had. Don't go before dark, however—the room itself will appall you. To 2 AM weekdays, Saturday to 3 AM.

Top of the Rock, Prudential Plaza, 120 East Randolph (east of Michigan), MI 2-7676

The Prudential is an office building and empties early. Hence, the crowd here is mainly tourist, and the bar, run by Stouffer's, is closed on Sunday. Otherwise, from 11:30 AM to midnight; Saturday to 1 AM.

Crown Room, United of America Building, 1 East Wacker Drive, 321-0502

A glass-walled drinking-dining room in which all customers have window seats, thanks to the location of the kitchens in the center of the room. Take your choice of four different views; from the north window wall, with binoculars, you can look directly into the top apartments at Marina City. Recommended for drinking only, because the food is not what it should or could be.

Tip Top Tap, Allerton Hotel, 701 North Michigan, SU 7-4200

Handy if you're on North Michigan Avenue and want to get above it all.

... WITH VARIOUS KINDS OF ATMOSPHERE

Wrigley Building Bar, 410 North Michigan, WH 4-7600

The place for members of the broadcasting and advertising fraternity. As such, noisy, convivial, full of shoptalk. Famous for extra-dry 4-oz. martinis at 75¢ (a little more if you specify a brand, but the bar gin is thoroughly respectable). Bar bourbon here is bonded 100-proof. Pre-lunch drinking starts at 11 AM, and the cocktail mob arrives shortly after 4 PM. By 5:00 it's a happy madhouse, but by 7:00 the crowd begins to thin. Since the bar closes with the restaurant, everything's over by 10 PM. Closed all day Saturday and Sunday.

Kon-Tiki Ports, Sheraton-Chicago Hotel, 505 North Michigan, WH 4-4100

Lush atmosphere, room after room of it, plus a waterfront atmosphere barroom called **Singapore Joe's.** Rum drinks a specialty here, and very good Cantonese cocktail tidbits.

Don the Beachcomber, 101 East Walton, SU 7-8812

Exotic and familiar rum drinks are the specialty here, too, with top honors going to the Navy Grog. Two floors for dining or drinking plus one of the most hospitable bars to be found. Superb Cantonese hors d'oeuvres. From 4 PM daily to 1 AM; Saturday to 2 AM.

Sage's East, Lake Shore Drive Hotel, 181 East Lake Shore Drive, WH 4-1557

The barroom in this restaurant is handsome, dark and intimate enough for assignations, and tucked away as though that's what management had in mind. Sometime between Christmas and New Year's Eve, owner Gene Sage throws a champagne party on the house. If you happen to wander in on the right day, you're as much a guest as the regulars who know in advance when the party will be.

Bivouac, Sheraton-Blackstone, South Michigan and East Balbo, HA 7-4300

At night, this is the most relaxing place to drink at the south end of the Loop.

Berghoff Men's Bar & Grill, 17 West Adams, HA 7-3170

An enormous brass-railed mahogany bar accepts 45 gentlemen comfortably but manages to accommodate three times the number during the lunch and predinner crushes. Famous for its age (pre-turn of the century), its great Berghoff beers, its staunch men-only tradition. Opens at 10 AM daily; closes at 10 PM. Sandwich bar and hard-cooked eggs available. Closed Sunday.

Binyon's, 327 South Plymouth, 341-1155

A jolly hideaway on the second floor of a three-story restaurant. The pro behind the bar is Tommy Tajiri, better known as Tommy O'Leary, a natural conversationalist celebrating his seventeenth year at Binyon's. Open 11:30 AM to 10 PM. Closed Sunday.

LATE HOUR DRINKING

Chicago's liquor licensing regulations are generous. Imbibing is allowed in all public places until 2 AM weekdays, 3 AM on Saturday (which, you realize, is three o'clock Sunday morning).* Chicago's historical disdain for blue laws (tried once, hastily rescinded) means that all bars are open on Sunday until 2 AM Monday. Any bar owner willing to pay a stiff fee every six months for the privilege of staying open until 4 AM may do so; for a still higher fee, until 5 AM. Most nonhotel bar owners are willing indeed. On Glitter Gulch (Rush Street) the late-late bars are every bit as busy at 4 AM as they are at any other hour—sometimes busier, because the crowd only appears after other spots close. Most neighborhood bars stay open until 4 AM, too. Though they're almost indistinguishable from each other (they're all furnished with the latest in blacklighted point-of-sale material given out by liquor distributors), it doesn't matter because neighborhood drinkers are generally oblivious to decor. If you can be, too, you'll find the local saloon friendly, even gregarious.

So you might try the **East Inn,** 206 East Superior, DE 7-9482—a cavernous double basement with jukebox dancing (rock 'n' roll) which caters to the students at nearby Northwestern University's downtown campus, and to the interns, residents, and nurses at the surrounding hospitals—Chicago Wesley, Passavant and Veterans Administration; or **Connolly's Tap** at 1445½ West Devon, 274-7303, a sliver of a bar jammed with Irish workingmen who come both for the Irish import beers and because Seamus McWilliams, the leprechaun who owns Irish Imports next door, will make his famous pork sausage sandwiches for them until the wee hours. Other neighborhood bars have atmosphere—of sorts. The most notable features of the **Comeback Inn,** at 1913 Lake, Melrose Park, FI 3-7490, are a working fireplace and a moose whose front half calmly surveys the crowd in one room and whose back half protrudes into another room. The atmosphere here is checked tablecloth, and good short order food is available.

Mariner's Club, on the riverfront at Elston and Division (SE corner), is hard to find because the river is far below grade, but if you look carefully you can spot the sign from the street. It's a Hell's Kitchen atmosphere in the shadow of the Division Street bridge—a wooden shack for workingmen in the area with a jukebox in continuous top-decibel operation and a pool table ditto. In summer you can take your beer outdoors to one of two weathered picnic tables or carry it along while you pick your way over the rubble-strewn riverfront to wander about the North on the River Boatyard.

Bars in Old Town and on Rush Street are of two kinds. The first are generally long-established neighborhood places that function almost as meeting grounds and "clubs" for single young residents of the area. The others are spots geared for conventioneers, tourists and non-neighborhood Chicagoans

---

* The law also allows bars to open at 7 AM, but a lot of neighborhood spots unlock their doors at 6 AM. It's illegal but it goes on all the time, thanks to clout. As explained by the City Collector's office which issues the liquor licenses, "They know somebody."

out on the town. **Pat Haran's** at 1007 North Rush, 337-8280, and **Larry's Lounge** at 1035 North Rush, MI 2-8252, are typical of the former. The drinks are generous and relatively inexpensive, and bartender and customers are generally friends of long-standing. Almost everything else on Rush (as on Wells) falls into the second category, even the **Stork Lounge,** across the street from the Playboy Club, at 59 East Walton, DE 7-2514, where bunnies go after they've finished their stint at the club.

CHARACTER BARS

The phrase can be interpreted to mean characters at bars. Or characters running bars. Or bars with offbeat character. Here are a few of Chicago's most remarkable:

Billy Goat Tavern, 430 North Michigan (lower level, entrance on Hubbard Street), 222-1525

Impossible to say which of the two Billy Goats is the greater institution—the tavern or proprietor Billy Goat Sianis—but both provide Chicago newsmen with a special kind of sustenance. The tavern is *the* hangout for reporters, editors, columnists, pressmen, truckers from the four nearby dailies, wire service reporters and every cop and Andy Frain usher in the vicinity. The proprietor is their friend and round-of-drinks buyer, a twinkling gentleman with a neat white goatee, fine Greek accent and the illusion that he ought to speak like a broken-down newsman, in staccato sentences. He gears the economics of his place to his people (a good rib eye steak sandwich from the grill is just 75¢) and runs the joint with perfect democracy. A bum coming in for a cup of coffee gets the same courtesy as a columnist; a confused new copyboy finds a place where he, too, is accepted as a member of the Fourth Estate. Billy Goat won his own newspaper credentials about 1909 when, as an immigrant kid, he got a newspaper route; he solidified them later by living through and surviving the era of the bloodiest circulation wars that ever wracked a city. Drop in some night between 11 PM and midnight; if you're lucky you'll find the big names of the Chicago news world on the premises in a scene that's the closest one can come to the now legendary (and demolished) Schlogl's. At 7 AM, you can join the block-long line for coffee and donuts. Open to 2 AM daily, Saturday to 3 AM.

Eagle, 5311 South Blackstone, HY 3-1933

Out front, an eagle shingle. Inside, to the right, one of the best pubs in the city; to the left, a dandy little bare-scrubbed-floor dining room. The Eagle came into being when University of Chicago sociologist Professor Philip Hauser convinced Harold Metcalf, Dean of Students of the Graduate School of Business, that a good off-campus pub was an absolute necessity. To the ever-

9

lasting credit of the university administration, it not only approved of one of its deans running a saloon but proudly and publicly talked it up.

The pub boasts one of the sturdiest lengths of mahogany bars going, and quite possibly features more highbrow types of liquor here than does any other drinking spot in this city. It is best known for its W. C. Fields Martini, 3½ oz. of good gin mixed ten to one at 75¢. It is second best known for the quality of dialogue exchanged here—intellectual, sometimes argumentative, always provocative. The bar is presided over by Pete Katos, another of the three partners who joined forces with Dean Metcalf.

The dining room features high, dark wood wainscoting topped by two preposterous vintage 1920's wall murals—highly romanticized and dubiously accurate paintings of the New York and Chicago skylines as seen from the water. Since the Statue of Liberty rises in the foreground of the Battery, the artist evidently felt the necessity of treating Chicago the same; hence the Chicago foreground is filled with *Miss I Will*, a lady carried over from the Columbian Exposition of 1893, intended to symbolize Chicago's restless energy and spirit. She carries a sword in this version (the original was a carpenter's square) and wears in her hair a phoenix with outstretched wings. Her breastplate says "I Will."

The menu at the Eagle is limited but satisfying. Soup—different each day —when they have it. Onion-bedecked sirloin strip steak with an enormous salad, rolls, excellent French fries. Steak or bratwurst sandwiches. Hamburgers. French-fried shrimp platter. Also a daily special at $1.50. And little niceties such as imported Grey Poupon Dijon mustard and marvelous coffee served in legitimate coffee cups. Noon to 1 AM Monday through Friday. Saturday to 2 AM. Sunday, 5 PM to 1 AM.

John Barleycorn Memorial Pub, 658 West Belden, DI 8-8899

It's a pub more in attitude than actuality—a great barn of a room decorated with some Victorian outrages and anything else that happened to appeal to owner Eric J. Van Gelder, gentleman of wit and warmth. Though he says that John Barleycorn is "dedicated to early 19th Century England where drunkenness was so common as to go virtually unnoticed," he runs his pub essentially as a place to congregate; the well-stocked bar is subservient to conversation. The congregation is postcollege and older with a sprinkling of artists, law and seminary students, even church groups after meetings. A girl alone or two girls are welcome and will be protected by the bartender, who will also refuse to serve customers who are loud.

Along with its gentleman's air, the pub is famous for its continuous showing of slides against a background of serious music. The Ektachromes are on just one subject—great works of art. The collection runs well above 2,000, and friends keep adding to it. None of it is catalogued. Van says, "We can't show requests except by the happy chance of spotting them immediately. We have 76 Van Gogh slides. Did you know Renoir was a dirty old man?"

Open from 11 AM to 2 AM. Businessman's lunch; rare roast beef and hamburgers at all hours. Also international hors d'oeuvres, including tacos and guacamole.

Sage's, 1 North La Salle, FI 6-2950

When former owner Gene Sage took over his father's conservative restaurant and bar, he rocked LaSalle St. by turning a middle-aged lawyer's lunch haven into a swinging after-hours phenomenon. If you're single, under 40 and in the Loop at 5 PM on a Friday evening, this is where half the action is. (The other half is at the **Bankers Building Lounge** in the Bankers Building, 105 West Adams (Clark), AN 3-7376.)

Throughout the year, Sage's host throws annual, zany, on-the-house parties which are announced in advance via table placecards and are open to anyone who hears of them and wants to join in: a Valentine's wine-tasting party; an income tax party in April (free drinks plus aspirin); the annual indoor June picnic, when the downstairs room is swept clean of furniture, a portable swimming pool brought in, and there's free beer and box lunches. Bastille Day is celebrated as close to July 14th as the calendar allows, with a wine-tasting party and a door prize—a date with a French model. September, the football kickoff, with raffled tickets to Bears' games. Christmas—the annual champagne party—44 cases were opened on the house this year. From October through April every Saturday morning (for the gang that has to put in office time), free coffee and donuts. There's more, but this is enough to make the point. Closed Saturday and Sunday.

Mr. T's, 5244 North Sheridan, SU 4-7927

Mr. T's is a neighborhood place, though it doesn't necessarily draw on its own neighborhood; rather, it gets people who prefer neighborhood spas to all others. As such, it's a kind of outstanding example of Chicago neighborhood camp. It features singer Sam Barrie, who accompanies himself on electric guitar and a foot pedal mike. The pedal lets him create his own echo chambers, and the mike has enough amplification for an opera house. The crowd, which knows and appreciates Sam ("Beautiful, beautiful," are the murmurs after every song), consists mainly of couples who nostalgically recall "The Donkey Serenade" as sung by Alan Jones—that's Jack Jones's dad—and who love to sing it with Sam.

IN PLACES IF YOU'RE NOT OUT BECAUSE OF AGE

The one group of Chicagoans that habitually meets for drinks after work are the young singles (ages 21-30) who frequent a handful of lunatic asylums on the Near North Side. The places are somehow unique to Chicago; though there are similar meeting places in other cities and equivalent crowding in bars at ski resorts, those who've sampled widely say they don't compare—though they can't tell you why. In any event, most people come stag since the point is to meet and be met in an atmosphere where, as writer Clifford Terry once observed, "the population per square foot would give India the creeps." Literally, it's a case of wall to wall people pressing body to body and screeching over the uproar in order to be heard. The big nights are Friday, Sunday, Wednesday, in that order; the fourth choice is Saturday afternoon, fifth is Sunday afternoon. During the dinner hour there's a hiatus everywhere, but the action is guaranteed to start up again after 9 PM.

Butch McGuire's, 20 West Division, DE 7-9080

Butch opened in 1961, claims his bar to be the first of its kind in the country and is probably correct. Sole entertainment is a juke box hypoed for maximum sound. No dancing, no food except weekend afternoons from about 2:30 on. Then a nickel buys a hot dog on a bun or a bowl of well-seasoned chili. One thing about Butch's, there's always a bevy of good-looking girls around—stenos, stewardesses and young teachers, whose backgrounds include the word *lady*.

The Spirit of '76, 26 West Division, 944-5995

Beer is the big Friday night drink, what else? Push your way past the people at the door and you'll find a huge back room with a rock band for dancing. $1 admission ticket on weekends includes a $1.05 meal ticket good Monday through Thursday. Spirit is now **Mother's**—it's too soon to report.

Melvin's, 1116 North State (Cedar), 664-1671

Hamburgers and steak sandwiches, and an enclosed sidewalk cafe with an unobstructed view of Rush Street for people-watching. The place used to be part of a whorehouse, but it doesn't show. Upstairs room now is as innocent as a room with a pool table can be.

Irvings?, 20 East Bellevue, 664-7010

Since it's also owned by Melvin's, it gives the proprietors a nice way to work both sides of the street, and there's room to dance. A pool table also turns up on the second floor.

The Store, 1036 North State, WH 3-7360

Two floors with a bar and a jukebox on each. Most of the dancing takes place on the second floor, where a band alternates with the jukebox at various times. As with the others, it's open until 2 AM.

The Store Annex, 937 North State, DE 7-7878

More of the same and just as big.

After 2 AM, follow the crowds to the **Filling Station,** 12 West Maple, 944-9837, or the **Rally Alley,** 1017 North Rush, 944-4179. (The names may change but the places will still be there. The turnover of ownership is frequently swift.) In summer, when the dancing becomes horribly perspiry, the 5 AM closing is often greeted with a cheer because somebody suggests running across to the lake for a quick swim. Go—you'll be just in time for the sunrise—and the lake is splendid at that hour.

WHERE CHICAGOANS DINE

2

Nine in the Chicago Tradition
Fashionable Dining
Continental
Seafood
Far East
Private Supper Clubs—Big on Lunch

CHAPTER 2

WHERE CHICAGOANS DINE

In the 1880's Chicago was famous for two kinds of restaurants—the civilized elegance of places like Kinsley's and Rector's, and the lusty steak house-whiskey-gambling establishments that reached their zenith at Chapin and Gore.*

Oddly, almost a century later, Chicago isn't famous for any particular kind of restaurant (though it could be), and, odder still, its most fashionable places are rarely those that offer the finest service and food. Smart promotion has built their reputations—not *haute cuisine* or the amenities.

Yet, there is a restaurant tradition in the city—and a worthy one. It has to do with standards and a basic honesty on the part of the founders of perhaps a dozen places, the belief that, wherever their establishments fitted into the hierarchy of restaurants, they would be the best of their kind. If a steak house, the owner would offer the best beef available. If a restaurant with a European accent, a genuine accent. Decor? The proprietors (many of whom established their restaurants years ago) scarcely knew the word, and most of them ignore it today. The exteriors of their buildings are likely to be so unpretentious as to dismay the fainthearted; the interiors are just as likely to be plain. But the linens are fresh. The glassware and silverplate have been pol-

---

* Chapin and Gore was a man's restaurant to which women were never admitted. It broiled its steaks over an open hearth, and if a patron could not find a cut to his liking, management promptly dispatched a cab to the stockyards with the order to procure and return immediately with the wanted cut. Such service attracted as regular customers Philip D. Armour, Gens. Phil Sheridan and Nelson A. Miles, Col. William F. Cody, actor Joe Jefferson, Long John Wentworth, John W. "Bet-A-Million" Gates, Allan Pinkerton, Florence Ziegfeld and the like. During the racing season every bookie in the city headquartered in the place; the word was, if a bookie couldn't be found there he was either in a hospital or dead.

ished. The service is good. The food is excellent. The prices are right. The waiters are probably as old as the restaurants—and proud of it. The chefs have been around since the beginning—and they haven't lowered their standards a whit. The proprietor or his now-grown son is still on the premises—the first man to arrive, the last one to leave. He knows his patrons by name and likes them as individuals; he greets new customers with equal warmth and courtesy. He's proud of his achievement, and he maintains his restaurant's reputation because he knows that if that goes, his integrity is shot. He is owner and host and he has no peer.

The other kind of restaurant that few visitors to the city get the chance to discover is the good little spot tucked away in the back room of a saloon or neighborhood tavern, or in quarters improvised out of a converted storefront, or in a weathered turn-of-the-century structure in which the rooms above are still the owner's home. The actual number of these restaurants is unknown, but Chicago has more of them than any other city you can name, and each time a new one is discovered it's a matter of triumph. If you're willing to adventure you can have some delightful and memorable dining experiences at prices that will more than offset car rental or cabs.

A few other realities about dining in Chicago are:

Don't look for *haute cuisine*. The natives won't, as a rule, pay the price it requires, and neither the expense-account crowd nor the 1,300,000 conventioneers who meet in the city annually want it. Neither, it seems, do most of the six-million-yearly tourists.

Don't dine in a fashionable place on Saturday night. This is the Midwest, and Saturday night is still *the* night for most city dwellers and suburbanites to go out. They flood the fashionable places, and the restaurateurs prepare for the onslaught by extending dining hours to accommodate three seatings instead of the usual two and, where physically possible, by increasing the number of tables and chairs by as much as one-third. Unfortunately, they do not increase kitchen or serving staffs—a policy that swells profits but makes dining out pure horror. Head for little, unknown places, listed mainly in Chapter 3.

Note: Negro visitors will find themselves welcome at most restaurants in this city. The exceptions will be some of the smaller ethnic restaurants in the following chapter. Conversely, whites will find themselves welcome at middle-class Negro restaurants but, depending on the temper of the times, perhaps not at some of the soul food stations because of their locations in the ghettos.

Make reservations everywhere—as far in advance as possible, on weeknights as well as on weekends. You're in competition with hordes.

Know that places change, especially those run by chain or absentee management.* With luck, you may find them to be exactly as reported, but it can't

---

* Places also go out of business. The restaurants recommended here have been in business at least three years, so their continuing success is likely.

be guaranteed. Restaurants owned and run by experienced individuals or families are likely to remain constant: pride of ownership and individual traditions generally assure continuity.

This is a time of rampant inflation, so prices may not be precisely as given here—but higher. For that reason, the following categories are used:

Expensive. This means dinner at $8 to $10 per person or higher, exclusive of cocktails, wines, tips. If "expensive" keeps you from trying a restaurant you're aching to visit, go after 10:30 PM and order from the supper menu, which is always an a la carte menu and which will offer after-theatre or late-show dining at reasonable prices. Sunday brunch is another alternative.

Reasonable. Dinner is in the $4.50 to $7.50 range.

Moderate. Dinner is under $5.

On page 67 you'll find a list of moderately priced family restaurants that serve standard American dishes and also go out of their way for children. Elsewhere, (F) indicates restaurants at which children will not be out of place.

The fashionable dining hour in Chicago is 8 PM or later, though all restaurants are open by 6 PM and many as early as 5 PM.

Tipping. Twenty percent in a first-rank restaurant at lunch and dinner. Fifteen percent everywhere else. Nothing if you've been treated shabbily and have the nerve.

This being Chicago, you can assume that every restaurant listed here and in the next chapter has a bar. Exceptions are noted. You can use the restaurant bar to great advantage—and not just for drinks. If you arrive at a place and are told that it will be 20 minutes or whatever until you can be seated, say that you'll wait at the bar. Willingness to spend money will usually get you a table sooner. The phrase, "Open daily," used with restaurants and elsewhere in this book, means open seven days of the week.

NINE IN THE CHICAGO TRADITION

They are not necessarily the most glamorous restaurants in the city, but they are among its most distinguished. What sets them apart from other places is their strong individuality and the fact that each retains its tradition—the best food of its kind, the best service possible and fair prices.

Binyon's, 327 South Plymouth (off Jackson, just west of State), 341-1155

Chop house atmosphere on the main floor, a quietly-lit, formalized French provincial dining room above, and a separate barroom run by one of the best known bartenders in the city. Binyon's caters to sports figures and fans at night and to federal judges, attorneys, brokers and insurance executives at noon. Mr. Hal Binyon, Sr., opened his restaurant in the 1920's and served simple, hearty German fare. Today, a few of the old specialties still appear on the menu, but Binyon's reputation for outstanding food rests on its prime beef, triple-rib chops and sublime seafood—Binyon Turtle Soup, Cotuits, New England Oyster Stew, New England Clam Chowder, Manhattan Clam Chowder, Broiled Red Snapper, Fish Chowder, Baked Shrimp Binyon (the original Shrimp de Jonghe recipe inherited from the de Jonghes when they closed their place). It's also known for its Russian salad dressing, which is the only Russian dressing in Chicago that tastes the way it should; for its feathery strudels baked on the premises; and as the only restaurant in the city that serves honeydew melon when every other restaurant swears melon is out of season.

And it has its own house rules and traditions: free chartered round trip bus service to all night games of the White Sox and Blackhawks; waiters who make certain you get to theatre or Orchestra Hall on time; regular hours on Saturday for men who come into the Loop to open their offices. The place is an oasis in more ways than one on Saturday—it's one of the few where you can dine on a short reservation that night.

Luncheon, dinner, a la carte, to 8 PM on the main floor, to 10 PM upstairs.
Closed Sunday and holidays. Reasonable unless you get carried away.

The Berghoff (F), 17 West Adams, HA 7-3170

The Berghoff tradition has its roots in the last century and offers a nostalgic excursion into another period of Chicago's convivial restaurant past—the era of bustling, cheerful German *brauhaus* when good food and drink could be had at moderate prices. (They still can in this restaurant, in complete lunches or dinners for less than $2.)

Except for enlarged menus and additional rooms, the tradition, the Men's Bar (page 7) and the original dining room are now what they were then. The beers Grandfather Herman Berghoff brewed and made famous are still on draft—Dortmunder (light) and Dortmunder Doppel (double dark). The Men's Bar still bars women; the black-tuxedo-white-apron-clad waiters still pay for customers' meals in advance, with brass chips bought from the cashiers, and race to serve you.

If you can pass up the fine German specialties, you'll get as good a steak, as fine a fish dish, as can be had anywhere. But who can bypass Sauerbraten that has been marinated in wooden barrels; or one of the four kinds of ragout; or Natur Schnitzel with imported pfifferling; Kassler Rippchen; gschnaetzlets and other schnitzels; or frog legs Orly in a beer batter?

The restaurant celebrates four annual festivals: Bock Beer in early spring; May Wine Time, when the fresh young wines that have been steeped in woodruff arrive (they're served in traditional *roemers* with fresh strawberries); the Lager Bierfest (October), when the restaurant is decorated in sheaves of barley and bierfest specialties such as Bratwurst, Huhn im Topf and Wiener Rostbraten are added to the menu; and the great season leading to Christmas. This last starts about Thanksgiving, and the restaurant turns into a Graustarkian hunter's lodge. Up go the greens, the tree, the old-fashioned wreaths. Out come the waiters bearing roast goose, hasenpfeffer, rehpfeffer (venison stew), rehbraten (venison roast), pheasant, clams, oysters. It's not to be missed.

Note: The Berghoff family also runs the new Berghoff at 123 North Wabash, opening late 1968.

Luncheon, dinner to 10 PM Monday, Thursday; to 9:30 PM other days. Moderate. Sandwich counter in Men's Bar closes at 8 PM. Closed Sunday.

Atlantic Hotel (F), 316 South Clark, WA 2-2646

From its founding at the turn of the century and until World War I, it was the Kaiserhof; generous areas of its imperial grandeur are still to be seen outside (stand across the street and marvel at that baroque facade) and inside, in what was originally the Ladies' Cafe but is now the main dining room. It's Victorian German schmaltz, but the crowd that lunches here (LaSalle Street bankers, brokers and lawyers) wouldn't have it any other way. The dining room offers enough viewing to occupy a full lunch hour—you find yourself studying the intricate carvings, making one joyful discovery after another among the friezes and column tops (flowers, fruits, apes, nudes, maidens, small animals, a bas relief of Bacchus and a high relief of the Emperor Frederick Barbarossa over the entrance), and underneath, breaking at intervals into the old wood-paneled walls, the most awful romantic oils.

Judging from the chairs and the ages of some of the waiters, the place hasn't changed since it was founded (it's run by the sons of the owners, Messrs. Ernest C. Roessler and Frederick C. Teich, and more glory to them for it). German dishes are a specialty: Thuringer and Fresh Sauerkraut, Wiener Schnitzel a la Holstein, Cold Smoked Westphalian Ham, German Apple Pancake Glacé and, when available, Broiled Lake Huron Trout. For any who long for the once justly-famous Lake Michigan trout (it disappeared with the advent of the seaway and the lampreys), this from the sister lake is an agreeable substitute.

Lunch only, 11 AM to 2 PM. Most moderate. A great place to dine if you're on the architectural tour at the south end of the Loop (see page 101).

Fritzel's, 201 North State (Lake), AN 3-7100

Fritzel's is an institution, with its counterpart in Lindy's or Reuben's in New York, but with a luncheon life that is strictly its own. From noon to the end of the three-hour lunch necessary to those businesses that require them, it's a showcase and meeting ground for celebrities, columnists, models, feature writers, public relations men and moguls in advertising, TV and radio. An efficiency springboard; gregarious, noisy, another aspect of Chicago. If you can get a lunch reservation, don't change your mind at the last minute—go.

Go with the knowledge that you're about to see a spectator event, that you're going to eat some of the best food imaginable, and that you're going to be part of a slice of Chicago life that can't be captured as fully at any other restaurant in town. Go, hoping to meet the man who until recently owned it and now hosts it—Joe Jacobson, one of the grandest gentlemen in the business. Nobody beats him as a fund-raiser for worthy events or as a teller of hilarious anecdotes. He frankly takes care of his celebrities and his regular customers first, and makes strangers respect him the more for doing so. If you can claim his attention, ask him why Eggs Benedict was once listed on his menu under "Soups" but is now to be found under the equally unlikely category of "Hot Sandwiches." The story concerns chanteuse Patachou and Maxim's—the Paris Maxim's—and every word is true.

If Fritzel's had a house specialty, it would be Eggs Benedict, but the fact is, there are no house specialties except "everything that's not on the menu."* That menu romps happily through six homemade soups, including Matzo Ball; twenty-one appetizers, including Chopped Chicken Livers, Gefilte Fish and Shrimp Scampi that would put many an Italian to shame; four kinds of herring; incredible salads** (order a fresh fruit salad, and the salad chef should drop dead if there's one piece of canned fruit in it); seafoods; steaks; fat columns listing hot sandwiches, Fritzel's Suggestions, broiled, sautéed, fried entrées, eggs, omelettes and savories; and, finally, some thirty desserts. Like the menu, whatever you order is always more than you can eat.

Saturday night at Fritzel's (late, after theatre) is eclectic Jewish, a scene right out of *Marjorie Morningstar* or any expensive bar mitzvah. Elaborately minked and jeweled ladies spend most of their time running from table to table, kissing each other, sampling the other's food, chattering volubly about shopping or their children; the men knot in their own world of business, and it's as if wives and husbands never knew each other. If you're not Jewish, you're going to feel like an outsider, but as author Harry Golden wrote, "Enjoy, Enjoy!"

Open every day but Christmas. Luncheon, dinner, supper to 1 AM; Saturday, 2 AM. Surprisingly moderate.

Wrigley Building Restaurant (F), 410 North Michigan, WH 4-7600

One of the best Continental-American restaurants in town, or anywhere, for that matter. It's bright, cheerful and busy—the sounds of U. S. business executives dominate the place at lunch, and if lunch is any gauge, the prospects of American business are not nearly so gloomy as the Republicans would have you believe. Those Republicans who are regulars at the Wrigley usually

* What Mr. Jacobson means is that if you can't find anything you want on the menu or have a taste for something not listed, it'll be made to order on the spot.
** There's another salad that's absolutely the best thing that ever happened to artichoke hearts, hard-cooked eggs, bibb lettuce, hearts of palm, cold asparagus—large chunk delicacies with a Fritzel special salad dressing that miraculously combines Durkee's, Worcestershire, capers, sugar, oil and vinegar.

look quite satisfied with everything, including the restaurant's famous Lake Superior Whitefish; My Salad (a lovely julienne of turkey and other comestibles done up in a bleu cheese salad dressing—on Friday it's listed on the menu as Your Salad because the turkey abdicates in favor of tuna); Chicken Clemenceau; Walleyed Pike with Almonds and White Grapes; omelettes that are as light and runny as any in France; veal offered in some fifteen different versions; Shrimp or Crabmeat Rockefeller, which only Julia Child or M. Andre Ballestra, the tireless manager, could describe adequately. His description: *"La reconnaisance du gandre*—the gratefulness of the stomach," and one's is.

Advertising, broadcasting and newspaper executives generally lunch in the grill area; junior execs lunch in the bar; celebrities are generally seated up front, where you're likely to be. Jo, a lady with an incredible memory, is famous for checking as many as 200 hats at noon without offering a single ticket; Bob Turney, the head barman, is famous both for his martinis (see page 6) and as presiding Resident Psychologist of the Wrigley Bar.

Reservations absolutely essential at noon and advisable in the evening. Make yours no later than 10:30 AM for the first seating at noon. This is another spot where, if you tell your waiter you're going on to theatre, he'll see you get out in time.

> Open Monday through Friday only, to 10 PM. Complete dinners and a la carte. Moderate to very reasonable. Free parking in Rush Street lot behind the Wrigley Building.

Whitehall Restaurant, Whitehall Hotel, 105 East Delaware, WH 4-6300

Tourists never learn of the Whitehall because owners Sidney and William Keller zealously avoid ordinary newspaper column mention and Duncan Hines-type recommendations. The reason is their clientele—the Old Guard of Chicago and the North Shore. Hence the restaurant, to the right of the lobby, is quite like a fine old home: comfortable but not highly decorated, leisurely, and noted for exquisite pre-World War II maid service.

The menu has a happy disregard for calories. Cream of tomato soup is thick and rich because it's made with incredible amounts of fresh cream. Eggs Sardow are a great favorite, likewise Chicken-Vegetable Salad; Breast of Chicken Martinique; Corned Beef Hash (Marshall Field II sent his chauffeur for it from his Lakeview apartment every Friday night he held a poker game). Petite Hamburgers are made of sirloin ground only after you've given the waitress your order. They're on the luncheon menu (and this is a fine place to lunch if you're shopping on North Michigan Avenue) along with more than a dozen rich, inventive sandwiches. The Whitehall's fresh hot fudge sauce is unquestionably the best in the city but don't ask for the recipe—it's been a secret for 40 years.

The restaurant's standards are carefully maintained. It's not for a young crowd, nor for touring families who seek informality. Children are welcome, but they're expected to have proper manners and be properly dressed—little boys wear Eton suits and little girls are in pinafores. At noon during symphony season (Tuesday and Friday matinees) it may be hard to get in because season ticket holders also have luncheon tables reserved here; it's part of a pattern, a way of life that for Chicago's leisured class is unduplicated elsewhere in the city—except at private clubs (see page 448).

Luncheon, dinner to 9 PM. Closed holidays only. Moderate.

Gene & Georgetti's Restaurant, 500 North Franklin, 527-3718

Echoes of Chapin and Gore here—the best prime aged steaks in the city, accompanied by huge rounds of cottage fried potatoes; also fine Italian specialties, including Lobster Diavolo; noise and banter and gin rummy games in the afternoon.* The restaurant is housed in an off-center 1870's structure onto which various additions were grafted over the years (they have to be seen to be believed—view the whole from across the street). A tiny glass pane in the heavy front door bears testimony to its speakeasy days. In true Chicago style, the kitchen was added after Repeal to accommodate the drinkers. Mr. Alfredo Fedrighi, co-owner and head chef for some 25 years, now comes in only on Saturday, Sunday and Monday to create his Florentine versions of Chicken Vesuvio, Veal Scallopini and Chicken Cacciatore—you might try dropping in on a late Sunday afternoon ahead of the evening mob. Both owners insist it's possible to get a bad steak on the premises but it's not likely.**

Stay away during massive conventions (Shoes, Chemical, NBA, Housewares) when the place is a madhouse. On the other hand, you can sometimes make it in on a Saturday night without a reservation and not have to wait more than 20 minutes at the bar, over which a marvelously improper young Bostonian presides.

Luncheon, dinner to 1 AM. A la carte only. Steaks, reasonable; Italian specialties, moderate. Closed all holidays and Sunday in summer.

Corona (F), 501 North Rush, 527-5456

It's probably the only restaurant in Chicago that's made the transition from storefront operation to its own handsome building without having a lot of other things change too. Except for decor and the fact that it's no longer a speakeasy, it's still the Corona that the late Harry Moroni opened shortly after World War I—still a great, informal place to dine.

Back in the old days, the first customers were from the *Chicago Tribune,* the sports and financial page writers and columnists. Then John Cuneo, later

---

* No poker because the law doesn't allow you to put out money where it shows.
** "Sure, you could get a bad steak here. Take a loin. The first three steaks are wonderful, but the fifth, sixth and seventh can be bad because the animal had a bruise. People say, 'I've been coming here fourteen years and I got a bad steak.' I say, 'After thirteen and a half years you're complaining?'"—Gene Michelotti, co-owner.

to make a fortune in Hawthorn-Mellody Dairies and the National Tea Company, discovered it. He was a produce man at the time, and he brought in customers from the market; the place began to thrive. His father, a realtor who was hooked on buying corners, and who possibly owned more corners than anyone else in the city, brought in the limousine trade, and business bloomed. Harry got in the habit of feeding the chauffeurs in the kitchen, but that largesse created such a traffic jam that it forced him to open a little back room with nineteen stools—and that's how the original, famous old Corona Annex began. Julio, long known as the original *disgraziato,* presided over the Annex; some "unfortunate"—he retired to Italy in style years ago. The Annex was always crammed with chauffeurs, cab drivers, pressmen from the *Tribune,* in their funny square newspaper hats, and anyone else in a hurry who could squeeze in. Harry Moroni finally had to take care of the rush hour overflow so he opened a room where you ate standing in front of individual tables four feet high. You can still lunch that way downstairs at the present restaurant and get soup, a main dish like roast beef, or corned beef and cabbage, plus good coffee, for under $1.

The main dining room menu is the same menu Harry concocted years ago, with Family Soup (a delicious minestrone crammed with alphabets) leading the list of specialties. Italian dishes are as fine as any in town; so are the steaks and double chops and everything else on the menu. It's the only place where you can order a carafe of wine by the litre or half-litre, and where Jumbo Louisiana Shrimp on Ice, if ordered by several people as an appetizer, are served as a mountain on one huge platter. It's the only restaurant in the entire category of restaurants in this chapter where, despite the elegance and formality of the room, a gentleman is welcome without a tie and a woman wearing the sightseeing clothes she put on that morning won't feel ill at ease even on a weekend. That's the kind of place it is, and Harry's sons and nephew who now run it intend to keep it that way.

> Downstairs room lunch only. Main dining room open for luncheon; dinner; late suppers. Full dinners and a la carte. Closed only on Christmas Day. Though you rarely see children here, they're welcome. Moderate.

The Bakery, 2218 North Lincoln, GR 2-6942

The Bakery is the shining example of Chicago's restaurant forte—the superbly run little restaurant off the tourist circuit, almost indistinguishable from its surroundings, in this instance, on the remnants of a commercial street desperately in need of a total beautification program. Except for a narrow, faded red and white striped canopy and the chauffeured Lincoln Continentals parked in front, you could drive past it at 25 mph and never know it was there.

The Bakery is the creation of its owner and head chef, Mr. Louis Szathmáry, a gentleman of ample girth, great drooping red mustaches, and fine

Hungarian wit. He is Chicago's most famous restaurateur, and to his establishment stream the cognoscenti of the country to be fed five elegant courses in what was once a harness shop.*

The tiny Japanese lady with the marvelous smile of greeting is Mrs. Szathmáry. The table at which she'll seat you is covered with immaculate linen, graced by a single fresh rose and meticulously set with a wild assortment of service plates and heavy old table silver, none of which match. With a fine European sense of what is and is not important, Mr. Szathmáry furnished his restaurant in the best odds and ends he could find, figuring that matched place settings weren't nearly as important as superb cuisine and an enormous staff of skilled European waiters and chefs. To this day he has kept his sense of proportion—and the mismatched silver.

There are no menus. Dinner begins with a *pâté maison*, French bread mixed and shaped by hand, and sweet butter. Soup ladled from a caldron at table—a very European soup. Then salad—in winter, an exotic like cooked, marinated celery root, in summer, the freshest greens. Next, your choice of entrées, any of which will be excellent. Filet de Boeuf Wellington is a favorite of many patrons, but the Duckling with Cherry Sauce, the Chicken Paprika cooked in sweet Hungarian paprika, and the Turbot are equally memorable, served with side dishes of vegetables you won't find elsewhere. Game in season—pheasant, venison, breast of guinea hen. Perrier water on request. The choice of desserts drives you wild.

The Bakery functions beautifully sans bar or service bar. Wines are available; patrons are equally welcome to bring their own, and after-dinner brandy as well. For reasons that defy all logic, the *in* room is the kitchen. Though the vast old range that roasted the ducks has been moved elsewhere, the dishwasher (human) is still very much in evidence, casually smoking cigarettes between bouts in the suds, the waiters race past you, the waitresses whirl at their tasks, chefs emerge and vanish. The ambiance of this kitchen is surely not to be found anywhere else.

> Dinner only, from 5 PM till 11 PM. One price, $7. Closed Sunday and Monday.

FASHIONABLE DINING

Maxim's de Paris, Astor Tower Hotel, 1300 North Astor, WH 3-1111

A French import sponsored by *the* Maxim's at 3 Rue Royale, Paris. The decor is a delicious copy of the original's sensuous dark polished woods, mir-

---

* You never know who you'll be seated next to because Mr. Szathmáry gives his patrons complete anonymity and never reveals to the columnists the names on his reservation list. Ambassador Stevenson was a regular; so now are his sons and daughters-in-law. The Neiman Marcuses, Mayor Lindsay of New York, cartoonist Bill Mauldin, Nelson Algren, Eartha Kitt, Federal Judge Parsons, all the French consular people and, one night, six Nobel prize winners together at a table in the kitchen.

rors and fanciful metal ribbons and petals—one of the great triumphs of Art Nouveau. There's even a small dais for the musicians, and potted palms.

The menu is as enchanting as the illusion—at first glance. For on it is the famous Billy-bi, a cream of shellfish soup to order cold or hot; Cotes d'Agneau Edouard VII (lamb chops with *fois gras*), braised endive, braised celery and cepes, those heavenly mushrooms of France for which this country yields no parallel; souffles are to be found among desserts, and the dessert cart is almost always glorified by a *croquembouche,* that towering concoction of small cream puffs filled with *crème pâtissiere,* layered up, up like a pyramid, drizzled with glaze, one of the most heavenly desserts ever devised and faithful to its name—melt-in-your-mouth.

Yet, it's Maxim's, Chicago, not Maxim's, 3 Rue Royale. The atmosphere is indelibly Midwest, and Paris is 4,133 miles away. The tradition and authenticity of the original Maxim's are exclusive with the original and can't be built-in here any more than in the Tokyo Maxim's. You'll dine well at this Maxim's —and perhaps even graciously—and the wines are magnificent. But you'll be disappointed if you expect it to re-create one of the incomparables. It just can't be done.

> Luncheon, dinner, late suppers. Sunday, dinner and late supper only. A la carte only. Expensive. Closed only Christmas Day. Christmas Eve is a gala night to dine here.

Camellia House, Drake Hotel, 140 East Walton (Michigan), SU 7-2200

No longer the handsome old Dorothy Draper room that hosted top-drawer Chicago for so many years, but something else with a heavy southern accent. The menu reads like a tourist folder of Charleston place-names, though there's nothing especially southern about the food, which is best described as excellent hotel. In the room's heyday, guests were not admitted unless in evening clothes; it's still a place where black tie seems appropriate, since it offers one of the best society dance bands in the city, along with a name entertainer in two evening shows.

> Dinner, late supper and a la carte. Expensive. Closed Sunday and Monday, except for Sunday brunch and dancing from noon to 4 PM.

Pump Room, Ambassador East Hotel, Goethe and North State, SU 7-7200

It's the kind of theatrical room that could exist in only one other city in the country, but a Chicagoan thought of it first so it's here, not in Los Angeles. It sports deep blue felt walls, glittering Waterford crystal sconces and chandeliers (in which some candles are inevitably askew), a striped gazebo over the service entrance, early Jean Harlow white leather banquettes, white armchairs, white telephones at table and four monstrous supporting pillars marching dead center down the length of the room to the little dance floor.

Waiters are decked out in hunting pinks and black satin knee breeches; coffee boys in emerald green perspire under heavy, plumed, white satin turbans; a curry boy zips around in cloth of gold; the sommelier affects white satin and a flowing Windsor tie. Meats are borne flaming from the kitchen, skewered on heavy fencing foils. Desserts are blazed in chafing dishes. The total effect is camp—and everybody loves it.

The famous Booth One (immediately to your right inside the entrance) is reserved for celebrities, VIP's and tycoons. The Shirley Booth (the Pump's best pun) is directly across the aisle and can be had by anyone who phones early enough to reserve it. It's just as desirable since it also faces the entrance, and thus, those who dine in it will always be seen.

What with all the goings-on you might expect the food to be a kind of sideline, but the fact is, it's excellent. The menu is extensive and reflects awareness of the time to stop clowning around. The one fault of the Pump Room is its service, which is not just less than enthusiastic but downright inexcusable. Plan to make an evening of it when you dine here. You'll have to, in any event.

> Luncheon, dinner, late supper. Reasonable if you order an entrée which arrives with accompaniments; otherwise, expensive.

Red Carpet, 28 West Elm (Dearborn), MO 4-2788

Of all Chicago restaurants, it comes closest to giving New Yorkers a sense of being home, partly because it's housed in an old brownstone on the Near North Side, partly because of owner-host Jerry Kovler and partly because half its regular patrons are New Yorkers in Chicago on business.

As with many another venerable brownstone, the walls in this one need fresh paint, and the color scheme and draperies could be improved. But in the same tradition the atmosphere is intimate, the table appointments are perfectly splendid, and the menu is fun to explore.* Originally, it was Haitian Creole, but now it fans out in enough other directions to rate as international. Salmon is flown fresh from Scotland, turbot fresh from the English Channel.

This is one restaurant where it's wise not to skip soup, unthinkable to bypass the famous Boula Boula or the chilled avocado soup, sad if you allow yourself to become so satiated you've no room for the cheese tray which is honored by rarities for this city—Brie, for instance, or La Grappe.

Should your reservation turn out to be in The Room At The Top, you'll pass a 250-pound brass lady on the stairway wearing only pearls and a 1920's cloche.** One regular patron who reserved a table in the new room shortly after it opened, passing the statue on the way up, stopped dead on a tread and

---

* The gold- or silver-plated water goblets you get just may bear the initials of the distinguished regulars to whom they've been presented. Mr. Kovler will interpret initials on request.

** The brass lady is the late Edith Rockefeller McCormick, a daughter of John D., and for many years if not Chicago's leading eccentric, right up there contending for the title with her cousin, Col. Robert R. (Bertie) McCormick.

said to his wife, "My God, this cannot be! That's my aunt, nude and three feet high!"

> Dinner only. A la carte only. Expensive. Closed holidays and alternate Sundays.

Consort, Continental Plaza Hotel, 909 North Michigan (Delaware), WH 3-7200

The crowd is the kind that makes a woman wish she'd dressed or undressed to the bone. It's a polished group and always seems to include more devastating young women in short, smashing décolleté than any other restaurant in town. Illusion, of course; that the dance band switches roles during the evening to become a string quintet, and a long-stemmed rose is placed by every lady's napkin, testifies to the fact that much older couples dine here regularly.

The room itself has the deep good looks brought on by candlelight against dark purple walls, tall plate-glass windows through which the lights of the city twinkle, comfortable white leather banquettes. The menu is far more extensive and interesting than you would expect it to be, despite eccentric spelling of hors d'oeuvres, such as Terrine de Fois Gras de Strassbourg. Service is excellent.

> Luncheon, dinner and a la carte. Luncheon not recommended, since all the splendor fades in daylight, implausible Austrian shades are drawn against the view and the lunch menu is frankly a bore. Expensive.

Biggs, 1150 North Dearborn (Elm), SU 7-0900

Curiosity about the way Chicago rebuilt after the Fire can be partly satisfied by dining at Biggs. The mansion that houses the restaurant was designed and built in 1874 by Edward Burling, the architect of St. James Cathedral. For a family named De Koven he produced equivalent grandeur—exquisite parquet floors; high ceilings; ornate hand-carved burl oak moldings and wainscoting above and below matched burl paneling; Italian marble fireplaces in some of the rooms; and carved wood fireplaces in others. It's like dining in an elegant old private home—under a candlelit Baccarat chandelier in one room, by footed candelabra in the others.

No menus—a captain or waiter offers a verbal choice of cocktails, wines from an excellent cellar, hors d'oeuvres, soups, four entrées, salads, desserts and footed silver compotes of fresh fruits and chocolates.

Too good to be true? Right. Some nights every course is superb; other nights one suspects the entire kitchen staff has the sulks. Actually, the trouble is that Biggs is part of a local chain with centralized buying, centralized decisions. It hampers the individuality of this, the one outstanding restaurant of the group. Nevertheless, go for the atmosphere, the sense of *luxe*, the gamble, because the odds are with you.

> All dinners $8.25 or $7.75, depending on entrée. Dinner only, 5 PM to midnight. Closed Monday.

Seventy-One Club, Executive House, 71 East Wacker Drive, FI 6-7100

A private business lunch club by day, it welcomes all comers from the cocktail hour on, offers an urbane 39th floor glass curtain-wall setting; a spectacular view of the lake, the river, skyscrapers old and new, including close-ups of Marina City and the fanciful Greco-Roman temples that adorn the Pure Oil Building; extra-dry martinis in goblets big enough to drown in; a fine menu, basically American but with light Italian touches, and a harpist whose music is good.

Start with Cannelloni as an appetizer or Fettucine Alfredo (both rarities in this city), proceed to steak, bird or seafood, fresh vegetables in baskets to view and select from; more baskets of fresh fruits served with cheese or the famous little paper-wrapped Amaretti di Saronno macaroons, unknown in Chicago except at Seventy-One. The last page of the menu lists available brandies and liqueurs under the lovely (and by this time essential) title of Digestives.

> Mainly a la carte, though steaks come with relishes, baked potato and salad. Mainly expensive. Closed Sunday and holidays.

Note: For hotel dining rooms that have shows and dancing, see page 77.

Champs-Elysées, 260 East Chestnut, 645-0666

A newcomer. As of the moment, it offers as authentically French a menu as you'll find in this city, intimacy in a small balconied room, beautiful appointments, and service (the waiters have been pirated from the best restaurants in the city; the busboys are so new to the United States they scarcely speak English). Fish—pompano, Dover sole, turbot and a half-dozen seafoods —are rapidly becoming the specialty here, though you'd be wise to specify Dover sole and pay a premium for it if necessary in the Fillet of Sole Veronique; the Veronique is exquisite, but what comes from American waters as sole does not do it justice. Meat-eaters will not be able to fault Le Carre d'Agneau aux Primeurs or the Chateaubriand, with its ruffles of tiny vegetables. The wine list is excellent; you are urged to take your time—and so you should, enjoying every moment of a restaurant that plays at least some recorded Bach as background music and prepares almost all dishes to order.

> Luncheon and dinner. A la carte only. Expensive. Closed Sunday.

CONTINENTAL

Like *trompe l'oeil,* most of the Continental restaurants in Chicago are interesting frauds. That is, the extent of their Continentalism lies in the single dimension of a printed menu gussied up in French or other European phrases. The results have been occasionally hilarious, like the following examples (from a restaurant with a fine French name): Chicken Livers Lyonnaise and La King

Crabe Miramar. The first is defined as "sauté with onions, wild rice," and the second as "Alaskan King Crab Legs wrapped in bacon and broiled." The French may know their onions, but the restaurateur who devised those glorious phrases doesn't know his—or the art of Carême, or native American grains and shellfish.

One authentically Continental restaurant was the Hartford Plaza **French Room.** A fire gutted it and the other restaurants in the Hartford Plaza Insurance Building, at 365 West Monroe (Wacker) CE 6-0971, in the spring of 1968; with luck, it will reopen by fall. Hopefully, it will be as fine as ever with Swiss-trained captains and Swiss gas carts wheeled to tables for final cooking, sautéing or flambéing of traditional dishes. The carts were new to Chicago when they were introduced in 1961 by maître d' Pierre Schmidt, who was lured to the Midwest from his position as assistant maître d' at the Four Seasons in New York. At the time he said, "Anyone can dim the lights and make a big flame. We do it for better food." He spoke truth. The French Room had the best Continental food in the downtown district for anyone willing to allow two hours for the preparation and consumption of a fine dinner.

> Luncheon, dinner in the French Room a la carte only, reasonable to expensive. Closed Sunday.

Sasha's, 914 Ernst (between Walton and Delaware, half block west of Michigan), SU 7-2183

Sasha's has innumerable things going for it, not the least of which is its owner, Alexander Vereschagin Sasha, a lusty, roaring host, a raconteur who slips from Russian to faultless English without a pause, sings at the top of his voice after 11 PM and does all the cooking for Wednesday luncheon, when a reservation is an absolute must.

With Louis Szathmáry of The Bakery, Sasha is Chicago's only other Maître Chef in the Confrérie de la Chain de Rôtisseurs (there probably aren't more than 16 U.S.A. Masters in the entire Society, which dates to 1248). His Wednesday lunches are basically indigenous Russian dishes—a classic beef-pickle soup, Siberian Rassole, such entrees as Beef Moussaka, Breast of Chicken Chablis, Lamb Shanks and Winekraut. Dinners are Continental Russe—the cuisine introduced into Russia when the grand dukes brought Parisian chefs to St. Petersburg and Moscow:* Duck Korniloff, fresh duck, roasted, dismembered, nested in a bed of winekraut, served with a Russian sauce; Chicken Kiev (the Muscovite version stuffed with pot cheese and chives); Beef Stroganoff, an authentic Molhovetz (the Escoffier of Russia) recipe.

---

* Ask Sasha to tell you about The Cuba, "the greatest restaurant in the world, sixteen master chefs, each earning 250,000 rubles per year, installed and supported by the grand dukes, who also paid a prix fixe of one hundred rubles for dinner ($50 U.S.) because the restaurant couldn't support those salaries; the ultimate of debauched restaurants—nothing like it before or since."

Hors d' oeuvres range from pots of domestic caviar to Beluga, and include meat-filled Piroshki. Soups include Borsch, hot or cold; entrées extend to lamb in several Continental Russe styles, steaks, shellfish and Firebird, a roasted Cornish game hen bathed in brandy. Desserts include Baklava and some flaming specialties. The coffees are marvelous. Decor is suitably dark and brooding, and the atmosphere pre-1917 Russia. Supper menu available after midnight.

A la carte only. Reasonable to expensive. Closed Sunday. No luncheon except Wednesday. Bar opens at 4:30 PM.

La Chaumiere, 1161 North Dearborn, MI 2-6654

French even to the traditional menu, hand-penned in purple ink. It was a first-rate Provençal charmer when it opened, but success went to management's head; though the food is still French and still fine, you'll have to put up with the kind of insane overcrowding that means the elbows of other diners at the tables on either side bumping yours, and their conversation intruding just as annoyingly.

Luncheon Monday through Friday, prix fixe $2.40 and $3.85. Dinner Monday through Saturday, prix fixe $8. Closed Sunday.

Should you phone for a reservation at La Chaumiere and it's suggested that, since all reservations are taken, you dine at management's new **La Brasserie de Strasbourg,** do not feel slighted—it will be an advantage. La Brasserie, in the North Park Hotel, 1936 North Clark (corner Armitage and Lincoln Park) WH 4-2232, is much larger, far pleasanter, and you won't feel rushed. Only warning you need here is to extract the promise, when you make your reservation, that you won't be seated at a table for two on the narrow balcony in the main dining room. It's central to heavy waiter traffic.

Onion soup, almost a meal in itself, comes in the deepest French casseroles this side of Provence; hors d'oeuvres include *souffle au fromage,* though because this is France-in-Chicago you'll have to pay a ridiculous price for it.

A request for the wine list produces a small textbook including maps and vintage charts for wines up to 1963 (one wonders why it stops there—the restaurant opened in June '67). Wines are rated on a scale of ten, from *useless* to *very great.* The restaurant stocks the five top categories, so you won't go wrong.

Dinner at $7.50 only, except for a few specialties somewhat higher.

Kungsholm, 100 East Ontario, WH 4-2700, once the proudest of Scandinavian restaurants. Since the restaurant no longer hews to the once-magnificent standards set by the original owner, it is not especially recommended except for its still beautiful decor and remarkable puppet opera (page 184).

Luncheon from $2.50. Dinners reasonable to expensive. Evening smorgasbord expensive. Closed Monday.

Seven Continents, Chicago-O'Hare International Airport, 686-6100

As a rule, airport restaurants are merely to sustain life or to conquer bore-dom. Seven Continents is an exception, and the best time to dine here is Saturday night, when air traffic is generally minimal and you're not forced into competition with travelers who have just 40 minutes between flights. (Tues-day is the next most leisurely night.)

Along with a lot of visual elegance, Seven Continents provides a sweeping view of airfield activity, and the menu (primarily Continental) expands a little on Saturday nights to include specialties that can't be rushed, flambées, for instance. However, whoever makes up the menu is eccentric—some evenings the choice of vegetable accompanying fish is turnips and boiled potatoes, and that's the entire choice. French bread is baked on the premises; so are elabo-rate desserts such as Meringue Glacé and Baked Antarctica.

Park in O'Hare's huge lot (four hours, 35¢) or stop at Valet Parking near the ramp leading to Arrivals and use its service ($1.75). Your waiter will phone for your car when you're ready to leave.

> Seven Continents is located behind a red and blue canopy on the Arrivals level between American Airlines and United. Luncheon, dinner to 9:30 week-nights, to 10:30 Saturday. Sunday, noon to 9 PM. A la carte only. Expensive.

Overrated is the word for a clutch of Near North Side restaurants with French names. Jacques, Mon Petit, Maison Lafite, Cafe La Tour, Cafe de Paris. Jacques and Cafe de Paris have little to recommend them. All suffer from ownership that attempts a vaguely Continental cuisine on a mass basis. Evi-dently the owners have found a success formula based on the old meat-and-potatoes theme: serve it in sophisticated surroundings at reasonable prices, and nobody will mind. For those who won't, the addresses are:

Jacques, 900 North Michigan, WH 4-4795

The famous garden is almost roofed over now, and the great old interior that looked like an Italian undertaking parlor has been redecorated—which is a pity. Lunch and dinner daily.

Mon Petit, The Churchill, 1255 North State, WH 4-1383

Smallest and handsomest of the group and the one with the best service. Dinner only. Closed Sunday and Monday.

Maison Lafite, The Churchill, 1255 North State, WH 4-1445

Across the hall from Mon Petit, a room of baronial dimensions. Closed Tuesday. Dinner only, on Sunday from 4 PM.

Cafe La Tour, Outer Drive East, 400 East Randolph, 527-1144

If you can get a window table, the view from this 40th floor restaurant is breathtaking. Luncheon, dinner, on Sunday from 4 PM.

Cafe de Paris, 1260 North Dearborn, WH 3-6080

If it hasn't been redecorated, its authentic 1920's interior can go a long way toward compensating for the food. Dinner only, on Sunday from 4 PM.

La Maisonette, 3445 Dempster, Skokie, 679-0444

Off the tourist beat and very comfortable. Via Edens Expressway, scarcely more than 20 minutes from the Loop. Luncheon, dinner. Closed Mondays.

SEAFOOD

The two great native fish from Lake Michigan, whitefish and trout, have been all but wiped out by lamprey infiltrating the lake via the St. Lawrence Seaway. If you see whitefish on a menu, be sure it's preceded by the magic words Lake Superior, for then the fish will indeed be superb. Otherwise, the fish was caught in Lake Huron and not worth ordering. The same is true of pike. Pike in these parts is pickerel unless it's specified as Walleyed Pike. Walleye is wonderful eating.

Visitors from coastal areas are advised to check with captains or waiters as to whether the selections they've made are fresh or frozen. There's a very real difference in flavor, and anyone who's been brought up on fresh catches, with their lingering taste of saltwater, isn't going to be happy with frozen finneys. Even oysters, lobsters, and shrimp flown in fresh in seaweed aren't quite the same, though they'll come as close as time and distance allow.

Cape Cod Room, Drake Hotel, 140 East Walton, SU 7-2200

An old Chicago favorite with a checked tablecloth, mounted-catch, fishnets-and-floats atmosphere that is the kind you wish you could find on the Cape but rarely do. Specialties of house are Bookbinder Red Snapper Soup, Steamed Whole Baby Lobster, Rocky Mountain Speckled Brook Trout flown in fresh each morning, and small catches of Lake Michigan Trout, when available, though, alas, not stuffed and baked in the classic manner. Resist the temptation to fill up on the crackers and rolls, even though the accompanying sweet butter is marvelous. The Cape Cod menu is extensive, and it's almost impossible to leave room for dessert. A small oyster bar within the restaurant offers a jolly time at noon.

Luncheon, dinner. A la carte only. Reasonable.

Note: If Cape Cod can't take your reservation, you can order from its menu in the hotel's Raleigh Room.

Nantucket Cove, 1000 North Lake Shore, WH 3-1600

A handsomely fashioned, new, beam-plank-and-antiques seafood establishment from the owners of Nantucket Cove in St. Louis. All seafood is flown in to be served fresh; trout swim lazily under the waterwheel in the entrance, waiting to be netted by you or your waiter; lobsters are really alive and fighting in saltwater that duplicates the ocean brine from which they came; and the oyster bar has the same varieties of clams and oysters you'd find along the Massachusetts coast.

Of the four dining rooms, Capt. Mendell's Cabin is the least pretentious and the room most reminiscent of Nantucket. Unadorned Block Island Swordfish is one of the best items on the menu; Yellowtail Snapper Veronique one of the poorest. The menu has some eccentricities. The rule of thumb for dining here is that the simpler the dish, the closer it is to its origins, and the better it's likely to be. For instance, all lobsters are steamed unless you request a different preparation. Desserts are rich and fantastically good.

Luncheon, Monday to Friday only. Dinner, all nights of the week. A la carte only. Expensive. Closed holidays.

L'Epuisette, 21 West Goethe, WH 4-2288

A small, handsome room of pickled and bleached woods and elegant murals. The fish and shellfish offered are generally well prepared, but their accompaniments leave much to be desired; for instance, you really don't expect creamed au gratin potatoes served with crabmeat-filled crepes. Furthermore, if you like fruit for dessert after fish, and melon is out of season, the captain will offer "grapefruit or fruit cocktail," which generally isn't what one has in mind. Dine here for surroundings more than anything else.

Dinner only. Closed Monday. Reasonable.

For excellent Filet of Sole with Tartar Sauce, any restaurant in the **Palmer House** on Friday—even the Coffee Shop.

For fine Finnan Haddie, the **Water Tower Inn** at noon on Friday.

For the best freshwater catfish to be had, see Creole House, page 45.

FAR EAST

This section is concerned with authentic Far East cuisine, not with Chinese-American restaurants, which you'll have no trouble finding on your own. The Chinese Restaurants advertise in all the hotel giveaway publications, and their gaudy neon signs make Wentworth Avenue between 21st Street and 24th Place South as bright as Old Town. With youngsters along, Chinatown probably is your best bet, since it also offers gift shops, a Chinese bakery, and enough peripheral sightseeing to occupy children for at least an hour or more. Otherwise, the following:

Don The Beachcomber, 101 East Walton, SU 7-8812

The most reliable and one of the finest Cantonese restaurants in the country, with waiters in No. One Boy uniforms, and a Polynesian island decor of complete charm. No restaurant will ever top the Beachcomber's Egg Roll (many a couple has made a full meal of appetizers alone—they're that good).

The Beachcomber was the first of its type and, as the original, sets the standard for fine Cantonese cuisine in sophisticated surroundings. Any further praise would be superfluous. Service is excellent; if you don't know what to order, trust your waiter's suggestions. Reservations absolutely essential except on the rare Sunday night when no conventions are scheduled for Monday. Stay away on Saturday night.

> Dinner only, to 1 AM week-nights, 2 AM Saturday. A la carte only. Closed Christmas and Thanksgiving. Moderate mainly, but drinks push up the tab considerably. Note: One of the restaurant's great customs is its suggestion that rather than tipping, you make cash donations in its boxes marked for special charities.

Kon-Tiki Ports, Sheraton-Chicago Hotel, 505 North Michigan, 527-4286

Travelers who know and love Japan will be enchanted with the little Tempura Bar that opens late in the afternoon in the Lanai Room, one of Kon-Tiki's ports of call. Voyagers who want exotic surroundings will be delighted with the spectacular Saigon Room (silk-paneled walls, tinkling fountain, antique statuary); the Macao Room (teak floors, inlaid mother-of-pearl ebony tables, heavy carved Oriental chairs); the Papeete (lush foliage, waterfall, idols); and the brass-rimmed hatches that serve as cocktail tables in Singapore Joe's Waterfront Tavern. Everywhere, the decor is beautiful and welcomes scrutiny. So does the menu, especially when you forsake the various international offerings for Cantonese and Indonesian specialties. Among the former, some of the best shrimp imaginable; for the latter, consult a captain, but insist the food be seasoned correctly—otherwise, because this is the Midwest, the kitchen may decide you'll be happier with Indonesian-American. You won't.

> Luncheon, dinner to 2 AM weekdays, Friday, Saturday to 4 AM. Open Sunday from 4 PM. A la carte only. Reasonable to expensive. Again, lavish rum drinks (of which a Mai Tai is one of the best) can run your tab up.

Dragon Inn, Glenwood Plaza, 18431 South Halsted (183rd Street), Glenwood, 756-3344

The only wholly Peking (North Chinese) restaurant between the coasts. The food is magnificent, and if you haven't discovered the difference between Mandarin and ubiquitous Cantonese, the drive to Dragon Inn is more than worthwhile. Mandarin cooking is an exquisite art, concerned with presentation of dishes as well as preparation; it's also much more varied and infinitely subtler—a cross-play of textures, colors, seasonings in ways that make most Western cooking taste heavy-handed.

The finest way to dine here is to call ahead a day or two and ask to have a dinner prepared for you. Miracles can be accomplished on a single day's notice if price is no object—two days brings the prices down considerably. Typically, you will get as starters three or four appetizers, including, perhaps, shrimp toast and sesame chicken (slender fingers of white meat dipped in batter and deep-fried)—the huge platters will be decorated with flowers, such as edible chrysanthemums that a chef has carved from abalone, each petal tipped with pressed egg yolk. When the Chinese couples dining at the next table turn to look at the dishes, you know each is special.

What follows might well be winter melon soup; delicate chicken breasts; pike filet with bamboo shoots and tomatoes; aga-aga, a Japanese seaweed salad; a thin-sliced beefsteak mushroom; Peking duck; eventually, a fantasy dessert of fresh pineapple and other fruits and litchi nuts flamed in brandy. All courses are open to discussion—anything you want, including sharks' fins, can be had—but you can leave everything to the owners with absolute confidence.

The owners, incidentally, are five North Chinese college graduates whose husbands are professional men (one physician, three Ph.D. scientists, one structural engineer). The wives, collectively known as the Dragon Ladies, are enchanting and, with persuasion, might be willing to take you through the kitchens where the chefs (none speak English) cook like madmen, tossing what they don't want on the floor, and the stir-frying is done in huge Mongolian copper chafing dishes over charcoal.

> Dinners and a la carte. From the menu, reasonable. To order in advance, a sliding scale (up from reasonable) depending upon the number in your party and the amount you're willing to pay. Items ordered in advance are never found on the menu. Luncheon, dinner, weekdays to 10 PM, weekends to midnight. Take Dan Ryan Expy to Tri-State Tollway, then to Halsted Street exit, continue south one mile to the Glenwood Shopping Plaza on left side of road.

For informal Chinese restaurants, page 63.

The two best-known, most decorative Japanese restaurants are Azuma House and Naka-No-Ya, both of which have now sacrificed tradition for popularity. Midwesterners, unfamiliar with the delicate, mannered dining traditions of the Japanese, failed to appreciate them; the restaurants, in turn, no longer insist that their waitresses maintain the paced rituals of at-table hibachi cooking and serving. The food is still good, the menus are ample, but what's missing is the very thing one went there to get in the first place—the pace and flavor of the best of another way of life. They're also overpriced. **Azuma House** is located at 5120 North Broadway, LO 1-2448; **Naka-No-Ya** at 2100 North Lincoln Park West, LA 5-4567. The latter is also open for lunch.

Far more interesting is **Senba,** a relatively new restaurant catering to Japanese patrons. Senba serves the best and most varied kinds of *sushi* in town (raw fish filets to be dipped in soya sauce). Its soups are excellent (stir with your chopsticks before drinking so that the seasonings and bits of meat and vegetables rise from the bottom of their lacquer bowls). The tempura is fine, and the menu abounds in various teriyaki, sukiyaki and noodle dishes. There's a bar and a *sushi* bar, and you'll be waited on by one of the prettiest kimono-clad young women in town. Senba is implausibly located behind a bead-and-bamboo-curtained doorway in the Granada Hotel, 525 West Arlington Place, LA 8-1200, and it's unpretentious—oilcloth tablecloths, for example, but always fresh flowers on top. Customer parking at the Lincoln Park Ritz Garage, 2427 North Clark Street. The hotel, a vintage residential establishment, has a tranquil garden off the main lobby that you'll enjoy.

Open nightly. Moderate.

PRIVATE SUPPER CLUBS—BIG ON LUNCH

These are clubs solely for expensive (and often expense-account) dining, with memberships held by men all over the country. Entry is always possible through your banker, who may be a member, or a banker or businessman in Chicago whom you know. (You pay cash in these circumstances.) Lunch hours are apt to be long and liquor-laden; dinners can consume the better part of an evening. Since membership has little to do with social pedigree, it's not only all right but desirable for women to look chic.

Key Club, 150 East Ontario, WH 4-2880. The first of the supper clubs; in the 1930's, one of the most social and socialite places in the city. It still swings, and the food is fine.

Barclay, Ltd., 906 North Huguelet, SU 7-7281. Situated in a converted two-story town house in an alley—so you know it's good.

Boyar, 58 East Delaware, SU 7-6005. Even smaller than Barclay, and just as well-known a hideaway.

International Club, Drake Hotel, 140 East Walton, SU 7-2200. Famous for its beef and chops. You may select your own if you wish, but it's not necessary since no one has anything but praise for the chef's choices.

Whitehall Club, Whitehall Hotel, 105 East Delaware, WH 4-6300. The finest French and Continental dining in Chicago. With Lutece, New York, the only other American restaurant to be included in the exclusive little Paris annual, *Passeporte Gastronomique—Les Restaurants Traditions et Qualite de France et de l'Etranger*. Men only at luncheon.

Several dozen clubs are run for members who share a profession or a national background. Accept all invitations to the Bar Association; the Swedish Engineers Society of Chicago in a fantastic old Chicago home on Wrightwood, where a St. Lucia feast is held on December 16 that is smorgasbord with all the stops pulled out; or the Swedish Club of Chicago on North LaSalle Street. Chicago Press Club has reciprocal arrangements with the Overseas Press Club of New York and other press clubs around the country. Use it for drinks only—the bar has a fine view of the lakefront.

WHERE CHICAGOANS EAT

3

Fine American Food
Steak Houses
Adventures
Quick, Reasonable Lunch in the Loop
Quick Lunches in North Michigan Avenue Area
Restaurants That Go Out of Their Way for Children
All-Time Great Hamburger and Barbecue Spots
Sunday Brunch on the Near North Side
Sunday Brunch Elsewhere

CHAPTER 3

WHERE CHICAGOANS EAT

The difference between places to eat and places to dine is not a snobbish difference but merely has to do with formality or time. Most of the restaurants in the preceding chapter are quite formal, specialize in cooking to order, and expect you to spend the better part of the evening on the premises. The restaurants in this chapter can get you in and out before half the night is over and are often shirtsleeves-informal. The symbol (*F*) indicates places children will not be out of place.

Price categories are the same as in the preceding chapter:
Expensive. Dinner from $8 to $10 per person or higher, exclusive of cocktails, wines, tips.
Reasonable. Dinner is in the $4.50 to $7.50 range.
Moderate. Dinner is under $5.

FINE AMERICAN FOOD

English Room, Pearson Hotel, 190 East Pearson (Seneca), SU 7-8200

A small English gentry room—walnut paneled, properly faded chintz, dark wood tables, leather-upholstered brass-studded armchairs, and a fireplace so large that if management burned the baronial-size logs it could accept, guests would be roasted right out of the room. Happily, roasting is confined to entrées, and the fireplace merely sports a cut-glass fire log. The room features American grill dining at its best—fish, fowl, steaks, chops, excellent roast beef and, at luncheon, a few specialties, such as chicken a la king. Always available: the biggest and finest shrimp cocktail in Chicago and the restaurant's hallmark, trays of hot English muffins slathered in butter.

Luncheon, dinner. Reservations essential. Moderate. Open daily.

Harlequin Room, Playboy Building (ex-Palmolive), 919 North Michigan, DE 7-0606

The Palmolive Building has so recently become the Playboy Building that it's hard to tell whether the Harlequin Room restaurant will maintain its dignity or change to accommodate the Bunny Empire editors, art directors and secretaries who are already jamming its bar. At the moment, it's still a gracious restaurant with deft waitresses, excellent American-Continental food and a good wine cellar.

Luncheon Monday through Friday only. Dinner and a la carte Monday through Saturday to 9 PM week-nights, Friday and Saturday to 10 PM. Closed Sunday. Moderate to reasonable.

Harvey House Grill (F) across the lobby is an informal room offering charcoal-grilled specialties, marvelous waitresses and *Playboy* magazine personnel six deep at the bar.

Luncheon, dinner to 10:30 PM. Moderate.

Raleigh Room (F), Drake Hotel, 140 East Walton (Michigan), SU 7-2200

A fine hotel restaurant with carefully prepared food. Friday night features a shore dinner; Sunday, a buffet.

Open daily and holidays. Reasonable.

Stouffer's Restaurants (F), The chain that's nationally known for its fine drinks, extra-dry martinis and special children's menus, in that order. All Stouffer restaurants are closed Sunday:

Top of the Rock, Prudential Plaza, 120 East Randolph, MI 2-7676. It offers a marvelous view of the city and a more adventuresome menu than one usually associates with the chain. A number of ad men from agencies in the building eat in it regularly, and one of them sums up the atmosphere as follows: "You wouldn't think of getting drunk here—it would be an insult to the waitresses."

Luncheon, dinner, late supper. Reservations essential. To midnight Monday through Thursday, Friday and Saturday to 1 AM. Reasonable.

Gibraltar Room, same building. The appointments are beautiful, and dining is by candlelight. Luncheon, dinner to 9 PM. Reasonable. Breakfast also available at Stouffer's **Beaubien,** on the lower level, same building, 7:30 AM to 11 AM.

Stouffer's in the Loop, Randolph at Wabash, ST 2-3711 (has a separate men's dining room); also at 24 West Madison, FR 2-7156.

Barney's Market Club (F), 741 West Randolph, AN 3-9795

No restaurant could be more American. Barney's atmosphere is as boisterous and informal as reputation has it. The steaks, prime rib, live-broiled lobster, casserole dishes and various entrées are first-rate; portions are huge (a side order of French fries will swamp you); and if you want to sing along with the pianist, you do, encouraged by the management. The tradition of greeting every customer with the title *Senator* dates to the restaurant's origins in 1910 behind the Polk Street railroad station. Washington-bound politicians between trains were frequent customers, but because owner Barney Kessel couldn't remember names, he adopted the greeting, "Yes sir, Senator, how many?" The pols were pleased, the non-pols flattered, and that's how traditions are born.

Luncheon, dinner. Also a la carte. Reservations essential. Reasonable to expensive. Monday-Thursday, 11 AM to midnight; Friday and Saturday to 1 AM; Sunday, 4 PM to midnight.

Bull n' Bear, 315 South LaSalle, 939-0945

A typical Chicago financial district spot not known to tourists, who will find it convenient to a walking tour of the Loop. The place is big on London broil, steaks and seafood. Lower level is men only at noon except on the day before a holiday.

Luncheon, dinner to 10 PM weekdays. Closed weekends. Reasonable. Reservations at noon a necessity.

Cafe Bohemia, 138 South Clinton (Adams), AN 3-8310

When owner Jim Janek's stepfather opened Cafe Bohemia 30-some years ago, he regularly supplemented the menu with game he shot in season. Today the restaurant is famous for its year-round selection of elk, moose, venison, broiled bear steaks and chops, buffalo steaks and buffalo burgers, braised African hippopotamus strip steaks, roast native beaver (three-hour notice), pheasant, roast mallard duck (three-hour notice), whale steaks, deep-sea turtle, northern Arctic char.

Bear is gamey. Buffalo coarser than beef. Beaver is best described as somewhere between roast pork and roast duck, but it's also been described as "Now you know how the Indians ate, and nobody's ever claimed they ate well." Hippopotamus won't put Wrigley out of business, but it's a good chew for your money. Char is similar to whitefish, comes in under the auspices of the Canadian government during a short 30-day season. The catch is limited; Canada uses the proceeds to further Eskimo education—which makes char the most worthy item on the menu, if you want to look at it that way.

Another house specialty: half a well-roasted domestic duck served with an enormous dumpling and wild rice. Steaks and chops are cut extra-thick. All portions are enormous. There's even a 60-oz. porterhouse that Yogi Berra eats without difficulty.

The crowd is interesting—a mixture of pols and sports figures, truck drivers, trainmen, jazz musicians and hockey fans. No reservations are accepted for two, so couples should expect to wait at the bar, which isn't a hardship, since the drinks are as big as the portions, and a request for a Gibson on the rocks produces a tankard and a jigger of cocktail onions.

Luncheon, dinner and a la carte. Reservations mandatory except at lunch on Saturday—the one time when you can walk in and be seated instantly. Closed Sunday and holidays. Reasonable.

Gold Lion, Union Station, South Clinton and West Jackson, ST 2-6722

An elegant-looking restaurant in the same neighborhood as Cafe Bohemia —red and brass against a background of mahogany paneling. Noted for its champagne dinner (reasonable), which includes a complimentary service of French champagne or sparkling Burgundy. Standard entrées—beef, fowl, lobster tails and lamb chops. Very convenient to the Opera House and the Civic Theatre.

Luncheon, dinner to 8:30 PM week-nights, 10 PM weekends and holidays.

Pinnacle, Holiday Inn, 644 North Lake Shore Drive, WH 3-9200

A split-level room with a slowly revolving elevated central section that gives diners a 360°-view of the city, the kitchens and the waiters, anxiously trying to find tables which aren't where they were when the orders were taken. As if this weren't enough, the room is decorated in Flamboyant Motel, but the table appointments are good-looking. If souvenir hunters haven't decimated the collection, this is the only restaurant in Chicago that considers a pepper mill per table standard equipment. Chops, steaks, fowl, seafood mainly, along with a few specialties, such as calves' liver. A good place when the convention load is light.

Luncheon, dinner, late supper. Open daily to 12:30 AM, Friday and Saturday to 1:30 AM. Dinners on the high end of reasonable.

Mayor's Row (F), 131 North Dearborn, 332-0224

A restaurant that has a lot of fun perpetuating old Chicago history, especially the image of its wild, wide-open gangster days. The decor is an improbable mélange: pictures of Chicago mayors, violin cases containing automatics, a machine gun over the piano in the Speak-Easy Lounge, the city's first voting machine, Egyptian murals from the Columbian Exposition, old sheet music adorning some of the walls. Among several dining rooms, The Levee, with dinners at reasonable prices, and the Mayor Edward J. Kelly Thrifty Thirties Room, with nickel beer, nickel cigars and a $1 blue plate special, such as corned beef and cabbage. The bar is a good spot for lunch—big sandwiches at $1.50. Because of proximity to theatres and hard-ticket (reserved-seat) movie houses, reservations are essential, although sometimes on a Saturday night you can walk right in.

Luncheon, dinner. Week-nights to 2 AM, Saturday to 3 AM. Closed Sunday and holidays.

The Cottage (F), 3147 North Clark (Belmont), WE 5-1557

An unpublicized hangout for professional athletes—players, coaches, referees of the Cubs, Bears, Blackhawks, plus major league ballplayers from visiting teams and avid "in" fans. The pros are protected in anonymity by Cottage owner Fred Hattenberger, who has refused to let articles on the place appear simply because he doesn't want his customers badgered by requests for autographs or invitations to "have a drink on us." Mr. Hattenberger has monumental respect for training rules, never pushes drinks, consumes only coffee (to set a good example), and would far rather see all his customers lost in conversation than in liquor—which almost all of them are.

Even in this sports-minded city it's hard to think of another place where you'll hear more conversation on a single subject. The atmosphere is equally single-minded: photographs of the greats line the walls, and sports memorabilia is everywhere, from signed baseball bats and hockey sticks to caps and footballs, even a home plate autographed by the Cubs in 1955.

The menu is wholesome American, ranging from hamburgers to Lobster Newburg. Prices are geared to accommodate pro players' daily meal allowance of $12.50. Highest a la carte item is $4.50; all other prices are well below.

> Open 3:30 PM to 2 A.M. Closed Monday and holidays. A madhouse after any of the Bears' games, when players and fans flood the place.

22 East, 22 East Jackson, WE 9-8543

One of the most interesting little restaurants in the Loop, the only remaining building of the few that survived the Chicago Fire in the downtown district. This one was the Henry Horner stable,* and its total floor space is consumed in an area 20' x 20', which allows room for just six tables and a bar on the main floor and ten tables in the room at the head of the narrow flight of stairs leading to the second floor. For years following the Fire, it was Abson's English Chop House, one of the city's best-known gathering places for bon vivants. Today, an advertising crowd jams it at noon, making it all but impossible to get in at conventional lunch hours. Try breakfast or supper instead. The smallish evening menu is a surprise—French and Italian dishes dominate. The breakfast menu is just four items: French Toast, with the proper accessories; Creamed Eggs and Beef on Baking Powder Biscuits; Ham- or Bacon-Stuffed Crepes; Eggs Benedict. With fresh fruits or juice and coffee, from $1.95.

> Monday to Friday, 8 AM to 11 PM. A la carte only. Reasonable. Dinner, $4.50 minimum.

Governor's Table, 3106 South Halsted, VI 2-2253

On Halsted Street, the old Bridgeport section** of Chicago has become a

---

* Henry Horner was a grocer and flour merchant and grandfather of a later Illinois governor. He built the stable in 1863; his home was around the corner on Wabash.

** So called because the south branch of the Chicago River encircles it, and the only way in is via the bridges.

dreary area of warehouses, small manufacturing plants and weathered frame houses. The last thing you'd expect to find is a first-rate, tastefully decorated restaurant—which is precisely what Governor's Table is. In the main dining room, wood paneling, starchy white linens, candles and small winestands of demi-bottles of a Beaujolais, a Pouilly Fuissé, a Chablis, a Médoc and a rosé. Your choice of any one for $1.25.

The menu features Chicago Stock Yards steaks, a variety of fish, chops, chicken, and some of the finest barbecued Canadian baby back ribs to be found. Drinks are far more generous than at most places; import beers are on draft. Specialty a la carte items may be ordered as part of the gargantuan dinners, which include appetizers in unlimited amounts, soup, salad, breads baked on the premises, fantastically good hashed brown potatoes, and bowls of fresh-chopped scallions and a buttery cheese sauce for baked potatoes. If you can somehow save room for desserts, do. The ice cream is homemade, parfaits glisten under swirls of real whipped cream, coffee is excellent and a bowl of hard candies arrives to help finish the meal and you.

The restaurant has a dandy history behind it; ask Mr. John Mamatis, one of the owners.

> Luncheon, dinner. Open Monday through Friday and Sunday, 11 AM to 2 AM; Saturday 11 AM to 3 AM. Reservations essential on weekends. Night owl selections. Seven-course dinners and a la carte. Moderate. Free parking at Enco and Sinclair Service Stations. Closed holidays.

Creole House, 324 West Armitage (2000 north, just west of Clark), 348-8571

Behind the drapery-hung windows of a converted storefront, find a delightful little candlelit restaurant serving the best Creole and Deep South food this side of New Orleans. Partners Guy Cucci, Jr., (the genius in the kitchen) and Al Branch (he'll probably wait on you) are ex-musical comedy singers turned restaurateurs and admirably suited to the latter occupation.* Their specialties can quite honestly be described as marvelous—shrimp, chicken or Creole House Jambalaya, Fried Louisiana Prawns, Fried Chicken and Corn Fritters, Bayou Chili, Creole Gumbo, Shrimp Remoulade, and what must surely be the finest freshwater catfish in the country. The recipes are authentic; dishes are delivered piping hot; the simple accompaniments—hush puppies, made with beer to make them fluffier, for instance—are wholly satisfactory. Mr. Cucci also offers Peanut Soup, salad with an elegant oil and vinegar dressing that he mixes himself, and desserts he spends the morning baking—bourbonized Sweet Potato Pie, Pecan Pie, Chocolate Devil's Float, ice cream pies and so forth, served with coffee in honest coffee cups. Bring your own bottle.

---

* Mr. Branch was with Fred Waring for years, then branched out into musical comedy and musical reviews. The partners met when they toured the country in one of the last of the blackface acts. You might also ask Mr. Branch about the joke with the punch line, "No wonder you're cold, lad, you've kicked off all your dirt."

Open 5 PM to 10:30 PM weekdays, to 11:30 PM weekends. Reservations essential on weekends. Closed Monday. Moderate.

Town and Country, 5970 North Ridge (between Clark and Peterson), ED 4-5345

Big, noisy and always crowded with North Siders because the menu is good, solid American and the prices are right. Steaks are dressed in a butcher shop on the premises, and pastry comes from the restaurant's own bakery. (The retail shop is right here, too.)

Breakfast, luncheon, dinner, and a la carte. 7 AM to 1 AM weekdays, later on weekends. Moderate to reasonable. Free parking.

Court of the Lions, 6935 North Sheridan, 973-6600

A restaurant that also counters the dearth of good restaurants on the Far North Side of the city. Its specialty is open hearth broiling and fried chicken, but it offers other standard fare as well. A pianist supplies mood music.

Luncheon, dinner. Open daily. Moderate to reasonable. A la carte also available.

STEAK HOUSES

The truth about Chicago steak houses is that it's practically impossible to differentiate one from another. All are good, but almost none are outstanding. The trouble is their copycat adherence to a formula that has proved successful in the Midwest: a charcoal-broiled steak with a baked potato (mushy) and sour cream, rolls and a salad, served amid surroundings that are all too frequently the most overblown Edwardian trappings the decorator could find. However, the steak houses asterisked below are the ones in this city that blithely created their own image and retain a certain individuality.

Gene & Georgetti's Restaurant, (page 23)

Erie Cafe (F), 658 North Wells (Erie), WH 4-9101

Forty-some years old and delighted to be exactly what it is—an Italian restaurant that specializes in steaks and outstanding Italian food. The decor in the main dining room is mainly fake overgrown vineyard, but it's right for the Erie, and you wouldn't want it any other way. The beef is aged and it's good. A T-bone for one person is one-inch thick; for a couple, two inches thick; for three persons, three inches thick, and so on, up to a thickness of seven inches for seven persons.

Erie also offers excellent spaghettis, pastas, various veal and chicken dishes, and a sensational version of Coffee Diable prepared at your table: coffee, coffee beans, cinnamon stick, vanilla bean, Cointreau, brandy and orange curaçao, blazed. It's the creation of co-owner Ernie Fontana, and it's a great shame one can't get it on Sunday as a fortifier for a Bears' football game.

Jammed weekdays, but Saturday nights can be slow, and you can often get a reservation at the last minute.

Luncheon, dinner, a la carte. Reasonable. Closed Sunday and holidays.

Pete's Est! Est!! Est!!!, 535 North Wells, WH 4-1535

Another old establishment with one of the finest examples of extant Chicago camp—a gilded nude clutching a bunch of grapes. She's vintage early Busby Berkeley and stands on the bar. Steaks are aged, T-bones are available and the house specialty is cottage fries.

Luncheon Monday to Friday only. Dinner daily, on Saturday, 5 PM to 11:30 PM. Reservations required. Closed Sunday.

Little Embers, 1034 North Dearborn, MO 4-1458

A chic little room which serves only prime rib and filet mignon with excellent standard accompaniments. Reservations absolutely essential. The same management offers **Embers on Walton,** 67 East Walton, WH 4-1005, with a menu expanded to include a variety of steaks and seafood, and **Embers on the Park,** 2136 North Lincoln Park West, LI 9-6400.

Reasonable to expensive. Dinner and a la carte. Open 5 PM to 2 AM daily, except Embers on the Park, open 5 PM to 11 PM daily.

Al Farber's, Belden-Stratford Hotel, 2300 North Lincoln Park West, LA 5-7375

Two rooms here: Chateau le Boeuf, which serves only roast prime rib and prime T-bone steaks with suitable accessories; and the Steak Room, which offers a gamut of steaks, chops, broiled chicken, fish, and calves' liver. Both rooms serve some of the best beef in the city and offer good wines. The crowd is well-heeled and sedate and can afford the insane appetizer prices.

Entrée includes salad and potatoes. Everything else a la carte. In Chateau le Boeuf this takes you out of the reasonable category and into expensive. Open 5 PM to 2 AM. Closed Sunday.

Brass Bull (F), Sheraton-Chicago Hotel, 505 North Michigan, WH 4-4100

More than a steak house in the range of items it offers—chicken Maryland-style, for example, and roast rack of lamb.

Closed Sunday and holidays. Reasonable. Children's portions of house specialties (not steak), $2.75.

Don Roth's Blackhawk (F), 139 North Wabash, 726-0100

Everything is relative. In a small city in the South, this would be *the* place.

Open daily. Reasonable. Free parking sometimes—ask about it when you phone for a reservation.

Palmer's Steak House (F), Palmer House, 17 East Monroe, RA 6-7500

With typical Hilton grandissimo, the Steak House menu attempts to include all and therefore goes far beyond steak and prime rib. As in any Palmer

House restaurant, try to leave room for dessert, specifically the famous pre-Hilton Palmer House Chocolate Ice Cream, than which there is no finer.

Luncheon, dinner, late supper. A la carte only. Open daily. Reasonable.

Sirloin Room, Stock Yard Inn, 4178 South Halsted (just south of International Amphitheatre), YA 7-5580

Excellent beef. You can select and brand your own steak from an on-ice display of sirloins, entrecôte sirloins, tenderloins and double tenderloins. Steaks are served with good salads, half-loaves of sourdough bread, French-fried onion rings and beautifully baked potatoes. Drinks are good, service is good. Also at the inn, the Matador Room (menu and prices comparable to the Sirloin Room) and the Stockyards Grill.

Open daily. A la carte only. Reasonable. Free parking. (Drive through the brick pillars that flank the entrance to the stock yards and park in the lot. Have waiter validate your ticket.)

Alexander's Steak House, 3010 East 79th Street, SO 8-6555

The best-known steak house on the South Side, and the steaks, chops and ribs are good. So is the atmosphere—wood paneling, white tablecloths. Alexander's is well known for the special house salad dressing that people are always carting home in jars.

Moderate to reasonable. Open 11 AM to 2 AM daily.

Shabazz, 616 East 71st Street, 487-9800

A Black Muslim restaurant (you can't smoke) in a Negro neighborhood. Ultra-clean and very kind to everyone. Shabazz handles steaks magnificently and is famous across the country for its Bean Pie.

Tiger Steak Bar & Dining Room, 642 East 79th Street, 224-3513

The other superb Negro steak house in the city (all meats are dressed in the restaurant's own butcher shop by a butcher who works with the skill of a surgeon). The Tiger is big—cocktail lounge, dining room, char-grill and private dining room for top echelon businessmen and celebrities, such as Dick Gregory. The main room is a hangout for Negro newsmen.

Luncheon, dinner, a la carte. Open daily. Moderate.

ADVENTURES

The Chicago rule, never retreat from an unpretentious restaurant exterior, might well be repeated here. You're about to be introduced to a great many restaurants in old ethnic neighborhoods and on business streets, and most of them look terrible, especially on the outside.

British Restaurants

Atlantic Fish and Chips Shop *(F)*, 5614 West Chicago, 261-9349

Gingham-checked tablecloths and a row of artificial flowers planted single file above vintage cove lighting do their best to transform an old 1930's grill into a semblance of home. The food is cooked by two delightful Britishers, a man and a young girl, and the fish in Fish and Chips is the finest English cod that can be imported. Also offered: Pie and Peas, Irish Bacon, Irish Sausages, Sausage Rolls and Welsh Pasties, all of which are delicious. On weekends, an Old Country Grill is served from 10 AM—sausage, bacon, eggs, tomatoes, black pudding, tea; otherwise, hours are from 5 PM. Extremely moderate. Closed Monday. For other points of interest in the surrounding neighborhood (English, Irish, Scotch, Welsh), see page 355.

The best Irish restaurant in the city is a long way from an ethnic neighborhood, but a great deal more convenient as a result. It's **Tipperary Inn** at the Pick-Congress Hotel, 520 South Michigan, HA 7-3800, and it's authentic, right down to the cinnamon in Mary Flynn's Beef Stew, the whiteness of the gravy in Dublin Stew, the mixture of uncured ham, sauerkraut, onions, mushrooms, bacon and apples in Irish Hunter's Stew, and the Irish whiskey and spices that limber the capon in Cock-of-the-North. Two wonderful broths, ladled from cast iron pots by the colleens who serve you, butter in tubs and bread in nice fat loaves. Irish Harp beer and Guinness Stout on tap, Irish whiskeys and tankards of Half & Half or Black and Tan, and Irish Coffee, Whiskey Pie, Apple Puddeny Pie. The room is warm and pleasant and has the only air-conditioned fireplace in the city.

Luncheon, dinner. A la carte only. Moderate. Closed Sunday.

Alas, there are only a few Scotch dishes in the **Royal Scots Grill** in the same hotel.

Italian Restaurants

Italian restaurants in Chicago are informal and great fun, and if you include pizza parlors, there are hundreds of them. Most are run by first or second generation Calabrians, whose menus feature the pastas characteristic of Naples and the southern end of the boot—steaming dishes of spaghetti, mostaccioli, ravioli, with slow-simmered sauces redolent of tomatoes, oregano, garlic and laurel (bay leaf).

Harder to find are restaurants run by Italians from Tuscany, but if you're willing to venture, there are some simple, delightful spots that serve indigenous home cooking and, typically, treat their admirable pastas as side dishes to accompany meats, seafood, chicken.

Missing entirely are the kind of splendid establishment you'd visit in Florence, Milan or Rome; on the other hand, you can find some highly expressive Sicilian restaurants here that you couldn't find there. One of the best of these (in Old Town) is described on page 51. If you have a car and want to find others, take the Eisenhower Expressway west to Melrose Park, a suburb solidly Sicilian in places, and try any of the cafes along 25th Street or Broadway—you almost can't go wrong.

In the 2400 block on South Oakley (one block east of Western Avenue) find a small, wholly intact Tuscany neighborhood of old Chicago-style frame houses with high flights of stairs leading to entrances one floor above ground level and steep gabled roofs that look exactly like the kind a child draws.* Also, as a child might draw them, nicely spaced trees in tubs along the sidewalk—like the homes, apparently freshly painted each year.

Find on the block two restaurants that cater to the neighborhood (you may well be the only "foreigners" the night you come here); a supermarket filled with Italian specialties, including onions in seven different sizes; an Italian delicatessen (Amy's) that specializes in homemade sausage and *panetone, panforte* and Florentine candies; the Fontana Bros. Bakery, which is open all night and pleased to sell its various kinds of fresh-from-the-ovens bread at any hour; and:

Bruna's Cafe (F), 2424 South Oakley, VI 7-8875

Mrs. Bruna Cane (pronounced *cah'nay*, or call her Mama Bruna) and her late husband opened their small, spotless restaurant behind the barroom some 35 years ago. Mama Bruna does all the cooking; her daughter and two other young women tend bar and serve. Her minestrone is out of this world, and the temptation to make a meal of it is all but irresistible. Her Sunday specialty of Roast Chicken, with oregano and other herbs tucked under its wings, would take prizes in any chef's competition; so would her fresh spinach, with its subtle flavor of fine olive oil. Her pastas are delicious; her broiled red snapper, halibut and shrimp are fresh, not frozen; her Friday specialty is Calamari e Polenta (squid cooked in cornmeal); and on goes the menu with a variety of chicken and parmigiana dishes. Desserts include a plate of her home-baked cookies (on the house), fresh fruits, and *canonelli*. Her wines are imported from northern Italy and they're good.

Open daily 5 PM to 2 AM. A la carte only. Moderate.

Riccardo's Restaurant, 437 North Rush, WH 4-8815

Mr. Richard (Rick) Riccardo hasn't changed the decor an iota since his father's day, so the restaurant still has its pleasantly timeless atmosphere—strolling guitarist, accordianist and singing waiters—and the bar still swings under its famous Seven Lively Arts murals, each the work of a different artist, one of whom was Ivan Albright and another Aaron Bohrod.

---

* Old Chicago neighborhoods are filled with these houses; the second floor entrances came about generations ago when the city raised the streets to grade.

The menu is first-rate Piedmont and, in true Piedmontese fashion, begins to approach French food and Continental cuisine. The sauce for Chicken Riccardo, for instance, is very like a French white sauce of wine, lemon and mushrooms in which the chicken has been literally steeped. House specialties include Saltimbocca, Trippa alla Livornese, Lobster Fra Diavolo and Cannelloni (the meat-stuffed pasta, not to be confused with *canonelli,* the pistachio-flavored ricotta-cheese-filled pastry. A salad called Millefiore (one thousand flowers) is a luncheon delight—greens, shrimp, chicken, eggs, anchovies, tomatoes and more. The wine cellar offers both Italian and French selections; the espresso is good. On warm evenings the little sidewalk cafe is open for drinks.

Luncheon, dinner, a la carte. To 1 AM week-nights; Saturday to 3 AM. On Sunday, open at 4 PM. Moderate mainly.

Mama De Luca's Sicilian Specialties, 1612 North Sedgwick (North Avenue), 337-2223

There's only one way to eat here—by phoning at least one day in advance, making reservations for four or more, and asking the De Lucas to take care of the meal. Given such authority, the family—husbands, wives, cousins, and in-laws (Mama lives above the restaurant and supplies all the recipes)—will provide a feast. Mr. Pat De Luca, self-appointed host, will comb the wholesale market for fresh snails; fresh clams to be steamed or baked; *gardini,* a celery-like vegetable deep-fried in a glorious egg batter; fresh artichokes to be baked and stuffed, the stuffing tucked delicately between every leaf; finnochio (fennel); and cauliflower that will arrive at your table hot from the broiler. Along with these, fava beans in a delicate sauce, marvelous lasagna, Sicilian sausage broiled in lemon and butter sauce; *splendini,* a rolled and stuffed beef skewered and broiled. Figure about $6.50 per person and $2 for a pitcher of wine. Pay attention to your reservation hour—the De Lucas will, and the procession of dishes is timed to the hour you've reserved. Don't look for decor—this is a small, dark, paper napkin place. Do persuade Concrete Sammy, a young cousin who drives a cement mixer during the day, to bring out his guitar and sing songs of love, tragedy and simple joys.

Open 11 AM to 2 AM. Closed Monday and holidays.

Piccolo Mondo, 3517 Dempster, Skokie, 679-2993

Handsomest exterior of any Tuscany restaurant in the Chicago area and thoroughly pleasant interior decor. Piccolo Mondo offers the best Cannelloni alla Romano imaginable; fine Fritto Misto (chicken, veal, vegetables and fresh mushrooms dipped in eggs and flour and sautéed in olive oil), excellent Linguine with Clam Sauce; and an ingratiating list of Italian desserts, including Zabaglione, Italian cakes, melons, Biscuit Tortoni and more. A number of dishes, such as Linguine, are cooked to order and require a half-hour of patience. You might wait at the bar and make the acquaintance of Stoney, a bartender-raconteur who's equally at home in Italian or Yiddish. Pizza bread available in the bar at cocktail hour on Wednesday.

Luncheon, dinner to 10:30 PM weekdays, 11:30 weekends. Sandwiches, eggs and omelettes available after 10 PM. Closed Monday. Free parking.

Club el Bianco (F), 2747 West 63rd Street, RE 7-2662

Its name means Club of the White, and since it borders a Negro neighborhood, it makes its meaning clear. The room under the striped Armenian tent is the most colorful, its brick walls decorated with huge sombreros and strings of peppers and garlic, Christmas-tree lights strung in fake lemon trees, a fireplace-less mantle bearing two lamps and a clock, and a general air of festivity throughout.

What everyone comes for is the Fiesta Dinner, served family style. Borrow a family, if necessary, or come in a group of at least five or six. Otherwise, you'll miss the half of the show that consists of gargantuan offerings of everything—relishes, by the pound, bowl after bowl of different salads, a vast platter of appetizers, a tureen of minestrone, plate after plate of various meats and vegetables and side dishes of mostaccioli and lemon ice. Eventually, gorged beyond belief, you look up, only to be confronted by a cart bearing tubs of nuts and sweets. The price for overeating on this level is $7.50 per person.

Italian Village, 71 West Monroe, DE 2-7005

Actually three restaurants under one roof, each with its own kitchen and its own atmosphere, but still a total of 500 people dining at the same time. The Florentine Room is the most luxurious; a number of dishes are prepared on gas carts wheeled to your table, and the Italian wine cellar is the best in the city. Because of the restaurant's proximity to theatres, the first question you're asked is not if you'd like a drink but whether you're going to theatre—in which case, everything is timed accordingly. A la carte only. Expensive. Closed Sunday and holidays.

Upstairs the Village offers a huge multi-paged menu with almost every Italian dish you can name. During the Lyric season, it also offers the chance to see opera singers offstage. Mainly a la carte and moderate. Open every day but Christmas.

LaCantina (The Wine Cellar) is a grotto that hums busily during the week especially and is good for a quite late supper. Closed weekends and on holidays. All three restaurants serve lunch and dinner and all are a must.

Gennaro's Tavern, 1352 West Taylor, CH 3-1035

One of the smallest and finest Italian restaurants in the city, family owned and operated by the kind of family that puts up a sign announcing, "We will be closed ten days for our daughter's wedding—we hope you understand."

The menu informs you that the Gennaros do not serve precooked pastas, but cook them to order, and further, that Mrs. Gennaro makes the spaghetti, noodles, gnocchi, ravioli and manicotti fresh daily. Her manicotti, with its meat and cheese filling, is marvelous; her pizza dough is thin and crisp (two people cannot demolish a large pizza unless they haven't eaten in two days); her Chicken Vesuvio calls for lyrical descriptions. The service is a little haphazard, but that's to be expected in a restaurant that caters primarily to old friends—the liquor commissioners and cronies, pols, newsmen, news photographers, Chicago Blackhawks, Detroit Tigers (when they're in town) and so forth. Be sure to try the anchovy-cheese-salami salad, so bountiful that newcomers inevitably think it's the antipasto.

Lunch, dinner to 10:30 PM weekdays. Saturday, 5 PM to 12:30 AM; Sunday 5 PM to 10:30 PM. Closed Monday. Except for steaks, the lowest prices in town.

Seven Hills, 6025 North Lincoln, 743-4362

Quite possibly the best Italian restaurant in the city, run by a man who used to cook for Sinatra and the Pack in Miami. Regardless of what you order, its preparation demonstrates care and flair—where else in this city are you likely to find, every day of the week, Stuffed Mushrooms and Cold Fish Salad among the appetizers, or Shrimp Broiled with Olive Oil and Lemon, or Linguini with White or Red Clam Sauce? The restaurant is also one of the rare places that automatically includes fresh fruit and a tray of Italian cookies with dinner.

Moderate through reasonable. Open for dinner only, weekdays to 1 AM, Friday and Saturday to 2 AM, Sunday to midnight. Open on all holidays.

New Capri, 662 West Diversey, 549-0210, offers Chicago-Italian fare in robust portions at very moderate prices. Closed Monday. **Gino's East,** 160 East Superior, WH 3-1124, has fine pizza at the bar on the main floor; the restaurant upstairs can be overlooked, however. There's also a **Gino's** at 932 North Rush, 337-7726, and the pizza's just as good. The two most famous pizza parlors in the city are **Pizzeria Uno,** 29 East Ohio, WH 4-9555, and **Pizzeria Due,** 619 North Wabash, WH 3-2400. Uno is a tiny English basement establishment that's always jammed; Due is larger, noisier and okay for families with children.

Chicago is stuffed with pizza parlors—for those beyond the Near North Side, check the "Pizza" pages—four of them—in the Yellow Pages.

German, Austrian, Hungarian, Czech Restaurants

German restaurants divide into those that concentrate exclusively on what's coming out of the kitchens in the way of food and those that also offer entertainment. The entertainment is lowbrow, not cabaret, and generally consists of accordion players in lederhosen clowning about with madchen in Tyrolean costumes. If you like thigh-slapping horseplay and yodeling, try Johnnie Held's

Brown Bear (F), 6318 North Clark (Devon), 274-1200. Good food, entertainment nightly, and singing waiters on the weekend.* Make reservations for weekends.

Red Star Inn (F), 1528 North Clark, WH 4-9637, is a turn-of-the-century favorite with character of quite another kind, dignity. The menu is extensive—and as eccentric as the waiters, for it translates most of the German dishes but leaves you helpless in the face of Leberklosse with Spec Sauce, Konigsberger Klops with Caper Sauce and Zwiebelfleisch au Gratin (liver with bacon, meatballs, and meat with onions, in that order). The German chefs are famous for their Lentil Soup, Sauerbraten, Hoppelpoppel (eggs flipped with frankfurters, mushrooms, onions) and fantastic Apple Pancake. The old waiters are famous for pained expressions, as if their feet haven't stopped hurting in the last 30 years.

> Open 4 PM to midnight. Closed Christmas. A la carte only. Moderate mainly. Reservations recommended on Saturday.

Golden Ox (F), 1578 North Clybourn, MO 4-0780

An old-timer endangered by urban renewal; the area is badly in need of help. The Ox, however, is as *gemutlich* as ever; the old murals, scenes of German mythology, and cuckoo clocks, have been recently restored, and old patrons still flock to dine. Or, as one waitress says, "I'm waiting on people I diapered." The food is excellent and cooked to order; house specialties are indicated as such on the menu—Wiener Rostbraten (potted steak with mushrooms), Hasenpfeffer (in season), Kassler Rippchen with Burgundied Red Cabbage, and a range of German salads hard to find elsewhere. A little old lady from Bavaria makes all the strudel; if she's ill, you're out of luck, but the chocolate icebox cake is a fine, rich substitute. Zither music every night but Sunday by Martin Andreas, the man who recorded "The Third Man Theme" for the movie of the same name. The Golden Ox at the intersection of Archer and Kostner avenues is owned by the same management.

> Luncheon (jammed with executives from factories in the neighborhood) and dinner to midnight. Special family style dinners on all holidays. Moderate.

Schwaben-Stube (F), 3500 North Lincoln, DI 8-8856

A cheery little checked-tablecloth restaurant with a small but thoroughly satisfactory menu, marvelous lentil soup, fresh, juicy bratwurst sandwiches at

---

* A good middle-aged band, but odd instruments: accordion, violin, trombone, plus a lady who plays bass and also sings. The music is rousing drinking songs, marches and sentimental stuff; the trombone goes boom-boom for the marches, and the violin handles the hearts and flowers, and for only four instruments they make a lot of music. Brown Bear has an annual *Oktoberfest*, the place decorated with fall leaves and waiters running around in red or green Bavarian hunters' caps and lederhosen.

noon and, on weekends, succulent roast duck. Portions are enormous. It's the best possible place to lunch if you're touring the WGN television studios nearby. Soup, entree, beverage for a top of $1.55.

Luncheon, dinner to 2 AM week-nights, Saturday to 3 AM. Closed Monday. Mostly moderate.

Heidelberger Fass (*F*), 4300 North Lincoln, IR 8-2486

A spotless middle-class German restaurant with patterned tablecloths and china, fresh flowers, and buxom Bavarian waitresses. Cocktails get quite fancy and quite German—a dash of Asbach Uralt brandy in a Manhattan, for instance. The menu may drive you wild since it affects a continuous and silly use of the German preposition *mit* ("mit above orders we serve . . ."), but the food is good, especially the veal dishes and the Hackepeter Sandwich (steak tartare), and the atmosphere is relaxing. Special dishes for children and ginger ale cocktails for them on the house; imported draft and bottled beers by the glass, stein, schooner or two-litre *Krug;* also good German wines.

Luncheon, dinner, and a la carte. Moderate. Closed Tuesday.

Muenchner Hof, 3700 North Clark, BI 8-1624

It's a good place if you're going to a game at Wrigley Field since it's just north of Addison Street. It's also a good place for lunch on a snowy Saturday: simple, unaffected, family-run. German records on the jukebox; three imported beers on tap: Dortmunder DAB, Hofbrau Dark and Pschorr (a Munich favorite). Order a bratwurst sandwich and you'll get a platter of sliced sausage with hot potato salad and more rye bread than you can eat. Soups are homemade; there are seven kinds of herring; the rest of the lunch menu is other sausages and import cheese sandwiches. An interesting decoration here is a life preserver from the "Leabeth," a freighter out of Hamburg—the crew swiped it from the ship and presented it to the restaurant one night.

Luncheon, dinner served 11:30 AM to 1 AM. Bar open 11 AM daily; noon on Sunday.

Otto's, 7212 Washington, Forest Park, FO 6-0298

A fine place to go the day you tour Frank Lloyd Wright homes in Oak Park and River Forest, since all three suburbs are adjacent. Otto's has been in its location since 1890, and though it added American dishes over the years, it's still basically Teutonic—thüringer, boiled back ribs, pork shanks, schnitzels, roasts, stews, goulashes and the like.

Luncheon, dinner to 1 AM daily, to 10 PM Sunday. Moderate.

Schwarzwaldhaus, 8840 North Waukegan (Dempster and Route 43), Morton Grove, 965-3113

The best small German-Austrian restaurant in the entire Chicago area and well worth the drive for Chicagoans or suburbanites, who will lose their minds buying the German specialties in the adjoining meat and imports market. (See Black Forest Finer Foods, page 370). The menu is limited but outstanding, partly because the kitchens are set up for what the young Tschurtz family calls "small pot" cooking, and partly because all the sausages are made on the premises. Anna Tschurtz is head chef, and her soups are tremendous. Entrées include Wiener Schnitzel, Kassler Ribs, Bratwurst Dinner (the best bratwurst you'll ever eat unless your loyalties are to Sheboygan, Wis.); steaks at bargain prices—a 20-oz.T-bone at $3.25, a 12-oz. prime Delmonico at $3.

To visiting Austrians, Germans, Hungarians and Yugoslavs, Mr. Robert Tschurtz extends a special welcome in the form of lunch or dinner as guests of the restaurant; use your passport or visa for identification.

Lunch, dinner to 9 PM. Closed Monday. Bring your own liquor, beer or wine—half the suburb is dry.

Lutz's Continental Pastries and Candies, 2458 West Montrose, IR 8-7785

A spotless German pastry shop that expects you to eat at least some of the goodies on the premises and therefore provides a tasteful small cafe and, in pleasant weather, an outdoor garden cafe behind the store. The garden is charming—two stately camellia trees, ivy-clad walls, a tinkling cherub fountain, pots of red geraniums, a tiny forest of pine and evergreens, and a rose garden encircling a fruit tree.

On the menu: soups, several kinds of open-face sandwiches, the prettiest ice cream desserts in the city, an assortment of rich butter cakes and coffee cakes, whipped cream pastries and that Viennese glory, Kaffee mit Schlagsahne. Also, imported beers, wine, and champagne in the small bottles Europeans call *piccolos* (the size you'd order for breakfast—just enough to get your mouth cold).

Absolutely mobbed with European customers on Sundays, so the place won't take reservations then. Bakery open 6:30 AM to 10 PM. Cafe and garden, 11 AM to 10 PM. Closed Mondays and holidays. Moderate.

Hunter's Horn, 3410 North Clark, 935-5313

Finest Hungarian restaurant in the city, with food and atmosphere that's best described as *igazi.** It's very *igazi;* the kind of place where you want to dine slowly and, in fact, are expected to do so. Dinners begin with a delicious liver appetizer, followed by homemade soup—perhaps Potato Soup with Sour Cream, Paprika and Chives served from a large tureen lovingly tucked in the waiter's arm. Salad with a typical Hungarian vinegar dressing—clear, light, slightly sweet; then crisp Roast Duckling with Cherries, or Hunter's Stew, or Veal Tokány, or Hortobagyi Rostelyos (steak), or Sautéed Turbot, all with vegetables and edible garnishes. Finally, desserts and coffee—every

* Genuine.

course delicious, and served so nicely that you want to come right back the next night. The crowd is mainly European intellectual, conversing with much animation and mirth in German or Hungarian.

> Dinner from 5 PM to 11 PM. Bring your own bottle. Closed Sunday and Monday. Moderate.

Epicurean, 316 South Wabash, WE 9-2190

Good everyday Hungarian food in the Loop—Stuffed Cabbage, Beef Goulash, Hungarian Thuringer, Chicken Paprikash with Spaetzles, Sauerbraten, Székély Goulash, and a taster platter of three of the above for people who can't make up their minds. There's none of the lovely European charm of the Hunter's Horn—the place is far too crowded for that, the tables too close, the diners (all of whom seem to be going on to theatre or Orchestra Hall) in too much of a hurry. But the entrées and desserts (blintzes, filled pancakes, strudels) can't be faulted; the crowd, if noisy, is also convivial; the prices are right.

> Luncheon, dinner to 9:30 week-nights, to midnight Saturday. Closed Sunday. Moderate.

Golden Prague (F), 2727 North Clark, 525-4111

Authentic Czechoslovakian food in which every dish has a subtle flavor of its own. Among the specialties: Svickova (pickled beef tenderloin), Game Hen with Apple Dressing (excellent) and, in season, Leg of Venison with a Madeira sauce that puts most wine sauces to shame. Genuine Czechoslovakian pilsners.

> Dinner from 2 PM Sunday, from 5 PM Monday through Saturday. Moderate mainly.

Swedish Restaurants

Ann Sather's (F), 925 West Belmont, DI 8-2378

Ann Sather's Swedish Meatballs are the best in the city; so are her fresh-baked breads and pies. She runs an immaculate neighborhood restaurant with neighborhood prices—the highest item on the dinner menu is Roast Beef at $2.80. *Lutfisk* from Thanksgiving through January. No liquor, and not the place to bring your own.

> Luncheon, dinner to 8 PM daily. Closed holidays.

Villa Sweden (F), 5207 North Clark, ED 4-1883

In the heart of Andersonville, a Swedish community (page 358), and the favorite family restaurant in the area. A simple smorgasbord is offered Thursday evening, Friday at noon, and all day Sunday. For children, special dinners and special smorgasbord at $1.50. No liquor, but all the good strong coffee you want, and the entire Andersonville area to browse in afterwards.

> Luncheon, dinner daily to 8:30 PM. Moderate. Reservations essential.

Svea, 5236 North Clark, 784-9539

An informal little eatery run by the Engstroms primarily for Andersonville's working class who want Swedish home cooking without having to dress up. Thursday specialty is Yellow Pea Soup; Friday, Salmon Loaf with Egg Sauce. At Christmas, *Lutfisk* and a free mug of *glogg* to everyone who comes in. Swedish pancakes any hour of the day. Sandwiches and coffee to go.

Open 5:30 AM to 8 PM. Closed Sunday and holidays. Most moderate.

Wholly Ethnic Adventures

Istanbul (*F*), 2619 North Clark, WE 5-3100

There are only 230 Turks in Chicago, so Mr. George C. Lukidis runs his restaurant for Americans and has softened the seasonings in certain dishes accordingly. His food is delicious: Tarma, a fine appetizer of red caviar whipped with olive oil and fresh lemon juice; Shish Kofte, marinated ground sirloin of beef that arrives in small, finger-length pieces; Tass Kebab, Turkish goulash seasoned with oregano; Chopped Kebab, ground sirloin of beef seasoned with cinnamon, mixed with pine nuts and currants and snuggled inside *phyllo* leaves; Eggplant Iman Bayildi (baked with good olive oil). You'll have a fine time working your way through the menu and ending with Turkish coffee and Baklava or Kadarif for dessert. Decor is authentic—all the antiques and silver filigree work came from Mr. Lukidis' family home. Free parking at Wrightwood Garage, 2569 N. Clark.

Open daily and Sunday, 5 PM to midnight. A la carte only. Moderate, mainly.

Casbah (*F*), 514 West Diversey, WE 5-7570

You ought to read *The Forty Days of Musa Dagh* before coming here, but if you can't, the meal will send you away eager to grab a copy. Proprietors Mr. and Mrs. Varousan Vartanian are Armenians born in Syria, and their cooking is a nice commingling of the two once-warring cultures: thick Pita Bread to be dipped into various appetizers; Lahmejun, an Armenian version of pizza; Egg-Lemon Soup; lamb and beef entrees, including Shish-kabab; and a rich Syrian version of Baklava for dessert. Prices are moderate, and reservations essential on weekends, when it's packed with a young crowd. Free parking in Stop & Save parking lot across the street and at Rienzi Garage, 554 West Diversey.

The city's two best-known Greek restaurants offer *bazouki* bands, belly dancers, and singers along with the food, so you can easily make an evening out of a trip to **Hellas Cafe,** 340 South Halsted, 263-0767, or **Grecian Gardens,** 404 South Halsted, 263-9006. **Athens on Rush,** 940 North Rush, 337-3500, is the Rush Street tourist version of the same thing—and if you don't insist on authenticity, you'll enjoy it.

For a Greek restaurant for Grecian customers, try **Deligiannis Bros., Inc.,** 766 West Jackson (enter from Halsted), 782-9855, and find behind the grocery store a tiny vine-hung *tavernaki* of ten tables with one elderly gentleman to serve all. He loves conversation and, if he likes you, will give you a full course in Greek liquors and brandies. You might try Omega, a 40-year-old brandy that goes down like velvet but fires away inside for a long aftermath. To start a meal, order double ouzo. Proceed to Avgolemono Soup (lemon and egg); lamb, fish or chicken dishes, side orders of Pastichio (baked macaroni) and Spanakotiropeta (spinach in *phyllo* leaves—out of this world). If you've room for them, Greek pastries of all descriptions or a light custard called Creme Caramele. It's like dining in the hills behind Athens, and you'll remember it for a long time.

Luncheon, dinner. Moderate. Closed Sunday.

For a Yugoslavian meal, the **Belgrade,** 1443 North Milwaukee, HU 6-9270. The food reflects the influences of nearby countries (Stuffed Cabbage, Smoked Pork, Moussaka, Beef and Sausages Shish-kabab), plus a great native addiction to sweet peppers in everything they can legitimately be put in. Desserts are tortes, such as Dobosh, and coffee is Turkish. Belgrade is a storefront operation with wonderfully native decor—multitudes of fake roses and an ikon in a place of honor, wreathed in flickering Christmas-tree lights. Reasonable, spotless and friendly.

Nabil Scherief, an internationalist from Baghdad, combines a menu of authentic Middle East dishes with such outlanders as Tartar Dumpling Soup, Chicken Curry, Corned Beef on Rye and Lamed Jume, a sandwich he may have invented that consists of ground beef, red pepper, allspice and good fresh parsley served on unleavened Syrian bread. His entertainment is equally one-world: flamenco dancing nightly and, on weekends, a belly dancer. This totally improbable blend is at least as workable as the UN and is to be found in the **Red Fez Cafe,** 1959 West Lawrence, 784-9527.

Luncheon, dinner. Moderate.

Serbian Club, 1928 West Evergreen, HU 9-2860

Not much English spoken here and not much in the way of decor, either, but a club, nevertheless, for elderly Serbian gentlemen, who come in nightly. The food is their food: Pork Sausage, served with fresh chopped onion and tomatoes; veal on skewers, Musaka od Kromjura (a cousin to Greek moussaka, served with potatoes); Biftek; Kajmak (Serbian butter used as cheese); Becha Smela sa Garnirungom (wiener schnitzel); and Pljeskavica (hamburger). For dessert, Policinchika (filled pancakes) and Turkish coffee. The menu is printed entirely in Serbian, so either take this book along or be willing to work slowly with the waitress, who is charming but not as familiar with English as you. One item she can't translate, *Srpski.* Whatever it is, it costs only 40¢ and may be your only chance to see five consonants in a row that spell something. Reservations essential on weekends when the whole neighborhood piles in. It's a neighborhood saloon with a small restaurant, and it's hard to find. Look for the only Dab beer sign on the block; it's under that.

> Open weekdays to 10 PM, Friday to 11 PM, Sunday, noon to 9 PM. Moderate.

For Ukrainian peasant dishes, **Sophie's Ukrainian-American Restaurant,** 2132 West Chicago, AL 2-9625. It's a sparse little storefront place with Formica-topped tables, but you'll get Old World courtesy of the finest sort from the Old World owner—unless you ask him about his Russian dishes. That will bring on a tirade and a history lesson; despite territorial annexation, Ukrainians are as fiercely anti-Russian as ever. Get here fine homemade beet, cabbage or chicken soup, homemade potato dumplings, Ukrainian spareribs and the like.

> Open daily from noon to 10 PM, on weekends to midnight. Very moderate. No liquor.

Ponor's, 2301 West Chicago, EV 4-9892, is good for Ukrainian blintzes and cabbage rolls on Sunday and for American and Ukrainian dishes the rest of the week. A jukebox and a TV set fight it out in the bar (imported beers on draft), but the din isn't too awful in the restaurant behind. Again, very plain atmosphere. Moderate.

Latin American Beat

La Hacienda del Sol, 1945 North Sedgwick, MO 4-6812

A beautiful restaurant, with a tile floor, growing green plants, and carved stone fountain dripping water in the center of it all. It is owned and run by a young man, nephew of a Mexican senator, who brought north some magnificent Mexican antiques to be part of his hacienda. He also brought north the head chef of the International Club in Mexico City, who converted simple national dishes into more cosmopolitan specialties. On Thursdays, a mariachi band marches about—trumpets pure and piercing, bass guitar, violins, standard guitars, a singer—a band that puts the Tijuana Brass in second place. A strolling trio appears all other nights.

> Open 5 PM to 1 AM daily and Sunday. Saturday to 2 AM. A la carte only; moderate for the most part. Free parking in an open lot catercorner across the street.

Also across the street (it's a triple intersection formed by Armitage, Lincoln and Sedgwick) is **El Sarape,** 2024 North Clark, BU 1-9813. Sarape has none of the splendor of its neighbor but it offers superb Margaritas in the bar and a swinging Latin American dance band on weekends. Tourists rarely come here; hordes of Latin Americans do. From 11 PM to the 5 AM Saturday closing, you're lucky if you can squeeze in. Week-nights, the music is supplied by a jukebox stuffed with Latinized versions of North American folk, rock and show tunes. The menu is satisfactory Mexican, with Puerto Rican overtones. Dancing from the bar.

Open daily and holidays at 5 PM. A la carte only. Moderate. On band
nights, a minimum equivalent to two drinks per person.

Su Casa, 49 East Ontario (Wabash), WH 3-4041

Su Casa's Mexican-colonial decor is richly beautiful, and the prevailing motif, the Su Casa angel, is a contemporary design with enough character to support 300-year-old hand-carved doors, 17th-Century Mexican cupboards,
16th-Century ceiling-hung church bells, antique statues, two panels painted by
the fabled contemporary Mexican artist Orozco, and a bar mural studded with
semiprecious stones and pre-Columbian artifacts. Table linens are hand-embroidered, troubadours sing and strum nightly, conventioneers throng to the
place—which may explain the North American management's total disinterest
in the quality of the food. The restaurant is open for lunch and dinner but you'll
be happier if you go for drinks and atmosphere only.

Closed Sundays. Moderate.

Cafe Azteca, 210 West North, WH 4-9854

A storefront restaurant with a charming garden that opens the first warm
day of spring and stays open as long as the weather holds. Specialties indoors
and out are Steak Zapoteca, owner Federico Camacho's lilting marimba playing, and the annual Posado (page 437), a wonderful Old Town tradition.

Open 4 PM to 1 AM daily. Closed Monday and holidays. Moderate.

Cafe La Margarita, 868 North Wabash (Chestnut), 645-0120

A handsomely furnished English basement, the kind a Julie Christie type
would choose if she wanted to drag out all her past. Non-Christie types will like
it because it's warm, hospitable, happy, and offers a menu featuring 78 dishes
from all sections of Mexico. Come on a week-night if possible; otherwise, even
with a reservation, you may find yourself waiting outside to get in.

Luncheon, dinner, daily and holidays. Musicians every night but Monday. A la carte only. Moderate for the most part. Recipes of favorite dishes
available on request.

Mexico Taqueria, 1350 South Halsted, SE 3-9295

An authentic Mexican restaurant located in the heart of a Mexican neighborhood and catering to it. The food is hotter and spicier than at the preceding
restaurants, seasoned for Mexicans who believe that the best way to end an
evening of drinking is with a bowl of Menudo (pepper-hot soup), and the best
way to begin it is with Caldo de Res o Gallina, a soup with big chunks of beef
and vegetables. Tacos are a house specialty, and they're marvelous. If you want
tortillas made of corn, ask for them specifically, or you'll get them made of
flour. The place is pleasantly furnished, operates on a round-the-clock basis all
year, including holidays. No bar but food orders to go. Very inexpensive. Very
little English spoken by anyone, including the waitresses. No liquor.

For Mexican home cooking in a home with FM string quartet music in the background, **Joe's La Siesta** (F), 6201 North Caldwell, RO 3-9482. Señor J. Ramirez does the cooking, and his food has a pleasant regional difference since he's from Morelos. Enchiladas, for instance, have a light frosting of mole sauce under the cheese and onion topping, and Chili con Carne is diced pork tenderloin only, with seasonings. Be sure to ask for tortillas if you want them; otherwise, they're not forthcoming. No liquor, but a freezer of house specialties to buy and take home with you.

Closed Monday. Very moderate.

Liborio, 4005 North Broadway, 549-8723

A Cuban restaurant housed in one of the fancier storefronts. The hospitality is exceptional and the food authentic. A marvelous Paella is brought to table in a huge casserole; unlike the Spanish version, the rice base is dry. It's always cooked to order, takes 35 minutes to prepare, so phone ahead if you know it's one of the things you want. Arroz con Pollo takes the same length of time and should also be ordered ahead. The rest of a meal can be ordered on the premises. The menu is extensive, and though it helps if you read and speak Spanish, there's always a host about who can translate for you. Bring your own wine or beer. For cigar smokers: a case filled with cigars of Cuban tobacco planted in Honduras and made in Miami by Upmann.

Luncheon, dinners and a la carte seven days of the week. Also, Cuban sandwiches (two slices of French bread five inches thick and crammed with sweet ham, roast pork, cheese, mustard, butter—75¢). Everything else very moderate.

Soul Food

Soul Station: A place where the atmosphere resembles that of a Negro household and where the little extras done to food in a Negro home are carried out. The table silver may not match, but the food is unbeatable for its kind.

Gladys Holcomb's Home Cooking, 4527 South Indiana, 548-6848

A soul station with hot fresh cornbread always ready, fine ribs, chili, chitlings, hot biscuits at breakfast, grits with everything, and a menu catering totally to Negro preferences. A favorite place of Joe Williams. Open around the clock, and very moderate.

H & H Cafe, 125 East 51st Street, AT 5-5262

House specialty at this soul station is country-style steak. The rest of the menu is similar to Gladys'—ham hocks and greens, sweets, white beans and corn muffins with everything. Service can be eccentric, but it has never discouraged visiting celebrities, like Oscar Brown, who drop in regularly when in town.

Moderate. Open around the clock. Free parking.

Far East Ethnic

Lee's Canton Cafe, 2302 South Wentworth (Chinatown), CA 5-4838

The restaurant is the cleanest of places—the food some of the best to be found anywhere, with such delicacies as Steamed Whole Yellow Pike in a fresh ginger sauce; Triple Dragon (roast pork, white meat of chicken, lobster, mushrooms, vegetables); Chow Lone Harr (jumbo lobster in its shell); War Sui Gai (pressed chicken with almonds and a ham sauce). Not on the menu but available: Chow Ta and Em Sum, two fine appetizers; a steamed, crustless, meat-filled sweet that's served somewhat like a sandwich with sauce; and Young Chow War Mein, a kind of Chinese gumbo containing meat, chicken, fish, shrimp, lobster, noodles, vegetables—one large bowlful serves two generously.

> Open daily for lunch and dinner, to 2 AM weekdays, Friday and Saturday to 5 AM. No liquor. A la carte only. Very moderate.

Harry Moy's Fong Yuen Restaurant, 216 West 22nd Place (Chinatown), CA 5-1558

Harry Moy is from North China, and although his menu is essentially Cantonese, he always has a few North Chinese dishes on the menu, plus a few that aren't. His restaurant is nondescript, and it's not like dining at Dragon Inn, but the food is fine. Just ask for the North Chinese dishes available that night and you'll eat well, even though the Moys deplore the fact that the one North Chinese ingredient they can't get is the traditional chicken blood. You won't miss it.

Wing Yee's Chinese Chop Suey, 2556 North Clark, DI 8-9748, is the best Cantonese restaurant on the North Side; on weekends you have to fight your way in. Takeouts. It's closed Monday.

Ding Hoe Chop Suey, 105 West Division, 944-8433, is the best storefront Cantonese restaurant on the Near North Side. Closed Tuesday.

For Filipino food, the **Shanghai Restaurant,** 406 South Clark, 939-3766, where you'll have to insist you be given the Filipino menu because no one will at first believe you really want it. Even the young Chinese waiter who finally brings it is full of misgivings, convinced that Americans don't like Filipino food, but that if they do they "only like the Pansit; Bangdoong is no good for American people—too soft." He is not entirely correct in his judgment; Sotanghon (soft noodles) with Barbecued Pork and Shrimp is delicious. The menu is written in Tagalog with English translations, and you can make out well, even though almost none of the staff are accustomed to speaking English.

> Very moderate. Lunch and dinner on a seven-days-a-week basis.

Matsuya, 1122 North Clark, WH 4-8351

A storefront Japanese restaurant with excellent Beef Nabe, Teriyaki, Sushi and Sashimi. The place is a favorite with Japanese and Nisei, and for $1.45 you can come away absolutely stuffed. **Miyako,** 1152 North Clark, WH 4-8278, is another hole-in-the-wall, but it serves the very best Tempura of them all. Closed Wednesday.

Jewish Delicatessens

A good Jewish delicatessen is a joyous assault on your senses—a conflict of spicy aromas and noise, samplings and staccato verbal familiarities flying across the counter from proprietor to customers, countermen to customers and countermen to each other. Under the banter, a friendliness that includes every stranger so that the newcomer, forced to shout over the heads of those in front of him, "Where do I stand for phosphate?" may hear, "Listen, wherever you stand, you got a lucky spot," but a sweeping gesture will also point the way.

Braverman's Cafeteria & Restaurant (F), 1604 West Chicago, HA 1-3979

It's the only delicatessen in the city that processes and cures its own corned beef and pastrami, and it offers mountainous sandwiches of each or both combined on fresh rye, onion rolls or Kaiser rolls for 95¢. People don't believe proprietor Sam Braverman's claim of seven lean, absolutely fat-free ounces of meat in every sandwich until they watch him trim and build the sandwich, and even then they stare around until they're convinced that the same size sandwich is what the regulars get too. (It is.) Mr. Braverman doesn't believe in portion control and never will. ("I give away more tastings and think nothing of it than most people sell. We're running a live show here. If we're slow on an item, we give it away at the end of the evening. We have too many potato pancakes, we say, here, try one—no cost to you. If I had you at my home I couldn't treat you any better.")

Nor could he. Behind the steaming vats of homemade soups (chicken, matzo ball, kreplach); the mounds of fresh chopped chicken liver; the heaping plates of hot dishes; the generous side orders of kraut, cabbage, potato salad, cottage cheese and sour cream, potato pancakes with apple sauce or sour cream—there's Mr. Braverman's pride of ownership and respect for his customers. He runs the best short order house in town.

> Closed Sunday. Open 6:30 AM to 7:30 PM weekdays. Restaurant open for lunch only. Takeout orders, of course. Parking is a problem, but there's a city garage around the corner on Marshfield.

Ashkenaz Restaurant & Delicatessen, famous for its home-baked pastries and blintzes, is at 1432 West Morse, HO 5-5392.

Ricky's Restaurant, famous for its chocolate sodas, is at 3181 North Broadway, LI 9-3136. Neither of these places offers the same counter atmosphere, but they have a deli flair nevertheless.

QUICK, REASONABLE LUNCH IN THE LOOP

These places are above-average restaurants where you can get lunch in less than an hour at moderate prices. The symbol (C) indicates places that also have counter service.

Cafeteria and Gavel Room in the Civic Center. Open 8 AM to 4 PM Monday through Friday. Stews are the specialty in the Gavel Room, served from individual iron kettles.

Tynan's, 1 North LaSalle. A beef, fish, chop house in a club atmosphere. Good drinks and very good fish.

Bowl & Bottle, 71 East Jackson. A Fred Harvey restaurant in a most convenient location.

Men's Grill, Carson Pirie Scott & Co., State and Madison (Wabash entrance). Where the rising young executive eats before he's invited to join a private club. Very fast at noon and the food is good. It's on the 8th floor. Buffet and regular menus; also liquor. Women welcome on Saturday with male escorts.

Champlain (C), 54 East Monroe. The best short order restaurant in the Loop. Separate bar features Michelob draft beer at 25¢, is accordingly crammed with personnel from airline row.

Harding's Erin Room, 21 South Wabash. Small, dark, masculine, crowded. Arrive before noon or have a reservation.

Wieboldt's Men's Grill, State & Madison. Strong, masculine atmosphere, and enough regular patrons to make every Loop restaurant envious. Women welcome if accompanied by gentlemen. Monday through Friday only, except the five weeks before Christmas when it's open on Saturday, too.

Crane Restaurants (C), 75 East Washington and 69 West Washington. The first is at ground level at the corner of Michigan and the second is in the lower level of the Brunswick Building. Food is first-rate, salads fresh and crisp, everything served is attractive. New England specialties abound.

Bamboo Inn, 11 North Clark. Chinese food reached via a faintly mysterious stairway to the lower level. Any number of LaSalle Street lawyers swear by the place.

Pittsfield Building Coffee Shop (C), 55 East Washington. An exceptional coffee shop, always jammed. Chili is especially good, soups fine, sandwiches generous. All pies and pastries homemade and delicious.

O'Connell's (C), 141 South Wabash; 60 West Adams; 132 South Dearborn; 104 West Monroe. Clean, quick and first-rate.

QUICK LUNCHES IN NORTH MICHIGAN AVENUE AREA

Ink Well, 226 East Ontario, WH 4-8232. Lunches under $1. Thick roast beef and turkey sandwiches, good frankfurters served in baskets with potato chips. Actually, the place is mainly a bar, but management doesn't care if you don't drink at noon. Crowded with staff from a nearby textbook publishing house. Make a reservation; you'll never get in without one.

Imprint, 235 East Ontario. Same kind of place as Ink Well, same low prices, same small, dark atmosphere.

Knight Cap, 152 East Ontario. All you can eat for $1, which includes two draft beers or two soft drinks or one cocktail. Food is spread out on a table in the back of the small bar: spaghetti on Monday; franks and beans on Wednesday; sandwiches, salads, potato chips other weekdays.

Luncheonette at the Drake Hotel (C) (in the drug store), East Lake Shore Drive and North Michigan. Small, quick, cheerful.

Coq D'Or, Drake Hotel, East Lake Shore Drive and North Michigan. One-price luncheons ($2.50), plus some handsomely concocted sandwiches in the $2 range.

Musket & Henriksen, 123 East Oak. In the back of an excellent pharmacy find a first-rate lunchroom that stays open to midnight every night.

Brief Encounter (C), Michigan at the Bridge (SW corner). Run by the owners of London House, it gets its pastries from there.

Pick Restaurants in present Time-Life Building, 540 North Michigan. The lobby Courtyard is self-service for coffee and Danish pastries from 7:30 AM to 10:30 AM, hot meat sandwiches from 11 AM to 2 PM, cocktails from 4 PM to 6 PM. The lobby is the famous Holabird & Roche lobby described on page 114.

St. Regis Hotel, 516 North Clark. An "in" place with artists in the neighborhood and AMA and IBM people who long ago learned that the hotel's scruffy exterior conceals a restaurant that serves far-above-average food. The place specializes in lunch items you'd scarcely expect, considering the area—sautéed chicken livers and fresh mushrooms on rice, for instance, or a half cantaloupe stuffed with fruit salad and topped with sherbert. Also prime steaks at extremely modest prices.

O'Connell's, (C), 618 North Michigan. *The* short order house for advertising, marketing, public relations and editorial executives along this section of Michigan Avenue. Open 8 AM to 8 PM. Closed Sunday and holidays.

Streets of Paris Coffee Shop (C), Allerton Hotel, 701 North Michigan. The counter is always open; the cafeteria in back serves lunch from 11:30 AM to 2:30 PM and supper from 5:30 PM to 9 PM. Closed Sunday and holidays.

RESTAURANTS THAT GO OUT OF THEIR WAY FOR CHILDREN

Harding's Colonial Room, 21 South Wabash, ST 2-1133

The waitresses like children and let them know it. The management likes children, serves special ice cream on their behalf, and has a treasure chest on the premises which kids dip into on the way out. Lunch and dinner. Reservation at noon essential. Closed Sundays.

Mickelberry's Log Cabin, 2300 West 95th Street, BE 8-6400

A good place to eat if you're exploring the Southwest Side or the Palos Park Forest Preserves. Red-checked tablecloths in a log cabin setting, with Indian, frontier and Civil War mementoes everywhere. Special children's plate at $1.40; adult specialty is roast prime rib dinner at $3.25. Roast beef and chicken dinners family style on Tuesday nights. Reservations essential for Sunday brunch and Sunday dinner. Moderate.

Tast-E Hast-E Dog, 5446 North Milwaukee

It advertises a 35¢ meal in a bun and means it. The meal is prepared in a ramshackle yellow shack that had its origins in a 1946 one-man stand on wheels. Now, five perspiring young boys put the meal on the bun assembly-line style. The first plunks down a frankfurter, the others add in succession what amounts to a vast salad of shredded lettuce, sweet peppers, cucumbers, sliced tomatoes, pickle slices, pickle relish, mustard, onion and hot peppers. You can get Polish sausage done up the same way for 65¢. Corny signs kids love are plastered all over the place. There's also a jar of free plastic toys—two per kid. Open daily from 9:30 AM.

All **Burger Kings** are better-than-average drive-ins; the claim "Home of the Whopper" is true; a Whopper with everything piled on is literally a meal.

Red Balloon, 5960 Touhy, Niles, 647-9600; also at the intersection of Central, Mt. Prospect and Rand Roads in Des Plaines.

Short order spots that are extremely clean and attractive and wonderfully easygoing about exuberant kids. Free helium-filled balloons for all of them, good drinks for exhausted adults. Red Balloon, Niles, is convenient to the Edens Expressway, since Balloon is only a mile west of it by way of the Touhy Avenue exit.

Ivanhoe, 3000 North Clark, GR 2-2771

Good for children who are properly awed by its catacombs filled with the sounds of rattling chains, blasts of cold air, and nooks of old bones. The restaurant is very big on children's birthday parties at reasonable prices.

Golden Dinner Bell, 8520 Fernald, Morton Grove, YO 5-4546

It ought to hang up a sign saying, "good home cooking," because that's exactly what you get, served with little customs, Guy Lombardo background music and invented superstitions that have a lot of folksy charm. It's a cheerful place—a low board-and-batten affair painted dark barn red on the outside—and it gives you a tremendous amount of food for the money. Dinners are in the $3 and $4 range; lunches at a single price of $1.45. Sunday turkey dinner is a specialty, and every Christmas there's a cookie tree that's a kind of reward tree for good children. No liquor, but you're welcome to bring your own.

> Dempster turnoff from Edens Expy, west to Fernald, south two blocks. Closed Monday.

ALL-TIME GREAT HAMBURGER AND BARBECUE SPOTS

Hackney's (F), on Lake, 1514 East Lake, Glenview, PA 4-7171; on Harms Road, 1241 Harms, Glenview, PA 4-5577; at 241 South Milwaukee, Wheeling, 537-2100

Visitors usually head for Hackney's on Lake Street since it's bigger, newer and the waiting isn't as long. Regulars consist of people who look as if they dropped their garden tools and rushed over, sweat and all, so a rumpled, equally sweaty sightseer will feel very much at ease. Hackney's on Harms is the one that started the trend in the Chicago area for big hamburgers served on big slices of black bread. In summer, have your cocktails outdoors under beautiful old willow trees. Hackney's in Wheeling is the newest of the three. Luncheon, supper.

Glass Dome Hickory Pit, 2724 South Union, VI 2-7600

During political conventions at the Amphitheatre it's wild since it gets all the spillover. The rest of the time it's crowded with politicians of the 11th Ward and people who've discovered its excellent hickory-smoked ribs, French-fried chicken, fantastically good French fries, and hot, crusty French bread. The only thing not to order here is a martini; the bar caters to a crowd that eschews them.

> Because of the Stevenson Expy, the approach route is circular at best. Take Archer Avenue west to Halsted. Turn left to Union and left on Union two blocks. Monday through Friday, 11 AM to 8:30 PM; Saturday to 10 PM; Sunday, 3 PM to 8:30 PM. Takeout service available, but the problem is where to take it other than the stockyards.

Homestead (F), 12126 South Vincennes, Blue Island, FU 5-2570

Outstanding ribs cooked over hickory so pungent you can smell it a good two blocks away. Enough people think the Homestead is worth the long trip, and they consume 1½ tons of ribs here weekly, driving in from Skokie and beyond. It's not a fancy place, but it's comfortable, wood-paneled and friendly. Ribs are all back ribs. An order of them is $3 and a slab is $3.50; no woman could finish the slab. The waitresses are wonderful, especially Dorothy, who's been here 19 years. Have a birthday and they'll all line up and sing "Happy Happy to you." Also steaks and chicken dinners at moderate prices; a good bar.

Open every day but Monday from 5 PM to 12:30 AM. Sundays and holidays, 1 PM to 10:30 PM. Reservations not accepted, but there are take-outs. Dan Ryan Expy to Calumet Expy to 115th Street. West to Vincennes, then left to the restaurant. A new connecting throughway is under construction and may be open by the time you read this. Check your map.

Elliott's Kitchen, 534 West Garfield (55th Street), LI 8-2348

Famous old South Side spot for huge barbecued beef, ham and pork sandwiches with strong sauce; hefty hamburgers, good fried chicken and plates of doughnut holes for dessert. Elliott's is housed in an ancient once-white diner in a neighborhood that's even more dilapidated. Ignore everything but the food, which is first-rate.

Free parking. Orders to go. South Side delivery.

SUNDAY BRUNCH ON THE NEAR NORTH SIDE

At the following restaurants, brunch is served in urbane surroundings with a considerable degree of formality. Brunch hours are from noon to 3 PM. Because many Near North Side churchgoers have standing reservations, phone to make your own as early as you can.

English Room, Pearson Hotel, 190 East Pearson (Seneca), SU 7-8200. Specialties are superb Bloody Marys, Eggs Benedict, the lightest of French pancakes. Prices from $2.25 to $5.

Drake Hotel, 140 East Walton (Michigan), SU 7-2200. **Camellia House** specialty is Chicken with Sweetbreads Under Bell, and Chuck Cavallo's orchestra for dancing. From $3.75 up. **Raleigh Room** in the same hotel is a less formal room with an east view of the lakefront and a westward view to Michigan Avenue, below. Specialties are Creamed Chicken with Mushrooms and Beef Stroganoff with Wild Rice. $2.50 and $3.50 mainly.

Pump Room, Ambassador East Hotel, East Goethe and North State, SU 7-7200. Outstanding libations, nice ways with eggs, and the famous Pump Room Chicken Hash. $3.85 and up. Noon to 4 PM.

Whitehall Restaurant, Whitehall Hotel, 105 East Delaware, WH 4-6300. It's got even more Old Guard flavor after church on Sunday than the rest of the week (see page 22), but that, of course, is a major part of its charm. The food is splendid, from $2.50.

Coach and Four, Water Tower Inn, 800 North Michigan, WH 3-5600. Specialties are calves' liver, chops, corned beef hash. When you make your reservation, ask for a window table. The view is of Chicago's famous old castellated Water Tower and the Sunday strollers. Brunch prices mainly $3 and $4.

For casual Sunday breakfast in the atmosphere of the Near North Side as a residential neighborhood, try **O'Connell's,** 1031 North Rush. It's a gathering place for the area and has been famous for years for its scrambled eggs. **Musket & Henriksen,** 123 East Oak, 944-3001, is another good spot for informal Sunday breakfast. The young crowd swarms to **Melvin's!** 1116 North State.

For breakfast in Old Town, try the **Pickle Barrel,** 1423 North Wells, 664-6647.

SUNDAY BRUNCH ELSEWHERE

Fritzel's, 201 North State, AN 3-7100. The bar serves some notable morning bracers, and the brunch portions are up to the restaurant's usual ample style. Brunch prices start at $3.25. From 11 AM to 3 PM.

Try a Chinese breakfast at the **Chiam Restaurant,** 2323 South Wentworth (Chinatown), CA 5-6336. The Chiam operates without a printed breakfast menu, so tell Mr. Wong, the gentleman who greets you, that you want the Chinese breakfast. Your order will be given in rapid-fire Chinese to your serving boy, and, shortly, there will be set before you a number of dishes, the only recognizable one being the pot of tea. Though many items vary from one Sunday to the next, you can count on being served Dim Sum, a delicious broad noodle dough wrapped around chopped meat with raisins; Bow, an enormous, just-barely baked yeast pillow stuffed with barbecued beef or pork; Hai Kow, a chopped shrimp concoction in a gray gelatinous dough; Shaw Mine, tasty little meatballs and onions served on a bed of black mushrooms; Rice Cakes, thick slices of very sweet, sticky dough made from rice flour; and, if you're lucky, Curry Kow, curried beef baked in triangles of western-tasting dough (like a Chinese piroshki). All this, plus a dish of plum sauce (for dipping) and another of hot mustard, will run to $3.45 per couple. For the money, it's obviously one of the best bargains in town. Served Sunday only between 11 AM and 2 PM.

Morton's Steak House, 5555 South South Shore Drive, BU 8-7400, features moderately priced breakfast steaks, chops, eggs with chives, eggs with chicken livers, pancakes, and it serves from noon to 3 PM. **Surf and Surrey,** 4920 South Chicago Beach (50th Street at the lakefront), MI 3-4900, doesn't serve late breakfast or brunch, but lunch items and salad-sandwiches are attractive, and the bar is a good one. At the **Woodlawn Club,** 1315 East 79th Street (Kenwood near Sears Roebuck), BA 1-6223, on a cold Sunday on the South Side, you can get a hearty Swedish peasant breakfast. Helen Widen, the owner of this modest tavern, serves a filling, home-cooked breakfast of fried herring or fried salt pork, boiled potatoes in cream sauce, sautéed onions, hardtack and butter. All that, and Helen's hospitality, for 75¢.

WHERE THE ACTION IS

4

Cabaret Entertainment
Dinner Shows and/or Dancing
Dancing Only
Burlesque
Banjo Bands and Folk Singing
Jazz—The Renaissance
Big Bands
The Blues
Films—Art, Underground, Experimental and Classic
Old Town

CHAPTER 4

WHERE THE ACTION IS

> There is something you must do. You alone can stop your girls from going straight to the devil. You *must* make them stop smoking cigarettes.
>
> *Antitobacconist and temperance fighter*
> *Lucy Page Gaston to Minna Everleigh**

Back in the corset and bustle era Chicago was known as the Gomorrah of the West, a scandalously lawless town. The anonymous author of an 1893 guidebook was hypocritically aghast at the section of Clark Street called the Levee, which he denounced as "the great wallowing ground of the pet vices of Chicago—gambling, drinking, and licentiousness, thrust as all three are, to the notice of passengers, by open, flaunting sign."

Flaunting or not, entertainment in that era had elements of genuine grandness. The Everleigh Club was a sumptuous establishment, and its girls behaved, in all ways but one, like ladies. "Be polite," Miss Minna told them, "and forget what you are here for."

The Everleigh Club made no pretense about what it was—the most expensive, most lavishly furnished brothel in the world. The best the Playboy Club can offer are three floors of faintly suggestive atmosphere and a pastime that most people leave behind with their childhood "let's pretend."

As a matter of fact, the notion of "let's pretend" is indigenous to all the city's tourist traps. Places that advertise topless and bottomless waitresses or

---

* Miss Gaston was not unaware, but she was terribly naïve. She knew Miss Everleigh's girls were whores, but she was enough of a Chicagoan for it not to bother her. "Girls will be girls," she told Miss Minna.

acts are pretending that the flesh-colored nylon bras with pasties and bikini bottoms with fringe their girls must wear don't exist. Places that advertise Oriental Dance Sensations are indulging in outmoded 19th-Century fantasies about the enticements of seraglios; to the last girl, the Sensations are merely overfleshed belly dancers. Places that splash the following words across their ads or marquees are probably kidding themselves as much as anyone, but that's no reason why you have to be taken in by *World's Only . . . World's Most . . . Sensational . . . Exotic . . . An Adult Show . . . Continental Acts . . . No Cover Charge.*

The *No Cover Charge* announcement is a sure tip-off to the fact that the place will hit you with a minimum after you're seated—usually a two-drink minimum at the going rate of $1.50 per drink, cola or beer at the same prices or just slightly lower. The absence of any advertised reference to cover or minimum means both are integral to every Chicago nightclub's policy. Ask, when you phone for a reservation. You've every right to know.

For current information about acts or shows, check the local newspapers. Friday *Chicago Sun-Times* carries a special section called *The Weekender;* *Chicago Tribune* offers *Weekend* on the same day. *Panorama* in the Saturday *Daily News* yields similar help, and traditional entertainment sections are to be found in the Sunday papers. *Chicagoland* (formerly *Omnibus Magazine*), a monthly concerned exclusively with the city and its suburbs, prints a fairly well edited and complete events calendar for the entire month. *Chicago,* a quarterly magazine, has a visitor's guide in each issue. Chicagoans who subscribe to the monthly *WFMT Guide* will find a complete and well edited entertainment section in it. Don't rely on the hotel-motel giveaway magazines. They're promotional pieces put together on a *quid pro quo* basis with their advertisers. Examine them and you discover that the so-called current entertainment listings contain only the names of advertisers. Following the old Chicago maxim, "Don't discourage business," they also meticulously avoid any mention of cover charges, minimums, admission fees.

CABARET ENTERTAINMENT

Mister Kelly's, 1028 North Rush, WH 3-2233

A sophisticated supper club with an a la carte supper club menu that runs to good steaks, lobster tails and the like. Still, the food is incidental to the acts, which consistently present some of the best talent in the country. You

---

* Will Leonard, the *Tribune's* Entertainment Editor, recently surveyed the entire nightclub scene, found Thursday to be the slowest night in the week at most places and advises "the man who craves lots of elbowroom" to pick that night above all others.

go to Mister Kelly's to hear Shelley Berman, Mort Sahl, Shecky Greene, Jack E. Leonard, Woody Allen, and such singers as Carmen MacRae, Dorothy Loudon, Lainie Kazan—in other words, whoever is in the top echelon of current entertainment.

The new padded, plastic, leopard-spotted tablecloths scarcely replace the elegance of the starched white linens that covered the tables before the now-famous Mister Kelly's fire (the building was gutted in 1966), but they may be one way to avoid using crime syndicate-owned laundry service. Shows nightly at 9 PM and midnight and three times on Friday and Saturday. Reservations absolutely essential, with a per person cover of $3.50 to $5, expensive drinks ($1.65 per); food range, moderate to reasonable. The bar is the best entertainment bargain in town. A two-drink minimum is all that's required, and you can see the entire show. Get in long before the show you want to see begins, because everybody else has the same idea.

Cautionary note: Don't drive into the Rush Street area and hand over your car to any nightclub doorman. All the car jockeys drive like dragsters. The flashier a car, the flashier the exhibitionism; the more modest a car, the more likely it is to be returned with dents earned in contempt for its lack of pizzaz. Also, don't park on the street. The area is the worst in the city for car thefts. The neighborhood hasn't enough parking lots, and they're expensive when you do find one. Use your head and a cab.

The truth about the rest of the Rush Street area nightclubs is that they're scarcely ever worth the money it costs to get in. This isn't a matter of singling out some names and carefully not mentioning others: the *area* is a tourist trap.

Playboy Club keyholders (the club is on 112 East Walton, just west of Michigan) can see some of the best acts booked in anywhere—but will also be hustled out of whatever room they're in the moment the show ends so that seating can be created for the next contingent.* If you don't have a key to Playboy you can apply for a club membership at the door ($50) and get a cash key for the evening. For whatever it's worth, this is the original Playboy Club —the proving grounds for semivoyeurism, bunnies, the whole bit. The club is on four levels, with the VIP dining room a formal showcase of elegant appointments, butlers in livery and a menu that rolls from French to English and back again in a funny, pretentious way. All dinners in this room are $8.50 or $12.50. Meals in other rooms are mainly steak and potatoes, masterfully portion-controlled. Actually, the best way to use the club is to stay on the main floor, have some drinks and then help yourself to the $1.50 buffet table. If you

---

* "Bunnies are reminded there are many pleasing ways they can employ to stimulate the Club's liquor volume. . . . The key to selling more drinks is . . ." *(Playboy Club Bunny Manual).*

don't overdrink, you can come out with a reasonable tab. After midnight, the buffet becomes as good a breakfast buffet as any in town. Open 11:30 AM to 4 AM nightly. Closed on holidays.

Playboy bunnies do hop to after-hour hangouts in the neighborhood, but the hutches keep changing. The last word was the **Stork Lounge,** directly across the street from Playboy, but don't count on it.

Gaslight Club, 13 East Huron, is the granddaddy of all the key clubs. You've got to have a key in order to get in the place, which bills itself as a private saloon. Once inside, find raucous gaslight-era entertainment in a huge, old mansion. Piano players or small combos are in all the rooms; a cowboy in the Last Chance Saloon engages customers in beating him to the draw; the Gaslight girls in the Speakeasy Room shimmy and Charleston; a main room lets you make your own nickel and dime sandwiches. All in all, far less blatantly commercial than Playboy and more fun. Hours are 4 PM to 3 AM Monday through Friday, Saturday to 4 AM, closed Sunday and all holidays.

Another place just off Rush to hear a good singer is the **Grapevine Lounge,** 14 West Elm. June Ives Rapp hasn't a great voice, but she does have an extremely sensitive way of interpreting lyrics. She's her own accompanist, and she's especially fine on ballads and show tunes and has a splendid repertoire of specialty numbers. North of Rush Street at **Mon Petit** in the Churchill, 1255 North State, Norman Wallace (he was Hildegarde's arranger for years) plays piano and sings through a repertoire that ranges happily from as far as "When the World Was Young" (in French) to all the little and most loved show stoppers.

For a list of Rush Street spots for the postcollege crowd (not tourist traps, but not for visitors over age 30 either), page 11.

Second City, 1616 North Wells (Old Town), DE 7-3992

Second City was born in 1959 in a converted Chinese laundry, with enormous creativity and a firm sense of what it was creating, but not much else. The first rehearsals took place during the conversion of the laundry, with a restless cat pacing back and forth amid two-by-fours and mountains of plaster dust, and the only thing to sit on other than raw lumber was the seat of an uprooted toilet with a cracked bowl.

Today, its performances are by an augmented company of eight in larger and more comfortable quarters but it's still an original, a cabaret theatre where satire has been honed to a fine edge, skits are fast and furious, and the material is always topical. Political satire is one of its fortes; biting commentary on race relations, people relationships, the foibles and prejudices of Americans everywhere and mores peculiar to Chicago and the Midwest.

What elevates Second City above other satirical acts in the country is its freewheeling use of improvisation. Second City never has had a book— director and actors discuss the nature of skits, and every actor is a defined character who adapts his role to each situation, but few actual lines are set and everyone is expected to improvise. If you don't believe that the show you're seeing is essentially improvisation, go on a week-night for the 9 PM show and stay for the improvisations that follow: members of the audience suggest topics or phrases or even single words, the cast plots for no more than five minutes, and a second show based on the suggestions takes full shape before your eyes.

Drinks available throughout the show, as well as a few short order accompaniments like hamburgers. No improvisations on weekends because the cast performs three times per night. $2.50 admission week-nights; $3 Friday and Saturday. Make weekend reservations at least a week in advance; other times, a phone call early in the day is sufficient. The Second City is closed Monday.

Game Theatre, 1935 North Sedgwick, MI 2-4198

A spin-off of the Second City improvisation technique in which an audience of 80 becomes involved in improvisation of its own performance. Miss Viola Spolin,* who uses the games technique to coach the actors at Second City, can bring the most resistant nonparticipant into the spirit of creating a kind of Second City performance. The games are not like the manipulative games people play in Dr. Eric Berne's book and, in terms of acting technique, are diametrically opposed to Method acting. Saturday night only from 8 PM to midnight; admission, $2.25; no liquor.

College of Complexes, St. Regis Hotel, 516 North Clark

The College of Complexes is Bughouse Square with a roof, walls, and drinks—a kind of mid-20th-Century town meeting in which, for $1 admission, anybody can speak after the main speaker. The pattern is: controversial subject, a speaker who may be cruelly logical or merely emotional, then a Q. and A. period in which everyone expresses his opinions on everything—all of it washed down with schooners of beer. The crowd is mixed but always includes serious girls in horn-rimmed glasses, some yippies, some well dressed middle-aged types, some young men in motorcycle jackets, a man with a tie, a man with a twitch, and so forth. Topics range from "Does the American Male Enjoy Emasculation?" to discussions of pornographic literature, adultery, irreligion, LSD, politics. The place is run by one of Chicago's pleasant eccentrics, Slim Brundage, and the whole evening is kind of lunatic. Arrive well before 9:30,

---

*Amateur actors will be interested in her book, *Improvisations for the Theatre*, Northwestern University Press, 1963.

otherwise you won't be able to squeeze into the room behind the bar that houses the antics.

DINNER SHOWS AND/OR DANCING

Cafe Bonaparte, Sheraton-Blackstone Hotel,* South Michigan and East Balbo, HA 7-4300

An elegant room with good entertainment nightly, mediocre food, a dance trio on Friday and Saturday, and a splendid polished copper dance floor. The bar is in the same room, and you can dance from it. No cover or minimum.

Isle of Capri, Pick-Congress Hotel, 520 South Michigan, HA 7-3800

Dancing in an intimate little cocktail lounge to the music of Dick Sarlo, who's been holding down the podium for 15 years. His range, from fox trot through Latin American rhythms to the frug, is always keyed to the immediate crowd. From 8 PM to 2 AM. No cover or minimum. Closed Sunday and Monday.

Boulevard Room, Conrad Hilton Hotel, 720 South Michigan, WA 2-4400

A glittering ice show, dinner, dancing. For details, page 316.

Empire Room, Palmer House, State and Monroe, RA 6-7500

A splendid green and gold room with top-drawer entertainment, dancing, and Fritz, the city's favorite maître d'. Tony Bennett, Maurice Chevalier, Jack Benny, Ray Bolger, Phyllis Diller and Guy Lombardo are among the stars who glitter here regularly, and it's fun to see the different crowds each attracts. When it's Tony Bennett, you find tables of four to eight women alone and wives forgetting they're with their husbands. When it's Phyllis Diller, the men go wild. Dinner and supper shows. Sliding cover of $4 to $8, depending on the current talent. What with food and entertainment tax and the price of drinks and tips, it can be an expensive evening. Even without food, four people having only three drinks each can spend $60. Open to 2 AM. Closed holidays only.

College Inn, Sherman House, Clark and Randolph, FR 2-2100

Multi-act revues and dancing in the redecorated old room, aptly described by *Chicago Daily News* columnist Virginia Kay as "a symphony of red plastic, wood paneling and patterned accoustical tile." Week-nights, $3 cover charge; $4 weekends. A la carte menu starts at $5. Drinks $1.25. Shows at 8:30 and 11:30 PM. Closed Sunday.

---

* For hotels where the food is equal to the show, page 25.

Cantina, Continental Plaza Hotel, 909 North Michigan, WH 3-7200

Noisy Las Vegas-type shows with constantly alternating acts. From 5:30 to 7 PM. you pay for drinks only at $1.50 each. After that there's a $2 cover Monday through Thursday and $2.50 Friday and Saturday. Closed Sunday. No dancing.

Mangam's Chateau, 7850 Ogden, Lyons, 447-4900 (Chicago 762-0500)

Dinner, big floor shows and the last chorus line in the area. It's almost the way things were in the 1930's—only expensive. Cover $1.50 Sunday through Friday, $2 on Saturday, dinners from $3.95 to $13.50. However, you can cut prices considerably by dancing from the bar. Two shows week-nights, three on Friday and Saturday.

Ogden (US 34) west to door or Eisenhower Expy to Harlem Avenue (Rt 43), south to Ogden intersection.

Willow Brook, 8900 Archer, Willow Springs, TE 9-1000 (Chicago LU 1-1676)

The place for couples who want to dance to Guy Lombardo, Jan Garber, Wayne King and other Mickey Mouse bands, though on Saturday night a rock 'n' roll combo is added and alternates. Willow Brook is a big ballroom, serves dinners from $3.25 to $5.75; drinks only 80¢. For dancing only, $1.25 admission Wednesday, Friday and Sunday. Saturday cover charge, $1 for diners, $2 for dancers who don't eat. The premises also include two bars and a soda fountain for nondrinkers and those under 21. Closed Monday and Tuesday.

Stevenson Expy south to LaGrange Rd. South to Archer Avenue sign (79th Street). Archer to the door.

DANCING ONLY

Charade a Go-Go in the Palmer House, 17 East Monroe, is the Town and Country Restaurant by day but a spot to dance to rock 'n' roll combos by night. Open to 1 AM. No cover, no minimum; and it's okay to nurse a beer. Go-Go girls on the weekend. Closed Sunday.

Pussycat, downstairs in the Happy Medium, 901 North Rush, DE 7-1000. Bugaloo and rock in a discotheque atmosphere. Admission $1 week-nights; $2 on Friday and Saturday. Drinks $1.50 each.

For rock bands in an entirely different atmosphere, see *In Places If You're Not Out Because of Age,* page 11.

For an authentic Latin American band, **El Sarape,** page 60.

Rock bands and dancing on weekends at three wild roadhouses lined up

78

on Old Skokie Road just south of Gurnee—the **Mouse Trap, Chez Francois** and the **Cat's Meow.** They're about 40 miles north of Chicago.

BURLESQUE

If you can't conceive of a visit to Chicago without seeing burlesque, that's a pity, because it's all third-rate. The places where you'll find it range from passable to raunchy, but they're not necessarily inexpensive; they tend to be half-strip, total clip. Phone before going so as to get the cover charge, minimum and price of drinks. If you're heading into what you suspect is a grunchy area, don't take more cash than you think you'll need. The tired old **606 Club,** 606 South Wabash, has burlesque; **Pigalle Cocktail Lounge,** at 56 East Delaware, has it; **Backstage,** at 935 Wilson, has it (the neighborhood is rough), and any cab driver knows where to take you in Cicero,* or to Impersonators Row (female) on West North Avenue. The **Follies Theatre,** 450 South State, has burlesque and a feature film; so does the **Burlesque Theatre** at 546 South State. Lots of luck.

BANJO BANDS AND FOLK SINGING

Red Garter, 21 East Pearson, WH 4-2630

You've got to be 21 to get in, but there's no age limit at the upper end. Conventioneers enjoy it, groups of grandmothers have the time of their lives, but mainly the crowd is young: girls alone; boys to meet girls; businessmen; couples lined up on weekends waiting for seats.

Sing-along is the big feature, and everyone does, with a band consisting of a preposterous combination of instruments; banjos, tuba, washboard, ricky-tick piano, sometimes a really great trumpet. The songs also have to be heard to be believed. The range is from turn-of-the-century stuff to the Mickey Mouse Club theme song. The washrooms are located under a sign that promotes Coolidge for President, and the band plays under another that commands DRINK MORE BEER. The Garter is beer and peanuts—you can spend an evening in it without spending more than $5. Monday and Tuesday are Ladies' Nights—beer at 10¢ a mug. Friday and Saturday $1 admission. Otherwise, no cover, no minimum, no entertainment tax. Open 8 PM to 1 AM, Sunday through Thursday; Friday and Saturday, to 2 AM. Closed only on Christmas and Election Day.

---

* Cicero dives are crime syndicate-owned. To avoid inspection of their books, several of them recently surrendered their liquor licenses. Fizzless grape juice has replaced champagne at $25 per bottle; soda pop for B-girls is $2 per glass.

Your Father's Mustache, 865 North State, 329-0193

More of the same, but on a smaller scale in a setting of World War I posters, Tiffany lamps and Victoriana. Admission 50¢ on weekends.

Earl of Old Town, 1615 North Wells, MI 2-5206

Folk singers nightly in a typical Old Town establishment of brick walls and fireplaces. Sometimes the entertainment is only a cut above amateur, but other times it's outstanding, as when Bob Connelly and the other two musicians of the New Wine Singers switch over into New Orleans jazz. Mr. Connelly is one of the few white men who can play it like a black man, and he is very good, indeed. Steak sandwiches, hamburgers, beer, bratwurst, Irish coffee and booze. Open daily, noon to 4 AM; music from 9 PM. There's a $1 listening fee when the entertainment starts, and beer goes up at the bar to 75¢.

Old Town School of Folk Music, 909 West Armitage, LA 5-7472, offers folk seminars and concerts on almost an every-other-Sunday basis. The student government at the **University of Chicago** runs a full Folk Concert Series during the year, bringing in some of the best singers in the country. Concerts are usually at Mandel Hall, 5706 University Avenue; tickets $2.50 and $2. For a schedule, call MI 3-0800, Ext. 3272.

JAZZ—THE RENAISSANCE

Some of the old Chicago jazzmen will tell you that jazz is still at low ebb in the city. In terms of steady bookings at scale pay, that's true.* But the pendulum is at the edge of the upswing, and the renaissance has to do with the rebirth of the blues. Urban blues, country blues, funky blues, "dirty lowdown" blues, bucket blues, gut blues, rent-party blues—by any name the blues are talking to a new young generation that's tuned in.

The parents of that generation usually prefer a different kind of jazz. For them, the first three places listed below are the spots they'll most enjoy; the jazz comes in familiar forms and comprehensible surroundings. For European jazz buffs of any age and the young, all the others, plus the first three.

London House, 360 North Michigan (Wacker Drive), AN 3-6920

It's not merely a Chicago institution but about as indigenously Chicago as you can get. Walk out of it after the late show in the dead of winter, snow blowing raw across your face, driven by the wind that howls along the vast expanse of Wacker Drive and the Chicago River, and you know you're in Chicago, no place else.

---

* So a solid blues pianist like Sunnyland Slim drives a cab for a living, and Little Brother Montgomery plays in a saloon in an Irish neighborhood where not one of the regulars at the bar knows the glory of what he's hearing.

London House is possibly the most sophisticated meat-and-potatoes spot in town; a completely integrated supper club—a showcase for topflight modern jazz musicians like Ramsey Lewis, Oscar Peterson, Cannonball Adderley, Errol Garner, Cy Coleman, Stan Getz, Peter Nero, Jonah Jones and one of the great unsung creative jazz pianists, Eddie Higgins, who, with his trio, alternates nightly year-round with the visiting bands.

One of the secrets of the London House success is that you can come any way you please just as long as you're decently dressed: women with other women—at least for the dinner show; young people and kids, especially kids after the prom; oldsters aged 70 are comfortable, assuming they like a jazz milieu. The bar faces the band but has visual obstructions; still, for a two-drink minimum you can absorb as much jazz as those seated at tables. The food is first-rate; steaks, mainly, in the reasonable range. A $2.50 cover after 8:30 PM, $1.50 for drinks. The one real drawback is the acoustics. If you want to hear jazz without the surrounding clatter of knives and forks, go for the late (1:30 AM) show when, on a week-night, the room may be half empty but the audience is reverential, and every musical nuance can be heard. Also open for lunch weekdays (no music, but a big advertising agency crowd that creates a driving tempo of its own).

Jazz, Ltd., 164 East Grand, SU 7-2907

Over the years, many of the great traditional jazzmen played it for long stretches (Sidney Bechet, Muggsy Spanier, Joe Sullivan, Sidney Catlett, Georg Brunis), and it's one of the few jazz spots known around the world. French and English visitors head for it; so have those two internationalists, Marlene Dietrich and Noel Coward. About five years ago, it went Dixieland with a house band: club owner Bill Reinhardt on clarinet, Dave Rasbury on trombone, Freddie Kohlman, drums, Emanuel Sayles, banjo and guitar, Quinn Wilson (he played with Jelly Roll Morton's Red Hot Peppers back in the 20's) on sousaphone and bass, Don Ingles (Red Ingle's son) on trumpet, Dave Phelps at the piano. Once in a great while you can still catch Georg Brunis here. The charming Eurasian hostess with a tough Brooklyn accent is Mrs. Reinhardt, and she means it when she says no women at the bar, all men in jackets. Don't give her a bad time over it either, because you'll lose. Dancing, for those who can dance to Dixieland. Minimum of $2.75; drinks $1.50 each. Open to 2:30 AM nightly. Closed Thursday and Sunday.

Showboat Sari-S, 500 West Ontario, SU 7-3383

It's an authentic old Mississippi stern-wheeler, brought up from Natchez under her own steam. She's moored in the north branch of the Chicago River; if you're driving, go west on Ontario, avoid the ramp leading to the expressway, and keep going west into what looks like and is an abandoned railroad siding.

Sari-S jazz policy keeps changing; sometimes it's Dixieland and some-times it's modern jazz like Marian McPartland, and still other times it's groups like the Function Junction Five, a kind of sing-along band. The weekly Friday Jazz At Noon Club welcomes anybody from a washboard player up to sit in. If any professionals are sitting in, the sessions are first-rate—Louis Armstrong when he's in town, Jonah Jones, Pete Fountain, Jimmy McPartland, and George Brunis, who is now close to 70 and semiretired in this city. The best of the regular Chicago jazzmen include amateurs of pro caliber as well as pros. Among them are Ralph Blank; Father Robert Owen (the Night Pastor of Rush Street); John Defauw, (son of conductor Desire Defauw); Remo Biondi; disc jockey Eddie Hubbard; almost all the members of The Salty Dogs, the group that came out of Purdue; Joseph Marsala; Earl Murphy, (trumpeter Norman Murphy's son); Ted Butterman; Chauncey Elsesser; society band leader Freddie Wacker, Jr., and a group of Chicago bankers that are as swing-ing a group of cats as you'll hear. Sessions start at noon and run to about 2:30. Admission, $1.50; buffet lunch $2.50. At night, $2 cover. On Saturday, a la carte dinners from moderate to reasonable. Dancing and a show tune pianist in the dark piano bar. To 2 AM week-nights, Saturday to 3 AM. Closed Sun-day.

Out of the city, **Glenview House,** a suburban bar at 1843 Glenview Road, just west of Route 43 but east of the railroad tracks, has open Dixieland ses-sions on Friday nights. The musicians, mainly in the communications business, are close enough to pro to play with a fine old-fashioned thump. The group shifts weekly, depending on who shows, but sometimes you can catch trum-peter Nappy Trottier playing in a combo of two trumpets, a cornet, two slide trombones, one valve trombone, one clarinet, one soprano sax and, for the rhythm section, banjo, guitar, piano, drums and tuba. Stein of beer at 25¢ is the admission, plus the beers you buy for the band (it's their only pay).

Scotch Mist, 875 North Wabash, MI 2-3100

Jazz and some fairly big-name entertainment, such as the Buddy Rich Orchestra or Esquivel, but you'll feel like a pigeon if you pay the Mist's prices. The weekend cover charge runs between $4 and $6, depending on the act, plus a two-drink minimum. Drinks are $1.60 per, and you'll never get to the ice because the waitresses scoop up half-empties with a skill just this side of sleight of hand. Even prices of the nonalcoholic Sunday matinee show for the very young are outrageous: $4 admission per person and $1 for each soft drink.

Jack Mooney's, 1360 North Sandburg Village (Schiller and Clark), DE 7-8090

Progressive jazz jam sessions on Sunday afternoons from 3:30 to about 7 PM. Dixieland on Saturday night; Judy Roberts at the piano week-nights.

Plugged Nickel, 1321 North Wells, WH 4-2420

Modern and mainstream jazz by big musicians such as Harry James, Kenny Burrell, Thelonious Monk, Lionel Hampton, Jimmy Smith, singer Anita O'Day, and occasionally big bands like Stan Kenton and Woody Herman. The place is unimpressive and the tables are too small, too close together. But it's a good place for black and white to mix comfortably, with jazz the common meeting ground. Two-drink minimum per person plus $2 door fee. Drinks at $1.25 each. Sunday matinee, nonalcoholic, and no soft drinks, either, for those under 21. Admission, $2.50.

Sauer's Brauhaus, 311 East 23rd Street, CA 5-6171

Contemporary big band music on Friday and Saturday nights in a handsome big barn of a room. Good draft beer—30¢ a stein for domestic Peter Hand Reserve, 50¢ for Henninger import. Small *brauhaus*-type menu and the chance to drown in sound from 8:30 PM to 2 AM. Admission, $1.50. The place is also open for lunch and supper without music the balance of the week, 11 AM to 10 PM; Sunday, 3 PM to 9 PM.

McPartlan's Tavern, 5110 North Broadway, 784-9493

Thursday through Sunday, Little Brother Montgomery plays here. He's one of the last of the great 1920's rent-party pianists, sings in a voice that sounds like an early recording with a scratch, but it suits his walking bass and sad syncopation. He's a man to be cherished—there probably aren't ten like him any more, anywhere in the country. The Irishmen who frequent McPartlan's don't care what they're hearing—it's the outsiders coming in who listen reverently to Little Brother's self-taught, somewhat primitive, down-to-earth style (you can hear the origins of boogie-woogie in it). Two of his own pieces, "Vicksburg Blues" and "Freeport Farewell," are triumphs of that style. Request them. The price of a beer (called a draw, here, not a draft) is all you pay. Hamburgers and cheeseburgers available until 11 PM, and a picture of the Golden Gate Bridge strung in real lights to contemplate between Little Brother's sets. Saturday he plays 10 PM to 5 AM, to 4 AM the other nights; sometimes Bob Skiver, the saxophonist from his old band, joins him.

Mich-Boul Lounge, 162 East Superior, SU 7-7715

Ted and Wanda Glowinski run a small neighborhood oasis for graduate students in the schools of Northwestern's downtown campus and the nurses and interns from the triumverate of hospitals just to the east. On Friday and Saturday night Madonna Martin comes in to play piano and sing. The kids don't know what they're hearing and neither do the Glowinskis, whose real talents lie in creating a home away from home for the kids. What you'll hear is Billie Holiday style, Billie in her last years (Miss Martin's inflection is iden-

83

tical), plus Dinah Washington numbers, old Pearl Bailey hits and 1920's rent-party blues with a little walking bass that's beautiful. Sometimes Miss Martin's blues are as funky as you'll find anywhere; sometimes you hear the same 1920's blues on the verge of evolving into boogie-woogie inherent in Little Brother Montgomery's style. Price of admission is a drink. The Glowinskis dispense beer in 15-oz. goblets at 50¢ each, with enough free popcorn to put themselves permanently in the red. To 2 AM Friday, Saturday to 3 AM. Closed Sunday.

Lurlean's, 319 East 75th Street, 224-8937

Lurlean Hunter, one of the finest modern jazz ballad singers, is Chicago's own. This place is her own, or rather a partnership with her husband, who handles the bar. Miss Hunter sings in a distinctive throaty style—she'll remind you a little of Sarah Vaughan. She's not on every week-night, but a good trio and a comedian are. The crowd, half University of Chicago and half Lurlean fans from all over the city, is absolutely silent when she performs. Open to 4 AM nightly, Saturday to 5 AM; entertainment Friday and Sunday to 4 AM, Saturday to 5 AM. Drinks $1.25.

BIG BANDS

Big bands can currently be heard at three places in the city, one essentially a white club and the other two Negro, but anyone is welcome at any of them.

Club Laurel, 5246 North Broadway, 275-0932, gets Count Basie, Woody Herman, Stan Kenton and the like, usually on a weekend or one-nighter basis. The rest of the time it's rock or soul bands for dancing. Open seven nights a week, 8 PM to 4 AM, Saturday to 5 AM. Two-drink minimum; cover charge depends on who is booked in.

On the South Side, **The Club,** 5523 South State, 684-3020. It's the old Club deLisa, a huge barn of a place that gets the best of the big bands and singers in the country on weekends. Count Basie packs it; Cannonball Adderley records for Capitol in it; B. B. King, who's often been called the only straight blues singer in America, plays it; any stars in town, white or Negro, make it out here after their own shows are over. Shows here are long, with very little time between them. Policy here is you buy a bottle and setups; it's just as well—the service is often bad. Open seven nights a week, 1 PM to 4 AM; cover charge depends on who's booked in, but usually ranges from $1 to $2.50. Don't be surprised if you're gently searched for knives or guns; it happens here, a kind of impersonal but efficient patting down. Parking available.

Regal Theatre, 4719 South King Drive, AT 5-9585, the last movie house in the city where you can also find stage shows. The Regal's are 90 minutes of big-name entertainment and big bands—the Drifters, Aretha Franklin, James Brown, the Temptations, for instance. Shows are well-advertised, but you can phone during the day to learn who's booked in for any given date. Open weekdays at 5:30 PM and weekends at 1:30 PM. Admission $2 adults, 75¢ children. Parking lot for drivers; otherwise, take the Jackson Park or Englewood El to 47th Street, a block away.

THE BLUES

Time correspondent Robert Anson once observed that "blues and soul music are so intertwined as to make them interchangeable. Without souls the blues wouldn't be, and maybe without blues the souls wouldn't be worth having." Since "soul" is the one inalienable possession of the Negro, the one thing whites may comprehend but can never possess, it's perfectly natural that the places to hear the blues nightly are in the Negro ghettos of the city.*

Because the Illinois Central Railroad runs up to Chicago in a direct line from Mississippi, the blues you'll hear at the shrines are Mississippi blues, the Negro folk tradition of the Delta backcountry, the howl that characterizes Howlin' Wolf, the pure emotion of Muddy Waters, the subtle rhythms of the rural south projected by Jimmy Cotton. A younger generation of blues singers —Junior Wells, Buddy Guy, Otis Rush, Otis Spann, B. B. King, Jimmy Rogers, Hounddog Taylor—born in the South but come of age in urban slums, have added to the blues a technical polish absorbed by exposure to other forms of music and the hard, driving, hurting sound of inner-city pressures.

As of this writing, anyone of any color is welcome at the Negro blues shrines. The audiences are mainly Negro, of course; the atmosphere can be very mixed, but it's always loose and easy; and soul—the raw emotion, the pain of being black—is not withheld. People stomp and shimmy in their seats and call out to the singer. And if Buddy Guy says to the crowd at Theresa's, as he did one night, "People, hold on to me" and begins to sing "I'm hurtin'," and halfway through his song, begins to cry, the audience will be crying, too. It's like Robert Anson said, "Blues is the anthem of the working class, the unemployed, the hustlers, and there's no attempt to deny the obvious misery of being a Negro. [The shrines] are places of honesty personified." So it's where you go to hear and begin to understand through the blues your fellowman.

Note: White or black, you can get picked clean, so don't carry a lot of cash.

Silvio's, Lake and Kedzie

In the heart of the West Side ghetto, where, since the riots of 1966, signs on all the neighborhood bars read *Cool It, Baby, Soul Brother.* Silvio, a nice

---

* The Regal Theatre is an exception since its audiences are multiclass. But as bluesman Willie Davis says, "Sometimes people are ashamed to accept the blues because it gives away part of their past." Most educated Negroes in the middle class avoid or simply don't know of the blues shrines in the same way that middle-class whites rarely frequent or know of the white workingman's taverns.

old Italian who has decorated his place with some mounted deer heads, has two or three uniformed special police on the premises. If Howlin' Wolf and Muddy Waters are in town at the same time, you may get the chance to hear both men and their bands alternating. Ribs and the like by way of food. Admission of 50¢ to $2.50, depending on who's playing. The neighborhood is rough; use the Lake Street El, get off at Kedzie; you're practically at the door. **Smoot's** is just a little farther up the street under the shadow of the El tracks. The bands play in an area under an ivy-hung ceiling that's somewhat like the inner court of a Spanish tavern. **Kansas City Red's** is in the same area, also under the El. Kansas City Red is a blues drummer; his place is about as nitty-gritty as you can find.

Theresa's Tavern, 4801 South Indiana, is a basement spot where you'll hear Buddy Guy and Junior Wells after 10 PM, when they're not booked out by the State Department for overseas tours. Buddy Guy, an auto mechanic by day, a self-taught musician (who pulled wires from a window screen to make his first guitar), is, by general consensus, the finest blues guitarist in the city, if not in the jazz world. He plays lead guitar for Junior Wells and also sings. The biggest night here is Monday, when every musician in town who can make it sits in.

Turner's Blue Lounge, 4012 South Indiana, KE 6-9530, in the South Side Negro ghetto, is another place to hear low-down funky blues. Sunday afternoon is the time for sit-ins here.

Pepper's Lounge, 43rd Street and Vincennes, has been home to everybody, including Muddy Waters; on Sunday the blues sound like a religious service, with Junior Wells using his harp (harmonica) and his voice to lead his audience of roughly fifty in an almost-ritualized participation in the blues.

Though the **Earl of Old Town** is essentially a folk-singer's haunt, it sometimes books in an upcoming bluesman like Terry Collier, whose own guitar is backed by a second guitar and a cello. The instrumentation is very good, and when Terry Collier lets loose with a song like "Mam'selle Marie," a not irreverent cry for help from the Virgin Mary ("Have pity on me, oh ma'am, have pity on me"), that's soul, baby.

To locate two Chicago jazzmen that many visitors to the city ask about: Art Hodes, the pianist and bandleader who's best-known as one of the early musicians who plays the blues "as well or better than any white man who's learned to play them," is currently staying out of nightclubs and playing at private parties and public events. If you're reasonable about the hours you phone (noon to 6 PM), he welcomes calls and will tell you where you can hear him during any given week. Phone 748-8666. Drummer Red Saunders, equally famous as the man who finally integrated the Chicago Federation of Musicians (it was the Negroes who resisted integration for so long), is following approximately the same route, plus giving college and theatre concerts. Call him at the federation at noon (ST 2-0063) if you want to learn where he's playing during a given week.

Mother Blues, 1305 North Wells (Old Town), 751-8575

Currently, the only place other than the South Side or West Side Negro ghettos to hear Howlin' Wolf, chief linguist of "dirty, down and out" back-country blues; Muddy Waters, the number two country bluesman; Otis Rush, famous for his "I Can't Quit You Baby"; Junior Wells; and Paul Butterfield, one of the few young white bluesmen who's played in enough South Side blues bands to absorb the feeling of the blues. Few of the bluesmen play here on regular gigs, but generally it's Monday night for Otis Rush, Tuesday night for Howlin' Wolf or Muddy Waters if they're not touring and not playing at **Silvio's** or **Smoot's.** Phone to verify.* Friday and Saturday shows from 8 PM to 10 PM for the generation that can't buy liquor; after that, as on week-nights, open to 4 AM to anyone with a valid ID. Dancing on a little floor behind the band. $2 admission.

A group of experimental musicians, the Association for the Advancement of Creative Musicians, performs in regular concerts at the **Abraham Lincoln Community Center,** 700 East Oakwood, DR 3-6600. The center is famous as Frank Lloyd Wright's first public building (dedicated 1905), a six-and-one-half floor structure built initially for a Unitarian church. The association is famous for its groups of jazz musicians who regularly play here on Sunday at 6 PM ($1.25 admission), and at Ida Noyes Hall, University of Chicago, on Tuesday nights (8 PM) as members of the Joseph Jarman Quartet, the Roscoe Mitchell Ensemble, the Alfred Fielder/Anthony Braxton Quartet, and so on. Typically, the groups are known more to readers of *Down Beat* and certain Canadian, British and French jazz magazines than to Americans.

Their music is hard to define, but you might call it Found Sound, instruments played as far out as they can go to produce sounds you hear daily but ignore because they normally don't come from instruments. The sounds played by association musicians are signals, as if the musicians aren't so much playing their instruments as themselves, talking to you. Their music is enormously compelling, sometimes reminiscent of Ornette Coleman, and sometimes derivative of preaching blues and the talking drums of Africa, but most often entirely of the present and a way of putting forth valid claims to leadership in contemporary jazz. Recordings are available at the Jazz Record Mart.

---

* Neither Silvio's nor Smoot's have phones, so you can't call to verify. However, *Down Beat* magazine, published in Chicago, may list them. If not, Bob Koester, owner of the Jazz Record Mart, 7 West Grand Avenue, 222-1467, will know.

THE ROARING CITY

FILMS—ART, UNDERGROUND, EXPERIMENTAL AND CLASSIC

Film Censorship: Chicago, wide open in so many ways, is one of the two cities in America in which films are subjected to censorship. (Dallas is the other.) Censorship appears to be imposed on the size of the film's budget in inverse proportion. Maybe Chicago is better off than was London in the 1930's, when for five years the film censor was physiologically blind, but one wonders.

The best place at the moment to see underground and experimentals is at **Aardvark Theatre,** 1608 North Wells, starting at 8 PM every evening. Depending on supply and the rate they're eating up undergrounds and experimentals, you may find a preponderance of foreign and classic features rather than the films of Kenneth Anger, Robert Nelson, Andy Warhol, Peter Weiss, Ron Nameth, Norman McLaren, Peter Weiner et al., but Aardvark will have them if anyone will. The phone is DE 7-4654.

Old silent film classics can be seen every Tuesday night at **Melvin's,** State and Cedar, in a saloon atmosphere of the young, tap beer and giant hamburgers ($1.25). One-hour showings at 6 PM, 8 PM, 10 PM. The price of a beer is all you have to pay, and if you're dressed in a business suit, you're overdressed.

World Playhouse Theatre, 410 South Michigan. It dates to the 1920's, and for twenty years was the city's only art movie house, the only place to see Flaherty, for instance, and the early post-World War II Italian films. It is still the leader, takes films of exceptional merit even if they have no potential box office. The **Cinema,** just east of Michigan Avenue at 151 East Chicago, will also occasionally stick out its neck on extraordinary films. Its owner has a nose for non-run-of-the-mill successes, such as *David and Lisa,* which ran seven months here, *Lord of the Flies,* and *A Man and a Woman* which ran well beyond the one year mark.

The **Esquire,** 58 East Oak just west of Michigan, and the **Playboy Theatre,** 1204 North Dearborn (Division), are two plush houses that run art films. The **Village,** 1548 North Clark, frequently runs them, but you're advised its washrooms are a disgrace. On the South Side, the **Hyde Park Theatre,** 5310 South Lake Park; on the North Side, the **Bryn Mawr Theatre,** 1125 West Bryn Mawr, deserves the biggest pat on the back for running art films not much later than anyone else at a 50¢ admission. The Bryn Mawr (it also shows opera films) is always jammed with intellectuals, not people who can only afford 50¢ for a movie. The **400 Theatre,** 6746 Sheridan and the **Coronet** in Evanston (817 Chicago) help ease the hunger for films of excellence on the Far North Side and the North Shore.

The **Clark Theatre,** 11 North Clark, is the most interesting film exhibition experiment in the city—and a successful one. The Clark runs a different double feature every day of the year, generally predicated on a weekly or monthly theme. It might be the entire cycle of John Wayne pictures or early Russian films, or the classics on the theme of war and peace. Hours are also unique: doors open at 7:30 AM and the late show starts at 3 AM.

A fine mix of revivals, some underground, some experimentals and classics can be seen at the following colleges and universities. Prices are sometimes most reasonable, usually 50¢ or $1.

Mundelein College, the Auditorium at 6363 North Sheridan, AM 2-8100, ext. 88.

Northwestern University Film Society, Fisk Hall, Evanston, 1845 Sheridan, 492-5665.

Roosevelt University Student Senate Films, 430 South Michigan, WA 2-3580, ext. 351.

Center for Film Study, DePaul University, DePaul Center Theatre, 25 East Jackson, WE 9-3525.

Chicago Illini Union, University of Illinois, Circle Campus, 828 South Wolcott, 663-7770.

Illinois Institute of Technology Union Board, Hermann Hall Auditorium, 3241 South Federal, 225-9600, ext. 530.

University of Chicago, film locations vary, MI 3-0800, Dept. of Public Relations.

For popular foreign language films: the **Avon,** 3327 West Fullerton (Greek and Italian); the **Davis,** 4614 North Lincoln (German); the **Senate Theatre,** 3128 West Madison, the **San Juan,** 2046 West Division and the **Puerto Rico** at 3912 North Sheridan (Spanish). The **Senate** not only has Mexican films, but Mexican film stars fly in to perform on the stage every weekend. **Las Americas,** 8 North Ashland, has occasional stage shows in addition to the films.

The **Pan American Council** runs Spanish language films on Saturday afternoons in winter at Thorne Hall on the Chicago Avenue campus of Northwestern University. You don't have to belong to the council to attend.

For Chicago's International Film Festival in mid-November, see Annual Events.

OLD TOWN

Old Town as a place to live, a part of Chicago history, is one thing. The Old Town you've heard about is something else—six blocks of complete physical and mental derangement on a street named Wells. (For your purposes, Old Town's south boundary is Division Street and its north boundary St. Paul; where Wells intersects North Avenue, the lunacy also spreads west.)

Basically, Wells Street consists of an improbable conglomerate of shops, saloons, restaurants, nightclubs, jazz joints, snack stands, hopelessly filled parking lots, some 2,000 hopeful drivers every Friday and Saturday night inching their way down the streets, trapped in the small area for more than half an hour (once in on wheels, you cannot get out simply because you wish to) and, on the same nights, upwards of 20,000 human beings moving along the sidewalks, as if in a trance, knotting in clumps to watch sidewalk artists painting imprecise portraits at apologist fees, gawking at the yippies who paddle barefoot through the sidewalk litter, dodging the greasers on motorcycles, pouring in and out of the stores—and generally having a great time. The farther from either side of 20 you are, the more fun you'll have. The quieter the life you normally lead, the more the total assault on all your senses will add to the unreality of it all.

The Sounds of Wells Street haven't yet been recorded, but it's only a matter of time before someone captures on a grooved plastic disc that will sell for $4.95 the man-and-machine-made uproar. The Smells of Wells are fortunately noncapturable, except for the duration of your visit. By the end of the evening you'll have absorbed all the world's carnival odors combined: buttered popcorn, pizza spices, charcoal broiling, grilled hot dogs, the greasy odor of deep-fat fried doughnuts, stale beer on human breath, stale beer in joints, car exhaust, unwashed bodies—the entire gamut of unmentionables swirling about in the private air pollution that is Wells Street's own.

The attraction of Old Town is that it's escapist *now*. Its ideas are those of the moment—the fads that catch on instantly from coast to coast. One season it was computerized handwriting analysis, and then came the buttons and posters shops; long before you get there, another half-dozen inspirations of the moment will have come and gone.

So will at least one-third of the shops and night spots, for they have an unsettling habit of appearing overnight and disappearing overnight. Many deserve their fast oblivion: like yesterday's newspapers, nothing is duller than last season's paper dress promotion. Or the places may be there, but their names and merchandise will have changed. Once, all the shops sold merchandise that was unique and attractive. Today, most sell *kitsch*—the kind of overpriced novelties and hoo-ha that turns up across America wherever a country eating spot has a gift shop on the premises. It doesn't matter. Shops are jammed with suburban ladies who drive in to make an afternoon of it; evenings they're crammed with the spillover from the 20,000 sightseers. If you're in the city with children, visit Old Town a little before noon, when it's just opening in time to serve lunch. Without children, pick a week-night (all shops are open until 10 PM and many until midnight) or try a Sunday afternoon.

The page numbers following the shops listed below are the pages where you'll find descriptions of their contents. These are Old Town's most interesting and most permanent stores. They were in the area before it became honky-tonk, and they are good places to browse and buy.

The **Town House** and the **Emporium** just south of North Avenue sell amusing nonsense at serious prices. Both specialize in delightful nonessentials, mainly decorative.

The most interesting places to eat aren't the overcrowded, Victorian-artifact-crammed elaborations but the following, which feature reasonable prices and some obviously calculated but genuine charm:

Bratskellar, 1608 North Wells

A swinging spot run by three young entrepreneurs who retired from junior executive positions in LaSalle Street firms. The big features on their menu are Shrimp Boiled in Beer, Bratwurst and Hamburgers. The bar features 173 kinds of liquor, and there isn't a second-rate brand of anything in stock. Decor is Middle Period Goodwill, and the enormous bar is made from doors. Noon to early morning.

Chances R, 1533 North Wells

One of the first establishments in the area, a veritable old-timer, vintage 1961. It specializes in good charcoal-broiled hamburgers, good draft beer, and bowls of peanuts on every table. The whimsy of expecting customers to throw peanut shells on the floor started here. The place was fashioned out of a garage or something like a garage, and the decor features what *Institutions* magazine calls about "$25,000 worth of calculated dilapidation." Open daily, 11:30 AM to 1:30 AM; Saturday to 2:30 AM.

Pickle Barrel, 1423 North Wells

Excellent corned beef and pastrami sandwiches in an improbable yester-year decor. Kids adore being brought here since every table offers not just a barrel of pickles but a salad bowl full of all the free hot popcorn they can eat.

A genius balloon blower creates and gives them animal balloons as souvenirs. Open from noon to 1 AM nightly, Saturday to 3 AM.

Paul Bunyan of Old Town, 1355 North Wells

Chicago's biggest log cabin aggressively decorated in logging camp paraphernalia and subject to great swings in menu. One year the big specialty was pancakes and northern fried chicken; another year it was oysters, clams, shrimp—all you could eat. The food isn't gourmet, but you can't go away hungry, and the prices are moderate. 11 AM to 2 AM.

Soup's On, 1246 North Wells

An absolutely charming spot designed by one of the owners who happens to be Mr. Eldon Danhausen, associate professor in the Department of Sculpture at the Art Institute. Your choice of a steaming bowlful of one of four kinds of soup (they change daily) and French bread with butter, or sandwiches. $1 brings either, and since a soup bowl holds sixteen ounces, you can't walk out wishing you'd had more to eat. No liquor, but you won't miss it. Hours are noon to 1 AM. Closed Monday.

Geja's Wine & Cheese Cafe, 1252 North Wells

A little flamenco spot (flamenco guitars on weekends, reasonably quiet weekdays) where you can get cheese, wine and some of the best homemade chili in town.

Twin Anchors Tavern, 1655 North Sedgwick

Long before there was an Old Town, the college crowd discovered this one—an old neighborhood tavern that at some time in its past added a kitchen as a kind of afterthought. The old-timers who spent their evenings and weekends at the bar and rightfully regarded the place as *theirs* weren't very happy about the squeeze, and for years the air was thick with the impact of two totally different groups mutually trying to claim the same space. The neighborhood diehards survived, of course, and still sit on their barstools carefully ignoring everyone but their own cronies. Ribs and good black bread are the reason for coming here.

The yippy hangouts of Old Town aren't nearly as obvious as you hope they will be and look pretty scruffy when you do find them. Columnist Mike Royko says the chili served at the **Garden Tavern,** 1429 North Sedgwick, is "the best and the cheapest in town" and that the kitchen is operated by one Cannonball Campa, "the basketball immortal from Chihuahua State Teachers College in Mexico." Cannonball also makes hot tamales. You have to push past a lot of sullen, oddly-assorted individuals at the bar, and you'll feel like an outsider; but the place is reasonably genuine yippy, and if that's what you're after, push in and don't comment about what you're seeing until after you're back outside.

There's also a crime syndicate side to Wells Street—the money pouring in was too much to be ignored. Some of the fanciest restaurants are either Syndicate-owned or controlled, and the signs are more obvious than at other places in town. There's also an increasingly rough element moving into the area, and there have been muggings and purse snatchings on the dark side streets. The good suburban ladies who come in coveys during the day may have the right idea when they come then: whatever they witness in daylight may look bizarre, but it's harmless.

There's one place in Old Town that unnerves a lot of people. It's **Piper's Alley,** a shopping arcade. Essentially, the Alley is a narrow, block-long, roofed-over store squeezed between two buildings, sharing common walls. Crowds ooze through about as fast as cars on the Eisenhower Expressway during rush hour, making their way back toward the cul-de-sac restaurant at the far end. It's no place for anyone who has claustrophobia or who worries about fires and panicked hordes. Some people play a devastating little game on the premises—counting the number of meaningless exit signs.

PART II: City of Surprises

SHOWCASE CITY

5

The Story of the Skyscraper
Walking Tours of the Loop
A Bus and Walking Tour Through Streeterville
Famous Buildings on the South Side
Illinois Institute of Technology Campus
University of Illinois at Chicago Circle
Frank Lloyd Wright in Oak Park and River Forest
Not To Be Missed

CHAPTER 5

SHOWCASE CITY

Why Chicago ignores its one unique contribution to the world is a mystery, but it does. No hall of fame or permanent exhibit of any kind is to be found here explaining Chicago's impressive role in the creation of modern architecture. History's first metal skeleton buildings were created in this city in the 1880's, and the skyscrapers that were the result of the invention not only changed the skylines of cities everywhere but made possible modern business and whole new industries, and helped change America from an agrarian to an urban society. In short, the achievement of the third great turning point in the history of architecture changed the world irrevocably.

The typical Chicagoan knows none of this. Nor does he know that his city alone is a living museum of modern architecture, world-famous for its buildings, or that 100 of them were designed by two of the three giants of modern architecture—Frank Lloyd Wright and Ludwig Mies van der Rohe.*

It's a fairly safe bet that no Chicago schoolteacher ever took school kids to the building that's now Sears, Roebuck, on State Street in the Loop, and said, "This building is famous because the man who designed it was the first man to build a metal frame to support the entire weight of the building. It's only eight stories high but it's a great granddaddy of all skyscrapers and high rises. See the windows? They're probably the first windows in a commercial building designed to let in as much light and ventilation as possible."**

This chapter, with its self-tours, is planned for adults who are curious about the development of modern architecture, who've heard about the First and Second Chicago Schools of Architecture, and who want to know how both came about.

---

* The third: Le Corbusier.
** If such a teacher has taken grade or high school classes on such a field trip, the author would like to know about it.

THE STORY OF THE SKYSCRAPER

The forerunners of skyscrapers as we know them were developed in Chicago as a direct consequence of the Great Fire of 1871. The Fire leveled the city's entire business district (the Loop) and thus created the same climate for re-building that the destruction of Berlin stimulated after World War II. The dif-ference was that the engineer-architects who rebuilt Chicago had the chance to build a totally new city without also having to digest a crumbling past.

There was no past. The city was only 38 years old. But it was a booming commercial city, and it needed commercial buildings that would give investors the greatest return and the maximum amount of rentable space for the least money. Height with light was the answer, and for the first time in history height was practical because the one invention crucial to height had been in-vented in Chicago the year before the Fire—the mechanical (hydraulic) ele-vator. C. W. Baldwin, its inventor, deserves to be listed with the giants who created skyscrapers: William Le Baron Jenney, Daniel Burnham, John Wellborn Root, William Sooy Smith (who conceived the ideas for most of the new foun-dations developed in Chicago, including the caisson foundation that Dankmar Adler worked up), William Holabird, Martin Roche, Louis Sullivan and Frank Lloyd Wright. These men, engineers by training and architects only informally, except for Sullivan, invented the kind of buildings that became known as Chicago Style and, later, as the First Chicago School of Architecture. Their in-ventions were primarily technological; the buildings they designed evolved during the last decades of the 19th Century from the technology which mas-tered iron and steel—and sheets of glass.

For 5,000 years, until William Jenney invented metal framing on which the entire weight of buildings could be hung, all buildings were erected with masonry walls. The walls carried the load. The higher a building went, the greater the wall thickness had to be in order to support the weight. Ten stories of height was about the limit; otherwise, the base walls became so thick as to be impractical. Chicago's Monadnock Building is famous because it went to 16 stories on masonry load-bearing walls, but it's the exception that proved the point: each base wall is six feet thick. Monadnock is a one-of-a-kind triumph, never duplicated. In the face of metal skeleton framing it made no sense.

At the time they were built, the skyscrapers of the First Chicago School looked very strange indeed. Essentially, they were the expression of height based on engineering principles, and steel and glass; and because they were created from the inside out (from Jenney's metal skeleton frame), they had an unheard-of directness and simplicity. They very clearly proclaimed their func-tion, which was commercial—offices, warehouses, stores—and their exteriors were relatively free of ornament, just as a good steel and glass building is today. They were not disguised temples or disguised anything else. They were wholly original—and wholly ignored at the time.

Elsewhere, architects of the era were indulging in an orgy of monument-making. The results are visible across America and in Chicago as well: banks, museums and libraries built to look like Greek temples, armories in rusticated Romanesque, hotels and railroad stations that look like Roman temples or French palaces, private homes ditto or in Italianate Renaissance. Furthermore, the architects mixed styles. The result was the worst hodgepodge imaginable,* but at the time the mix spelled culture, and to a nation scarcely 100 years old, culture implied respectability.

The World's Columbian Exposition of 1893 was Chicago's first public display of its Second City complex. The real reason for the fair was not that Chicago was hell-bent on celebrating the 400th year since Columbus landed, but that it wanted to show the world it was just as refined and had just as much culture as any older city along the Eastern Seaboard. To Daniel Burnham and John Root, classicists at heart, went the task of designing the exposition. Root died suddenly during the project; Burnham, who was one of the best promoters of his era, promoted the construction of a "Great White City" of Roman classic buildings and brought in eastern architects to execute the grand design.

It was very grand. The buildings were imposingly classic and uniformly white and so awed some 27 million visitors that from then on, neoclassic architecture was the rage. Louis Sullivan, whose Transportation Building was the only contemporary building on the fair grounds, mournfully predicted the fair would set back the development of modern architecture by 50 years. Burnham said to Frank Lloyd Wright, who was a draftsman for Sullivan at the time, "Frank, the fair shows our people the beauty of the classic—they will never go back." Nor did they—for the full 50 years Sullivan prophesied.

The ideas of the First Chicago School of Architecture didn't die overnight, but increasingly the Chicago skyscraper was gussied up in ornament and period styles. You have only to look at most of the buildings erected in the Loop and on the Near North Side in the period from the fair to the early 1930's to see neoclassicism rampant. The white terra-cotta Wrigley Building went up as a Spanish Renaissance skyscraper. The Tribune Tower (a newspaper plant) marched up as a stretched-out Gothic cathedral, replete with buttresses in the sky. The tower of the American Furniture Mart is a blue tile and gold leaf copy of the Renaissance bell tower of San Marco in Venice. What is now the Stone Container Building, at 360 North Michigan Avenue, got crowned with a fanciful Greco-Roman temple. Lincoln Tower next door wears ascending layers of

---

* One of the funniest examples of what came to be known as eclecticism is the Illinois State Capitol in Springfield. It has rusticated Romanesque foundation walls, Italianate Renaissance windows, Roman Corinthian temple front, Georgian Corinthian pilasters, Byzantine Romanesque arcaded windows, French mansard roof, and an Italianate Renaissance dome and lantern.

Gothic stonework. The University Club, at 76 East Monroe Street, is capped with Tudor Gothic pediments and penthouse. There are dozens more, all grandiose and utterly anachronistic. The only exceptions are some 20 buildings designed by the sons of Holabird and Root and erected in the 1920's, when "modern" meant a certain sleekness, a heavy, smooth, polished look. The Palmolive (now Playboy) Building is one of them; 333 North Michigan is another. Once you become familiar with their hallmarks, they're easy to find.

From the mid-1930's to the mid-1950's there was very little building in the city, but there was something else—the electrifying presence of Ludwig Mies van der Rohe. Mies, who came to Chicago in 1938, brought back from the Continent, where they had been kept alive, the early Chicago ideas about modern architecture—but refined and dazzling. Mies single-handedly created the Second Chicago School of Architecture and gave the city the skyscraper penultimate—soaring, serene, a glittering length of glass and steel, a creation of his own intellect, of a lifetime devoted to one objective—the definition of the "architecture of our time."

Chicago has a staggering collection of more than 40 Mies buildings, another 20 or more designed in the same idiom by his students or disciples, and it is all of these together that make the central part of the city today the architectural wonder that it is. Mies said, "Less is more," and the aphorism is the key to the best of Chicago's new buildings.

Each of the self-tours that follow will give you several views of Chicago. The two walking tours of the Loop will take you to the origins of the skyscraper, the interim years when Chicago wanted and built monuments, and the present decade in which the Loop, especially Dearborn Street, is transforming itself. Chicago's real showcase street is not the so-called "Magnificent Mile" but Dearborn, anchored by the Monadnock Building at its south end and the twin towers of Marina City to the north. Dearborn exhibits some of the world's most exuberant modern office buildings—and may well be the most architecturally significant mile in the United States.

If you've never taken an architectural tour, start with the Loop tours. They offer a little of everything.

A WALKING TOUR OF THE LOOP—PART I

At first glance many of the early skyscrapers will not look like skyscrapers because they're not very tall. The fascination the early buildings of the First Chicago School holds for architects is what they represent—engineering genius that led to an entirely new way of erecting buildings (eventually, with no limitations of height)—buildings flooded with natural light for the first time— buildings that could be equally functional as offices, warehouses or hotels.

Most of them are black with soot. Some are squeezed by elevated tracks

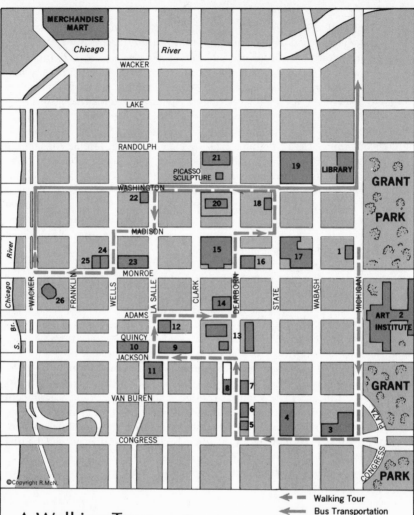

A Walking Tour
of the Loop

1. Gage Building
2. Art Institute of Chicago
3. Auditorium
4. Leiter Building II
5. Manhattan Building
6. Old Colony Building
7. Fisher Building
8. Monadnock Building

9. Continental Illinois National
   Bank & Trust Co.
10. Federal Reserve Bank
11. Board of Trade
12. Rookery Building
13. Federal Center
14. Marquette Building
15. First National Bank of Chicago

16. Inland Steel Building
17. Carson Pirie Scott & Co.
18. Reliance Building
19. Marshall Field & Company
20. Brunswick Building
21. Chicago Civic Center
22. 30 North LaSalle Street
23. Northern Trust Company
24. Leiter Building I
25. 210 West Monroe
26. U. S. Gypsum Building

or much taller buildings. But one aspect will emerge after you've seen five or six of them—their blunt simplicity. They were commercial and they almost never pretended to be anything else. And somehow they express the direct-ness of Chicago, which is a city of almost no pretentions, in a way nothing but buildings can do.

Note: Landmark buildings are indicated as such with (L). You won't find the Landmark Commission plaques on many of the buildings. Owners have been fearful of putting them up because legislation just might prevent the building's sale or destruction.

1. Gage Building (L), 30, 24, and 18 South Michigan; Architects: Holabird & Roche, 1898

Start at the northeast corner of Monroe and Michigan. The three build-ings directly across Michigan Avenue to the right of the University Club are collectively known as the Gage Building. Those at 30 South Michigan and 24 South Michigan display pleasant examples of the famous Chicago Window, which was the first window in commercial buildings to bring in real light and sufficient ventilation. British critic Reyner Banhan has said that the Gage Build-ing(s) "Epitomize the splendors and miseries of the First Chicago School." They do. They are all steel framed, and the frames are articulated on the out-side, though concealed with facades of stone. Eighteen South Michigan wears a Louis Sullivan facade. Though the big ornaments at the top now seem rather arbitrarily stuck on, like two brooches glorifying a pair of suspenders, they were originally balanced by some of Sullivan's exquisite metal ornament and a delicate, glass-enclosed marquee. But the Commission on Chicago Land-marks obviously sees them in a different light. Like the commission, you've got to overlook the banal storefronts which were added in the name of "modernity." Many of the most famous old buildings have been desecrated in this manner; Chicago has never tried to govern the preservation of its great heritage.

The Chicago Window is characterized by a wide central pane of glass flanked by movable panes. The central pane is often much wider than any window found in contemporary buildings, and in Sullivan's Carson Pirie Scott store it is vast, but also beautifully scaled. Once familiar to you, you'll recog-nize it many times in Loop buildings. It evidently was a Holabird and Roche innovation but was used extensively by other architects of the First Chicago School because it was practical—and practicality was the *leitmotif* of all their buildings.

Architects will debate endlessly as to whether the true Window is a mat-ter of proportion or shape. Whichever, it was a giant step forward, and as with many of the radical ideas created here, it came from the technology of the 1880's, in this case the invention of wide sheets of rolled plate glass. The fact is, the men who rebuilt Chicago after the Fire seized each technological invention as fast as it came along. Jenney, for example, built his first skeletons of iron, but with the 1884 invention of rolled sections of steel he abandoned iron for the far superior structural material.

2. Art Institute of Chicago, Adams and Michigan; Architects: Shepley, Rutan & Coolidge, 1892

The Art Institute is a perfect example of the classic palace of culture that Chicago built to impress visitors to the World's Columbian Exposition. (It housed the Congress of Religions during the fair, then reopened as the Art Institute in December, 1893.) A Boston firm of architects, Shepley, Rutan and Coolidge, was given the commission, probably because its designers were masters at adapting classic styles and had done the Library of Congress in Washington. For Chicago, they decided upon Italianate Renaissance. The two immense new wings have been added quite recently by two different Chicago architectural firms. They don't help any—they seem to be holding the building up.

Walk south to Congress Street, past Daniel Burnham's surprisingly delicate Orchestra Hall, 212 South Michigan (1904), and S. S. Beman's Studebaker Building, 410 South Michigan (1884), with its original cast iron facade but now mutilated top and ground floors. Congress is the street which Burnham chose as the central axis of the downtown area when he created his famous Plan For Chicago in 1909.* One can see why he chose it: on the northwest corner of Michigan and Congress, running back the full width of the block to Wabash, stands the most phenomenal building of the late 19th Century:

3. Auditorium (L), 70 East Congress; Architects: Adler & Sullivan, 1889

It was the most talked-of building in America, the largest and most complex, the first multipurpose structure, with office tower, hotel and theatre buzzing with life. It is still one of the most powerful buildings of any age. Its exterior is not beautiful, although the arches give it a rugged simplicity of undeniable appeal; its interior is exquisite in the manner of its day. The floors are mosaic, more than nine million little tiles in all. The pale gold theatre, recently restored, is still one of the great theatres in America, acoustically perfect and with sight lines that allow anyone in an audience of more than 4,000 to see perfectly no matter where seated. By contemporary standards the interior is extensively ornate (the counter color is red, main floor and box seats

---

* The plan was important for many reasons, above all because it was one of the first examples of a business community commissioning an architect to show it what could be done for a city. When L'Enfant created Washington D.C., there was no established city and he worked like a developer with raw acreage. But when Chicago bankers and businessmen wanted a plan, they were in effect saying, "Create a city out of an already thriving city." Burnham's plan did just that. It was a grandiose scheme, almost European in concept, and it said, "tear down here, build up there"—it was city planning as we understand it today.

are upholstered in gold velvet), and the romantic poetry Sullivan inscribed on the walls ("A great life has passed into the tomb and there awaits the requiem of winter's snows") is either embarrassing or confusing, depending upon your point of view. But none of that matters once you become aware of the tremendous genius of both architects (Adler was the acoustical genius) creating a theatre unsurpassed for sight and sound and of a building as anticipatory of combined functions as this one. Even the fact of getting the incredible weight of the total structure to stand erect in Chicago's oozy mud base is an engineering marvel, easy to appreciate when you look at the thickness of the load-bearing walls. Group tours only, at this time, though an individual is welcome to join any group scheduled for a tour. Fees (to cover cost of lighting and heating the theatre) are $2. Student rate, $1. Phone 922-2110.

See also Roosevelt University, page 335.

4. Leiter Building II, Congress and State; Architect: William Le Baron Jenney, 1891

Two blocks west on Congress, hard by cheap burlesque houses and dingy cigar stores, stands Jenney's Leiter Building II. It's Sears, Roebuck now, but if you look above the remodeled facade, you can see the relationship between engineering construction and architecture that characterized the First Chicago School of Architecture. Here, an eight-story steel skeleton of columns, girders and beams supports all the weight of the building. Jenney, an engineer with a mania for light and ventilation, let these considerations and the skeleton frame dictate the architecture of the building. The result is a structure as grand in its severity as it was innovative, but unappreciated for 55 years. To architects in the East, the simple exterior said "commercial building," and commercial buildings didn't have to look like anything. In their eyes, this one didn't, and they saw only that Jenney had proved with this building that a metal skeleton structure cost less than masonry supporting walls, could rise higher because it was lighter, and could be erected easily and quickly. The simplicity was not understood at all.

5. Manhattan Building, 431 South Dearborn; Architect: William Le Baron Jenney, 1890

Walk west one block on Congress to see the first tall (16-story) building with metal skeleton construction throughout. Jenney built it in his usual practical fashion and placed projecting window bays on the central floors to bring in as much natural light as possible.

6. Old Colony Building, 407 South Dearborn; Architects: Holabird & Roche, 1884

Two young engineer-architects, William Holabird and Martin Roche (Roche trained under Jenney) probably best represent the core ideas of the First Chicago School of Architecture. Their Old Colony Building is a metal skeleton on which the two longest sides are emphasized with vertical piers and the short sides given an expression of horizontality by continuous sills under the window groupings. Notice the huge window bays on the southern exposure that anticipate 20th Century glass curtain-walls.

7. Fisher Building, 343 South Dearborn; Architects: D. H. Burnham & Company, 1896

Though Daniel Burnham trained with Jenney, he had also worked in the offices of an eminent Gothic revivalist whose influence shows here. The Fisher's basic Chicago School simplicity is hidden under Gothic ornament—even the corner piers became Gothic piers through Burnham's use of engaged moldings. Yet, despite these historical reminiscences, he succeeded in giving the building great lightness and airiness and one is aware of its skeleton structure.

8. Monadnock Building (L), 53 West Jackson; Architects: Burnham & Root, 1891

The Monadnock is actually two buildings. The original Burnham and Root structure fronts on Jackson Boulevard and is the Landmark Monadnock, the highest traditional brick masonry construction in the world, the building that proved masonry could support height if one overlooked vast impracticality. Despite its thick base walls, the Monadnock is wonderfully proportioned and, though solid as a castle, not static as it rises from its heavy curve above the baseline. The harmonious southern metal cage addition to the original was designed by Holabird and Roche in 1893. Walk west on Jackson to LaSalle Street and you're at the south end of Chicago's financial district. Here the old banks look like Greek temples and there is a fine money-god distinction between federal and local dollars; elaborate Corinthian columns characterize the **Federal Reserve Bank** (No. **10** on map), and less pretentious Ionic, the **Continental Illinois National Bank and Trust Company** (No. **9**).

11. Board of Trade, 141 West Jackson; Architects: Holabird & Roche, 1930

Board of Trade is one of the 20 Holabird and Roche anomalies among Chicago skyscrapers. The buildings are not Chicago School, nor are they classic, despite a few places where you find a restrained Pompeian influence. They are basically masonry-clad skyscrapers with very little structural expression but with a fine sense of the era in which they were built. They tend to make you think of F. Scott Fitzgerald-era formality, when tuxedos represented the new casual formality over the older Edwardian tails. The architects literally pioneered a style which is just beginning to be recognized for what it is and were the only men in Chicago to use setbacks and towers. Their buildings represent skyscrapers, as most of us use the word, more clearly than any other buildings do. The statue on top of the building is Ceres, the Roman goddess of agriculture.

12. Rookery Building (*L*), 209 South LaSalle; Architects: Burnham & Root, 1886

The Rookery's major importance is inside—the lobby that Frank Lloyd Wright remodeled in 1905. Walk up the staircase a flight or two and then look down for a view of the court and the perfectly beautiful early Wright detailing. The dome over the lobby court was glass but has been painted over. The Landmark citation is "in recognition of its pioneering plan in providing shops and offices around a graceful semiprivate square and the further development of the skeleton structural frame using cast iron columns, wrought iron spandrel beams and steel beams to support party walls and interior floors." The ornament is Chicago style because it eschews classic derivative for ideas wholly its own. The building got to be called Rookery because of the excessive pigeon population that roosted on it shortly after it was built. Building management shrugged good-naturedly and adopted the name. Because of the Rookery's inner good looks, rental space in the building is at a premium.

13. Federal Center, Dearborn (both sides) from Jackson to Adams, west to Clark; Architects: Mies van der Rohe; Schmidt, Garden & Erikson; C. F. Murphy Associates; A. Epstein & Sons, Inc., 1964-69

Three buildings will ultimately comprise the Federal Center. The first is the United States Courthouse and Federal Office Building on the east side of Dearborn; the second, a 45-story office building across the street; and the third, a low United States Post Office Building. What you see most clearly here are some of the qualities in which Mies is unrivaled—articulation, modulation (the relation of buildings to each other) and proportion (exquisite scale—the buildings never ask you to look up, but you do, and that's scale in the hands of a master). The buildings are formal and restrained, but the restraint creates excitement. The plaza is a triumph, not merely bold open space in the central part of a city, but space superbly related to its buildings and therefore of almost equal significance.

14. Marquette Building, 140 South Dearborn; Architects: Holabird & Roche, 1895

Another strong example of the kind of skyscraper erected by the architects of the First Chicago School, and of the kind of problem the famous Chicago Window could create. The width of the window flooded buildings with natural light (an unheard-of extravagance for commercial buildings) but created a dilemma in partitioning the space behind the expanses of glass. In this building, you can see what happened when partitions came as they must, rather than at column lines—many of the windows are quartered. If, at this point, you're desperate for a washroom, go west one block to the Harris Trust and Savings Bank at the corner of Clark and Monroe. Downstairs, next to the vaults, are some of the nicest facilities in town. Upstairs, on the lobby floor, take a moment to look at the old bank on Monroe Street as well as the new

Skidmore, Owings and Merrill corner addition. It's one instance where modernizing added not just space but an impressive new dimension to the weighty old forebear.

15. First National Bank of Chicago, Monroe to Madison, Dearborn to Clark; Architects: C. F. Murphy and Associates; Perkins & Will Partnership. Building completion, 1968; plaza completion, 1971

Throughout 1968, you'll be able to see both the old building on Clark Street, designed by Burnham, and the new First National rising along Madison and Dearborn. When completed it will be 850 feet high, the tallest building in the Loop, sweeping up from a base almost twice as broad as its upper stories. When the old bank is demolished, the space it occupied will be turned into an open plaza of several levels, with reflecting pool, restaurant and shops. (For those who enjoy odd facts, this block is the exact center of the Loop.)

16. Inland Steel Building (L), 30 West Monroe; Architects: Skidmore, Owings & Merrill, 1957

A spectacular building, sheathed in stainless steel, demonstrating clearly the ability of Skidmore, Owings and Merrill architects to innovate within Miesian concepts and Mies' sense of discipline. The innovation here is the seven load-carrying columns on Dearborn Street, expressed emphatically on the outside of the building (whereas a Mies column is always part of the structure) and by the creation of a separate, windowless shaft to house elevators and stairs. Be sure to walk completely around the building to see how the architects created a sense of space and beauty in an alley, then enter the lobby which contains a Richard Lippold wire construction suspended like a great sunburst over a shallow pool. Lippold was commissioned to design a construction specifically for the building; the lobby design was altered somewhat to accommodate it, and it's a good example of the results that are possible when architects and artist work in tandem.

17. Carson Pirie Scott & Co. (L), Madison and State; Architect: Louis H. Sullivan, 1889

Carson's occupies most of a city block, but it's the building at Madison and State that is considered Sullivan's masterpiece and the ultimate achievement of the First Chicago School. What you most want to see here (and what is hardest to do because of traffic) is the way the floors and columns are expressed above the lower floor ornament while the in-fill is all glass—the Chicago Window at its best. The building is the essence of directness, and one marvels at Sullivan's self-restraint, because he adored ornament. But he confined it to the first three floors, where you'll find a propagation of cast iron foliage seen most abundantly over the five arches at the rotunda entrance on

State and Madison. It takes time to discover what all the vegetation is about, yet it's worth the effort because you can trace the way Sullivan developed ideas from a simple organic starting point, such as a leaf, into the beautiful design for which he's famous. Burnham and Company built the second section of the store in 1906. Holabird and Root added the last in 1961. Wander inside, through the remodeled interior to any back stairways you can find. They're marked with exit signs and they still have their original Sullivan balustrades and cast iron elaborations; they are lovely.

18. Reliance Building (L), 32 North State; Architect: D. H. Burnham & Company, 1895

One of the happiest expressions of the First Chicago School, if you can ignore the crass neon signs and vulgar "modernizing" of the main floor facade. The building above flows from window to window between slender columns, piers and mullions which are tied together with the nicest possible use of spandrels. In many ways, the building is Burnham being joyful, something one suspects the old promoter wasn't often.

You are now half a block from Marshall Field and Company, a good stopping place. Field's famous tearooms will provide rest and sustenance.

A WALKING TOUR OF THE LOOP—PART II

19. Marshall Field & Co., State to Wabash, Randolph to Washington, 1892-1914

The great department store which encompasses an entire city block is actually a number of buildings constructed at different times. The earliest of these rose on the northwest corner of Washington and Wabash—nine stories, designed by Burnham. Architects in his firm added subsequent buildings in 1902, 1906, 1907. Between 1904 and 1906, Graham, Anderson, Probst & White built the North State Street building with its enormous classic columns.

20. Brunswick Building, 69 West Washington; Architects: Skidmore, Owings & Merrill, 1964

An interesting example of the Second Chicago School working on the foundations of the First School. The Brunswick Building actually has load-bearing exterior walls of concrete, hence the little sweep above the base looking like and performing the same task as the greater sweep of Monadnock, to spread the load. There are internal structural differences, of course, since 70 years separates the two buildings, but somehow one is more aware of similarities. From the lobby floor of this building or the Civic Center across the street, you can escalate down to an underground walkway and proceed east to emerge at Field's. The labyrinth is the start of a growing underground city of little service shops and restaurants along the way which is being planned for various sections of the Loop. It will be interesting to see how the underground idea develops and whether it goes beyond a mere repetition of street level facilities.

21. Chicago Civic Center, Washington to Randolph, Dearborn to Clark; Architects: C. F. Murphy Associates; Skidmore, Owings & Merrill; Loebl, Schlossman & Bennett, 1965

A number of architects consider it not only the most brilliant public building in Chicago but the most important piece of civic architecture in the country. It is innovative (only three bays but each 80 feet long, a size tried only once before in the United Airlines Executive Office Building and Training Center, Mt. Prospect, Ill.). Mr. John Entenza, director of the Graham Foundation for Advanced Studies in the Fine Arts, engagingly describes it as "the Second Flood rising to its peak, Miesian in the strongest and most honorable sense, Mies spread to new horizontal possibilities." The structural steel frame is Cor-Ten, a new low-alloy steel developed by U.S. Steel that will gradually weather to a soft black with a warm brown undertone—unless Chicago's air pollution interferes.

The center's sweeping plaza is a gem—first and foremost a ceremonial plaza for civic functions and, secondly, a great breath of fresh air for the downtown district. The design for the sculpture is Pablo Picasso's gift to Chicago, an abstraction that is open to interpretation as you wish, since Picasso has remained silent as to its meaning. The thing to do is walk around it more than once and allow it to make its presence felt. It's a remarkable experience.

22. 30 North LaSalle; Architects: Adler & Sullivan, 1894

Under the west wall of the building, originally the Chicago Stock Exchange, is the world's first true caisson foundation, which solved permanently the old problem of the irregular or excessive settling of a building. The idea came from William Sooy Smith, engineering consultant to the Stock Exchange, but Adler gets the credit for making it workable. The relief in the left medallion represents the house of P.G.W. Peck, 1837, which stood on the site; the numerals in the right medallion merely tell when construction of the present building started. A special Louis Sullivan room inside contains original ornament, including the elevator grills. It's open during regular office hours.

23. Northern Trust Company, 50 South LaSalle; 1906, 1930, 1965

The old four-story pseudoclassic bank was built in 1906 by Frost and Granger and may well be more notable for its foundation to bedrock than anything else, since in 1924 the city engineers cut the Number One City Datum Mark into the granite at the southeast corner and proclaimed, "There is no likelihood that the building will ever sag, so the mark is stationary." It may not have settled, and all building heights continue to be measured against it. The next two floors were added in 1930 by Holabird and Root. Behind the building (on Monroe) is the new addition, more interesting for its drive-in plaza than anything else because the planting gives dingy old Wells Street its first pleasantry in years. C. F. Murphy Associates were the architects.

24. Leiter Building I, 200 West Monroe; Architect: William Le Baron Jenney, 1879

It is now the Morris Building, and you have to look around the outside fire escapes and above some awful remodeling of the first story to see it, but it's interesting because it anticipates Jenney's own steel cage. Here Jenney hung the roof and floor loads from timber joists and girders, which were in turn supported by cast iron beams. The brick piers support only themselves. Thus he could reduce their width and place them where he chose—widely, as you see, in order to gain a sense of openness. In so doing, Jenney also antici- pated the Chicago Window of the next decade.

25. 210 West Monroe; Architects: Adler & Sullivan, 1881

This is the first building in which Sullivan used the vertical emphasis for which he became famous in his later skyscraper designs. He seems to have gotten carried away with ornament at the top, however. Because the original entry and main floor facade have been ripped away in favor of a slab of "modernization," it's impossible to know how he balanced his ornamentation.

26. U. S. Gypsum Building, 101 South Wacker Drive; Architects: Perkins & Will Partnership, 1963

Probably the most remarkable fact about the Gypsum Building is that its architects placed it at a 45° angle to Chicago's insistent 90° grid. For some rea- son, that placement has made Gypsum one of the most controversial buildings in the city, even though it is a refreshing change from the norm and gives office workers inside far more natural light than could a conventionally placed building. The design is the basic form of a gypsum crystal. Gypsum, worth the extra short walk to see, gives you a chance to look at another down- town area undergoing transformation, and if you want to continue directly on the next tour, you can hop on CTA bus No. 157 here and be driven to it.

A BUS AND WALKING TOUR THROUGH STREETERVILLE

Streeterville is the informal name of the area north of the Chicago River and east of Michigan Avenue to Oak Street. The name comes from one of Chi- cago's balmier squatter-citizens who commandeered the area's lakefront for his own. His story is on page 451. This tour begins outside Streeterville at the Chicago Public Library. The library stands on the site of part of the old reservation of Fort Dearborn and sports a bronze marker with an appropriate, oddly written bit of early Chicago history: "On this site, then the Lake Shore, Jean Baptiste Beaubien, Chicago's second civilian, in 1817 built a 'mansion' to which he brought his bride, Josette Laframboise. It remained their home until 1845." The library is an 1897 palace of culture designed by Shepley, Rutan and Coolidge of Boston. Its interior is Carrara marble, and its main floor plan duplicates part of the main floor of the Library of Congress, but as such is almost unrecognizable due to the innumerable partitions added to accommodate more books.

Just inside the Washington Street entrance find one of Louis Tiffany's great shows of mosaics which, along with the two leaded glass domes in the building and the bronze work, stands as one of his finest achievements. The public relations desk on the main floor has folders describing the architecture in some detail, texts of the mural and clock inscriptions and a code to the early printers' marks which are part of the interior decoration in a number of areas.

At the bus island on Washington Street just across from the library, catch CTA bus No. 157 going east.

1. 333 North Michigan Building; Architects: Holabird & Roche, 1928

You can't see the address as the bus approaches it, but it's on the southeast corner of Wacker, and the best view of it is from north of the bridge. The Tavern Club on the top floor, a private club for businessmen, is notable for its membership, good food, dining terrace on a conveniently provided, typical Holabird and Roche setback, and the spectacular view of the lakefront—from the men's washrooms. See also page 451.

2. The construction on the riverside site just east of the 333 building is to be a new office building by Ludwig Mies van der Rohe. The address will be 111 East Wacker Drive.

3. Equitable Building, 401 North Michigan (north bank, Chicago River); Architects: Skidmore, Owings & Merrill; Alfred Shaw, Associated, 1965

Despite its fountains and tracery planting at the river's edge on the lower level, its plaza is a good example of what happens when space is not integrated with a building. This and the lumps of decorations haven't improved it. The plaza space just sits there and becomes a murderous wind trap for raging storms.

4. Chicago Sun-Times, Chicago Daily News Building, 401 North Wabash (north bank, Chicago River); Architects: Naess & Murphy, 1957

Two of Chicago's daily newspapers are published here, and from lobbies and walkways throughout the building you can stand and watch the presses roll.

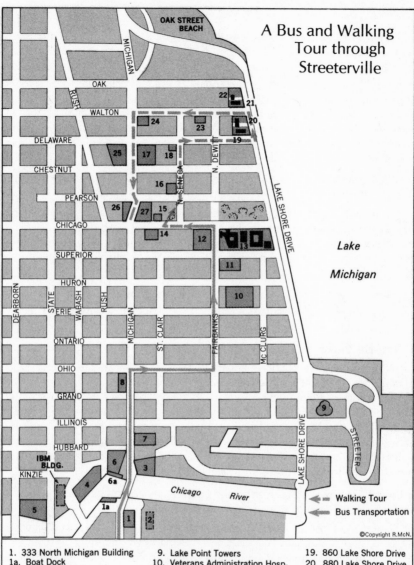

A Bus and Walking Tour through Streeterville

Lake Michigan

Legend:

- - - Walking Tour
- - - Bus Transportation

©Copyright R.McN.

1. 333 North Michigan Building
1a. Boat Dock
2. 111 East Wacker Drive
3. Equitable Building
4. Sun-Times, Daily News Building
5. Marina City
6. Wrigley Building
6a. Boat Dock
7. Tribune Tower
8. Time-Life Building
9. Lake Point Towers
10. Veterans Administration Hosp.
11. Passavant Memorial Hospital
12. Chicago Wesley Mem. Hosp.
13. Northwestern Graduate Schools
14. American Dental Assn. Building
15. Engine Company No. 98
16. Pearson Hotel
17. John Hancock Center
18. The Casino
19. 860 Lake Shore Drive
20. 880 Lake Shore Drive
21. 900 Esplanade
22. 910 Esplanade
23. 227 East Walton
24. Playboy Building
25. Fourth Presbyterian Church and Parish House
26. Water Tower
27. Pumping Station

5. Marina City, 300 North State (north bank, Chicago River); Architects: Bertrand Goldberg Associates, 1964

Merely to be noticed now, in the distance, and examined later. With all its faults, it is an engineering feat in concrete, using a technique long devoted to the building of grain elevators, applied for the first time in buildings used for living. The Marina towers demonstrate some of the most beautiful concrete work you'll ever see. The significance of Marina City is its combined facilities for living, working and recreation in a downtown area, giving a business area life on a 24-hour basis.

6. Wrigley Building, 400 North Michigan; Architects: Graham, Anderson, Probst & White, 1924

A Spanish Renaissance skyscraper, as already noted, a design based on that of the Giralda Tower in Seville, Spain. What is more important is that it was the first office building north of the river and was responsible for the subsequent development in the 1920's of North Michigan Avenue as a shopping and business center.

7. Tribune Tower, 435 North Michigan; Architects: Howells & Hood, 1925

The ultimate in skyscraper Gothic. The labeled rocks imbedded in the facade just above eye-level were collected at the owner's request.

8. Time-Life Building, 540 North Michigan; Architects: Holabird & Roche, 1930

It was built as the Michigan Square Building, later became the Diana Court Building, may get still another name after the new Time-Life Building, rising east of Michigan Avenue, is completed. Its superb central lobby is given over to a bi-level area that is splendidly "modern" in the chrome and marble style of the late 1920's. The upper level is a circular rim of shop entrances, the center well holds a tinkling fountain, with a Carl Milles sculpture of Diana, and a restaurant. Currently, you have to look past the lower level restaurant decor to see that the lobby is absolutely smashing.

9. Lake Point Towers, 505 North Lake Shore Drive; Architects: Schipporeit & Heinrich, Inc.; Graham, Anderson, Probst & White, 1968

Catch a glimpse of it as the bus swings east on Ohio Street and again at the next stop by looking back. It's a 900-apartment building of concrete sheathed in bronze-finished aluminum, with curtain walls of bronze-tinted glass.

10, 11, 12, 13. Veterans Administration Hospital, Passavant Memorial Hospital, Chicago Wesley Memorial Hospital, Northwestern Graduate Schools of Medicine, Dentistry, Business, Law

A melange of various architectural styles built since the 1920's. Leave the bus at Chicago Avenue and Seneca and walk west to:

14. American Dental Association Building, 211 East Chicago; Architects: Graham, Anderson, Probst & White, 1965

One of the least anxious precast concrete buildings in the city—it simply flows. One wonders if it was capped with its massive slab roof to keep it from flowing away. The lobby, unfortunately, repudiates the fine exterior.

15. Engine Company No. 98

Here you'll find one of the city's friendliest little one-engine firehouses, a miniature castle with a crenelated parapet and unlikely beer-hall bottle-end windows on the east wall. It was obviously designed to fit in (more or less) with W. W. Boyington's Water Tower and Pumping Station to the immediate west, which you'll see on the return at Nos. 26 and 27.

16. Cut through the adjacent dollop of park, emerge in front of the **Pearson Hotel,** which is a hotel typical of 1920's style of graciousness. Walk north on Seneca past Chestnut Street and the garage of the John Hancock Center.

17. John Hancock Center, Chestnut to Delaware, Michigan Avenue to Seneca; Architects: Skidmore, Owings & Merrill, 1969

A 100-story complex—in which the first five floors are shops and commercial quarters, the 13th to 44th floors are offices, and the 45th to 92nd floors are apartments. Official Chicago has been crowing about the Hancock ever since it was announced (the tax revenue will be something), but the neighborhood and concerned citizens view it with dismay as it is totally disproportionate to the area, will add approximately 14,500 persons to a neighborhood that already has the highest human density in the city and will daily glut the area's streets with as many as 500 delivery trucks. The diagonal beams are a contemporary form of windbracing, and they will obstruct the view from a good many apartments. They also make it possible to build a 100-story building for the equivalent unit cost of a normal 40-story framed structure. Tour the model apartment at Seneca and Chestnut if you're curious. When the center is completed late in 1969, an observation deck will open on the 94th floor and restaurants on the 95th and 96th. The view will undoubtedly be extravagant.

18. The little brick building painted gray at the northeast corner of the Hancock site (195 East Delaware) is Chicago's most society-minded private club— **The Casino.** When it refused to sell to the Hancock site developers, it became a kind of monument to individuality and human dimensions, since the Hancock might have been even larger and more ominous had the builders been able to develop the full block.

Walk east on Delaware. New Yorkers will feel right at home on this street, for it, like LaSalle, feels like a Manhattan canyon. The buildings here are built right to the street-side lot lines, something you don't find elsewhere in Chicago.* Ahead, as you continue toward the lake, is the focal point of this expedition—the first expressed steel and glass curtain-wall skyscrapers built, not for commercial use, but for living, and the four most photographed apartment buildings in the country.

19, 20, 21, 22. 860 and 880 Lake Shore Drive (L), **900 and 910 Esplanade Apartments;** Architect: Ludwig Mies van der Rohe, 1961 and 1965

Architects have a phrase for great buildings; they say you can experience them. What they mean is a heightened awareness of a building, a feeling of its presence, as though it were alive. 860 and 880 Lake Shore Drive, which are the work of genius, can be experienced, more the second time than the first, more the fortieth than the second. They are extremely disciplined buildings and totally serene. They also have a profound effect on the people who live in them or near them—towers of calm strength above the endless, nervous traffic of Lake Shore Drive. At the time they were erected, they shocked natives, who called them "boxes," and hooted derisively and only grudgingly admitted one advantage—that Mies had found a way to eliminate the long detested lobby floor apartments. Be sure to cross the drive to see all four from the lakefront. Mies sat on a bench there daily, watching the construction of 860—"When it was twelve stories, I wanted them to stop. It was perfect at twelve but—" he grins, "it was planned for twenty-six so it could not stop."

The chairs in each lobby are his famous Barcelona chair, designed in 1929 for the German Pavillion at the Barcelona Fair. Like his signature, they're in the lobby of almost every apartment building he has erected in Chicago.

Eight-sixty is a masterpiece of innovation. It was not only the first glass apartment building in America, but it solved the problem of enclosing skeleton-frame buildings with glass curtain-walls. Until 860, glass either acted as in-fill or was hung in front of the skeleton. Mies set his glass between columns and spandrels and kept the surface of all three contiguous by introducing projecting steel mullions at the quarterpoint of each bay and on the column surfaces—as Carl Condit says, "the final dissolution of a wall into glass."

23. 227 East Walton; Architects: Harry M. Weese & Associates, 1955

A small apartment building that is in the idiom of the First Chicago School, by the contemporary architect who leads most of the citizen battles to preserve Chicago's historic buildings. His building is notable for the way he made the most of an extremely narrow lot on a relatively narrow, dark street, and also the way his concrete-frame construction hints of Auguste Per-

---

* Chicago zoning ordinances give developers a premium for *not* building to their lot lines. The farther back a building is set from its lot line, the higher it can go. The ordinance is unique and supplants the stringent setback regulations found in other cities. It also explains why Chicago skyscrapers rarely have setbacks and do not create canyons.

ret, the pioneer Frenchman. The interior design recalls the old Chicago five-room flat, in which rooms stretched back one after the other rather than clustering.

24. Playboy Building, 919 North Michigan; Architects: Holabird & Root, 1929-30

A building (originally the Palmolive Building) that is even more effective at night because its floodlighting is superb. Unfortunately, the great view of it from the Water Tower looking north has been sliced off by the Continental Hotel and the John Hancock. The only way to see it now in full splendor is from Lake Shore Drive north of Oak Street.

25. Fourth Presbyterian Church and Parish House, Michigan at Delaware; Architects: Ralph A. Cram; Howard V. Shaw, 1912

One of the most beautiful examples of Gothic revival in Chicago. Church and parish house flank both ends of the block between Chestnut and Delaware; the link between is a cloistered garth, planted with the utmost restraint, the better to display the austerely elegant fountain. On a warm summer night, the garth looks like a setting for a rich Elizabethan drama, and the glimpse pedestrians sometimes have of a young couple holding hands merely deepens the impression of a segment of life wistfully perceived.

26, 27. Water Tower and Pumping Station, Michigan, between Chicago and Pearson; Architect: W. W. Boyington, 1869

One rare survivor of the Chicago Fire (the pumping station was erected in its image in 1920) and significant only as such. The best description of the Water Tower is in Arthur Siegel's *Chicago's Famous Buildings,* "An imitation of Gothic architecture so naïve that it seems original at points, as in the cut-stone 'battlements' at the top of the lower wall sections."

From the Water Tower you might stroll south on Michigan Avenue, back to the river. Somewhat surprisingly, the buildings along Michigan are relatively low and inconspicuous; but if you look at details and roof treatment, you'll find a lovely old late 1920's formality which, more than most people realize, is what gives this section of Michigan Avenue its decidedly urbane air.

FAMOUS BUILDINGS ON THE SOUTH SIDE

Robie House (L), 5757 South Woodlawn; Architect: Frank Lloyd Wright, 1909

Robie House is perhaps the most famous private house in the world—Wright's Prairie House adapted to a narrow city lot, brought to perfection in the middle of a city. This is the house that shot Wright into the international limelight long before his genius was recognized in this country. In 1911 the Robie House drawings and plans were published in a German architectural

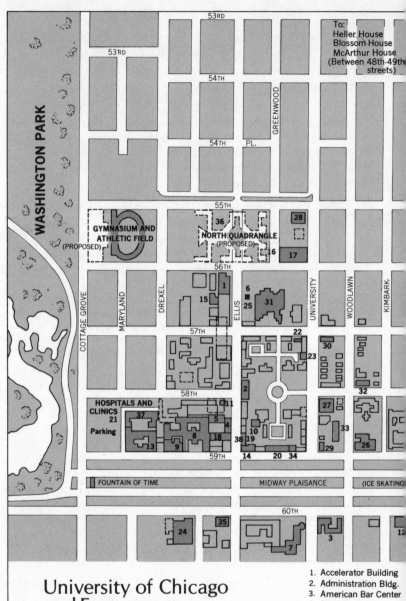

University of Chicago and Famous South Side Buildings

1. Accelerator Building
2. Administration Bldg.
3. American Bar Center
4. Argonne Cancer Research Hospital
5. Philip D. Armour Clinical Research
6. "Atomic Birthplace"

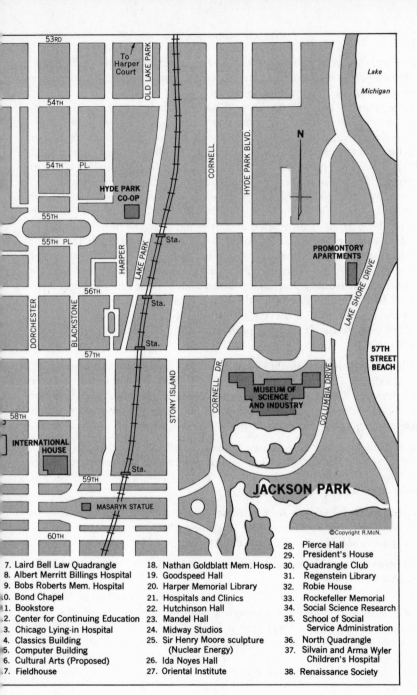

7. Laird Bell Law Quadrangle
8. Albert Merritt Billings Hospital
9. Bobs Roberts Mem. Hospital
10. Bond Chapel
11. Bookstore
12. Center for Continuing Education
13. Chicago Lying-in Hospital
14. Classics Building
15. Computer Building
16. Cultural Arts (Proposed)
17. Fieldhouse

18. Nathan Goldblatt Mem. Hosp.
19. Goodspeed Hall
20. Harper Memorial Library
21. Hospitals and Clinics
22. Hutchinson Hall
23. Mandel Hall
24. Midway Studios
25. Sir Henry Moore sculpture
     (Nuclear Energy)
26. Ida Noyes Hall
27. Oriental Institute

28. Pierce Hall
29. President's House
30. Quadrangle Club
31. Regenstein Library
32. Robie House
33. Rockefeller Memorial
34. Social Science Research
35. School of Social
     Service Administration
36. North Quadrangle
37. Silvain and Arma Wyler
     Children's Hospital
38. Renaissance Society

119

magazine and the accompanying editorial material praised Wright to the skies. When the magazine reached Japan the Far East discovered him, thus came the commission to build Tokyo's Imperial Hotel.

Robie House is one of America's 48 national landmarks, officially designated as such by the Department of the Interior. Only four houses in the country are in the group; of these, Robie House is the only one cited for purely architectural reasons. It is also the only modern building in the entire group.

What did Wright build that brought Secretary of Interior Stewart Udall to say: "There is no house in the United States that matches its importance. . . . It is one of the great statements by an American architect "? Briefly, it was the first house in the world to be built on a slab foundation; the first house in America to have garages constructed as part of the structure; the first house in which the overhangs were calculated on an astronomical basis for maximum natural light in winter and maximum shade in summer (prior to Wright, a roof overhang was a matter of architectural whim or sense of design). It was the first house to put laundry and utility rooms above grade; the first house in the world to use indirect lighting; the first to use rheostat lighting—the list goes on and on. The Adlai E. Stevenson Institute of International Affairs is now housed in Robie House. Tours by appointment. Phone Director of Public Relations, 684-3200.

Other Wright houses in the immediate area are: **I. Heller House,** 5132 South Woodlawn (1897); the nudes on the molded frieze are by sculptor Richard Bock; **G. Blossom House,** 4858 South Kenwood (1892); **L. McArthur House,** 4852 South Kenwood (1892); **Dr. A. W. Harlan House,** 4416 South Greenwood (1892).

In the University of Chicago area, see: **Laird Bell Law Quadrangle,** University of Chicago, 1121 East 60th, Eero Saarinen (four building complex, 1960); also his **Women's Dormitory** at Woodlawn and the Midway (59th Street, across the street from Rockefeller Chapel).

School of Social Service Administration, 969 East 60th, Ludwig Mies van der Rohe (1964). Also his **Promontory Apartments,** 5530 South Shore Drive—the first apartment he built in Chicago (1949).

J. J. Glessner Residence and Stables (L), 1800 South Prairie; Architect: H. H. Richardson, 1886

The Glessner residence is the last remaining building in Chicago built by H. H. Richardson; a monolithic 35-room Romanesque house of granite, it is considered his finest work. The house is built as an inward-turned L with all main rooms facing the quiet courtyard. It is being restored by the Chicago School of Architecture Foundation, which is now housed in it and maintains a museum, library and an information center on Chicago architecture. For information, call 326-1393.

Prairie Avenue is now one of the shabbiest of streets. In its day—from 1870 to a little after the turn of the century—it was *the* residential street in Chicago. The Marshall Fields I, the Marshall Fields II, the George Pullmans, the Philip Armours, Clarence and Kate Buckingham, the M. M. Rothschilds, and the W. W. Kimballs (pianos) lived here—and so did almost all the rest of Chicago's millionaire business and social leaders—70—on both sides of the street. The only house which retains any of its former glory is the Kimball mansion at 1801 South Prairie, a fanciful Solon Beman (1892). Coincidentally, the Glessner and Kimball houses mark the approximate site of the massacre of the small garrison, women, and children of Fort Dearborn.*

ILLINOIS INSTITUTE OF TECHNOLOGY CAMPUS

Ludwig Mies van der Rohe came to Chicago in 1938 to accept the directorship of the Armour Institute (later to become IIT) School of Architecture, which, at the time, was housed in an attic of the Art Institute. His first great project was the master plan for the IIT campus (see map, page 374), and though it took 25 years to build, its sense of order is remarkable. The buildings are low; extremely limited funds dictated the structural materials—brick, glass, steel. The method of construction is skin and skeleton—the skin is glass, except in the chapel where it is load-bearing brick. When you know that a slum had to be cleared for the project and consider the year in which construction began (1943), you can imagine the isolation of that first building—a type of geometric structure Chicago had never seen, standing in the middle of an absolute wasteland. Crown Hall, which houses the Department of Architecture, Planning and Design, is a gem. Its great roof, 120 by 220 feet, is suspended, and at each end of the building it projects 20 feet beyond the trusses. There are no interior supports. You may get a campus map at Crown Hall, also the Department of Architecture's list of outstanding Chicago buildings. It's the most complete list to date; it has maps but no interpretive material (50¢). Crown Hall also has continuous exhibits of architectural interest. 9 AM to 5 PM weekdays.

Mies designed and built the following buildings on the campus:

Crown Hall, Architecture, Planning & Design Building, IIT, 3360 South State, 1956;

Metals Research Building, Armour Research Foundation, 3338 South Federal, 1943;

---

*When the little band evacuated the fort for a land march to Detroit during the War of 1812, it followed a route south along present Michigan Avenue. The lake was at the group's left, a low sand dune at its right (you have to remember that everything east of Michigan Avenue is fill) and from behind the dune, the Potawatomi descended.

It was all over in 15 minutes; the Potawatomi marched the survivors back to the fort and there butchered the walking wounded.

Engineering Research Building, Armour Research Foundation, 55 West 34th Street, 1946;

Chemistry Building (now Perlstein Hall), IIT, 3216-3253 South Dearborn, 1946;

Metallurgical & Chemical Engineering Building, IIT, 10 West 33rd Street, 1946;

Alumni Memorial Hall, IIT, 3216-3244 South State, 1946;

Boiler Plant, IIT, 3440 South Federal, 1950;

Administration Building, Association of American Railroads, 3140 South Federal, 1950;

Institute of Gas Technology, IIT, 17 West 34th Street, 1950;

Test Cell, Armour Research Foundation, 3454 South Federal, 1950;

St. Saviour Chapel, IIT, 32nd Street and Michigan, 1952;

Mechanical Engineering Research Building I, Armour Research Foundation, 3422 South Dearborn, 1952;

Carman Hall, IIT, 60 East 32nd Street, 1953;

Mechanical Engineering Building, Association of American Railroads, 3100 South Federal, 1953;

Commons Building, IIT, 3200 South Wabash, 1953;

Bailey Hall, IIT, 3101 South Wabash, 1955;

Cunningham Hall, IIT, 3100 South Michigan, 1955;

Physics and Electrical Engineering Building, Armour Research Foundation, 3440 South State, 1956;

Metals Research Building Addition, Armour Research Foundation, 3300 South Federal, 1957;

Electrical Engineering & Physics Building, IIT, 3300 South Dearborn, 1957.

John Crerar Library, 35 West 33rd Street, and the **Student Union,** 3241 South Federal, were erected by Skidmore, Owings and Merrill.

Michigan Avenue or Dan Ryan Expy to 35th Street exit (there's parking on the campus), see map, page 374. Or, North-South subway; Englewood A train; or Jackson Park B train to 35th Street. CTA buses, State No. 36A, Wentworth No. 22A stop along the campus.

UNIVERSITY OF ILLINOIS AT CHICAGO CIRCLE

It's a new, almost instant, campus, not yet finished, a commuter campus without dormitories or a faculty row. Designed by Skidmore, Owings and Merrill, it is a huge maze of precast and poured concrete scaled to superhuman dimensions that will either leave you feeling disoriented or triumphant, depending on the way you've gone through it. Best way is on a student-guided architectural tour, which can be had any hour between 10 AM and 3 PM Monday through Friday. Phone Tour and Information Office, 663-8686. Tours run one to two hours; if you want a two-hour tour, make your reservation a week in advance and request the best guide to be had. Free, but the tour office hopes you'll compliment your guide if you feel praise is due. These kids work hard to improve their architectural knowledge and like to know when they've done a good job. They'll furnish maps and also give you insight into student life on a commuter campus. Also see page 333; and map, page 374.

> Kennedy Expy or Dan Ryan Expy to the Roosevelt Road exits. Campus is one block west and north of the exit ramps which are marked as campus exits. CTA buses Harrison No. 7, Roosevelt No. 12 or Taylor No. 37. Congress subway trains A and B stop at U. of Illinois-Halsted stop on the West-Northwest subway. Campus is one block south of the station.

FRANK LLOYD WRIGHT IN OAK PARK AND RIVER FOREST

Chicago itself has approximately 15 homes and apartment buildings by Frank Lloyd Wright. Ten of these, including his masterpiece, Robie House, are on the South Side, while Charnley House, which he's believed to have designed while at Adler and Sullivan, is at 1365 North Astor. Architects planning to visit the Graham Foundation for Advanced Studies in the Fine Arts at 4 West Burton (L), will find Charnley House just three short blocks away (corner of Schiller). The Foundation has splendid architectural exhibitions. Phone SU 7-4071 for information.

Another dozen Wright homes are scattered through the North Shore suburbs.

But Oak Park and River Forest were Wright's proving grounds and have between them 31 of his buildings. The one house and stable he built in 1893 for William H. Winslow (**515 Auvergne**) was considered so radical that its owner finally avoided rush-hour commuter trains because he simply could not stand any more comments from his neighbors. Winslow House is considered the first clear statement of Wright's architectural themes. It was his first independent commission after leaving Adler and Sullivan, and the arched entrance to the stable is very Sullivan-like, and also more prophetic than the house, which is Wright doing his independent best.

Wright was one of the most inventive, prolific, imaginative architects of our time. Ideas came by the dozens, including open plans, casement windows, car ports, free flowing interiors, and exteriors that were integral parts of the landscape—hence, Prairie Houses. He influenced Mies in Europe as early as 1910 with a Berlin exhibition, and Mies still speaks of him as the Master. Yet, except for his students, no architects follow his path, though all have adapted his major ideas.

Like all the men of the First Chicago School, he was trained as an engineer, and the training was as helpful to him as it was to the others. He was experimental; he had a tremendous sense of scale. If you're unfamiliar with his work, discover him first in Oak Park and then see Robie House, which isn't really comprehensible without some background.

The Oak Park Public Library, 834 Lake, EU 3-5030, has compiled an illustrated booklet, *A Guide to the Architecture of Frank Lloyd Wright,* of his buildings in Oak Park and River Forest; a map plots a compact tour of both suburbs. Send a check for $1.15 to the library for a copy in advance, or stop at the Circulation Department when you arrive in Oak Park. Library hours: 9 AM to 9 PM Monday through Friday, Saturday to 5 PM.

To get to Oak Park:

> Eisenhower Expy to Oak Park, or the Lake Street elevated train, which can
> be boarded at any Loop elevated station. Austin Boulevard is the dividing

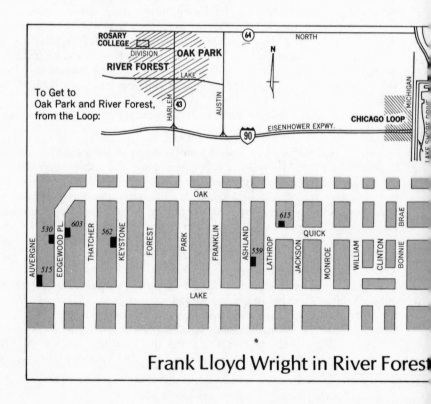

Frank Lloyd Wright in River Forest

line between Chicago and Oak Park where north and south street numbers begin at North Boulevard. In River Forest, the numbering system is identical to Chicago with Madison Street as the dividing line between north and south blocks.

Map shows locations by street numbers of the 31 Wright buildings, plus three others marked EH; these three are the homes Ernest Hemingway lived in as a boy. The house at **339** (was 439) **North Oak Park Avenue** is the one he was born in, a typical middle-class late Victorian Queen Anne. From 1905 to 1906 the family lived in the house directly north of the Oak Park Library, then moved into their newly built home at **600 North Kenilworth,** a large plain gray stucco house which Mrs. Hemingway was forever remodeling. Hemingway lived here until he was 17, and he hiked along the Des Plaines River and through Thatcher Woods at the western boundary of River Forest.

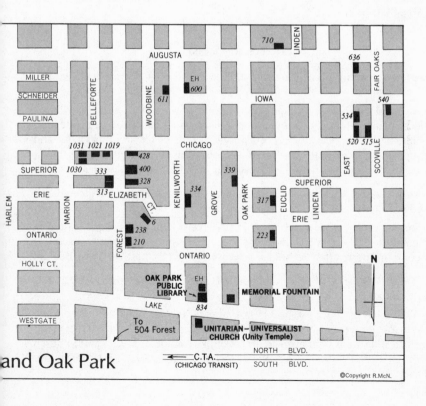

and Oak Park

Two Wright buildings in Oak Park are open to the public: his Unitarian-Universalist Church at **875 Lake,** built as Unity Temple, and the house and studio he brought his bride to, at **951 Chicago Avenue.** The Clyde W. Nookers, who've lived in it some 20 years, open it to the public every day but Monday, 10 AM to 5 PM. Tours are conducted by architectural students. Admission, $1.25. All other Wright buildings are private homes in use; the owners will be grateful if you do not ring their bells and ask admittance or mouse around the premises.

The house at **603 Edgewood Place,** originally of stucco, was remodeled in brick, under Wright's supervision, in 1955. The house at **530 Edgewood** is a style he never repeated. The house at **6 Elizabeth Court** (1909) was the progenitor for his famous Falling Water House in Bear Run, Pennsylvania (1936). The house and stable at **333 Forest Avenue** is a half-timbered Tudor inspiration which was completely alien to his thinking but what a client demanded. Wright hated it; when it brought requests for similar houses he was furious. When a fire gutted this one in the early 1920's, he managed to work in a number of his then-current ideas; the combination produced some unconsciously whimsical effects.

NOT TO BE MISSED

Interior of the Arts Club of Chicago, 109 East Ontario; Architect: Ludwig Mies van der Rohe, 1951

An exquisite background for art exhibitions and small concerts, plus a gracious members' dining room. Go up the suspended stairway to the second floor; the exhibition hall (open to the public) is directly ahead of the stairs, and a lounge with a stage is at your left. If anyone still thinks that modern architecture negates the use of antique furnishings, the lounge will be a revelation.

Five Row Houses, 1826, -28, -33, -32, -34 Lincoln Park West; Architect: Louis H. Sullivan, 1884

Simple, warm, brick row houses in Old Town kept in excellent condition by their present owners. Sullivan built them for a Mrs. Ann Halsted, probably as income property after he built the house she lived in at 440 West Belden.

Holy Trinity Russian Orthodox Cathedral, 1121 North Leavitt; Architect: Louis H. Sullivan, 1903

Almost out of *Dr. Zhivago,* this small, beautifully simple little cathedral no larger than the average church. The Byzantine ancestry of much Russian architecture shows through, even to an onionlike "dome." If you can attend an Eastern Orthodox service here, you'll be glad you did. (See Easter under *Annual Events.*)

For Sullivan's famous Getty and Ryerson tombs in Graceland Cemetery, see page 386.

Henry B. Clarke House, 4526 South Wabash; Architect: unknown, 1836

The oldest Chicago house still standing comes as a surprise to everyone. You expect to see a mangy log cabin or, at best, a shack; instead, the Henry B. Clarke house reveals not only the spaciousness of the city's first elegant homes but the way the early settlers (mainly New Englanders) brought their own architecture with them; the Clarke House would look at home in any New England town. The original porch and tall shutters have been removed, and the house itself has been moved from its original site near 16th and Michigan.

MUSEUMS

6

CHAPTER 6

MUSEUMS

Like the great European capitals and like Washington, D.C., and New York, Chicago is rich in museums. At least six of its 28 rank with the major museums of the world; a dozen, though not major, are unique; the rest fall into the category of delightful esoterica. But large or small, they're all so specialized that no single museum is *The Museum*. In this city, *The Museum* is literally all over town.

Paradoxically, Chicago's two best-known museums, the Field Museum of Natural History and the Museum of Science and Industry, have come to be thought of as children's museums, which they're not. That they're currently overrun with schoolchildren is as much the result of the cultural explosion as anything; the only way to avoid swarms of children is to confine your visits to Sunday mornings or, in summer, to any late hours offered. Certainly if you're here with very young children, you'd be wise to save the giant museums for another trip: the Field Museum and Science and Industry are too vast, their exhibits too sophisticated, for children much younger than eight.

Equally paradoxical is the fact that the Chicago Historical Society is Chicago's only museum of American history, while no museum exists in which you can discover the great, unholy side of Chicago history—the Everleigh sisters and their gold piano, Bathhouse John and the Levee, the saloonkeeper who gave the world the phrase "a Mickey Finn," the people idolizing Capone.*

But if you want to see the famous Baedekers that guided visitors of the 1880's and '90's through Chicago's roaring vice districts, you'll have to do li-

---

*The closest thing to a public exhibit of this last are the gruesome life-size wax effigies portraying the St. Valentine's Day Massacre in the Old Town branch of the Royal London Wax Museum, a display that might correctly be called the St. Capone Diorama. See Glossary.

brary research or wangle an invitation to the Tavern Club, which has a set on display. The Gaslight, a key club, has a simpering marble nymph from the Everleigh Sisters' fabulous brothel, but she's only on the premises as a joke. The missing museum is not a joke—it's missed.

A word of caution: Because the Field Museum, Adler Planetarium and Shedd Aquarium are a trinity near Roosevelt Road and the lakefront, local propaganda inevitably suggests you visit all three on the same day. Don't even try. All that can come of such folly is the grim feeling of a forced march and aching feet. You do *not* owe it to any city to polish off three museums at one crack; besides, it's not possible. However, you *can* take advantage of their proximity to a sightseeing boat that docks in the harbor just north of the aquarium, and combine the pleasant contrasts of one museum with a lakefront cruise. You can also combine a free Grant Park open-air concert in the evening or an event at Soldier Field with an afternoon-early evening visit to the Field Museum or the planetarium, since both keep late hours in summer. The Field Museum's cafeteria will feed you decently enough, or you can get hot dogs and soft drinks at the band shell northward in the park. The concerts are outstanding, and CTA buses wait at the ready just south of the band shell as the performance ends (see map, page 159).

To reach the Field Museum, Adler Planetarium, Shedd Aquarium, take bus No. 126 (marked *Planetarium* or *14th and Lake Shore*), or State Street shuttle bus No. 149. Illinois Central commuter trains stop at 12th Street—walk east across the bridge over the tracks to the Field Museum. By car, Lake Shore Drive from North or South sides of the city. Free parking at north side of the Field Museum; 25¢ parking at south entrance. Parking also available at the planetarium.

On the following list of museums to be found in this chapter, asterisks indicate those of international renown.

Field Museum of Natural History*

Adler Planetarium and Astronomical Museum*

John G. Shedd Aquarium*

Chicago Academy of Sciences

Museum of Science and Industry*

Oriental Institute*

Chicago Historical Society

Museum of the International College of Surgeons

Lizzadro Museum of Lapidary Arts

Museum of African-American History

Polish Museum of America

Maurice Spertus Museum of Judaica

Morton B. Weiss Museum of Judaica
Freedom Hall of the Institute of Human Relations
Balzekas Museum of Lithuanian Culture
Ukrainian National Museum
Grand Army of the Republic Memorial Hall

Art Institute of Chicago, Museum of Contemporary Art, Arts Club, and Renaissance Society will be found beginning on page 153.

Morton Arboretum and the Botanic Garden, both outdoor nature museums, are described on pages 388 and 390.

Hinsdale Health Museum, Frontier Museum, and Timke's Indian Museum are museums especially for children and will be found beginning on page 311.

The war museums at Fort Sheridan and Cantigny are described on pages 321 and 322.

Field Museum of Natural History, Roosevelt and Lake Shore Drive, 922-9410; *E. Leland Webber, Director*

Marshall Field I created it; his nephew Stanley Field and his grandson made it the remarkable institution it is today. As with every Field endeavor on behalf of this city, the Field Museum belongs to Chicago in a special way and is the closest thing to *The Museum* you will find here. Even Chicagoans who haven't visited it in years, or who may only have wandered through a few of its galleries, think of it as such and regard it as one of their city's greatest possessions.

Rightly so, for the Field Museum is devoted to natural history and anthropology on a worldwide scale. In this country it's outranked only by the Smithsonian Institution and the American Museum of Natural History. Here, the story of mankind is not merely western man's story, but it embraces the civilizations of China and Tibet, the ancient cultures of the Near East,* Indians of the Americas, peoples of Oceania, the African heritage. The African collection contains some 400 pieces of Benin art, hundreds of artifacts and a Cameroon king's house, which can be the single most memorable exhibit if you buy the marvelous little booklet *The King's Day* (35¢) at the museum bookstore.

The point is, you could spend days in the galleries displaying the story of mankind without ever getting into the other seven acres of exhibits devoted to natural history—the planet Earth, prehistoric life, the plant world, the animal kingdom. So, to enjoy the museum, you have to be selective. On the way in,

---

* The Egyptian collections overlap those of the Oriental Institute, and art of the Far East crosses with the Art Institute, so if you're planning to visit those museums you may want to skip them here.

ask for current free maps, folders, and descriptive material highlighting the major exhibitions.

What the folders can't tell you is the degree to which you'll be amused by small carved and painted figures in the Primitive Artists Look At Civilization Exhibit. They're tongue in cheek caricatures of European colonials and delicious little private jokes created by observant natives who could view the bwanas with amusement as well as anger. Nor have the folders space to describe the superb exhibit of precious gems and Etruscan and Greco-Roman jewelry. This museum removes centuries of tarnish and encrustation from its antiquities and restores them all to their original splendor, thereby creating exquisite, like-new antiquities.

Everyone wants to see the unbelievable Chalmers blue topaz—and it would be hard to miss: 5,890 carats revolving slowly in a bath of light, its facets shooting brilliance that neon signmakers would give their eyeteeth to duplicate.

The sculptures in the Hall of Man tend to stop some people cold, because they purport to delineate mankind in 92 separate types, a notion anthropologists have proved false. So it helps to know that the museum itself now regards the sculptures merely as a series of beautiful representations of human beings by a recognized 20th-Century sculptress, Malvina Hoffman.

There are more dinosaur skeletons in the natural history museums of Pittsburgh and New York, but if your children have never seen any, the skeletons shouldn't be missed. They're located near the superb displays of realistic stuffed animals in their natural habitats. (Su-Lin, a mounted giant panda is there; also Bushman, Chicago's famous gorilla.) These displays, in turn, aren't far from the life-size dioramas of prehistoric humans, a collection so utterly realistic that young children are often convinced that these are real people who got stuffed, too.

The American Indian collection is one of the greatest in the country, comprising not merely tools and weapons and artifacts but molded figures of Indians, with elegant features, wearing the costumes of their tribes, working in the various tasks that characterized daily life among the Plains, Pueblo and Woodland tribes. Maps and background legends tell almost, but not quite, as much as you want to know.

On the second floor are three collections that will make your head swim. The unrivaled ethnological exhibit of the Chinese Ch'ing Period embraces the full range of the culture, not merely its art. Nearby is the jade collection, an old exhibit, but absolutely magnificent. Across the hall stands the world's largest collection of plant models—rare and unusual plants, useful plants, fossil plants—and a hall of North American trees. If *Kon-Tiki* aroused your curiosity about Oceanian culture, head downstairs for the Pacific Island halls. They're as large as an average museum and so filled with exhibits and information that *Kon-Tiki's* author, Thor Heyerdahl, comes to study them.

Recently the museum unveiled its own great auk. The bird is extinct, and specimens of it are so rare that the museum had to trade almost 2,000 specimens of American birds for it.

More recently, the museum mounted an exhibition of paintings created by three talented chimpanzees. The chimps painted for their own pleasure, and their work shows a surprising talent for composition and control. The art is, naturally, "nonrepresentational and lacks informational content." The museum uses the ape art to show how man added symbols to his pictures to provide the content.

Adult film lectures each Saturday in March and April, October and November at 2:30 PM. Special programs for children—see page 311. And for qualified scholars and researchers, one of the greatest specialized libraries anywhere—160,000 volumes dealing with the museum's particular fields.

> Open daily (except Christmas and New Year's) 9 AM to 5 PM; in summer, open Wednesday, Friday, Saturday, Sunday to 8 PM; other days to 6 PM. Free. Cafeteria opens at 11 AM; you can also use the cafeteria in Park District headquarters, the building just south of the museum on 14th Street.

Adler Planetarium and Astronomical Museum, 900 East Achsah Bond Drive (Northerly Island), WA 2-4488; *Joseph M. Chamberlain, Director*

Of all Chicago museums, this one may be the most unexpectedly rewarding. Most people assume its exhibits will be too "scientific" for them, but that's not true. The whole purpose of the museum is to explain as simply as possible the awesome mysteries of space and time.

Begin at the information desk. Ask for whatever literature is available and for the time of the next planetarium lecture. Head for it—the other exhibits will make more sense later. The fascinating star show, conducted by a member of the astronomy staff, takes place in the large chamber (some chairs have special equipment for deaf visitors) under the museum's domed roof. There the great Zeiss Projection Planetarium (it's an instrument, not a building) re-creates the vast sky, the 9,000 stars visible to the unaided eye, the sun, the moon, planets, meteors, the Milky Way, the aurora borealis. During the hour show you are moved back in time 26,000 years or forward to the 26th Century. Or you are taken to the North Pole, the South Pole—even Bethlehem the night Christ was born.

Astronomy is the oldest of the sciences, and its origins lie in ancient religions and philosophies which you learn about during the lecture. The observations men made centuries ago are yours to discover, too, and the ways men began to conceive of time and the instruments they created to measure space and time.

Those instruments (the earliest is a Babylonian tablet from 2000 B.C. showing a constellation) form the second largest collection (Oxford first) of antique instruments in the world, some 500, including the famed Mensing collection, begun about 1600, and the Strozzi collection, begun by a Florentine family some 400 years ago. The exhibit is as much art as science since many of the elaborate, exquisitely designed instruments of brass, bronze and silver were made for royalty and aristocracy, somewhat in the manner of "gentleman's toy boxes." You'll find mechanical planetaria; celestial globes; armillary spheres (one with an inscription, "Cabinet Du Roy Versailles"—and the king was Louis XIV); astrolabes, octants, sextants, sun dials (including dials by Christopher Wren and President Thomas Jefferson); hourglasses; compasses; telescopes; clepsydras (water clocks) and other early clocks.

In other exhibits: oversized photographs and transparencies of the earth (taken from U.S. and Russian space flights), the stars, sun, moon, galaxies. Farther along, the huge Rand McNally geophysical relief globe, its diameter of 75 inches representing the earth's diameter of 7,917 miles (the scale is one inch = 106 miles). The view you get is comparable to the view astronauts in space have of Earth.

The museum also offers outdoor stargazing parties in July and August, each Friday night from 9 PM to 11 PM (also during eclipses); an outstanding library (open to anyone who has a serious project in astronomy); free courses in basic and advanced astronomy, navigation and celestial navigation; a special weekend program for children; a unique workshop for amateur telescope-makers of all ages; and a wonderful bookstore and shop.

> Summer hours: 9:30 AM to 9:30 PM except Mondays (to 5 PM). Winter
> hours: 9:30 AM to 5 PM but Tuesday and Friday evenings to 9:30 PM.
> Closed only on Thanksgiving, Christmas, New Year's. Museum and lecture
> hall admission always free, Planetarium Chamber, 50¢.

Note: Don't call the Museum about UFO's. The staff will not get involved in the endless argument.

John G. Shedd Aquarium, 1200 South Lake Shore Drive (Roosevelt), WE 9-2426; *William Braker, Director*

The aquarium can be viewed in several ways, and you may find one more interesting than another. One view is architectural—a basically Doric structure of white marble with magnificent bronze doors, its calm, white, classic interior enhanced with aquatic animal motifs. Even the clock is in character—aquatic animals rather than numerals.

The second way to look at the aquarium is as a place to be entertained. It is the largest aquarium in existence and gives you a chance to view a fish and aquatic animal population of 5,000 to 7,500, including almost 400 species of fish, turtles, invertebrates, sea horses, three birds (penguins), one mammal (porpoise) and one of the prototypes of the mermaid myth—the manatee. The aquarium's manatee is enormous, and you'll wonder how any ancient mariner —even one who'd been at sea for years—could possibly have fantasized a mermaid out of the creature. The assumption is that sea distances, a roseate sunset, and the fact that female manatees use their flippers to hold their young and lie on their backs while nursing made it possible.

The third way is to visit the aquarium as a place to learn something *interesting* about fish; but there are no tours or even prerecorded information in front of the well-maintained tanks. However, you can help yourself: buy a copy of Walter Chute's *Guide to the John G. Shedd Aquarium* ($1.50) at the aquarium store. Or, if you're lucky, you may meet the director, who has a headful of enchanting, offbeat knowledge about fish, such as: The drab brown Australian lungfish that sits on the bottom of its tank is almost a living fossil; his body structure has remained unchanged 250 million years. He surfaces to breathe and takes in air through a fish lung . . . . The horseshoe crab goes back 350 million years and is another living fossil, the only survivor of an earlier, once larger, group of animals . . . . The dolphin is a toothed whale but not a true whale . . . . It's almost impossible for the aquarium to keep an octopus because he's sensitive and doesn't like to be handled. He probably also doesn't like captivity (he has the largest brain of any mollusk) because he won't adapt to it and at most will live in captivity a week to three months . . . . Barracuda pike are *not* man-eaters, and the only time they're dangerous is when you swim in murky water wearing the white tennis shoes you've been told to wear or a bright ring which no one ever suggests you remove. In either instance, barracuda will strike. However, there's some comfort in the fact that their long sharp teeth are for grasping and holding but not for chewing.

> Open daily except Christmas and New Year's. May through August hours, 9 AM to 5 PM; spring and fall hours, 10 AM to 5 PM; winter hours, 10 AM to 4 PM. Free Thursday, Saturday, Sunday; adult admission 25¢ all other times.

Chicago Academy of Sciences, 2001 North Clark, LI 9-0606; *William J. Beecher, Director*

For years the city's oldest scientific museum was also its gloomiest and dullest. Founded in 1857, 11 years after the Smithsonian, it was known as "the first museum of the West." Today it's one of the most visually exciting small natural history museums in the country, thanks to its splendidly eccentric director, who may well be the only scientist capable also of serving as chief architect, chief photographer, art director and display director of premises that were admirable in 1893 but impossible when he came to them in 1958. One can visualize Dr. Beecher stalking through the old institution with a sense of mounting indignation at the sheer deadliness of everything that then confronted him and making his decision to accept the directorship on the basis of the immensity of the challenge. Anyone else in his right mind would have immediately said No, thank you; Dr. Beecher shed his jacket.

The result of his furious energy is natural history brought to life with every modern display idea Dr. Beecher could borrow—and create. In this museum you enter a dense coal forest (complete with the sounds of flies and bugs) that was the Chicago area 350 million years ago. You walk around a corner and are suddenly in a rain forest where tropical birds attack a boa constrictor. On the second floor, where the emphasis is on the natural history of the Great Lakes region, a tree trail* leads to the great Indiana Dunes exhibits. On the third floor, dioramas and walk-in exhibits of the origins of the world, of life on earth, of the appearance of man; a vast globe of the world houses a small planetarium (the Atwood Celestial Globe, designed in 1913) which shows the skies as seen from Chicago. The planetarium is cozy and eminently satisfactory for children.

Also ask about the museum's free week-night lecture series, films and Saturday field trips which give you the chance to discover the natural wonders of this region in the company of leading biologists, botanists, zoologists. Field trips are free except for bus fares. The museum's library may be used by scholars and science students. A Junior Curator Program and the Junior Academy are open to talented Chicago area students who want to become scientists.

> Open 10 AM to 5 PM daily. Free. CTA buses No. 76, 153 or 156 to Stockton Drive and Armitage; or No. 22 or 36 to Clark and Armitage. The museum is just east of Clark Street in Lincoln Park and can be combined nicely with a trip to the Lincoln Park Zoo.

Museum of Science and Industry, East 57th Street and South Shore Drive, MU 4-1414; *Daniel M. MacMaster, Director*

It's Chicago's show-off museum—the one every native insists you must see. It's a vastly entertaining, informative, and ever-changing place, one of the world's few museums where you can come to grips with time, motion, energy, atomic energy, electronics, mathematics, sound, aspects of computer sciences, and enjoy every minute of it. Its major purpose: to show "the meaning of science translated by industry into terms of living, to show how the combination of science and industry produces the American way of life." If that second clause seems both grandiose and ethnocentric, ignore it in favor of the museum experience itself, which is like being turned loose in a gigantic, ingenious laboratory where you're free to experiment with everything in sight. Display after display says to you, "Push the button and watch what happens."

Discerning visitors are often bothered by the museum's Barnum and Bailey approach to science and the free publicity to certain industries. The museum operates on the theory that museum-going needn't be a stuffy, hushed-voice experience. But in recent years, things have gotten out of hand. Perhaps it *is*

---

* The tree trail illustrating the 30 trees that grow in this region came into being when Dr. Beecher discovered he could not uproot the museum's obstructive supporting pillars. Beneath each plaster bark (cast from latex molds made on living trees) find—marble.

time that somebody in authority put the reins on the stampede of undisciplined, fun-loving youngsters. It's perfectly true that millions of visitors go through the world's first diesel train engine, through a captured German submarine, a re-created coal mine purely for enjoyment and don't relate them to scientific or technological innovation or to anything else. What you get out of the museum is up to you.

As to the second criticism, a science and industry museum can't exist without collaboration. At one time, each exhibitor was limited to a single small name plaque; lately the regulation has been relaxed. One reason: the U.S. State Department uses the museum as a Midwest showplace. By bringing official visitors to it, the State Department can, in the words of a museum official, "eliminate the tours of factories and scientific laboratories; our industrial exhibits show what's going on in one fell swoop."

Expect to spend the better part of a day here. The place is enormous; you're not going to be able to see all of it. Get a museum guidebook and map at the information desk; plan to lunch in the cafeteria or luncheonette (retired people in the neighborhood eat in it regularly—its prices are that reasonable). Smoke cigarettes anywhere on the premises. Be sure to see the great Foucault pendulum demonstrating the earth's rotation. Regular lecture-demonstrations daily. Special lectures in the auditorium on weekends, concerts off and on during the year—outdoors in a lagoon setting in summer (see page 174).

> Open every day but Christmas. Summer schedule: 9:30 AM to 5:30 PM Monday through Saturday; on Sunday and holidays, 10 AM to 6 PM. Winter schedule: 4 PM closing on weekdays, except during the annual Christmas exhibit when the museum is open to 9 PM. Illinois Central commuter train to 57th Street, walk east; the museum is at the entrance to Jackson Park. By car, South Lake Shore Drive. CTA buses No. 2, 5, 55, but they all take much longer than the Illinois Central.

Oriental Institute, 1155 East 58th Street (University of Chicago campus), MI 3-0800, Ext. 2471; *George R. Hughes, Director*

The Oriental Institute specializes in the exploration of ancient civilizations of the part of the world we now call the Near East,* and its museum displays the astounding results of those explorations and archeological digs. In truth, you will find more antiquities here from more places in the Near East than in any other museum in the country, including the Metropolitan in New York.

To see ancient Egypt from its beginning through all the dynasties, you have to come here. To satisfy curiosity about the civilizations of Sumer and

---

* When the institute was founded, the phrase "Near East" had not come into use. So Dr. Breasted used the European designation "Oriental" for the lands immediately east of Europe—Egypt, Nubia, Turkey, and the countries that are now Libya, Iraq, Iran, Israel, Jordan, Syria.

Akkad, Babylonia and Assyria, or those of Palestine or Persepolis, or the collections rescued from Nubian cemeteries that have now disappeared under the backup waters of the Aswan Dam, find them here. The whole point of the institute since its founding by Dr. James Henry Breasted has been to rescue all possible original evidence on the history of human culture and to interpret and present it as the earliest story of civilization. The effect of the evidence (it dates from 3000 B.C.) is better than a tranquilizer. You begin to feel that if man could come this distance, as he indeed has, he may possibly survive the violent wrenchings of our century which mark the end of 5,000 years of an agrarian civilization and the beginning of the technological age.

You can't look at bricks such as the Children of Israel made without gaining that kind of perspective. You can't view the collection of delicate Sumerian statues without feeling that, like the Children of Israel, man's sense of beauty also endures. In one large hall, go far back in time to discover the original Great Bull that guarded part of the entrance to the palace of Sargon II, greatest of all Assyrian kings. The Great Bull with his fifth leg is part of human legacy, too. Like the Sumerian statues, there is no collection anywhere of antiquities duplicating these, just as there is no equivalent Nubian collection outside Cairo. Near a model of the Tower of Babel (it fascinates Fundamentalists) are old tiles from the Ishtar gate. Around a corner is the only Dead Sea scroll jar in the U.S., with fragments of the scroll it contained.

The Egyptian wing, dominated by a reconstruction of the enormous stone portrait of Tutankhamen, contains art and artifacts: musical instruments, gaming boards, an adult's bed that stuns everyone by its smallness (but the ancient Egyptians were only four to four and a half feet tall). Out of Tutankhamen's tomb came the astronomical instruments on display. The contents of other tombs form exhibits of jewelry; cosmetic jars; mummified eggs, bread, cheese, chickens, ducks; gold mummy cases; painted mummy cases; mummies themselves, with skins the color of dark leather, all their features intact.

Volunteer guides will explain steps of mummification and how the Rosetta Stone hieroglyphics were deciphered. At a temple statue of Horus, the god who took the form of a falcon, you learn that priests worked ropes to move the falcon's beak, speaking from behind him as the voice of a god. You learn that ancient sculptors could not depict children, so they made small adults, finger to mouth to indicate children, sidelocks if the children represented were boys. You learn that the first chairs were made not for comfort, but to elevate an important person, an idea carried through centuries and which you'll come across in the form of an African chieftain's stool at the Museum of African-American History (page 142).

One facet of the institute's research worth knowing about: the compilation of the Assyrian dictionary, an act of scholarship and dedication that has not only involved the accumulation of nearly two million file cards, but already has consumed the life work of a platoon of scholars. The dictionary will be published in 26 volumes, of which ten have now appeared; the only parallels to the effort involved were the German government's Egyptian dictionary, which took 50 years to compile, and the Oxford English dictionary. Yet, the differences are crucial. Though the Assyrian language was spoken for 2,000 years, the number of universities with Assyrian studies is so limited that only 900 copies of each volume will be printed. That's scholarship at the University of Chicago.

> Open Tuesday and Wednesday, 10 AM to noon, 1 PM to 5 PM. Thursday through Sunday, 10 AM to 5 PM. Closed Mondays and holidays. One hour tours at 10:15 AM, 11:15, 1:15 PM, 2:30. Free. Illinois Central commuter train to 59th Street. Walk west to University Avenue or hop the University bus that rumbles (at terribly infrequent intervals) along 59th Street. Better yet, take a cab from the station.

Chicago Historical Society, North Avenue and Clark, MI 2-4600; *Clement M. Silvestro, Director*

If you're familiar with and fond of the museum pattern of privately supported historical societies,* you'll enjoy this one since it is so much grander than most such endeavors. Its building is stately, the exhibits are meticulous. Though it has a great many typical collections of Mrs. So-and-So's silver and her equally prominent sister-in-law's clothes, it goes well beyond such donations. Find the Civil War, a superb Lincoln collection that includes artifacts of national significance, a variety of American period rooms, copies of the inaugural gowns of all the U.S. Presidents' wives, a fine early gun collection and suitably dramatic displays of the Fort Dearborn Massacre and Chicago Fire.

The society lists itself in the Yellow Pages as a "Museum of American, Illinois and Chicago History." It is, yet it never makes the same clear statement of purpose on any of its descriptive literature, and the omission leads a great many Chicagoans as well as visitors into thinking that perhaps the Chicago Historical Society is the missing museum, the one with the material that will show you how Chicago got its international reputation for lawlessness and gangsterism. And so it does—upstairs in the library where you may dig it out in research.

That library is one of the great public resources for the history of Chicago, and it is almost as big on the histories of the Midwest, Illinois, the Civil War, and sports. The first four collections are the more impressive for the fact that the original 100,000 manuscripts, maps, books, newspapers, relics, histories of the various Indian tribes who formerly occupied the Illinois prairies, and the original draft of the Emancipation Proclamation, were destroyed in the Great

---

* The key descriptive word is *genteel*. The key opportunity to visitors is the chance to snoop through collections that show how the First Families of a community lived.

Fire. The collection was matchless; it had been started when the historical society was organized (with a fine awareness of Chicago's future) in 1856 when, you realize, the city was just 23 years old. The present library is open to all visitors and high school students; the remarkable print collection is accessible to qualified researchers.

> Open 9:30 to 4:30 Monday through Saturday; Sunday, 12:30 to 5:30. Closed on Thanksgiving, Christmas, New Year's. Free to children, students, teachers at all times and to visitors on all weekdays except Memorial Day, July 4th and Labor Day, when admission is 25¢. Fine old Hollywood films are shown every Sunday at 2:15. CTA buses No. 36 or 22 to North Avenue and Clark. Or Nos. 76 or 153 to LaSalle Drive in Lincoln Park. East entrance of the building faces the park. Parking facilities in Lincoln Park lot one-half block north.

International College of Surgeons, 1524 North Lake Shore Drive, MI 2-3555, *Judith Toedte, Secretary, Hall of Fame*

Two elegant old mansions on Lake Shore Drive serve as United States headquarters for the organization and its museum.* Both were founded by Chicagoan Dr. Max Thorek, who was also an author, linguist, distinguished photographer, and specialist in Napoleonic history.

The museum is based on the history of surgery and allied sciences, the progress of medicine, the development of surgical instruments, the history of healing herbs. If your stomach is strong enough, there's a fine exhibit of the history of bloodletting and another of 2,000-year-old trephined Peruvian skulls.

The libraries of the college may be used by serious researchers and medical students upon request. The monthly winter lecture series at 8:00 on Tuesday evenings is open to anyone interested in attending. The subjects are not always what you'd expect—"Mozart's Death from a Medical-Historical View," or "Sex in Scandinavia and How It May Affect . . . Sexual Morals in the U.S." being as typical as an evening devoted to "The Growth of Forensic Pathology in Illinois."

> Open Monday through Saturday, 10 AM to 4 PM. Guided tours available on request. Free.

Lizzadro Museum of Lapidary Arts, 220 Cottage Hill (Wilder Park), Elmhurst, 833-1616; *John Lizzadro, Director*

One of the two new museums in the Chicago area built on a single private collection—this one of gems (precious and semiprecious), fossils, minerals and art objects carved from jades, ivories, corals, such as an Imperial Chinese screen, a birthday gift to the emperor Ch'ien Lung in 1736, and a pi (a prayer wheel, pronounced *bi*) of the Chou dynasty more than 2,000 years old.

---

* The building at 1524 is a stone-for-stone replica inside and out of Le Petit Trianon at Versailles.

A spectacular mass of uncut jade weighing 1,300 pounds flanks the museum's entrance. Inside, brilliantly lit display cases hold rubies; sapphires; emeralds; tiger eyes; topazes; lapis lazuli ranging in color from sky blue to violet; a phoenix bird of agate; Scottish jewels of agate; three solid gold elves working on an uncut emerald; an ivory ceremonial elephant solidly encrusted with gems; a coral Kwan Yin figure; a madonna of rutilated smoky quartz; the Last Supper carved, in the last century, of ivory.

A wall of dioramas shows gem animals in their natural environment—obsidian bears and an agate timber wolf in the North Woods, jade alligators in the Everglades, bloodstone dinosaurs in a forest of 100 million years ago, jasper and agate mallards in a cattail marsh. Fossils tell the early history of our earth; thunder eggs from Oregon (the Indians believed they were hurled by angry gods) bring the story up to the 20th Century.

Slide lectures downstairs seem to be continuous, and though tours lasting about 45 minutes are by appointment only, an individual can tag along if the group is not too big. Catch lectures on earth sciences at 2 PM the second and fourth Saturday of each month from September through May, and closed-circuit TV gem-cutting demonstrations every Sunday at 3 PM. Lapidary classes offer Chicagoans and suburbanites four phases of jewelry making. The museum shop contains everything from small uncut gem samples, such as tourmaline and garnets, to stone-polishing kits ($1.75), dinosaur gizzard stones (35¢), fairy stones from Virginia (50¢) and jewelry up to $75. A special collection of fine jewelry can be seen on request—and if you want to spend $10,000 on a necklace, the shop can accommodate you.

> Closed Monday and major holidays. Saturday, 10 AM to 5 PM. All other days, 1 PM to 5 PM. Admission 25¢ Wednesday and weekends. Free all other days. Eisenhower Expy to Route 30 (Roosevelt Road). West on 30 to York Road, north on York to St. Charles Road (two blocks) and right two blocks on St. Charles. There's a nice restaurant almost directly across the street—Cottage Hill, 117 West First. Standard American food at very moderate prices.

Museum of African-American History, 3806 South Michigan, 624-7910; *Mrs. Charles Burroughs, Director*

It's one of the few African-American museums in the United States, and the hope is that one day it will be among the finest. Right now, it's still getting started, needs to define its purpose more clearly, and must get more financial support from well-wishers than has been forthcoming. The almost desperate need for funds is obvious once you walk past the magnificent, bigger-than-life bust of Jean Baptiste Point du Sable (Chicago's first settler) which guards the front door of the old graystone mansion* that houses the museum. Until the

---

* Once the home of the contractor who built Union Station, donated for its present purpose by the Quincy Club, a Negro organization of railroad men.

house can be remodeled the collections of art, artifacts, and significant historical material are in small rooms burdened with Victorian golden oak—and the oak wins.

Even so, there's enough material to warrant a visit: African masks, some good sculpture, a row of old clocks on a mantel to remind visitors that the first clock made in the United States was made by a Negro, Benjamin Bannecker. Bannecker, an extraordinary mathematician, among innumerable other endeavors compiled some of the best almanacs of his day and wrote a plan for universal peace that is absolutely contemporary. He also did L'Enfant's surveying for the grand plan of Washington, D.C.

There are some primitive paintings and some extremely sophisticated Charles White etchings; some crude but interesting dioramas; models of inventions made by Negroes, such as the shoe-lasting machine. There are collections of jazz recordings, including at least 500 rare Bessie Smith 78's, a tape library based on James Baldwin tapes and a series of discussions on *The Last Citizen—The Negro in American Society*. For researchers there's a film library (slides and motion pictures), a photography collection, a clipping file, a Negro bibliography, a good nucleus library on the history of Negroes in the Midwest.

Before the museum opened, Curator Charles Burroughs (it's his wife, Margaret, an art teacher at DuSable High School, who is the museum's founder and tireless director) wrote to each of the African delegations at the UN, telling them of the new museum and asking for flags of their countries and loans of representative art. The flags arrived promptly, but so also did letters explaining that the newly created nations were so new (this was in 1961) that they did not yet have museums of their own from which to loan anything. Then they somehow sent enough to fill the front parlors—carvings, masks and a wonderful reproduction in wood of an African elephant stool—the age-old symbol of a chieftain who was elevated above his subjects in more ways than one.

Open noon to 4 PM weekdays; 1 PM to 5 PM weekends. Children 25¢; adults 75¢. CTA buses No. 5, 6, 38 stop on Michigan Avenue almost in front of the museum. If you've come by car, you might plan to drive to nearby Stephen A. Douglas tomb, monument, and park. See page 444.

Polish Museum of America, 984 North Milwaukee, 384-3352; *George C. Walter, Director*

Another museum that needs a stronger orientation, especially if it expects American visitors of non-Polish descent to comprehend either the fierce history of the Poles in Poland or their contributions as citizens of the United States. It also needs overall lighting equal to that in two new exhibits on the history of Polish science and technology and 16th-Century ethnic development (models of the work of Copernicus, like the celestial globe he made and used and a 17th-Century Amsterdam edition of his major work, *De Revolutionibus*

. . . *Orbium Coelestium;* models of the contributions of Mme Marie Slodow-ska Curie, the discoverer of radium and polonium).

The museum has a wealth of material: early 18th-Century Polish-American primitive art; a large Ignace Jan Paderewski exhibit with one of his pianos and a heady mixture of manuscripts of his two great interests—music and freedom; marvelous items on and by the two great Polish heroes of the American Revolution and the 1792 insurrection against Russia: Brigadier General Tadeusz Kosciuszko, the artillery specialist who contained the British by his fortified blockade of the Hudson at West Point, and young Count Casimir Pulaski, Father of the American Cavalry, hero of the battle of the Brandywine and the siege of Charleston. There are dozens of original manuscripts by both men, plus one of the few original copies of General Kosciusko's brilliant military work, *Manouevers of Horse Artillery* (1808). There is the huge oil of Count Pulaski, who was mortally wounded at the siege of Savannah (Mrs. Eleanor Roosevelt unveiled the painting at the 1933 Century of Progress); there are personal items and the correspondence between the general and Thomas Jefferson.

Elsewhere find Polish national costumes, two of which are particularly impressive—the heavy hand-woven, hand-embroidered wool of the Tatra Mountains in southern Poland, and the national costume worn in Lowicz (central Poland) during the Corpus Christi processions. Its colors are so remarkably like those used by Navaho Indians that anthropologists always ask, Who took from whom?

The library centers on the history of Poland and the history of Christianity in Poland—some 30,000 volumes, a scholar's windfall.

> Closed Saturday. Open 1 PM to 4 PM all other days. Closed Sunday July and August. Free. CTA Milwaukee bus No. 56; Logan Square subway to Division or Chicago Ave Station (museum three blocks from each); by car, Kennedy Expy to Augusta Blvd exit.

Maurice Spertus Museum of Judaica, College of Jewish Studies, 72 East 11th Street, HA 7-5570; *Moshe Davidowitz, Director*

A fine collection of ceremonial objects, artifacts and manuscripts, including the largest and finest collection anywhere of Yemenite manuscripts. The museum is a good place to study Jewish art from North Africa and the Near East or simply to enjoy the contrasts of Jewish art through the ages. Ceremonial and ritual objects range from pottery through textiles, ivory, bronze, silver and gold; the workmanship is often dazzling. Modern art includes a number of pieces donor Spertus commissioned, such as three collage paintings by Nehemia Azaz, who first exhibited in the Israeli pavilion at Expo 67 and whose bronze exterior sculpture distinguishes the facade of The Loop Synagogue, 16 South Clark Street, Chicago. Open 11 AM to 3 PM Monday, Wednesday, Friday, Sunday, but check; hours are expected to be extended.

Morton B. Weiss Museum of Judaica, Temple Isaiah Israel, 1100 East Hyde Park, WA 4-1234

A small but unique collection housed in an exquisite, contemporary display room behind the altar of the Byzantine temple. At the entrance there is always a loan exhibition of sculpture; within find some items that are frankly memorabilia donated by members of the congregation, but also a scholarly collection of antiquities from Persia (Iran). Many of these are the gift of Dr. John Rust, an Episcopalian donor ("I wanted them to be in a place where there was reverence for them") and a professor of pharmacology at the University of Chicago. Dr. Rust assembled them while on Fulbright scholarships to Iran. From the towns of Tehran, Mashhad, Resht, Shiraz, Esfahan, and Hamadan (the burial place of Esther and Mordecai) he brought 400-year-old *ketubahs* (marriage contracts) of ornately inscribed brass, and illuminated parchment contracts from the early 18th Century. Their recurring symbols of lion and sun were Babylonian derivatives brought by the Jews into Persia at the time Queen Esther persuaded Xerxes to release the Jews from Babylon. The tree of life and the doves came from the Assyrian captivity; the elaborate, intertwined, colorful designs show their Persian origins, and if you can translate the Yemen marriage contracts you'll find they sound much like their Moslem counterparts.

Roman tomb fragments date back to the time of the Maccabees. There are old silver prayer cups and a 17th-Century edition of *The Book of Shulchan Aruch* that contains the 613 proscriptions of ritual code by which 16th-Century Orthodox Jews were supposed to live.* Most charming of all are the ornate spice boxes of silver, silver filigree, ivory and wood which contained the spices used to separate the sacred from the profane week—when a family said farewell to the Sabbath on Saturday night. One wishes the descriptive cards beside each object bore more than a date and a donor's name; however, the guide who escorts you has a headful of facts and welcomes questions.

> Open every Friday evening and Saturday morning after religious services; by appointment at all other times. Free. By car, South Lake Shore Drive to Hyde Park Blvd (51st St.), west to temple at corner of Greenwood. Or, Illinois Central commuter train to 51st Street, then cab or any bus going west on boulevard.

Freedom Hall, Institute of Human Relations, Oak Park Temple, 1235 North Harlem, Oak Park, EU 6-3937; *Mrs. Herbert Brockway, Curator*

Freedom Hall is a small, handsome exhibition room of historic manuscripts, letters, autographs, signed documents, and nicely related items, such

---

* It was written by a young 16th-Century Spaniard who, though he had to flee the Inquisition, was evidently every bit as fanatical as any of the Spanish Roman Catholic dogmatists.

as costumes, photographs, memorabilia that unify each exhibit and deepen its theme. So you might find a historic American exhibit on the Civil War, or America's heroes, John F. Kennedy, the family life of Abraham Lincoln, or an exhibit on Winston Churchill. Whichever, it will be of national or international importance, since all the items come from a private collection of such major proportions that its owner was recently awarded an honorary degree by Rutgers University "in recognition of his collective achievement." The owner, Philip D. Sang, has assembled his collection with love and respect, and each exhibit he installs is planned to give history an extra, human dimension.

Exhibits are changed twice yearly. Mrs. Brockway will serve as your guide. She was a schoolteacher, and it shows in the way she keeps fresh supplies of coloring books and crayons for small fry too young to be interested in the displays.

> Open Sunday afternoon from 1:00 to 5:00, and occasionally by appointment. Phone Mrs. Brockway at 386-8016 weekdays. Closed July and August. By car, Eisenhower Expy to Harlem Avenue, north on Harlem.

Since you'll be near the heart of the Frank Lloyd Wright houses in Oak Park and River Forest, you can easily combine both kinds of sightseeing in an afternoon. See page 123. You're also close to Brookfield Zoo (page 387).

Balzekas Museum of Lithuanian Culture, 4012 South Archer (Pulaski), 847-2441; *Stanley Balzekas, Jr., Director*

Except for the Lithuanians, few people know that the now small Baltic country was one of the largest states in medieval Europe or that, in the 15th and 16th centuries, it was the center of Eastern European arts and culture. If Americans think about Lithuanian culture at all, they think of peasant art, which explains, at least in part, the director's incentive to build the first museum of Lithuanian culture in the United States. It happens to be located next door to the showrooms of his business (car sales), but except for a common wall, there's no connection between the two.

The museum is new, handsome, and filled with surprises—like the full suit of intricately etched 16th-Century armor, its helmet jauntily plumed. Surrounding it, a display of medieval weapons—thrusting daggers designed to penetrate chain mail, swords, crossbows, a child's crossbow, an early (1680) wheel-lock rifle. Nearby, a collection of amber believed to be the largest in the world. Only part of it is on display, but it includes pieces of extreme rarity —dark green, black, red. The case explanations are wonderful, and from them you learn that amber began as a gum or resin 60 million years ago, oozing from pines growing mainly on the land that ultimately became Lithuania. There are, here, pieces of amber found in cave dwellings in Switzerland, excavations in Egypt (the Pharaohs ground it and used it as aspirin) and in Assyria and in ancient graves in Greece.

Elsewhere find much of the social history of the country told through collections of every coin produced in Lithuania since the 12th Century; household articles, carvings, wall shrines, icons, gesso-and-gold-leaf wall figures of SS Peter and Matthew from the late 18th-Century Church of Lesciai, household and farm equipment, and Stone Age implements found in the land.

The 10,000-volume noncirculating library is well on its way to becoming a major source for rare Lithuanian books (in Latin as early as 1662, in German from 1761 on), plus a collection on Lithuanian geneology and heraldry. Special exhibitions at Christmas, art exhibits all year-round for Chicagoans, continuing lessons in an old Lithuanian art—straw-ornament making. For nearby Lithuanian shops and restaurants, see page 356.

> Tuesday through Sunday, 1 PM to 4:30 PM. Free. By car, Stevenson Expy to Pulaski Exit, south on Pulaski to Archer. CTA bus No. 62 Archer (board at State Street) stops at door.

Ukrainian National Museum, 2453 West Chicago (Western), AR 6-6565; *Volodymyr Pomirko, Director*

For years, the sign on the front door of the old brownstone that houses the museum spoke only Ukrainian. What it said was that the museum is open only on Sundays from noon to 3 PM or by appointment. What it never said was that to make the appointment you must contact Dr. Elias Mula, museum president, at his office at 2301 West Chicago Avenue, HU 6-3132. Would-be visitors who persisted often got night appointments, found the house had a delightfully conspiratorial air, since black-suited gentlemen sat around in the sparsely furnished first floor, spoke no English and tended to regard Americans as intruders. Eventually a guide with some knowledge of English arrived— and he still will—to lead you up a narrow flight of stairs to a museum where Victorian-size rooms, bad lighting, and undramatized displays are likely to give a first impression of not being worth the bother.

But they are, because they portray both the ethnic life of peasants in the Ukraine and the history of centuries of Ukrainian-Cossack warfare against Russia, told in a series of splendid oil portraits and informative dialogue by your guide. The earliest oil is of a crown worn by a 13th-Century prince. Two of the most striking are of Bohdan Khmelnystsky, a 17th-Century rebel hetman (a Cossack leader) who fought against the Poles in 1648, and of Ivan Mazeppa, hero of a Byron poem and head of a Ukrainian state that was also a forced Russian protectorate. Prior to the futile uprising Ivan Mazeppa made against the Czar, he built Cossack baroque and Byzantine churches, nicely represented here by pictures from old manuscripts.

The paintings lead to old guns and swords, flags, money and insignia from the two proud years of independence (1917-19), when the Ukraine had not only its own army, but a navy in the Black Sea; medals and souvenirs of General M. Hrekiv, whom the Russians exiled to Siberia for ten years (there's even a spoon from a Siberian prison camp), and uniforms of Ukrainian soldiers.

In the ethnic representation are samples of wood carvings, the work as intricate as inlay: plates, crucifixes, vodka sets, candelabra, models of country equipment, a model of a church in the Carpathian Mountains, the masonry of Byzantine architecture adapted into wood; Ukrainian national costumes; musical instruments—a six-foot-long ceremonial trumpet fashioned of tree bark, *cymbalys* (for dances), a bandora, the Ukrainian national instrument (it's like a big lyre); an extraordinary collection of elaborately decorated Easter eggs; beautiful sculpture by the very contemporary Serge Lytwinenko. You may well come away wishing that at least a little Ukrainian history were taught in American schools.

Chicago Avenue CTA bus No. 66; by car, west on same street. Free.

Hall of Fame, DoAll Company Test Center, 254 North Laurel, Des Plaines, 824-1122

A striking exhibit hall of industrial and machine tools chosen to dramatize the Industrial Revolution, the conversion from doing by hand to doing by machine, and the advantages of the change, especially the way it freed men for the first time in history from spending all their waking hours solely to meet their basic needs. The prize exhibit is a James Watt steam engine, built in 1799, that operated mill machinery from 1799 to 1945 in England and was still in good working condition when replaced by a diesel engine. It's the only original Watt engine in America and is now operated by a concealed electric motor. The other six machine tools basic to the Industrial Revolution are also on display, including the only full-size replica of John Wilkinson's boring mill, the first machine tool, constructed from Wilkinson's original drawings which DoAll found in Birmingham, England. Elsewhere, original 1798 and 1812 Eli Whitney muskets—the first products made using interchangeable parts, which process Whitney fathered, and without which mass production could not exist.

The company welcomes visitors but only by appointment, since the museum is also used for business seminars. Phone Mr. Milton E. Hlava, Director of Educational Research, for appointment between Monday and Friday, 8:30 AM to 5 PM.

North Western Railroad to Des Plaines or Kennedy Expy to O'Hare turnoff. Take River Road into Des Plaines, cross the North Western tracks, turn left onto Miner Street (Rt. 14). Just past third stoplight at a fire station, make a sharp right onto Laurel Avenue; follow DoAll signs.

Grand Army of the Republic Memorial Hall, Chicago Public Library, Washington and Michigan, CE 6-8922

Southerners will be pleased to know that the Confederacy is represented in this Civil War collection by three important flags: the Confederate Naval Ensign, the Battle Flag of the Confederacy and the Stars and Bars—the first flag of the Confederacy. Civil War buffs of either leaning will find that the

Grand Army of the Republic collection runs mainly to flags, uniforms, sashes, badges, curios, bronze busts, relics, Presidents Lincoln and Grant material and "other valuable mementoes."

Among the more interesting items: one of the few remaining copies of the War Department circular, issued in 1865, offering a $100,000 reward for the murderer of President Lincoln; a case of Civil War weapons, including a Colt six-shooter, the most widely used revolver of the war; Matthew Brady photographs, one with a macabre caption—"A Conspirator About To Die"; the bronze plaque of the governmental order creating Memorial Day on May 5, 1868; a collection of Civil War drums, including one used by young Billy Nevans, "the drummer boy of the Rappahannock." But the single most interesting item has to be the extra edition of the July 23, 1885, *New York Evening Telegram,* headlined: "GRANT DEAD! THE GREAT GENERAL SUMMONED TO HEADQUARTERS ABOVE."

Open 9 AM to 5 PM Monday through Saturday. Free.

ART AND PERFORMING ARTS

7

Museums of Art
Sculpture in Chicago's Parks
Art Galleries
Music: Symphonic, Chamber, Choral, Liturgical
Opera
Theatre
Ballet

CHAPTER 7

ART AND PERFORMING ARTS

We have boasted long enough of our grain elevators, our railroads, our trade . . . our business . . . let us now have libraries, galleries of art, scientific museums, noble architecture, and public parks . . . otherwise there is danger that Chicago will become merely a place where ambitious young men will come to make money and achieve a fortune, and then go elsewhere to enjoy it. You must have culture, taste, beauty, art, literature, or our city will become a town of mere traders and money-getters; rude, unlettered, hard, sharp and grasping . . .

> Hon. I. N. Arnold, President, Chicago Historical Society, to the members of the society at their first meeting in their new post-Fire building, 1877.*

The president of the society was right about the need for taste and beauty, right in his concerns for Chicago's future, wrong only in thinking that the contents of certain buildings would automatically create culture. Thanks to the efforts of a devoted few, the money of a few more and the interests of a few thousand, the museums got built, the parks were created under an elegant plan, and the architecture ultimately turned out to be far greater than anything he could have foreseen.

Yet beneath the surface, Chicago didn't change. It is now what it always was—a business city. Its arts lend it status and prestige, but they're far down the list of concerns. When Mayor Daley, the city's official spokesman, says that "There's nothing to beat city living," he explains why in terms of noncultural facilities exclusively—a proposed airport in the lake, for instance. When asked

---

*The Chicago Historical Society, an Unconventional Chronicle, Paul M. Angle, Rand McNally, 1956.

to enumerate the accomplishments of his years in office, he refers solely to facilities like "the accelerated expressway system" [and] "O'Hare airport—talked of for seven years; in six months after we came in we straightened out the contracts." For those Chicago parents who think one of the few remaining advantages of bringing up their children in the city happens to be the accessibility of art museums and symphony orchestras in live performances, 50,000 other Chicago parents see no advantages whatsoever and annually move to the suburbs.

Perhaps the great nations of the world can only support one art capital each. What is missing in Chicago is the belief cherished in London, Paris, New York, that the arts are as essential as commerce or government. Chicago has the arts—often in surprising numbers—but it is not involved with them, not in love with them. That is why the city, viewed from afar, so often gives the impression of a culturally deprived city, which it is not. But to the degree that it roars along without *needing* the arts, it will continue to seem parochial despite the considerable attainments won for it.

MUSEUMS OF ART

Art Institute of Chicago, Adams and Michigan, CE 6-7080; *Charles C. Cunningham, Director*

With monumental indifference to all discussions about culture, the Art Institute goes about its business of building one of the world's great collections of art. As an institution it is oblivious to sniping and to battles over its individual shows. As a museum it is aloof and conservative and has for years been accused of domination by a small social aristocracy. (Director Cunningham is exempt from this criticism, since he did not arrive on the scene until the summer of 1966.) It also makes arbitrary decisions that often infuriate its membership-at-large. But despite, or perhaps because of these very qualities, it has managed in less than a century to become one of the country's four most significant museums of art.

So you can visit it with maximum expectancy for its Renaissance oils, French Impressionists (one of the world's greatest collections) and post-Impressionists, Oriental (Far East) galleries, primitive art, prints and master drawings, photography and modern art.

Among the Art Institute's triumphs: Correggio's "Madonna and Child"; El Greco's "Assumption of the Virgin," his "St. Francis" and his "Feast in the House of Simon"; Rubens' "Holy Family with Infant St. John and Elizabeth"; Velázquez' "Saint John the Baptist"; Rembrandt's "Girl at an Open Half-Door"; David's "Portrait of the Marquise de Pastoret"; Seurat's "Sunday Afternoon on the Island of La Grande Jatte"; Matisse's "Bathers by a River"; Caillebotte's "Place de l'Europe on a Rainy Day"; Grant Wood's "American Gothic"; Chagall's "The Praying Jew."

Actually, you can take signatures at random from the museum's total investment of art, and the names spin out like a golden litany: Tintoretto, Van Dyck, Rubens, Veronese, Reynolds, Turner, Goya, Delacroix, Corot, Pissarro, Monet, Manet, Degas, Cézanne, Redon, Morisot, Renoir, Gauguin, Van Gogh, Toulouse-Lautrec, Picasso, Kollwitz, Klee, Beckmann, Pollock, Calder, Arp, O'Keeffe, Magritte, Davis, Tobey, Balthus, Brancusi, Giacometti. And these are but a few. All the giants are represented, often by as many as four or five major works, often to the extent of a dozen Degas, eight Gauguins, seven Van Goghs, 11 Manets, 19 Renoirs, 29 Monets and 16 Picassos.

Oriental art encompasses Japanese, Korean and, in greatest depth, the last two Chinese dynasties, Ming, 1367-1644 A.D. and Ch'ing, 1644-1912. There are scrolls, prints, ceramics, porcelains, lacquer, pewter, jades, bronzes, sculpture,* furniture and costumes—imperial robes and priests' robes woven in colored silks and silver and gold, opulent beyond belief.

The primitive art collection, on its way to becoming one of the finest in the world, deliberately does not duplicate anything at the Field Museum but presents spectrums of African and middle American art, the latter including especially famed Peruvian and pre-Columbian collections.

Sections of the galleries of decorative arts have followed the Philadelphia museum's system of incorporation into handsome room settings. The system is ideal and is being extended to early American art. Further expansion depends on space—such rooms require an unholy amount of it.

To see period rooms in profusion, visit the Thorne Rooms, 68 European and American miniatures (scaled one inch to one foot) exquisitely and authentically detailed by a private citizen of great antiquarian knowledge, Mrs. James Ward Thorne. They're probably the most sophisticated dollhouses in the world.**

You'll need a map—stop at the information room. The calendar of current activities will undoubtedly list at least one special exhibition since at the Art Institute they're almost continuous. In early autumn you may catch the **Bi-Annual Artists of Chicago and Vicinity Show.** It's always furiously controversial. The 1967 ACV achieved notoriety as well as controversy by the museum's refusal to hang one of the prizewinners on the grounds of visual pornography.† Everyone screamed, but with the customary self-possession that allows it to ignore criticism the museum went calmly about its affairs.

In summer, lunch in McKinlock Court under its yellow umbrellas and leafy trees encircling Carl Milles' "Fountain of the Tritons." (Also open for

---

* The 12th-Century seated Buddha who now dreams over a calm pool was discovered in south India, seated against a water tank, his back serving as part of the tank's outside walls.

** See page 241 if you want to own a similar miniature room.

† It was justified in its decision but also had to swallow the fact that one of its curators had served on the jury.

dinner on Thursday night.) In winter, use the cafeteria or the handsome dining room. (All are closed on Sunday—and are always liquorless.)

Free lectures on the collections each Sunday at 3:30 PM; Tuesday and Friday at 12:15 PM; Thursday at 6:30 PM. "Meet the Artists" lectures for youngsters each Saturday at 11:30 AM from October through June. Get permission at the information room to use a camera or to sketch. Free art and fine arts authentications every Tuesday by appointment. Write or phone Mr. John Maxon, associate director, for these. Burnham and Ryerson libraries here can probably satisfy any art or architectural research requirement: combined, they have nearly 80,000 bound volumes, 20,000 pamphlets, 65,000 photographs, 52,000 slides, almost 20,000 color prints and 54,000 postcards.

> Open daily, 10 AM to 5 PM; Thursday evenings to 8:30 PM, and sometimes for a major exhibition, Tuesday evenings as well. Sunday, holidays, 1 PM to 6 PM. Closed only on Christmas Day. For Goodman Theatre, also part of the Art Institute, see "Too Late For Press" sheet, museum store, page 267; Junior museum and Library, page 312. Free except for admission to special exhibitions, and Thorne Rooms (25¢).

Museum of Contemporary Art, 237 East Ontario, 943-7755; *Jan Van der Marck, Director*

From the opening exhibition, "Pictures to Be Read/Poems to Be Seen," the shows at the museum have been deliciously upsetting. The truth is that the museum claims to be serious about its exhibitions but at the same time refuses to be solemn about them. (In the Midwest, if you're not solemn about art, people suspect you're putting them on, the reaction to the Picasso at the Civic Center being a case in point.) What unnerves conservatives is that not once since the museum opened in November, 1967, has it exhibited nicely framed canvases and carefully mounted pieces of sculpture. Instead, it has presented collage art that stretches the entire length of walls; art shaped into boxes, cubes, balls and prisms; art fashioned of plastic, paper, neon tubes; art that can be walked into (and in at least one instance, walked on); art that includes the use of commonplace objects such as telephones; art that refuses to be a polite background for anything; art that disdains to be looked at reverentially; art that intrudes and insists you recognize it even if you don't understand it. In short, art that's like life itself—unpredictable, exuberant, flamboyant, sassy, vulgar, challenging, generally more transient than transcendental, but dynamic and strangely moving.

The museum has two commitments. The first is to present to its audiences the best of contemporary international art; the second is to be experimental. Romping about in its exhibitions (the whole place is one vast setting for an Environment) is a joyful experience. And you're supposed to romp. This isn't a museum where you get points for walking about wearing a sober expression and speaking in whispers. The exhibits are chosen as much for their humor as for any other reason. Victorians wouldn't understand the art or the philosophy, but anyone who's learned how to use laughter to cope with the lunacy of his era will feel right at home.

Tuesday, Friday, and Saturday, 10 AM to 5 PM. Thursday to 8 PM. Sunday, noon to 5 PM. Closed Monday. Admission, 50¢.

Arts Club of Chicago, 109 East Ontario, SU 7-3997; *Mrs. Alfred P. Shaw, President*

Of all private clubs in the United States, the Arts Club may well be the most public-minded, since it opens all its art shows to the public. Its membership is equally unique, consisting of Chicago's intellectual elite as well as its leading professionals in architecture and the arts. And, as a club, it has a purpose other than social; "to encourage . . . and develop higher standards of art."

Part of that encouragement has been to fill a gap the Art Institute could not fill—the introduction of major new art movements. Through the Arts Club, Chicago and the Midwest discovered the French post-Impressionists and American Modernists in depth. Early in the 1920's, the club held the first one-man display of sculpture by Rodin presented west of New York; the first large exhibit of drawings by Picasso to be held in this city (Picasso himself made the selection); the first one-man shows in Chicago of Braque, Toulouse-Lautrec,* Lachaise, Vlaminck, Utrillo, the first large Brancusi exhibition in the United States, 38 pieces of sculpture and 20 drawings.**

Early, it hung Picasso's "Guernica" and his studies for it; gave the first one-man shows in the city of Max Ernst, Hélion, Chagall, Matta Echaurren, Hofmann, Lipchitz, Lam, Léger, Dufy, Pollock, Graves, Davis, Motherwell, Tobey, James Thurber. For members, its programs included Sergei Prokofiev in a recital of his own compositions, assisted by Mme. Prokofiev; Harold Kreutzberg and Martha Graham in dance recitals; Massine making his debut as a solo dancer; Buckminster Fuller introducing his fundamentals of dymaxion design; Fernand Léger showing his film *Ballet Mecanique;* the first performance of Schoenberg's *Kammersymphonie,* the first performance of Stravinsky's *Octuor* for wind instruments, conducted by Stravinsky and Hans Lange; the first Chicago recitals of William Kapell, Claudio Arrau, Martial Singher, John Cage with percussion orchestra; lectures by Bertrand Russell, Aaron Copland, Leonard Bernstein, Sir Thomas Beecham, Virgil Thompson, Jean Dubuffet.

If you're a friend of a member, you may attend any recital or lecture as a guest; without knowing anyone, every show in the club is open to you.

Open 9:30 AM to 5:30 PM Monday through Saturday. Free. Closed July to mid-September.

---

* "The Circus Rider" was purchased from the show by the Art Institute.

** "The Golden Bird," now in the club's permanent collection, came from that show.

Renaissance Society at the University of Chicago, 1010 East 59th Street (Ellis), MI 3-0800, ext. 2886; *Mrs. Elizabeth S. Daniels, Director*

One year older than the Arts Club, the Renaissance Society is also a pioneer of contemporary art and ideas and offers some of the most original exhibitions in the Midwest. Its gallery is housed at the university but is independent of it. (Go through the Classics Building, use entrance to Goodspeed Hall.)* Because of the society, Chicagoans saw in the early 1920's comprehensive showings of Picasso, Matisse, Rouault, Brancusi, Lipchitz; in the 30's, some of the earliest one-man shows of Calder, Albers, Gris, Miro, Mondrian, Moholy-Nagy.

The society is innovative, has, for instance, upset popular notions about art shows with such esoterica as "The Artist Looks at the Scientist's World— Raw Materials of the Laboratory," and examining "The Spiritual Condition of Modern Man," a religious art show, without religious art or iconography. It also gives traditionalists a breather with gems like "Northern Renaissance Art In Shakespeare's Time" and "Baroque Portraits"—elegant changes of pace that have given the society a justly deserved reputation.

The Young Collectors' January exhibit is always a selling show, and the Christmas Sale, the most unusual sale of its kind anywhere (see Annual Events, page 434), has induced the cooperation of galleries everywhere to put special lower-than-normal prices on art sent to this sale.

Open 10 AM to 5 PM Monday through Friday; Saturday, 1 PM to 5 PM. The location is convenient to Wright's Robie House, could be combined with a tour there, with the university itself, with the famous Midway Studios and with the Oriental Institute, if you really want to make a day out of it.

ART IN PARKS

No image of Chicago encourages the idea that it's a city of great outdoor sculpture and fountains—but it is, and many of the works are monumental indeed. The Chicago Park District alone lists 58 pieces of sculpture and fountains throughout the park system; with all other outdoor sculpture in the city, there are more than 100.**

The city's most obvious fountain is the one Miss Kate Sturges Buckingham, a strong-willed Chicago heiress, gave to Grant Park in 1927. It's modeled after

---

* The society will be moving to the Midway Studios (page 168) so check address before visiting.

** You can get the complete Park District list free; ask for "Monuments and Memorials." It gives names, locations, etc., but in at least one instance, confuses things by including a small memorial fountain which turns out to be a drinking fountain. Nor does it state where in Norwood Park you'll find a Gilbert Stuart portrait of George Washington, but presumably it's in a field house and not hung under trees.

Versailles' "Latona" but on a much bigger scale, because that's the way Miss Kate did everything.* It's too well-known to need describing, but you might keep in mind that nightly at 9 PM in summer it puts on a show involving great spraying cascades of color-lighted waters. Location is Grant Park at Congress Street, just west of Lake Shore Drive.

Compared to Buckingham, the crowns of water dotted about the rose garden to the north and to the south are mere fountainettes. Nevertheless, they're lovely—Leonard Crunelle's winsomely sculptured "Crane Girl" (her crane spouts), "Dove Girl" (the dove spouts) and two lads, "Turtle Boy" and "Fisher Boy." Almost directly west across Columbus Drive, half hidden by magnificent flowering trees and shrubs, is Augustus Saint-Gaudens' last work, his massive seated Lincoln centered in a sweeping exedra, one of the most beautiful public seating accommodations in the entire city. South a few blocks at 9th Street and Michigan Avenue is his poetic equestrian bronze of General John A. Logan; the best time to see it is in the early morning with eastern light behind; at sunrise, it's absolutely lyrical.

A few blocks north along Michigan Avenue are Ivan Mestrovic's abstracted American Plains Indians mounted on Arabian stallions. Mestrovic, a naturalized citizen, may well have created the two most heroic equestrian bronzes of all time, and one can't fault him entirely for his romanticized European notions about American Indians and their steeds since no Hollywood Western shown in movie houses abroad likely ever used the kind of horses the Indians actually used—spavined and very short in the leg.

The Art Institute landscaping includes Lorado Taft's heroic "Spirit of the Great Lakes," five classic maidens symbolizing the lakes, the highest maiden (Lake Superior) spilling the waters of a basin into another held by Lake Michigan who in turn empties hers into Huron, Erie, Ontario. At the north mall there's a modern new pool with three crowns of water. At the broad entrance to the Art Institute proper, the two famous Kemys lions that wear spectacular green wreathes around their necks each Christmas and, for certain festivals, jaunty gold crowns; and, at the head of the stairs, dwarfed by the Italianate facade, a copy of Jean Antoine Houdon's George Washington in regimental dress. It's a curious fact that whether in history books or sculpture, the Father of Our Country never comes through as the bigger-than-life figure he actually was. He is always remote, impersonal, and overshadowed, even

---

* Miss Kate also commissioned the nine-foot gold leaf statue of Alexander Hamilton in Lincoln Park near Diversey. When asked by sculptor John Angel why it had to be nine feet she said, "Because Lincoln's statue is that big." The Art Institute got in on some of her largess when she moved into a cooperative apartment at 2450 Lakeview. Her architect wired Miss Kate from Europe that he had options to buy two complete rooms of a Gothic castle. Miss Kate cabled that she'd buy both, "One for the Art Institute and one for the apartment you are building for me."

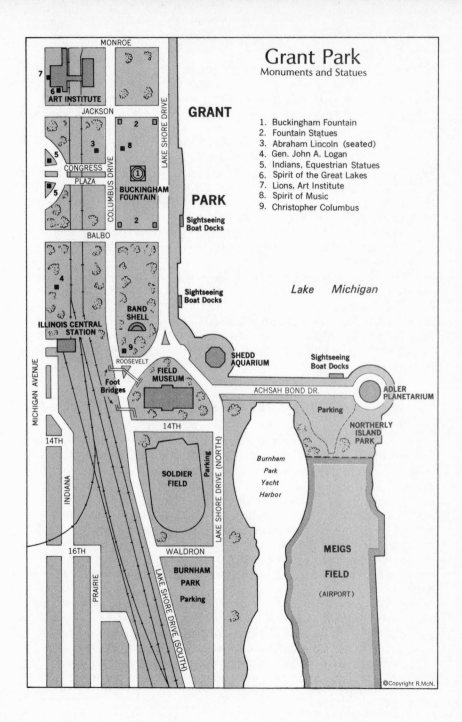

Grant Park
Monuments and Statues

1. Buckingham Fountain
2. Fountain Statues
3. Abraham Lincoln (seated)
4. Gen. John A. Logan
5. Indians, Equestrian Statues
6. Spirit of the Great Lakes
7. Lions, Art Institute
8. Spirit of Music
9. Christopher Columbus

MONROE

ART INSTITUTE

JACKSON

CONGRESS

PLAZA

BUCKINGHAM
FOUNTAIN

BALBO

ILLINOIS CENTRAL
STATION

BAND
SHELL

ROOSEVELT

Foot
Bridges

FIELD
MUSEUM

14TH

MICHIGAN AVENUE

14TH

INDIANA

16TH

PRAIRIE

COLUMBUS DRIVE

LAKE SHORE DRIVE

GRANT

PARK

Sightseeing
Boat Docks

Sightseeing
Boat Docks

Lake   Michigan

SHEDD
AQUARIUM

Sightseeing
Boat Docks

ADLER
PLANETARIUM

ACHSAH BOND DR.

Parking

NORTHERLY
ISLAND
PARK

SOLDIER
FIELD

Parking

Burnham
Park
Yacht
Harbor

LAKE SHORE DRIVE (NORTH)

WALDRON

BURNHAM
PARK

Parking

LAKE SHORE DRIVE (SOUTH)

MEIGS

FIELD

(AIRPORT)

©Copyright R.McN.

159

when he is the central figure as in the Lorado Taft-Leonard Crunelle trio at Heald Square (a tiny plot of traffic-dividing land at Wabash Avenue and Wacker Drive) where, holding hands with Haym Solomon and Robert Morse, the financiers of the Revolution, he is imposing, yet not nearly as human as the two bare-headed heroes.

At Olive Memorial Park, the beautiful new park surrounding the Ohio Street-Lake Shore Drive Filtration Plant (the building boasts Milton Horn's "Hymn to Water" on its facade), five simple pool fountains jet water in great arching plumes the year-round, five to ten stories high even in winter. A bronze plaque of the hero for whom the park was named honors Medal of Honor winner Pfc. Milton Lee Olive III, the 19-year-old Negro who in 1966 threw himself on a hand grenade in Vietnam to save the lives of four comrades. "Man," he'd said to one of them shortly before he sacrificed his life, "you gotta *care*."

The rest of Chicago's statues, as widespread as the city itself, are listed wherever they appear in relation to other places of interest. Those in Lincoln Park, for instance, will be found in Chapter 17, and you'll have to visit them on foot, except for Gutzon Borglum's equestrian statue of General Phil Sheridan. General Phil on Rienzi, rearing away from a high-rise called Harbor House, at the intersection of Belmont Avenue and Sheridan Road, is visible from bus or car.

ART GALLERIES

As devotees know, there's no selling venture quite like an art gallery. It's a free enterprise, if ever there was one; yet if it's a serious gallery it has far more than the profit motive going for it. What it has is an owner who chose the field primarily for the rewards of working with art, discussing art, introducing customers to good art. All those nonprofit motives can make gallery-going a delightful experience because the serious owner not only welcomes your questions but makes you feel that your presence and interest is adding an extra dimension to his day. He will generally also be most obliging if you want to arrange time payments, or if you want to try art in your home before making a final commitment, or if you want to exchange one purchase for another.

As to the quality of art sold in Chicago galleries, the critics generally agree that it's somewhere midpoint between New York and West Coast offerings. New Yorkers won't find the depth or variety that Manhattan offers as an international art center, nor will they find any gallery as august as Knoedler, or the Wildenstein, which is virtually a museum and sells to museums. West Coast collectors won't find as much far-out art as they're accustomed to, but they will discover that individual gallery shows are likely to be more substantial. Currently, no gallery displays art representing a Chicago art movement, but that's because there isn't one. What there is, is the best art that can be assembled between the two coasts—and it's very good indeed.

There is a kind of semiracket in art here as elsewhere that demands a caveat emptor warning. "Fantastic Original Oil Paintings by Upcoming Masters of This Century—$5 to $125—None Higher" read ads you'll see in Chicago newspapers and hotel giveaway magazines. The oils are originals, all right—cranked out by European art students and maybe even wistful amateurs. None of them show any appreciable talent; most of the canvases are imitations of works of recognized artists currently in vogue—Buffet, for instance. If you do browse in one of these places and decide to buy a painting, the price is probably fair enough for the meager talent involved, but you shouldn't lug your selection home with any hope of having it ultimately increase in value. It won't, because the kind of gallery at which you bought it is selling merchandise, not art.

The galleries listed here are the legitimate galleries of Chicago—and the most interesting. When their owners introduce new artists it's because the art has genuine content, talent is unmistakable, and the owners are willing to lend their prestige and stake their reputations on giving the works deserved exposure. You may not always agree with their choices, but you can trust the reasons for the selection.

Chicago galleries cluster around three locations: the Loop, Ontario Street and North Michigan Avenue, and on Oak Street. Ontario is as central an art gallery street as 57th Street in New York, though here most galleries are housed in modernized brownstones or on the second floors of office buildings.

> Unless otherwise noted, gallery hours are 9:30 AM to 5:30 PM, Monday through Saturday. However, some are open Wednesday evening; check by phone. In July and August, many galleries close on Saturday; again, check by phone. Galleries have recently begun to experiment with evening hours. In the winter of 1968, a number stayed open on Wednesday till 8:30 PM. Check newspaper listings under "Art Exhibits" for current policy.

Ontario Area Galleries

B. C. Holland Gallery, 155 East Ontario, MO 4-5000

Mr. Holland opened his gallery in 1959 as the local torchbearer for the avant-garde and the champion of the abstract expressionists, but found himself going deeper into established masters as time went on. Still, his is one of the city's three most avant-garde galleries (Pollock, de Kooning, Rothko, Arp, Calder, et al), and his back room is the most famous art dealer's office in the city, with exhibitions of great quality—if you're a serious collector you'll be invited in. Drawings throughout the gallery normally start at $500, though there are always some specials by young artists of stature in the $150 range.

Allan Frumkin Gallery, 620 North Michigan (Ontario), SU 7-0563

Mr. Frumkin was the first major gallery owner in Chicago to specialize in modern art, made a roaring success of it, and paved the way for everyone else. New Yorkers now get far more opportunities to talk with him than Chicagoans do, since he spends most of his time in his establishment there. They're lucky. He's an authority on German Expressionism and primitive African art. The gallery here specializes in major 19th- and 20th-Century French and German art. You can go back as far as Delacroix among the former and through all the German Expressionists—Klee, Beckmann, Barlach, Kirchner, Kollwitz, Munch. Art is available in all media. Graphics* range from $50 to $500; prices on oils and sculpture are those serious collectors pay.

Richard Feigen Gallery, Inc., 226 East Ontario, SU 7-0500

New Yorkers will also know Mr. Feigen; he's now in their city more often than he's here. This gallery, run by the knowledgeable Mrs. Lotte Drew-Bear (she'll give you an entire art education if you give her the chance) handles major paintings, sculpture and drawings by 18th-, 19th- and 20th-Century masters, represents a number of the better-known members of the avant-garde, and because it's especially interested in working with major Chicago architects, gears many of its special exhibitions of large outdoor sculpture and modern tapestries to the architectural community as well as collectors. Graphics by recognized young artists for as little as $25, master drawings as low as $200, expected prices on major works.

Richard Gray Gallery, 620 North Michigan, 642-8877

The Gray gallery is becoming an extremely important gallery in Chicago. Mr. Gray, a nonpracticing architect of taste and wit, specializes in notable 20th-Century drawings, paintings and sculpture, much of which is nonobjective, but all of which he insists will make sense to anyone who will not merely glance at it but will take the time to see. He's also delighted to provide verbal explanations whenever he and you have the time. Be sure to see his shaped canvases by John Pearson—fascinating. Saturday hours start at noon. Closed in August.

---

* Graphics refers to woodcuts, etchings, engravings, drypoint, lithographs, aquatints, linoleum cuts and serigraphs in limited editions, usually but not always numbered and signed. It does not mean mechanical reproductions, such as the museum reproductions you can buy at the Art Institute and in stores.

Kazimir Gallery, 620 North Michigan, 337-2236

Gallery owner Kazimir Karpuszko has a master's degree in art education and an educator's passionate interest in giving a recognized new art form maximum exposure. Relief constructions are the form: nonobjective designs with surfaces at two or more levels, part of the Constructivist movement that goes back to the Russian movement of 1912 and the Dutch group that included Mondrian (sometimes the constructions look like three-dimensional Mondrians). Unless you're a confirmed traditionalist, you'll enjoy the works of trailblazers Henryk Stazewski and Jean Gorin and the structurist artists Professor Eli Bornstein and Dave Barr.

Fairweather-Hardin Gallery, 101 East Ontario, lower concourse, Martin-Marietta Building, MI 2-0007

One of the happiest galleries in Chicago, it focuses on contemporary American art in all media, is run by two of the most joyful gallery owners you can meet. Mrs. Fairweather and Mrs. Hardin have done as much to encourage contemporary art collecting as anyone in this city and go out of their way for younger collectors. Artists here lead off with Max Kahn, George Buehr, Robert Natkin, Eleanor Coen (Mrs. Max Kahn), Margo Hoff, Joyce Treiman, sculptor Harry Bertoia and Stanley Edwards, the young popster. At least twice each season the owners present wild, tongue in cheek Op or Pop or whatever is the current "in" thing, plus one or two new discoveries, like Fay Peck—a socialite who surprised everyone by being not only a serious artist but a strong one.

Lo Giudice Gallery, 157 East Ontario, WH 4-2200

A new gallery next door to Holland that has started out in much the same way Holland did—by specializing in drawings and attempting to establish its reputation with these. The gallery is off to an exemplary start. Mr. Lo Giudice, who learned from Mr. Holland, is a former collector who found his hobby so expensive he turned pro. He believes in showing whatever he feels is worth seeing, and leads from the conviction that art, if it's good, isn't limited to the 19th and 20th Centuries. Hence, the time span of drawings and graphics is considerable, primitive art is currently a big part of his exhibits and the star of his stable of painters is José Luis Cuevas, a young contemporary whose work, like Léger's, is not really of any school but unique. Weekdays the gallery opens at 10:30 AM; Saturday at 11 AM.

Dell Gallery, Ltd., 620 North Michigan, MI 2-0630

Gallery owner Marjorie Dell, cordiality itself, specializes in very avant-garde artists and sculptors and is always surrounded by dozens of them. Your chance of meeting an artist in a gallery (other than at a formal opening) is quite probably better here than anywhere else in town.

Phyllis Kind Gallery, Inc., 155 East Ontario, MI 2-0047

Graphics, sculpture, paintings in a gallery run by the wife of a professor of humanities at Illinois Institute of Technology. Mrs. Joshua Kind offers a fine range of art; in 1969 gave Chicago its first California art show.

Deson-Zaks Gallery, Inc., 226 East Ontario, SU 7-0005

Run by two University of Chicago faculty wives, it deals almost exclusively in contemporary Italian artists in all media—Enrico Baj, founder of the group known as the nuclear movement, Kiky Vinces Vinci (kinetics and paper reliefs), Fontana, Boccadasse and others; also sells hard-to-find art books. Prints start at $40. Open Tuesday-Saturday. Closed mid-July to September.

Vincent Price Art Gallery, 140 East Ontario, 265-6176

This is Sears, Roebuck and Company selling some very good original art, with collector Vincent Price lending his name, prestige and services as art buyer and consultant. The gallery is new, offers enough kinds of art to please a range of tastes. More important perhaps, because it *is* Sears, Roebuck, visitors who have never been in a gallery will find it a comfortable introduction to the heady world of art galleries and original art.

Main Street Galleries, 642 North Michigan, SU 7-3301,

Offering a range of art from conservative 19th Century through Hans Erni and on to Op and Pop, Main Street has substantial gallery artists, interesting cubists and puts on bright, solid shows. It also has a room of fine paintings for collectors who can make major investments. Graphics from $25. Paintings to $15,000. The gallery is expanding, will be worth watching to see what new directions it may take.

International Galleries, 645 North Michigan, 943-1661

International has handsome—and expensive—19th- and 20th-Century art, mainly traditional, and for reasons best known to Texans, it is their favorite Chicago gallery. Owner S. C. Johnson had several outstanding shows yearly—the 1966 Léger Retrospective was the most comprehensive gallery exhibition ever given Léger in this country. Since Mr. Johnson's death, Mrs. Johnson has continued to run the gallery along its established lines.

Conrad Gallery, 46 East Chicago, WH 3-1542

Gallery owner Conrad Burck grew up in an art milieu (his parents are artists), knows what he's doing and does it well. He specializes in established Illinois and Midwest artists, such as painters Lawrence Stafford and Ed Pashey, painter-sculptor Jacob Burck, and sculptors Egon Weiner and James Clow, whose life-size figures in plaster are sometimes even more startling than Frank Gallo's. Art may be rented here; paintings and sculpture may be brought in for crating and shipping. Be sure to visit the sculpture court in warm weather. It's large and is used primarily for monumental pieces and commissions. When a life-size piece titled "The Nun," and recognizable as such, was out there she became a wayside shrine for Rush Street inebriates who made loud confessions to her in the early morning hours; at least half the time the neighbors were enchanted.

Oak Street Area

Benjamin Galleries, 900 North Michigan, Suite 318, DE 7-1343

One of the extra dividends of this gallery is the opportunity it gives you to see art the way you're going to display it—in a private home. Except for a few pieces of sculpture in her permanent collection, all the art in Mrs. Benjamin Krohn's serene apartment is for sale—it's like having a friend take a painting from her own wall for you. Mrs. Krohn specializes in 20th-Century French and American art in all media, has excellent graphics (Albers, Chagall, Giacometti, Matisse, Picasso and so forth). Among her gallery artists are Leonard Baskin and sculptor Sorel Etrog. Graphics from $50 to $1,000; rare paintings and sculpture, much higher, of course. Open Wednesday through Saturday, 11 AM to 5 PM. Other afternoons and evenings by appointment.

Gilman Galleries, 103 East Oak, DE 7-6262

Contemporary American art in a two-story gallery with a sculpture garden. Owner Mack Gilman shows both nonobjective and representational art in all media, ranging from the meticulously detailed Wyeth-like landscapes of Alan Gough and the mysterious gem-colored paintings of Richard Wilt to the controversial life-size figurative art of Frank Gallo. Gallo's medium is epoxy resin, and his nude women, sprawling in floating sling chairs (disconcerting if you've never seen them), are being bought by major museums in this country and abroad. Here also you'll discover a selection of really fine African sculpture, less than astronomically priced.

Just east of Gilman on Oak are the galleries of **Frank Oehlschlaeger** and **Distelheim,** favorites with people who want art to be decorative as well as art-for-art's sake. At Oehlschlaeger, be sure to see the work of Aaron Bohrod, Herbert Davidson and Phil White—the portraits of children by the last two are exceptionally sensitive.

At the easternmost building entrance on Oak (the address is 952 North Michigan), discover the **Kovler Gallery** on the second floor. In a remarkably short time it's gained a fine reputation for outstanding graphics by 19th- and 20th-Century artists and is developing into a gallery of considerable importance. Be sure to find and explore the contents of the back rooms off the main gallery.

Jacques Baruch Gallery, 154 East Superior, MI 2-9328

A new gallery run by a Polish-born architect, who specializes in Polish artists and ikons. The gallery is in the Baruchs' home, so phone for appointment.

Loop Galleries

Wally Findlay Galleries, 320 South Michigan, WE 9-4481

Not only *the* downtown gallery for traditionalists but also Chicago's oldest and largest gallery. Findlay has 12 rooms of art, including French Impressionists, post-Impressionists and Fauve painters, is the exclusive U.S. representative of Buffet. Miss Helen Findlay, the unpretentious, charming sister of the owner, is in charge of the 2,000 or more selections here, also displays the only complete collection of Dorothy Doughty birds owned by a business establishment. Art prices begin at $200.

Guildhall Galleries, Ltd. South, 406 South Michigan, WE 9-2964

Guildhall makes a specialty of paintings and sculpture by established European artists from countries other than France or Italy; it first brought Henk Bos, Brochet, Conti, Hennessy and Rijlaarsdam to the attention of American collectors. You can make some interesting discoveries here.

Two Loop galleries that specialize in sophisticated religious art are **St. Benet Book Shop Art Gallery,** 300 South Wabash, and the **Center for Religious Art,** 180 North Wabash. One example of the degree of sophistication: a St. Benet show last year, called "Ecumenical Art," featured the works of five widely acclaimed artists of varied faiths—Misch Kohn, Egon Weiner, Gerald Hardy, Brone Jameikis and Sister M. Rembert. St. Benet also shows the works of Sister Corita

Sergel Gallery of Original Prints, 86 East Randolph, RA 6-5814

One of the best places for serious print collectors. Though Sergel deals mainly in contemporary prints—Chagall, Miro, Maillol, Motherwell and the like, it also offers Goya, Daumier and Vasarely, Japanese woodcuts and some occasional razzle-dazzle Pop-Op. Every November, Sergel offers its annual Eskimo Show—prints and little carvings, each piece one of a kind, far more worldly and beautiful than you expect Eskimo art to be. Prices range from $5 to $500, with a pleasant 10 percent discount to students. Monday through Friday only.

Off the Beaten Path

The South Side, especially in the University of Chicago area, has a number of galleries; if you're driving by and one catches your eye, slide into the nearest parking place and drop in. **Harper Court** (page 271) has at least three galleries. On 31st St., between Cottage Grove and South King Drive, you'll find three galleries that specialize in Negro paintings, sculpture and photography. Mid-North there's **Silverman Gallery,** 2433 North Lincoln, 477-0069. It's the biggest loft gallery in town, specializing in Op-Pop-Hard-Edge-and-Shock—whatever is currently "in." Mr. Silverman is serious, however, and gives avant-garde artists, such as David Hickman, Peter Bodnar and Daniel Davidson, a chance to be seen. Art here may also be rented. The gallery is flanked on one side by the old Biograph movie house where Dillinger was shot, on the other by a meat market that sells Australian rabbits. Seeing art here is somewhat like walking into a happening, but without the revolving lights.

Serious art collectors share a common wish when traveling—the opportunity to see a great private art collection in a city they're visiting and the chance to meet its leading artists or at least visit the studios where they work. In Chicago, both wishes are grantable. Mr. Arnold Maremont, an industrialist, has built a notable collection of post-World War II art, beginning with Jackson Pollock. Much of the **Maremont Collection** is spread through four floors of halls, sculpture court and executive offices in the Maremont Building, 168 North Michigan. Visitors genuinely interested in wholly contemporary art may phone AN 3-7676, ask for the president's office and request an appointment to see the collection. Corporate pressures will occasionally result in polite refusals, but for the most part your chances are good. The lobby of the building, open to anyone during business hours, houses a Roszak, a Calder, and a César sculpture collage.

Contemporary Art Workshop, 542 West Grant, LA 5-9624, is the largest non-subsidized art workshop in the country, and there really isn't any place like it—a permanent workshop of 30 well-known artists, jewelry designers, and craftsmen, including Barbara Aubin, Claude Bentley, Ralph Bornmacher, and John Quintana, who rent space from sculptors Cosmo Campoli and John Kearney. The workshop is internationally famous and visited not only by artists from all over the world but by official State Department visitors to Chicago. It's not a place to visit merely because you're curious—it's full of plaster dust and scrap metal and will wreck any pair of high-heeled shoes. But it is the place to come if you want to commission work. Mr. Kearney, its official spokesman, will see that you get to the right person, and if the right person isn't part of the workshop group, he'll send you to the best artist for your needs in an 11-state area. If he has time, he'll also show you his own work (he's a gold- and silversmith as well as a prominent metal sculptor) and give you the opportunity to see the premises. The main floor is primarily for sculpting, welding and bronze casting; the second floor houses potters and craftsmen; the skylighted third floor shelters the painters. By appointment only.

Midway Studios, 6016 South Ingleside, AT 5-7614

Lorado Taft's famous sculpture studios—the central room a one-time brick barn with great wide doors, timbered ceilings and huge skylights—now a registered National Historic Landmark Building and the fine arts studios of the University of Chicago. Taft's plaster casts and working models are here; also continuous exhibits, graduate and undergraduate students at work, their art for sale at the end of each quarter (December, March, June, August). This is one place where you are likely to discover student work of real talent. If you want a conducted tour just ask for it at the information desk. Otherwise, wander about on your own.* The studios have been renovated and are exceedingly handsome.

> Open Monday through Friday, 9 AM to 5 PM; Saturday and Sunday, 10 AM to 4 PM.

Exchange National Bank of Chicago, 130 South LaSalle (Adams), DE 2-5000, has installed an exceptional permanent collection of photographs by 20th-Century greats like Alfred Stieglitz, Edward Steichen, Ansel Adams, Henri Cartier-Bresson, Edward Weston, Brett Weston, Aaron Siskind, Arthur Siegal, Eliot Porter, Walker Evans—more than 40 photographers in all. Their work hangs throughout the bank—over check-writing desks on the main floor, over executive-client conference centers on the upper banking floor, in the board room and private dining rooms of the 14th floor and along corridors everywhere. The entire exhibition is open to visitors who are expected to roam about during regular bank hours discovering some of the most sensitive photography imaginable—a collection that Beaumont Newhall, curator of Eastman House (Rochester, N. Y.) and consultant to the bank, agrees is comparable to those at Eastman House and the Museum of Modern Art. So you find the memorable Yousuf Karsh portrait of Casals taken from behind the cellist as he played; Walter Evans' rainwashed Saratoga Springs Main Street, taken in 1931; the blades of grass and cobwebs Harry Callahan shot at Aix-en-Provence, looking more like drypoint than drypoint itself; Robert Doisneau's portrait of Picasso and Francoise Gilot; and Lewis Hine's documentaries of immigrants and child laborers in the early 1900's. The range of subjects is as varied as the 250 photographs that have turned the bank into a showcase for another art form.

> Drive-in parking on the Adams Street side of the bank. Open 9 AM to 5 PM Monday and Friday, to 4 PM Tuesday, Wednesday, Thursday. Closed weekends and on banking and other holidays. Free.

For art fairs, see page 419. For fine picture frames: **Armand Lee & Co.,** 350 West Erie, **Newcomb-Macklin Co.,** 400 North State, or **Charles Quint & Associates,** 615 North State, DE 7-5631.

---

* Groups must arrange for tour in advance; may also request demonstrations of various media, such as lithography or ceramics.

MUSIC: SYMPHONIC, CHAMBER, CHORAL, LITURGICAL

Chicago is one of the world's most musically rich cities. The keystone to the city's exceptional output is the 109-member **Chicago Symphony Orchestra,** third oldest in the country, preceded only by the New York Philharmonic and the Boston Symphony. Stravinsky calls Chicago's orchestra the finest in the world; conductor Seiji Ozawa says it consistently produces the warmest sound of any orchestra anywhere; the praise it received from eastern critics on its 1966 tour of the seaboard cities was almost embarrassing—"an orchestra that can do anything" and "absolutely glorious."

It was founded in 1891 by the remarkable Theodore Thomas, who brought music to America as no other individual ever did, and gave Chicago his ultimate gift of a symphony strong enough to grow and an orchestral hall acoustically brilliant enough to nourish it. The hall, the first one in America built exclusively for a symphony orchestra, turned out to be far too brilliant for early recording techniques; only when high fidelity recording came into being were non-Chicago purchasers of Chicago Symphony Orchestra recordings able to discover what the years of acclaim were about.

Thomas' first violinist and assistant conductor, Frederick Stock, took the podium in 1905 and held it for 37 innovative years. He introduced youth concerts (page 316), popular concerts, the Chicago Civic Orchestra (the country's only professional training orchestra maintained by a symphony to provide musicians for its own ranks), guest conductors, tours by the orchestra, new music and, to celebrate the orchestra's golden anniversary, commissioned works from Stravinsky, Milhaud, Miaskovsky, Roy Harris, Kodály, Glière, Casella and Sir William Walton. Because of Stock's longevity as musical director the Orchestral Association (governing body of the orchestra) went into a tailspin at his death, and the orchestra, subjected to a dismaying version of musical-directors' chairs and guest conductors, glissandoed from high C attainments to BBb doldrums. Fritz Reiner (a man of astounding musical charisma) finally rescued the orchestra from the shambles it had become, restored it to its former glory, created the Chicago Symphony Chorus and introduced regular performances of oratorio and concert versions of opera into the symphony programs.

His death brought in Jean Martinon, who revived the elegant tradition of giving concerts of chamber music in the ballroom (foyer) on the second floor of Orchestra Hall, a suitably glittery and acoustically accurate setting for the Symphony String Quartet, which is drawn from the orchestra's first and second strings. Mr. Martinon then inaugurated the June Festival, thus extending the season here into a month that is generally nonmusical in most cities. Mr. Martinon left at the end of the 1967-68 season. Mr. Irwin Hoffman has been appointed acting music director; his first concerts have been greeted by the critics with acclaim.

As with all great orchestras, this one has some exceptional musicians; the waves of applause that flood Orchestra Hall at the end of a performance are often as much in appreciation of the strength of individual contributions as for the orchestra as an entity—Victor Aitay, first violin and assistant concertmaster; Milton Preves, first viola; Frank Miller, first violoncello; Donald Peck, first flute; Adolph Herseth, first trumpet; Ray Still, first oboe; Donald Koss, timpani; Edward Druzinsky, harp.

Immediately following the last of the season's performances, the orchestra plays a three-week June Festival of Baroque music and other specialties at Orchestra Hall. It then moves to the handsome outdoor Ravinia Pavilion on the North Shore where it performs until mid-August.

Orchestra Hall, 216 South Michigan, 427-0362, seats 2,546 on the main floor, in boxes, tiered balcony and gallery. It was completely renovated and refurbished in 1967 and is a beautiful concert hall. Big night is Thursday, the major subscription night. As many as 30 guest soloists perform during the series, and perhaps a half-dozen guest conductors take to the podium during the season. Friday afternoon subscription concerts repeat the Thursday program, and there's been a pattern of a third identical performance on alternate Saturday nights (alternate with Pop Concerts) and at some of the Tuesday matinee subscription concerts. For tickets: box office, or Ticket Central, 212 N. Michigan, or write.

> Michigan Avenue buses stop at the door. To catch northbound buses in bad weather, walk through the Grant Park Underground Garage (directly in front of Orchestra Hall) to Washington Street exit. Special parking arrangements have been made with the garage for concerts and theatre. Pay $1 in advance, park from 6 PM on for the entire evening.

Grant Park Concerts, Music Shell at 11th Street between Columbus Drive and Lake Shore Drive, HA 7-5252

For 31 years, the Grant Park concerts were mainly pleasant, free, open-air performances highlighted from time to time by outstanding guest soloists. In 1965 Edward Gordon became full manager of the concerts and began to revolutionize them with imaginative programs, including Schoenberg, Webern, an evening of Ernest Bloch, and a spectacular concertized version of Verdi's *Masked Ball*, with New York Metropolitan Opera singers in the leading roles; there is a minimum of four adventuresome concerts weekly from late June to the end of October.

It's true that you and the orchestra have to fight overhead noise from planes, the orchestral shell is a disgrace (too shallow for decent acoustics or even to protect the musicians and their instruments—when it rains, the performance ends), but the music is free and of the first rank.

About 600 seats are reserved for each performance, but some 1,800 persons write for them so make your request as early as possible for major concerts. Send self-addressed, stamped envelopes for each performance to Chicago Park District, Public Information, 425 East 14th Street, Chicago 60605. Season programs are often available by March. About half the audience will bring picnic suppers and will listen to the concerts from the grass. Ballet is performed in the band shell by leading dancers from the American Ballet Theatre or New York City Center, usually in pas de deux but occasionally as solo performances in early August, and it's generally very good. Young People's Concerts are scheduled for late mornings, usually Thursday, and you're welcome to attend any rehearsal in progress whenever you wander by.

Free parking across the street in front of and behind the Field Museum of Natural History (see map, page 159). For various CTA buses, phone MO 4-7220. Jackson Blvd. eastbound bus marked *Planetarium* goes directly to the band shell. Buses are waiting just south of the band shell at the end of each concert.

Ravinia Festival, Ravinia Park (adjacent to south end of Highland Park), ST 2-9696, or box office, 273-3500

Ravinia is the nub of Chicago's heady summer concert season. It offers a beautiful outdoor setting for music, 3,000 seats under an acoustically superior pavilion, and 36 acres of lush, beautifully maintained grounds for picnickers who upend the folding chairs the park supplies and use them as backrests during performances. Musically, it offers the Chicago Symphony under Resident Musical Director Seiji Ozawa, at least until the end of the 1969 season; guest conductors and soloists; alternate evenings of jazz, folk singers and rock artists, the Sunday Four O'Clocks (always controversial, always the most exploratory new music to be heard outside of the University of Chicago); Young People's Programs (see page 316); an annual week in mid-August of the New York City Ballet; drama at the Murray Theatre on its grounds; an annual art or arts and crafts exhibit at its Casino; and open-air dining in the Carousel.

Ravinia opened in 1903 as an amusement park, by the 1920's had evolved into the most spectacular opera "house" of its time. That golden age lasted until the Depression; then it stood dark. The full story of Ravinia is usually printed in its programs—a history flashing with highlights of and nostalgia for a fabled musical era.

There is a standard gate admission of $2 for all evening performances ($1 for the Four O'Clocks and $1 to hear daytime rehearsals from seats at the edge of the pavilion) plus a sliding range of pavilion seat prices up to $5. At these prices Ravinia attracts a stylish audience. Picnicking is part of the scene, and the society editors of Chicago's newspapers make an awful to-do about it; the way they report contents of picnic baskets and elegant accouterments you'd think nobody went to Ravinia for any reason but box-supper competition. The truth is, even the largest crowds listen raptly. The Chicago Symphony commands that kind of respect and can be heard well anywhere in the park, thanks to an excellent albeit storm-quirky amplification system. Although a true pianissimo isn't really possible outdoors, and humidity affects the timbre of the strings and horns, and the North Western sends at least two trains roaring through every performance, and air traffic can be heavy, a Ravinia evening is a Chicago event not to be missed.

The weather along the North Shore can be variable. Women should bring sweaters no matter how hot it may be in town. In case of sudden downpour, put up your big black umbrella or head for the Murray Theatre along with everyone else—the balance of the concert will be piped in.

> Pavilion reservations can be made in town by phoning ST 2-9696; you can pick up tickets at the Ravinia Festival Association offices, 22 West Monroe Street, at Ticket Central, 212 North Michigan Avenue, or ask to have them held at the reservations kiosk inside the park. Chicago and North Western trains go direct to the gates. Driving from town, use Edens Expy north to Lake-Cook turnoff (marked Ravinia Park) and follow the crowd. Or, overshoot Lake-Cook to the next exit (Clavey), take it east to Blackstone Place and then swing south on Green Bay to the park entrance. It's a couple of miles longer but often some 20 minutes shorter.

Performances to Watch For

The **University of Chicago** offers audiences the chance to hear remarkable contemporary, Baroque and Renaissance music performed on a regular basis by three distinguished groups. Its Department of Music, under the distinguished Leonard B. Meyer, is ranked with the best in the country, and it has three leading composers on its faculty—Easeley Blackwood, Ralph Shapey and Richard Wernick. During a 30-week season it sponsors an average of 1.5 concerts per week, performed by its own musicians and stellar visitors.

The **Contemporary Chamber Players** is composed of graduate and postgraduate fellows in the department plus Chicago-area musicians who, as associates, are under contract for the season. Its level of performance is exceptional, and its music perhaps the most exciting contemporary music to be heard anywhere. "One of the shining things that has happened in Chicago," said music critic Donal J. Henahan. Performances are generally at Mandel Hall, 1131 East 57th Street.

The **Collegium Musicum,** a group of 25 musicians, plays Renaissance and Baroque music with reproductions of ancient instruments of the two eras at **Bond Chapel,** 1025 East 58th Street. The **University Orchestra,** a 90-instrument symphony orchestra of students, is usually to be heard at Mandel Hall, as are most visiting musicians and chamber or symphony groups. For information, phone the concert office, MI 3-0800.

The **School of Music** of Northwestern University, Evanston, is one of the oldest in the country, has a conservatory, and graduates composers, performers, teachers and theorists. Its standards are high, and any student performances you attend will be well above average. The musical organizations on campus that perform are the symphony orchestra, the 35-instrument chamber orchestra, the marching and concert bands (the latter of exceptional merit), an a cappella choir, glee clubs and a chapel choir. **Cahn Auditorium,** seating 1,200, is the hall for the major orchestral, band and choral concerts. **Lutkin Hall** is the appropriate little setting for chamber music and the annual spring master classes in vocal literature, which Lotte Lehman flies from Santa Barbara to teach (the public may attend). **Alice Millar Chapel** hosts organ recitals by distinguished guests as well as faculty and students. **Deering Meadow,** in front of the massive Gothic library on Sheridan Road, is the summer setting for outdoor symphonic and concert band performances. Almost all performances are free. Dates of most performances are listed in the entertainment sections of Chicago newspapers; or phone the concert manager at the School of Music, 492-7575.

Roosevelt University, housed in Sullivan's Auditorium Building at Congress and Michigan, has incorporated the famous old Chicago Musical College and now offers almost-weekly free concerts of chamber music and recitals at 1 PM on Wednesdays in Rudolph Ganz Recital Hall (Room 745). Performances are by faculty, graduate students, undergraduates or guests, and are usually jammed. Evening symphony concerts are announced at regular intervals. For information, WA 2-3580.

Chicago Strings, conducted by Francis Akos, one of the Chicago Symphony Orchestra's leading violinists; the **Chicago Chamber Music Society,** which presents daytime concerts at the Arts Club; the **DePaul University Symphony;** the occasional performances of the **Chicago Businessmen's Orchestra,** a fully-instrumented group of above-average amateurs; recitals by touring virtuosi booked through Sol Hurok or Harry Zelzer's Allied Arts (every Sunday afternoon during the fall-through-spring season at Orchestra Hall, often simultaneously at the Civic Opera House). The **Pro Musica Society** brings in chamber groups, some of them exceedingly prestigious, as the Amadeus Quartet of London, the Juilliard Quartet, etc. The **Society of Contemporary Music** and the **Fromm Music Foundation** (both specialize in commissioning new music) sponsor several concerts each season.

Touring concert artists and musical groups of differing sizes are also booked for performances by local colleges and universities, notably the University of Chicago, Northwestern, Illinois Institute of Technology, University of Illinois Circle Campus, Rosary College, and DePaul University.

Chamber Music

The **Fine Arts Quartet** is internationally recognized as one of the world's finest string quartets. Now in its 20th year, and part of the faculty at the University of Wisconsin, it regularly performs seven concerts at the Goodman Theatre in Chicago and seven at the Howard Junior High School Auditorium in Wilmette. The quartet is especially renowned for its performance of Mozart, Haydn, Beethoven, Schubert and Mendelssohn, and the complete string quartets of Bartok. It frequently adds guest soloists of the caliber of the late clarinetist Reginald Kell and pianist Leon Fleisher. For the past two years, it has sold out on subscription to its Monday night concerts at Goodman Theatre, but tickets are turned back just often enough to make a phone call to its headquarters (446-3831) worthwhile. The Howard Auditorium may seem like a crazy place for chamber music, but its acoustics are excellent, and with almost 1,200 seats you can generally get last-minute tickets.

The **Chicago Chamber Orchestra,** a resident chamber ensemble that is actually a small symphony orchestra of professional musicians (most of them also play in the Lyric Opera and Grant Park orchestras) performs under Dieter Kober almost every Sunday afternoon at several locations within the city—inside in winter, outdoors by lagoons or the lake in June and September. An interesting new performance site is the Lincoln Park Zoo. Though it's not an orchestra to be described in superlatives, it performs seldom heard music and ably fills a musical gap. All concerts are free. For information on location and programs, phone 779-4779.

Choral and Exceptional Liturgical Music

The **Chicago Symphony Chorus,** directed by the gifted Margaret Hillis, performs major oratorio and opera in concert form at regular performances of the Chicago Symphony Orchestra. Do not miss these. The chorus sings great music with authority and style.

Rockefeller Memorial Chapel, on the campus at 59th Street and Woodlawn, is the spectacular Gothic setting for the annual fall-winter-spring oratorio series that presents in close to original form significant and seldom performed great works of choral literature. The chapel is endowed, has its own musical staff of some 36 to 40 voices under the direction of Richard Vikstrom; accompaniment is provided by members of the Chicago Symphony Orchestra. Choral works performed here are so masterful it's a pity that they're never recorded. Concerts are on Sunday afternoons at 3:30; ticket prices range from $2.50 for students to $4.50 for reserved seats. For telephone inquiries, MI 3-0800, ext. 3387.

The 150-voice **St. Mary of the Lake Seminary Choir** under the direction of Father Stanley Rudcki is an inspired group that performs at Orchestra Hall annually in early May. Fr. Rudcki's goal is to reverse the image of a seminary as cloistered and project it as one which makes a cultural contribution to its community. The choral works he presents do just this—the Midwest premieres of Bernstein's *Chichester Psalms* and Britten's *The War Requiem,* the Verdi *Requiem* (still considered too secular for church use) and the *Messiah,* which Fr. Rudcki treats in a moving *concerto grosso* style. The spirit of all his performances is one of love and reverence.

For outstanding liturgical music in houses of worship: the **Cathedral Choristers** and the **Quigley Plain Chant Choir** at 10 AM Solemn High Mass at Cathedral of the Holy Name (Roman Catholic—the Cardinal's Cathedral, to be closed for renovations till mid-1969); **Edward Mondello's** splendid organ music at services and recitals at Rockefeller Chapel, which also holds recitals by visiting organists; **Benjamin Hadley's** organ music at Church of the Ascension (Protestant-Episcopal); the excellent choir which sings at all Sunday services at Temple Sholom (Reformed Jewish); the inspired organist at Northminster Church in Evanston—**David Porter Sackett,** who also composes some of the music the choir sings; and **Marlon Allen's** special choral programs at Christ Church in Winnetka (Protestant-Episcopal). Metropolitan Opera tenor **Richard Tucker** flies yearly to Chicago to serve as cantor during the High Holidays (September or early October) at Park Synagogue Shaare Shalom in the Sheraton-Chicago Hotel.

The **Apollo Music Club** (oldest choral group in the city) performs at least three major oratorios each year, and at Christmas there are a bewildering number of performances of Handel's *Messiah*—one of the most extraordinary is the Rockefeller Chapel performance, which is as close to the Baroque *Aufführungspraxis* as can be found (small chorus, Bach-size orchestra without the added Mozart woodwind parts); the recitative is bone-dry and brilliant.

OPERA

Chicago has had a long and remarkably sophisticated opera tradition which began in the 1850's, when the city was still in its infancy. Though Chicago opera also has a tradition of coming apart at the seams, it had one of the world's most glorious eras of grand opera from 1910 to the early 1930's. The Auditorium Theatre was the original setting of the Chicago Opera Company and the background for Mary Garden's famous debut in *Salome,* a performance that, when she went into the Dance of the Seven Veils, stirred up one of the all-time great storms among the self-appointed moralists of Chicago. The Chief of Police spat that her performance was "Disgusting. Miss Garden wallowed around like a cat in a bed of catnip."

Miss Garden retaliated by saying that she always bowed down to the ignorant and tried to make them understand, "but I ignore the illiterate," a put-down that one suspects went over the Police Chief's head.*

Opera flourished until the Depression; the remnants of the Chicago Opera Company gave up the ghost in the late 1940's. But the fact that it had been grand opera and had set magnificent standards was the main strength of the triumverate (Carol Fox, Nicola Rescigio, Lawrence Kelly) that organized the Lyric Opera Company in 1953—Lyric would be grand or not at all. And it has been, though, true to Chicago tradition, the latest seam-ripping being the cancellation of the 1967 season. The instrument was the musicians' union; its inability to compromise its demands (the most demented of which, that *it* set the length of the operatic season) not only deprived Chicago of opera but left approximately 400 musicians and affiliated stage and opera personnel without work. However, Lyric had its 1968 season—and its comeback was remarkable.

Through its first 13 seasons at the **Civic Opera House,** ** 20 North Wacker Drive, FI 6-0270, Lyric's reputation grew steadily, especially for its willingness to introduce European and Latin American stars in their North American debuts (Maria Callas, for instance, Nicolai Ghiaurov, Alfredo Kraus), for its chorus which gained the reputation of being one of the best in the world, and as an experimental company willing to tackle difficult operas such as *Wozzeck* and Prokofiev's *Angel of Fire*. The company survived the year's hiatus, and patrons again heard an opera company that is neck and neck with the New York Metropolitan in bravura performance. Productions are ably mounted—Lyric does not rely wholly on the old Chicago Opera Company sets but exchanges sets with other companies and even imports them. The orchestra is excellent. The audience, rapt. In short, all the elements of grand opera exist at this opera house.

A number of amateur and semi-professional local opera companies perform from time to time in and around the city. Of genuine significance is the **Apollo Opera Company,** 281-1862, which performs three or four times each year. The Apollo uses a professional orchestra of about 20 musicians from Lyric's orchestra, has Giulio Favario, one of Lyric's assistant conductors as its

* For a fine, gossipy history of Chicago opera, read Emmett Dedmon's *Fabulous Chicago,* from which the above anecdote has been paraphrased.

** Samuel Insull's famed building, the third in Chicago to combine an opera house with an office building (the Auditorium and Uranus H. Crosby's much earlier opera house of 1866 preceded it). The opera house is unbelievable—the elevator that carries scenery is, for instance, 75 feet high; the house itself is scaled to dizzying heights; boxes are so far in the rear that opera glasses are a must. Mary Garden insisted that it was more like a convention hall than an opera house, and all performers agree that the size of the place tends to defeat communication with the audience. That Lyric as well as the earlier Chicago Civic Opera Company have succeeded here is a major triumph.

conductor, hires professionals to design and make scenery, costumes and so forth, spends up to $3,000 to mount a single performance—yet is in business not for profit but to give dedicated young singers the one thing that's hardest to get—a showcase. Singers, chosen by audition, are graduate and advanced students from the best conservatories in the city and from Northwestern University's Opera Workshop. Not only are their voices good, but they can be heard in the 1,000-seat or larger auditoriums Apollo rents for performances.

The **Opera Workshop** at Northwestern University can also be recommended for the quality of voices, good sets, full orchestra and more than reasonable air of professionalism. Furthermore, NU offers audiences a chance to hear offbeat period and contemporary operas, such as Mozart's *Idomeneo*, Stravinsky's *The Rake's Progress*, Benjamin Britten's *Albert Herring,* and Aaron Copland conducting his own opera, *The Tender Land.*

Two groups that annually put on joie de vivre, full of beans performances of Gilbert and Sullivan are the **Savoyaires** and the **Gilbert & Sullivan Opera Company.** Musical Director of the Savoyaires is Frank Miller, first violoncello of the Chicago Symphony, who has been a G & S buff since he was an adolescent playing in a pit orchestra. Mr. Miller has conducted some 350 G & S performances (which is probably more than any other conductor in this country); he's also studied every performing group anywhere, and any performance he conducts will be a delight. Leading roles are usually sung by professionals; architects design scenery and costumes; the theatre is the new Niles North High School next to Old Orchard Shopping Center, Old Orchard Road and Edens Expressway. The Gilbert & Sullivan Opera Company performs at Mandel Hall.

THEATRE

To visitors it may be only a matter of passing concern but to Chicagoans it's a matter of cultural inferiority—theatre here simply isn't like theatre in London or New York.* The big shows are elsewhere and Chicago is left out. Left out of the razzle-dazzle of openings, the celebrity game, the taken-for-granted right of the West End and Broadway to make or break plays, authors, new actors, stars. When it comes to professional theatre, Chicago is scarcely better off than any other road-show city in America—it takes what New York producers decide will make money outside New York.

The fault is Chicago's. The plays it makes most profitable for New York producers are the musicals and the broad comedies such as *Barefoot in the Park* and *The Odd Couple.* Serious drama, the cultural basis of the enviable

---

* It isn't even spelled the same way. Chicago usually insists that the word is *theater.*

177

theatre of London and New York, is rarely sent from Broadway to Chicago because the financial risks are too great. The risk exists in New York, of course, but there it's offset by the vast prestige accorded a producer, whereas in Chicago there's no similar compensation. The implication of the intellectual snub is obvious: Chicago is just another hicksville in the eyes of New York.

Yet there is serious theatre here, especially if one is willing to venture beyond the Loop into "off-Broadway" theatre. Chicago has some first-rate community theatres and university theatres where you can see plays of content, well produced and ably performed. Chicago also has William Robert Sickinger's wonderfully experimental Hull House theatres; it has the famous Second City which, though usually listed in newspaper,entertainment sections under "Revues," has actually created a new kind of theatrical experience based on improvisation, satire and wit (see page 75).

There is also a kind of theatre here you won't find elsewhere—dinner theatre. It's a package deal: dinner followed by a light comedy you watch from your table. Often if the food is good the performance isn't, or if the performance is the food isn't, but if you're not too critical you can have a good time.

Professional Theatre

Since Loop theatres are open or closed according to what's booked in, only their names need be mentioned here. The **Blackstone,** 60 East Balbo, CE 6-8240 (next door to the Sheraton-Blackstone Hotel and across the street from the Conrad Hilton Hotel), is the handsomest of the Loop theatres, the most intimate, the most like a fine old New York house. Its sight lines are good, and you'll be able to see and hear well from almost any seat in the house.

The **Studebaker,** 418 South Michigan, 922-2973, is larger, but except for its loges, which are at right angles to the proscenium (which means an angled view), and its upper balcony, its sight lines are fairly good. The **McVickers,** 25 West Madison, 782-8230, is a converted movie house, so big that it generally only carries musicals, but they're amplified so you can hear anywhere in the house. Its side seats in the balcony should be avoided if possible. The **Shubert,** 22 West Monroe, CE 6-8240, is equally huge and even more awkward, and its second balcony is so remote from the action on the stage that opera glasses are essential. The Shubert also has load-bearing pillars in front of some seats, but since no Shubert ticket seller will ever volunteer that information, it's up to you to make sure you don't buy behind them.* The **Civic Theatre,** 20 North Wacker Drive, FI 6-0270, is another 1920's-handsome small

---

* All Loop theatres have near their box offices diagrams showing seat locations. If after checking location you're not happy with the tickets you've been given, exchange them immediately.

theatre but suffers from the same exaggerated height and depth Sam Insull built into the Opera House, in the same building. The **Auditorium Theatre,** 70 East Congress, 922-2110, has 4,000 seats for large-scale musicals, visiting opera and ballet. Architect Dankmar Adler's superb engineering skills (see page 104) assure you of perfect sight lines and acoustics wherever you sit.

Goodman Memorial Theatre, 300 East Monroe (Columbus), CE 6-2337, is a little gem of a theatre of 744 seats. Goodman is an old and distinguished part of the Art Institute's School of Drama and, as such, is a training ground for young actors, actresses, stage designers and costume designers. But to the degree that its plays are always headed by at least one and frequently two outstanding professionals—Morris Carnovsky, for instance, or Sam Wanamaker, Leo G. Carroll, Eugenie Leontovich, Jerome Kilty—performances are often at an exceedingly high level. In the last few seasons director John Reich has tackled increasingly ambitious plays—*Marat/Sade,* for instance, which was done with distinction. Goodman patrons gobble up seats on subscription, and your best bet for tickets may very well be on a week-night. Ticket prices are considerably lower than elsewhere (generally a top of about $4.50), and the theatre itself is considerably more elegant than most. Sight lines are generally excellent.

Ivanhoe, 3000 North Clark, 248-6800, is a new theatre in the square in which no seats in Sections 2 and 4 are more than five rows from the stage. It has a certain charm, and its professional casts are always headed by a star, but it deserves better plays than it gets. The old Ivanhoe Restaurant is next door; you can dine in it before the play or stop in afterwards for dining and dancing until 2 AM on weekdays, 2:30 on weekends. Parking lot for those who drive; Clark Street CTA buses stop at the door.

A new professional theatre has opened in Wilmette, and it's gotten off to a good start. It's the **Academy Playhouse,** (Loyola Academy), 1100 Laramie, Wilmette, BR 3-4040. Marshall Migatz produced several outstanding plays in it during the summer of 1967 and has booked the theatre for the summer of 1968.

Mr. Migatz specializes in theatre of a most distinguished kind, casts the best professionals he can find, brings in New York directors when necessary— Theodore Mann, for instance, who directed the haunting, beautiful *Hogan's Goat.* Goat's author, William Alfred, who of course saw both the original off-Broadway production and this one, found the Chicago performance superior in every way. The kudos are Mr. Migatz's.

Theatre Tickets

When the grump at the box office tells you he's sold out for a performance of something you want to see, try **Joe's Cigarstand** at the Pearson Hotel, SU 7-

8200 (ask for Tickets). You'll pay about 25 percent more than box office prices, but the seats will be excellent and you can count on them being so. Joe also handles tickets for special events, opera and some sports events.

Community Theatre

Probably the most astonishing dramatic achievement in Chicago is the **Hull House Association,** which began with a single theatre in 1963 and by 1968 had become the biggest amateur theatre program in the country. If theatre were to acknowledge the sports term *Pro-Am,* it would be apt here, for nothing Hull House does is amateurish.

When William Robert Sickinger created the initial project, he based his choice of plays on the idea that somewhere in the city there were enough people to support serious contemporary and experimental drama. He tried community theatre at a variety of levels and, depending upon the neighborhoods in which he established his theatres, offered plays to audiences whose intellectual demands were high, to audiences of moderate tastes and to audiences who had never seen any drama at all. His first theatre was:

Hull House, Jane Addams Center, 3212 North Broadway, 348-5622

In an unpretentious structure Chicago first got bold, provocative drama—plays by Albee, Gelber, Beckett, Murray Schisgal and Frank Gilroy's first venture, *Who'll Save the Plowboy?* What Mr. Sickinger didn't and still doesn't have in the way of funds for slick productions is unimportant compared to the snap of his productions—taut, electrifying, challenging. Because of his predominant choice of plays, the theatre has come to be known as Sickinger's Theatre-of-the-Cruel. It's off-Broadway theatre at its finest, and though you may be puzzled and even discomforted by what you see, you'll be involved. The house seats 140; performances are every Friday, Saturday, and Sunday night. All but 40 seats for each performance go to subscription holders, so phone your reservations as far in advance as you can. Top ticket prices are under $5.

Hull House Parkway Theatre, 500 East 67th Street, HY 3-1306, is a purposeful little three-quarter stage theatre in a Negro neighborhood. It's the second of the Hull House theatres, plays to racially mixed audiences who more often than not come from outside the area, uses integrated actors in plays of significant inter-racial drama. Simply as a community experience Parkway commands interest. But it also offers poignant drama. Furthermore, it's community in the best sense of the word—on week-nights it opens its door to other forms of entertainment, such as folk singers and African dancers, and has also added a Children's Theatre. Tickets top at $3; special student rates on Friday.

Hull House Playwright's Center, housed at 222 West North, WH 4-9679, is now in its fifth year of working with playwrights (about 100 of them) and monthly offers the public the chance to sit in on readings and actual performances of plays coming out of the workshop. Some of the plays have become prizewinners and have been produced elsewhere—Toronto and New York. Performances on Friday and Saturday evenings; tickets generally at about $2.

Hull House-Leo Lerner Theatre, 4520 North Beacon (south of Wilson), has a horseshoe stage and specializes in musicals. As it seats only 140, it gives you the chance to enjoy musicals in close-up. Top prices, about $5.

Mr. Sickinger has also developed a touring theatre road show that visits schools, colleges and other organizations in nine states. Another group, **Chamber Theatre,** gives professional play readings before organizations and in private homes. Chicagoans who would like to have a Chamber Theatre reading should contact Miss Bea Fredman, 477-8009. The plays are avant-garde; the fee of $5 per listener is donated to the Hull House Association. The programs also include audience participation discussions led by volunteers in psychiatry and the arts. Chicagoans who want to be on the Hull House mailing lists will have to contact each theatre individually, since no overall schedule is provided.

Old Town Players, 1718 North North Park, 645-0145, the oldest community group in the city, recently converted an Old Town church into a handsome theatre with a variable thrust stage and a tiered arena. Every seat is 12 inches higher than the seat in front of it, and you're never more than six rows away from the stage, so sight lines and acoustics are perfect. The seats are directors' chairs, which means you have 24 inches, instead of the standard 19, in the most comfortable chairs ever invented.

Old Town Players tackle ambitious plays—*The Balcony, Little Foxes*—and do them with style and wit. Furthermore, Resident Director Frank V. Carioti is constantly expanding the notion of community theatre. In addition to the plays there are offerings of the Children's Musical Theatre Workshop, madrigal singers, jazz, an actors' workshop, dance recitals, poetry readings; Mr. Carioti has ably produced at least one opera and by the time you read this may be offering the Association for the Advancement of Creative Musicians (page 87) as well. For plays, tickets top at $2.50.

Theatre First, Inc., 2936 North Southport, LA 5-9761 (in the Atheneum just off Lincoln Avenue), has a season from September to mid-June, is quite experimental and will plunge into Ionesco with as much fervor as it will tackle a musical. Scenery and costuming are always first-rate and acting is often very polished.

The **Village Players,** Oak Park-River Forest Civic Theatre, 447 South Boulevard, Oak Park, 383-9829, have great imagination, ability and offer a wide variety of productions. For instance, they'll do *Dylan* and follow it with a musical version of *The Christmas Carol,* and follow that with *A Man for All Seasons.* Theirs is a three-quarter stage, the setting is intimate, and you can hear every word of a musical as well as every word of a play. Everyone troops over to Hogan's Bar at Oak Park Avenue and Roosevelt Road after performances. Go along with them—you'll be welcome.

Lincoln Park Players, 2021 North Stockton, DI 8-7075, perform on the second floor of the Lincoln Park Boathouse above Cafe Brauer. Two recent productions were really knockouts—*Toys in the Attic* and *Rope Dancers.* The players are almost always among the winners in the Chicago Park District's annual competition for all Park District drama groups who are entitled to perform in summer at Theatre on the Lake.

Theatre on the Lake, Fullerton Pavilion, Fullerton and the Outer Drive, DI 8-7075. Summer season only here since the Pavilion is an open one. The plays are the best plays produced by all Park District groups during the previous winter. Because performances are inexpensive ($1), the reserved seats sell out on subscription, but there are always about 50 unreserved seats, and everyone who waits in line seems to get in.

Dinner Playhouses

You'll need a car to reach these since they're either at the outskirts of the city, in the suburbs or even farther out. They all follow approximately the same pattern—a package price for dinner and the play, and a professional cast usually headed by a Hollywood star.

Drury Lane Theatre, 2500 West 94th Place, Evergreen Park, PR 9-4000, is the big entertainment spot for the Far South Side of Chicago. It has a plush Miami Beach decor, and people get dressed up to go to it. You can attend only the play if you wish, since the theatre is separate from the dining room. You can also order a la carte or from a sandwich menu. Drury seats 792, but no seat is more than 50 feet from the arena stage. Then there's **Candlelight Dinner Playhouse,** 5620 South Harlem, Summit, GL 8-7373, which specializes in musical comedies, seats 600 around its stage, stays open for dancing afterwards. **In the Round Dinner Playhouse** is located at 6072 Archer (two blocks west of Central), 581-3090. **Country Club Theatre,** Old Orchard Country Club at Rand and Euclid, Mt. Prospect, 259-5400, offers smorgasbord as well as dinners and an arena stage no more than 25 feet from any seat. **Pheasant Run Playhouse,** Pheasant Run Lodge, Route 64, St. Charles, 312-584-1454, is part of a handsome lodge that includes seven restaurants, shops and nightclub entertainment in addition to the dinner theatre. Its stage is three-quarter round, and dinner tables are on several tiers. **Shady Lane Restaurant and Play-house,** three miles west of Marengo on US 20, 815-568-7218, can be reached in slightly more than an hour from the Loop via Eisenhower Expressway to Northwest Tollway and US 20 turnoff. It offers a nicely rural setting, really fine country dining, a deluxe converted barn theatre, intermissions long enough to whomp up a good bar trade, shops and an Hassafrass Room for after-theatre corned beef and pastrami. **Ivanhoe** (page 179) also offers a package rate for dinner and theatre.

University Theatre

Court Theatre at the University of Chicago, MI 3-0800, ext. 3581, has one of the most charming outdoor settings in the country—the court of Hutchinson Commons, part of the original university quadrangle at 57th Street and University. University-area audiences picnic here with jugs before the play; everyone rents lawn chairs (25¢) or sprawls on blankets on the grass. The ivy-covered Gothic surroundings are perfect for Shakespeare and the classics, and if a play calls for a crowd scene it will be spectacular, with perhaps 100 costumed performers bearing flaming torches and entering the action from all sides. If the weather turns, Court Theatre moves into Mandel Hall—a graceless old hall that not only formalizes everything but magnifies faults you happily overlook outdoors. Pray for good weather. Season is July to mid-September.

Northwestern University's Annual Summer Drama Festival, (July, August) is also performed outdoors in the tree-outlined Garden Theatre at 1905 Sheridan, next to the School of Speech. Plays range from Anouilh's *Ring Around the Moon* to Sheridan's *School for Scandal* and frequently Bernard Shaw. Casts are advanced and graduate School of Speech students.

Barat College School of Drama, at the Drake Theatre on the Barat campus, Lake Forest, CE 4-3000, sponsors fall and spring productions, uses students at all levels of the four-year program, and fills male roles from the faculty or other drama schools. Plays range from the classics through contemporary drama.

BALLET

Just as Chicago gets every play booked out of New York for the road, so it gets every international ballet company that tours America, as well as New York's touring companies. Some years the calendar is crowded with one major company after another at the Auditorium or the Opera House. **Harper Theatre** on the South Side, 5238 South Harper, BU 8-1717, brings in smaller modern dance groups, many of which are worth seeing.

Two resident companies certainly deserve attention: the famed **Sybil**

Shearer, one of the best-known dancers in the world, though now in semi-retirement here, can still be seen in occasional performances as can young dancers tutoring under her. The **Phyllis Sabold Dance Company,** a professional group in residence at Barat College, has as artistic director Mr. Eric Braun, former principal dance and ballet master of the American Ballet Theatre. The company is adventurous and capable, and among its finest ballets are three which Miss Sabold choreographed: *Missa Luba,* to music from an authentic Congolese Mass; *Canterbury Tales,* which is pure delight; *Hats on to Stravinsky,* danced to his *Suite for Small Orchestra,* quick and full of romping fun. The company performs in the stylish new Drake Theatre on the Barat Campus in Lake Forest, CE 4-3000.

Ruth Ann Koesun and John Kriza, principal dancers of the American Ballet Theatre in recent years, are now artistic directors of the Hull House Dance Department.

PUPPET OPERA

Kungsholm Miniature Grand Opera, Kungsholm Restaurant, 100 East Ontario, WH 4-2700

For opera almost any evening you choose, take in the famous Kungsholm puppet opera, which is grand opera performed by authentically costumed 13-inch puppets to outstanding opera recordings against settings copied from La Scala and the Metropolitan Opera. The intimate little theatre in which you view the proceedings was copied after the gilt and plush Royal Opera House in Copenhagen, complete even to boxes, small balcony and inscription across the procenium "Ej Blot Til Lyst," Not Only For Amusement.

The illusion of live opera is splendid. Houselights dim, a 52-piece puppet orchestra rises into view, the puppet maestro mounts the podium, raises his baton, and, on the downbeat, one of several dozen favorite operas unfolds. Tosca throws her fan to the floor; Mimi drops her muff; Hansel and Gretel dance together; the crystal chandeliers in the ballroom scene of *La Traviata* twinkle as brilliantly as the Met's, and the vocalizing is naturally flawless. Broadway musicals are also performed so if you missed *Man of La Mancha* or *Oliver* you can catch puppet interpretations to the voices of the original cast. Matinees Tuesday, Thursday, Saturday at 2 PM, Sunday at 3 PM. Evening performances nightly at 8 PM and a late Saturday performance at 10:15 PM. Closed Monday. Tickets are free to restaurant patrons but should be reserved in advance.

Note: If you're writing to Chicago theatres for tickets in advance of your arrival, the *New Spectator's Guide* ($1) shows floor plans for all Loop theatres, the Opera House, Auditorium and Chicago Stadium. Available through Griffin Publishing Co., 1002 North State, Chicago 60610.

PART III: Sports in Chicago

SPORTS FOR SPECTATORS

8

Baseball
Football
Hockey
Basketball
Soccer
Racing
Polo
Cricket
Junior Tournament Tennis
Championship Golf
Horse Shows
The Mackinac and Other Regattas
Sports Areas—Where They Are

CHAPTER 8

SPORTS FOR SPECTATORS

At no time is the jingoism of the native Chicagoan more evident than during a discussion of his city's professional teams. Though these rarely deliver championships, the Chicago fan's emotional commitment to them is like nationalism—intense and blind. Furthermore, fan enthusiasm is not confined to one stratum of Chicago society but peppers it like shotgun pellets. One incident will prove the point:

In 1959, officialdom in the person of the Fire Commissioner got a flash report that the White Sox, in a night game against Cleveland, had just won the American League pennant. Immediately, the Commissioner ordered Chicago's entire air-raid warning siren system turned on for a half-hour citywide celebration.

Not for a moment did it occur to the commissioner that a citizenry attuned for years to air-raid siren testing only at 10:30 on Tuesday mornings might think of a nuclear attack rather than White Sox when the sirens screamed about an hour before midnight.

Yet once the fans recovered, they went wild, and an estimated 3,000 of them descended on the airport to greet the returning victors.

Only a little of this attitude can be explained easily, but it has something to do with the sheer number of places scheduling sports events—two open-air ball parks, six racetracks, three indoor arenas, two stadia, a suburban sports core, an armory and some lesser locations which needn't be listed at this moment but which will be found with the addresses of all facilities on page 197.

Because of the spread of playing fields, there is considerable pressure for a glossy new catchall indoor-outdoor sports arena, one that will top Houston's Astrodome, of course. The pressure comes from the *Chicago Tribune* and from promoters whose main selling point is the convenience of centralization, not especially from fans.*

PRO BASEBALL

Just as Americans everywhere are exposed to advertisements for Wrigley chewing gum, so Chicagoans, at the home base of the Wrigley empire, are exposed to a local slogan—"Beautiful Wrigley Field."

The slogan is true. P. K. Wrigley maintains the last major ball park in America to bear legitimate resemblance to a park. His **Chicago Cubs** play in an environment of ivy-clad walls and lush green outfields from which all billboards, night-lights and crazy scoreboards are banned. The idea of an attractive ball park is now so singular that it may account in part for the myth that P.K. doesn't really care about baseball. Cubs fans are continuously grumbling that he doesn't even attend home games, but they're wrong. P.K. simply eschews a conspicuous box for anonymity elsewhere in the stands.

The Cubs were organized in 1876, are now the only charter member of the National League. P.K.'s father bought into the team in 1916 and became a majority stockholder three years later. Under father and son the Cubs won 16 league championships and two World Series, but in the years from 1947 they set some kind of league record for longevity in the second division— before rebounding to a third-place finish in 1967. Yet, they're never without notables, and the current big names are Ron Santo, Billy Williams, Ernie Banks (who in 1958-59 became the only player in National League history to win the Most Valuable Player award in two consecutive seasons) and, in a different way, peppery manager Leo Durocher.

You can see good baseball at Wrigley Field; you also can place bets in the right centerfield stands. Even on an off day, the park is one of the nicest places to spend a summer afternoon. For complete schedule of home games, see the last page of the Yellow Pages. It also lists ticket information and starting times.

Across town are Arthur Allyn's **White Sox,** an entirely different kind of team. The White Sox always threaten to win the pennant but almost always end in second or third place. They've won the league pennant five times, most recently on the memorable occasion of 1959, and the World Series twice— like more than 50 years ago.

The team is great on pitching, running and hustling, but batting is some-

---

* Not even from the ladies who write endless letters to the editor complaining about litter and inadequate washrooms. Visiting ladies might try using the First Aid Station instead. The trick is to rush in looking distressed—the nurse won't dare say no. Thus you get a toilet that *flushes,* two kinds of water in the wash basin, soap and *plenty of paper towels.*

how beyond them. When a batter does manage to get a scrawny little hit into the infield the hustle is something to see—a brave but usually hopeless attempt to turn a weak single into a double on legwork.

White Sox Park is freshly painted and relatively neat. It seats 46,500 and has an enormous outfield. The variety of ball games played here is a promoter's dream—day games, double headers, ladies' days, holiday night games, twin night doubleheaders, and ladies' nights. There is also former owner Bill Veeck's famous manic-depressive scoreboard. Let the Sox score a home run and the thing explodes in an hysterical whirl of fireworks, rockets, bombs and a bit of the "Hallelujah" chorus from Handel's *Messiah (Hallelujah! Hallelujah! Hallelujah!)* It goes depressive and mute when opposition scores.

Sox Park concession stands sell fried chicken, hamburgers and the like, and there are picnic tables under the stands where you can watch the team practice while you're munching. You can also bring in box lunches from outside. For schedules, ticket information, etc., see the last page of the Yellow Pages.

PRO FOOTBALL

In fall the big Sunday sport in this city is pro football, with the **Chicago Bears** as the attraction. The Bears play at Wrigley Field to capacity audiences, some 34,000 of whom are season-ticket holders. They're one of the oldest teams in pro football (National Football League), and Papa Bear George Halas, their founder, gave up coaching in 1968. They got their name when Halas brought them to Chicago from Decatur, Illinois, in 1921. Wrigley Field was available for a home field, and Wrigley had the Cubs—hence, Bears. The team plays seven regular-season home games starting in October. The Bears also sponsor and play the annual Armed Forces Benefit Game on the first Friday in September, usually against the St. Louis Cardinals. The team has eight world championships to its credit, the most recent in 1963.

A funny notion has been circulating for years about the seating capacity of the field. The Bears claim 47,000 seats. The Wrigley people say the actual seat count is 36,644. Though east stands are erected (blocking out some of the bleachers), nobody seems to know precisely what the net gain is, but it does not add up to an additional 10,500 available seats, and tickets are the devil to come by. As a last resort, scalpers are your best bet—in the Loop on weekdays or outside the field on game days. Or use your business contacts in Chicago, who reserve chunks of seats for each season.

Chicago weather can be murderous during the final games of the season —wear everything you own. A clutch of rinky-dink bars in the neighborhood will welcome and warm you after the game. Fans have grinned for years at the sign over **Mike's Cellar Lounge** on Addison—"Good and Bad Whiskey," but no one has ever been poisoned there.

The **St. Louis Cardinals'** summer training camp is at Lake Forest College, Lake Forest. Phone the college, CE 4-3100, if you want to watch drill or practice sessions between mid-July and the first week in September.

COLLEGE FOOTBALL

At Dyche Stadium, west of the **Northwestern University** campus in Evanston, Big Ten football in a Big Ten stadium that seats 55,000 cheering fans. Most of them are wildly enthusiastic students and alumni, but if the only seats you can get are up on the west rim, don't complain; you'll also have a splendid view of the leafy suburb to the east.

The College All-Star football games were born at NU, as were the NCAA basketball championships. Though recent NU teams have not been outstanding, they play against the best. They also have beautiful cheerleaders, a spectacular marching band and all the college spirit one could wish for. The one game for which tickets are always scarce is the match against Notre Dame—too many alumni of both universities in the vicinity.

Evanston is dry, so bring your own jug.

COLLEGE ALL-STAR ANNUAL GAME

Always the first Friday in August at Soldier Field, and always a game between June graduates who were outstanding varsity players and the champion of the National Football League of the previous season. There are obvious pitfalls in putting together a team that's had only a few weeks of practice and hurling it against a pro team in which members have played together for years; final scores are often hopelessly lopsided. Still, it's a good chance to see the Big Ones in action, and the price of the tickets goes to a good cause—the *Chicago Tribune* Charities.

PUBLIC AND PAROCHIAL HIGH SCHOOL CHAMPIONSHIP FOOTBALL

Soldier Field also hosts the runoff Saturday games between Chicago's Roman Catholic and public high school teams. The final game is known as the **Mayor's Championship,** and it's always on the first Saturday in December. Good football and worth seeing.

PRO HOCKEY

Led by Bobby Hull and Stan Mikita, the **Chicago Blackhawks** barreled through the 1966-1967 season to win their first title (after 44 seasons), with their hysterical fans screeching them on. The Hawks have a reputation for rough and dirty fighting, and their fans are every bit as bad, stomping about the aisles and throwing anything that isn't nailed down when they disagree with a referee's decision to stick a Hawk in the penalty box. Since they disagree with every decision, the violence in the stands usually matches that on the ice. Before midseason in 1966-67, the city's Fire Commissioner angrily ordered extra lieutenants into the stadium and complained bitterly about the way his 50 men were being treated.

As might be guessed, the Hawks (National Hockey League) play to capacity crowds. The Chicago Stadium seats 17,000, and tickets are scarce; often your best bet is a theatre broker, who charges about $1.50 to $2.00 over the box office price. Commercial parking facilities exist, but barely. Most spectators look for on-the-street parking and fend off intimidation from little self-appointed car watchers who offer to guard the car for one dollar or more. A refusal brings loud threats of airless tires and other nasty tricks. One regular has solved the problem by carrying a Polaroid with a flash at the ready. Threatened, he just snaps the shutter and warns the kid that if there's anything wrong with *his* car when he returns, the police will know who to look for. The man hasn't paid a cent in parking fees or protection for years.

PRO BASKETBALL

Pro basketball failed several times in Chicago but came back with a smashing start in 1967. The new team—the **Chicago Bulls,** mainly young athletes just out of college—won more games than they were expected to win and made pro basketball here look very big. Their game is fast, racehorse basketball, all offense and a constant rush from one end of the court to the other. The Bulls play at the Chicago Stadium week-nights, weekends and Sundays. Their first year saw 36 home games between October and March. Get tickets at the box office or from Bull headquarters, 221 North LaSalle Street, RA 6-0335.

COLLEGE BASKETBALL

Doubleheaders on Saturday nights at the Chicago Stadium from December through February and the chance to see some outstanding college basketball. Last year, **Loyola** played one of the games each week, and two visiting teams played the other. In other years, **DePaul** and Loyola alternated during the season. Visitors include teams such as Duke, Kentucky, Michigan, UCLA and Notre Dame.

Northwestern plays Big Ten games from mid-December through March, plus intersectional games before the season with squads from the East, the West Coast and the South. All Northwestern games at McGaw Memorial Hall, north of Dyche Stadium in Evanston. For schedule and ticket information, call 492-7070.

PRO SOCCER

Arthur and John Allyn's **Chicago Mustangs,** organized in 1967, compete in the 12-city North American Soccer League and have the official sanction of the International Football (soccer) Federation, which governs the sport world-wide. Soccer is fast and rough and tumble. Halves run 45 minutes with no time-out, so action is continuous as opposing teams vie for single point goals. The Mustangs played exhibition games with Europeans their first year, began their first league season April, 1968. They're at White Sox Park with 16 home games scheduled for dates the Sox are on the road.

AMATEUR SOCCER

Chicago's had soccer for years in the form of ethnic groups playing some of the toughest games to be seen. To see the diversity of Chicago nationalities, go to the amateur soccer games. Amateur teams are all over the city and meet and compete on a year-round basis.

Schwaben and **Hansa** are German teams. The **Lions** are Ukrainian, the **Maroons** Italian, the **Olympics** are Greeks, the **Eagles** are Polish, the **Spartans** are Czech and, though it's not commonly known, the **Norwegian-Americans** also include Swedes. The **Vikings** are a 40-odd-year-old Swedish team, and the **Kickers,** newcomers mainly German, followed tradition and captured the 1966 United States Amateur Championship. The **Tanners** and **Necaxa** are South American teams—their fans are some of the most ardent you'll see. See Sunday newspapers' sports sections for the location of games scheduled that day.

Following games, most players troop off to their clubs. If you want to drink with them, drop in at the **Hansa Soccer Football Club,** 3501 North Hermitage (Lincoln), LA 5-5251, or the **Eagles Athletic Club,** 1340 North Ashland, HU 6-9587. Swedish players eat regularly at **Verdandi Swedish Restaurant,** 5017 North Clark, LO 1-5697. The food is authentic and inexpensive.

RACING

There's thoroughbred and harness racing at six different tracks in and around Chicago. Some of the purses are as rich as you'll find anywhere; the richest races are at **Arlington Park, Washington Park** and **Sportsman's Park.** Arlington's $150,000 Arlington-Washington Added Futurity in September, the last stake of the meeting, is the richest race for thoroughbreds in the world. Though off-track betting is illegal, handbook operators abound—in bars, behind news-stands, in elevators (the operators), and behind cigar stands, and they charge 20 percent to place each bet. The season at the tracks is as follows:

Thoroughbred racing opens mid-April at Sportsman's Park (25 days), moves to Arlington Park in mid-May for 103 days, on to **Hawthorne** in mid-September for 35 days, then back to Sportsman's for the end of the season (24 days).

Harness racing starts on or about February 22 at Washington Park and runs there until mid-July. Sportsman's Park picks up on the next day, goes into the first week in September. Washington Park gets harness back again from September until mid-October; **Maywood Park** takes over mid-October to the end of November. **Aurora Downs** opens December 1 and runs at least to the middle of February.

POLO

If you've never seen polo, **Oak Brook** has it, complete with canopied refreshment stands. Formally, Oak Brook is known as the International Sports Core; the rest of the time it bills itself as a high spot on the list of the international jet set. However, it's not true that only second- or third-rate titles play here—a lot of other people who also crave publicity play at Oak Brook. The polo season is late April to mid-October with games on the weekends.

Major tournament trophies include the Maharaja of Jaipur Trophy, the Kimberly Cup, the Maltese Cup and the Illinois Governor's Cup. Saturday games are played on the Pan American Field and Sunday games on International Field. Games both days start at 3 PM. For daily field and weather, phone 654-1550. Practice matches free. Regular games viewed from grandstands, $1.50. If you're a guest in a box, you won't feel well dressed unless you're in the latest thing in *Vogue* or *Gentleman's Quarterly;* if you're in the stands, pants, sweaters and sweat shirts will do, regardless of sex, and sunglasses are a must since the afternoon sun is strong.

On the North Shore, at Onwentsia Country Club, the four teams of the **Onwentsia Polo Club** play indoors from October to mid-April, when they move outside to the field. Its entrance winds westward from 300 North Green Bay Road in Lake Forest. The public can watch at any time.

AMATEUR CRICKET

Though few Chicagoans and almost no sportswriters seem to know that Chicago has cricket, there are six teams in the area and they have the aura of the great days of the British Empire—players in traditional whites, red leather ball, Empire terminology (pitchers are *bowlers,* the field is the *pitch,* batsmen run between *wickets* and the catcher is the *wicket keeper*).

Of the six teams, four are members of the U.S. Cricket Association. The membership is primarily West Indian, with a sprinkling of East Indians, and they play 40 matches during the season (mid-May to mid-October) in Washington Park. Matches start promptly at 1:30 PM every Sunday—at least two are played simultaneously on adjacent fields and sometimes as many as four. Take the Outer Drive to 55th Street, drive west to Cottage Grove and into Washington Park. The pitches are between 53rd and 55th Street, east of South King Drive. Baseball diamonds surround them; just work your way around these to the center of the park.

The **Winnetka Cricket Club,** composed mainly of Englishmen, an East Indian or two, and a handful from other Commonwealth countries, plays on Saturdays and Sundays at the Skokie Playfield at Hibbard and Pine streets in Winnetka. The club dates back to 1928 and is unaffiliated so that it's free to travel to other matches whenever it wishes. Some weekends it will not be playing home games. Call Skokie Playfield, HI 6-2397, for starting hour and dates.

The **Northwestern University Cricket Club** is a member of the Midwest Cricket Conference. It plays on Wells Field, immediately north of Dyche Stadium, Evanston—Ashland Avenue is the western boundary. The team is a mixture of British, Australian, West and East Indians, and it plays 40 weekend matches from May to Labor Day. For current schedule of games and starting time, call the Director's Office, Northwestern University Physical Education Department, 492-7314.

JUNIOR TOURNAMENT TENNIS

The National Clay Court Championships have left Chicago, but the River Forest Tennis Club, which hosted these, still sponsors the **Junior Invitational Tournament** for young people ages 12 to 18. Daily during the first full week in August, some 360 youngsters in the junior division of the U.S. Lawn Tennis Association compete in singles and doubles for trophies and ranking in what is one of the biggest and most exciting junior tournaments in the country. Admission is free. No grandstands, so visitors sit on the grass. The clubhouse canteen is open for sandwiches and soft drinks. Tournament hours are 9:30 AM to 5 PM. The club is located at 615 Lathrop Avenue, River Forest.

> Take Eisenhower Expy to Harlem turnoff, north to Lake Street, west to Lathrop.

CHAMPIONSHIP GOLF

The **Western Open** is played in Chicago sometime between the end of June and early August—the date is loose because some 45 tournaments for pros precede it. The Western Open is the second oldest tournament in the country (est. 1899) and is one of the 24 offering a purse of $100,000 or more. Spectator fee is $5 weekdays, $6 on Saturday, $7 on Sunday. For location and exact dates call Western Golf Association, KE 9-4600.

The **Illinois Open** is played early in May. The **Illinois State Amateur** is played the end of June, and the **Chicago District Amateur** in mid-July. For exact dates and locations, call the Chicago District Golf Association, 943-5022.

Annual Children's Memorial Pro-Amateur Golf Tournament, at Onwentsia Country Club in Lake Forest, teams leading pros, such as Billy Casper, Gay Brewer, Jack Nicklaus, Doug Ford and the rest, with wealthy and very social Chicago executives in a best ball 18-hole meet. Each executive will have contributed $500 to the Children's Memorial Hospital Fund, and the pros divide a purse of about $15,000. Tickets may be purchased at the club gate or at the hospital, which is in Chicago. Admission: $10 for adults, $9 of which are tax-deductible, and $5 for children. Always the Monday following the Western Open Tournament, starting at 8 AM.

> Edens Expy to US 41. East on Deerpath, south on Green Bay to club entrance, 300 North Green Bay Road.

HORSE SHOWS

Oak Brook again, about one show each month from May through November. There's a schooling show in Mid-May, a **Northern Illinois Arabian Activities Club Horse Show** in mid-June, a **Grand Prix** show in mid-July, two big fall shows and, in November, the **Chicagoland Hunter Trials,** beautiful to watch despite the preponderance of competing amateurs. The course is excellent with fences consisting of brush, natural rails, stone walls, aiken gates, logs and coops. Hunters are shown in seven classes, all for full championship points. For dates and weather information, phone 654-1550.

After a pause of several years, the **Onwentsia Horse Show** is again annual— with events during the second week in July. Open to the public. Look for signs at 300 North Green Bay Road in Lake Forest, the entrance to Onwentsia Country Club.

THE MACKINAC AND OTHER REGATTAS

Every weekend during the sailing season there are course races on Lake Michigan, part of which, at least, can be seen from the lakefront. The biggest race of all is the internationally famous 333-mile **Chicago to Mackinac Island Race,** the longest freshwater race in the world.

Upward of 160 racing yachts from some 35 clubs compete, including clubs on both coasts. During the week before the race as many as 100 guest boats come into the Chicago Yacht Club and Columbia Yacht Club (Monroe Street to Randolph), and the best place to see what some $8 million worth of racing yachts look like is on the docks on Thursday and Friday afternoons and evenings. The Chicago Yacht Club docks are open to the public when the race gets underway at noon on Saturday. Though the race starts immediately off the breakwater, you'll need binoculars to make any sense out of the melee since literally hundreds of sightseeing boats, Coast Guard cutters and the regular sightseeing boats are roiling the waters in a scene of total confusion. The Mackinac Race is always the second or third Saturday in July; the date alternates each year with those of the Port Huron race. The caliber of Chicago-area sailors is outstanding—in the last Olympics, for example, area racers took something like four out of five medals.

Of the one-design classes that race in the area on weekends, **Stars** race out of Jackson Park Harbor, Belmont Harbor and Wilmette Harbor; **Lightnings** and **Snipes** out of Burnham Park Harbor and Montrose Harbor, **Rhodes-19's** at Monroe Street and Montrose, **Dragons** out of the Columbia Yacht Club, **110's** and **Flying Thistles** out of Wilmette and **22 Sq. Meters** out of Belmont.

To see lavish yachts at lavish boatyards, go to **North on the River Shipyard,** 2315 North Elston, where more than 200 boats and racing yachts are quartered during the winter, or to **Grebe Yacht Sales,** 3250 North Washtenaw.

SPORTS AREAS—WHERE THEY ARE

Arlington Park, Northwest Hwy and Wilke Road, Arlington Heights, CL 5-4300
Kennedy Expy to Northwest Tollway. Exit north at Ill. Route 53. Also Chicago & North Western trains direct to track; also special buses to track.

Aurora Downs Racetrack, Route 31, Aurora, 896-3076
Northwest Tollway, exit at Route 31. Signs direct you to track.

Chicago Avenue Armory, 234 East Chicago, WH 3-4070
All Michigan Avenue buses stop at Chicago Avenue. Walk east one block to Armory.

Chicago Coliseum, 1513 South Wabash, WA 2-5862
CTA bus No. 4 on Wabash.

Chicago Stadium, 1800 West Madison, 733-5300
CTA Madison Street Bus No. 20 or Lake Street elevated train for speed.

Dyche Stadium, 1501 Central, Evanston, 492-7070
North and west of the campus. Edens Expy to Dempster, east to Ridge, north to Central; or, Sheridan Road north through Evanston to Central, then west, just follow the crowd. Or any CTA elevated train to Howard Street—transfer to

Evanston train to Central Sreet. North Western R.R. suburban locals also stop at Central Street, a few blocks west of the stadium.

Hawthorne Race Course, 3501 South Laramie, FR 2-0222

Eisenhower Expy to Laramie exit, south to 35th Street; or Douglas Park el-subway.

International Amphitheatre, West 43rd and South Halsted, 927-5580

At the Chicago Stock Yards. Dan Ryan Expy to 43rd Street exit, west to Halsted Street; or Outer Drive to Stevenson Expy and west to Halsted. Parking inside the Stock Yards. CTA bus No. 44 on State Street on weekdays; does not run on weekends. Use State Street subway to 43rd St. and get CTA bus No. 43.

Maywood Park, North and 5th Avenue, Maywood, MA 6-4816

Eisenhower Expy to Maywood. Exit on 5th Avenue, north to track.

Oak Brook International Sports Core, 1000 Oak Brook, Oak Brook

Eisenhower Expy to US 30 exit, turn immediately into US 20, exit on York Road. The Sports Core runs the length of York Road and the polo fields are on your immediate right. For weather and fields of play, 654-1550. Tickets and reservations, 654-2211; weekends, 654-3060.

Soldier Field Stadium, 425 East 14th Street, HA 7-5252

Outer Drive, just south of Field Museum and Park District administration building. Parking for 5,500 cars, or CTA bus No. 149 from State Street.

Sportsman's Park, 3301 South Laramie, BI 2-1121

Same directions as for Hawthorne.

Washington Park, 175th Street and Halsted, SY 8-1700

Dan Ryan Expy south, exit at Halsted. Paved parking. Or Illinois Central trains. Also special buses.

White Sox Ball Park, 324 West 35th Street, 924-1000

Dan Ryan Expy to 35th Street exit. Parking for 5,500 cars; also State Street A or B elevated train to 35th Street, transfer to CTA bus No. 35.

Wrigley Field, Addison and North Clark, 281-5050

CTA Clark Street bus No. 22; or State Street elevated B train to Addison Street stop.

SPORTS FOR PARTICIPANTS

9

The Beaches
Golf
Tennis
Yacht, Sailboat, Canoe, and Rowboat Rental
Sailing Instructions
Horseback Riding
Fishing
Ice Fishing
Ice Skating
Sledding and Tobogganing
Skiing
Bicycling
Bowling
Boxing Instruction
Archery
Skeet
Hunting
Sporting Goods and Equipment

CHAPTER 9

SPORTS FOR PARTICIPANTS

Blessed by a giant of a lake to the east and sports facilities in parks and forest preserves, Chicagoans can and do indulge in sports to the hilt. Given the first half-warm day of spring, they swarm outdoors to golf courses and tennis courts, pedal along the lakefront bicycle path, get their sloops and stinkpots into the lake, start a tan at the beaches. On a sunny midsummer weekend you can hardly find a healthy Chicagoan at home. (Nor on Wednesday afternoons in summer can you find a physician: to a man, they abandon their offices for the golf courses.)

Yet, there is nothing relaxed about the way Chicagoans play. They may be using leisure time, but they pursue their sports as if there were no time to lose.* The explanation lies not in the clichés about the city's driving energy but in the volatile climate which frequently lops off big chunks of the long-awaited summer by withholding at one end and foreshortening at the other.

The sports facilities described in this chapter are available free or for a daily fee. Chicago has superb private country clubs, but they're inaccessible except by invitation or influence.

THE BEACHES

Chicago has 19 public beaches along its lakefront, and anybody can swim at any of them. Officially, the season starts in late June when the schools close and runs to Labor Day; lifeguards are in attendance, and swimming is permitted until 9:30 PM. You can also swim before and after the season, and

---

* Visitors from both coasts are continually amazed at the number of golf invitations extended for 4:30 AM.

there's nothing illegal about it. Actually, it's better swimming, for at the first sign of waves overzealous lifeguards spoil the fun for real swimmers by confining everyone to the smallest patch of lake.* A parent with small fry may be grateful, but everybody else is furious. The obvious solution, a roped or fenced area just for kiddies, has for some reason eluded the Park District—but then it has never been noted for innovation.

Despite such annoyances, the beaches can be magnificent, and never more so than in late May or early June when only people in the immediate neighborhoods use them. The lake is cold but the sun does tan. By early August, the waters can be as tepid as consommé and will stay that way; you can swim into October if air temperatures hold.

Visitors are always surprised to see how Chicagoans on the Near North Side use Lake Shore Drive as an esplanade in summer. High-rise dwellers along the old Gold Coast think nothing of flipping over to the beach dressed for it—in bikini or shorts or robe, collapsible lounge chair under arm, plus jug, radio and something to read.

Some North Shore suburban beaches let visitors in for a fee. The **Wilmette Beach** in Gillson Park is probably the best beach along the entire end of Lake Michigan—ten spacious acres of good white sand, free of orange peel and refuse, thanks to a rule that picnicking must be done in the nearby picnic area. There's a beach house with toilets and cold showers, a first aid station and emergency vehicles at the ready. The beach opens the Saturday after the schools close and closes the day after they open. Daily fee: 50¢ weekdays, $1.50 weekends and holidays. Chicagoans may buy season tickets for $10 plus $2 for each family member. Hours: 10 AM to 10 PM.

The four smaller but equally immaculate Winnetka beaches also extend visitor privileges. Weekends: $1.50 for adults, $1 for children; weekdays $1 for adults, 50¢ for children. The beaches are **Elder Lane** at Elder Lane and the lakefront, **Tower Road Beach, Lake Front Beach** at Maple, **Lloyd Beach** at Lloyd and Sheridan. They open mid-June and close mid-September. Lake Front Beach has bathhouse facilities and a long diving pier.

Chicagoans also swim at the Illinois Beach State Park at Zion and at the Indiana Dunes State Park at Tremont, Indiana.

GOLF

Chicago is probably one of the best cities in the country for public and semi-public daily fee golf courses. Some 55 or 60 of these are in the area, easily

---

* Neither do they permit children or adults to use inflatable rubber rafts or sea horses. A recent newcomer from the East was astounded. "Heavens," she said, "it's not like a little lake where you'll be overcrowded—it's bigger than Long Island Sound!"

accessible by expressway. The *Chicago Tribune* Public Service Office offers a list of 53 locations by area but does not include ratings. The toughest courses according to current Western Golf Association ratings are:

Cog Hill, 119th Street and Archer, Lemont, CL 7-6251; #4 Championship is rated 74.7 and #4 Regular is rated 72.5.

Old Orchard, 700 West Rand, Mt. Prospect, CL 5-2025; from back of the tees, the rating is 71.2.

St. Andrews, Route 59, West Chicago, AU 7-7775 (Chicago phone) or 231-3100; #1 is rated 70.9; #2 at 70.3. Eisenhower Expy to East-West Tollway. Exit at Route 59, drive north to club.

Sportsman, 3535 Dundee, Northbrook, CR 2-0272; #1 rated 70; and #2, 69.

Mission Hills, 1695 Sanders, Northbrook, CR 2-0564; rated 69.9.

Skokie Playfield Golf Course, Oak, Winnetka, (west of Hibbard) is not rated but is an exceptionally lush, attractive course, one of the finest public courses on the North Shore—a par 70. The playfield also has a sporty little 9-hole par-27 course where you'll use every club in your bag. For information, Winnetka Park District, 446-9842.

The Chicago Park District operates four public courses.* The two that most visitors use are **Waveland,** in Lincoln Park, Addison Street at the lake (9 holes, par 36) and **Jackson Park,** two blocks east of Stony Island on Center (63rd Street), 18 holes, par 69. Both courses are jammed except during midweek mornings. The season is April to November, depending upon weather.

The Cook County Forest Preserves maintain five 18-hole courses and one 9-hole. There's no reservation system, but in midweek it shouldn't be much of a wait. For information, CO 1-8400.

If none of these seem tough enough, drive to **Brown Deer Golf Course,** 7835 North Green Bay Road, Milwaukee, Wisconsin. Brown Deer is a 6,800-yard course, the USGA plays on it, and it's rated at 73. For practice near the Loop, try the **Diversey Driving Range,** 141 West Diversey, Lincoln Park. It opens the second week in April and stays open to November 1. The pro will lend you clubs; $1 buys a bucket of balls. There's also a putting green. Open 7 AM to 11 PM daily.

For an indoor driving range, try **All-Seasons Golf, Brunswick Recreation Center,** 19 West 445 Roosevelt (Highland), Lombard, 627-6763. There are two 18-hole par-72 "courses." You shoot to a screen with a fairway scene; a com-

---

* Chicagoans can get golf lessons starting in January at any of a dozen park field houses. For information, HA 7-5252.

202

puter measures the angle, velocity, hook, slice, bounce, roll and stopping place of your ball. You dial a console to get the scene of the fairway where your ball landed and make your next shot. Greens shots are made on a mechanical green that adjusts to 18 different contours. Foursomes only—it takes two and a half hours to complete nine holes. Winter fees: weekdays to 5 PM, $2.75 per person; week-nights, $3.25; weekends and holidays, $3.75. Open 6 AM to midnight daily. Reservations essential. Take Eisenhower Expy to Roosevelt Road into Lombard.

TENNIS

Fullerton Tennis Club, 2315 North Sheffield, 477-0915. Weekday afternoons are your best time for getting on quickly since the club does not take reservations. Eight good composition courts open as early in April as possible. Weekday fee: 75¢ per hour singles, 50¢ doubles; weekends, $1 singles, 75¢ doubles.

To play on clay, **Northwestern University Clay Courts,** Colfax and Sheridan, Evanston, 492-3310. A dozen beautifully maintained courts in such demand it's essential to reserve several days in advance if you want to play on a weekend. Fee: $2 per hour per court; if you call far enough in advance you may reserve a court for several hours of uninterrupted singles or doubles.

Skokie Playfield, the boundless piece of real estate at Willow and Hibbard, Winnetka, has excellent grasstex coating over asphalt base courts (the bounce is similar to a clay bounce). Though the ten courts are primarily for Winnetkans, guests may play on a fee basis. Weekdays, 40¢ per person; weekends, 60¢; for lighted courts at night, 80¢ per person; 20¢ per for anyone under 18. Guest reservations taken only 24 hours in advance.

Wilmette Park District maintains four hard-surface public courts in Gillson Park just north of Bahai Temple and the Coast Guard station on Sheridan Road. Metered lighting for night games—25¢ turns them on. Also four non-lighted asphalt courts at 15th and Lake Street and four new concrete courts with a shelter in Thornwood Park, Kenilworth Avenue at Dartmouth. None of these last are lighted for night play.

Chicago Park District claims to maintain 605 public courts, but its ideas about what constitutes maintenance leave able tennis players wondering. The courts most convenient to the Loop—in Grant Park—are generally in indifferent condition, which doesn't make sense because they're almost under the nose of the Park District administration building. You can find two hard-surface courts in good condition behind the Chicago Avenue Armory and eight courts at Waveland in Lincoln Park* (between Irving Park and Addison).

---

* The nice clay courts immediately south are also Park District property, but you can't play on them because the district has allowed a private tennis club to take over.

Few Chicagoans know it, but there are some 28 *indoor tennis* courts scattered around the north and south suburbs. The most convenient are:

Skokie Racquet Club, 9444 Skokie, Skokie, 674-0211. The fees are ferocious but the five courts are plush cork turf, the lights are excellent, and you also get shower and locker-room privileges. Winter guest rates from October to May, $10 court fee per hour during prime time (7 PM to 9 PM on week-nights, weekends to 5 PM). Other hours, $6 per hour. *Plus* guest fee: $5 for men, $2 for women and juniors. In summer, guest fees are abolished and court fees drop to $6 per hour during prime time, $4 at all other hours. Open daily, 9 AM to midnight. If you reserve a court but can't play, you're on your honor to pay.

The **Orchard Twin Bowl** alleys (64 lanes) are on the same premises—55¢ a line.

Skokie Playfield has an excellent facility with four Hartru courts and a spectator gallery. Rates currently are $8 per 1½ hours of court time on weekends, $6 weekdays, and going up. Reservations essential, phone 446-9763. The courts are housed in the A.C. Nielsen building facing Elm.

South Side Racquet Club, 1401 East Sibley, Dolton, Ill., VI 9-1235. (Use the Dan Ryan Expressway and it's less than half an hour from the Loop.)

West Side Racquet Club, Route 83 in Villa Park, 833-1250 (18 miles from Loop).

YACHT, SAILBOAT, CANOE, AND ROWBOAT RENTAL

Rodi Chris-Craft, Inc., 2550 South Ashland, MO 6-6670

If you can indulge any whim, Rodi will be glad to rent one of its two 57-foot Chris-Craft yachts at $360 per day, including captain and mate. Each yacht sleeps ten, accommodates 30 for cruising, moors in Burnham Park opposite McCormick Place, is air-conditioned, fully equipped, has owner's stateroom and showers. Available any time to go anywhere between April and November, or you can simply party at the mooring. Two weeks minimum to reserve. Also available: 32-foot powerboats you skipper yourself if you can prove capability, $82 per day plus fuel.

Grebe Yacht Sales, Inc., 3250 North Washtenaw, KE 9-8300

Grebe is one of the two best boatyards in the city. Many of its regular customers make their boats available for charter during the season. Hence Ken Masters at Grebe can line up power yachts or sailboats almost any time. He also has two 35-foot sloops that go in and out of charter regularly. The fees depend on the owners but generally run about $100 per day, $800 per week. Both sleep four to six persons, and you may do your own sailing if you can prove experience. A 47-foot power yacht complete with skipper runs $600 per week plus fuel, and sleeps eight. Other boatyards, like **Eubanks Marina, Inc.,** 1400 Broadway, Blue Island, FU 5-7576, may offer similar possibilities. Check the Yellow Pages.

American Youth Hostels, Inc., 2210 North Clark, EA 7-8114

Any AYH member who has passed the AYH 12-lesson skipper course may rent one of five Rhodes-19's moored in Grant Park Harbor. Fees are $7 to $10 for five hours of sailing. AYH gives a skipper course in Chicago.

Chicagoland Canoe Base, 4019 North Narragansett, SP 7-1489

Canoeing is one of the fastest growing year-round sports in Illinois. One man in Chicago knows everything about it, and every explorable Illinois stream and river as well. He's Mr. Ralph Frese, and he'll not only rent you a canoe, but furnish the mounting gear for your car, give you a descriptive folder of places to paddle within and outside of the city, tell you what you can expect to find where, plot maps, and advise on gear—for exactly $8 per day rental ($24 per week). The man is mad, but he doesn't want to raise his fees because then he might outprice young couples just getting acquainted with the nearby Des Plaines River, Salt Creek, the old Illinois & Michigan Canal (which replaced the Chicago Portage in 1848 and is now closed to commercial traffic) and a host of rivers and tributaries that ultimately lead to the Mississippi River.

Mr. Frese builds his own fiber-glass canoes and kayaks and has more than 50 for rental. If you ask about his custom-made canoes you'll inspect replicas of Montreal traders (16 men and 7,000 pounds of pelts and supplies), North canoes (six men and 3,000 pounds of freight), Voyageur canoes, Man O' War canoes, sailing canoes and so forth. He also leads weekend canoe trips, which you can join, and is locally famous as the man who has taught a current generation of slum area American Indian boys how to build and paddle canoes.

A certain amount of patience is necessary when you phone. His line is almost always busy, and nobody's been able to persuade him to add another. Also, his shop is hard to spot the first time. It's between Irving Park and Cuyler on the east side of Narragansett, several doors north of the Irving Park-Narragansett intersection and behind his blacksmith shop. The shop (welding) is where Jacob Burck and other local sculptors cast their biggest pieces.

Canoe Trails Co., runs the concession at Skokie Lagoons. The seven lagoons spill into each other in a thoroughly satisfying way through a woodsy section of forest preserves. The rate is $2 per hour, and though people line up on weekends and holidays, there's rarely more than a 20-minute wait. Take Edens to Willow exit east. Turn north on Forest Way Drive, follow it to Tower Road. Stop where the crowd is. Open daily July and August, weekends only in May, June, September and October, 10 AM to dusk. No phone, but owner Don Dressler's home number is 825-5015.

Last summer there was a canoe concession at Salt Creek in Du Page County's **Fullersburg Forest Preserve,** which is lovely and remote-feeling. For information, phone 629-5700.

Rowboats can be rented at **Lincoln Park;** at **Skokie Lagoons** in the Cook County Forest Preserves; at **Fullersburg Forest Preserve, Herrick Lake** and **Mallard Lake** in Du Page County Forest Preserves. Respective phones are LI 9-6333; CO 1-8400; 629-5700.

SAILING INSTRUCTIONS

Pre-season and in-season instructions are offered by the following:

U.S. Coast Guard Auxiliary—dry-land lessons in sailing and power boating, primarily for people who've bought boats but don't know how to get the most out of them. Courses run eight weeks, two-hour sessions each, in Park District fieldhouses and in high schools. Free unless a school charges for use of a room. The auxiliary also conducts courtesy examination of boats to see if they're legally qualified for state and federal waterways. The decal it issues to qualified boats is recognized by state and federal authorities, and you won't be stopped if your boat displays it. For information in both categories, phone USCGA, YO 5-6574, ask for name and phone number of Public Education Officer of the CG Auxiliary.

Chicago Park District—lessons in dinghy sailing, using the dinghies in its Rainbow Fleet. Senior fleet moors at Burnham Harbor, junior fleet at Humboldt Park Lagoon. Senior fleet lessons (anyone over age 14) begin in early May, run through October. Junior fleet (youngsters 11 to 13) lessons run July 1 to August 30. Applicants are eligible for membership after passing swimming and seamanship tests. For information, call the craft supervisor, HA 7-5252.

Adler Planetarium and Astronomical Museum—evening lessons in celestial navigation. For information, WA 2-4488.

HORSEBACK RIDING

For more than 60 years, Chicagoans were able to rent horses within two blocks of the delightful Lincoln Park bridle paths which stretch from North Avenue (1600 north) to Hollywood Avenue (5700 north). In 1967 the last of the stables was demolished in favor of some quasi urban renewal. As of this writing, the bridle paths are unused, but check with the Park District.

Stables closest to Jackson Park bridle paths on the South Side are **Hyde Park Stables** at 742 East 61st Street, MI 3-5771, and at 6041 South Langley, NO 7-9563. The **Westown Stables,** 4815 North Clifton, Norridge, GL 3-9822, has horse rental and gives riding lessons (English and Western saddles).

The **Cook County Forest Preserves** offer 175 miles of winding trails through beautifully wooded areas. There are stables near all trails which will also sell the 50¢ license necessary to ride in the preserves. Last year, some 30,000 riders were licensed—ample testimony to the enjoyment of riding informally through some of the county's magnificent, wooded, completely natural forest preserves. For information on trail entrances, CO 1-8400 or FO 9-9420.

FISHING

Chicago Park District Lagoons are stocked with largemouth bass and panfish such as crappies, bullheads and bluegills, but each summer brings surprise catches. Last year, a man using dough for bait hauled a 32-inch, 18½-pound carp out of the Douglas Park Lagoon. Fishing is permitted from the banks of all lagoons but not from boats, landing piers or bridges. State fish and game rules apply; anyone under age 16 may fish without a license. The lagoons are:

Jackson Park, 2200 East 65th Street.

Washington Park, 5818 South Cottage Grove.

Sherman Park, 1301 West 52nd Street.

Columbus Park, 5701 West Jackson.

Douglas Park, West 19th Street and South California.

Garfield Park, 100 North Central Park.

Humboldt Park, West North at North Humboldt.

Marquette Park, 6700 South Kedzie.

McKinley Park, 2210 West Pershing.

Lincoln Park, North Stockton and West Fullerton.

Fishing is also permitted along the lakefront at the following piers: **North Avenue** (1600 North); **Montrose** (4400 North); **Loyola** (6900 North); on the South Side at **31st Street, 59th Street** and **63rd Street.** Other sections of the shoreline are open to fishermen if not in use for other activities. Best example of this is the little promontory at the southeast end of the Oak Street Beach, where sportsmen from the high rises directly across the street come down with Abercrombie & Fitch equipment to fish alongside low-income families from west of Clark Street who come because a catch means a free meal. On any summer evening, this little section of fishing waters (perch, mostly) is an interesting example of Chicago's diversity in the shadows of some of the most expensive real estate to be found. From mid-April to mid-June it's possible to catch coho salmon along the shoreline, although the best catches are from boats in offshore depths of 15 to 50 feet.

Cook County Forest Preserves stock 27 lakes, sloughs, quarries, lagoons, ponds and rivers. The preserves put out a fine annual fishing guide listing all waters open to the public, their location, size and depth, principal kinds of hook-and-line fish in each, public transportation where available, fishing and boating regulations, etc. The booklet also lists boat launching ramps and boat rental areas. For a copy, write to Forest Preserve District Headquarters, 536 North Harlem, River Forest, Ill. Or phone CO 1-8400 or FO 9-9420.

Du Page County Forest Preserves has ten fishing areas. For information, call 629-5700.

In Chicago's **Lincoln Park** you'll find a pier and free practice casting rings in the lagoon just north of the Fullerton Parkway Drive.

For a guaranteed catch of pay-by-the-pound fishing, take children to **Fisherman's Dude Ranch,** 9600 Golf, Des Plaines, 824-9821. Five ponds and a large lake are variously stocked with panfish, walleyes, bass, Northerns and rainbow trout. You can rent or bring your own fishing equipment, buy minnows or bring your own. One horrified father, whose daughter caught $16 worth of bass within an hour, swears the fish fight to leap onto your hook. Trout cleaned and filleted at 15¢ per fish; you're on your own with catches that also need scaling. Admission: 90¢ adults, 50¢ for children under twelve. Open all year, 9 AM to 5 PM. For ice fishing, bring your own auger. Closed Mondays in winter.

Hook-Line-Sinker Sport Fishing, 158th and Greenwood, is a similar facility, its lake stocked with bullheads, crappies, largemouth bass. **Larry's Fishing Hole,** one mile northwest of Lemont, stocks rainbow trout, largemouth bass, bluegills, green sunfish, bullheads; **Berryland Park,** Des Plaines, at the south end of Wonder Lake, has 12 ponds stocked with rainbow trout, largemouth bass, panfish, catfish; **Lake Julian Trout Farm,** Cary, has five ponds stocked with trout, bass, walleyed pike, panfish, catfish, bullheads; **O.W. Wold,** four miles east of Woodstock, has six ponds stocked with brook, brown, cutthroat and rainbow trout, largemouth bass, bluegills.

ICE FISHING

In 1967, Cook County Forest Preserves approved seven lakes for a sport two fishery biologists headlined "Idiots On Ice" in a how-to article written for the Illinois Department of Conservation.* Since locations each year may vary, depending on ice and other conditions, phone the Preserves for current sites.

A fully detailed booklet on fishing throughout Illinois is available free from the Chicago office of the Illinois Conservation Department, 160 North LaSalle, FI 6-2000. Ask for *Illinois Fishing Guide.*

---

* *Illinois Wildlife*, Vol. 17, No. 1, Dec., 1961.

ICE SKATING

The Chicago Park District floods a number of playfields each winter. Among the spots with warming houses are the **Lake Shore Athletic Field** on Chicago at Lake Shore Drive, two areas in **Lincoln Park,** and the great central depressions of the **Midway** at 59th Street between Kenwood and University on the South Side. When the lagoons in **Humboldt Park** and **Lincoln Park** are solidly frozen, skating is allowed. For information, HA 7-5252.

Ice skating is also permitted on all sloughs and ponds in the **Cook County Forest Preserves.** Ice thickness of four inches is mandatory. For ice information, CO 1-8400. **Du Page County Forest Preserves** offers three skating sites, including **Herrick Lake.** For information, 629-5700.

Northwestern University has an outdoor rink (small fee) next to McGaw Memorial Hall, just north of Dyche Stadium. It's well maintained and has a warming house. **Evanston** also floods its playgrounds for skating. **Winnetka Park District** maintains first-rate outdoor rinks at **Hubbard Woods Station Park, Indian Hill Station Park** and **Skokie Playfield.** All have heated shelters with rest room facilities. Daily fee for non-Winnetkans, 50¢. For adjacent coasting mound at Skokie Playfield (lighted for night use), the fee is 25¢. Children may coast on disks, sleds, whatever. Also two supervised runs for tobogganing. For information, HI 6-2160.

Marina City Rink at Marina City offers skating outdoors from October to mid-March or thereabouts. Because of its site and location, it's a little like the rink at Rockefeller Center in New York—pretty secretaries and overweight executives skating on their lunch hour during the week, schoolchildren and their mothers in the afternoon, an overflow of children on Saturday and Sunday, large groups of teens the same nights. Serious skaters should avoid weekends entirely. Numb skaters can get hot coffee from a machine and free Kleenex for sniffles from a box at the skaters' desk. Open noon to 2:30, 3:00-5:30; 7:30-10 PM daily. Closed Mondays. Admission: children 50¢ and 75¢; adults $1 and $1.50. Phone 527-0747.

Rainbow Ice Arena, 4836 North Clark, 275-5500. A big indoor rink, but the crowd on weekends is too rough for youngsters under 12 to have much fun. Sunday evening is adults only. Weekday hours are too varied to list here, so phone. Skates can be rented for 50¢. Admission: over age 16, $1.50; under, $1.00. Open from about the end of August to May, including Christmas Day.

SLEDDING AND TOBOGGANING

Any child may coast on a sled in any Chicago park. Families may bring their own sleds, saucers, disks, whatever to the Forest Preserves. **Brookfield Woods,** just north of Brookfield Zoo, and **Shiller Woods,** East River Road near Cumberland, have especially good coasting and hills.

In the following list of Forest Preserve sites, those marked with an asterisk have toboggan slides and will rent toboggans from 1 PM to 10 PM for $1. Deposit is required. So is a snowfall of at least four inches.

*Swallow Cliff, Route 83 west of Mannheim (about 99th Street south). This is a major winter sports facility. Open 10 AM to 10 PM daily.

*Jensen Slides, Devon east of Milwaukee.

Bemis Woods, Ogden west of Wolf.

Dan Ryan Woods, 87th Street and Western.

Deer Grove, at stone shelter, Grove No. 5, north of Dundee Road and west of Quentin.

SKIING

By mountain standards (Aspen or Stowe) there is no skiing around Chicago except for beginners or those who want intermediate slopes to get their ski legs. Chicagoans, living on terrain as flat as a tabletop and only 580 feet above sea level, are well aware of the limitations. So are the entrepreneurs who have built new or expanded pioneer ski facilities. Between bulldozers and earthmovers, the area will create a full-scale man-made mountain yet. Meanwhile, according to a ski editor, every entrepreneur is an exaggerator: the standard hill in the area is 200 feet, give or take 20 percent.

For one-day skiing within the Chicago area, try these:

Fox Trails in Cary offers beginner and intermediate slopes. So does nearby **Barberry Hills** at Fox River Grove, which throws in a second attraction—ice skating on the Fox River. **Buffalo Park** near Algonquin has rope tows and a couple of fairly challenging slopes. Then there's **Gander Mountain,** slightly northwest of Antioch, and **Wilmot** (Wis.), the granddaddy of close-in Chicago ski areas, with about the highest and best developed area facility, including lights for night skiing. It also has one of the best ski shops with first-rate ski equipment and chic imported ski wear. The little town of Wilmot is springing to life a la Aspen and has several atmospheric places to eat.

Chestnut Mountain at Galena claims a 485-foot vertical drop. It's vertical, all right—you think you'll plunge straight into the Mississippi sloughs below. The Link-Belt chair lift is classic. It was designed for Sun Valley by Link-Belt Company years ago—an adaptation of one of Link's banana loaders. Sun Valley eventually sold it to Caberfae (Mich.); eventually it wound up at Chestnut.

At Elkhorn, Wisconsin (west of Milwaukee), there's **Alpine Valley,** offering much more terrain to work on and one of the swankiest lodges about. It and Wilmot are the two most expensive ski locales of them all.

About 30 miles north of Milwaukee, **Little Switzerland** at Slinger has the only chair lift in the entire country that goes up one side of a hill and down the other. **Wunderburg,** about four miles north of West Bend, just ten miles from Slinger, has interesting terrain. **Majestic Hills,** at the southwest end of Lake Geneva, Wisconsin, used to be the Val-O-Will Chicken Farm, but the owner got out of chickens, built a challenging hill and an intermediate hill, turned one of his big brooder houses into a chalet until he could upgrade. He has, and it's a fine place. **Mt. Fuji,** at the east end of the same town, has a chalet built along the lines suggestive of a Japanese teahouse; don't ask why, nobody knows. Fuji got off to a bad start, but has been upgraded considerably and is now known as a place that swings. A rock band heaves to at 4 PM in the bar, and from then on there's as much activity inside as out.

The farther north you head into Wisconsin and Michigan, the more interesting the trails and hills become. For weekend skiing or information on places within 500 miles, phone the ski editor of any of the newspapers, ask whom he can refer you to for realistic information. The Chicago Metropolitan Ski Council (an organization of all ski clubs in Chicago) knows, but hasn't a phone as of this writing. Ski equipment can be rented from **American Youth Hostels Ski Shop,** 2207 North Sedgwick, BU 1-9826. Skis, boots, poles, $7.50 for a weekend plus $15 deposit for nonmembers. AYH is nonprofit, hence the low prices. The organization also arranges ski trips. Open Monday, Wednesday, Thursday, Friday, 5 PM to 9:30 PM.

For current rates at above-mentioned ski resorts, see "Skiing Centers & Resorts" in the Yellow Pages, which lists local offices of Illinois resorts. For Wisconsin resorts, phone the Wisconsin Official Vacation Center, DE 2-7275. Thursday and Friday editions of local papers generally list rates and snow conditions of area resorts. For last-minute snow report, dial CE 6-SNOW.

BICYCLING

Everyone who can bicycles along the lakefront because it is one of the most exhilarating trails to be found. The route follows the shoreline from Argyle (5800 North) south to the Jackson Park Boat Harbor at 67th Street. The east-west boundaries are the lake on one side, the city skyline at a discreet distance on the other. Like swimming off-season, bicycling here in early spring or quite late fall gives you solitude, winds, sand, water and gulls.

There are three bicycle rental shops in the Old Town-Lincoln Park area. Personnel will direct you to the nearby "Bicycle Path" signs at the edge of Lincoln Park. Follow them and arrive at the lakefront in minutes.

American Youth Hostels Bike Shop, 2207 North Sedgwick, BU 1-9826; open days and evenings except Monday.

Old Town Bike Shop, 1720 North Sedgwick, 664-5860.

Lincoln Park Bicycle Rental, 2437 North Clark, 327-1626, and also at 605 West Wrightwood, 327-9448.

The Park District has just completed a channel path along part of the Sanitary District Channel between Peterson and Lawrence avenues (3200 West). It's surprisingly scenic. For information, HA 7-5252.

Cook County Forest Preserves have one especially good bicycle trail through six miles of woodsy land. Starting point is between Wolf Road and the Tri-State Tollway just north of Ogden Avenue (U.S. 34) in Bemis Woods South. You end at the Brookfield Zoo. Bring your own bikes for this.

BOWLING

The Yellow Pages carry two pages of bowling-alley listings. Those most convenient to the Loop and Near North Side are **Spencer's Marina City Bowling Lanes** in Marina City, having 38 alleys with open bowling any time from 10 AM to 5 PM and 10 PM to 2 AM. The hours from 5 PM to 10 PM are frequently taken up by bowling leagues, but you can always inquire by phone. Thursday is the biggest night—the alleys are kept open until 3 AM. Shoe rental, 25¢; fee per game, 55¢. Cocktail lounge on the same floor.

BOXING INSTRUCTION

Johnny Coulon Physical Training Club, 154 East 63rd Street, PL 2-9890

Johnny Coulon, a bantamweight champion in his day, not only exemplified the finest in boxing (he was absolutely clean, never consorted with hoodlums) but came out of the ring as he went in—a gentleman. Retired, he began to teach boxing to boys in his neighborhood, and though he's close to 80, he still teaches daily. He takes any male from age eight up for boxing, body building or reducing. He does not have any exhibition bouts, but a father whose son is interested in the sweaty atmosphere of the boxing gymnasium might phone to see if he and his son could drop in. Weekdays, 11 AM to 7 PM; weekends to 2:30 PM.

ARCHERY

Chicago Archery Center, 3109 West Armitage, SP 2-9027

Regulation 60-foot indoor range can accommodate 20 or more persons at a time. Range fee $1.50 for as long as you want to shoot. The center will rent bow and arrows for $1, or bring your own. Open 8 AM to 9 PM weekdays, Saturday until 5 PM, Sunday, noon to 5 PM.

SKEET

Lincoln Park Gun Club, Diversey and Lake Shore Drive, LI 9-6490

It's a private club in Lincoln Park on the lake side of the drive, but it allows visitors to use its facilities for a fee. Only shotguns allowed; bring your own, buy the club's shells. Open 10 AM to 6 PM weekends, 11 AM to 6 PM weekdays. Closed Mondays.

HUNTING

Des Plaines Wildlife Area, 40 miles southwest of Chicago.

An Illinois Conservation Department refuge opened to hunters during the pheasant season for a $5 fee. You must apply in advance and may only apply for one permit. Write to Illinois Conservation Department, 160 North LaSalle, Chicago (FI 6-2000). No permits issued before September 1 (requests mailed long before this date are not honored).

> Interstate 55 (proceeding south), exit beyond Des Plaines River bridge at the sign "Joliet Army Ammunition Plant." Drive south on frontage road, parallel to Interstate 55, into Wildlife Area.

DAILY FEE HUNTING

The shooting preserves listed here are privately owned but operated under Illinois Conservation Department regulations. You hunt in tailor-made bird cover with no bag limits. The season is generally five months long, October 15 to March 15. Most preserves furnish trained bird dogs, but some allow you to bring your own. You must have a State of Illinois hunting license to shoot on all private preserves. The following are within day range of Chicago:

Huntley Game Farm, RFD #1, Huntley, Ill., 669-5600. Pheasant only.

Lakefield Farm, PO Box 37, Cary, Ill. Pheasant, mallard. A very expensive place, but beautiful and worth it if you can write off the charges to business entertainment. Owner George Bates insists upon furnishing everything—guides, dogs, even guns, all at fees.

Northern Illinois Game Farm, Inc., Rt. #2, Box 32, (Plato Twp.) Elgin, Ill., 742-3293. Pheasant and mallard.

Twin Ponds Hunt Club, Rt. #1, Box 50, Algonquin, Ill., 658-5784. Pheasant and chukar.

Wild Boar Ranch, mailing address Rt. #543, Itasca, Ill., 773-9600

Erl Svendsen has stocked a working ranch in Galena so heavily that you can just about count on a boar per acre. The beasts are everywhere, weighing

100 to 300 lbs., and averaging 175 lbs. You shoot with shotgun (slugs), rifle, pistol, or revolver of enough power to take a boar quickly. Bow hunting by special arrangement. Fee is 35¢ per pound. Guides will field-dress boars, if desired. The owner says the meat is good; he sends you to the Galena Food Bank for boar processing, which includes hickory-smoking the hams. He also says that a day is sufficient for a good hunt. Season runs to April 30.

Conquest Hunting Preserve, mailing address Box 84, Orland Park, Ill. The preserve stocks Spanish goats, Angora sheep, Marino rams and wild boar in Custer Park, 55 miles southwest of Chicago, on the Kankakee River. Going price has been $50 per trophy, and co-owners John Quinlan and Charlie Steele say the sporty way to hunt the area is with bow and arrow, though they allow guns. All hunters are guided, and guides will help field-dress game.

FAMILY RECREATION FACILITY

Shagbark, RFD #2, Alden, Ill., 815-648-2488. It's a private hunt club, part game preserve, part year-round family sports club. Owner Robert Tansill has turned 1,200 lush acres into a facility that includes ring-necked pheasant and partridge hunting preserves; a duck marsh and pond; ponds stocked with trout, bass and panfish; traps, firearm ranges; archery ranges and bow hunting course; horseback riding; canoeing, swimming, dinghy sailing; and, in winter, ice skating on the frozen ponds with shoreline bonfires; beginner skiing; ski *jorling*; tobogganing; bar and lodge. He also boards and trains hunting dogs and boards horses. Daily fee hunting by special arrangement only.

SPORTING GOODS AND EQUIPMENT

Abercrombie & Fitch, 9 North Wabash, CE 6-6700;
Gabby Hartnett Recreation Inc., 6676 North Lincoln, Lincolnwood, OR 4-1188;
Klein's, 185 North Wabash, 372-0826;
Marshall Field & Company Men's Store, 25 East Washington (Wabash), ST 1-1000.

You can buy excellent guns in Chicago, but a new ordinance requires registration of *all* firearms, even B-B guns.

Oscar Wastyn's Cycle Shop, 2221 North Milwaukee, EV 4-8999

Oscar Wastyn is the only man in the U.S. who makes unicycles and stunt cycles, such as high-wire and collapsibles. He also stocks more than 100 racing and touring cycles and does first-rate bike repair.

PART IV: Where To—How To

SHOPPING—THE NAME STORES

10

Loop Department Stores
Loop Specialty Stores
Fashion Shopping in the Michigan Avenue Area
Boutiques
Men's Stores
Custom Tailors
Chicago's Finest Jewelers
Fine, Absolutely Reliable Furriers

CHAPTER 10

SHOPPING—THE NAME STORES

Midwest conservatism must drive Chicago's prestige retailers wild. By instinct, a sophisticated retailer wants to display the latest ideas in his windows. In this city, each time he does, he's likely to terrify his best customers. Midwesterners take their time accepting radical style changes—as much as two years.

Essentially, Chicago is not a high fashion city and isn't for next week's fashions now. What it is for is a "nice" look (translate as "not daring"). On the North Shore, and in Barrington-Wayne country, and in the old Gold Coast, this attitude has produced a daytime uniform for women: in winter, a simple, well-tailored suit worn with a discreet pearl choker and good gloves; in summer, a linen skirt, matching cashmere cardigan and McMullen blouse. This goes a long way toward explaining why even the styles in Michigan Avenue shop windows may be very expensive and very quietly elegant, but are almost never *wow*. You have to get inside the shops to find those.

Shopping here is likely to irritate as well as delight you. Some stores consistently volunteer extra services and courtesy, but others tolerate rudeness and laziness in their salespeople to a degree that's shocking. The executive excuse is that "we can't get the kind of help we once could." Yet some stores still do, most notably Marshall Field and Company, Abercrombie and Fitch, Stanley Korshak, Martha Weathered, the best men's shops, the fine jewelers. A few Michigan Avenue shops still permit long-nosed attitudes toward customers; the way to overcome that nonsense is to borrow or rent a large status-symbol dog and sail in—the attention you'll get will be magnificent.

Note: For fashion shows, a daily occurrence in this city in department stores and restaurants, see the women's pages of any daily newspaper.

LOOP DEPARTMENT STORES

Store hours listed below are year-round except during the hysterical six weeks between Thanksgiving and Christmas, when all stores are open week-nights for late shopping.

Marshall Field & Co., 111 North State, ST 1-1000; Telephone orders and request for pickup through Personal Shopping, ST 1-1050

For more than a hundred years, one store in Chicago has been synonymous with shopping—Marshall Field and Company. Every visitor heads for it; most of the natives have charge accounts at it; in turn, the store is one of the great, promotable institutions of the city, and Chicago's pride in it is wholly justified.

Generations of Chicago women have spent some of their happiest times indulging in a very real Chicago tradition, "a day at Field's." A day is not only possible but probable, since the store has something like 955 selling sections, one more enticing than the next. Yet, it's not just the great range and variety of merchandise that makes Field's what it is—it's also the wealth of ideas, the displays, the careful attention to details, to the total shopping effort,* the really beautiful blending of old carriage-trade thoughtfulness with modern merchandising. Field's sets the standards against which Chicagoans measure all stores—in this city and elsewhere.

Obviously, it's impossible to describe the store in any detail here, but the way to see it is to take the escalators from floor to floor and wander across each. Start in the Luggage Department on the main floor—there's nothing like it anywhere, with the possible exception of Mark Cross in New York—and Mark Cross is not a department store. The Linens Shop is second to none in the city. Second floor bric-a-brac, near the paintings and porcelains, is like an international bazaar. The Toy Floor (see page 317) is not to be missed. Nor the Kitchenwares Department, where there are so many incredible gadgets that visitors from overseas have to be restrained from purchasing everything in sight to ship home.

Field's has floors of fashions at all prices—dresses from less than $10 to more than $1,000. The 28 Shop is designer fashions, has its own elevator tucked behind Main Floor Silver. The Sunningdale Shop is superb casual clothes. Globe-Trotter Shop is imports, and so on down to dresses on the

---

* Translators who speak more than a dozen languages and who serve as shopping guides are available. So are conducted tours of the entire store. Ask at the main floor information desk or at Personal Service and Information on the third floor, which will also get theatre and concert tickets for you. The third floor has marvelous conveniences—a postal substation, a place to check parcels, racks of out-of-town phone books, a magnificent, huge, old marble ladies' washroom, a refreshment bar (nonalcoholic) and still more.

Budget Floor—a floor where merchandise is as carefully chosen for quality as upstairs and where buys in bath towels, for instance, are exceptional.

It serves breakfast before the shopping sections open. Use the Randolph Street entrances as early as 9:00 AM for elevators to the most famous department store restaurants in the country. Expect to wait in line for lunch, even in the cafeteria.

But over and above everything else, enjoy that aspect of Field's that makes it an absolutely unique institution—its superb courtesy and helpfulness toward customers. Field's genuine concern for customers is as much a part of the character of the store as the two short phrases which, through the years, have been used by management and customers alike to define merchandise and the shopping experience: "That's Field's . . ." "That's not Field's."

Store hours: 9:15 AM to 5:45 PM; Monday and Thursday to 7 PM. For detailed information on special departments, antiques, silver, furs, jewelry, see Index.

Carson Pirie Scott & Co., 1 South State, 744-2000, Personal Shopping, 462-4747

Carson's can be compared to Field's in about the same way Princess Margaret can be compared to Queen Elizabeth II; Carson's is more likely to kick up its heels. It specializes in promotions that add flavor to the entire Loop by running the whoop-de-do outside the store as well as in. (When you see a red double-decker London bus zipping about the Loop, that's Carson's having a British Promotion.)

Annual events start with the January California or South of the Border Promotion. The store bursts forth in light, bright colors, brings in West Coast designers to show their own fashions, heats the sidewalks outside so that bathing suits can be modeled in the midst of snowstorms, reproduces Los Angeles' famous Farmers Market and turns a gloomy retailing month into a lively one.

April—the Scandinavian Show, dramatizing the Scandinavian Shop (home furnishings and furniture). The shop is the best of its kind in town and one of the best in the country. Biggest surprise is the moderate prices. September— British Fortnight for Men, distinguished by men's import clothes, the presence of Commander Whitehead (Schweppes) or his equivalent, and the London bus.

November—the Import Fair—imports from one country, such as Italy or France, or from several countries at once, say the entire Mediterranean. The event turns the entire store inside out—even special shopping bags, hangtags, lunchroom menus featuring the foods of the host country, import foods to take home—the works.

If you need gloves, Carson's has what is probably the largest glove department in the world; it certainly has one of the smartest glove buyers shopping for it. Inner Circle has marvelous clothes, and the dressing rooms alone are worth a visit—a Rome room, a Paris room and so forth. Little import shops are dotted throughout the store. A year-round For Men Only Shopping Service will do all a man's shopping for him—just ask for Billie Dargis. The store also makes term life, health and accident and hospitalization insurance available to all customers—and controls the quality of the insurance by owning enough of the insuring firm to guarantee it.

Prices throughout the store are generally a little lower than at Field's.

Store hours: 9:15 AM to 5:45 PM; Monday and Thursday to 7 PM.

Wieboldt Stores, Inc., State and Madison, ST 2-1500

A department store in the moderate price range, best known for services which have little to do with typical department store operations. Example: Wieboldt's gives Green Stamps with every purchase and has the biggest Green Stamp Redemption Center in the country—2,000 items always in stock.

The store also has an up-to-date book rental department, which more than one conventioneer's bored wife has discovered to her pleasure. On the main floor it sells exceptionally good, inexpensive candies. Liquor is available in its restaurants. Many women swear by its beauty shop. Store sales can be quite amazing; sample evening gowns, for example, marked down to $10 from $70.

Store hours: 9:15 AM to 8:30 PM Monday, Thursday, Friday; to 5:45 PM other days.

Goldblatt Brothers, Inc., 333 South State, WA 2-9800

Goldblatt's advertising hasn't changed much from the old days when it was a hard-sell, budget-priced department store, but the merchandise has. The store is trading up, though keeping its prices low. If you're in the market for import knits and know your merchandise, you'll find some at Goldblatt's identical to those stocked at Bramson's, Bonwit Teller or Martha Weathered—but at half their prices, i.e., $45 vs. $90, $150 vs. $275, and the knits will come from Portugal, Belgium, England, Ireland, Germany, Spain, Italy and Israel, which sends its knits decorated in suede. Beaded knits and things from Hong Kong are available at what the merchandise manager describes accurately as fantastic prices. Millinery is another department full of good buys, as is Coats, with suede coats from Spain. The basement stocks fashions from Florida shops at the end of the short Florida season; it also has Elizabeth Post cosmetics, which New York women swear are put out by Elizabeth Arden as a lower price line. Creamy lipsticks, for example, in current fashion colors and no-colors, are 39¢—the best lipstick buy in town.

Because the store image hasn't been changed by its advertising, it's still jammed in the afternoon by its regular bargain-hunting customers. Shop in the morning, when it will be a happier experience.

Visitors from overseas who would like to see an American retail version of **Sears, Roebuck and Company** will find one at 403 South State (Van Buren),

WA 2-4600. The biggest Sears of all, at operating headquarters, is located at 925 South Homan, 265-2500.

Montgomery Ward and Company has a Loop store at Adams and State; the headquarters store is at 618 West Chicago,* but most ordering there is done from the catalogs.

LOOP SPECIALTY STORES

Abercrombie & Fitch, 9 North Wabash (Madison), CE 6-6700

Fortunately for all shoppers, when A & F bought Chicago's famous old V L & A (Von Lengerke & Antoine) it had the good sense to leave the physical interior of the store alone. No amount of modernizing could improve its present air of a shop for Old Money and Old Families. Even its old-fashioned gift boxes (flying red ducks on a green background) are right for the *ne plus ultra* of sporting goods stores. Find here five floors of outstanding merchandise from sunfish sailboats to the kind of casual clothes and sportswear worn by men and women in *The New Yorker* magazine's best ads—the man who wants Grant's, the people who protect their nest eggs—those ads. The main floor has a grand assortment of gift ideas: drinking accessories decorated with sporting emblems, proper leather and canvas luggage, carving sets, elaborately fitted English wicker picnic hampers, pipe-smoking and gaming equipment, transistor television sets, shortwave radios for yachtsmen and so forth. Upstairs, men's and women's clothing—casual and deep country; a pet shop for sporting- and hunting-dog needs; a floor of camping and safari equipment, including tents, canoes, guns, rifles, fishing gear, tackle. Service at A & F is superb.

Store hours: 9:15 AM to 5:30 PM daily.

Charles A. Stevens & Co., 25 North State, RA 6-1500

One of the largest women's specialty shops in the country, with fashions at all price levels as in the big department stores, and much of the same merchandise you'll find at Carson's and Field's. A store policy that insists upon fast turnover of all merchandise (buyers are urged to mark down quickly as far down as they wish) gives Stevens an edge over competition since it can put current fashions on the sales racks long before competition does. The De-

---

* The Montgomery Ward Warehouse is famous architecturally—a vast, beautiful white warehouse stretching along the quiet west branch of the Chicago River, built in 1907 by Schmidt, Garden and Martin. Almost as famous is the dancing lady statue atop the tower who appears to be waving a trumpet or a crutch. It's neither—it's a caduceus, but nobody knows why. Ward's was the world's first mail-order house, established shortly after the Fire by a young man who'd lost everything but $65 and the clothes he wore in the conflagration—A. Montgomery Ward. Obviously the calamity didn't matter at all.

signer's Shop is especially famous for its sales—one store executive laughingly described the room as "kind of junky looking because the sales racks are out so much of the time." No customer enthralled with a whopping markdown has ever complained. The Junior Floor is wild young fashions sold against jukebox rock. The fifth floor lunchroom offers Continental breakfast from 9:30 to 11 AM, luncheon, midafternoon snacks and dinner on the two nights the store is open late.

Store hours: 9:30 AM to 5:45 PM; Monday and Thursday to 8:30 PM.

Brooks Brothers, 74 East Madison, AN 3-0100

Tradition insists that only items available in the men's department be carried in the women's, so the selection is limited to blazers, polo coats, rainwear, button-down shirts, sweaters, Bermudas and loafers, all with the unmistakable Brooks look.

Peck & Peck, 24 South Michigan, CE 6-6071; also 660 North Michigan, SU 7-2615

Moderately priced casual clothes for college girls and young women. Skirts, blouses, suits, sweaters, jumpers, daytime dresses and accessories with a pleasantly traditional, suburban air.

Johnson & Harwood, Inc., 37 North Wabash, CE 6-9864

Good-looking half-sizes and styles for mature women and an outstanding alterations department. Also classics in regular sizes. Prices are moderate to expensive.

Lane Bryant, 101 North Wabash, RA 6-9800

The store famous for maternity clothes and for its ability to fit any problem figure—the very short, the very tall, an overweight junior, a chubby girl, an extra slim, a girl who needs young half-sizes and a woman who needs adult half-sizes. Years ago, Lane Bryant merchandise had a wash-dress look; today, its fashions are thoroughly fashionable. Also millinery, shoes and lingerie in hard-to-find sizes. Except in the Crystal Room, prices are modest to moderate.

Open 9:45 to 5:45 daily, Monday and Thursday to 8 PM.

Capezio, 17 North State, CE 6-1911

Years ago the famous old ballet-shoe company added a nifty line of flats and little dancing slippers, now has kicky boots as well.

If you need two different size shoes, you can buy split sizes at **Perry Shoe Company,** 30 North Michigan, DE 2-1357. Prices are $20 to $50; all shoes are orthopedic. **Dr. Scholl** (see "Shoes" in the Yellow Pages for most convenient location) also makes split sizes from $28 to $150. Dr. Scholl's regular arch-lift shoes offer marvelous comfort and are carefully fitted from imprints of your feet. Prices from $13.

Pint-Size Shop, 17 North State, RA 6-3579, claims to have the largest selection of dress and suit sizes 1, 3, 5, 7, 9 in the city, and it may be true. Young stuff mainly—Mam'selle, Mr. Mort, Junior Sophisticate and so forth.

FASHION SHOPPING IN THE MICHIGAN AVENUE AREA

Store hours are generally 9:30 to 5:30, though some stores are open until 7 PM on Monday. Many are closed on Saturday during July and/or August.

Saks Fifth Avenue, 669 North Michigan (Erie), WH 4-6500

An old, able representative of the New York store, it can dress you from top to toe in several different price ranges. The Designer Shop, haughty but excellent, includes the entire Sophie of Saks Fifth Avenue ready-to-wear line. Sportswear is first-rate, millinery outstanding. The shoe department is the finest in the area and includes Roger Vivier imports; lingerie is delectable, the linen shop is stocked with exquisite merchandise. Young Elite Shop has the best contemporary fashions at moderate prices to be found anywhere—lots of summer dresses in the $23 bracket, for example. Additionally, it always has a sales rack of new merchandise that didn't move fast enough (Saks moves very fast) at knock-down prices. Every smart young Chicagoan in the size 8-to-12 range heads straight for it when she shops in Young Elite.

Bonwit Teller, 830 North Michigan (Pearson), WH 4-1600

A not so able representative of the New York store, mainly because of an inattentive sales force on the upper floors. The store is beautiful and the merchandise chic, and if you don't mind self-service it's the best place in Chicago for separates and Italian knit blouses and jerseys. Main floor has an excellent jewelry department staffed by friendly and attentive salesladies and a gift shop ditto. The Safari Shop is filled with bright, crazy clothes and sportswear and is the gayest department in the place.

Stanley Korshak, Inc., 919 North Michigan, DE 7-7766

A truly distinguished, carriage trade women's shop with a graciousness that makes you feel like the most welcome customer who's ever come through the doors. Everything is understated here—even the background of beige walls and carpeting. Clothes are exquisite. Mr. Korshak, Jr., goes to every Paris opening, brings back originals from the great French houses and also has adaptations made. He does the same with American designer clothes—you can get the original or a superb adaptation. Expensive—and worth it. Dresses begin at $160; suits and costumes start at $200. The Mr. Stanley Shop sells fashions for younger women at considerably lower prices: dresses from $70 to $125; coats and suits from $125 to $200. Korshak's also offers fine millinery, blouses, real and costume jewelry, at-home apparel, handbags, scarves.

Bramson, Inc., 700 North Michigan, ST 2-1080; also 160 North Michigan, 782-1080

Main floor specializes in contemporary young fashions from name designers; less expensive fun fashions are found on the second floor. Also millinery, handbags, robes, costume jewelry, very good fake hair chignons and hairpieces.

Martha Weathered, 950 North Michigan, ST 2-1080

A noted Chicago women's shop, though no longer run by the original owners. Main floor dresses start at $90, climax around $800. A special main floor department caters to youngish women with difficult figures—sizes to 22½. On the second floor find young classics and marvelous knits—the kind you wear for years, priced $30 to $145. Weathered also offers designer hosiery, millinery, beautiful lingerie and robes.

Beth Fritz of the Drake, 931 North Michigan (Walton), WH 4-7718

Stunning knits, dresses and classic suits for women and mature women.

Couture Ltd., 66 East Walton, WH 4-1218

A small apple-green-and-white shop in a converted Chicago graystone, owned and run by Danny McMahon, who does custom work on request, carries designer clothes and line-for-line copies of imports and also stocks moderately priced dresses starting at $55. Upstairs, a smashing at-home department and, in season, an aprés-ski shop. Young matrons and small chic women of any age are his main customers since the biggest selection is in sizes 6-8-10. One wishes the sales force and models wouldn't sit about gossiping in the reception room while new customers wait for attention, but, alas, they do.

Elizabeth Arden, 717 North Michigan, SU 7-6950

Designer dresses and evening gowns, including the full Castillo line, and consistently the prettiest lingerie, robes and dressing gowns to be found in Chicago. The specialty lingerie fabric is polyester georgette, a matte crepe, infinitely superior to nylon tricot, almost impossible to find elsewhere. Robes and peignoirs start lower than you'd think—about $35.

Pompian Shop, 550 North Michigan, DE 7-6604

New York and California coats, suits, dresses, sportswear, very contemporary but never extreme. Young women in their 20's shop here, so do women in their 60's. Prices are $30 to $95 for junior sizes; higher in misses.

T. Jones, 638 North Michigan, DE 7-1171

New branch of the New York shop of the same name—the one that's patronized by Jacqueline Kennedy. Clothes are the ultimate of chic simplicity

225

—currently a spare, lean look with a feeling of Courrege's tailoring. T. Jones offers approximately ten dress styles and a number of coats and dress/coat or dress/jacket ensembles, which come in all colors of the rainbow and almost as many fabrics. You order your selections in any color or material you want. Price range is about $80 to $120.

Model Mother Maternities, 670 North Michigan, DE 7-5160

Maternity clothes only—an entire storeful of them—and the place to find something smart for an expecting daughter or daughter-in-law.

W. Harvey Ltd., 43 East Oak, 337-2167

The country look in town at very reasonable prices. In an Early American setting find classic sportswear and accessories. Dresses $18 to $70. Suits $30 to $60.

Jax, 736 North Michigan, MI 2-4946

The skinnier you are, the better Jax clothes are going to look on you. Famous Jax slacks here and pants, little velveteen suits in season and interesting, extremely simple dinner dresses. Stock is small. If you have to order something you want that's not in stock, there's a 10 percent increase in price (20 percent for special order), which, as one bright young thing points out, means "you pay for their stupid merchandising." If you don't mind this sort of foolishness, you can have a dandy time selecting fabrics from three huge swatch books. Dresses $50 to $300. Coats $75 to $850 (mink-lined leather). Shoes $20 and $25. Also sweaters and bathing suits.

Ching & Co., 148 East Ontario, SU 7-0429

Oriental robes, lounging apparel, dresses in silks, wool, cashmere or cotton, children's pajamas, men's robes. Miss Ching will make to order for customers who can't find the size they want in stock. She goes to Hong Kong for fabrics woven and dyed to her specifications; brocades are handwoven in traditional designs. Her custom sewing is beautiful. Cotton dresses start at $25, silks at $50. Long robes $65, short $55. Also Oriental jewelry in 14-carat gold. Following a Chinese tradition, the shop never opens until noon, but you can call for an off-hours' appointment.

MILLINERY, SHOES, UNDERPINNINGS, ACCESSORIES

Bes-Ben, Inc., 938 North Michigan, WH 4-6691

Chicago's Mad Hatter, whose rare midnight sales have customers lined up outside the store for hours in advance, since Mr. Greenfield, the proprietor, literally tosses out every hat in the shop at a flat $5. The rest of the year he specializes in the expensive, zany window hats for which he's famous (trimmed with little animals, bumblebees, political party symbols and so forth) and some of the most becoming custom designs to be found.

Andrew Geller, 741 North Michigan, MI 2-3550

Fashionable shoes in a handsome, antique-furnished salon. Geller shoes fit best if you've a high vamp and a short last, but you can get sizes from 10 quad to 5 triple. Young shoes start at $16.95; regular lines at $26; alligators at $55 up.

Two big annual sales everyone watches for—immediately after the 4th of July and immediately after Christmas when prices come down about 40 percent. The shop had a terrific repair service, and demand may possibly bring it back. Meanwhile, for shoe repair, see page 304 or ask a salesman where Alex is located. Open until 6 PM.

Joseph Salon Shoes, 679 North Michigan, WH 4-1111; 50 East Randolph, DE 2-2772

Five well-known lines here: Margaret Jerrold, Herbert Levine, Martinique, Capezio, Nina. Also posh boots and a young boutique of fashions from Jr. Sophisticates, Teal Traina, Anne Klein of Mallory, Geoffrey Beane and Bonnie Cashin, plus coordinated avant-garde shoes. Lowest shoe price: $14 (flats); heels average $30.

Chandler's, 650 North Michigan, WH 4-9375, and **A. S. Beck,** 542 North Michigan, MI 2-1360, are well-known for copies of fashion shoes in a $12.95 to $18 range and for copies of those copies at $4.99 to $6.99.

Arnold's, 730 North Michigan, DE 7-2900

The specialty here is handbags in distinguished materials. Also gloves, umbrellas, luggage, costume jewelry, unusual little travel and gift items.

Mollye Lewis Foundations, 112 East Walton, DE 7-0320

The shop for bras, girdles, corsets, waist cinchers, etc. The stock is beautiful, and you're fitted with a knowledgeable concern hard to find elsewhere. Mothers bring their growing-up daughters here—and all customers have implicit faith in the personnel. Also, a year-round selection of bathing suits with matching beach jackets, custom-fitted and altered whenever necessary. Prices throughout are reasonable.

F. W. Woolworth Company, 676 North Michigan, SU 7-0427

The only convenient dime store outside the Loop, with a respectable lunch counter up front and canaries, parakeets, fresh house plants in the rear. Also excellent toy counters.

BOUTIQUES

Lencia, Inc., 70 East Walton, DE 7-1730

In a setting of antique furnishings, coffee service during the day and liqueurs in the late afternoon, find Chicago's most expensive boutique. Though clothes on the racks start as low as $70, prices rise to $500 for exotics which are shown only in the privacy of dressing rooms. The Princess Luciana Pignatelli of Rome line is here—casuals and at-home outfits. Also Odys men's sweaters from France and Chicago's own Sharon Davis-designed, Madge Friedman-handloomed at-home clothes, stoles and skirts. Sizes 6 to 14. Most clothes are too sophisticated for very young women.

Terry Kaplan, 224 East Ontario, 944-1038

Mrs. Kaplan, a bright, lively Englishwoman, runs her small boutique with British know-how, and she is fully aware that the one advantage a small shop on a side street has is that the customer is waited on by the owner—and the owner cares about the customer. Mrs. K. specializes in clothes for active in-town women who want things that will take them through the day—or through dressy little evenings. She shops yearly across Europe, also carries American lines. Find a few size 4's and a few size 12's and 14's, but most things are in between. Price range, $25 to $200. The annual post-Christmas sale culminates in a merry auction about January 15: customers come in during the week, try on auction items, bid for them on auction night. With luck, you get a $100 dress for $17.

I. Miller Galleria, 710 North Michigan, DE 7-1320

It's the I. Miller shoe store expanded to carry mad young imports and one-two-three-of-a-kind styles from small companies. Fine shoes still here, of course: I. Miller, David Evins, Andre Perugia, all starting at $40, and Ingenue shoes from $22.

La Colonna Imports, now at 1515 Sheridan, Wilmette (Plaza del Lago), 251-7535

A boutique in the true European sense of the word—young, worldly and, in this instance, Italian clothes and accessories. Owners Marcello and Barbara Franchini opened it in 1955 on Chicago's Near North Side, long before Americans knew what a boutique was. Signor Franchini, a Roman of exceptional taste and imagination, regularly wins AID awards for his window displays, which are built on imagination, not cash, like flowerpots filled with yellow tissue-paper tulips backgrounding yellow sportswear. As a matter of fact, all La Colonna windows except at Christmas are traditionally one-color displays. Find at-home clothes and sport clothes (more or less) from little-known Italian designers whom the Franchinis specialize in unearthing—"We keep discovering people who are eventually discovered by the large stores; finally they out-price us, so then we find more newcomers and develop them." Summer dresses start at $35, winter dresses at $45. Suits $100 to $200. Sizes 8-14. Also some delicious accessories, such as Fornasetti plates. One of the nicest shops you'll discover anywhere.

Horse of a Different Color Ltd., 1714 North Wells (Old Town), 664-7323

A shop currently promoting the total look—pants suits, for example, but no separate slacks; hostess outfits but no separate skirts. The shop is decorated in paisley, with owners Jeanne Cristofv and Nancie Link dressed to match. Clothes are amusing and terribly current. Dresses start at $30. Cocktail dresses to $200. Suits $70 to $150. Accessories, though limited, are chosen carefully to go with whatever is the current look—one glove style but in 40 colors, two kinds of boots in 30 colors. Customers are mainly career girls, models, young matrons who want high style. Horse never opens before noon but stays open until 9 PM weekdays and 6 PM on Sunday.

Caravan North, Inc., 1716 North Wells, 787-4801

Offbeat imports—caftans, burnooses, Mexican shifts of lace or embroidery. Also exotic fabrics which the shop will make up into any of its basic patterns. Dresses to $60, hostess gowns in the same category, theatre coats to $100.

City of Florence Shop, 450 West Diversey, WE 5-0045

Imports from Italy, France, Austria, Spain and Switzerland—Gino Paoli, Avagolf, Korrigan, Cortefiel (raincoats) and so forth. Three-piece knits start at $85, knit dresses at $65, Swedish cottons at $28.

MEN'S STORES

In the Loop, the better men's stores cluster around East Madison Street and Wabash Avenue; State Street stores are generally lower in price, far more promotional, and prone to fairly swift style changes.

Brooks Brothers, 74 East Madison, AN 3-0100

A fine branch of the oldest retail establishment in the country (1818), the store that's been Ivy League since its beginnings. Brooks reputation rests on the fact that its styles are changeless—quite possibly, the last major innovation was from the long jacket suit worn by President Abraham Lincoln at the time of his assassination. Its tradition—three buttons, natural shoulders, vests, narrowed trousers without pleats. University Shop carries summer suits from $45; the 346 Shop stocks winter suits $110 to $135; Maker Department (own make) $150 to $200; special cutting (when you can't be fitted properly off the rack and Brooks makes to measure from a regular pattern) is a standard $25 over rack prices: custom cutting, $310 to $350. Evening clothes, of course, and a complete line of furnishings—button-down shirts, robes, blazers, sportswear, shoes, hats, ties. On the main floor, an expanding gift department running to ships' lamps, ram's-head humidors, drinking equipment, English hunting horns, barometers, pewter mugs, magazine racks, jewelry, brushes and Brooks' famous Economist's Diary, which is one of the most useful appointment books ever designed.

Store hours: 9:30 AM to 5:30 PM Monday through Saturday.

Capper & Capper, 1 North Wabash, CE 6-3800

A conservative old Chicago store, now owned by Hart Schaffner and Marx, delivers your suit on a heavy, curved wooden hanger in a zipper bag. Appeal is mainly to older and sometimes heavier men; Walter Morton, for instance, is one of the biggest lines here. Special order also available and a full line of evening clothes. An excellent shoe department. Churchill hats. The main floor has a good gift and novelty gift department. Suits are in the $90 to $260 range. A Michigan Avenue branch should be open in the Continental Plaza Hotel by the time you read this.

Store hours: 9:30 AM to 5:30 PM Monday through Saturday.

Higgins, Frank & Hill, Inc., 65 East Madison, FR 2-5005

Another Old Guard store with an excellent selection of suits (Oxxford, Hill, Louis Roth), special order and custom, men's furnishings, shoes, plus some of the best salesmen in town who came over from Finchley when it closed. It's also *the* place to get a shoeshine, since Jimmy not only gives an excellent one but creates strong rhythmic effects and keeps a beat with the rag he slaps across your shoes. His chair is in the shoe department on the main floor.

Store hours: 9:30 AM to 5:30 PM Monday through Saturday.

Abercrombie & Fitch, 9 North Wabash, CE 6-6700

Correct sporting clothes for hunting, fishing, sailing, tennis, camping, etc., plus blazers and handsome suburban outerwear. Whatever A & F offers is good and looks right. (See also page 222.)

Carson Pirie Scott & Co.

The men's store at Wabash and Monroe includes an excellent University Shop with a subdepartment for young *au courants*. The entire men's store is preferred by many Chicagoans because, to quote one of them, "It offers Field's merchandise with Sears' merchandising"—which means that most of the goods are out on display and it's easy to browse.

Store hours: 9:15 AM to 5:45 PM daily; Monday and Thursday to 8:30 PM.

Marshall Field & Co., Men's Store, Washington and Wabash, ST 1-1000

Like the main store across the street, the five floors of the Men's Store offer a vast amount of merchandise, hence can fit almost all hard-to-fit men as well as customers of average height and weight. Everything is good here, and the custom-tailoring shop one of the best in the city and so is the shoe department.

Store hours: 9:15 AM to 5:45 PM; Monday and Thursday to 7 PM.

Jerrems, 11 North Wabash and 7 South LaSalle, RA 6-2200

Ownership has recently changed, but if the Jerrems tradition (it goes back to 1857) is maintained you'll find one of the best busheling departments (alterations and tailoring to fit) and the old Jerrems specialty of Scotch import fabrics. Hickey Freeman, Lebow, Burberry are featured. Prices start at $87.50.

Store hours: 9:30 AM to 5:30 PM Monday through Saturday. LaSalle Street store, same hours but closed Saturday.

Baskin Clothing Co., 137 South State, AN 3-1000

Retail outlet for Hart Schaffner and Marx. The hat department is outstanding. Also good for casual shoes.

Store hours: 9:30 AM to 5:45 PM daily; Monday and Thursday to 8:30 PM.

Broadstreets, Inc., 123 South State (Palmer House), RA 6-8902

Superior service in a State Street store. Featured lines are Kuppenheimer, GGG, Stein-Bloch, Saxony, Worsted-Tex. Also a full line of men's furnishings, somewhat lower in price and less luxurious than on Wabash Avenue.

Store hours: 9:30 AM to 5:45 PM; Monday and Thursday to 8:30 PM.

Saks Fifth Avenue, 669 North Michigan, WH 4-6500

Conservative basics of excellent quality, yet the store never seems serious about being a men's store, possibly because it's a supplement to the women's shop and draws in lady shoppers looking for men's gifts.

Store hours: 9:30 AM to 5:30 PM. Closed Saturday in July.

Gingiss Formalwear, Inc., 30 West Lake, 263-7071

Sells and rents evening clothes and formal wear for weddings. At whatever level you want, you'll get reliable advice and quality clothing. Open to 9 PM, accepts all national credit cards. See the Yellow Pages under "Men's Clothing" for other locations.

Brittany, Ltd., 642 North Michigan, MI 2-6551; 29 South LaSalle, FR 2-5985

One of the best younger men's stores in Chicago. Among its strong points, its exclusive Southwick Line and its own Brittany label on suits cut at the same place in Connecticut and in the same style as J. Press suits. Excellent casual clothes with a country look; fine imported tweeds. Gant and Hathaway shirts, Burberry raincoats. Generally, a beautiful collection of ties. Winter suits $90 to $145.

> Store hours: 9 AM to 5:45 PM daily; Saturday to 5:30 PM. LaSalle Street store closed Saturday.

Benjamin Clothing Co., 1150 South Clinton, WA 2-1536

An exceptional rack operation, with 21 tailors on the premises to make alterations. Benjamin is a family-run business with, as the chief Benjamin says, "a lot of pride." It specializes in men's suits, trousers, odd jackets, coats, raincoats and there's probably more merchandise on the premises in more sizes than in any other retail establishment in the city.

Benjamin isn't cheap; suits are $100 to $275—but regular customers and competitors say you can't beat the prices, usually 20 to 25 percent off the finest lines made, including Oxxford, Cellini, and the like. Benjamin also buys its own woolens and has different houses make its own label suits, which are understated and handsome. You can trust any salesman in the place, but what you really ought to do as a new customer is ask Mr. Stanley Benjamin to fit you in the same suit he wears.

> Store hours: 9 AM to 5 PM daily; Sunday, 10 AM to 3 PM. Free parking in front of the building.

Lucas Clothing Co., 322 South Franklin, HA 7-1132

A near-rack operation in the heart of the old garment district, with prices considerably lower than elsewhere. Immensely popular with young executives, since it racks Forbes Hill of New England, a line in the Brooks-Press-Chip tradition.

> Store hours: 9 AM to 5:30 PM daily; Saturday to 5 PM.

The entire, suitably dingy garment district has superior little old Jewish and Italian tailors tucked away in the upper reaches of its old buildings. If you have the time to ferret and are willing to take chances, you can get faultlessly tailored suits for about $80.

M. Hyman & Son, 215 North Clark (Lake), 346-6880, specializes in well-cut clothes and sportswear in extreme sizes (36-60). Fits extra-short, short, portlies, long portlies, extra-long, double extra-long (men over 6'7") big college men who want imports, and does a huge mail-order business across the country. Standard brands include McGregor and Haspel.

> Store hours: 9:30 AM to 5:30 PM; Monday and Thursday to 8:30 PM. Free parking.

232

Edward's Hats, 201 West Lake (Wells), ST 2-2245, has a good selection of men's hats at reasonable prices. **Harry Gold Shoe Co.,** 12 North Wells, DE 2-7955, gives you well-fitted shoes at reasonable prices. For handcrafted Italian shoes, **House of Italian Shoes,** 3836 West Chicago, DI 2-8281. It helps if you speak some Italian. **Florsheim Shoe** stores are all over the Loop (see Yellow Pages).

CUSTOM TAILORS

In contrast to custom work done at the preceding stores, the big-name custom tailors in Chicago tend to turn you out looking like a celebrity or a press agent who handles celebrities. **House of Duro,** 172 North Michigan, DE 2-2307, openly promotes the fact that Ray Milland, Cary Grant, Rex Harrison and Chicago's Mayor Daley have had suits made here. **Lawrence Pucci,** 333 North Michigan, DE 2-3759, is an old second-floor custom shop for the man who can afford $300 suits. **Strahorn, Inc.,** 620 North Michigan, 337-2785, another second-floor shop, is considered one of the best of the custom houses. **George Mashbitz, Inc.,** 547 North Michigan, DE 7-7979, seems to duplicate Sy Devore's place in Hollywood. **T. W. Simpson & Sons,** 29 East Madison, DE 2-0101, is a small, old establishment run on an entirely different level. T. W. came from Scotland; today, son Craig is the tailor and son Stewart both models and contacts. The house makes suits for men and women, and though Tallulah Bankhead and a number of equally important types have been or are customers you'd never know it. Prices start at $210, and styling is conservative.

OLD TOWN STORES FOR YOUNG MEN
WHO WANT THE NEWEST

Man At Ease, 1706 North Wells, 642-4700. One of the finest shops in the country for the way-out look.

Male M-1, 1608 North Wells (Piper's Alley), 664-0978. Like its neighbor, it specializes in whatever is newest, especially if it qualifies as fad. Clothes are good. Shoes are mostly boots.

CHICAGO'S FINEST JEWELERS

Spaulding & Co., 959 North Michigan, DE 7-4800

Chicago men who want their wives to wear outstanding jewels have patronized Spaulding since it opened in 1854. The firm has its own factory, its own designers, its own sources of import, and is famous as the originators of

14-carat and 18-carat gold jewelry set with precious stones.* Designs are exquisite, timeless, almost unduplicated. Spaulding is also one of the best places for sterling tea sets, trays, small serving pieces of all kinds, antique Georgian and Victorian silver, American and English flatware—the English sterling has its own Guildhall-registered London hallmark. Across the hall (the store is in the Drake Hotel Arcade) find china—Spode, Minton, Royal Crown Derby, Royal Worcester, Wedgwood, Richard Ginori Italian porcelain, and crystal—Waterford, Val St. Lambert, Baccarat, Lalique, collector's items and contemporary services. Back in the main shop, superb leather desk accessories, engraved stationery with the best selection of papers in town, handbags, and a large collection of small clocks. The repair department is excellent and will accept pieces not originally purchased in the store. All purchases are wrapped in the store's classic heavy white paper, tied in waxed black string, and sealed with black wax—a distinction that's hard to beat.

Tiffany & Co., 715 North Michigan, WH 4-7500

A small branch of the New York Tiffany with some of the most exciting fine jewelry the Midwest has seen. Tiffany has developed a new sense of jewelry design—there isn't an expensive but nondescript piece in the shop. Find here also a representative selection of the 1,000 china and crystal patterns carried in New York (any of which can be ordered, of course); Tiffany sterling, entirely handmade whether flatware or keychains; an "Under $10" table with small gifts as low as a $3 gold cross and, though not always in view, a little paperback book, *Tiffany Table Manners for Teenagers* ($1); you order stationery in a separate little room—Tiffany's own papers, own watermark, own engraving—a specialty unduplicated with the possible exception of Cartier, New York. The store keeps New York hours—opens at 10:30 weekdays, 11 AM Saturday.

C. D. Peacock, State and Monroe, CE 6-0065

The oldest store in Chicago, founded a few months before the city got its charter in 1837; it was then a tiny lean-to whose owner, Elijah Peacock,

---

* Until 1932-33 important diamonds, rubies, sapphires, and emeralds were always set in platinum. Mr. Gordon Lang, president of Spaulding, took his first gold-set pins to New York, to Mrs. Edna Wollman Chase, Editor-in-Chief of *Vogue* magazine, and to Frank Crowninshield, Editor of *Vanity Fair.* Both editors looked at the pieces with interest, said they liked them but that they didn't really know what they were looking at. Each, however, agreed to show them to their staffs for opinions. Both staffs went wild over fine jewelry at prices considerably lower than platinum settings and also with a kind of fashion appeal the Depression had killed. The pieces were mainly hearts, bows and arrows, shells, tassels—all the romantic symbols that had come down through the ages. Both magazines featured them; the rest is history.

made watches and ships' chronometers. Today, behind bronze peacock doors, in a green marble interior lit by crystal chandeliers, are superb diamonds and jewelry, elegant handbags, an astonishing stock of perfumes, baronial sterling. The second floor is given over to bridal registry, English bone china, crystal, leather goods, engraved stationery. Be sure to see the present Mr. Peacock's (fifth generation) collection of natural color diamonds in a diamond case on the main floor. Their size isn't impressive (they're arranged on a card scarcely larger than a postcard) but the color range makes the collection outstanding in the country—palest green to deep blues and lavenders, palest yellows to a diamond that is literally chocolate brown. A Michigan Avenue shop should be open at 900 North Michigan by the time you read this.

Carteaux, Inc., 31 North Wabash, ST 2-5375

Specializes in solid gold from a needle at $2.50 to any top price you care to name. Also carries the complete line of Omega watches. One rarely thinks of Frenchmen as immigrating to Chicago, but Mr. Carteaux's grandfather, a Parisian boilermaker, came here with his wife immediately after the Civil War. Their son started the firm and *his* son, the present Mr. Carteaux, grew up in the business. He's as charming an expert as you're likely to meet.

Trabert & Hoeffer, Inc., 940 North Michigan, SU 7-1654

The *forte* here is custom design, and the firm especially likes to create new settings for your own old jewels. The shop will give New Yorkers a distinct sense of *deja vu;* it was designed to duplicate Trabert & Hoeffer at 407 Park, a double-balconied, quiet room in which you are seated at one of several small tables for any discussion of jewelry. One difference—the Lalique fixture, the only one of its kind in the country and *not* for sale, though at least 500 customers have tried to purchase it.

Store hours: 9:30 AM to 5 PM Monday through Friday. Open Saturday during the pre-Christmas season.

Juergens & Andersen Co., 55 East Washington, ST 2-7240

The second oldest jewelers in Chicago (1854), though the first shop was founded by a family of silversmiths in Denmark some 300 years earlier. In the still smoldering ruins of Chicago after the Fire, a Juergens dug a conglomerate mass of gold and silver out of the ashes of the shop, raced to New York with the salvage, got $12,000 for it, and within a week of the disaster was back in business. About 1910 the firm originated the Add-A-Pearl necklace, still one of the most enchanting gift ideas of all time for a new baby girl. The shop is now both wholesale and retail.

Store hours: Open 9 AM to 4 PM; Saturday by appointment only, except during the pre-Christmas season.

Marshall Field & Co., 111 North State, ST 1-1000

It's always been known for its diamonds—loose and made-up pieces from all over the world. It's also the only department store in the world that carries Patek Philippe watches.

Nagatani Oriental Arts, 848 North Michigan, DE 7-5449

Superb Oriental jewelry and art objects at one of the finest shops of its kind in the United States. Find extraordinary cultured pearls, both unmounted and set into necklaces and rings, pendants of remarkable jades and quartz, earrings, cuff links, and so forth. Like his colleagues, Mr. Nagatani will make jewelry to order—but with one requirement: he has "to like the customer and sense real interest in having something made." See also page 243.

Kalo Shop, 222 South Michigan (Adams), 427-6540

Silver is the specialty here—heavy sterling silverware and jewelry designed and handwrought in the Kalo workrooms. Designs are simple, timeless and enchanting, styled with a rounded look that is unmistakably Kalo. Silverware includes bowls, serving pieces, flatware; jewelry includes enamel on sterling. If you have suitcase room for just the tiniest gifts, be sure to look at the Wedgwood medallions mounted in silver and at the shop's small enameled pins and thimbles. These last, in delicate floribunda designs, are just $5.

Uniques Gallery, 333 North Michigan, 346-0960

A wholly unexpected sideline of corporate enterprises that have no business relationship with jewelry other than the owners' interest in the fantastic designs of Frank E. Lowenstein, a sculptor who creates one-of-a-kind jewelry in a wayside studio in San Juan Teotihuacan, Mexico. His pieces are extreme, the next thing to Salvador Dali, yet they show an almost Louis Sullivan interest in organic forms—designs worked out of or around the shapes of the stones and Baroque pearls Mr. Lowenstein uses. Pins and oversize rings are likely to have moving parts, a pendant may be made of a wild boar's tooth ridged in emeralds and mounted from a gold drop. No piece looks like anything you've ever seen—on exotic tall women, they're magnificent. From $250 to $5,000. By appointment only.

Jade House, Suite 910, 25 East Washington Street, 641-0041

Find jade in the Loop in a shop that grew out of the hobby of George Van Hagen, who is available only on Saturdays, and then generally by appointment—the rest of the week an associate is in charge. You'll find jade in 50 colors from all parts of the world, including pieces that the intrepid Mr. Van Hagen has prospected himself on mountain expeditions. Uncut stones may be purchased here for lapidary work.

For Antique Jewelry, see page 242.

236

FINE, ABSOLUTELY RELIABLE FURRIERS

Marshall Field & Co., 111 North State, ST 1-1000

Has the biggest selection of furs in Chicago. The department is not a lease department but as integral a part of the store as any other.

R. G. Uhlemann Fur Co., 936 North Michigan, WH 3-5155

Chicago's oldest furrier, past its 90th anniversary. Caters to North Shore and city carriage trade that wants mink and sables in timeless styles.

Thomas E. McElroy Fur Co., 645 North Michigan, WH 3-7878

A relative newcomer but highly regarded. Emphasizes fashion-show furs and carries the Christian Dior line.

Carson Pirie Scott & Co., 1 South State, 744-2000

In the last few years it's featured mad animal furs, such as fox built in layers.

Charles A. Stevens & Co., 25 North State, RA 6-1500

Has one of the most respected fur buyers in town, who selects every item, piece by piece, never in lots. Mr. Gus Munson is also always available to talk with purchasing husbands. Schiaparelli designed furs are here.

Adolph Richman Furs, Inc., 30 South Michigan, ST 2-0675

A long-established firm with a number of one-of-a-kind and original designs, and some of the nicest people in the business on the premises. Milton Friesleben in charge of all.

Bonwit Teller, 830 North Michigan (Pearson), WH 4-1600

Gunther Jaeckel furs, as in the New York store, and scrumptious.

Saks Fifth Avenue, 669 North Michigan (Erie), WH 4-6500

Revillon here and, as in New York, utterly luxurious.

N. H. Rosenthal Furs, Inc., 666 North Michigan, WH 3-1365

Sophisticated, high fashion furs. Like McElroy, always the latest.

Alper Furs, Inc., 190 North State, RA 6-0485

Nobody sells furs with more enthusiasm than Mr. Alper, who is a mink expert and has an abiding passion for the creatures' pelts.

Sears, Roebuck & Co., 403 South State (Van Buren), WA 2-4600

It may come as a surprise, but Sears has exceedingly fine furs, a tradition that began with Mr. Roebuck, who started his business career as a fur trapper in Canada.

SHOPS—FOR COLLECTORS AND CONNOISSEURS
11

Antiques
Antique Shows
Auctions
Rare Books, Maps, Prints
Fine Book Binding and Restorations
Exceptional Garden Sources
Chicago's Finest Wine Merchants
Tobacconists
Florists

CHAPTER 11

SHOPS—
FOR COLLECTORS AND CONNOISSEURS

This chapter is for epicures who seek reliable sources of fine antiques, rare books, equally rare prints, maps, autographs, or manuscripts, and who would also like to discover shops that specialize in exceptional garden and house-plants, outstanding wines and tobaccos. People who collect buttons or medals, stamps, coins or old railroad emblems should not feel denigrated—the chapter has to stop somewhere, and the classical division between collector items and hobby items is where the line has been drawn.

There is a Chicago section of the National Button Society,* but there is no single good source for buttons. There are a great many stamp and coin dealers in the city, but, to a man, their reputation is one of charging what the traffic will bear. Collectors of Boehm birds will find them at **Field's** and at **C. D. Peacock.** Steuben is in the Steuben Room at **Field's.** Royal Copenhagen Limited Edition Christmas plates are at **S.P. Rasmussen,** 1618 North Rand Road, Arlington Heights, 259-4077, as are Hummel figures and the annual Lalique crystal plate. Rocks are available at the **Tom Roberts Rock Shop,** 1006 South Michigan. Mr. Lester A. Weinrott has one of the largest collections anywhere of old postcards, old Christmas cards, old valentines, advertising trade cards and old posters. Write to him at 645 North Michigan Avenue, Chicago 60611. Doll collectors might find it worthwhile to contact Mary Harvey at the **Mary Harvey Doll Museum,** 3139 West Palmer, DI 2-7161, since she has a collection of some 500 dolls in her home.

To locate sources for other highly specialized kinds of collections, contact the Tribune Public Information Bureau, 222-3232, or the public relations

---

* If you're interested, call Mrs. Milton Axberg, EU 3-6649.

office of a museum that has exhibits in your particular line of interest, or the Exhibitions Office of the Chicago Public Library, which frequently displays offbeat collections of items such as old flatirons and other Americana.

ANTIQUES

In Chicago, hunting for antiques often has more of the true character of a hunt than elsewhere. The reason, of course, is the city's age. Or lack of it. Until a city is old enough to have become venerable, it has few treasure resources of its own to draw upon. If a Chicago antiques dealer confines his scouting to the Midwest, the best he'll be able to offer customers is mid-to-late Victorian, or 19th-Century Farmhouse; this part of the country simply doesn't go farther back than that.

What this means is that even though the Yellow Pages carry eight or nine columns of antique dealers, the chances of finding an item of outstanding value in most of the shops are slim. If you had all the time in the world, the hunt might be worth it, but if your stay is limited and you want only antiques of exceptional quality, confine yourself to the shops listed immediately below and —if you're here when one is in progress—to the antique shows listed in this chapter.

Malcolm Franklin, 126 East Delaware, DE 7-0202

Superb English furniture (1650 to 1830 exclusively), chosen with exquisite taste and literally of museum quality—the Chicago Art Institute has at least six items which it selected at the shop. The shop has three distinct areas, for walnut furniture, mahogany, oak, plus accessories and some ceramics throughout. In an article on antiques as an investment, *Barron's* weekly qualified the treasures here as the equivalent of anything you'll find at Needhams or Stair and Company in New York. They are. The shop has its own cabinetmaker, but he only works on a piece *after* it has been purchased, and only after you know what repairs the Franklins think should be made. There's scrupulous insistence here that items be described solely by date of monarchical reign; hence, you won't find a piece of Queen Anne mahogany, since the only woods used in England during the brief years she ruled (1702-1714) were native—walnut, oak, yew—and the earliest known English use of mahogany was 1725. The miniature, authentic period rooms you may find here are made by Eugene Kupjack who did many if not most of the rooms in the Thorne collection at the Art Institute. They're $700 each and they're in tremendous demand. The genial overlord of the establishment is Mr. Franklin; his two extremely able lieutenants are his son Paul and his daughter, Mrs. Daniel Sullivan.

Walter H. Willson Ltd., 904 North Michigan, DE 7-5955

Noted for very fine English silver, ceramics and furniture.

Joseph E. Dimery Coach House Antiques, 60 West Erie, SU 7-3457

Country English furniture at surprisingly modest prices sold by one of the sweetest, gentlest, most knowledgeable proprietors of the Old School. Mr. Dimery and his sister Mary have been in business as long as most collectors have been alive, and there's very little in the way of fine antiques that hasn't passed through their hands. New shipments arrive constantly but, because of the exceedingly fair prices, are sold out as fast as they come in. The Coach House is especially well-known for its most marvelous Windsor chairs and amusing Victorian mementoes. Mr. Dimery lives on the premises but prefers to work by appointment only so that he can devote full attention to you. A phone call in advance to let him know you're coming over is all that's necessary.

Marie-Louise Farman, 118 East Delaware, SU 7-6333

The only dealer of Continental antiques in town. Very fine pieces and some extraordinarily early ones—sometimes as far back as the 13th Century. The proprietress knows and remembers every piece she's ever carried; if you bought from her once, ten years ago, she may not recall your name but she'll remember exactly what you purchased and, in all likelihood, the address she shipped it to. If you favor French furniture, ask her advice on decorating—she does superb interiors.

Marshall Field & Co., 111 North State, ST 1-1000

Fine antique furniture (at very "fine" prices), accessories, a distinguished clock collection, Georgian silver and Sheffield, antique jewelry and toys and superb old oriental rugs.

Russell Button, late dean of Chicago antique dealers, moved his shop to 955 Center Street, Douglas, Michigan. It's now operated by his partners, Mildred Berggren and Rudolph Leuser. The no-charge phone from Chicago is Enterprise 4731—put your call through long distance.

Charles Frank & Co., 154 East Superior, SU 7-0985

English furniture of the 18th Century and good collections of Dr. Wall Worcester and Chinese Export porcelain. The shop is known for its master drawings in pencil, ink, chalk dating back to the school of Michelangelo and proceeding forward through Rossetti, David Cox, Venet, George Yates.

ANTIQUE JEWELRY

Marshall Field & Co., 111 North State, ST 1-1000

Field's has one of the best antique jewelry collections in the country (mainly 17th and 18th Century), along with collectors' pieces from the Middle

242

East dating to pre-biblical times. The department is extremely cautious about misdating the latter, leans over backwards whenever there's a question of exact authentication.

Alexander Hamilton, 25 East Washington, RA 6-9153

Antique jewelry in the medium-to-better range, though you can find some charming Victorian stone-set rings for young girls here for as little as $20. Mainly, though, it's Third-Empire French and Victorian and a few Georgian pieces from about 1820. The shop is owned by two of the more interesting personalities in antique dealerdom—Mr. Hamilton, a splendidly outspoken one-time gold prospector and direct descendant of the first Secretary of the Treasury, and Mrs. Hamilton, who, with urging, may be persuaded to show her enameled little old lady fob seal, a very rare piece not for sale at any price. Among the treasures you *can* buy are also solid gold English men's watches with elegant repoussé, some earlier stem winds, small carriage clocks, very old dangle earrings, French Empire flexible 18-carat gold bracelets, and contemporary pins made of the most imaginative use of old stick- and tiepins to be seen anywhere.

Mark Ist, 1440 North Wells, WH 4-9212

The name is an acronym from the owner's name—Mark Furst. The shop specializes in old jewelry, especially rings, some antique, some merely antiquated, but all interesting and honestly priced. Armor and old guns may be found here. This, by the way, is one of the few reliable Old Town antique shops* (though, of course, any named in this chapter can be trusted implicitly) and to keep curiosity-seekers from cluttering up the small premises, Mr. Furst charges 25¢ admission.

ORIENTAL ANTIQUES

Nagatani Oriental Arts, 848 North Michigan, DE 7-5449

Some of the finest antique Oriental art from China, Japan, Korea, Thailand to be found in this country. The shop is hushed and quiet—a place for collectors sincerely interested in Oriental art objects, not for window-shoppers. In fact, Mr. Nagatani only turns on the case lights when he's convinced you're serious about his prizes. Among his carefully collected treasures are porcelain, enamels, carved alabaster and carved woods, antique scrolls, ancient small

---

* The trouble with most of the others is that they offer only authentic hoo-ha, or a lot of bourgeoisie bravado, or outrageous prices—or all three.

temple figures, bronzes, including Fu dogs, stone sculptures. Mr. Nagatani takes knowing. He does have the inscrutable air of the Orient and doesn't open up quickly. But should you happen to discuss one of his pet subjects, such as the Oriental art collection at the Field Museum ("much finer than at the Art Institute," he maintains), then you can establish the beginning of a good acquaintanceship and *then* you might find yourself the recipient of some of his vast knowledge and insights.

NAUTICAL ANTIQUES

Bern C. Ritchie & Co., 105 South LaSalle, FR 2-0363

Proprietor Arthur R. Sawers is one of a scant handful of U.S. dealers specializing in nautical antiques. He also has the largest selection and has become the referral source for museums. When the late President Kennedy wanted an authentic model of a sailing vessel that once plied between this country and Zanzibar (to present to the Zanzibar head of state following the country's new independence), the Peabody Museum in Boston immediately referred him here. Mr. Sawers had two models available, of the whaler "Morgan" and a very early Baltimore clipper, the "Ann McKim." He shipped both to the White House where an entranced President immediately purchased the "Ann McKim" for his own collection and the "Morgan" as the official gift. All this is by way of background to a collection that includes English, Dutch and some French ships' models; old binnacles; scrimshaw; 17th-Century figureheads running four to seven feet in length; iron pirate and Spanish Armada chests; some of the earliest known pocket sextants; shadow boxes made of waterline half-holds containing hand-whittled models of ships with as many as 27 exquisitely carved wood sails; and barometers—Georgian stick, gimbals, angle and four-liquid. The rest of the offerings are too varied to single out, but they're fascinating both as objects in themselves and symbols of an age which is no more. Monday through Friday only, 9 AM to 5 PM.

Captain's Walk, 56 East Walton, DE 7-3515

A delightful new addition to the city's shops for collectors. This one specializes in ship models and antiqued reproductions of nautical paintings, scrimshaw, decorative accessories, imported fishermen's sweaters and gift items. Open 10 AM to 7 PM daily.

ANTIQUE FIREARMS

Arnold Marcus Chernoff, 1941 North Mayfield, NA 2-0675

Mr. Chernoff, antique gun editor of *Guns & Ammo* magazine, shows his collection by appointment only, specializes in firearms from 1500 to no later than 1870, in edge weapons and in military antiquities—medieval weapons and armor. His collection of early American firearms is considered the finest in the country, and his personal collection, not for sale, is nationally known.

ANTIQUE ORIENTAL RUGS

Nahigian Brothers, Inc., 737 North Michigan, WH 3-8300

A very old and reliable firm with probably the largest stock of antique Orientals in the Midwest—at least 6,000 are always available for viewing. Nahigian opened for business in 1890; somewhere along the way, members of the family had a falling out, and Chicagoans are always amused by their advertisements. The ads of Nahigian Brothers described here always state, "Not connected with any firm bearing a like name"; the dissenters (H. C. Nahigian & Sons) proclaim their independence just as firmly. This Nahigian is possibly the only firm in the Midwest able to repair Orientals of museum quality.

A VARIETY OF ANTIQUES

Callard of London, 127 East Oak, DE 7-4320

Behind a newly remodeled shop front find a bubbling Welshman who came to Chicago at the bottom of the Depression and made very good indeed. His shop is heavy on old paintings, contemporary graphics and good antique accessories of the type called conversation pieces—old music stands, tole, small and large elegants in silver or brass. Mr. Callard is a fountain of slightly scandalous gossip about prominent deceased Chicagoans (but the soul of discretion about living natives); if you're curious about Chicago society in the 1930's and 40's, he might be persuaded to release a tidbit or two.

Lynstan's Antiques, 674 North Dearborn, WH 4-6433

Proprietress Lyn Plath trained under Malcolm Franklin and selects her pieces with the same fine eye to detail. She carries early English furniture—mahogany, walnut and oak; ceramics including Rockingham, faience, Sunderland lustre and Meissen; some Georgian silver but more Sheffield; very good quality English pewter.

Petrushka Art Studio Inc., 911 North State, SU 7-7874

The proprietor is one of Chicago's more charming White Russians. For years Mr. Sokoloff specialized in Russian ikons, enamels and Russian antiques, but such items are rare these years, and he has filled his shop with antique Mexican Santos—carved saints dating from the 17th and 18th Centuries. Also Russian samovars and some art objects.

Collectors Nook, 1712 North Wells, MI 2-4734

Pine and country furniture, wrought iron and country pottery, including Galena (Ill.) pottery. Edith Lipsky, the delightful proprietress, is also a teacher, so the shop has unusual hours. Phone to be sure she'll open at the time you want to shop there.

Edwardian Antiques, 619 North State, SU 7-0712

The name refers not to the period of the antiques to be found here but to the proprietor, Edward Wolbank, who is also a State Senator and not always available. Phone first to make sure he's in, if you're interested in French furniture of the period 1900 to 1920, especially chairs, occasional tables, cabinet pieces. Mr. Wolbank also amasses porcelain and bronze figures, and anything with French ormolu, the more ornate the better.

La Bourse, 45 East Walton, SU 7-3925

A small green and white shop operated as a scholarship fund-raiser by the Woman's Board of Chicago Medical College. Items are provided by Chicagoans, sold on consignment at the price the consigner asks. The board takes 40 percent for scholarships for medical students. Since many items come from old estates as well as attics, you can sometimes discover rarities in old silver, porcelain, prints, heirloom jewelry, sconces. Prices start at $5, and there's an annual sale in September with about 40 percent reduction on everything. Open on Saturday the year around.

111 Shoppe, 111 East Oak, 943-9563

Mrs. Adah Siegal sells Victorian antique jewelry and interesting accessories, such as scrimshaw. She's the kind of dealer who'll tell you precisely what's wrong with a piece as well as what's right about it, and why you should never hold opals up to the heat of an electric light (they'll fire there as they never will again). Her Victorian stickpins are most reasonably priced—a number of them are as low as $4.

Shatkins Importers, 25 East Washington, 372-4713

Morris Shatkin has recently moved from his old digs, where he just didn't believe in dusting the merchandise, of which there was an incredible amount crammed into the small shop. Along with jewelry he hoarded Georgian serving pieces and Sheffield, and if you knew what you were doing and weren't afraid of dust, you had a fine time. Presumably, he polished everything when he packed and moved, but who knows—the dust may have settled by the time you arrive.

There are also serious dealers on Wells Street between the Merchandise Mart and Chicago Avenue. Though a disappointing number of them proclaim

"To the Trade Only," the rest will, from time to time, have one or more fine English or old Continental pieces available to all. However, it's purely a matter of shipments and luck—that is, you're around when a shipment arrives and you get first crack at it—or you're not around and you don't. Two shops you may find interesting are:

Country Living Antiques, 618 North Wells, WH 3-7534

Prairie country as well as New England in the soft toned woods used so commonly at the time—butternut, for instance. Ownership has changed hands recently so the shop is mentioned without comment.

Stanley's Antiques, 666 North Wells, SU 7-9800

Five floors of old and not so old things, including art nouveau and a lot of imports from France, Germany, Austria and England. Mostly decorators and dealers buy here, so it helps if you know your periods since the shop is geared to those who do. Annual sales the first two weeks in August and the first two in February with 30 percent reductions.

ANTIQUE SHOWS

One of the best sources for antiques are the annual prestige antique shows which attract exhibitor-dealers from the East as well as the entire Midwest. All charge admission, about what you'd pay in a top movie theatre, except on preview night when the tariff is considerably higher. As a rule, attendance at previews is by invitation, but if there are unsold reservations, visitors are generally most welcome. These are quite dressy affairs, a great deal of fun, and offer a way to meet Chicagoans whose interests are similar to your own. Check with the sponsoring organization.

Early June: **Lake Forest Antique Show,** Reid Hall, Lake Forest Academy, CE 4-3210

The most prestigious of all Midwest antique shows, ranked as one of the top five shows in the country, with some $2 million worth of superb antiques on sale. The entire affair is a visual delight since it is held in the 19th-Century Italianate mansion* that was once the home of the late J. Ogden Armour, is now part of a fine prep school.

Outdoors, flags wave and bright red geraniums border the courtyard and balconies. Indoors, all school furnishings are removed for the show, leaving only the original paneled walls and marble fireplaces of the house as a splen-

---

* Elsie de Wolfe (later Lady Mendl) made decorating history here when she introduced her "chintz period" in the upstairs rooms of the 35-room mansion. The villa, designed by the late Arthur Heun, took four years to build (1904-08) and ranks with "The Breakers" at Newport as one of America's great houses.

did background for items ranging from, say, a solid door secretary dated 1750 to two Lowestoft bowls valued at $6,000 but displayed as casually as plastic ware. Luncheon and tea are served at buffet in the courtyard. Proceeds of the sale go toward academy scholarships.

Mid-September: **Hinsdale Antiques Show & Sale,** Hinsdale Community House, 415 West Eighth (Madison), Hinsdale, FA 3-7500

The setting is casual and country, and the antiques are mainly English and American primitive. A Blunder Shop stocks donations from local people—not rummage items but old and/or arty pieces, valuable enough for dealers to pick clean. By all means, head for the Blunder Shop first, preferably on the first day of the show. Luncheon served on the terrace, weather permitting. The show benefits the Community House, a not-for-profit organization.

Late September: **Chicago Antiques Exposition & Hobby Fair,** usually at the Conrad Hilton Hotel, 720 South Michigan, WA 2-4400

Mostly Victorian, but there are always one or two dealers with good antique jewelry. The character of the show is changing—hobby is becoming more important than antiques.

Fourth week of October: **Wilmette Antiques Show,** Woman's Club of Wilmette, 930 Greenleaf, Wilmette, AL 1-0527

Oldest of the suburban shows and one everybody enjoys. Lunch and dinner are served at the club.

Second week of November: **North Shore Antique Show & Sale,** North Shore Congregation, 1185 Sheridan, Glencoe, Chicago No. BR 3-3322

A newcomer with dealers of the caliber of those that show at Hinsdale. Allow time to stroll about the very contemporary Sunday school that houses the show, have luncheon on the premises and see the temple; Minoru Yamasaki's only building to date in the Chicago area is perfectly beautiful (see page 404).

Early March: **Greater Chicago Antiques Show & Sale,** sometimes at the Lake Shore Club of Chicago, occasionally in an old city mansion.

The show is run by the North Shore Junior Board for the benefit of Northwestern University Settlement House. For information check with Northwestern University Settlement House, 1400 West Augusta Blvd., Chicago, BR 8-7471.

Third week of May: **Evanston Antique Show,** Woman's Club of Evanston, 1702 Chicago, Evanston, GR 5-3800

Another very well-balanced antiques show, with about 30 dealers. Petite luncheon on the premises.

AUCTIONS

No auction house in this city bears comparison to Parke-Bernet, Sotheby's or Christie's, except for the hushed cathedral-cum-gambling-house tension during the auction of a major piece at Hanzel's.

Hanzel Galleries, Inc., 179 North Michigan, FR 2-4878, is the outstanding auction house here and its sales are attended by the cream, which means a mixture of shrewd and wealthy Chicagoans, antique dealers bidding for private customers of their own and a sprinkling of young marrieds or bachelors who are learning or have learned the value of finding good antiques in this way.* All Hanzel auctions are conducted by Swiss-born William E. Hanzel, a delightful man whose ethics are the highest and who will always state if a piece is a reproduction or has flaws. There are no plants in his audiences, and if you raise your hand to smooth your hair you won't find that you've just bought a Chinese vase for $650. Sales are not at set times, but there are always previews and, of course, catalogs. The merchandise is always quality, and most of it is very distinguished indeed. Any Monday night auction during a blizzard is bargain night since the crowd will be an auctioneer's nemesis—thin.

Archie Shore Galleries, Inc., 3318 West Devon, OR 4-6900, is known for his gun and rare coin auctions.

Pick Galleries, Inc., 886 Linden, Winnetka, HI 6-7444

Conducts estate auctions on their premises. The estates are mainly North Shore, and items put up for bidding can be very fine indeed.

There really are no other auction houses that can be recommended at this time.

In mid-November, usually the Thursday and Friday preceding Thanksgiving, the **Chicago Public School Art Society** holds its annual **Collectors' Auction.** Many of the items, often the entire furnishings of households that are being broken up, are donated, since auction proceeds ($10,000 to $20,000) support the society's public school program of Art Institute scholarships. A preview exhibition is always the day before the sale (conducted by William Hanzel), and though no catalog is printed every piece is numbered as well as appraised. Some amazing buys turn up—one year, for example, 15 exquisite 18th-Century

---

* If you've never attended an auction, go to the preview where everything to be auctioned will be on display. Get a catalog and mark the numbers of the items you want to bid on. Before the auction proper, decide if you can't live without the things you're planning to bid on and how much you can't live without them. Don't be surprised if Mr. Hanzel looks quizzical when he first hears you bid—he's very careful to make certain he's heard newcomers correctly.

rosewood and walnut small desks and writing tables. Location is usually at the Germania Club, 1536 North Clark, in a gold and white Baroque ballroom. For exact date, contact the society at its headquarters in the Art Institute.

Country Auctions are listed in the Sunday edition of the *Chicago Tribune* under "Auction Sales." Though many of the announcements concern auctions two weeks hence, a number of events are almost always scheduled on the Sunday at hand. They're held in authentic surroundings—old barns and the like, are wholly informal, and are good places to find rural mainline Americana from the late 19th to the early 20th Century. None of it may be of much value but you never can tell. Among the usual welter of ironstone jugs, tin milk gallons, dented kettles, nondescript kitchen chairs, stout old sideboards, headboards, clunky chests of drawers, a beautifully carved or turned rosewood sewing cabinet just may turn up.

House Sales, unknown in some parts of the country, are usually listed in the *Chicago Tribune's* classified advertising columns under "Private Sales." If the ad lists items of obvious taste and value, and if the address of the sale is the old Gold Coast area of the Near North Side or along Lakeview Avenue, and if it mentions that Mrs. So-and-So is in charge, grab your coat and go. All signs indicate an organized sale in a fine old town house or baronial 1920's apartment; attending gives you the opportunity to snoop without buying and discover firsthand how wealthy Chicago lives.

RARE BOOKS, MAPS, PRINTS

Kenneth Nebenzahl, Inc., 333 North Michigan, AN 3-3513

The proprietor's name so conjures fantasies of a wizened gentleman in a musty shop that you have trouble reconciling your fantasy with the tall young Harvard type who welcomes you to his modern, carpeted, air-conditioned suite with a superb view of Michigan Avenue and the crazy roof ornamenture atop the Stone Container Building directly across the street. Mr. Nebenzahl specializes in Americana of the western hemisphere from Columbus through the end of the 19th Century, and his collection is the finest in Chicago.

Mr. Nebenzahl also specializes in rare prints and maps. Among the former: naval subjects, the War Between the States, historic scenes, Indians (he still has some Catlins) and natural history, including some of the Elephant Folio Audubons. In maps: an excellent collection dating from the early 16th Century, including Mercator, and a set of hemisphere maps by Jean Baptiste Louis Clouet (Paris & Cadix, 1788-93). He issues four illustrated catalogs yearly: *The Compass,* for map collectors; *The Print Collector; Canada and*

Rare Americana (2 eds.) for book collectors. Cable address: Nebenbooks.

Hours: Monday through Friday, 9 AM to 5 PM; Saturday, 9:30 AM to 4:30 PM.

Hamill & Barker, 230 North Michigan, CE 6-9782

Miss Margery Barker and Miss Frances Hamill are general antiquarians of first editions and manuscripts, with emphasis on early English literature and beautiful leather-bound sets of the classics which, surprisingly, are purchased as frequently for wedding gifts as by collectors. Though both ladies stoutly maintain they are not specialists, theirs is the only rare book shop in Chicago that handles botanical subjects in depth.

Hours: Monday through Friday 9 AM to 5 PM; Saturday to 11:30 AM.

Abraham Lincoln Book Shop, 18 East Chestnut, WH 4-3085

In a high, narrow house built just after the Fire, find the only book business built on interest in a single personality, Lincoln, and a single war, the U.S. Civil. Lincoln expert Ralph Newman, who has crammed into the house the world's biggest stock of hard-cover and paperback Lincolniana (10,000 separate titles) and U.S. Civil War history (40,000 titles), has somehow also made room for the Civil War Round Table, which he founded; an apartment that he rents to a Civil War buff and the buff's wife; *and* a guest room. The Round Table welcomes any male guest interested in the subject; the guest room welcomes Mr. Newman's friends of either sex, so it's entirely possible you'll find Pulitzer prize winner Allan Nevins or singer Peggy Lee wandering around the premises. State governors may drop in to browse through the bookshelves; so may bus drivers—the common denominator is intellect and interest. Mr. Newman also has good collections of American history; manuscripts and letters; the entire 128 volumes of *The War of the Rebellion* (the official records of the Union and Confederate armies); and the *Weekly Compilation of Presidential Documents,* published every Monday by the Office of the Federal Register, National Archives and Records Service.

Hours: 9 AM to 5 PM Monday through Saturday.

Buckingham Book Shop, 65 East Van Buren, 939-7306

The two most interesting specialties in this small, pleasant shop are the collections of old sheet music and miniature symphonic scores and remainders of art and other gift books initially published for cocktail tables. Sheet music dates back to the Civil War. Large sheet music is available in all categories—popular, sacred, arias, foreign, studies for piano, violin, etc., and a surprising collection of old songs about Chicago. All of it is "used" music but in good or even fine condition. Also some Americana and back copies of *Horizon, Venture* and *American Heritage.*

Hours: 11 AM to 7 PM Monday through Friday; Saturday to 6 PM.

Richard S. Barnes, 1628 North Wells, MI 2-8005

It's the kind of specialists' bookstore that does 80 percent of its business with libraries seeking history, sociology and literature. Making your needs known to Mr. Barnes, a scholar's scholar with an M.A. in history, given to muttering and an absentminded way with customers, may require patience, especially if he's tracking down a library request. However, if you're serious about a particular book, persist, because once he knows you're inexorable he'll transfer that same fine concentration to your needs. He also runs a book-locating service, and though he's likely to insist that something you want can't be found, if it can he will, and you'll get it within six months, as a rule. The books you buy on the spot will be wrapped in newspaper and sealed with wide brown tape. If anybody but Richard Barnes tried it, the packages would look like remnants—but in his capable hands, they emerge with such neat square corners that you realize you've just watched a creative man take a commonplace and give it great style. While he's wrapping, peek through the side windows at the most remarkable city garden in Chicago, the imaginative work of the late Mrs. Barnes.

Hours: 10 AM to 6 PM, including Saturdays.

Owen Davies, 1214 North LaSalle, MI 2-6697

Mr. Davies describes his shop as one big exhibit, and he's correct. Old railroad lanterns, model planes, prints of various forms of transportation proclaim the house specialty: books on all forms of transportation, including balloons and trolleys. He insists his books aren't rare, yet if you want one of the earliest books written on trains, you'll find something that goes back to 1830. He has over 2,000 books on railroads alone and thousands of old timetables ("People like to read them and just dream"). He also has current timetables for all the railroads of the world, and for an unstated reason lawyers frequently consult them. Because of subject matter most of his customers are men, so women, when they do appear, get special treatment. Scholars and students may do reference work in the shop at a flat fee ranging between $15 and $20 per day, depending on Mr. Davies' mood and the type of work being done. He supplies a table and chair.

Hours: 9 AM to 5:30 PM Monday through Saturday.

For current books in general bookstores, see page 263.

FINE BOOK BINDING AND RESTORATIONS

Extra Bindery, R. R. Donnelley and Sons Co., 2223 South King Drive, 431-8000, and the **Bindery, Newberry Library,** 60 West Walton, WH 3-9090 (Gérard Charrière or Reginald Walker), for fine binding and restoration of volumes. Donnelley also does hand restoration of rare books and documents.

For regular book and magazine binding and also fine, hand-tooled leather binding, **Ernst Hertzberg & Sons Monastery Hill Bindery,** 1751 West Belmont, LA 5-4126. For fine binding only, **Cuneo Press,** 2242 South Grove, VI 2-2100 (George Baer or William Anthony); also, **Elizabeth Kner,** 608 South Dearborn, WA 2-3879.

EXCEPTIONAL GARDEN SOURCES

Plants Alive, 5210 South Harper (Harper Court), 667-2036

It's not a greenhouse, but the atmosphere is as moist and fragrant with green things growing as if it were. Find here some 400 to 500 species of houseplants—more varieties than are carried by all the florists in Chicago put together—plus herbs that thrive indoors. Proprietor Nathan Morris is a lively encyclopedia of plant knowledge (he's also editor of *Garden Talk,* the Chicago Horticultural Society's bimonthly) and gladly shares knowledge with you. He coordinates his plants with one-of-a-kind pots made by leading Chicago potters, sells them at the same prices you'd pay at their studios—$1 to $100. Plants start at 75¢, top at $150. You'll find lots of greenery at the $5 level and shrimp plants at $2. Bring your own containers to be planted if you wish.

Hours: 10 AM to 6 PM; Sunday, noon to 6 PM.

Mission Gardens, Techny, Highway 43 (Waukegan Road), three miles north of Glenview, 272-7669

Just to stroll through the gardens across the road from the Divine Word Mission is a joy. Brother Charles is the presiding horticulturalist here, known throughout the gardening world for his own magnificent strains of peonies, double peonies, tree peonies, iris and junipers. The gardens also yield 150 other kinds of flowers, ground covers, trees and shrubs, all of which may be ordered by mail. Catalogs on request. Closed Sundays.

Bello-Groppi Studio, 421 West Wisconsin (Old Town), WH 3-1557

Mr. Bello is a sculptor who both makes and imports fountains, classic garden sculpture (figures, urns, pedestals), birdbaths and the like. His prices are from $60 to $1,000, and he has a charming town garden attached to the studio where you can view his pieces in natural habitat.

Tuscany Studio, 163 West Ohio, MO 4-7680

Religious and classic-inspired statuary, benches, fountains and pedestals of cement for outdoor gardens and plaster for indoor use. Proprietor Mario Anichini does most of his business wholesale but welcomes individuals. A three-foot plaster figure is about $55; in cement, about $70.

Hours: 9 AM to 6 PM daily; Sunday to 1 PM (if you're late, ring the bell; if he's home he'll open for you).

Jeanette, 120 East Delaware, DE 7-6299

A little English basement shop in which Miss Jane Dunham, who grew up doing fresh flower arrangements, has turned her talents to flowers of silk, beads, wool and papier-mâché. The results are exquisite arrangements for small tables and centerpieces. Miss Dunham does almost all the arrangements for private parties at the Casino and private dinners in Old Guard homes. Currently, she still has a supply of the French flowers given to her by the late Mrs. Thorne (Thorne Rooms of the Art Institute). Arrangements begin at $6, go to $76, and come in semi-antique or amusing little pots. Imaginative decoupage (her own) also available.

Hours: 2 PM to 5 PM Monday through Friday and by appointment.

Almost annually, though it misses an occasional year, the **Chicago Horticultural Society** conducts a late May or first week in June sale of flower, herb and vegetable seedlings ready for transplanting. The sale is held in the gardens of a garden club member, usually an estate where the planting is exceptional, such as the Albert D. Farwell home in Lake Forest (famous not merely for its luxurious foliage but for Mrs. Farwell's gardens of healing herbs, biblical herbs, herbs mentioned in Shakespeare, and kitchen herbs). Demonstrations are scheduled throughout the day, which is run on an informal basis—wear sneakers and a cotton dress. Income from gate receipts and the extra-fine plant strains sold goes to the new Chicago Botanical Gardens. Call the Horticultural Society, DE 2-3495, for date and place.

Hlavacek's Flowers, 235 Ridge, Wilmette, AL 1-4400

Behind the florist shop are a large greenhouse and cold frames. On a bright day in late May fully half the North Shore ladies who garden will be here to buy herbs, strawberry and tomato plants and all the flowers they want to set out. To the best of anyone's knowledge, it's the only place in the Chicago area where you can consistently find young potted outdoor herbs. Catalog available.

CHICAGO'S FINEST WINE MERCHANTS

House of Glunz, 1206 North Wells, MI 2-3002

The oldest, largest, best-known wine merchants in the city (also the oldest Schlitz beer distributor in the country), still in the elegant quarters in which the Glunzes began in 1888. More than 600 wines here—plus fine spirits and the rare wines a connoisseur looks for, including, as of this writing, '37 Chateau Haut Brion, '43 Chateau Latour, and all the estate wines of the great years in the 1950's. Don't miss the small wine museum, the turn-of-the-century wine-tasting room (still used by Glunzes), the imaginative gift samples in all price ranges and one of the most unusual $100 gifts of all—sherry on tap in a 4½-gallon oak butt equipped with a hand-carved stand, spigot and bung; the sherry is Monte's Rare Cream (oloroso). Free parking in the Glunz lot.

Hours: 8:30 AM to 6:30 PM Monday through Saturday.

Stop & Shop, 16 West Washington, RA 6-8500

Very fine wines and spirits in the city's best-known gourmet shop (see also page 371).

Open 9 AM to 6 PM Monday through Saturday.

Marina City Drugs and Liquors, 300 North State, 222-1400

Proprietor E. Leonard Solomon is one of those rare wine men who didn't grow up in the business but knows almost as much about it as if he had. His wine stock is excellent and his recommendations (blunt, no-nonsense) will be appreciated by anyone above the novitiate level of wine lore.

Hours: 9 AM to 10 PM daily; Sunday, noon to 8 PM.

Le Petit Pavillon, Drake Hotel Arcade, 140 East Walton, SU 7-2200

A small but elegant stock of estate wines, eminently suitable as status gifts to a host or hostess.

Hours: 10 AM to 9 PM Monday through Saturday; Sunday, noon to 6 PM.

For the best selection of wines in both moderate and higher price ranges, consult Sig Langstadter at **North Gate Liquors,** 137 West North Avenue. Mr. Langstadter grew up in the classic tradition—apprentice winemaker for years, then salesman, finally wine buyer (see also page 279).

TOBACCONISTS

Rubovits Cigars, Inc., 306 South LaSalle, WE 9-3780

Connoisseurs order their cigars here because the selection is fabulous and Rubovits delivers. Standard and private label cigars, imported and domestic, mail order as well as retail. The big private label brand is La Perla Espanola. Top cigar price currently, $1.

Jack Schwartz, 120 South Dearborn, 782-7898

Another fine tobacconist, with imported cigars and a complete line of pipes and tobaccos.

Cellini Fine Pipes (Victory Pipe Craftsmen), 170 North Franklin, FR 2-4633

Cellini not only specializes in handmade natural briar pipes, but invites you into the factory on the premises to see how they're made. With tour or without, you'll learn as much about pipes and pipe tobaccos as you can absorb, come away with some genuine expertise. Ask for Mr. Silber, Sr., the owner, if you'd like to learn why mildness in pipe tobacco is the least desirable characteristic it can have. The shop believes it has the largest pipe repair service in the world, and it repairs yours while you wait. Catalog on request.

Iwan Ries & Co., 133 South Wabash, 372-1306

The shop dates back to 1857, is known throughout the world for its vast selection of imported and domestic pipes, tobaccos, foreign cigarettes and related smoker's items. Its antique pipe museum displays pipes more than 300 years old and has a separate room just for carved Meerschaums. If you've never bought or smoked a $500 pipe, here's your chance—a handcrafted affair made by Sixten Ivarsson of Denmark. You can also get French natural pipes as low as $6 and just about anything else in between. Ries's own tobacco pouches come in a fascinating assortment of leathers—baby gazelle, Sahara camel, kangaroo, etc., and fabrics (madras, Royal Irish poplin in regimental stripes, etc.). You're invited to sample Ries tobaccos, have your own pipe polished and sterilized while you look around. Catalog on request.

Alfred Dunhill of London, Inc., 534 North Michigan, 467-4455

Indulge yourself in Dunhill's humidor department or with an expensive, handsome, unnecessary gift: leather goods of all kinds, including small tables, lamps, chests, bar tables covered in goatskin (laminated and polished until it looks like marble); bar accessories; ornate chess sets; men's toiletries; women's handbags; and, of course, Dunhill lighters which, in 14-carat gold, are only $215, plus tax.

OUTSTANDING FLORISTS

Anna Flower Shops, 942 North Michigan and 101 East Oak, WH 3-1425

Anna does most if not all of the big weddings and has the kind of reputation that puts her shops in a class of their own. If you want to send an imaginative arrangement to a hostess, or a small but perfect bouquet, this is where to order it in the North Michigan Avenue area.

George Wienhoeber, 7 South Wabash, RA 6-3700

Quality houseplants and cut flowers at a convenient Loop location. Wienhoeber's make-good policy—when flowers that should last don't—is outstanding.

Mangel Florist: Drake Hotel, Palmer House, Conrad Hilton Hotel, Sheraton-Blackstone Hotel, North Western R.R. Station, 939-6200

Absolutely reliable. Flowers and houseplants ordered as gifts always arrive with a note requesting a phone call if there's a question of freshness.

Thomas Murray, 1127 North State, SU 7-2721, and **Jegen Florist,** 1149 North State, SU 7-8146, are two fine old neighborhood florists who always have the earliest flowers of a season. Murray is big on houseplants; Jegen always has the best daisies to be found. Both are convenient if you're invited to a home on the Near North Side.

For florists open on Sunday, see page 299; for bargain flowers, page 277.

SHOPS—ALL OTHER KINDS

12

The Best Barbershops
The Best Beauty Salons
General and Specialty Bookstores
Serendipity: Gift Shops Et Al
Furniture
Sight and Sound
Bargains of All Kinds

CHAPTER 12

SHOPS—ALL OTHER KINDS

If you have friends living in the city it's easy—they'll steer you to their own barber, hairdresser, camera shop, discount liquor dealer and the little shops for gifts and household items only Chicagoans could know about. If you know no one in the city, use this chapter as a surrogate friend; the places listed here are the best of their kind in Chicago. For shops that do emergency repairs, reweaving and the like, see page 303.

THE BEST BARBERSHOPS

Joe Lala Barber Shop, 333 South LaSalle, WE 9-7722. *The* place for young Chicago bankers, lawyers, stockbrokers. Ask for Nick. Haircuts, currently $2.50. At the opposite end of the Loop go to Kurt in the barbershop on the 8th floor of the 360 North Michigan Avenue Building. In mid-Loop, **International Barber Shop,** lower arcade of the Pittsfield Building, 55 East Washington, where eight barbers speak eight foreign languages as well as English. The **Ambassador Barber Shop,** in the Ambassador West Hotel, SU 7-7200, is highly recommended by its clientele, sometimes seems more like a club than a barbershop because so many Chicagoans with standing appointments have become old friends with the regulars in the chairs that flank theirs; also because the place serves drinks. **Henri VI** at Astor Tower (Astor and Goethe), 337-5313, specializes in English cuts. A $1 tip is minimum here and at the Ambassador. You can also trust the barbers in the Prudential Building, the Playboy Building, the Palmer House and the Drake Hotel not to ruin your head with the funny Midwest cut that wavers uncertainly and ruinously high across the back of a head.

If you want to know what male hair *styling* is all about, **Maestro Gerhard's Red Plush** in the Brunswick Building is probably as red plush a place to find out as any. For $9 stylist Maestro Gerhard ("I am the highest in Chicago, and if you find one higher then I will raise mine," he stated in a newspaper interview) will turn you out looking like U. S. Senator Charles H. Percy (R-Ill.), one of his erstwhile customers.

THE BEST BEAUTY SALONS

The luxury beauty salons are along North Michigan Avenue and on the Near North Side, but don't overlook those in Loop department stores—their work is good and their prices generally lower. Most hotels have beauty shops on the premises, but except for a couple of outstanding shops, such as Basil of the Astor Tower, Chicago women eschew them. No attempt has been made here to find above-average shops in neighborhoods or Loop or Near North Side office buildings, though there undoubtedly are a number of them. The reason is that most women on vacations or business trips want to indulge themselves. Prices are going up. Those quoted here were accurate when this book went to press.

The staffs of all beauty salons are given to unpredictable, explosive bursts of temperament; even the best has its sulky days. It's part of the big city tradition of American beauty shops, and if you run up against it you may justifiably volley back. As for tips: at least $1 to your hairdresser in a Michigan Avenue shop, $2 if he also cuts your hair; 50¢ to the shampoo girl; 25¢ to the girl who brings your smock and helps you out of and into your clothes; 50¢ to the manicurist. Incidentally, it's hard to get Friday or Saturday appointments in most places unless a standing appointment cancels. Aim for early or midweek and you'll get twice the attention you otherwise would.

Basil of the Astor Tower, (Astor and Goethe), WH 3-1111

If you've been to Chicago before, you knew him as Basil of the Ambassador; he simply moved east to the end of the same block. Cuts $4, shampoo/set $6. Also facials, wax treatments, manicures and pedicures. **Lilly Dache** now has the franchise for the Ambassador salon, and it's as good as ever except for Basil's absence.

Elizabeth Arden, 717 North Michigan, SU 7-6950

Behind the famous red door, find the only salon in Chicago where you can indulge the face and body for a full day—a Maine Chance Day at $50 which includes face treatment, body treatment, manicure, pedicure, hair styling, a half-hour makeup job and so forth with lunch brought in on a tray. Or try a half-day (Miracle Morning, $30), available under the same name in the afternoon.

Arden's is a sanctuary—you can request a private room for a cut/shampoo/set ($12) and get it, plus whatever else you want. Because it offers maximum privacy, many celebrities and Chicago and North Shore elite prefer it. Arden wigs and hairpieces are exquisite—and expensive—but a half-hour makeup is only $6.50. There's no such thing as a mediocre operator here but four people deserve to be mentioned by name: Ann, a gay little Englishwoman who's a genius at hair coloring; Gladys, who sets long hair to perfection; Arnold, long hair and superb cuts that hold their shape for weeks; Genevieve, his shampooist, has the same passion for clean hair that you do. You can also get any Arden service in your home or hotel room at about double the salon price.

Saks Fifth Avenue, 669 North Michigan, 944-6500, has a fine beauty salon. Cuts, $7.50; shampoo/set $7.50.

Fred Glaser Fashion Center, 740 North Rush, SU 7-3626

Fred Glaser is famous as the hair stylist who flies to Barbra Streisand to do her hair. His new shop offers all regular beauty shop services plus make-up, wigs and hairpieces and a fashion boutique in a setting reminiscent of the movie **2001.** Cuts, $10; shampoo/set $10.

John Garrison, 666 North Michigan, WH 4-7111

Having Mr. G will set you back $20 for a cut/shampoo/set, $7.50 for a shampoo and set, since he's in demand with Chicago's models and well-heeled young Near North Side wives. His staff is able and you can trust it—cut/shampoo/set $14; shampoo/set $6.50.

Salon de Paris, 646 North Michigan, SU 7-0324

Another shop with a number of top models among the clientele because makeup people and hair stylists for WGN-TV are also on the staff here. George, a young Cuban, does especially pretty things with your hairpiece. Shampoo/set, $6. Add $2 for long hair.

Michel Kazan, 846 North Michigan, WH 3-6400

The great one's in town twice yearly, but the rest of the time a highly competent staff turns out some of the prettiest heads in town. Try Mary or Ronnie if you want a soft, flattering set. Cut/shampoo/set, $10.50; shampoo/set, $6.

Kaye-Pierre Salon, 700 North Michigan, DE 7-3892

Marc-Benaim, the French *enfant terrible* of the Windy City, dominates the scene here. Your initial visit will run $25; after that it's merely $18 for a shampoo/cut/set. Cuts are almost imperative—Marc doesn't believe in long hair. You may also have to wait an unconscionably long time, like two or three hours; some women just don't mind.

Syd Simons Salon, 1015 North Rush (Oak), WH 3-2333

Syd Simons, an ex-Hollywood makeup man (Max Factor, Twentieth-Century-Fox) has adapted theatrical makeup techniques for everyday use, gives private lessons in these in his salon ($15 if he does it, $10 if by a staff member, three lessons for $35) along with hair styling, coloring, permanents, facial treatments, etc. Shampoo/set $7. Most customers, chic matrons between 30 and 50, have standing appointments. Your best chance to get Mr. S is the early part of the week.

For beauty salons open late at night, all night and on Sunday, see page 296.

In the Loop: **Wieboldt's** Budget Salon gives you a cut/shampoo/set for $5.50; its regular salon sets you back another dollar plus tips. **Carson's** regular salon charges $6 for cut/shampoo/set; $7 in the Styling Salon. **Field's** charges $7.25 to $9.25 for the same work and $5.75 to $6.75 to wash and set long hair. Field's alone in Chicago is realistic about what constitutes long hair ("long enough to sit on"), not merely shoulder length. Shampoo/set at Field's for short hair is $4.75.

GENERAL BOOKSTORES

Since Chicago isn't thought of as an intellectual's capital, it is something of a shock to discover that the city is positively stuffed with bookstores* and, furthermore, that among them is the largest bookstore in the world.

Kroch's & Brentano's, Inc., 29 South Wabash, 332-7500

It bases its claim on the total number of books within this one store—50,000 titles hardbound, 15,000 in paperback. (Foyle's, in London, which makes the same claim, probably does so on the basis of total number of books it owns, but you also have to go from building to building to find the ones you want.) In any case, K & B is one of the easiest bookstores in which to find fiction, biography, business books, science, art, foreign languages, reference, religion and marvelous children's books. The store is a Chicago institution, especially loved because it does not have compulsory retirement, and thus many of its old pros and specialists are around in their late 70's to serve long-time patrons. Papa Kroch's great interest was his rare book department, but in recent years the emphasis has changed to British bindings—that is, the store takes the sheets and sends them to Britain for binding. You might also

---

* More than 19 columns of them in the Yellow Pages.

want to look into the K & B First Edition Club, which offers autographed first editions to members; book search service available, too. The ten branch stores in the city and suburbs offer overnight delivery on any request for a current book not on the premises but somewhere in K & B stock. The two other most convenient K & B stores are at 16 South LaSalle Street and 524 North Michigan Avenue.

Paul Theobald & Co., 5 North Wabash, CE 6-3994

The place for art books—fine, applied, decorative, architectural, and if something you want isn't in stock, Mrs. Theobald (Spanish, delightful) will order it from anywhere in the world for you. The shop also has frequent art exhibits, always by ranking artists who are Mrs. T's friends.

Marshall Field & Co., see page 317.

Central Bookstore, 174 North Michigan, 332-4794

Publishers' overstocks (remainders), recordings and paperbacks in a shop that is most obliging.

Stuart Brent, 670 North Michigan, DE 7-6357

Parents who've bought *Mr. Toast and the Woolly Mammoth* and *The Strange Disappearance of Mr. Toast* for their small-fry will be pleased to know that the proprietor of this store is the same Stuart Brent who authored the above. Specialties of his bookstore, however, are psychiatry, philosophy, art. The premises may be in a state of grand confusion during some part of 1968. Mr. Brent is enlarging his quarters and remodeling them along the lines of Blackwell's in Oxford; that's worth any temporary inconvenience, as those who've browsed in Blackwell's will testify.

Walton Books, 172 East Walton, SU 7-7635

A delightful little shop that specializes in the latest best sellers in fiction, nonfiction and the arts. It also has one of the most agreeable lines of greeting cards in the city—the kind you don't feel slightly guilty over sending.

In the razzmatazz of Old Town find two very good bookstores, **Barbara's Book-Shop,** 1434 North Wells, MI 2-5044, and **Volume I,** 1608 North Wells (in the back of Piper's Alley), MI 2-2070. Both specialize in quality and egghead paperbacks. Additionally, Barbara's carries a lot of offbeat publications, such as all the New Directions books, City Lights Press, the top literary quarterlies, and monthlies—*Paris Review, Punch, The Humanist, The Realist, Partisan Review, Kenyon Review, Encounter, Commentary,* while Volume I carries publishers' overstocks, especially in books about films and art. Mrs. Lynn Wimmer, owner of Volume I, has a second bookstore at 54 East Oak Street called, appropriately, the **Oak Street Bookstore.** The feature here is the theatrical books center, something Chicago's needed for a long time.

A-1 Bookstore, 1112 North State (Cedar), 787-7830

Noted for great book bargains in used books of all kinds and a delirious method of cataloging. *Saratoga Trunk* is just as likely to be under Travel as not, Margaret Mead's *The Wagon and the Star* under Westerns. It's run by the Newmans, a dear couple who keep late hours (4 PM to 9 PM) for Rush Street-area browsers and also buy used books. Weekends 1 PM to 6 PM.

Vanguard Books, 1010 North State, 822-0066

A general bookstore in all ways but one—it's run by five young ministers of almost as many Protestant denominations and is headquarters for their off-the-street ministry program (page 288). What you get here are books, coffee, late-night hours, and conversation, but if you don't want that last, nobody's going to bug you.

For bookstores that deal exclusively in professional or technical volumes, or in denominational publications not mentioned above, consult those 19 columns in the Yellow Pages. For rare books, see page 250.

Economy Bookstore, 171 West Madison, DE 2-3366

The browser's favorite because occasional treasures do turn up among the used books. Also stocks new books and remainders.

SPECIALTY BOOKSTORES

Among the more interesting religious bookstores in the Loop are **Cokesbury,** 79 West Washington, which also carries general books; **St. Benet,** 300 South Wabash, which usually also has exhibitions of the finest contemporary religious art; **Thomas More Association,** 180 North Wabash, 332-1795, the world's largest Roman Catholic bookstore (it stocks every Roman Catholic book in print) and has a center for religious art; **Jewish Book Mart of Chicago,** 127 North Dearborn, specializes in Judaica, Hebraica and ceremonial objects, such as antique spice boxes.

Rand McNally & Co., 39 South LaSalle, FR 2-8836

The biggest map store of the largest commercial publisher of maps in the world, visited by some 100,000 people each year who range from Ph.D.'s in search of the latest projections to youngsters who want to learn how to lay out outline maps. It has a huge supply of trade and commercial maps, land and air navigation maps, topographic and detailed relief maps, base planning material, globes, atlases—not published just by Rand McNally but by all publishers in the field—private, government, domestic and foreign, including Freytag-Berndt, Vienna; Philip-Stanford, London; and Bartholomew, Edinburgh. Also stocks mappish guides, pictorial guides, city-street guides, even such lovely obscurities as a New York City theatre district guide, every *Guide Michelin* published, Baedekers, Blue Guides, Olson, Fielding, a fine array of guides from Hallweg and Kummerly & Frey, both of Berne, Switzerland. All Rand McNally books are also available here.

Navigation Equipment Co., 228 West Chicago, 944-3634

Coast and geodetic maps plus naval hydro and Canadian hydromarine and aeronautical charts, books, instruments in a shop appointed official charts distributor for the U.S. Navy Oceanographic Service, the U.S. Coast and Geodetic Service (Air and Marine Divisions), the British Admiralty, the Canadian Hydrographic Service. Proprietor Oscar Berman, who is also a lecturer in celestial navigation at the Adler Planetarium, offers the only service of this kind between New York, San Francisco, and New Orleans; his government maps are sold at official government prices. His book selection would fascinate anyone. In marine subjects alone it ranges from how to build a canoe to how to wire a ship to how to sail around the world alone. Instruments run the full gamut: hand-held instruments—computers, plotters, sextants and so forth; plus flares, ropes, safety equipment—everything but hardware.

U.S. Government Printing Office Bookstore, 14th Floor, Federal Office Building, 219 South Dearborn, 353-5133

The only store outside of those in Washington, D.C., where you can purchase GPO publications. About 1,000 of the best sellers are in stock, but catalogs listings the other 26,000 are available and orders are sent airmail daily to Washington (money payable in advance). Delivery to this store is on a priority basis—a week to ten days, which is roughly a month faster than if you order from Washington on your own.

Librería Broadbent, 14605 Poplar, Orland Park, 349-3644

Librería Broadbent has the best selection of books, from all Spanish-speaking countries, to be found west of New York City. Here are 6,000 separate titles in stock from 300 publishers, including French houses which issue books Franco won't allow to be printed in Spain. The stock is heaviest in the humanities, especially literature and literary criticism, but the proprietor can find almost anything you want, including rare old (18th Century) Spanish grammars and other texts; his antiquarian connections are excellent. The explanation for the contrast between his surname and his business is simple enough: Mr. Broadbent, an ex-naval intelligence officer, whose career included a number of years in Latin America, started the business because of his own frustration in trying to get good Spanish books. He now does a mail-order business that reaches to New Zealand and Jamaica. Box 1, Orland Park, is his mailing address. Phone before visiting him—both to make sure he's in and to be met at the junction of Highway 45 and 103rd Street, a gesture typical of the hospitality you will receive.

SERENDIPITY: GIFT SHOPS ET AL

Here are some of the shops Chicagoans consider special. Most will yield one-of-a-kind items, decorative, amusing and sometimes even useful.

Scholarshop of Roosevelt University, 430 South Michigan, WA 2-4677

The only shop of its kind in the country insofar as new, not resale, items are sold by volunteers as a way of raising scholarship funds. The shop abounds in gift items and the range is from tiny African carvings to large pieces of contemporary African sculpture, enameled bowls from Scandinavia, glassware, ceramics, jewelry—true serendipity. The price range is excellent— from 50¢ to $350 (for antiquities), but most things are at the lower end of the scale.

Museum stores yield unusual and generally inexpensive gifts that won't be found elsewhere since items almost always include museum reproductions. Try the **Museum Store at the Art Institute** for small antiques and reproductions of antiques—candlesticks, jewelry, tea caddies, English brass scoops, old glass paperweights, Leeds, and so forth. Also modern mobiles, cards and note papers, all kinds of books on art and architecture. Art subject Christmas cards in season and prints of the art collection all year round. The **Museum Store of the Field Museum** is rich with small gifts in the $1 range, tiny carved animals and South Sea Island jewelry, for instance. Also excellent natural history books for children and adults. The gift counter at the **Shedd Aquarium** sells beautifully made small plaster sculptures of animals that live in or on water, at trinket prices (60¢, 75¢), but the workmanship is superior.

The **Suq** (the word means bazaar) at the **Oriental Institute** specializes in marvelous reproductions of its own pre-biblical Middle East collections. Jewelry is mostly reproduced in gold plate with superb fake stones; statues as small as two inches, as large as 30 inches, and other tomb finds are equally intriguing. The Suq is highly selective and is run solely to further research done by the institute.

Darbe Accessories, 222 West Kinzie, 644-5811

Rita and David Segel shop England and Europe for one-of-a-kind items, such as small lined chests, brass fenders, lovely old tole lamp bases, odd brass pieces and small accessories, cigarette and end tables (all with levelers), old leather hatboxes that they converted into wastebaskets, plus accessories that

267

they reproduce in limited editions. No bargains here, but everything is so exceptional you'll feel the prices are justified. The Segels are frequently open on Sundays as well as weekdays.

Pique' Ltd., 700 North Michigan, 944-2333

The partners of this establishment scour the castles and châteaux of Europe for small decorative things, especially the antique boxes and miniature chests for which they're best known. Prices run from $3.50 to $750.

U. S. Accent on Mexico, 535 North Michigan, 828-9648

Owner Harriette Senge specializes in Mexican furniture, accent pieces, candelabra, jewelry, tiny crafted things and her own well-known sunflower art. All the furniture is Artes de Mexico and handsome. The shop has moved a couple of times recently, so you'd better phone to confirm hours and location. Currently Accent is open from 10:30 AM to 6 PM Monday through Friday.

House of Candles, 49 East Oak, 642-3290

The most attractive and sophisticated of all the candle shops that sprang into being in recent years. One reason: the displays here are designed so that you make continuous discoveries instead of being overwhelmed with clutter. Mrs. DeLee selects her candles with equal care and with an urbane town clientele in mind; you can, for instance, find black candles here—almost unheard of in suburban shops, and you can find imported candles nobody else stocks. The owner and her designer also do decorations for parties.*

In the same block, discover **Ginza,** 33 East Oak, MI 2-6921. Imports from the Orient, thoughtfully selected for quality as well as price. Kimonos, robes, sandals, scrolls, vases, chinaware, jade jewelry, art books and delightful children's novelties—tops, toys, puzzles, paper lanterns, small fans. Special sales every April and November.

Design Group, 126 West Kinzie, 467-4740, and 106 East Oak, 822-0298

Plexiglass cocktail and cube tables ($50 and up) are the big items at both stores, along with very contemporary architectural lamps and accessories and custom-tailored clothes made in Hong Kong. The Kinzie Street shop (it fronts the factory and may look dark but someone will always answer the bell during the day) also carries architect Howard Alan's Prototype Table, which is the most beautiful contemporary "butcher block" table going—a heavy slab beau-

---

* At a dinner for two debutantes at The Casino they carried out a peacock theme requested by the hostess, Mrs. Brooks McCormick—fans of peacock feathers for the debutantes; showers of feathers and ribbons as background and as table runners; candelabra of stained glass peacocks with spread tails of peacock feathers on the tables—the effect was dazzling.

tifully veneered in walnut with chromed steel legs; to order, as a dining, work or side table in any dimensions you wish.

Kinzie store open 9 AM to 4:30 PM Monday through Friday; Oak St. store, 11 AM to 6 PM Monday through Friday; Saturday to 5 PM.

Perfect Touch, 1538 North Clark, MO 4-0130

Great fake antiques and antiquities in the form of wall decorations, bas relief you'd swear had been excavated from the ruins of Athens, and free standing three-dimensional pieces, such as Corinthian capitals, which will serve admirably as table bases. Also period pieces of the 17th and 18th centuries, such as a triad of dolphins which can grace a garden or become a cigarette-table base. Everything in this marvelously fraudulent little shop is cast from a museum cast of genuine antiquity or from a cast made directly from antiques. The material is hydrocal, much harder than plaster and much more amenable to antique finishes. The owners of the shop keep experimenting with new ideas, recently found a way to mount and treat old prints on wood so that they look like fragments of old church frescoes. Prices are sometimes ridiculously low—a small piece of "paneling" at $3.50, a small urn-cum-cigarette cup at $4.50. The Corinthian capitals run $65 to $90, depending on the finish you want.

Hours: noon to 7:30 PM weekdays; Saturday to midnight; Sunday, 1 PM to 5 PM.

Caravan, 1606 North Wells, 664-7044

One of the three outstanding gift shops in Old Town with merchandise you won't see elsewhere: art objects from Africa and the Middle East, exotic jewelry from the same areas, a truly fine collection of primitive art, another of opals that you ask to see, East Indian fabrics, handloomed or hand-printed, animal skins (it's the place for zebra) and more—far more than can be adequately described here.

Hours: noon to 10 PM Monday through Thursday; Friday and Saturday, noon to midnight; Sunday, 1 PM to 8 PM.

Crate & Barrel, 1510 North Wells, SU 7-4775

The second outstanding gift shop in Old Town, specializing in contemporary crystal; glass; stoneware; porcelain; enamelware; stainless steel trays; wine racks of teak or rosewood; a few gourmet cooking extravagances, such as fish poachers and asparagus steamers; a few delightful children's toys; contemporary fabrics—all imported, all displayed against the crates and barrels they arrived in. The shop itself is a joy—beamed ceilings, red oak floors, the faint fragrance of packing-case wood throughout. Extremely reasonable prices for the most part, starting at $1.

Hours: 10 AM to 9 PM daily; Sunday, 1 PM to 6 PM

Cook's Cupboard, 1718 North Wells, 943-9085; 3300 North Broadway, IR 2-2951

The Bazaar Française of Chicago and the third of the triumvirate. This one specializes in import kitchen utensils and kitchen gadgets, all eminently worthy of a place in your own or a friend's home. Some things you'll discover here you simply won't find anywhere else—an Italian olive and cherry pitter, for instance. Also gourmet teas, coffee and spices in highly original packages.

Old Town hours: noon to 6 PM Monday-Saturday. Broadway shop hours: noon to 7 PM daily; 1 PM to 6 PM Sunday.

Sleepers Galore, 520 North Wells, 828-9679

Proprietor Max Marek, who until recently owned and ran a bar that looked like a Goodwill Resale Shop, has simply moved from one kind of ingenuous clutter to another. Now he haunts dealers, flea markets and secondhand shops for small pieces of furniture and bric-a-brac which he repairs and refinishes, currently specializes in bentwood chairs at $8 each, stained-glass windows, signed Tiffany lamps at $200 or more. Mr. Marek is the only man who ever knocked out Joe Louis (it was in their Golden Gloves days) and is probably the only ex-prize fighter who not only knows what a Tiffany lamp shade is but can tell you exactly how it was made and why it's worth its price. As a carry-over from his barroom days, he loves an audience and will be just as willing to entertain as to sell to you—puns, stories, sick jokes and dreadful Polish jokes, which he gets away with because of his ancestry. The German shepherd on the premises in the four-inch wide rhinestone-paved collar doesn't chew customers.

Hours: 10 AM to 5:30 PM Monday through Saturday.

Kohler's Trading Post, 638 East St. Charles, Lombard, 629-2330

Kohler's is where you go junking in old clothes. Three drafty big buildings contain some of the best junk imaginable, but all of it is dusty, much of it needs to be dug out, and the rest has to be climbed over or shoved aside. Among the navigational hazards are mountains of old wood-topped school desks; countless washtubs; barrels of used nails; rooms heaped with used furniture vintage Grand Rapids, 1912; old picture frames; oil lamps; miner's lamps; bird cages; the odds and ends of the entire Midwest. Yet prizes are ferreted out just often enough to make the effort worthwhile. Take Eisenhower Expressway direct to Lombard, a drive of about 45 minutes from the Loop.

Lee Schubert Floral Arrangements, 670 North Dearborn, WH 3-4225

Fake topiaries such as mock orange, flowering podocarpus, boxwood hedges for high-rise balconies and a great many other frauds, all well above the ordinary plastic stuff found elsewhere. The firm designed and made all the Camellia House (Drake Hotel) trees, the hedges at the Palmer House and the interior and exterior greenery at Corona Cafe, which is as good a set of credentials as a "fake florist" can produce. Custom order and rental, the latter an arrangement that should please any number of decorations committee chairmen.

For gift linens: **Field's** is superb. **Franklin Bayer,** 630 North Michigan, WH 4-4737, is a shop devoted to luxury linens, custom design, and coordinated bath and bedroom ensembles. Mr. Bayer maintains a limited but excellent hand-laundry service for his customers, offers free laundry service the first year on any $100 tablecloth.

On the South Side, the 28 shops in a cluster of faintly self-conscious, Southern California-type, white buildings, collectively known as **Harper Court** (52nd Street and Harper Avenue—see map of the South Side, page 119), are easy to visit on the same expedition that takes you to the nearby University of Chicago or the Museum of Science and Industry. The complex includes two restaurants, two bookshops, four art galleries, Nathan Morris' **Plants Alive; Fabyar,** a shop of unusual handcrafted fabrics; **The Clothes Closet,** where talented Marta Devins custom-makes dresses, suits, sportswear and also offers ready-to-wear from other young Chicago designers; **Sticks & Stones,** where, under a two-story ceiling, you'll find a fascinating assortment of imports, mainly from Africa and South America—carvings, skins, drums, bows and arrows, spears, shields, masks, jewelry, Siamese temple rubbings, and the persuasive scent of leather throughout. In the same community of shops, find Ray Williams' **American Designer Galleries,** which Mr. Williams stocks with contemporary one-of-a-kind: furniture, stoneware, tapestries, ceramics, art, and small handcrafted whimseys.

By car, use South Lake Shore Drive to 53rd St. By train, reach Harper Court via the Illinois Central—take any train that stops at 53rd St., which is just two blocks away.

If, after all this, you still haven't found the perfect gift, phone **Finders Inc.,** 8 East Huron, WH 4-7723. Barry Stone, a young ex-television-commercial writer, will find anything for you so long as it's outrageous enough. He won't bother with routine requests; does not locate missing persons or lost jewelry or obscure breeds of dogs. But if you want a dog that talks or a monkey trained to play Monopoly, he'll oblige. He's also great at finding Japanese rickshaws, retired railroad cabooses, replicas of Viking ships, etc. Additionally, you can rent Barry for parties or for party planning (outsize events, preferably, and always with some insane twist, which he'll provide). Lastly, he'll build anything that's big enough to be impressive—a birthday cake five people can pop out of, a life-size version of the Trojan horse, the Coliseum in Rome, or what have you. Finders are usually out of the store finding new lunacies, so don't drop in; phone. Mr. Stone has a 24-hour answering service, and he's good about returning calls promptly.

Craftsman Wood Service Co., 2727 South Mary, VI 2-0507, stocks unusual wood veneers; exotic solid woods, such as fiddleback maple; rosewood and musical instrument woods; inlay bandings and overlays; tools and patterns for those who are themselves craftsmen. **Decorator Supply Corp.,** 3610 South Morgan, 847-6300, offers fanciful pressed wood-fiber reproductions of 18th and 19th Century decorative and architectural ornamenture—unicorns, lions, griffins, fruit, *fleurs de lis,* moldings, cornices, etc. Write for their list of catalogs. **Drehobl,** 2847 North Lincoln, BU 1-2022, is an old family firm of leaded stained-glass specialists, stocks more than 500 colors of domestic, import and fine hand-blown glass, does some of the finest custom work in the country. **Erwin C. Gruen** is a blacksmith who specializes in hand-forged iron—chandeliers, furniture, etc. He's at 1302 North LaSalle, WH 3-3841. The Novotny family will custom-weave anything you want in wicker. The firm name is **Artistic Reed & Willow Mfg. Co.,** 420 South Kolmar, 533-8720.

FURNITURE

Field's entire eighth floor is stocked with it—antique to contemporary. **Carson's** has a marvelous Scandinavian department and a good Early American shop. **Wilson-Jump,** 608 South Michigan, WA 2-8765, an outstanding old Chicago firm, offers luxury traditional furniture and antique accessories, including lamps. The store is famous for its old-fashioned service to customers, as personalized as the furniture it selects. It also has a bona fide interior decorating service (at least six of the staff are as qualified as any individual decorators) and many of its long-standing customers start working with the decorator when a new home is still in the blueprint stage.

John M. Smyth, 12 North Michigan, CE 6-9400, a furniture store that's passed its centennial, offers good traditional, contemporary, provincial, colonial and modern furniture, plus a reproduction and import gallery. It also gives a guarantee that takes all the anxiety out of shopping: anything you've bought may be returned if you change your mind and no questions will be asked.

John A. Colby, formerly a landmark fine furniture store on Wabash Avenue, is now in Northbrook—bigger and more impressive than ever. The address is 1001 Skokie Boulevard, Northbrook (just off Edens) Chicago #273-2696.

Baldwin Kingrey, 105 East Ohio, 644-9103, is the place to find Knoll, Dunbar, Herman Miller, Georg Jensen, Jens Risom, Singer, and Hans Wegner. The criteria here are good architectural design and workmanship as well as practicality, standards that extend to accessory imports: handwoven area rugs, dinnerware, glassware, and so forth. If you want an unusual puzzle for children, be sure to see the Animal Suite, designed by Italian architect Enzo Mari—each piece is a different animal. The set comes in three sizes, the smallest $5.95, the largest $25.

Shops run primarily as interior decorator services always have some beautiful and unusual items and fabrics for sale. Among the best:

Mrs. Meredith T. Beals, 200 East Walton, SU 7-3753, who specializes in furnishing North Shore homes and in-town apartments in the finest 18th Century English (striped shades are her trademark). She travels all over the country collecting her pieces, and a phone call to her might be most worthwhile. **Watson & Boaler Inc.,** 712 North Rush, SU 7-1302, is an old, well-thought-of Chicago house. **Lubliner & Himmel,** 109 East Oak, 337-3973, is big on small antiques—English, French and Italian. **Cat & Fiddle,** 120 East Delaware, 944-2120, always has some choice little antique pieces and beautiful flower-print fabrics; and **Interior Design,** down the street at 132 East Delaware, DE 7-0250, specializes in luxury furnishings.

CAMERAS AND PHOTOGRAPHIC EQUIPMENT

The following shops are absolutely reliable, carry professional equipment and are patronized by professional photographers: **Altman Camera Co.,** 129 North Wabash, AN 3-0749; **Central Camera Co.,** 230 South Wabash, HA 7-5580; **Mid-West Photo Supply,** 65 East South Water, 372-4585 (also rents); **Norman-Willets Co.,** 316 West Washington, RA 6-8300; **K. Schlanger Co.,** 420 North Wabash, 467-4560.

For professional equipment only: **Bass Camera Co.,** 179 West Madison, ST 2-7410; **Burke & James, Inc.,** 333 West Lake, 372-5422 (also industrial equipment); **Standard Photo Supply Co.,** 43 East Chicago, SU 7-3124; **Cogan & O'Brien Co.,** 560 West Randolph, FR 2-8117. Amateurs will find **Wolk Camera,** 133 North Wabash, CE 6-4425, most satisfactory.

PROFESSIONAL ARTISTS' SUPPLIES

Near-North Guild, 63 East Chicago, DE 7-2668, and **Brudno Art Supply Co.,** 601 North State, 787-0300, are two of the best. Brudno also has a good line of picture frames. Both shops will cut mats for pictures. In the Loop, **Flax,** 176 North Wabash, MI 2-7612, and **Favor Ruhl & Co.,** 14 South Wabash, 782-5737, are old reliable houses with complete stocks and services. **Aiko's Art Materials Import,** 714 North Wabash, WH 3-0745, is the best source in the city for Japanese art supplies and Japanese rice and mulberry papers. Catalog available.

HI-FI, STEREO, TAPE RECORDERS, ELECTRONIC EQUIPMENT

Allied Radio is literally the world's biggest supplier of electronic equipment and components. The main store is at 100 North Western, HA 1-6800, and it's open Monday, Thursday, Friday 9 AM to 9 PM, Sunday from 10 AM to 5 PM, other days to 5:30 PM. Allied also has a branch store at the corner of Walton and Rush Streets, WH 3-1166.

MusiCraft, 48 East Oak, DE 7-4150, has four floors of hi-fi and stereo equipment, does custom design and installation and has a trade-in allowance policy. Its repair service is reasonable, trustworthy.

Toad Hall, 105 East Ontario, DE 7-4400, also 1444 East 57th Street, boasts the lowest prices in town, will refund the difference if you find an item for less within 30 days, and gives a five-year parts guarantee on everything. Like Allied, Toad Hall offers installation and repair service. Also rents everything in stock, including typewriters.

FOR MUSICIANS

Chicago is an outstanding source of musical instruments and sheet music of all kinds. The best-known stores are:

Lyon-Healy, 243 South Wabash, WA 2-7900. A distinguished old store (it was founded by two young Bostonians in 1864) that stocks literally everything in music—every instrument made in this country, its own harps,* sheet music, books on music, recordings, a collection of rare old import violins (for sale, but you have to ask to see them since they're kept in a vault). It also makes appraisals and offers instrument repair service. On Monday and Thursday, open until 8:30 PM.

Carl Fischer, 312 South Wabash, HA 7-6652. Between Fischer and Lyon-Healy, you can get anything in sheet music. Fischer specializes in it and in volumes, good foreign editions and musicological paperbacks. The store will also Gambelize sheet music that's falling apart.

For out-of-print music, **Buckingham Bookstore,** page 251.

Kenneth Warren & Son, 28 East Jackson, HA 7-7475, affiliated with Hill & Sons, London, makes, repairs, sells and appraises violins. **Fritz Reuter & Sons,** 1565 West Howard, 764-2776, are members of the Mittenwald Guild of Violin Makers, have an international reputation as master makers of violins, violas, cellos, basses, double basses and lutes; also repair, restoration, and appraisals.

---

* The firm is the only maker of harps in the western hemisphere.

On Wednesday evenings they're open to 9 PM. Take CTA elevated train north to Howard Street—the shop is one block east of the station.

Sid Sherman Musical Instrument Co., Inc., 226 South Wabash, HA 7-1796, rents and sells jazz instruments and is a hangout for jazzmen. You can also find old wooden clarinets, flügelhorns and mellophones here. **Frank's Drum Shop,** 226 South Wabash, WA 2-1300, is the big place for drums and percussion instruments of all kinds. Noisy but fun. **Chicago Guitar Gallery,** 334 South Wabash, HA 7-8434, stocks folk, classic and flamenco guitars and enough electric amplification equipment to satisfy all enthusiasts.

RECORD SHOPS

Discount Records, Inc., 201 North LaSalle, CE 6-2187, sells classical, jazz and import records at discount. **Lowe's Record Shop,** 212 North Michigan, 726-0980, does the same.

Jazz Record Mart, 7 West Grand, 222-1467, specializes in blues and jazz, has the biggest blues collection between the coasts. Also stocks out-of-print LP's, old 78's, obscure recordings of New Orleans and other jazzmen. Owner Bob Koester publishes a tightly-packed mimeo newspaper, *Blues News,* and rents films—early classics, shorts and jazz films. Classics include *Bill of Divorcement, The Fugitive, The Hairy Ape, The Phantom of the Opera* (1925), *The Return of Draw Egan* (William S. Hart, 1916). The shop is a hangout for jazzmen as well as collectors, and you're just as likely as not to find that the customer next to you is an early jazz musician who cut his last shellac in the 1920's or 30's.

If you want to make a recording, try **MBS Recording Studios,** 228 South Wabash, WE 9-0866. The studio has a Steinway and a Hammond Organ you can use, records on tapes, 78's, and 45 RPM unbreakables; it's air-conditioned, has echo chambers; also rents tape recorders. Closed Sundays.

BARGAINS OF ALL KINDS

Fashion bargains. A really astonishing number of smart Chicago women patronize a clutch of fashion resale shops on the theory that one woman's Dior might just as well be another woman's Dior. The kind of merchandise you'll find is almost exclusively high fashion—name designer dresses, evening gowns, ball gowns, coats, suits, shoes, millinery, handbags, furs, brought in by entertainers who can't appear in the same thing more than a few times and by Chicago's jet set or socialites who feel they can't either. Many garments will have been worn only once or twice. The bargains are real: a Norman Norell for which the original purchaser paid $1,000 will cost you $150. Prices frequently start as low as $35. The best of the well-established shops of this kind are:

Entre Nous Designer Resale Shop, 110 East Oak, DE 7-2919

Fashion Exchange Center, 121 East Oak, 664-1657

Margory Cowan Resale Shop, 32 North State, Room 1220, DE 2-3342

Y-Not Resale Shoppe, 646 West Diversey, 281-6636, which also carries fine shop labels at even lower prices—a pair of Andrew Geller Shoes at $4, a good Lord & Taylor suit at $13.

The Little Sparrow, 112 East Oak, 664-3322, a new shop that seems to know what it's doing.

The garment district, between Franklin and West Wacker Drive, Van Buren and Jackson, is dotted with little retail stores that offer handbags, nylon hosiery, lingerie, millinery and dresses at near-wholesale prices. For example: **Muriel Boutiques,** 325 West Jackson, Room 606, 427-6094, advertises factory-to-you fashions ranging from $35 dresses at $15 to $225; designer clothes (original samples) at $119.75. All sizes from 12 up, including half-sizes and custom sizes. **Hand-Moor,** 216 West Jackson, DE 2-1400, advertises juniors, misses, petites and half-sizes at 20 to 40 percent off. **Fred A. Block,** 337 South Franklin, 427-2944, sells dresses, coats, suits, junior coats considerably below retail. Styles are classics for the most part.

Goodman's, 410 South Wells, WE 9-5653, sells knitting yarns at near-wholesale prices.

For millinery supplies at near wholesale, go to **Fox Millinery Supply** or **Dan Fox,** two brothers who reputedly were once in partnership but no longer speak to each other and compete furiously in separate stores. One Fox is at 162 North State, the other at 6 East Lake, just up the block.

When **Carson's** has Dollar Day sales, wedding dresses can be marked down to $10.

Bryon, Inc., is a Kowloon, Hong Kong tailor (his Hong Kong shop is Peter Raney's). About three times a year, a representative comes to the Executive House with sample men's suits, women's fashions, fabric samples, accessories. You bring in pictures of any style you want made and the work is done in Hong Kong at about half the price you'd pay here, and some very well-turned-out Chicago women swear by the service. To get on the announcement list, write: Mr. Peter Raney, Vice-President, Bryon, Inc., P. O. Box 7159, Kowloon, Hong Kong, or the Byron, Inc., store at 344 North Beverly Drive, Beverly Hills, California 90210.

American School of Beauty Culture, 131 South Wabash, CE 6-5446, will give you a cut/shampoo/set for $3.50 and a permanent for $8. To avoid the beginners, ask for your appointment in the Model Shop since that's where you'll find advanced students and operators taking advance training.

Chernin's, 606-610 West Roosevelt (corner Jefferson), WE 9-4080

Shoes for men, women, children—odd lots and discontinued lots from fine sources such as Andrew Geller, I. Miller, Florsheim. You can save as much as 50 percent on high style brands. Also a selection of handbags and hosiery for women.

G. Fishman's Sons, Inc., 1101 South Des Plaines, WA 2-7250

For finds in yard goods and fabrics, Fishman's is unique. It doesn't have the biggest inventory in the country, but it has the most varied—yard goods from the world over, less than $1 per yard to $100 per (Vicuna), and the Fishman specialty: *all* the unused imported yard goods left from the current season's cuttings in the New York couturier houses—Ben Reig, Adele Simpson, Jo Copeland, Rentner, etc. The odds are 75 percent in your favor of finding the same fabric you saw made up and displayed in a Michigan Avenue window at Fishman's—and the original tags will be on the bolt to prove it. Every Chicagoan, suburbanite and female celebrity in town who sews shops here; on Sunday the place is pandemonium. Bargains even extend to the old-fashioned way all Fishman salesmen cut yard goods: customers inevitably get the benefit of the extra half-inch. The place is an institution—huge, immaculate, friendly —and you can trust implicitly any salesman's judgment about any fabric.

Home Fabrics, 3350 North Paulina, 281-3241

Mill ends, remnants, extra upholstery squares. A nice selection of materials and sewing supplies.

Flowers. **Amling's,** the florist shop on the main floor of Carson's (Wabash Avenue) frequently cuts prices on flowers (cash and carry) at the end of the day and always on Friday afternoons. **Wienhoeber,** 7 South Wabash, cuts prices on cut flowers every Friday and Saturday afternoon (cash and carry) and often cuts the price on certain blooming plants to $2. The small outdoor stand at the Randolph Street end of Garland Court (the wide alley that runs behind the Chicago Public Library) always has fresh flowers at bargain prices (50¢, 75¢, $1) and the flower stall downstairs in the Illinois Central (Randolph Street) Station specializes in fine flowers at reasonable prices. **John E. Maloney Co.,** 1359 West Devon, RO 4-1617, an undertaker, will let high school students who need floral decorations for proms have whatever is on the premises after the day's obsequies.

Household. Every May for the entire month, **Field's** Linens Department sells pillowcases made of Wamsutta 200-count percale sheeting at $1 each. Even the sales force looks forward to this one. In February, it's Penobscot sheets (Wamsutta seconds) at excellent reductions, often better than the January linen sales. On the 10th Floor at Field's find the **Clearing House,** a department that's never publicized but can be a gold mine for bargain hunters since it stocks furniture, radios, TV, rugs, etc., that didn't move during regular sales or which are slightly floor-damaged. **Carpet Barn,** 2163 North Lincoln, 248-0855, will cut to your specifications firsts of leftover installation carpeting (a 100 percent wool carpet, approximately 4'3" x 5'3", will run $10). Carpet Barn carries seconds in large sizes and reconditioned carpets which they will dye to suitable colors. The buys are unbelievable.

Hours: Tuesday and Friday, 11 AM to 5:30 PM; Monday and Thursday to 9 PM; Sunday to 4:30 PM. Closed Wednesday.

Red-Cliff Company, 1911-15 Clybourn, 248-1951, manufactures traditional pattern ironstone, china and Early American pressed glass patterns, and sells the seconds at considerable reductions. Most imperfections are scarcely noticeable. Stock includes stemmed glass goblets, full place settings, tureens, casseroles, tea and coffee sets.

Monday to Friday only, 10 AM to 4:30 PM.

Liquor. Happily for all, Chicago is one of the three cities in the country categorized in the liquor industry as a "dump city." What this means is that fair trade is ignored whenever a liquor dealer wants to move stock in a hurry—also that price skirmishes and wars are frequent. A chain drug or grocery store opening across the street from an old, established neighborhood liquor dealer will, if it has a liquor department, undercut the old-timer and keep on undercutting for years, if necessary. The old-timer can't and won't sit still for that, so he retaliates. This explains why Chicagoans driving through the business sections of the city's 76 neighborhoods pay more attention to window banners announcing cut rates than to stop signs. Four places that always sell below normal prices are:

Zimmerman's, 240 West Randolph (Franklin), DE 2-0012. It's the best-known liquor store in Chicago, the biggest individual store in the country, and consistently has the lowest prices because owner Max Zimmerman buys in quantities no one can match. Hence, it's the measuring stick for other dealers, i.e., if you know a specific Zimmerman's price and can quote it, other dealers will usually drop to the quote. Max Zimmerman has never been seen at work without his famous hat, is known accordingly as "Max, The Hat." He's one of Chicago's sweetest human beings, incidentally. Big free parking lot and a fine staff.

Hours: 8 AM to midnight; Sunday, noon to 9 PM.

North Gate Liquors, 137 West North (LaSalle), 337-1323. The only liquor store on the Near North Side that offers a free parking lot—just west of the store entrance on North Avenue—and cut prices on all standard brands of booze, plus weekly specials, and on cartons of cigarettes. As at Zimmerman's, the staff is just like the ads for your friendly neighborhood dealer.

> Hours: Weekdays 11 AM to 9 PM; Saturday to 10 PM; Sunday, noon to 7 PM.

Gold Standard, 3012 North Broadway, 528-6100; 3427 North Clark, 528-6220. Free parking at the first address, good prices at both. Open Sundays to 6 PM.

National Tea Co., 2500 North Clark, 327-1448, has to compete with every liquor dealer along Clark Street—and there are many, so it's like the example on page 278. No rarities at bargain prices, but favorite brands are good buys.

For bar supplies at semi-wholesale prices, try **Amann Bros.,** 623 West North. Bar glasses, the new throw-away plastic glasses, beer steins of all kinds, including old German lead-capped types, paper napkins and plates, hotel cooking ware, and utensils. Also rental of bar glasses and dishes.

Auctions. The **Chicago Post Office** conducts eight or nine auctions of unclaimed articles each year—the merchandise is as varied as the kinds of things people ship by mail: appliances; clothing, often in lots; cosmetics; kitchen utensils; phonographs; TV sets; electric shavers; stainless tableware; wristwatches; jewelry; sporting equipment; toys; etc. The biggest toy auction is shortly after Christmas and it's wild. All auctions conducted at 358 West Harrison, Room 400. Exhibition earlier in the week lets you glimpse merchandise behind wire lockers. Catalog available. For dates and times, call Dead Letter Office, WA 2-9200.

The **Chicago Police Department** conducts a dozen auctions yearly—six for bicycles (fabulous buys at these) and the rest for general merchandise, which often includes valuable jewelry, appliances, TV sets, tools, clothing, auto tires, wheels and hubcaps, etc. Much of the merchandise is stolen, some is recovered goods from stolen cars, some is abandoned merchandise, all of it, obviously, has never been reclaimed. Auctions are generally on Saturday at 10 AM with advance exhibition. Phone WA 2-4747, Chicago Police Central Services Division, for date and place.

Salvage and Surplus. **Underwriters Salvage Co. of Chicago,** 1032 West Washington, HA 1-6444. A huge warehouse of railroad salvage: furniture, damaged but reconditionable; appliances; toys; clothing; cameras; canned goods; cosmetics and so forth. Hours vary so phone before going.

Leon Korol Co., Inc., 3900 North Elston, 583-5484. Specializes in closeouts and surplus stocks of housewares, china, silverware, glassware, flatware, utensils.

Able Surplus Sales, 1737 East 87th Street, RE 4-1200. Drugs, cosmetics, toiletries, are the specialty here.

Federal Surplus Sales, 1245 South Wabash, 939-6235. Army and navy closeouts, camping equipment, tarps, toys, some gift items, clothing, shoes, novelties.

Edna and Jerry's Postal Auction & Unclaimed Items, 3041 West Irving Park, 463-8335. A little shop crammed to the ceiling with small buys, generally at less than half of retail since Edna and Jerry hound the Post Office auctions. Inexpensive toys and school supplies are two of the best buys here. Also glassware, lamps, lamp shades (usually at $1 regardless of size), garden items, salad servers, house paints, etc. Closed Wednesday and Sunday, 10:30 AM to 6 PM all other days.

Pets. The **Anti-Cruelty Society,** 157 West Grand, 664-8388, offers healthy household pets—male dogs $8, females $18 (includes cost of spaying, an enforced requirement to guard against a population explosion of strays). Male cats $3; females $13 (spaying again). Canaries and parakeets $1. Occasionally other kinds of animals are available. In late fall, after the hunting season, there's a plethora of sporting and other large dogs. Monday through Friday, 9 AM to 4:30 PM, Saturday to 12:30 PM. Groups may make appointments for four weeks of Saturday morning classes in animal first aid and care.

Thrift Shops. The city is dotted with them, and once in a while genuine finds are to be found. The most likely time for luck is mid-April through early May and mid-September through early October when stocks swell as the prologue to Chicago's traditional household moving times. Unlike their counterparts in Washington, D. C., Chicago thrift shops, run by women's boards as money-raising ventures for private schools, hospitals and charities, permit the volunteers who man the shops to get first crack at the best stuff that comes in. The volunteers are savvy—that's why the real treasures are few. Still, for furniture, china, glassware, the shops are worth browsing.

Oldest and most social is the **White Elephant Shop** of Children's Memorial Hospital, 411 North LaSalle. Also try **Michael Reese Hospital Service League Thrift Shop,** 54 West Chicago; the **Thrift Shop,** 729 North Clark, run for the benefit of the University of Chicago, as is the **Thrift Shop** at 11416 South Michigan; **Children's Asthma Research Institute & Hospital Thrift Shop,** 3708 North Broadway; **Christopher House Thrift Shop,** 1418 West Fullerton; **Gold Coast Resale Shop,** 866 North State; **Parker's Bazaar,** 2565 North Clark; **Catholic Salvage Bureau,** 3514 South Michigan; **Salvation Army Thrift Shop,** 509 North Union. Like these last two, **Goodwill Industries of Chicago** has a number of retail shops around the city, but the most interesting is the headquarters shop at the rehabilitation center, 120 South Ashland, 738-3860, where the leading item is fur coats for dogs made from old donated furs. The canine coats sell for $5, and when the weather turns brisk, the Cadillacs are literally lined up.

HELP!...SOME ESSENTIAL INFORMATION

13

Street Numbering System
Emergency Services
Regular Telephone Services
Local Transportation
Cross-Country and Global Transportation
Information Services
Six Services for Chicagoans New and Old
Services—Free and Fee

CHAPTER 13

HELP!...SOME ESSENTIAL INFORMATION

Chicago is undoubtedly one of the world's worst-informed cities when you want reliable information. The natives do their best to be helpful, but they almost never know with any degree of accuracy what services exist outside their own neighborhood. And Chicago is still a city of neighborhoods—76 of them.

The trouble is, there's no single central source of information in Chicago, no great official mother figure of a facility with computerized information spewing out sources of emergency services and all sorts of facts visitors need to save body and soul. There is a Visitor's Bureau in the Civic Center, but it's not open on Sunday. In summer there is a tourist information kiosk on State Street near Madison; it's not open on Sunday, either. The Visitor's Bureau at the Association of Commerce and Industry evidently makes no attempt to update the information in its files. Sometimes a Bell Telephone operator can be helpful; if she can't, ask for her supervisor and hope she is willing to go beyond the Bell system of rote answers.

STREET NUMBERING SYSTEM

Chicago's street numbering system has logic—yet is confusing. The downtown section has from the beginning been anchored to the area just south of the mouth of the Chicago River. The river divided the early city into a South Side, a North Side, and a West Side. Dead center for street numbering are State and Madison streets in the Loop, with every block continuing for 100 numbers, whether they are used or not. Furthermore, even numbers always indicate a building on the north or the west side of a street, while odd numbers always mean the location is on the south or the east side of a street.

Chicago Street Number Map

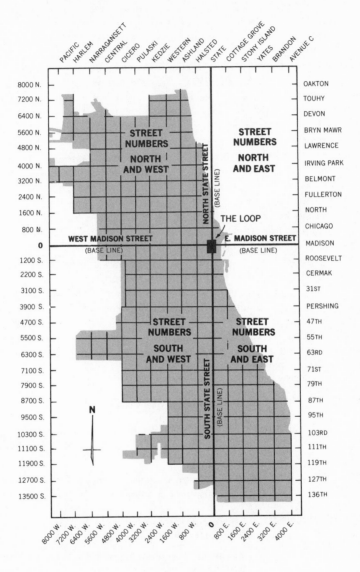

Note: Margin numbering denotes one mile intervals.
Corresponding street names appear in opposite border.

©Copyright R.McN.

Theoretically, all north-south streets south of Madison have the word "South" as part of their address, while those north of Madison include the word "North," i.e., North Michigan Avenue. In conversation, Chicagoans aren't always this specific, so get in the habit of asking whether they mean north or south. Otherwise, you may go miles in the wrong direction. If you're going to be here for more than a couple of days and expect to be driving around a great deal, get a *Rand McNally Chicago Street Guide,* which pinpoints the location of every Chicago street whether numbered or named. There's also a street guide in the front of the classified telephone book, the Yellow Pages.

On the preceding page is a map of the principal streets. To save time, use tollways rather than expressways. Tollway entry fees are 35¢ for passenger cars, and in a few cases where places are quite far out of the city, you'll pay another 35¢ en route. If you prefer to avoid those fees, use a map and plan an alternate route, but keep in mind that you may spend an extra hour driving.

Expressways are free. The expressway you'll use most often will be the Eisenhower. From the Loop you get onto it via Congress Parkway, which is 500 south, or from West Wacker Drive.

Chicago street signs are maddening. They bear a street number such as 31st Street or a name, but never in useful small print the cross street or the block number they're located at. Furthermore, street signs have been put up in a haphazard way. Sometimes they're on the right side of a street above a stop sign, but just as often they will be on the left side of the street so that you have to look back while driving to see what you've just crossed. On streets such as Ogden, Archer and Milwaukee, which are angle streets, you'll curse the entire system. So do Chicagoans.

EMERGENCY SERVICES

Police:	Dial **PO 5-1313***	Or, dial O for Operator,
Fire:	Dial **FI 7-1313**	ask her to connect you.

Hospitals: In a crisis, go directly to Emergency at one of these hospitals, the city's finest:

Near North Side: **Chicago Wesley Memorial Hospital,** 250 East Superior, **DE 7-6500**

Passavant Memorial Hospital, 303 East Superior, **WH 4-4200**

---

* Police Department Headquarters, WA 2-4747.

Near South Side: **Michael Reese Hospital and Medical Center** (also Sarah Morris Children's Hospital), 29th Street at Ellis Avenue, **CA 5-5525**

Mercy Hospital, 2520 South Prairie, **VI 2-4700**

South Side: **Albert Merritt Billings Hospital** (Also Wyler Children's Hospital), 950 East 59th Street, **MU 4-6100**

Mid-North: **St. Joseph's Hospital,** 2900 North Lake Shore Drive, **528-1000**

Near West Side: **Presbyterian-St. Luke's Hospital,** 1753 West Congress, **738-4411**

Far North Side: **Evanston Hospital,** 2650 Ridge, Evanston, **492-2000**

Physicians: To locate a competent physician, ask the switchboard operator at any of the above for names and phone numbers of staff members. All staffs at these hospitals will be specialists. If you think you have flu or feel terrible but don't know what's wrong, the specialist you want is an internist (internal medicine).

Ambulance: Dial **FI 7-1313** to get the finest, fastest service in Chicago. The Chicago Fire Department has 25 ambulances positioned throughout the city, guarantees that one can get to the scene of any emergency within three minutes. Fire Department ambulances are free, but will take you to the closest hospital— not one of your choice.

Dental Emergency Service: **RA 6-4321.** This is the telephone number of the Chicago Dental Society's 24-hour emergency service. It furnishes names of society members who are available for crises.

Northwestern University (Chicago Avenue campus) and the University of Illinois at the West Side Medical Center maintain dental surgery clinics in connection with their schools of dentistry. During clinic hours, anyone may appear for emergency treatment.

Poison: **Poison Control Center** is located at Presbyterian-St. Luke's Hospital **(738-4411)** and is open on a 24-hour emergency basis. During the day, a number of other hospitals offer identical help. Phone the center and ask for the name and location of one nearest to you.

F.B.I.: Dial **431-1333**

Night Pastors: When you need a pastor, a counselor, a friend or someone to talk to at night when no churches are open, turn to **Fr. Robert Owen, MI 2-5096,** the Episcopal priest known to everyone as the Night Pastor. His five-room office and chapel at 30 East Oak (located over a snack shop) is open between 10 PM and midnight every night; the rest of the evening and early morning, you'll find him making his rounds along Rush Street (8 PM to 10 PM and midnight to 4 AM) or even pounding out "When the Saints Go Marching In" in a basement dive in the area. You can ask the proprietor of any establishment if he's seen him, and you'll be directed to him without delay when he's on the street. The man is marvelous.

Vanguard Bookstore, 1010 North State, is both bookstore and ministry to the young. Hours are 11 AM to 4 AM. Call **822-0066.** No chapel but lots of free coffee, conversation and help from any of five young pastors who know what they're doing and can be friends indeed.

Travelers Aid Society— incorporating Immigrants Service League ST 2-0950. The society offers emergency help of all kinds to travelers and nonresidents who are in difficulty in Chicago. This includes people who are physically or emotionally ill, people who are in flight for one reason or another, or who've fled to Chicago without exactly knowing why. The professional staff and volunteers can handle 27 different languages and every legitimate crisis situation imaginable. Services include financial aid, hospitalization, guidance and counseling, food, and temporary shelter. The society maintains Travelers Aid areas at O'Hare Airport, Greyhound Bus Depot, and the following railroad stations: Union, Dearborn, Grand Central and Illinois Central. The offices are at 22 West Madison Street, open from 8:30 AM to 9 PM every day, ST 2-8771. An answering service refers phone calls after hours. Phone 686-7562.

REGULAR TELEPHONE SERVICES

Telephone Information Operator: Dial **411**

Recorded Time: **CA 8-8000**

Servicio Amigo: Dial **727-7878.** Get Illinois Bell Telephone's Spanish-speaking operators, who will handle emergency as well as regular calls of any kind.

Weather: **WE 4-1212.** Hourly U.S. Weather Bureau reports, often in sharp contrast to reality. As with radio station forecasts, it's as if that old-fashioned device, a window, were nonexistent.

Long-Range Weather Forecasts: 5-day weather forecast, maximum and minimum temperature forecast, and auxiliary information. **WA 2-3251**

Pilot Weather Briefing at O'Hare Airport: **686-2157**

Ski Weather Reports: **CE 6-SNOW** also **346-9554** (for ski conditions across the entire U.S.)

Sports Scores: **222-1234**

Stock Market Reports: **WE 9-1600**

Long Distance Operator: Dial **211**

Long Distance Information: To get the telephone number and address of any person or any business anywhere in the country, dial his (its) Area Code plus **555-1212.** The operator who answers will provide the information.

Western Union: **WA 2-7111**

Phone calls beyond the Chicago city limits: Toll charges to restaurants, museums, and other public places in the suburbs do not apply if the exchange starts with the letters **CO.** CO indicates a Chicago tie line, and 10¢ will put your call through. If the exchange is other than CO, dial **411** (Information) and ask the operator if the place you're calling has a tie line. Don't let her tell you there isn't such a thing—there is, and a suburban place may

289

have installed one since this book went to press. Furthermore, the current Yellow Pages indicates tie line numbers like this: Chgo#

Action Line: *Chicago Today* (daily newspaper) has an action line service (222-4444) which tape-records requests for information or action on citizen complaints. The service takes time because of the number of requests, but in crises, it tries to offer same-day help. **Beeline,** 321-1111, is the *Chicago Daily News* equivalent.

LOCAL TRANSPORTATION

CTA (Chicago Transit Authority), MO 4-7220. CTA operates all local bus and subway-elevated lines in the city. The personnel in the CTA's information department are helpful and will tell you how to get where, and whether you need to transfer. Personnel may also suggest you consult one of the free CTA route maps. The offer is well intentioned, but unless you're already thoroughly familiar with Chicago streets, you'll find the maps no more helpful than the ambiguous signs on the bus fronts. The problem with the maps is that they try to combine time and place on the single dimension of a drawing.

In summer, CTA expands its weekend bus schedule to include Adler Planetarium and the Caldwell and Dan Ryan Forest Preserves.

CTA shuttle-bus service operates up State Street to the Merchandise Mart, and from Grant Park parking facilities to the Loop. Depending upon time of day, commuter bus fares vary from 20¢* to 30¢. Assume a 20¢ fare; the driver will quickly correct you if you're wrong.

Continental Air Transport Co., Inc., 726-8720. This is the shuttle-bus service between O'Hare International Airport, 15 hotels in the Loop, the Near North Side, and Evanston. Schedules are realistic and the bus will get you to O'Hare almost as fast as a cab. Fees are less than half those of taxicabs, about $2.00. Between Midway Airport and the Palmer House it's $1.45.

United Motor Coach Co., FI 6-5000. This is a regular bus service to the western suburbs; O'Hare Airport is one of the route stops. For other suburban bus lines, check the Yellow Pages.

Illinois Central Commuter Trains, WA 2-4811, run to Chicago's South Side, and

South Shore Line, WA 2-0460, travels to nearby towns in Indiana. Both depart

---

*No Chicagoan has ever understood why suburban commuters get this break whereas the natives, whose tax dollars support the CTA, don't. Nor does anyone understand why the CTA fails to post schedules of the 20¢ time limitations on buses which have such.

from the Randolph Street Illinois Central Station at the southwest corner of Randolph and Michigan Avenue. Take ramp downstairs to underground station. These trains may also be boarded at the underground station at Van Buren and Michigan Avenue and at the grand old 1893 Romanesque Central Station at 12th Street, just east of Michigan Avenue.

Commuter Trains to the North Shore and western suburbs leave from Union Station and North Western Station. For a complete listing of all transportation to suburbs, and all city streets, get a copy of the *Rand McNally Chicago Street Guide* ($1).

Taxicabs. The service is good (you can phone for cabs in this city) but expensive. All cab company rates are identical under the Taxicab Code except for flat rates to 200 suburbs and communities in Illinois. Meters start at 40¢ before the cab pulls away from the curb and flick to 50¢ the moment it has traveled 1/5 mile. From then on they jump by dimes every 1/3 mile. There's also a wholly unnecessary 20¢ per additional passenger charge for each person in the cab over age 12.

Some examples of fares: from O'Hare Airport to the Palmer House (20 miles), approximately $6.50; from Marshall Field & Company to the Museum of Science and Industry, about $3.20; from Field's to Old Town, say, North Avenue and Wells Street, about $1.30. Plus 20¢ for each additional passenger. The suburbs that adjoin Chicago (Evanston, Oak Park, Dolton, Skokie, and so forth) are included in metered fares. Beyond these, the driver must phone his company for permission to take you deeper into suburbia and also to get the flat rate, $9 from Chicago to Winnetka, for instance. No cab may refuse to accept a passenger unless his "Not For Hire" sign has been showing. Use the following numbers to phone for a cab.

Yellow Cab Co., CA 5-6000. Operates 2,166 cabs, most of them new Checker Motor Company vehicles with sufficient headroom for the tallest passengers. Also has an extremely courteous, helpful lost and found department.
Checker Cab Co., MO 6-3700. Has 1,500 roomy cabs in operation and a good lost and found service.
American United Cabs, BI 8-7600; **Flash Cab,** LO 1-1444
These two firms have 460 cabs between them.

There are literally dozens of other cab companies with small fleets. See the Yellow Pages under "Taxicabs."

CROSS-COUNTRY AND GLOBAL TRANSPORTATION

Most flights are in and out of Chicago-O'Hare International Airport, but O'Hare is so jammed that old Chicago Midway Airport **(PO 7-0500)** has been reopened to accommodate the overflow. O'Hare, the world's busiest airport, takes advantage of its position and does not have a central telephone number for inquiries. For flight information, reservations and lost and found call the airline you're booked on. The airline companies are marvelous. They're service oriented and will provide full information about airlines other than themselves.

The following airlines operate in and out of Chicago as of this writing:

Domestic Flights

American Airlines, FR 2-8000

Braniff, FR 2-8900 (also international flights)

Continental, 686-6500

Delta, 346-5300

Eastern, 467-2900

Allegheny-Lake Central, 346-9020

North Central, 346-9860

Northwest Orient, FI 6-4900 (also international flights)

Ozark, 726-4680

TWA, 332-7600

United, 346-5700

International Flights

Air Canada, RA 6-3644 (operates from domestic terminal at O'Hare; you clear customs in Toronto)

Air France, ST 2-6181

Alitalia, 427-4720

BOAC, 332-7744

Irish Airlines (Aer Lingus), 236-7811

Lufthansa, AN 3-6670

Mexicana, HA 7-2585

Pan American, RA 6-6272

Scandinavian (SAS), HA 7-4200

Swissair, DE 2-4388

TWA, 332-1118

Most of the airline offices cluster around Monroe Street between Michigan Avenue and Wabash. Some also have hotel ticket offices which may be more convenient. Twenty-four foreign airlines that do not serve Chicago and domestic lines in the same position maintain convenient sales and information offices here. Check "Air Line Companies" in the Yellow Pages.

Commuter airlines come and go. When they're operational, it's mainly out of Meigs Field or Midway. Meigs, a small-plane airport in Lake Michigan just east of the Chicago shoreline, will know what lines are in service. Currently five lines out of Meigs service Illinois, Wisconsin, Indiana and Detroit. For information, phone 744-4787.

Passenger railroads and depots serving Chicago are:

Chicago & North Western Station, 500 West Madison, FI 6-7979; North Western trains and commuter trains only.

South Shore (underground) **Station,** 151 East Randolph, (Michigan Avenue), WA 2-0460: South Shore Line trains to Indiana and Illinois Central commuter trains.

Dearborn Station, Dearborn and Polk, 427-7500: Santa Fe, Chicago and Eastern Illinois, Erie-Lackawanna, Grand Trunk Western, Monon, Norfolk & Western railroads.

(Illinois) Central Station, 12th Street at Michigan Avenue, WA 2-2575: Illinois Central and two Penn-Central trains.

Grand Central Station, Harrison and Wells, WA 2-2211: Chesapeake & Ohio and Baltimore & Ohio railroads.

LaSalle Street Station, LaSalle and Van Buren, HA 7-4270: Rock Island Railroad (commuter lines).

Union Station, Adams at Canal Street, FR 2-6700: Burlington, Milwaukee, Gulf, Mobile & Ohio, Penn-Central railroads. Also commuter trains.

Chicago commuters flowing in and out of the North Western and Union depots use the stations' lost and found departments to great advantage during sudden downpours. What you do is step up and ask if a plain black umbrella with a plain wooden handle has been turned in. Usually some 40 umbrellas meeting the description are waiting to be claimed. If you're a gentleman, you return the umbrella the next day.

Steamships. At the moment, no passenger flagships serve Chicago, though 49 steamship lines.(freighters) provide regular overseas service from the Port of Chicago to 58 countries around the world. Since freighters often have accommodations for a dozen passengers, it's possible to book space on them. The three United States flag lines that have permanent route authority out of the Great Lakes and through the St. Lawrence are: American-Export Isbrandtsen Lines, ST 2-0535 (to Northern Europe, the Mediterranean); Farrell Lines, Inc., 427-9127 (African ports); and Moore-McCormack Lines, 346-6933 (Latin America). For foreign lines with sales offices here check "Steamship Companies" in the Yellow Pages. Use same listing for American companies with sales offices in Chicago.

Buses:

Greyhound Bus Lines Terminal Building is at the corner of Clark and Randolph streets, FI 6-5000. **Continental Trailways** is located at 20 East Randolph, RA 6-9500.

INFORMATION SERVICES

Chicago Tribune Public Service Office,* 33 West Madison, 222-3378; 435 North Michigan, 222-3232

A first-rate information office offering help in a number of categories. It is probably best-known for its telephone information service (222-3232) which

---

* Other services offered at the bureau are a Travel Bureau Service; Pamphlets Bureau; School, College & Camp Bureau; Etiquette Bureau; Motion Picture Bureau (2 films—*Trees to Tribunes* and the most recent All-Star Football Game).

was started in the 1920's. One woman handled it then; 17 are hard at work now.

It is almost easier to state what the telephone service won't do than what it can do for you. It will not do scholarly research or answer scholastic, medical and legal questions. It will not do a child's schoolwork for him. It will not help anyone win contests. But it will locate a business, advise on the right governmental agency to contact for help with a specific problem or furnish the name and address of any governmental department or agency at any level of government. It will answer questions about heads of government offices at all levels. It can handle a number of emergency questions, answer questions about the history of Chicago and events in the city, furnish directions within the city, provide general tourist information. It also has a reputation for its ability to answer any question about weight. For instance: Q. What is the weight of the world? A. Sixty-six sextillion, 588 quintillion. Q. Is that with or without people?

> Telephone information service hours: 8:30 AM to 6 PM Monday through Friday, to 5 PM Saturday. Michigan Avenue office open Monday through Saturday; Madison Street office open Monday through Friday.

Mayor's Office of Inquiry and Information, City Hall, 744-4000

When first established, its prime function was to answer questions about city services—Where do I go to get so and so? What department is responsible for such and such? It is also supposed to be able to answer questions about city government, provide information about city events and help persons who have been victimized by unscrupulous moneylenders or salesmen. It has been known to contact federal, state and county governments if necessary, and to this degree is more effective than the Better Business Bureau, which cannot take legal action on complaints. But overall, its main function is as a complaint department.

At the information booth in City Hall you can get material describing the functions of various departments of city government. A Spanish-speaking representative is available. A speaker's bureau is part of the service.

> Hours: 9 AM to 5 PM Monday through Friday; Saturday until noon.

Chicago Association of Commerce & Industry, 30 West Monroe, FR 2-7700

This is Chicago's Chamber of Commerce. It also happens to be the largest regional Chamber of Commerce in the United States, covering the eight counties that the U.S. Department of Commerce designates as Metropolitan Chicago—six in Illinois and two in Indiana. For businessmen thinking of Chicago as a possible market, it will provide all the necessary basic information.

Consulates and Other Foreign Government Representatives are listed as such in the Yellow Pages. Some 55 consulates have offices in this city.

Cercle Universitaire Franco-American is a group of French-speaking Chicagoans and French residents of Chicago ages 17 to 35. Members offer hospitality to visitors from France. To contact the current president, call the French Cultural Service, 919 North Michigan, 664-3525.

Marshall Field and Company has translators who speak 14 languages and who will take visitors from overseas through the store. The information desk on the third floor provides the service.

SIX SERVICES FOR CHICAGOANS NEW AND OLD

Chicagoland Community Guide. A guidebook of more than 200 pages for families moving here. It describes approximately 120 of the nearly 300 incorporated areas in Greater Metropolitan Chicago—population, distance from the Loop, driving time, tax rate, type of local government, median age, median income, fire rating, socioeconomic class of people in the community, vehicle tax, commuter ticket fares, etc. It's thorough and is revised annually for each edition. Available at Rand McNally map store, Kroch's and Brentano's bookstore, Marshall Field and Company, and from the publishers, Law Bulletin Publishing Company, 34 North LaSalle, Chicago 60602. Single copy price, $1.95.

Chicago's How To Do It Guide, A Directory of Human Needs. Despite its slightly ambiguous title, it's a very useful guide, listing major Chicago services for residents and ways to use them. It also lists city, county and federal facilities operated on behalf of citizens; names of ward committeemen, aldermen, state and congressional representatives; social and welfare services; civic information, including rights and responsibilities of landlords, tenants and home-owners. Updated yearly by the publisher, Back of the Yards Neighborhood Council. Single copy, 50¢, through Livingston and Associates Inc., 16 West Erie, Chicago 60611.

Community Referral Service, 123 West Madison, RA 6-0363

An exceedingly helpful service for Chicagoans at all income levels. If you don't know where to turn for guidance in marital, personal, family, child care, legal, psychiatric or financial problems, CRS does. It cuts through the confusing welter of available public and private agencies and directs you to the most appropriate one.

One of its most useful but least known services is the Homemaker's Service, which sends a qualified homemaker to a family when a mother is ill or has died, or when an individual living alone is bedridden. The homemaker is assigned on a day basis for as long as necessary, does everything but heavy-duty cleaning. Available to anyone regardless of income level; the fee slides according to ability to pay.

Chicago Police Department offers useful, free booklets: "Know the Law—For Newcomers to Chicago," "Know Your Chicago Police," "Help the Police Protect Your Home," and a booklet that tells women how to protect themselves. For copies, contact Public Information Division, Police Department Headquarters, 1121 South State, WA 2-4747, ext. 531.

Incidentally, the rate of city car thefts is high, but the Police Department rate of return almost matches. However, the Police Department is needed for other duties, and it's the height of folly in this city to ever leave a parked car unlocked. Don't, even in a supermarket parking lot.

In the light of a recent personal experience, the author retracts her once-glowing appraisal of the Internal Inspection Division of the Chicago Police Department. The IID has changed considerably since its inception by then-Superintendent of Police O. W. Wilson. It is supposed to provide redress for any citizen who feels he has been treated unfairly or been intimidated by a CPD cop. IID is probably best described in the words of one of its own men, Detective Jack Muller, who said: "[the IID is] a great big washing machine. Everything they put in comes out clean."*

Charity Fraud Division of Illinois Attorney General's Office will tell you whether the unknown charity that is plaguing you for donations is legitimate or not. Phone 527-5000.

SERVICES—FREE AND FEE

Banks: The four largest banks in Chicago are **Continental Illinois, First National Bank of Chicago, Harris Trust and Savings** and **Northern Trust.** They're all located in the Loop, have foreign currency exchange departments, can wire funds anywhere in the world, and will sell cashier's checks for cash. None will cash personal checks unless you know an officer who can vouch for you. All of these banks sell American Express Travelers Checks. There is no branch banking in Illinois.

Beauty Shops: Open Late Hours & Sunday **William's,** 49 East Oak, DE 7-0487, **Andreas,** 102 East Oak, 664-7522, and **Mr. Philip's,** 48 East Chicago, 337-9462. For regular beauty salons, see Chapter 12.

Box Lunches: **Gaper's Caterers,** a division of Stop & Shop, 16 West Washington, DE 2-4935. Superior box lunches, but you must order three days in advance. **Stop & Shop**

Chicago Sun-Times, March 14, 1968

offers carry-out roasted and fried chicken, cold cuts, salads, pastries, etc. A branch in the lower level of the 260 East Chestnut Building always has sandwiches, cold salads, hot dishes to go. See page 371.

Car Wash: **Red Carpet Car Wash,** 923 West Washington, MO 6-3750. Offers luxury service, uses a detergent so mild the car washers don't wear gloves. No steam guns—the owner doesn't believe in them. $2.25 Monday through Thursday; $2.50 all other days and day prior to holiday. Open 8 AM to 6 PM Monday through Saturday, to 2 PM Sunday. Standard Oil products for sale on premises. Also a gas now-wash later plan.

Charter: Executive cruiser bus may be chartered from **Continental Airways Transport.** Comes complete with bar, tables, stereo, hi-fi, TV, washroom and airconditioning. Charter planes and helicopters from any of two dozen firms listed under "Aircraft Charter & Rental Service" in the Yellow Pages. Sightsee over Chicago for an hour or take off on longer journeys.

Supplemental airlines, such as **Flying Tiger, American Flyer Corp.,** and **Corporate Air Transport,** are available for group charter to fly anywhere in the world. To charter yachts or sailboats, page 204.

Limousines for rent are listed in the Yellow Pages under "Livery Service." **Mack's Livery Service, Inc., Chateau Cadillac,** and **Union Club Motor Livery, Inc.,** offer chauffeur-driven Cadillacs. The two Cadillacs at the **University Club,** RA 6-2840, may also be rented, but there's often a long waiting list for them. One Howard Risner operates a one-man limousine service complete with television set, red carpet which he rolls out upon arrival at your destination, and a recorded victory march which plays simultaneously and very loudly thereby guaranteeing a grand exit. Phone him at NA 5-8820, if not home his answering service will connect you to his car phone.

For automobile rental see Yellow Pages.

Copy Service: Coin-operated copy machines of various kinds (25¢) are to be found in most banks; on the third floor of the **Playboy Building,** 919 North Michigan, 50¢; at **Marina City Copying Service** in the lobby of the office building at 300 North State Street (a Xerox). **Aims Services, Inc.,** makes Xerox copies (25¢ per) at three downtown locations and has pick-up and delivery service; phone HA 7-1880.

Repass Letter Service, Inc., 29 South Wabash, CE 6-4056, has a Xerox 2400 Copy Center, and coin-operated self-service machines. For others see "Photo Copying" in the Yellow Pages.

Delivery Services: **Railway Express Agency** and **Air Express** (same organization) will pick up and ship parcels. For rates and schedules call HA 7-9700. For pick-up service, WA 2-7214. **Greyhound Package Express** delivers to all stops on its routes and is good for small packages. Phone 346-6540. **Continental Trailways** has the same service, RA 6-9500. In both instances, you deliver and pick up. Bonded local messenger services will be found in the Yellow Pages. Chicagoans also use taxicabs—illegal but only slightly so, and often the fastest service available.

Dog Boarding: **Collar & Leash,** 810 North Wabash, SU 7-1751, takes all breeds of dogs to its Country Kennels for boarding; it has combination indoor quarters with outdoor runs. Depending upon size of dog and suite, daily fee is $2 to $3. Advance reservations usually essential. Kennels are on Route 45 at Half Day, Illinois, NE 4-3730.

Cliff Wallace, considered the all-time great trainer of springers and retrievers, boards and trains both at his Wadsworth, Illinois, kennels. **Val Christensen,** owner of Richmond Game Fields, a daily fee game preserve at Chain O'Lakes near Wilmot, Wis., also has good hunting-dog boarding facilities.

European Apothecary: **Merz Brothers Drugs,** 2921 North Lincoln, LA 5-0184 A true European pharmacy dealing in drugs and prescriptions only. There isn't a hot water bottle on the premises, though pharmacist Ralph Merz does have soft white cat pelts with brown markings on hand for ladies with low back pains. The shop was opened by his grandfather in 1875, on downtown

Clark Street, and came north as the city did. The pharmacy is immaculate and thoroughly modern except for a row of rocking chairs in graduated sizes for waiting patrons from age three up. Pharmacist Merz caters almost exclusively to transplanted Europeans; he and his staff speak nine languages and can accommodate anyone. Hundreds of herbals available, plus basics, and custom compounding, including ointments and tinctures no longer made by major drug houses. On any Saturday, the place is mobbed.

Film Processing, Professional: The three firms listed here do only custom processing and printing for advanced amateurs and pros. **Astra Photo Service, Inc.,** 6 East Lake, AN 3-6856; **Gamma Photo Labs, Inc.,** 319 West Erie, 337-0022 (both firms do b/w and color); **Color Technique,** 100 East Ohio, DE 7-5051.

Eastman Kodak has a processing lab and color print service at 1712 South Prairie, WA 2-9691. Everybody's film is accepted here. Hours: 8 AM to 4:30 PM Monday through Friday. Or leave films at one of approximately 30 authorized Kodak dealers in the Loop who'll send the film to this address for you.

Florists Open on Sunday: **Mangel Florist,** one of the finest old Chicago floral establishments, keeps its shops open until 1 PM on Sunday. They're in the Palmer House, Drake Hotel, Sheraton-Blackstone Hotel, Conrad Hilton Hotel. The friendliest florist on the entire Near North Side, Henry, who keeps his little **Esquire Flower Shop,** 1017 North Rush, DE 7-5674, open all day Sunday, and nights to 10 PM, is especially good on chrysanthemums and human relations—when you become a friend, you have to fight to keep him from giving you the flowers you want to buy. He's also the only florist known to sell Queen Anne's lace. For other florists open on Sunday in outlying neighborhoods, see the Yellow Pages.

Formal Wear Rental: If Chicago men don't rent from **Gingiss Brothers,** 30 West Lake, 263-7071 (page 231), they rent from **Seno & Sons,** 185 North State, ST 2-1115.

Women's formal wear rental is offered by **Estelle Nye,** who also rents bridal gowns, furs and bridesmaids' gowns. Miss Nye is at 3534 West Montrose, KE 9-0566.

Fur Rental: **Hertz,** 3355 North Drake, 583-5858, offers a weekend of full-length mink for $50 plus free pick-up and delivery service. **Seno** (above) rents white fox shrugs and mink capes and stoles. For others, see the Yellow Pages.

Health Services: **Northwestern University** has a free Glaucoma Test Center on the Chicago Campus, 303 East Chicago. Open 5 PM to 7 PM Wednesday. Free and low-fee health services offered by the **Chicago Board of Health** include clinics, infant welfare clinics, cancer prevention center, dog-bite center, VD clinics, etc. Phone Central Office in the Chicago Civic Center, 744-4346.

Senior Citizens: **Little Brothers of Notre Dame,** 500 West Division, 337-0626, are young Frenchmen who came to Chicago a few years ago. They specialize in aid to senior citizens of all nationalities, including visits to those who are housebound and help to the poor and ill.

Maid Service & Domestic Help: You can rent maid service by the hour from a number of firms listed in the Yellow Pages. **Perry Maid Service, Inc.,** 782-7642, has a staff of insured and qualified employees who also cook, do odd household jobs and party service. **Jane Estabrooks Household Registry** is one of the oldest top-drawer registries in the city. Also very snooty. You call it only for live-in help, trained to estate living, and child nurses or governesses. A firm in Pennsylvania listed in the Yellow Pages locates full-time, live-in domestic help from overseas.

Newspapers, Out-of-Town & Foreign: Most hotels and the newsstand at the southwest corner of Michigan and Chicago carry the daily and Sunday *New York Times*. The stand on the northwest corner of State and Randolph carries out-of-town papers from all over the country. So does a stand at Quincy and State.

Post Office News, 37 West Monroe, RA 6-4386, carries airmail editions of overseas papers and magazines from all over the world. Also recent back issues of magazines. **Astor Tower Hotel** gets daily editions of *Figaro.*

Magazines, Back Issues: Three stores in the 400 block of North Clark are dingy old places largely inhabited by mice, but also crammed with back issues. If you ignore the atmosphere (typically, the owners seem to resist your wanting to do business with them), you can find just about anything you're looking for. The stores are: **Gallery Book & Magazine Shop, Acme Book Store** and **ABC Magazine Service.** Their phone numbers are listed in the Yellow Pages under "Magazines, Back Number" but not here because experience has proved it's hard to get much information by phone.

Movers, household and furniture: **Pat Ryan,** 3038 North Wilton, LA 5-8388, is not only absolutely reliable but charges somewhat less than other movers because Mr. Ryan does all the estimating. His is a family business run with all the pride of such an operation, and the crews have been with him for years. If you have an ear for American regional speech patterns, you'll be fascinated with those of Mr. Ryan's crews.

Party Planners: **Gaper's** (page 296) for superior catering and serving. Barry Stone of **Finders, Inc.,** (page 271) for outrageous party ideas (944-7723), and a long list of firms listed in the Yellow Pages. One **Charles Napolitano,** GL 3-3645, (he has the balloon concession in Lincoln Park) can handle large orders for helium-filled balloons. **Astor Tower Hotel** will rent its French Roof Garden for parties. **Rainbo Paper Favor Works,** 116 West Illinois, supplies paper favors for large parties and conventions. Go to **Kroch's and Brentano's** on Randolph (page 320) for items for smaller affairs. Suburban Norridge, just west of Harlem Avenue, is headquarters for stables renting hayracks, stagecoaches, covered wagons, sleighs, rooms with fireplaces for square dancing or whatever. Among these are **Westown Stables** (riding lessons and horse rental only), 4815 North Clifton, GL 3-9822, and **Rocking H Stables,** 8500 Lawrence, GL 3-9721. The

Country Boys, Route 22, Prairie View, NE 4-3633, has an old-fashioned party barn, a picnic grove, and seven or eight pioneer-type vehicles, such as a Wells Fargo overland stagecoach, scaled to child-size. Dandy place to hold children's parties, winter included, because the owners then bring out horse-drawn sleighs. Between June 1 and Labor Day you can hold a party for children under eight in the Party Tent at the **Lincoln Park Zoo.** It's located to the east of the central bird enclosure in a fenced-in area of its own. The Zoo Society provides party hats and favors and the Park District donates the services of a recreation leader to help supervise the patting of small animals such as rabbits. The area also contains play equipment. Fee for Zoo Society members, $5. For nonmembers, $15. Reserve by phoning 935-6106.

Post Offices, 24-Hour Service: The **U.S. Post Office** straddling the Eisenhower Expressway is Chicago's Main PO and is open around the clock. Enter at 433 West Van Buren. Phone is 353-2420-1-2-3-4.

The **AMF** (Air Mail Field) **O'Hare** PO keeps the same hours. It's hard to find the first time (phone for directions—686-2120), but is worth the trouble because airmail goes out on the next plane.

Private dance lessons: **Joseph Regets** gives private dance lessons in your home, in town as well as in the suburbs. His phone is 432-8950; 304 Green Bay Road, Highwood.

Rental Firms: **Hertz Rent-All,** 583-5858, rents everything from baby carriages to sitz baths; ski equipment, TV sets; air conditioners; all the necessities for a party—including matching china for as many as 1,800—each piece sterilized and delivered to you in a polyethylene bag (you can return it *dirty*); inhalation and therapy equipment; office machines, etc. This is a telephone business with same-day delivery. **Associated Rent-All, Inc.,** in Highland Park, ID 2-6333, rents party and guest needs, including garden awnings. Harry Oppenheimer's **H.D.O. Productions, Inc.,** in Highland Park, rents striped tents with bars, tables, chairs, dance floors to go under them, uniformed and insured car parkers. For others, see the Yellow Pages.

Repairs* of All Kinds: **Field's** main floor repair desk takes watches, jewelry, handbags, umbrellas (but only sentimental ones because repair is costly), luggage, silver and brass for replating, some china repair, some lamp repair, camera repair, and will also reline ice buckets and sharpen scissors. Free estimates. Field's also does excellent dry cleaning, especially of laces and other fine items.

Repairs, art objects, fine lamps, fine china and crystal: **Kankuro Matsumoto,** 226 South Wabash, WA 2-4110. Amid a hodgepodge of lamps, bowls, goblets, find the Matsumoto whose china and crystal repair is the finest in the country; you literally need infrared to see the repairs once made. Bonwit Teller and Field's refer customers here and also send in Boehm birds for work. People in every state in the Union send fine items to Mr. Matsumoto and have never yet been disappointed. **Carson Pirie Scott** has a very reliable crystal and glass repair shop on the eighth floor.

Repairs, eyeglasses, contact lenses: The three top firms in the city are **Almer Coe Optical Co.,** 10 North Michigan and 666 North Michigan; **House of Vision,** 30 North Michigan, 700 North Michigan and 135 North Wabash; **Uhlemann Custom Opticians,** 65 East Washington and Prudential Plaza. All three firms have additional locations. See "Opticians" in the Yellow Pages. All can make emergency repairs and fast lens replacement if you have a copy of your prescription with you.

Repairs, furniture, antique furniture: **Hannibal, Inc.,** 1919 North Sheffield, LI 9-7180, and **Art Furniture,** 2054 North Larrabee, MI 2-1299, do excellent repair, refinishing and restoration of antiques. **William Paul & Associates,** 411 West Armitage, 664-3887, does restorations, caning, weaving. **Industrial Workshop for the Blind,** 1850 West Roosevelt, run by Lighthouse for the Blind, does recaning and rushing at very reasonable prices but may need three to four months to do your work. The Novotny

* Repair services listed by name have been tried and proved reliable.

family of **Artistic Reed & Willow Co.,** 420 South Kolmar, 533-8720, custom-weave almost anything in wicker. **Hawk and Handsaw,** 733 North Wells, 944-5990, strip paint and varnish from anything.

Repairs, handbags, shoes:

Capitol Handbag Co., 55 East Washington, AN 3-6430, is a good place to take expensive handbags. **Schultz & Mark Bag Repair Shop,** 25 East Washington, CE 6-1156, make, repair and duplicate fine handbags, including petit point and needlepoint.

Sam the Shoe Doctor has five Loop shops, does good work and also reglazes leather purses. **Zoe's** in the Steven's Building Arcade at 16 North Wabash is a shoe shop that also restyles and dyes and does handbag repair. **Parisian** does good tinting, dyeing and shoe remodeling—17 North Wabash, DE 2-2311. On the Near North Side, **Lake Shore Shoe Repair Shop,** just west of Rush Street, 61 East Chicago, MI 2-1070, does excellent work and gives excellent shines. **Wabash Avenue Shoe and Valet Service,** 157 North Wabash, cleans and shines shoes (fine shines) and presses trousers while you wait. **Alex,** the expert who does Andrew Geller's work, is in the basement at 154 East Erie, MI 2-3569. He specializes in dyeing, rebuilding, custom making, and orthopedic adjustments. Open 8 AM to 6 PM Monday through Friday, to noon Saturday.

Repairs, sculptures:

Ralph Bornmacher, Contemporary Art Workshop, 542 West Grant Place, LA 5-9795, is a sculptor who also restores and mounts sculptures—all the art galleries in Chicago send their pieces to him.

Repairs, special automotive:

Ronnie Kaplan, an automotive engineer, has a shop at 5915 West Grand, and specializes in performance work on racing machines and passenger cars. **Paul Emerling** at Totoh Company, 2157 North Lincoln, specializes in restoration of vintage cars and foreign and sports cars and does beautiful work on both. All mechanics at Totoh are as dependable as any foreign car mechanics in the city.

Repairs, garments, textiles:

Stitch in Time shop is no more, but the two ladies who ran it for so long in a calm, unpretentious example of what integration is all about, still accept in their homes, knits, wools, linens, laces and tapestries for reknitting, reweaving, and repair. Miss **Josephine Wilkins** can be reached at 764-3601; her mailing address is 1139 Lunt Avenue, Chicago, 60626. Miss **Lillian Boling's** phone is 667-4651; her address is 6226 South Eberhart, Chicago, 60637.

Repairs, watch: **Alfred Blum,** 55 East Washington, DE 2-1166; **Ingolf Pedersen,** 7 West Madison, ST 2-9340.

Emergency Repair Services: (known but not tried) Handbag repair, one-day service including zippers—**Becker's Leather Mfg. Co. Inc.,** 27 East Monroe, AN 3-1364. Zipper repair, handbags, luggage, garments, **A-Ability Leather Repair Service,** 7 West Madison, FR 2-7754. **Ace Leather Goods Repair Service** offers the same service, 32 North State, AN 3-3946. Cane and umbrella repair while you wait, A-Ability. Reweaving in two-hours, **American Weaving Co.,** 5 North Wabash, DE 2-1693.

24-Hour Service Station: **Ontario-Dearborn Shell Service,** 30 West Ontario, WH 3-1711.

Dearborn & Erie Service Station, 659 North Dearborn, SU 7-8164.

Congress & Dearborn Service Station, 51 West Congress, 939-7724.

24-Hour Towing: **State & Pearson Sinclair Towing Service,** 813 North State, MO 4-2100.

Out-of-Town Telephone Directories: **Marshall Field & Co.,** has a full set on the third floor near the waiting room. So has **O'Hare Airport,** in the international terminal. **Chicago Public Library** has phone books from all over the world. Every hotel has a Manhattan directory. **Illinois Bell Telephone** general offices will sell you out-of-town directories provided you're not planning to use them for mail-order solicitation; offices are located at 212 West Washington, RA 7-9411. You can also find directories from 1876, the first year of publication in this city. Open 9 AM to 11 AM and 2 PM to 4:30 PM.

TV Rental: **Color King TV, Inc.,** 56 West Division, WH 3-7171. Also rents hi-fi and stereo.

Tickets: **Ticket Central,** 212 North Michigan (back section of Lowe's Discount Records) 782-7023, handles tickets to all events in Chicago except Blackhawk and Bear games. There's a 25¢ charge, but it's worth it in view of the accessible location. Open 9:30 AM to 9 PM Monday, Thursday, Friday, to 5 PM alternate days. Closed Sunday. See also page 179, Joe's Cigarstand.

Taxidermists: Two of the best are **Wanke Bros.,** 4543 North Lincoln, RA 8-1440, and **Acme,** 3845 West Grand, SP 2-2828, which also does handsome safari game mountings and sells exotic fur rugs.

Wig Rental: The name of the place is **One Touch of Glamour, Inc.,** 6130 North Broadway, SH 3-8100. Wigs are of 100 percent human hair, sterilized. Rental is $4 per day, three-day minimum rental. $2 each additional day.

PART V: The Undiscovered City

LIONS' TAILS AND ANGEL'S TOE—
A CHILDREN'S CHICAGO

14

The Best Museums for Children
Children's Theatre
Music for Children
Showbiz—Loosely Used
Other Entertainments
Shopping—For and With Children
Expeditions

CHAPTER 14

LIONS' TAILS AND ANGEL'S TOE—
A CHILDREN'S CHICAGO

Like an indulgent mother, this city lets children play on the grass in its parks, climb into its trees and onto its monuments. No child has ever been told he may not touch the big toe of the Wynken, Blynken and Nod guardian angel statue in the Lincoln Park Zoo—or that he must not swing from the tails of the noble lions flanking the entrance to the Art Institute. So, bronze toe and tails are as bright as the day they were cast, though overall the sculptures are green-black with age and oxidation. Chicago expects children to *be children*.

Parents who bring their youngsters here naturally think of summer as the ideal time to come. Yet gray November is just as rewarding. The city's pace zooms, and a child is swept up in its energy. A Christmas visit is a heady experience—glittery department store windows, Santas and Salvation Army bell ringers on every corner in the Loop, the feeling of snow in the air and, if a child is lucky, a snowfall, the early 4:30 dusk with its sense of things-about-to-happen, and enough Christmas happenings for children to surfeit them (See Christmas in Chicago, page 435).

Picnics in the park are not solely the prerogative of Chicagoans—any delicatessen will pack a box lunch for you. Beaches welcome you and provide bathhouses, snack stands and lifeguards. Bookstores are as easy to find as dime stores. Hotels provide baby-sitters. Three hospitals are solely for children: **Children's Memorial Hospital** (DI 8-4040), Mid-North; **Wyler Children's Hospital** (MU 4-6100) at the University of Chicago on the South Side; **Sarah Morris Children's Hospital** (225-5525), part of the Michael Reese Medical Center, mid-point between the two. (All hospitals offer emergency room care.) Baby carriages and strollers can be rented from **Hertz Rent-All,** 3355 North Drake, 583-5858, and if the carriage you brought with you breaks down, the **Baby Carriage Hospital,** 2633 North Milwaukee, BE 5-2222, has free pick-up and delivery service, along with parts and repairs.

THE BEST MUSEUMS FOR CHILDREN

Most children from age ten up are fascinated equally by the mummies at the Oriental Institute, the uglier species of fish at the Shedd Aquarium, the cozy little skyline planetarium at the Chicago Academy of Sciences, the greater display of all the heavens at the Adler Planetarium and the special weekend children's stars shows, and that part of the Lincolniana collection at the Chicago Historical Society that displays the bed in which Lincoln died—an item of inexplicable appeal.*

Field Museum of Natural History (see also page 132), Roosevelt and Lake Shore Drive, 922-9410

Its Self-Guided Journeys are designed to help children get the most out of exhibits. Each journey, part of a series, highlights specific interest. For example, "Who's Who In The Prehistoric World?" explores the age of dinosaurs with a quiz. Chicago children take these to earn titles and awards.**

If the current journey does not seem suitable for your children, ask for a descriptive folder of the museum and head for the exhibits you think they'll most enjoy—perhaps the precious gems collection or the American Indian galleries. Two tape-recorded tours are also available—one on the world of nature and the other on the story of mankind. The cafeteria opens at 11 AM; the bookshop has excellent natural history books for children and inexpensive young collectors' items of all kinds (page 267). In summer, free films, far above average, like *Water Fun, Yellowstone and Its Bears, Potlatch Country*. Generally on Thursday at 10 AM and 1 PM, but check.

Chicago Academy of Sciences (also page 136), 2001 North Clark, LI 9-0606

If your child has never been to a natural history museum, a visit here should supercede the Field Museum since the academy's exhibits are capsule versions of some at the Field Museum, and not as overwhelming. The academy also offers free science films for children on Saturdays at 2:30 PM. Some deal with life in faraway places, others with life in America, with animals, outer space, the universe. Films are highly rated.

---

* It also had great appeal for an inebriated robber on one occasion who hid under it shortly before the museum closed, then emerged to steal two pistols from the gun collection. He was caught by two policemen who found him at Damen Avenue drunkenly waving the pistols and bragging about duels with Western sheriffs. But according to a news story, what gave him away was not that he was waving the pistols but that he was waving pistols of obvious antiquity, dated 1846.

** Four tours successfully completed give a child the title of Museum Traveler. Further journeys graduate him to Museum Explorer. The last journey in the series, the Voyage of the "H.M.S. Beagle," bestows membership in the Discoverers' Club and a host of rewards.

Junior Museum and Little Library, Art Institute of Chicago (page 153), Adams and Michigan, CE 6-7080

It's great. Its exhibits appeal to very young children, hold the attention of older youngsters: the simplicity evolves from a judicious use of space, the sophistication from the selection of art on display. None of the art is childish.

A series of small galleries scaled to small persons offers art to be viewed and ideas about art to try. For instance, a child can experiment with the concept of chiaroscuro in a wall-hung display that invites him to move plastics of black, white and clear until he produces a design that pleases him. A second exhibit lets him create Mondrian-like patterns; elsewhere, gold paper squares let him recreate in a single dimension Bertoia's "Construction After Enjoyment of Mulberry Tree."

In the Rainbow Gallery he learns about color from an imaginative audio-visual display. In another gallery, he learns how artists use size to create rhythms, surprises, a sense of power, a sense of mystery—and that "size can be small but the measure is delight." The art that illustrates these concepts is prize art—a 19th-Century Japanese screen, a Magritte, a Baule ancestor figure, a Westermann wood sculpture, and some tiny carved figures.

In the Junior Museum Auditorium, an older child has the time of his life being entertained (and taught) by artists who give demonstrations from October through June (Meet The Artists—Saturdays at 11:30). In the Little Library he finds books beckoning from three walls and sink holes with sunken pedestal tables where he may sit to read. Children who can read alone are allowed to stay here alone; one finds them totally engrossed in books written at grade and high school levels on the visual arts, Indian crafts and lore, archaeology, art history, theatre, costume history and so forth. Leave your avid readers here while you view the art collections upstairs.

Open daily, 10 AM to 4:30; Thursday to 8:00; Sunday, 1 PM to 4:30. Free.

Museum of Science and Industry (page 137), East 57th Street and South Shore Drive, MU 4-1414

It's often called the greatest push-button museum in the world. Even if it isn't, there are enough self-operative mechanical marvels to keep children over eight busy a full day. Naturally, they have to push every button, turn every crank—and sometimes they stay in front of an exhibit long enough to learn something from it.

In addition to the ubiquitous animation, there's a captured World War II German submarine to explore and a working model of a coal mine that is so realistic a number of visitors have congratulated the museum on its luck in discovering the mine under its foundation. There is the Colleen Moore Fairy Castle—a sumptuous dollhouse complete with plumbing and electrical system. Its gem-laden interiors were designed in a style the decorator calls "Early Fairy." A souvenir brochure is available.

Yet, the single most absorbing exhibit is one that has nothing to do with levers or fairy tales. It is the miracle of reproduction in the glass-walled incubator where one hundred ready-to-hatch chicks do so daily. To children, who literally must be torn from the railing because it is time to leave, this is the greatest "do-it-yourself" of all. And, of course, there is a museum store (all Chicago museums have these).

Hinsdale Health Museum, 40 South Clay, Hinsdale, FA 5-1900

Its name could scarcely be more inappropriate, since "health" to Americans either conjures up dreary notions about nutrition or scary ideas about disease. Neither kind of exhibit exists here. The HHM is a wholly contemporary museum about human life—one of the finest you'll ever visit.

Literally any questions children have about the human body are answered satisfactorily by a person or an exhibit at HHM. The displays are three-dimensional with push buttons, levers, lights and phones for self-instruction. A child can hear his own heartbeat, test his lung capacity, learn how a baby is born. Films and a lecture by the HHM's famous talking glass lady also help a child understand the human body—"the house we live in only once." In terms of self-tours, the exhibits are superior to those at the Museum of Science and Industry.

Two remarkable high school biology teachers are the entire lecture staff. Their sex education discussions cannot be praised highly enough. They start with a question—how does human life begin? The answer is explicit, beginning with an exhibit of a whale, a man, and a mouse, and the indisputable proof of the fact that all three mammals originated from egg cells of exactly the same size. Then follows a discussion about reproduction.

The lectures are simple, unsentimental, realistic. The birth of a human baby is shown with cutaway models. The inevitable question about Siamese twins is answered. There are no questions the instructors cannot answer satisfactorily—even the one always raised by Roman Catholic schoolboys accompanied by nuns: Why is masturbation a sin?

Because school demands get priority and lectures are now booked a year ahead, the only way your children can hear one of the sex education lectures is by phoning in advance to ask if a group at their age level is scheduled on the day you plan to visit—and if you may join it. Excluding Easter week, the director's office will do its best to accommodate you.

> Open daily 9 AM to 5 PM; Sunday, 1 PM to 5 PM. Closed holidays. Free. Eisenhower Expy to Route 83. South on 83 to Chicago Ave. East to Clay St. South ½ block to the HHM's free parking facilities. Or by Burlington train from Chicago Union Station. Trains leave at about one hour intervals. The museum is 5 blocks west of the Hinsdale Station.

Timke's Indian Museum, Haddow & Francisco, Downers Grove, 968-1234

What began many years ago as one man's hobby has become a three-generation family involvement with the first Americans. Part of the involvement has led to a collection of more than 1,000 items from 70 Indian tribes; part has led to a quiet but steady collection of clothing, food, toys and cash for distribution to American Indian centers across the country.

Though the collection is informally housed in the Timke home, it bears no resemblance to the so-called roadside "museums" that are generally little more than dismal collections of trivia. The Timkes are avid researchers, interested in accuracy: "We want to be sure everything we tell the children is true." So a visit here includes 45 minutes of cultural anthropology presented informally by Mrs. Timke (Sr. or Jr.), who explains the designs of ceremonial blankets, Cochiti drums, kachina dolls, the magic number eight, the thunderbird and the turtle.

The Timkes also sell authentic, contemporary American Indian crafts (proceeds go to American Indian centers), Western gear, and saddles, bridles, tack. Outside, the family is building an authentic tepee village and a false-front Western town—bank, saloon, stable and store. Their horses and dogs are meant to be petted. Their grounds are available for picnics, and with a little advance notice they'll furnish hamburgers, cheeseburgers, hot dogs, potato chips and soft drinks at 75¢ per person. On Sunday afternoons, when weather permits, the head of the household, once a rodeo rider, puts on an outdoor show—trick roping and bullwhip stunts—and introduces visiting Indian chiefs. Show hours are at 1 PM and 3 PM on Saturday and Sunday for family groups. Museum admission is 50¢ for adults, 25¢ for children. Closed Mondays and for an unscheduled two weeks sometime during the year when the Timkes take their annual trip through Indian country to add to their collection and visit tribes. Otherwise, open 10 AM to 8 PM, but it's best to call for an appointment.

> Eisenhower Expy to Highland Ave. exit. Left on Highland to Ogden, right
> on Ogden to Belmont Road. Left on Belmont approximately one mile to
> Haddow. Right on Haddow five blocks to Francisco.

Frontier Museum, Illinois Route 25 just south of Illinois Route 72, East Dundee

Robert R. Beyer, a middle-aged bachelor, is another individual who's turned a hobby into a first-rate museum collection—in this case Americana from 1800 to 1910. Like the Timkes, his knowledge about his collection is sound, stems not from formal education but from personal interest and a lot of rooting about through the Midwest. His museum, an authentic red barn at the edge of a horse pasture, includes a country store, post office, jail, Conestoga wagon, barbershop and a blacksmith shop with one of the biggest collections of smithy fittings in the country. His hundreds of smaller items include dolls and toys, pioneer musical instruments, *ladies'* shaving mugs, gold panning and mining equipment, household possessions, early gambling devices, pine coffins, snake oil and patent medicine bottles, frontier dental equipment—the list is endless.

Propelled by his own enthusiasm, the proprietor bounces about from exhibit to exhibit, certain you're as enthusiastic about his collection as he. And you are, for the entire social history of the frontier comes to life here.

At present, the museum is open only on weekends from spring through late fall. Phone before driving out: PE 6-3448 (Mr. Beyer's Chicago home phone).

Northwest Tollway (US 90) to Ill. Rt. 25. North (right) on 25. The museum is on the west side of the road just south of the Higgins Road intersection.

CHILDREN'S THEATRE

Newspaper entertainment listings of theatre for children generally do not specify whether performances are by professionals or by little amateurs enrolled in neighborhood drama schools. The latter have their largest appeal to prideful relatives who will overlook even the camp-chair seating. Professional children's theatre is to be found at:

Goodman Memorial Theatre, Monroe & Columbus Drive, CE 6-2337

The Goodman performances September through May are by adult actors. The performance level is excellent, the repertoire appropriate—*Androcles and the Lion, Treasure Island, Jack and the Beanstalk, Puppet Prince, Winnie-the-Pooh.* The theatre is small and handsome; the demand for seats high. Tickets must generally be reserved two to three weeks in advance; only in a blizzard are you likely to get same-day seats. Main floor $1.25 and $1.50. Mezzanine, 75¢. In summer, Goodman generally offers two plays at the Civic Theatre; write to Goodman address for advance information of these.

Second City Children's Theatre

To date, the able performances have been at several theaters. Check entertainment sections of newspapers or phone Second City, DE 7-3992.

Hull House Children's Theatre, 3212 North Broadway, 348-5622

Competence here, too, in plays of above-average interest.

Ivanhoe Children's Theatre, 3000 North Clark, 248-6800

Sunday afternoon performances, generally at 3 PM. Children's classics mainly for ages 5-13; *Cinderella, Rumpelstiltskin, Hansel and Gretel,* etc. Tickets, $1. The theatre is next door to the Ivanhoe Restaurant, long known for Elizabethan atmosphere, "catacombs" filled with fake skeletons and bones, and Sunday children's birthday parties—paper crowns, souvenirs, birthday cake. Children's dinner $2.50; special banquet menus available. Moderate-priced meals for adults. Free parking.

Pheasant Run Children's Playhouse, St. Charles, 584-1454 or 584-6300

Dinner theatre at noon—lunch followed at 2 PM on Saturdays by a good performance of a children's classic—seen from your lunch table. Pheasant Run is a complete resort, about 45 minutes from Chicago. Arrive early enough to browse through its Bourbon Street shops and explore the premises.

MUSIC FOR CHILDREN

Since 1918, Chicago mothers and grandparents have taken their children to the Tuesday afternoon **Youth Concerts** at Orchestra Hall. Besides the chance to see and hear one of the outstanding orchestras in the country, each season brings new delights: an opera, a drawing contest based on Ravel's "Mother Goose" Suite, a special performance by young soloists and more. Youth Concerts also sponsors an annual competition in the fall for student soloists, composers and conductors—a professional competition with auditions and the submission of original scores written for orchestral accompaniment. Any interested music student may get application forms by calling the Chicago Symphony office, 427-0362, or by writing to the General Manager, Chicago Symphony Orchestra, 217 South Michigan, Chicago, 60604.

For program information, phone the ticket office at the above number. If you can't bring children to a matinee concert, try the Saturday evening Popular Concerts—an excellent alternate.

In July and August, the outdoor **Ravinia Festival** (page 171) programs special Saturday concerts for children: symphonies, an opera performed by the Northwestern University Opera Workshop, a hootenanny, brass and percussion ensembles from the Chicago Symphony Orchestra, a special matinee performance by the visiting New York City Ballet. Concert-goers sit in the modern outdoor pavilion or on the acres of well-maintained lawns (picnicking permitted). Lunch and soft drinks available at the Carousel Restaurant in the park. For time and programs, phone the Ravinia Festival Assn., ST 2-9696, or the ticket office (summer phone only), 273-3500. Suburbs, ID 2-1236.

Edens Expy (US 41) to Lake-Cook Road. East to Green Bay Road and Ravinia Park. Chicago & North Western trains stop at the gates.

Also in summer, special outdoor children's concerts in Grant Park, usually on a weekday morning at 11 AM. Free. Check time and dates with Park District, HA 7-5252. For children with strong musical backgrounds, also see Music, page 169.

SHOWBIZ—LOOSELY USED

Ripley's Believe It or Not Museum, 1500 North Wells, DE 7-6077

A commercial museum that is a triumph of a display artist's skill. You think you've gone through 92 miles of exhibits only to find you've been backtracking and upping and downing in a space scarcely bigger than a postage stamp. The artist has used interesting new architectural installations, and youngsters under 12 are impressed by the random curiosities displayed therein, like a model of a ferris wheel made from 30,000 toothpicks; a microcircuit that can slip through the eye of a needle; a five-pound hairball from a cow's stomach; old tombstones with quirky death sentences, like Robert Yeast's stone ("Pardon me for not rising"); a shrunken heads department; and, most fascinating of all to a four-year-old, the Iron Maiden "who has a funny man inside—he has long red hair and spikes all around." Admission: $1.25 for adults and 75¢ for children. A good place for a gloomy Sunday afternoon. Open from noon on.

OTHER ENTERTAINMENTS

Bernard Horwich Jewish Community Center, 3003 West Touhy, RO 1-9100

·Sunday afternoon and midweek matinee entertainment—folk singers, plays, professional ballet, etc., in programs selected especially for youngsters five and over. Modest admission fees vary with performers.

Chicago Public Library, Michigan at Randolph, CE 6-8922

Children's Hour every Saturday at 2:15 PM, October through April. Programs include stories, films, recordings for children ages 4 to 12. The library prefers that children attend without their parents, keeps them for you about one and a half hours. Free, but you need tickets. Reserve them by phone or request by mail.

Chicago Historical Society, Lincoln Park at North Avenue and Clark, MI 2-4600

Excellent free film programs, with lots of documentaries and fictionalized American history, three times daily on Tuesday and Wednesday in summer. Reservations necessary. Winter schedule offers Sunday feature films. Admission fee 25¢ on Sunday only.

SHOPPING—FOR AND WITH CHILDREN

Marshall Field & Co., 111 North State (Washington), ST 1-1000

Not many stores are able to devote a full city block to children. Field's can and does. On the fourth floor you can completely outfit any child, furnish a nursery and squander a savings account as you progress through aisle after aisle of dolls, stuffed animals, toys, antique toys, hobby sets, games, art and craft material, indoor and outdoor play equipment. It is impossible to cross this floor without going happily berserk—with the result that Field's has probably made more children happy than any other store in history.

As if the fourth floor weren't enough, there's the children's book department one floor down—13 different display counters of children's books, including one for old favorites you thought were long out of print—*all* the Oz books, for instance.

With children in tow, have breakfast or lunch at Field's—another tradition that reaches its zenith at Christmas when the entire store turns into a glittering fairyland. Randolph Street entrances admit breakfasters at 9 AM weekdays, 8:00 on Saturday. Shopping starts at 9:15 AM.

Sugar 'n Spice Shop, Carson Pirie Scott & Co., State and Madison, 744-2000

Take the escalator to the third floor, walk under a wildly imaginative papier-mâché sugarplum tree—doves, birdcalls, confections—emerge in an irresistible children's boutique. The shop is a showcase of gift suggestions—cuddle toys, children's luggage, beach sets and clothes.

With children, stop at the Old Fashioned Ice Cream Parlor, a turn-of-the-century goodies shop that brews coffee for exhausted adults. Or treat children to Moon lunches at Heather House (under $1) with souvenir Happy the Monkey kits.

Brooks Brothers, 74 East Madison, AN 3-0100

This branch of the East Coast establishment has both a boys' and a university department, and stocks Eton suits with matching caps for sizes 4 up. In youth sizes it offers polo coats, British warms (military coats), blazers, madras jackets, button-down oxford cloth shirts (girls and women regularly raid the department for these), ties, sweaters, shorts, knit shirts, khaki and corduroy trousers and outerwear. The Brooks look for boys is unmistakable, and the store has a proper Brooks air.

Saks Fifth Avenue, 669 North Michigan, WH 4-6500

Three shops on the children's floor here, infants to young teens. All the merchandise is handsome and very Saks Fifth Avenue—with prices to match. French and Swiss imports are exquisite; American markets are combed for dashing young styles. Chicago mothers pounce whenever the store has a sale, and the place is bedlam. If you can take it, the bargains are worth it.

Little Bramson, 700 North Michigan, 782-1080

The owners state frankly that Little Bramson is run exclusively for indulgent grandmothers. Unfortunately, the sales force interprets this to mean only grandmothers in sable and pearls. For these grandmothers there is courteous service.

Patsy Rue Children's Shop, 10th floor at 17 North State, DE 2-3480 or DE 2-9874

Mothers who do not choose to wear their status symbols while shopping will enjoy buying children's clothes from Miss Myrtle Kaplan, owner of Patsy

Rue. As one mother puts it, "Her staff always restores your faith in people." Concern for all customers has been Miss Kaplan's reputation for 35 years, and it explains why every mother who can afford it brings her youngsters to be outfitted here.

There are two shops, one for infants and children, the other for girls to size 15. The children's line begins at $6, skips along to Florence Eisman Originals at $50 and leaps to Piccolino Knits (made by a division of Gino Paoli) at $100 and more. Other imports from Portugal, Switzerland, Israel bring prices back within reason. So do the moppet styles made in this country by Gay Sprites, Merry Mites, Danskin, et al.

Les Enfants, 64 East Walton, MO 4-5222

A bright little shop in the English basement of an old brownstone on the Near North Side. Specialty is Belgian knits, infants to size 10, beautifully tailored and with enough adjustable features and extra wearability to justify their above-average prices. Also Swiss cottons and batistes, and a line of American styles in which summer dresses start at $5. Boys' sizes go to 6X.

Young Gentleman, Inc., 509 West Diversey, EA 7-4892

The boys' clothes here are Ivy League styles—suits, jackets, raincoats, coats, sweaters, shirts, slacks in sizes 6 to 20 at prices comparable to department stores. What makes the shop noteworthy is the owner's willingness to help outfit boys who need husky or extra slim beanpole sizes. Though there isn't a large stock of these on hand, anything you want will be gotten immediately for you. Alterations, such as shortening pants and sleeves, taking in seats and waists, are free.

Boys' Haircuts

Danny, in the men's barbershop at the **Ambassador West Hotel,** SU 7-7200, specializes in the cut known in England as the Prince Charles and in this country as the John-John. Almost all the lads from nearby Latin School are sent here to get their heads shaped. Downtown, the barbershop in the **Pittsfield Building** basement, 55 East Washington, 726-2466, does more conservative work. A barbershop in Morton Grove (**Chuck's,** 9103 Waukegan) has a 200-gallon oil storage tank on the premises stocked with a largemouth bass, some bluegills and crappies. Children are allowed to catch the fish (barbless hooks) but must return them for the next sportsmen.

Granny Goodfox, Inc., 1525 North Wells, 787-2762

A toy shop in Old Town with Field's taste and imagination in the selection of toys. Granny's shop is small and intimate, with display counters and shelves dropped down to child height—a cunning ploy that rules out any chance of saying "No" to a child who is eyeball to shelf with a Discovery. Two specialties almost impossible to locate elsewhere can be found here—children's paint smocks and handmade rag dolls. Granny is expensive, but her merchandise is equal to her prices.

Nik Klein, 2934 North Lincoln, GR 2-7633

Handmade rocking horses with real horsehair hides and hair manes, leather saddles and reins made by an old German craftsman who learned his trade as a boy. The rockers and frames of his horses are of hand-carved wood, come in sizes up to five feet high. New Yorkers have seen the horses in the past at F.A.O. Schwarz, where they sold for just about twice the prices asked here—$45 to $250. Mr. Klein is past 70; he speaks no English but his daughter will take your order and translate for him.

Kroch's & Brentano's, 62 East Randolph, DE 2-7500

Shop here for children's party favors and decorations and, downstairs in the craft center, for paper and styrofoam craft items for children to make. The children's book department in the store on Wabash Avenue is filled with carefully chosen selections; the children's book buyer is a real pro in the field.

EXPEDITIONS

Chicago Police Department, Central Headquarters, 1121 South State, WA 2-4747. This incredibly efficient new building is not only a marvel of electronic controls and instant data processing, but the reason why Chicago police efficiency is now the envy of every city in America. *Central Headquarters* is open on a 24-hour basis. Visitors are welcome any hour of the day or night. Just stop at the Inquiry Desk for a self-tour sheet and a short taped telephone briefing by Supt. of Police James Conlisk. Visit the Communications Center, Data Processing and, until 5 PM weekdays, the Crime Detection Laboratory. On Sundays from 1 PM to 5 PM the Canine Department performs.

Guided tours daily, 9 AM to 4 PM. Write for reservations, if possible a month in advance, since demand for these is excessive. Visitors who can't plan that far ahead may ask to join a tour going through; if the group isn't too big, you're welcome.

Chicago Fire Academy, 558 West De Koven (1100 south), 744-4000

Its site helps interpret Chicago history, for it's near the O'Leary barnsite where the Great Fire of 1871 began. Stand at the Egon Weiner cast bronze memorial flame, look east to the Loop: this is the path the Fire first took. Map, page 441.

The Fire Academy houses the CFD's School of Fire Instruction, and it's possible to watch firemen drill here in the early afternoon. There are no set days for drills, but a phone call at noon should furnish information about the day's schedule.

320

In the six-story drill room you watch firemen get the kind of training they're most likely to need—ladder work, hose work on fire escapes, jump-net practice, Pompier ladder and snorkel practice, and caisson practice with oxygen tank, flashlight and lowering rope.

In the main lobby, see the photographic display of famous Chicago fires (Chicago history is filled with them) and a brass-fitted redwood hand pumper fire engine dating back to 1835.

At the southwest corner of Illinois and Dearborn Streets (just north of the Chicago River) find Chicago's largest fire station housing three engine companies, two hook-and-ladder trucks, a snorkel, a rescue squad and offices of the central area Fire Prevention Bureau.

Fort Sheridan, Highwood, Illinois, 432-5000

A typical old Army base now a STARCOM and MARS facility, and Fifth Army Headquarters as well. At present, anyone can drive through the gates without an official pass and request a tour.

The base shelters an airstrip for light craft, a rifle range, a soldier's cemetery and a museum. The museum contains an assortment of military documents and paraphernalia, a coach once used by General Phil Sheridan, for whom the fort was named; rare Civil War surgical instruments; weapons and uniforms dating from the Civil War and the Spanish-American War.

Open house on Armed Forces Day occasionally produces some kind of special event, but you can't count on it. A phone call to the Public Information Office will let you know what's scheduled.

Tour hours: 7:30 AM to 3 PM Monday through Friday. Sheridan Road (Route 42) north leads directly to Fort Sheridan. Next-door Highwood has several good restaurants—see page 404.

Great Lakes Naval Training Center, Great Lakes, Illinois, 688-3500

At 2 PM every Friday from May to October watch 2,000 young sailors graduate from induction training at Great Lakes. The impressive outdoor ceremony attracts spectators by the thousands who come to watch pomp and ceremony—intricate drill maneuvers, a march on the colors, presentation of medals, and the final passing in review.

Great Lakes is headquarters for the nation's largest naval district—the mighty Ninth. It trains more than half of all the Navy's recruits and, as if to prove its efficiency, gets along as the only naval district without a seacoast or a harbor for Navy ships. (Its Corn Belt Fleet drops anchor in Lake Michigan ports elsewhere; two ships are in Chicago.)

Except for occasional weekends when you might run into an impromptu tour, guided tours are offered only to groups of 20 or more by prearrangement, include lunch with the men in the largest mess hall in the Navy. Families may ask for a pass and a map for a self-tour on Friday and may eat in the Navy Exchange Cafeteria.

Glenview Naval Air Station, Glenview, Illinois, 657-1000, is probably best known for its squadrons of Lockheed Neptunes and Grumman Trackers (the Fleet's carrier-based submarine-killing specialists). Unfortunately, Glenview isn't open to single families—except the annual Open House, often near Labor Day—but only to groups of 20 to 50 who have made a written request 60 to 80 days in advance. Request must include the total number of persons in the group, date and time of expected arrival, and two alternate dates. Tours are conducted by naval personnel, cameras are permitted, and you get close-up viewing of the antisubmarine planes, helicopters, A-4 Douglas Skyhawk jet bombers, weather station facilities, and sometimes the firehouse and parachute loft. Tours Friday, Saturday and Sunday (holidays excluded) after 1:30 PM.

Chicago-O'Hare International Airport, between Mannheim, Touhy, Irving Park, and Cumberland. Chicago phone, 686-2200.

The action at the world's busiest air terminal is continuous. It's so busy that the tower men can work only stints of less than an hour. During peak traffic hours, 4 PM to 8 PM, flights are logged in and out at two per minute. Landings and takeoffs are simultaneous, since O'Hare has parallel runways, NE to SW and SE to NW.

This crossroads-of-the-continent airport handles international and domestic flights, and some of the glamor jets of the world can be seen here each day. There are two observation decks; a dime gets you into either (groups on tour, free). Twenty-three places serve food—from snack bars to the posh Seven Continents (page 32).

O'Hare statistics are staggering. For example: 1,700 to 1,800 daily flights, 104,569 travelers on the Monday of any three-day holiday and an absolute madhouse. The airport was named for young Lt. Commander "Butch" O'Hare, a World War II hero, posthumously awarded the Medal of Honor. Two plaques near the entrance to the main building tell his story.

Kennedy Expy to O'Hare. Or hop on a Continental Air Transport limousine at any of 15 Loop and Near North Side hotels.

For *boat cruises* on Lake Michigan, see Chapter 17.

For overnight and weekend *expeditions by train,* look into the Burlington Railroad's escorted tours to Mark Twain country in Hannibal, Missouri. Tours include guides, lectures, an overnight stay at the Lincoln Hotel in Quincy, all meals and some noteworthy sightseeing. Adults, $35; half fare for children under 12. Another tour, to Galena, Dubuque and Prairie du Chien, includes a stern-wheeler boat trip on the Mississippi River. With luncheon and dinner, $14; less for children under 12.

Cantigny, 115 Winfield Road, Wheaton, MO 8-5161

Colonel Robert R. McCormick, late owner of the *Chicago Tribune* and one of Chicago's leading eccentrics, served briefly in the First (Rainbow) Division

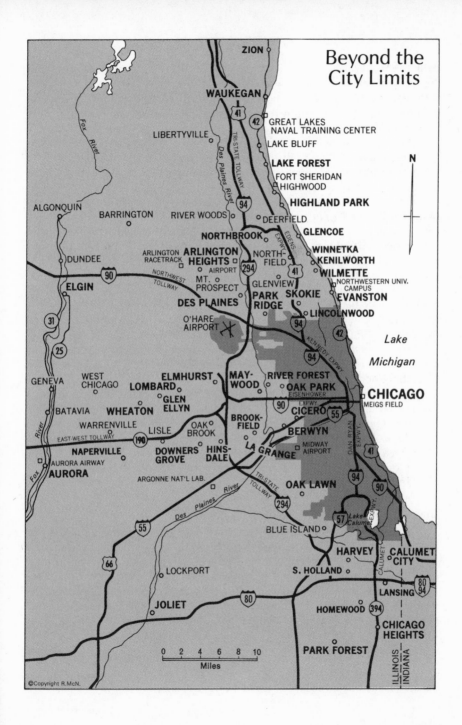

Beyond the City Limits

ZION

WAUKEGAN
41
42 GREAT LAKES
NAVAL TRAINING CENTER
LIBERTYVILLE LAKE BLUFF
LAKE FOREST
FORT SHERIDAN
HIGHWOOD
94 HIGHLAND PARK

ALGONQUIN
BARRINGTON RIVER WOODS DEERFIELD
GLENCOE
NORTHBROOK
ARLINGTON ARLINGTON NORTH- WINNETKA
RACETRACK HEIGHTS FIELD KENILWORTH
DUNDEE AIRPORT 294 WILMETTE
ELGIN 90 MT. 41 NORTHWESTERN UNIV.
PROSPECT GLENVIEW CAMPUS
NORTHWEST DES PLAINES PARK SKOKIE EVANSTON
31 TOLLWAY RIDGE
O'HARE LINCOLNWOOD
25 AIRPORT 94
42 Lake
KENNEDY EXPWY
94 Michigan
GENEVA ELMHURST MAY- RIVER FOREST
WEST LOMBARD WOOD OAK PARK
CHICAGO GLEN EISENHOWER CHICAGO
BATAVIA WHEATON ELLYN 90 EXPWY CICERO 55
WARRENVILLE OAK BROOK- MEIGS FIELD
EAST-WEST TOLLWAY LISLE BROOK FIELD BERWYN
190 LA GRANGE MIDWAY
NAPERVILLE DOWNERS HINS- AIRPORT
AURORA AIRWAY GROVE DALE 41
AURORA ARGONNE NAT'L LAB. OAK LAWN
94 90
TRISTATE
TOLLWAY
294 Lake
Des Plaines River 57 Calumet
55 BLUE ISLAND
66 HARVEY CALUMET
LOCKPORT S. HOLLAND CITY
80
JOLIET 80 94
HOMEWOOD 394 LANSING
CHICAGO
HEIGHTS
PARK FOREST

N

CHICAGO

0 2 4 6 8 10
Miles

ILLINOIS
INDIANA

©Copyright R.McN.

during World War I and never got over his peculiarly romantic notions about the glory of military life; he was *Col. McCormick* to the end. When his first wife died, he buried her on the estate with full military honors, including a riderless saddled horse with reversed stirrups and blinders, and a 20-gun salute from a military detachment. His own funeral was scarcely more spectacular.*

When the Colonel died, he left his 500-acre estate as a park and museum of his life interests. One of his major interests was war, and Cantigny, despite its formal gardens and greenhouses and "museum," is essentially a glorification of man's need to butcher his fellowman.

On most estates, trees line a mall; at Cantigny, it's tanks and large pieces of field artillery swarming with youngsters. The War Memorial Museum is filled with martial music at the highest decibel level, and the "sights and sounds of world war." So states a piece of promotional literature, and it's all too true. You're under bombardment in a replica of a dugout and trench in No-Man's-Land. You're at the diorama battles of Cantigny (France) and Normandy, where, to the canned, overamplified roar of war, animated troops advance and retreat, the town blazes and burns and, if you can stick it out to the end, there's undoubtedly a victory of some kind to cheer. Elsewhere, a photo exhibit of the Colonel's ideas of the causes leading to World War II; a war library; a half-size replica of the memorial statue of the Normandy Beach which could be quite moving except that the original inscription has been replaced with the Gettysburg Address.

The Colonel's home is open and features conducted, detailed tours. A small picnic area in an oak grove is also open. Various patriotic ceremonies are held on the estate during the year, but anyone who both hates mobs and recalls the Colonel's super-patriotism would probably be wise to stay away.

Open May-September 9 AM to 5 PM; October-April 10 AM to 4 PM.
Closed Mondays, Thanksgiving, Christmas and New Year's. Free.
Eisenhower Expy to intersection with East-West Tollway. West past sign "Cantigny Memorial Next Exit."

Graue Mill and Museum, York Road, Oak Brook, 654-9703

Come here to find tranquility after the barrage at Cantigny. The old mill perched beside Salt Creek in a quiet woods and water setting dates to the late 1840's and an early farm community in Illinois. Fred Graue, a young German, hand-built his waterwheel mill to serve farmers in Du Page County and the tiny village of Brush Hill (now Hinsdale). He scarcely got the mill in operation when he turned its cellar to another use—a station on the Underground Railway for slaves fleeing north along what is now US Route 34 to freedom in Chicago.

State legislator Abraham Lincoln stopped in the area on at least one

---

* Both tombs are guarded by carved dogs whose once living prototypes are also buried with the Colonel and his wife on the estate grounds.

occasion; visitors today see more than he because the mill is now a Civil War era museum (upstairs) as well as the last working gristmill in Illinois.

A miller in the expansive white apron of his trade and helpful ladies from the nonprofit Du Page Graue Mill Corporation demonstrate, guide, sell fresh-ground cornmeal and give free recipes.

Outside, stroll through some of the prettiest grounds imaginable, past a short waterfall and along Salt Creek, which rushes through stone-bottom rapids. Alas, the creek is poison-green here from the sewage dumped into it by suburbs to the north, but it serves at least one purpose: a firsthand confrontation with the meaning of present-day water pollution.

> Open mid-May to late October. Monday through Saturday, 1:30-8:30 PM, Sunday and holidays, 11 AM-8:30 PM. Admission: 25¢ adults, 10¢ for children 8 to 12. Free to educational and civic groups with leaders on weekdays if reservations are made in advance. P.O. Box 293, Hinsdale, Ill.

The **Village Gate,** across the creek, is an old tavern serving hickory-cured ham sandwiches for 50¢. Also Polish sausage, braunschweiger, kosher corned beef. Wash down with imported Pilsner-Urquell beer and refuse to be irritated by the grumpy proprietor who saves all pleasantries for his regular customers.

> From Cantigny, take US Alt. 30 to York Rd. going south. Or, for a country drive, Winfield Rd. south to Warrenville, east to East-West Tollway, and Tollway east to York Rd. turnoff. From Chicago, Eisenhower Expy to York Rd. going south.

The famous **Cook County Forest Preserves** (chains of connecting forests maintained in their natural condition, teeming with wildlife indigenous to this area) are filled with delights for adults and children alike. In addition to all the sports facilities described throughout Chapter 9, the preserves offer the chance to roam over the sites of old Indian villages; follow trails to the sites of chipping and signal stations; explore ponds, sloughs, lakes that in fall are havens for migrating waterfowl; wander in woods that in spring offer the earliest wild flowers of the area; find blackberry, dewberry and raspberry patches, the berries ripe for picking in July (you're allowed to pick them and also gather fruits, mushrooms and nuts provided you're not destructive).

The **Little Red Schoolhouse** nature center is a place where a family can spend a full day between the indoor exhibits and the self-guiding nature trails. Also telescopes for watching bird life. It's one mile west of U.S. 45 and one-half mile south of 95th Street at Willow Springs Road (104th Avenue).

Sand Ridge emphasizes the earth history of the Calumet area—marsh, woods, open water, wooded sandy ridges with a trail and observation mound. It's on Paxton Avenue, two blocks north of 159 Street, South Holland.

Palos Park Farm is a working farm where children can feed and pet animals. It's at 127th and Southwest Highway, Palos Park. Phone first (448-2056) to be sure the day isn't reserved for school groups. **Trailside Museum,** designed for short visits, is located close to Forest Preserve District Headquarters at Thatcher and Chicago avenues, River Forest. It's worth stopping there for brochures with maps, pictures and descriptions of all facilities at every forest preserve division. Or, write or phone for a set: Forest Preserve District of Cook County, 536 North Harlem Avenue, River Forest, Ill. 60305. CO 1-8400. Headquarters has brochures at cost (generally 10¢), describing various flora and fauna at the different preserves.

Note: The vast majority of the 15-million people who visit the preserves do so on 17 Sundays and holidays. Most of them are picnickers; but if your goal is to get away from humanity, go on a Saturday or a weekday.

Animal Kingdom, Inc., 2980 North Milwaukee, CA 7-6410

Exotic animals in a pet shop that both rents and sells them—a baby elephant at $4,000, a tiger cub at $2,000, a lion cub at $250 and, more reasonably, kangaroo rats at $4.95, mice at 98¢ and water newts at 45¢. Priced somewhere in between are South American monkeys, African chimpanzees, boa constrictors, lesser snakes (physicians and their sons are the big purchasers of these), exotic fish, ducks, chickens.

Owner Bernie Hoffman grew up in a pet shop, has spent his life working with animals and can advise on the care and feeding of any purchase. He will also advise against ordering: (1) a llama, unless it can be given as much room as a horse; (2) a giraffe, unless it's guaranteed at least 18 feet of head room. He rather favors boa constrictors because they're quiet—at least the neighbors won't complain about noise. Chicago-area children find all the pets they've seen on TV—Bingo the chimpanzee, Sheba the lioness, and Chelveston, a notable, trained white duck.

> Monday through Friday noon to 9 PM; Saturday 10 AM to 6 PM; Sunday noon to 6 PM. School groups that give advance notice of a visit will get a special tour and discussion of animals. Visits by the animals to a school may also be arranged.

Hawthorn-Mellody Farms, Route 21, approximately 2 miles south of Libertyville, and South Milwaukee Avenue, EM 2-4193

Hawthorn-Mellody is a local dairy, and its farm has a demonstration milk barn filled with a moist, milky smell and cows on an assembly-line basis, milked automatically, then fed and washed. Children can watch the entire proceedings, including the flow of milk from the cow's udders into plastic tubes. They'll also get gobs of giveaway literature. Outside, there's a children's zoo and a miniature train pulled by a steam engine across a field to Hawthorn Gulch, a facsimile Western ghost town.

> Open daily and Sunday 10 AM to 5 PM. Picnic area on the premises. Edens Expy to Tri-State Tollway north. Exit west at Half Day Road (Rt. 22) to Rt. 21 (Milwaukee Avenue). North on 21 to farm.

INTELLECTUAL OASES

15

Colleges and Universities
Medical Schools and Centers
Libraries

CHAPTER 15

INTELLECTUAL OASES

For all its basic Midwest distrust of intellectualism, Chicago is a major center of pure research and education. For all their pragmatism, enough Chicagoans willingly contribute funds and their wholehearted support to underwrite the costs of theoretical research in an astounding number of wholly experimental, intellectual ventures. No city in America has more of these and possibly none close to the number here that exist solely on behalf of the search for truth.

Maybe it could have happened only in the Midwest where the land stretches out to infinity. Adlai Stevenson said, "Maybe because Illinois is flat and people can see in all directions, they can see farther." Chicago's research and educational institutions are unique. And they welcome visitors, particularly those whose curiosity about the world or man's position in the world is equally unsatisfied.

COLLEGES AND UNIVERSITIES

University of Chicago, roughly 55th Street to 61st Street between Lake Park and Cottage Grove, MI 3-0800; *Edward H. Levi, President; Quadrangle Enrollment, 8,475*

The University of Chicago was founded by the most prodigious young academic overachiever of the 19th Century and by one of the century's most prodigious multimillionaires. William Rainey Harper (1856-1906) was a high school graduate at age nine, a college graduate at 13, a college teacher at 16, a Ph.D. and the principal of a Tennessee college at 19. Before he was 30 he had become the country's leading instructor of Hebrew and had made the study of Hebrew a national challenge. He raced around the country conducting seminars; gave courses in the English bible to undergraduates; instituted correspondence courses in Hebrew and wrote the textbooks; originated and published the *Hebrew Student* and *Hebraica;* founded the American Institute of Hebrew; lectured at Chautauqua and became a Yale instructor whose daily mail was larger than Yale's.

Harper was born a Presbyterian but became a Baptist. As that denomination's leading young theologian, he came to John D. Rockefeller's attention, and Rockefeller, in turn, came under Harper's vision of a great nondenominational university to be founded in Chicago.* The one they built opened as one of the first full-scale universities in the country with the strongest faculty in the country, including eight former college presidents whom Harper had enticed from other campuses.** At the same time it offered the first reduced faculty teaching load that allowed adequate time for research; faculty salaries as much as double the prevailing scale; the four-quarter system; the first Jewish theologian in a Christian university; the first professional football coach (Amos Alonzo Stagg).

It was Harper's university all the way, and the impetus he gave it never slackened. Sociology was born on this campus. John Dewey established and formalized progressive education here. The Nuclear Age was born here. Thorsten Veblen wrote *The Theory of the Leisure Class* here. The nation's first Nobel laureate in science (physicist Albert A. Michelson) was on its faculty; 27 Nobel prize winners studied or taught on the campus. Its college leads the nation in the number of graduates who subsequently earn doctorates.

It is the richest and most prestigious private institution in the Midwest, a world of its own, not just in the great quadrangle but along all the surrounding streets. There are guided two-hour walking tours of the campus every Saturday (10 AM from Ida Noyes Hall, 1212 East 59th Street), but it's not difficult to tour on your own. Use the map on page 118 or get a larger version from the Office of Public Relations, 5801 South Ellis.†

South of the Midway, see Mies van der Rohe's **School of Social Service Administration Building** and Eero Saarinen's **Law School** complex (page 120); on the north side of the Midway: the original **Quadrangle,** the **President's** home at 5855 University, **Rockefeller Memorial Chapel**‡ (page 174); the **Orien-**

---

* Rockefeller's initial gift was $60,000. Harper organized the university on a scale of about $50 million. Rockefeller ultimately contributed $35 million and his foundations about $45 million.

** In the Harper tradition of simplicity and forthrightness, no Ph.D.'s at the university are called "Doctor" except for Doctors of Medicine. On this campus some of the world's most learned professors are addressed as Mister.

† In the same office get copies of the current calendar of events and booklets, *The First Pile* (an AEC reprint) and *The Hyde Park-Kenwood Urban Renewal Years* by Muriel Beadle, wife of former president George Beadle. It's the success story of the first major attempt in the U.S. to integrate and upgrade a changing urban community. The university spearheaded the program. Mrs. Beadle's booklet is a small gem.

‡ Carillon recitals every Wednesday at 5 PM, Sunday at 12:15 PM.

tal Institute (page 138); **Robie House** (page 117); Lorado Taft's **Midway Studios** (page 168) and his great **Fountain of Time** at the west end of the Midway. The fountain was suggested by Austin Dobson's aphorism: "Time goes, you say? Ah, no. Alas, time stays. We go." The colossal mounted knight at the east end of the Midway is the mythical Czech **Knight of Blanik,** erected in 1949 as a symbol of the spirit of Thomas Garrigue Masaryk, liberator of Czechoslovakia and its first president. Lunch at **Hutchinson Commons,** a replica of Christ Church Hall, Oxford, or in the cafeteria at **International House.**

Every campus has its tales of eccentricities. The story of **Pierce Hall,** a men's dormitory, named for the alumnus who left his estate to the university, is this: when Pierce died in 1960, the executors found in a safe in his garage a blank check which bore a notation on one side, "If anything happens to me over." The other side read, "Dig under paper bag in the garage, under barbed wire in the garage and dig under Bartlett Pear Tree at the southwest corner of house. Surveyor's pipe very hard to find." A crew of diggers, supervised by bankers and attorneys, shoveled through six inches of snow into the soil until they found more than 6,000 United States twenty-dollar gold pieces crammed into pickle jars and canvas containers from the Federal Reserve Bank. A full Treasury Department and Secret Service investigation had to be made to establish that the coins were part of the deceased's legitimate coin collection. Finally exempted from confiscation, they were appraised, cleaned, put on display, and finally sold at private auction to the highest bidder. Pierce Hall was built with the proceeds.

One block south and half a block west of Pierce on Ellis, between 56th and 57th streets find **Sir Henry Moore's** epic sculpture commemorating an event which for years was symbolized only by a small plaque attached to a tennis court fence: the first self-sustaining nuclear chain reaction. The ominous 6,000-pound bronze, related to Moore's helmet heads, is named "Nuclear Energy."

The university also administers **Argonne National Laboratory**, 9700 South Cass, Argonne, 739-7711. Argonne, 27 miles from Chicago, is one of the country's major atomic energy research and development establishments and is open to visitors. Almost all of the work done by the 1,300 scientists and engineers on its staff is unclassified, so you may drive through the vast 3,700-acre facility to visit some of the buildings housing reactors, atom smashers (particle accelerators) and the meteorology station. A guided tour must be arranged in advance through the Department of Public Information; otherwise, any time from 7:30 AM to 6 PM. Argonne specializes in the development of nuclear reactors, high energy physics and radiation biology and is a permanent national laboratory funded by the AEC.

From the Loop, Stevenson Expy to Ill. Rt. 55 to Cass Ave.

Northwestern University, Sheridan Road between Church and Central, Evanston; Chicago Campus, East Chicago Avenue, Chicago, 492-3741; *J. Roscoe Miller, President; Enrollment of both campuses, 15,356*

Once—until recently, really—you could immediately distinguish Northwestern undergraduates from those at the University of Chicago by the all-American prettiness of the coeds and the expensively casual look of the fraternity men. Despite its stern Methodist origins, Northwestern became one of the rah-rah Big Ten colleges noted more for its spirited football marching band, plush fraternity and sorority houses, annual Waa-Mu show, its students who came out of the School of Speech and made good in Hollywood (Warren Beatty, Jennifer Jones, Charlton Heston, Patricia Neal, Charlotte Ray, Ann-Margret, Gregory Peck, Paula Prentiss) than for undergraduate scholarship. Though old Big Ten accoutrements still exist, and the coeds are as pretty as ever, undergraduates now are part of the new breed that goes to college for serious reasons and works furiously once enrolled.

Northwestern was staked out on the lakefront in the early 1850's. The site was an oak grove reached via an Indian trail above the sandy, pebble-strewn beach. "We were delighted—some of the brethren threw up their hats. We had found the place," so wrote one founding father. Their cheers were for the chance to start from scratch with a model Methodist community; they could in effect draw a line around the land and say, "no liquor, no gambling, no dancing" and be far enough removed from Chicago (15 miles) to isolate themselves from its sinful influence.*

The model community was named Evanston in honor of Northwestern's principal founder, John Evans (a physician as interesting and full of interest as Harper), and the town was laid out: church, hotel, Chicago, North Shore and Milwaukee Railroad passenger station, and the first college building, a small, Victorian, wood structure with a chapel with plain pine benches, six classrooms, a library, a museum, a room for the literary society and two attic rooms to house the students (it now houses the headquarters of the School of Education). On November 5, 1855, four of the first ten students, together with the university's two teachers (a professor of math and a professor of Greek) and three of the founding trustees, celebrated opening day.

Today, the campus runs a mile along the shoreline, and its science department is expanding into the lake on a 170-acre landfill. Its Technological Institute has some of the nation's most advanced facilities for education and research in nuclear engineering, astronautics, biomedical engineering, and computer sciences. NU now ranks among the first ten undergraduate schools in the country and first 20 graduate schools.

The campus is lovely: wooded, slightly rolling, with pathways winding

---

* Chicago's population of 29,000 was swinging in the best frontier boomtown style.

along the lakefront and dipping in and out of leafy groves. Walking tours guided by members of the Wildcat Council start at 2 PM Monday through Friday and at 11 AM Saturday from the Admissions Office, Rebecca Crown Center, 633 Clark. Phone 492-7271 at least one hour in advance. For self-tours, go also to the Admissions Office or to the Activities Center on the second floor of **Scott Hall** (corner Chicago and Sheridan) for maps and the current calendar of events on campus: there's something scheduled almost daily. Or tour the new **Lindheimer Astronomical Research Center** (the twin milk-white towers you saw thrusting up from the lakefront if you drove north from Chicago along Sheridan Road; one houses a 40-inch telescope and the other a 16-inch scope). Conducted tours of the **Technological Institute** start in the lobby at 11 AM every Saturday. **Dearborn Observatory,** 2131 Sheridan, has night programs the first four Fridays of each month—tours followed by telescope viewing of the skies (program cancelled if raining). Phone 492-7651 to reserve tickets. Hours vary according to the time of year. **Deering Library** always has two book-oriented exhibits; library hours are 8:30 AM to 10 PM Monday through Friday, to 5 PM Saturday, 2 PM to 10 PM Sunday.

Don't miss the **Shakespeare Gardens,** just east of Sheridan Road and north of Howes Chapel on the grounds of the Garrett Theological Seminary, planted with all the flowers Shakespeare mentioned in his plays. The garden is probably at its prettiest in mid-June but at its most fragrant in September when the herbs—rosemary, thyme, lovage, tansy, lemon balm, chives—are beginning to dry.

You can easily make a day of sightseeing at Northwestern and in Evanston proper (page 400). Lunch on campus in the grill at **Scott Hall,** a student union; off-campus at **Michelini's,** a student hangout at 2001 Maple, at the small outdoor cafe in front of the Hotel Orrington. For dinner, **Fanny's,** 1601 Simpson, (see page 401).

Illinois Institute of Technology, 30th to 35th streets between Michigan Avenue and Dan Ryan Expy., CA 5-9600; *John T. Rettaliata, President; Enrollment: 7,885*

The completely mid-20th-Century campus—no Gothic, no Victorian—is the result of Mies van der Rohe's Master Plan (page 121) for the outstanding technologically-oriented education and research center of the Midwest.

Half ITT's roots lie in the Armour Institute of Technology, founded in 1892 by Philip Armour, the Chicago meat-packing magnate.* In 1890, the

---

* The other half lies in Lewis Institute, a polytechnic school, came into existence through the will of one Allen Cleveland Lewis, who died in 1877, leaving his estate in trust for its establishment, and for the education of "respectable females." God only knows what other kind of females he thought would want the kind of education he was willing to provide. In any event, when the two institutions merged in 1940, IIT was the result.

Reverend Frank W. Gunsaulus reached eloquent heights one Sunday in his church sermon on the need for an educational institution to serve a rapidly growing industrial society. According to all versions, Mr. Armour marched up to him at the conclusion of his sermon, saying, "Give me your time and I shall furnish the money." Actually, he furnished something better than cash—row after row of new income-producing apartment buildings on property he held.

ITT now consists of the colleges, the Departments of Architecture and of City and Regional Planning, the Institute of Design founded by Laszlo Moholy-Nagy in 1937 as the successor to the Bauhaus in Germany, the Graduate School, the Evening Division (this is the largest engineering school in the country where night students can earn degrees), the million-volume John Crerar Library (page 342), and research affiliates.

Guided tours every Saturday, September through May, 10 AM, starting from Admissions Office, Room 101, Perlstein Hall. High points to visit on your own: **St. Saviour Chapel** at 55 East 33rd Street, program center for foreign students featuring continuous exhibits; the **Teller Brass and Copper Collection** of more than 1,500 artifacts—antique and modern, European and Oriental (Perlstein Hall); the inventive student design exhibits in **Crown Hall** (architectural and industrial design), which alternate with traveling exhibits. The monthly calendar of events provides information on current art exhibits, films, plays, recitals and seminars or lectures open to the public.

In the same vicinity: the Museum of African-American History, South Commons, the row of Negro art galleries on East 31st Street, Michael Reese Hospital & Medical Center. (See map page 374.)

University of Illinois at Chicago Circle, between Eisenhower and Dan Ryan Expys, Roosevelt Road (12th Street) and Morgan; Tour and Information Office, 663-8686; *David D. Henry, President; Enrollment: 15,000*

"Instant campus" it was called when it opened in 1965, and it was. In a little less than two years the massive concrete commuter campus of one of the largest state universities* had been created on land obtained through urban renewal. Construction is still going on to meet enrollment needs. The new campus is worth touring, not merely to see an architectural achievement in concrete (page 122) but as a chance to see a full-scale commuter campus.

Its focal point is a raised, open-air, central courtyard with a dramatic 2,500-seat amphitheatre. It also forms the roof of an enormous teaching center which you reach through a forest of concrete piers or raised walks. The traffic jam on the walks at the ten-minute breaks between classes was created by the architects, deliberately, in the hope of offsetting the sense of isolation stu-

---

* The University of Illinois is located in Urbana-Champaign, downstate, was created as a land grant college in the last century.

dents at commuter campuses usually feel. If at no other time, students and faculty are at least physically close during the hourly shift from classrooms in one building to another.

Guided tours are offered so frequently that they're recommended. Or get maps and information at the main desk in the lobby of the **Chicago Circle Center**—open from 6:30 AM to 10:30 PM Monday through Thursday, to midnight Friday and Saturday, and from 11 AM to 7 PM Sunday. Don't overlook the Book Center in the same building, with 20,000 titles beautifully arranged. You're free to browse and read the books in an adjacent lounge whether you buy or not. If you want to come in and copy a recipe from a cookbook or dates from a history book, the Book Center couldn't care less. Eat in the student cafeteria of Building No. 18, the **Pier Room;** or **The Brown Bottle,** 1014 West Taylor, a self-service student hangout—sandwiches, pizza, hamburgers, bratwurst boiled in beer, Italian beef and draft beer. Decor is semi-Old English pub. Or there's **Al's Bar-B-Q,** 856 West Van Buren, a droopy old shack with a scrupulously clean counter inside and one of the jolliest proprietors anywhere. Al specializes in Italian beef and Italian sausage sandwiches and, in summer, outdoor picnic tables, ice-cold watermelon and clams. Late hours here—as busy at 3 AM as at any other time.

Not to be missed: the restored buildings of Jane Addams' famous **Hull House,** 800 South Halsted. The original building is a Victorian house built in 1856, one of the few to survive the Fire. Compared to the mass of new concrete behind it, it looks like a little 19th-Century sentry box. It was built by a remarkable Chicagoan, Charles Hull—lawyer, physician, successful real estate dealer, who, in his own way, anticipated Miss Addams. He visited the Bridewell jail to teach prisoners, founded a home for alcoholics, aided newsboys and bootblacks, helped poor families acquire homes at decent prices and foreshadowed the social philosophy Miss Addams made explicit by saying: "All charities, public and private, in the support of the poor merely increase pauperism. They are the nurseries of poverty and crime. We should help them (the indigent) to help themselves."

What Jane Addams and Hull House stood for after 1889 (she bought the house from Hull's secretary, and by then it was in the middle of a polyglot neighborhood of impoverished immigrants) was a social force that had not existed previously in America. Hull House served the immediate needs of the immigrants in the neighborhood, but under Miss Addams' leadership the forces it put into motion reached across the United States. The field of social welfare came into being here, and the ideas this inspired woman put into action helped establish the United States Children's Bureau, got the U.S. Child Labor Law passed, abolished sweatshops and established the first juvenile court in the city. The name Hull House keeps popping up across this city on community houses, neighborhood social centers and community theatres, all of which in one way or another follow the leadership of the original. Miss Addams' Hull House is part museum and part center for university seminars and conferences. Phone Miss Mary Lynn McCree, curator, MO 3-2793, for daily tour hours.

Other sightseeing in the vicinity: the West Side Medical Center, just three-quarters of a mile west (page 374); Chicago Fire Academy (page 320); the remnants of the old Greek Harrison-Halsted section of Chicago (page 351) and, on Sunday, Maxwell Street (page 377).

Roosevelt University, 430 South Michigan, WA 2-3580; *Rolf A. Weil, President; Enrollment: 6,500*

Housed in the building that was once the world-renowned Auditorium Hotel, the school was founded in 1945 with no funds, no physical plant, but possibly the finest national press ever given a new college. Drew Pearson's column of November 15, 1945, gives the reason:

> Behind Mrs. (Franklin Delano) Roosevelt's dedication of Roosevelt College in Chicago today is a unique story. Formerly, Chicago's YMCA College, a low-cost institution in the Loop, was supervised by leading Chicago banks. Suddenly they awoke to the fact that 25 percent of the student body was Negro, asked President James Sparling to put a quota on further Negro students. He refused, then handed in his resignation. . . . Simultaneously, 92 percent of the faculty resigned plus 97 percent of the students. The bankers found themselves without a college. . . . Marshall Field (III), the Julius Rosenwald Foundation, plus Chicago citizens then raised half a million to found a new low-cost college in the Loop. The old YMCA College is no more and Roosevelt College begins today. . . . It's the first time that both students and faculty walked out simultaneously. (From Washington Merry-Go-Round, Bell-McClure Syndicate.)

Roosevelt University was not merely a pioneer in equal education, but it gave a degree of freedom to its faculty that is still unique—appointments and upward mobility to full professorial rank based on merit alone, without regard to sex, race or creed, and the expectation that some of the faculty will always be on the Board of Trustees. (It is.) Though a commuters' university, Roosevelt now has 150 students from 45 countries and an even larger number from 40 states of the union. Among its academic strengths: the College of Business Administration; Department of Education (it trains more teachers for the Chicago school system than any other private university in Illinois); and the renowned Chicago Musical College* (founded in 1867 by Florence Ziegfeld, Sr.), which merged with Roosevelt in 1954.

---

* Among its alumni: Jack Benny, Benny Goodman, Irene Dunne.

For a conducted tour, phone the Admissions Office, WA 2-3580. Only with a guide can you see the fully restored Louis Sullivan Room, once the Ladies' Parlour in the Auditorium Hotel. Sans guide, you may visit the Murray-Green Library, originally the famous Auditorium Restaurant (the library stacks are housed in what were kitchen and laundry rooms); see the exhibition of Auditorium Theatre mementoes in the Reading Room; and Fainman Memorial Hall on the second floor, once the hotel's main lounge, now a student lounge. Its recently restored ceilings reveal the original Sullivan stencil designs hidden for years under 20 coats of paint. The elaborate plaster decorations were also conceived by Sullivan, with Frank Lloyd Wright probably doing most of the actual renderings. On the seventh floor, see the Rudolph Ganz Recital Hall, formerly a banquet hall-ballroom. Its restoration includes the gold leaf in the window arches, stained-glass windows, gold and green stenciling, and the wood paneling; the 1 PM Wednesday concerts are performed here or in Miriam Mesirow Marks Recital Hall. To see the Auditorium Theatre restoration, follow procedure on page 104.

For schedule of current and special events, check with the Information Office, WA 2-3580. For Scholarshop, page 267.

Mundelein College, 6363 North Sheridan (Devon), AM 2-8100; *Sister M. Ann Ida Gannon, BVM, President; Enrollment: 1,470.*

The most interesting aspect of Mundelein, a women's college of liberal arts, is the two-year investigation it made of itself (1962-64), after 32 years, to answer the question, "Do we deserve to exist?" The answer was, "Yes—if drastic changes are made." Starting at the top, Mundelein made them—turned full control over to a lay Board of Trustees and became the first Roman Catholic college in the United States to elect a Jew to Chairman of the Board. It totally revised its curriculum (now exceedingly liberal); upgraded its teacher standards; changed its student admissions policy; turned from a local, parochial college into one that draws students of all races and creeds from this country and others, is now ranked among the top Roman Catholic colleges in the United States. Its Degree Completion Program for college dropouts accepts life experiences as credits toward a degree whenever a student can satisfactorily prove that she has already achieved the objectives of a given course. The program has so successfully served community needs that a second program for teachers who need certification has been added.

Mundelein's Fine Arts Program offers the public an almost continuous round of art exhibits (generally in Galleries 4 and 8 in the Main Building), auditorium recitals, lectures, a performing artists series and a foreign film series in the College Theatre. For current events, check with the Public Relations Office. For guided tours of the campus, contact Mrs. Jeanne Carroll Cass, Public Relations Office, several days in advance.

DePaul University, Lewis Center, 25 East Jackson, WE 9-3525; College of Liberal Arts and Sciences, Lincoln Park Campus, 2323 North Seminary, 549-6000; *John R. Cortelyou, C.M., President; Enrollment: 7,982*

The first Roman Catholic university in Illinois, the first in the nation to become coeducational (1911) and the first to introduce a modified elective system supplanting the rigid curricula then in vogue. It turned control over to a lay Board of Trustees in 1967.

DePaul is noted for its School of Commerce, College of Law, and Music Department, which has seven members of the Chicago Symphony Orchestra on its faculty; conversely a half-dozen of its graduates are Chicago Symphony members. DePaul University Community Symphony Orchestra performs at Orchestra Hall under the chairman of the department, Dr. Leon Stein; its percussion ensemble, concert band, opera workshop and soloists perform during the season at DePaul Center Theatre in Lewis Center.

The university's combined library facilities are open to the public for research (page 345); its philosophical symposia are open to anyone who wishes to attend: discussions led by men of the stature of Walter Kaufmann of Princeton University on "Reflections on Atheism"; Abraham Kaplan of the University of Michigan on "The Self and Its Identity"; Thomas J. J. Altizer of Emory University on *"The Death of God."* For schedule, the Admissions Office or the Chairman, Department of Philosophy.

College of Jewish Studies, 72 East 11th Street, HA 7-5570; *David Weinstein, President; Enrollment: 330*

The small college, established in 1925, rapidly outgrew its original purpose of providing a basic Jewish education for high school graduates, added departments of Hebraica and Judaica and is becoming *the* Department of Judaica for all colleges and universities in the area. The college is also accredited by the State of Israel (graduates can teach there without examination).

Two outstanding facilities are its Leaf Library of Judaica (page 345) and the new Maurice Spertus Museum of Judaica (page 144).

Loyola University, 6525 North Sheridan Road, BR 4-3000; Lewis Towers, 820 North Michigan, WH 4-0800; Medical Center, Maywood, Ill.; Bellarmine School of Theology, 230 South Lincoln Way, Aurora; *James F. Maguire, S.J., President; Enrollment: 12,651*

Unfortunately, you cannot tour Loyola. The great gates at the entrance to the lakeshore campus—looking for all the world like one's childhood notion of the gates to heaven—are indeed like the gates to heaven—closed to visitors except by special arrangement. A pity, because Loyola is the largest Jesuit university in the world, with ten schools and colleges, four campuses in the Chicago area and a fifth in Rome.

MEDICAL SCHOOLS AND CENTERS

Medicine as a science and Chicago as a city came of age together. Each helped the other take long strides forward from 1845, when what was possibly the town's first "hospital" was established.* The County Pest House was for people with infectious diseases, but since little was known in the way of treatment, one suspects the Pest House merely sheltered the victims of the town's recurrent waves of cholera and typhoid, and they either recovered or they didn't.

When the great obstetrician Dr. Joseph B. DeLee pioneered the first lying-in hospital for maternity patients with its separate pavilion for those with infections, the idea of a separate unit was no longer a death sentence, but a matter of healing; the gap between the County Pest House and Chicago Lying-In was a matter of only some 40 years.

Medical pioneering has been a continuing hallmark of the city's five medical schools and three major medical centers. Out of Chicago has come fundamental work on environmental diseases, such as lead poisoning; the isolation and classification of a great variety of streptococci; the concept of focal infection; the establishment of the importance of chemical factors influencing changes in the human body, even death; the use of ethylene gas in anesthesia, replacing ether, chloroform and "laughing gas." Chicago researchers discovered the carrier of Rocky Mountain spotted fever and the louse as the transmitter of typhus fever. The first major encyclopedia of pediatrics was compiled here (it's still in demand); all kinds of contributions to the care of premature infants; fundamental research on the causes of epidemic influenza; a long string of advancements in surgery; vast new knowledge on bone pathology; the discovery and popularization of vagotomy; the cure for blue babies; some of the earliest pioneering in the field of psychoanalysis and the establishment of a vast body of knowledge fundamental to the treatment of emotional illness and psychosomatic disorders.

The **University of Chicago,** both medical school and medical center (12 hospitals) is perhaps best known today as a center for cancer research, and its **Argonne Cancer Research Hospital** is considered the first atomic hospital in the country. Enrico Fermi's contribution as a physicist cross-fertilized medicine and led to the use of radioisotopes in the treatment of cancer. The medical school was from its inception a research and education department, and if you arrive at any of its hospitals with an illness the department is researching, you'll get a case history work-up and in-depth medical staff concentration second to none.

---

* A free dispensary existed as early as 1839, the forerunner of the present Presbyterian-St. Luke's Health Center, but the first hospital as such was Mercy, established by the Sisters of Mercy in 1849.

Northwestern University's Medical and Dental Schools are equally well-known for the amount and quality of research they conduct. The medical school pioneered the acceleration of medical education, instituting in 1961 a new curriculum that allows top high school students to enter and complete work for an MD degree in six years. Neither medical nor dental school have hospitals of their own (though they have clinics), but the rather newly organized Northwestern University Medical Center coordinates the functions of the medical school with leading hospitals—Chicago Wesley Memorial, Passavant Memorial, Veterans Administration Hospital, the Rehabilitation Institute of Chicago, Children's Memorial Hospital, Chicago Maternity Center and Evanston Hospital.

The **University of Illinois School of Medicine** is one of the three largest in the country in terms of students—225 in each class yearly. The university also has schools of dentistry, pharmacology and nursing, plus its own hospitals of research and education. The entire complex is part of the West Side Medical Center, which also includes Presbyterian-St. Luke's Hospital; Illinois State Psychiatric Institute; Illinois State Pediatric Institute; West Side VA Hospital; Chicago Medical School; and Cook County Hospital.

Cook County Hospital, a Victorian behemoth, is the largest single hospital in the nation, giving rise to some staggering statistics: more than 4,500 beds; more than 100,000 patients in those beds annually; another 250,000 patients yearly in Fantus Clinic; another 350,000 in its diagnostic clinics. It's easy to see why for years it has been a prize hospital in the country for internship or residency: by sheer numbers, the patients offer a variety of clinical problems unduplicated elsewhere.

You can't tour County, but you can tour the University of Illinois classrooms and the clinics that emphasize student-faculty-patient relationships. Contact Tour Service, Office of Public Relations, University of Illinois at the Medical Center, 663-7680. West Side Medical Center is bounded by 13th Street and the Dan Ryan Expressway, Ashland and Oakley—a ten-minute drive from the Loop via the Eisenhower.

Two other medical centers worth knowing about: the **Institute for Psychoanalysis,** 180 North Michigan—a pioneering institution that is at once a low fee clinic, a research center and two schools; and the **Michael Reese Hospital & Medical Center,** 2929 South Ellis. By virtue of its staff and research, Reese is one of the outstanding private medical institutions in this country. After World War II, Reese found itself in the center of one of the city's worst slums. Together with **Illinois Institute of Technology** and New York Life Insurance Co., it undertook a huge program of urban renewal, brought into existence the city's first private efforts at integrated housing (the complex of attractive apartment buildings known as **Lake Meadows** and **Prairie Shores** on South King Drive between 26th and 35th streets. The area is worth exploring by car as an example of enlightened self-interest that not only reclaimed a part of the city once thought to be a total loss, but stimulated still further building: the new Mercy Hospital at 26th and Michigan and a two-phase private housing development known as South Commons.

South Commons is the first attempt to build a community for both lower- and upper-middle-income families. Whether 3,000 people of widely different income levels and diverse education, mores and interests can be part of a single harmonious preplanned community is anyone's guess; but the concept is intriguing. The first buildings are up, and much landscaping has been done in the area bounded by East 26th Street, East 31st Street, South Michigan Avenue and Prairie Avenue.

G. D. Searle & Co., Searle Parkway, Skokie, Illinois, OR 3-3200

Searle ranks number 12 in the country among pharmaceutical houses and will arrange tours for anyone with a legitimate interest in learning how a manufacturer tablets, codes, packages and processes drugs. To arrange a tour, write Joseph K. Bartulis, Director of Personnel, P.O. Box 5110, G. D. Searle & Co., Chicago 60680.

Abbott Laboratories, 14th and Sheridan, North Chicago, Illinois (Lake County), 338-1600

Abbott is fifth or sixth largest pharmaceutical manufacturer in the U.S.; it employs some 4,700 persons at this plant. It specializes in anesthetics, sedatives, and antibiotics, does chemical and biological research, and is developing drugs for heart disease, cancer and mental illness. Tours are tailored to fit need, but a general tour will show you what goes on in a modern pharmaceutical research building and in light drug operations. The full length tour will take four to five hours. Write Professional Guest Relations, Abbott Laboratories, North Chicago, Illinois 60064. Be sure to explain the reason for your visit.

> Chicago & North Western Railroad has a North Chicago stop or, driving, Kennedy Expy to Edens Expy to Rt. 41, north to the laboratories, which will be on the right side of the highway.

LIBRARIES

Within days after the Great Chicago Fire, a long-forgotten Englishman issued a circular urging his fellow Londoners to rally to Chicago's aid by donating books for a public library. Whether Mr. A. H. Burgess knew that Chicago had never had a public library, or whether he believed that one of the city's essential resources had been demolished along with its (now outstanding) private collections, is not entirely clear. Whichever, he put in effect the civilized notion that books were the single most precious gift England could send to help the stricken city.

Only the English would have thought of it, and the list of contributors (and what follows is only partial) reads like Burke's Peerage and literary England combined—Her Majesty; Mr. Burgess; the Duke of Argyle; the Lords Comms of Admiralty; the British Museum; Cambridge University; the Camden Society; Lord Alfred Churchill, M. P.; Mr. Disraeli, M. P.; the Archbishop of Dublin; Mr. Evelyn; the Royal Geographical Society; Mr. Gladstone, M. P.; Sir Charles Trevelyan; the Patent Office; Sir R. Palmer, M. P.; Oxford University; Macmillan and Company; Lord Romily; the Social Science Assn.; Mr. Herbert Spencer; and a list of barons, marquesses, earls, lords and book publishers from all sections of the British Isles.

The first packet of books arrived from Glasgow on December 4, and shipments continued to arrive throughout 1872. Faced with such embarrassing new riches, the city fathers converted an old iron water tank into the Chicago Public Library. The tank remained in service until 1897, when the present building on Michigan Avenue was opened. Despite its auspicious beginnings, its current status as a public library is deplorable. As aspects of its architecture have already been admired (page 112), it needs no further attention here.

Newberry Library, 60 West Walton (Dearborn), WH 3-9090; *Lawrence W. Towner, Librarian*

The Newberry, one of the country's great, privately endowed* research libraries, ranks with the Morgan, the Folger, the Huntington. It is a library of the humanities with its major strengths in the history, literature and music of western Europe and the Americas. Its vast collections of Americana include the Edward E. Ayer collection of 90,000 printed books and manuscript pages documenting the earliest exploration of the western hemisphere and the reciprocal effects of the meeting of the Indian and the white man; printed copies of letters from Columbus to the Spanish monarchs describing his voyages; early maps and atlases showing geographic knowledge at the end of the 15th and subsequent centuries; paintings, drawings, early photographs of Indian tribes; and grammars and texts in various Indian dialects. The Everett D. Graff collection of Americana dovetails with the Ayer and includes accounts of pioneer journeys across the plains and Rockies, personal narratives

---

* Its founder was Walter Loomis Newberry, who came to Chicago from Connecticut in 1833 as a young man, helped build the city, made a fortune in land speculation (tracts he bought by the acre he later sold by the foot) and returned to the city half his fortune in the form of a bequest upon his death. His death was rather strange; it occurred on a Europe-bound liner, and the captain, instead of burying him at sea, placed his body in a cask of Medford rum that was part of the cargo and eventually returned cask and corpse to Chicago for burial in Graceland Cemetery.

of the gold rushes and broadsides and pamphlets bearing witness to the spread of law, order, commerce and culture across the expanding nation. Because of the Newberry's policy of collecting in depth in the fields it chooses to cover, the Ayer and Graff collections are not the only ones of Americana— merely the biggest and best-known.

Scholars also know the Newberry for its extraordinary library of 13,000 volumes on the history of linguistics, built by Prince Louis-Lucien Bonaparte; the books of Henry Probasco, a Cincinnati bibliophile, which included the first, second, third, and fourth Shakespeare folios and much incunabula; the music collection of the Florentine Count Pio Ressi, who specialized in books of early music theory and practice; and the John M. Wing Foundation library on the history of printing—more than 10,000 books and manuscripts demonstrating the technical and aesthetic development of the craft, including about 2,000 incunabula.

Since the Newberry is a scholar's research and reference library, it offers resident fellowships and grants-in-aid, mainly to Ph.D.'s, occasionally to one or two doctoral candidates working on their dissertations. To Chicagoans and others who are associate members, it offers a remarkable series of lectures and exhibitions throughout the year; memberships are open to anyone interested in becoming an associate member for a yearly fee of $50. To visitors, the Newberry offers main floor exhibitions of materials from the collections and, in a small room off the central lobby, a library store which sells facsimile Newberry publications in print, such as *Narratives of Captivity Among the Indians,* reprinted from the Ayer Collection; reproductions of maps in the Newberry collections; an English translation of the first letter of Columbus of March 14, 1493; and a series of charming greeting and Christmas cards that are reproductions of art elements from various library possessions. Admission to the library's reading rooms requires formal application to the Admissions Secretary and a precise statement of the work one plans to do. The splendid reference room on the second floor is more easily accessible, though an admission permit is given only if the books you need are not in the Chicago Public Library. Open 9 AM to 9:30 PM Monday through Saturday. Special collections reading rooms close at 5 PM.

John Crerar Library, 35 West 33rd Street (IIT campus), CA 5-2526; *William Stone Budington, Librarian*

In an authorized history of the John Crerar Library is a delicious statement: "Mr. Crerar's life was not an eventful one except in the rapid accumulation of wealth." Perhaps not, yet John Crerar was one of the most influential Chicagoans during the town's great formative years. And though his daily life had a marked pattern and he died a bachelor, the statement just doesn't fit the man who left $100,000 for a colossal statue of Abraham Lincoln (Saint-Gaudens' seated Lincoln in Grant Park) and $2 million to found a public library. The surprising part of his bequest was its lack of specification other than that a free library be created in his name and that the first Board of Directors be the men he named in his will (they included Marshall Field I and Todd Lincoln).* Since the Chicago Public Library was already established as a broadly general repository, Newberry was to specialize in the humanities, the Crerar became a library of science and technology. For example, not only is it the single free public library in the United States with a major medical collection, but it has the largest collection west of the Alleghenies covering all of the biomedical sciences and all fields of clinical medicine. Certain gifts have made it especially strong in cardiology, ophthalmology, obstetrics, gynecology and pediatrics, and its rare medical books, dating from the late 15th Century, are one of the greatest collections in the world.

When Crerar was chartered in 1894, technology was so new that it was called the Useful Arts, and almost all of man's knowledge of the Useful Arts was contained in books. Today, the real strength of any scientific library is in its periodicals—the journals in which scientific developments are reported. Crerar's uniqueness lies in its complete coverage of scientific journals in approximately 50 languages. The Crerar is likely to have anything current in print. The present collection numbers about one million books and 13,000 current serials and periodicals. A quarter ton of mail daily increases the number by 150,000 issues yearly.

Anyone may use Crerar on a noncirculating basis. Anyone may avail himself of its special departments—research information service, photoduplication service, and the Special Libraries Association Translations Center—by reimbursing costs. Business firms can subscribe to a "current awareness service," and any firm contributing more than $1,500 annually can reserve permanent workrooms here. In fact, the industrial community knows more about Crerar than the general public does—except for high school students who flow in on Saturdays.

For visitors: such main floor exhibits as a Robert Fulton display or three-dimensional exhibit on bridges, canals and roads going back to the construction of the Appian Way in 312 B.C. Upstairs, a display room with deep,

---

* The final provision of the will read: "Recognizing the fact that I have been a resident of Chicago since 1872, and that the greater part of my fortune has been accumulated here, I give . . . my estate . . . for the . . . creation . . . and endowment of a Free Public Library to be called the John Crerar Library and to be located in the South Division of the city inasmuch as the Newberry Library will be located in the North Division. . . . I desire the building to be tasteful, substantial and fireproof . . . the books and periodicals . . . selected with a view to create and sustain a healthy moral and Christian sentiment in the community, and that all nastiness and immorality be excluded. I do not mean by this that there shall be nothing but hymn books and sermons but I mean that dirty French novels and all skeptical trash and works of questionable moral tone shall never be found in this library. . . ."

upholstered chairs, an Oriental rug and the chance to savor a marvelous display of rare books. Open daily 8:30 AM to 10 PM; Saturday to 5 PM. Closed Sunday.

Library of International Relations, 660 North Wabash, SU 7-7928; *Eloise Requa, Director*

The nation's first free public library specializing in international politics, political science, economics and social issues was founded in 1932 by a young woman who was at least 20 years ahead of her time. Eloise Requa, a Bryn Mawr graduate fresh from graduate study at the School of International Studies in Geneva, foresaw the growing need for such a library and, despite the Depression, organized it and got it going in space provided by the Crerar. It is still the only public library of its kind in the country, has no endowment, lives from month to month through the efforts of its distinguished Board of Directors (of whom the late Adlai E. Stevenson was one), and deserves far more support than it gets.

There's no free library like it for information on the current internal situation of practically every country of the world. It has so much material that it is compelled to publish a quarterly annotated bibliography of current sources, scholarly analyses and significant commentaries on contemporary political, economic and social developments of more than 100 nations.

It has a complete collection of State Department publications and is a depository for all United Nations publications and documents, all publications of the European Common Market, European Coal and Steel Community, European Atomic Energy Agency, International Court of Justice, International Labor Office, Organization of American States, World Health Organization and Food and Agriculture Organization.

Along with its collection of more than 200,000 books, documents, pamphlets and magazines, it offers language records and texts for Arabic, Chinese, French, German, Italian, Japanese, Russian, Spanish and Turkish; it maintains an information service that answers inquiries from all over the world and sponsors the prestigious annual Consular Ball, which it inaugurated —a formal expression of appreciation to the members of the Consular Corps in Chicago and a way of focusing attention on U. S. relationships with other countries. Open Monday through Friday 9 AM to 5:30 PM. Noncirculating.

Municipal Reference Library of Chicago, Room 1005, City Hall, 744-4992; *Joyce Malden, Librarian*

A first-rate reference library containing all documents issued by the City of Chicago and by other municipalities throughout the country: codes; annual reports of the agencies, departments and bureaus of local governments; special reports of local governments. It also contains an excellent representation of historical material about Chicago; city council proceedings; Illinois House and Senate bills; a newspaper clipping file; old telephone directories and long-out-of-print city directories. Its librarians are wonderful and can answer almost any question about the city. Open Monday through Friday 8:30 AM to 4:30 PM.

Leaf Library of Judaica, College of Jewish Studies, 72 East 11th Street, HA 7-5570; *Sara Dayan, Librarian*

One of the most specialized libraries of its kind in the country, with more than 56,000 volumes, periodicals and academic publications. Among its collections of Hebraica, Judaica and rabbinica are the 1,500-book duplicate collection of Hebraica and Judaica that was part of the 12,000 volume library presented by Ephraim Deinard to Harvard College (rare books from the 16th through the 18th centuries); the private library of Joseph Mann of Cincinnati, which ranges through Jewish literature on the Bible, biblical Exegesis, Talmud, Talmudic commentaries, Hebrew belles lettres, historical chronicles and responsa; the American Jewish Society's duplicate Yiddish collection of 1,000 books, considered one of the outstanding collections of Yiddish materials in the nation; the Herbert Reichner collection of Jewish medievalia; the 42-volume set of the transcript of the Nuremberg Trials *(Major War Criminals of Nazi Germany)*; and all Israeli government publications. The Chicago Jewish Archives are also housed here. Open 1 PM to 9 PM Monday to Thursday; 9 AM to 3 PM Friday; Sunday, 9:30 AM to 5 PM. Closed Saturday.

De Paul University Library houses the Otto J. Lemke Napoleon Library, a collection of some 4,000 books, pamphlets, letters, memoirs, maps and very rare items, such as broadsides. Open to anyone for research purposes. Bibliography available. The Law Library has a small (50 items) but elite St. Thomas More collection, of which the most significant volumes are a first edition of *The Workes of Sir Thomas More Knight, Sometyme Lorde Chancellour of England,* and *The Non-Utopian.* The collection also includes a letter about Sir Thomas from Erasmus of Rotterdam to Ulrich Hutter and a portrait by Hans Holbien engraved by Bartolozzi in 1793. Open to anyone for research. There's also a fine likeness of More memorialized in the stained-glass window of the Miraculous Medal Chapel on the first floor of Lewis Center. See also page 337.

Burnham Library, Art Institute, Michigan and Adams, CE 6-7080; *Ruth Schoneman, Librarian*

A superb architectural library, having on microfilm original drawings of many of Chicago's famous buildings, and the library of Fontaine, architect to Napoleon. Though primarily for members, students and alumni of the Art Institute, researchers and visiting architects may use it by appointment. Write in advance, if possible. Monday through Friday 10 AM to 5 PM; Saturday to 12:30 PM. Use of the **Ryerson Library of Fine and Decorative Arts** at the Art

Institute, with its separate department of slides and photographs, is subject to the same restrictions as the Burnham Library.

Mead Library of Ideas, 20 North Wacker (41st floor, Civic Opera Building), FI 6-1822

A handsome little gallery maintained by the Mead Corporation, a firm manufacturing paper. Exhibits relate to graphic designs on paper for commercial use and will probably be of greatest interest to art directors, advertising and public relations people, printers and art students. Recent exhibitions have included business letterheads, campus graphics, financial communications, graphics of travel, house organs, menus, paper sculpture, record albums. Annual shows include the New York Type Directors exhibit, Creativity on Paper exhibit, Annual Reports, and the Mead Show of Shows, in which all designs have been printed on Mead papers. The library also has files of printed samples catalogued by industry-user and graphic design. Monday through Friday 9 AM to 5 PM.

Hild Library for the Blind, 4536 North Lincoln, LO 1-6298

A regional branch of the Chicago Public Library and also a regional library of the Library of Congress Department for the Blind and Physically Handicapped. Hild has 7,000 titles in fiction, biography, philosophy, law and history in Braille, plus 4,500 talking books and 40,000 recorded tapes. It has the *World Book Encyclopedia* in Braille (144 volumes), about 20 recorded periodicals, such as *Reader's Digest, Newsweek, Atlantic Monthly, Harper's, American Heritage, Good Housekeeping.* It will circulate as many as 15 or 16 volumes of a book to a single person and provides special government labels for return of books by mail free of postage. It has no large type books. Monday through Friday 9 AM to 5 PM.

Sterling Morton Library of the Morton Arboretum, Ill. Route 53, Lisle, WO 8-0074; *Mary K. Moulton, Librarian*

A horticultural library including agriculture, forestry, conservation, it offers an outdoor garden in which to read and a large collection of prints and photographic slides of the arboretum's specimens as seen at different seasons. Open Monday from 9 AM to 5 PM and 7 PM to 9:30 PM. Tuesday through Saturday, 9 AM to 5 PM. In design, it's a beautiful library, and the reading garden is a total charmer. So is a sign on the library door which states: "Readers Welcome All Day"; Sightseers' Hours 11:30 AM to 1:30 PM and 4:30 PM to 5 PM.

Marquis Biographical Library Society, 200 East Ohio, SU 7-2008; *Joanne Edwards, Librarian*

A biographical library—dictionaries of biography, manuscripts of unpublished biographical data, and all volumes printed by Marquis Who's Who Inc., since its founding in 1897—*Who's Who in America, In the East, In the Midwest, South and Southwest, In American Women, In Commerce and Industry* and *Who's Who in the World.* Monday through Friday 8:45 AM to 4:45 PM.

National Library of the Theosophical Society in America, 1926 North Main, Wheaton, MO 8-1571; *Helen Loenholdt, Librarian*

A 15,000-volume library of theosophy, life after death, reincarnation and karma, astrology, extrasensory perception, healing, mysticism, occult fiction, yoga, major religions, Eastern and Western philosophy and music. One of these days, the new young converts to East Indian mysticism are going to discover the place and it will probably never be the same. Reading room open to all, but nonmembers must fill out an application and pay a $5 deposit in order to take books home. Bibliographies available on request along with library rules and application forms. Free public lectures, followed by tea, on the fourth Sunday during October, November, and January through May. Weekdays, 9 AM to 5 PM; Sunday 2 PM to 5 PM. Closed Saturday.

For library of the Chicago Historical Society (Margaret Scriven, librarian), page 140. For museum libraries, Chapter 6 or Index. For the many smaller libraries in the Chicago area, consult the *Directory of Special Libraries* in the Reference Room of the Chicago Public Library. For librarians: the modern new executive offices of the American Library Association are on the Near North Side at 50 East Huron, WH 4-6780.

Adult Education Council of Greater Chicago, 332 South Michigan, HA 7-2670

Many of the council's meetings and programs are open to the public, generally for admission of $1 or $1.50. Phone for schedule of current program. For Chicagoans: The council publishes a very complete monthly arts calendar that includes fairs, special events, exhibits, art shows and lectures in Chicago and the suburbs. Phone for subscription. It maintains a speakers bureau and is a prime source for information on education.

Chicago Council on Foreign Relations, 116 South Michigan, RA 6-3860

The largest Council on Foreign Relations in the country has a continuous program of luncheon and dinner meetings, lectures by leading politicians, news analysts and top government people from abroad and in this country, followed by open discussions. Often there are as many as three or four of these meetings a month, including Headliner Luncheons, Business Executives Luncheons, Young Adult Suppers, Background Luncheons, and Lecture Seminars. Phone for schedule of events. Meetings are open to the public for the price of luncheon or dinner and a small admission fee.

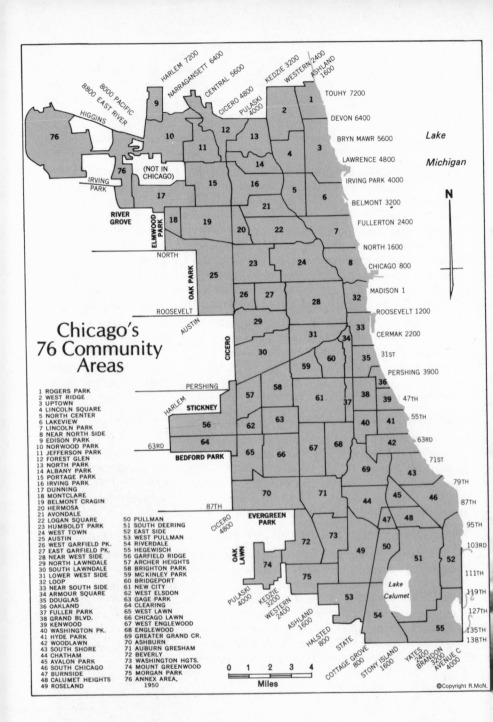

Chicago's 76 Community Areas

1 ROGERS PARK
2 WEST RIDGE
3 UPTOWN
4 LINCOLN SQUARE
5 NORTH CENTER
6 LAKEVIEW
7 LINCOLN PARK
8 NEAR NORTH SIDE
9 EDISON PARK
10 NORWOOD PARK
11 JEFFERSON PARK
12 FOREST GLEN
13 NORTH PARK
14 ALBANY PARK
15 PORTAGE PARK
16 IRVING PARK
17 DUNNING
18 MONTCLARE
19 BELMONT CRAGIN
20 HERMOSA
21 AVONDALE
22 LOGAN SQUARE
23 HUMBOLDT PARK
24 WEST TOWN
25 AUSTIN
26 WEST GARFIELD PK.
27 EAST GARFIELD PK.
28 NEAR WEST SIDE
29 NORTH LAWNDALE
30 SOUTH LAWNDALE
31 LOWER WEST SIDE
32 LOOP
33 NEAR SOUTH SIDE
34 ARMOUR SQUARE
35 DOUGLAS
36 OAKLAND
37 FULLER PARK
38 GRAND BLVD.
39 KENWOOD
40 WASHINGTON PK.
41 HYDE PARK
42 WOODLAWN
43 SOUTH SHORE
44 CHATHAM
45 AVALON PARK
46 SOUTH CHICAGO
47 BURNSIDE
48 CALUMET HEIGHTS
49 ROSELAND

50 PULLMAN
51 SOUTH DEERING
52 EAST SIDE
53 WEST PULLMAN
54 RIVERDALE
55 HEGEWISCH
56 GARFIELD RIDGE
57 ARCHER HEIGHTS
58 BRIGHTON PARK
59 MC KINLEY PARK
60 BRIDGEPORT
61 NEW CITY
62 WEST ELSDON
63 GAGE PARK
64 CLEARING
65 WEST LAWN
66 CHICAGO LAWN
67 WEST ENGLEWOOD
68 ENGLEWOOD
69 GREATER GRAND CR.
70 ASHBURN
71 AUBURN GRESHAM
72 BEVERLY
73 WASHINGTON HGTS.
74 MOUNT GREENWOOD
75 MORGAN PARK
76 ANNEX AREA, 1950

©Copyright R.McN.

NEIGHBORHOOD CITY

16

CHAPTER 16

NEIGHBORHOOD CITY

Despite the city image it has attained in the Loop and along Lake Shore Drive, Chicago is really an aggregate of 76 neighborhoods, almost no two alike. Chicagoans even think in neighborhood terms. Ask them where they live and they tell you in Rogers Park or South Shore or Near North. The neighborhoods aren't arbitrary subdivisions; it's the other way around. Chicago grew through annexation of townships, villages and unincorporated communities; despite subsequent population shifts, the neighborhoods remain intact.

Some of them are very much what they were around the turn of the century when immigrants were pouring into the city by the hundreds of thousands, accounting in large part for the city's population leap of one million between 1900 and 1920. These immigrants came poor and they spoke no English, and they felt far more alien than the Irish and German and Dutch and Scandinavian immigrants of pre-Civil War years who were pioneering a new town. At the time of the Great Fire, half of Chicago's 300,000 citizens were foreign-born. But the latter-day immigrants came to an established industrial city, and the welcome was not warm. So they moved into neighborhoods where a few of their own kind who had arrived earlier already lived, and they built their own churches, established their own banks, opened their own shops and taverns and funeral parlors, established one or more newspapers in their own language and, when radio came along, set up their own native language radio stations. They created their own social clubs, athletic clubs, fraternal organizations, cemeteries. Along with their Old World holidays and festivals, they brought Old World prejudices and fears. Eventually, thousands of them became mobile and moved into outlying communities where they bought or built their own homes. But they still clustered, and you can see the patterns of cluster in every local election when huge areas of the city vote as nationality blocs. They still return to the church in the old neighborhood for the major holidays and festivals. They are still in-group, narrow and possessive, and never more so than over home ownership. The awful battles over the right of a Negro family to move into an all-white neighborhood occur most often in the neighborhoods where first- and second-generation Americans live. The demonstrations led by the Reverend Martin Luther King in 1966 were staged deliberately in many of those neighborhoods to expose the hostility, the fear, the hysteria which were scarcely different in this northern city than in Oxford, Mississippi.

Depending upon the kind of visitor you are, Chicago's nonviable ethnic neighborhoods may prove at least as interesting as the city's Lake Shore Drive-Michigan Avenue facade. West of the drive is where the city lies; mile after seemingly indistinguishable mile of old homes, old Chicago Cottages, old 1920's bungalows, standard old Chicago three-flats and six-flats in neighborhoods studded with factories and foundries, crisscrossed by railroad tracks at grade. The hallmark of the community is always an uninspired business district just big enough to keep the neighborhood self-contained. The neighborhood is flat and graceless except in summer when trees are green and small lawns thrive. Yet the old neighborhoods have much to offer: the chance to see what the city looked like 50 years ago, the chance to discover a variety of ethnic and non-English-speaking communities, the chance to delve into the whole complicated fabric of the city—a melting pot set over a very slow flame.

As to Negro ghettos like North Lawndale, Woodlawn, Douglas, Oakland, parts of Englewood—you can avoid them entirely, as most Chicagoans do, or you can drive through them because there's something you want to learn. The tour may shake you. And if you wonder why a guidebook urges you to undertake it, the answer on the simplest level is: *you* don't have to live there, but, by white America's refusal to look, Negroes do.

HALSTED STREET: GYPSIES AND GREEKTOWN

More than one visitor has happily ridden the Halsted Street bus from one end of the line to the other simply because the ugly old street is main street for one ethnic group after another and sometimes, as in the Maxwell Street area, for several vastly different cultures that mingle but keep their separate identities. The long ride is worth taking if you have the time; if not, try a condensed version by boarding a southbound CTA No. 8 bus at Lake and Halsted. Within three blocks the bus lumbers across Skid Row, and shortly, it's into what's left of Greektown, then out across land created by urban renewal for the Univer-

sity of Illinois Circle Campus.* At Roosevelt Road the bus plunges into a human goulash—Mexicans, Puerto Ricans, Negroes, Romany Gypsies, each
group as identifiable as an ingredient in a stew but not as compatible.

This is the Maxwell Street area that is one kind of place on Sunday (see
page 377) and another kind the rest of the week. Leave the bus at 16th Street
and start walking back along the crowded, inhospitable sidewalks, past a department store called **The 12th Street Store,** which has been on Halsted forever
but never, within anyone's memory, at any location other than 14th Street;
past the jumble of easy-credit shoe and clothing shops, the no-money-down
furniture and appliance stores, the dingy-looking storefront restaurants, the
best of which is **Mexico Taqueria** (page 61); the narrow door leading to the
Vienna Sausage Company, where you can buy corned beef, pastrami, pepper
beef, beef frankfurters and salami; and past—if they're around when you are
—Gypsies in storefront homes.

Fully half the stereotypes about Romany Gypsies are true. They do live
in storefronts, the old women do tell fortunes and bless your wallet and
gently, while blessing it, lift some of the contents; the children do sell paper
flowers or real but bruised gardenias, and they are a lot greedier about money
than the old crones: they heist wallets. The men don't work, and the only time
a *gadzo,* a non-Gypsy, will ever see the young men doing anything other than
tinkering with their cars is on Easter Eve in an Eastern Orthodox church, such
as Holy Trinity, when they bring their Easter baskets to be blessed (page 413).

Almost everything these nonconformists do turns out to be illegal, like
the living in storefronts. Building inspectors, truant officers, the police are always after them, hence the 200 or so Romany families in the city are always on
the move. Mainly they shuttle between Halsted Street and West Madison.
Evicted from a storefront in one locale, they simply take down the flowered
curtains and religious chromos and put them up in another equally temporary
home. Ordered to send the children to school, they do—for about a week.
Taken to court for fortune-telling, they show up as a tribe with an expressive
and expensive lawyer, and what with enough wailing to the judge and the
payment of a $25 fine, they're back on the street telling fortunes in a matter
of hours. Because they're illiterate they haven't a chance, but because they're
originals and unconformables, they add another dimension to the city, and
nobody really wants to see them vanish—except, perhaps, some weary judges
and angry Chicagoans or visitors who've been had.

---

* The land on which nothing has been built, as well as the land under the U. of I.,
held the homes of the oldest Greek and Italian colonies in the city—people who had
lived there three and even four generations. Their diaspora obviously was not nearly
as necessary as the city's Dept. of Urban Renewal made out at the time; and though
the community organized and resisted with great courage, in the end it was literally
bulldozed by the Establishment.

The Romany Gypsies emigrated from Russia, Serbia and Romania about 1900. Some 3,500 Hungarian and Austrian Gypsies, who preceded the Romanies by a third of a century, now live on Chicago's Northwest Side; though they're a tight ethnic group with close ties to all other Hungarian and Austrian Gypsies across the nation, they're urbanized and indistinguishable from their neighbors. The men work; fully 90 percent are professional musicians, and you hear them in hotel dining rooms and restaurants—Maxim's, for instance, where violins are a basic part of the ensemble. Their only link with the Romany Gypsies is the secret Gypsy language, a form of Sanskrit, diluted and altered in the 1,500 years since the first Gypsies left northwest India but still intact enough to be the common language they call Romany.

Greektown is restaurants (page 58), the seductive 9-8 rhythm of recorded *bazouki* bands, grocery stores (page 366), a coffeehouse, a clutch of gift shops stocking small import items—inlaid backgammon sets, woven goods, traditional red slipper-shoes with black pom-poms, water pipes; brass Turkish coffeepots, dolls, guitars, goatskin rugs, ceramic plates and jugs, art reproductions, Greek newspapers and Greek recordings. But this Greektown is just a remnant of what used to be the center of life for all Greeks streaming to the .city, home for those who got their first jobs as dishwashers. They learned enough English to become counterboys, able to chant the litany that author Harry Mark Petrakis, who grew up among them, calls the "Song of the Pies—'Stromberry pie, peacha pie, happula pie, pinehappula pie. . . .' " That Greektown was an area of restaurants with vine-hung gardens fragrant with the mingled scents of small roses and thyme; coffeehouses by the score; pastry shops and bakeries where the loaf you bought was wrapped in newspaper, and everybody sensed that newsprint was sanitary, even if it did occasionally rub off. Urban renewal (all too often in this city a thin disguise for land grabbing) decimated it all; and though a new Greek neighborhood is emerging at Lawrence and Western, that area is too bright, too garish, too many other things, for the old Greek community to ever be the same.

Celebrations: Easter (celebrated on the Eastern Orthodox calendar). Greek Independence Day, March 25, but because of weather not celebrated publicly until May, when a large parade forms and marches down State Street. Day of No, October 28, is celebrated at St. Demetrius Greek Orthodox Church, followed by a parade, dinner in the church, a speech by the Greek Consul General.

CHICAGO AVENUE: UKRAINIANS, SICILIANS, BRITISH ISLANDERS

Chicago Avenue is a gray, faceless thoroughfare bisecting the city from east to west. The Ukrainians occupy the territory from 2000 to 2500 west, and their neighborhood is at its most interesting just before Easter, when the shops display baskets full of magnificently decorated eggs; when bakery counters are heaped with two-foot-high loaves of *Pasca* bread; when the florist shop is a triumph of floral crucifixes; when the entire neighborhood swarms with housewives shopping furiously after the long Lenten fast, in preparation for the greatest holiday of the year. It may well also be the longest Easter of all, for half the population celebrates Easter as Roman Catholics and the other half as Eastern Orthodox. Since the two Easters coincide only about every five or six years, the season has a decided stretch. The dates for the next few years, on the reconciled Eastern Orthodox calendar, are: 1969, April 13; 1970, April 26; 1971, April 18; 1972, April 9. For a description of the special celebrations in both churches, see Chapter 18.

Stop in at the **Ukrainian American Publishing & Printing Co., Inc.,** 2315 West Chicago. It turns out to be one of the most interesting import shops in the neighborhood, offering coloring books for children, greeting cards, beautifully embroidered peasant blouses and linens, Ukrainian postage stamps, recordings, magazines and what is likely to be the largest assemblage of French embroidery silks in the city—more than 200 colors in all.

At 3200 West Chicago (Kedzie), you enter a wholly Sicilian neighborhood, in which almost nobody ever seems to speak English. **Salerno's Market,** at 3511 West Chicago, specializes in pastas, olive oils, aromatic sausages of all shapes and sizes. **Sialas Fisheries,** at 3523, carries wholly recognizable clams, oysters, snails, but the fish runs to varieties you've probably never seen, like *lupini* and squid. **Joe Berlin's Peoples Food Mart,** at 3513, does a bustling business in "fresh-killed" [sic] winter and spring baby lamb, baby goats and rabbits. He's open only on weekends, which may account for the jam-up inside. **Italia Food Mart,** at 3658, is vegetables and fruits and always a daily special, such as good, firm tomatoes at 15¢ lb. **Sicilian Bakery,** at 3557, sells pizza, three kinds of breads, all sorts of Italian cookies. **Flowers by Ferdinand,** at 3649, specializes in weddings, funerals and corsages for a neighborhood that likes its bouquets bright and its floral arrangements big and sentimental. If one judges by the window displays Mr. Ferdinand surely leaves competition far behind. Two blocks west a bakery displays some of the most fanciful towering wedding cakes imaginable. The **House of Italian Shoes,** 3836 West Chicago, is exclusively men's and boys' footgear from $10 to $65 (for alligator). You can play bocci evenings at **Mazzini Club,** 4014 West Chicago, CA 7-9130. Phone first. And so it goes, shop after shop—everywhere a babble of rapidly spoken Sicilian, outbursts of laughter, and flashes of temperament. In this neighborhood, especially on a hot August day, Chicago's Loop is far more remote than the arid Sicilian hills.

For Italian festivals, see pages 412, 422, 425.

Keep going west to Central Avenue (5600), and you run into a tight little island of Scotch, Irish and Welsh—the reason for the **Atlantic Fish & Chips Shop** (page 49), the Watney's Ale and Old Country Bitter Ale at **Sullivan's** and at **Carnahan's** taverns and **Gaelic Imports,** at 5931 West Chicago, which caters to the combined tastes of the neighborhood. Up in the front of the shop are plaids, kilts, clan crests, chevrons, tartans; racks of Welsh and Scotch histories, dictionaries; volumes of *Welsh* and *Gaelic Self-Taught,* road maps of Ireland and England; enamel and marcasite jewelry; chanters and drones for bagpipes; imported tinned foodstuffs, including at least a dozen brands of Irish fruitcake, Scotch brose meal, Christmas puddings, plum puddings. In the rear of the store get Scotch meat pies fresh from the ovens, Cornish pasties, Irish bacon, beef sausage, fat loaves of Irish soda bread, potato scones.

Ask the proprietor how, aside from the taverns, the neighborhood entertains itself, and you're invited to the **British Club,** 5156 North Leavitt. "Go and sing on the piano," he says, "meetings every Friday night." He then invites you to the **Hebron Welsh United Presbyterian Church,** services in Welsh on occasional Sundays in winter, and, if one is scheduled anywhere in the city, to an Irish *Feis.*

CHINATOWN

The Chinese began migrating to the Midwest from California before the turn of the century, and when they got to Chicago they settled along Clark Street south of Van Buren in an exotic colony that prompted guidebook descriptions like the following:

> The wonderful signs of the Celestial, almost invariably of white lettering on a red painted board, stare one out of countenance from every other doorway. Celestials, in the unvarying costume of their country, haunt the sidewalks, lounging much in the fashion of their occidental neighbors, but with their taper hands concealed in the flowing sleeves or under the equally flowing skirts of their wonderful coats. They come up the steep narrow stairs from the basements that carry—for revenue only—the sign of a laundryman, but which are plainly the habitat of the national *bungloo,* or the equally exhaustive pastime of *fan-tan.* They are weary-eyed and silent, passing their countrymen without the faintest vestige of recognition, and disappearing in the quaint tea stores or tobacco stalls of the heathen.
>
> Opium smoking-rooms, popularly called "joints" are hidden away in Clark Street, but it is dangerous to visit them, as the police are likely to raid them at any moment . . . the price of "hitting the pipe" is $1. The habit has spread outside the Chinese quarter. . . .

The colony moved south along Clark until it reached its present location at 22nd and Wentworth, and until recently it was a genuinely ethnic neighborhood. But somebody decided the area needed jazzing up, so it now looks like a promoter's neon scheme for Chinatown, U.S.A. The shops are stuffed with trinkets made in Formosa and Hong Kong; mercifully, most of them are inexpensive enough to indulge children who want everything in sight, including—shortly before the Fourth of July—miniature firecrackers and tiny flares.

Gourmets will find the grocery stores the most interesting shops of the area, the one aspect of Chinatown that hasn't changed over the years, since they still cater to an immediate Chinese population of 2,500 persons. The shops are old and dark and crammed with barrels and crates of dried and boned whole ducks, squid, sea cucumbers; Chinese-style bacon; water lily roots; ginger roots; bitter melons; Oriental grapefruits; Chinese cabbage, spinach; *bak toy,* the pale green vegetable vaguely related to celery. The produce is pale and luminous; the dried meats and fish are brown and shrively and smelly. The shops themselves are dark enough to start a train of fantasies, and if you look up at the top shelves you may still find the forbidding glass jars of leeches and the ground rhinoceros horn the old generation of native Chinese uses for medicinal and other purposes.

Celebrations: October 10, a parade throughout the area to celebrate the day China became a republic; Chinese New Year, parades, firecrackers, a dragon in the streets, lots of excitement for a full week. Dates are: February 17, 1969, Year of the Rooster, 4667 on the ancient Chinese calendar; February 6, 1970, Year of the Dog; January 27, 1971, Year of the Pig.

For time, location, etc., phone Mrs. Helen Wong Jean at the Chinese American Civic Council, CA 5-0234. She also arranges group tours through the area and is a gold mine of information about it.

THE LITHUANIAN COMMUNITY

The largest Lithuanian population in the country is in Chicago, and it numbers close to 150,000. The Lithuanians started coming in the 1880's and came steadily until World War I. And because they had come from a land of forests and fresh air and the jobs they found were on the South Side in the stockyards and at the Pullman Company, they settled in what was then an open suburban area bounded by 67th and 71st Streets, Western and California.

The place to start your tour is actually at the edge of the area, at the **Balzekas Museum** (page 146). It's a fine introduction to a culture almost no one except other Lithuanians knows about. Afterwards, drive into and around **Marquette Park,** a lovely city park with a rose garden at its south end (beautiful even in late October), a nine-hole public golf course and a monument erected by a Lithuanian memorial fund committee to honor two young Lithuanian-American army officers who, in 1933, tried to fly to the homeland in a single-engine plane, crossed the Atlantic with no difficulty, but crashed in a forest in Germany. Yearly, there's a little neighborhood parade to commemorate them.

On 69th Street, find the huge **Holy Cross Hospital,** erected with Lithuanian funds; the **Vosylius Food Mart,** where you buy various kinds of Lithuanian sausage and the best Canadian bacon in town; **Tulpe,** a tiny family-operated restaurant in a storefront at 2447 West 69th. Father works the counter, mother and grandmother the kitchen and a pretty young daughter, who introduces herself as Miss Blinstrubas, works both.

Go to the Tulpe with an appetite; portions are mammoth, as though the family is convinced each meal might be everyone's last. So you work your way through huge bowls of steaming soup, perhaps Sauerkraut Soup with a side dish of potatoes, and entrées like Cepaelinai (beef-stuffed potato dumplings dotted with bacon, gray and glutinous looking but worthwhile so carry on) or Kugelis (grated potatoes mixed with bacon and eggs, poured into a mold and baked). Or very good fried chicken, or one of several daily Lithuanian specials. Everything is served with homemade rye or sweet white bread with raisins; salad, canned fruit desserts and coffee, and the price for all this just a few months ago was $1.45.

Lithuanians also recommend two other restaurants in the neighborhood—**Palanga,** at 6918 South Western, and **Ruta,** at 6812, a couple of doors away. There are several gift shops in the area: **Jonas Karvelis Gifts,** at 2501 West 71st, specializes in amber, crystal and wood carvings; **Terra Import Center,** 3237 West 63rd, is somewhat along the same lines.

ASSIMILATION

It's fairly well-known that Chicago has a Polish population second only to Warsaw's and a Bohemian (pre-Czech) population that blankets five adjacent suburbs—Cicero, Berwyn, Lyons, Brookfield and Riverside. As late as 1946 much of the old Polish community was intact; what is left now consists mainly of two splendid Baroque churches, the first, **St. Stanislaus Kostka,** at Evergreen and Noble, just west of the John F. Kennedy Expressway and immediately north of Division Street, and the second, **Holy Trinity,** at Noble and Haddon, a huge brick structure with copper domes and stone gargoyles. A third church, **St. Hyacinth,** 3636 West Wolfram, is the one to visit to see the blessing of the Easter baskets (page 413). Milwaukee Avenue in the vicinity of Division Street and Ashland Avenue offers a few gift shops, a bookstore, a couple of restaurants which are thoroughly acceptable but not steeped in any Polish gourmet tradition. You might try **Polish Villa,** 1249 North Ashland—good soups, *pierogi,* stuffed cabbage, etc.

In Chicago—an area within South Lawndale bounded by 22nd Street on the north, 32nd Street on the south, Albany on the east and Kostner on the west—find the heart of the Chicago Czech community known as the Little Village. As recently as 1962, the only language you'd have heard here was Czech, but with the incoming of Mexicans and a kind of hysterical concern over the nearness of Negroes in Lawndale proper, as much as 40 percent of the community has moved to Berwyn and Cicero. One fine small restaurant with all the flavor of "Old Czech" remains—the **Club Moravia,** 4142 West 26th Street, LA 2-9310. It's absolutely authentic, small, clean, and very good. The weeknight menu is printed in Czech and English and on the weekends the menu is English only, so depending on when you come, you can order Pecená Kachna, Knedlik a Zeli, or roast duck, dumpling and sauerkraut. The Pickled Beef with Sour Cream Gravy (Svickova) is memorable and so are the soups— Liver Dumpling, for instance, or Tripe Soup, which are both about as Czech as you can get. Pilsner beer and all bar whiskies available; full dinners that even people with big appetites can barely finish for as little as $2.10.

Open 4 PM to 8:30 PM daily; Sunday, noon to 7:30 PM. Reservations necessary on Thursday and Saturday nights. Closed Monday.

Try the **Czech Lodge,** 2519 Des Plaines, North Riverside, which is handsomely furnished and very convenient to Brookfield Zoo, or the **Old Prague,** 5928 Cermak Road, Cicero, or **Klas,** 5734 Cermak Road, Cicero.

The great German communities were assimilated generations ago except for one on North Lincoln Avenue from 4000 to 5000, known as Sauerkraut Boulevard. Put the emphasis on sour and forget about it. Good German food stores exist elsewhere, however—see Ethnic and Gourmet Food Shops, this chapter.

The old Swedish colony around Belmont and Clark is gone except for a Swedish delicatessen (page 370) and a fine little gift shop. **Dalkullan Imports,** 3252 North Clark, is the oldest Scandinavian shop in the city, stocks peasant craft items and contemporary gifts, like heavy, expensive Orrefors crystal, bright enamel kitchenware, pewter Norwegian blazer buttons at 25¢ each. It's always Christmas in some old rosewood cases toward the rear: they're filled with little decorative items to buy and put away for the holidays. And because customers of Swedish descent are regular patrons, the shop still rents gold wedding crowns. You might ask to see them—they're fairy-tale crowns for young brides.

Farther north on Clark, where Swedes settled a community called Andersonville, there's been considerable promotional activity to create the Swedish-American equivalent of Chinatown. Shops, and restaurants as already mentioned, are on Clark Street north from 5100.

The **Swedish Pioneer Historical Society** is located at 5125 North Spaulding (North Park College Campus), and you will delight Professor E. Gustav Johnson if you show an interest in it. If you know any families of Swedish descent in Chicago, speak up and ask for a chance to see the **Swedish Engineers Society**

of Chicago, 503 West Wrightwood, a fantastic old Baroque mansion that's at its best during the annual St. Lucia Festival on December 13; an incredible smorgasbord, Christmas songs by Swedish choral groups, and the crowning of the St. Lucia queen. Incidentally, no invitation to the **Swedish Club of Chicago,** 1258 North LaSalle, should be ignored; the food is in the best Swedish tradition.

Unlike the worldly Dutch merchants who founded New York City in the 17th Century, the Dutch who emigrated to the Midwest in the 19th Century were farmers to the last man. Those who settled south of Chicago around Lake Calumet were members of a single denomination, the very strict Calvinist Christian Reformed Church. The two communities they settled have always been called "onion country" but are formally known as South Holland and Roseland. The settlers built 12 churches, and life still revolves around their Calvinist services—at least two on Sunday. Though onion growing has given way almost entirely to general truck farming, roses and trees, nothing else about the communities except the buildings seems to have changed in a hundred years. Dutch who have come to Chicago since the end of World War II refer to both communities as Dutch ghettos, but except for the churches and one store, the Dutch in Roseland and South Holland are completely invisible and impenetrable as an ethnic group.

The store is worth visiting—import foods and gift items. An enormous stock of cookies, wafers, honey cakes, toffees, candies, glaces, 50 kinds of chocolate, soups, vegetables, spices and all the famous Dutch cheeses. Gift items run to Dutch cigars and pipe tobaccos, traditional blue Delft, silver jewelry and flower bulbs—daffodils, tulips, hyacinths, crocuses. A catalog for mail orders is available, also travel posters and some other items for school display. Tours can be arranged for schools and clubs. Contact the proprietor, Tom Vander Vliet, **Hollandse Winkel,** 11036 South Michigan, Chicago, 60628, 785-9250. Use Dan Ryan Expy to Wentworth exit, 99th St.

The **Holland Dutch** store in Berwyn, at 6700 West Roosevelt Road, carries similar merchandise, plus wooden shoes, for a smaller and more integrated Dutch community in Berwyn.

For a short time after World War II there was a Japanese-American colony, but its members are already assimilated as the 7,000 Chinese who don't live in Chinatown. Before World War II, Chicago's Japanese population numbered 300 persons. Forced resettlement drove it up to 25,000; now the population has leveled off at 15,000 and lives in little pockets throughout the city. Its Christian churches generally have English-language services in the morning and Japanese-language services in the afternoon. You might try the **Congregational Church,** 701 Buckingham; the **Methodist Church,** 900 West Sheridan Road; and the **Presbyterian Church,** 3500 North Sheffield. There are several Buddhist temples in the city; the most convenient one is in Old Town, **Midwest Buddhist Church,** at 1763 North North Park. It sponsors two impressive late-summer street festivals, the Ginza (page 425) and the Obon (page 422). For Japanese import groceries, page 371.

There never was a French colony here, though there are French. The sizable group of Serbians is spread out, too, except for the little neighborhood off Milwaukee Avenue where the restaurants (page 59) are. Italians can be found in clusters everywhere. The time to share their way of life is during the *festas* and the patron saint holidays that draw them back from wherever they live to the churches (see Annual Events).

THE MEXICANS

The largest number of Mexicans by far are in South Chicago in the vicinity of the foundries and mills. The second largest group is probably the one in the vicinity of Blue Island and 18th Street. It's an ancient section of the city, with decrepit firetraps—a slum. A number of small storefront restaurants dot the area; a gigantic *supermercado* at 18th dominates it. The store, owned and run by two jolly Italians, caters also to Puerto Ricans and East Indians and is a lively place to shop (page 366). **El Nopal,** down the block, bakes twice daily, at 5 AM and again at 11:30 AM and on Saturday is sold out before 2 PM. A Mexican mail-order outlet, **Casa La Barata,** is filled with inexpensive and colorful dry goods and clothes. **San Fernando** is the pharmacy for the entire neighborhood, does a big business in herbs, *yaceites, medicinas.* In summer the entire street has some of the feeling of a Mexican market square; evenings, the young men of the neighborhood lounge around **El Burro,** the local nightclub, watching the girls go by. But in winter, when the impoverished neighborhood shivers through Chicago's endlessly raw days, one wonders what distorted tales were heard back home to lure so many to a harsh climate, an inhospitable city, and victimization by their own shrewder countrymen.

Celebration: Mexican Independence Day, September 15. A long and colorful parade down State Street, one of the best from a spectator's point of view.

Parents who want to give their children a firsthand introduction to the kinds of people who make up big cities beyond the groups cited here can easily find other little neighborhoods of foreign-born families. Use the Yellow Pages to find the churches that list foreign-language services and work out from those. Go to the food shops—page 365, this book. Their counters and shelves are filled with the specialties of other cultures, and if you shop with the idea of wanting to learn, a proud proprietor will generally give you a great deal of information about his culture and upcoming events that can be shared. Use the "Annual Guide to Gourmet Shopping" that's a tear-out section of

Chicago magazine. Its list of shops will take you all over the city, and almost always, wherever there's a foreign food shop, there's an ethnic neighborhood nearby.

INTEGRATED AND NEGRO NEIGHBORHOODS

When the Department of State sponsors official foreign visitors to Chicago, two neighborhoods are high on the sightseeing priority lists. The first is the Lake Meadows-Prairie Shore developments (see map, page 374): a modern complex of high rises, town houses and shopping center planned to become exactly what it is today—an area of middle-income integrated housing for about 9,500 people. The second is Hyde Park-Kenwood, the nation's outstanding example of integration and urban renewal in an area where a prime goal was neighborhood conservation of rambling old Queen Anne houses of the 1860's and 70's and mansions and spacious apartments that were constructed from 1900 on. The area runs from about 47th Street on the north to 59th Street on the south, and west from Lake Shore Drive to Cottage Grove. It's worth driving through if only to see what an old, substantial, fully integrated neighborhood of families in upper-middle- and middle-income brackets looks like. The great houses on Greenwood, Woodlawn, Kimbark and Kenwood between 48th and 50th streets are perhaps the most startling of all, not simply because they're estate-sized homes in the heart of the city, but because of the human mix. For instance, the owners and occupants of homes in the 4800 block on Woodlawn include the Dean of the Law School at the University of Chicago, the Reverend Clarence H. Cobb of the First Church of Deliverance, cartoonist Bill Mauldin, an order of priests, the Reverend Elijah Muhammad, leader of the Black Muslims, and, in the house guarded by two 300-pound Bangkok temple lions, an architect and his family.

Chatham, farther south, is a showplace for visiting Negroes, since it's almost entirely a middle-income neighborhood, containing a subneighborhood known as the "Golden Rectangle," famous both for its custom-built homes and their owners—people of the stature of Mahalia Jackson, for instance. The Golden Rectangle is bounded by 79th and 99th streets, the Dan Ryan Expressway and South King Drive—a residential community of unusually wide streets and pleasantly shaded lawns, fine old churches and a good school. To everyone except Negroes, the obvious pattern of well-heeled middle class living (Saturday afternoon devoted to raking the lawn, for instance), generally comes as a surprise. So does the statistic that 44 percent of all Negroes in Chicago own their own homes.

On a political and economic basis, Negroes in Chicago achieve more power than elsewhere in the country, as proven by their numbers in politics and in the ownership or control of major businesses. There is a Negro Establishment and there are also Negro rackets; and for every level within the white social hierarchy there is a similar, if not identical, level in the Negro community. You could not, for example, name Chicago's most prominent scientists without including the names of Drs. Percy Julian and T. K. Lawless. Or name leading educators without immediately including John Hope Franklin, Chairman of the Department of History at the University of Chicago. Or leading artists without naming sculptor Richard Hunt and Pulitzer Prize-winning poet Gwendolyn Brooks, who is now also the official Illinois state poet.

If you talk about the few major consumer magazines published here, you find that the leading publishers are Hugh Hefner (*Playboy*), John Johnson (*Ebony*) and Leonard Evans (*Tuesday,* a newspaper magazine). If you talk about newspaper publishing, this city has five, not four dailies, and the fifth is the *Chicago Daily Defender,* which has been published since 1905 and is bought by at least 36,000 Chicagoans.

Before the Picasso sculpture was unveiled at the Civic Center at least a couple of white aldermen who weren't happy about nonobjective art insisted that art and the city would be served better by a representational sculpture of Ernie Banks of the Cubs. They weren't being facetious—in this sports-happy town Mr. Banks is a Chicago hero.

The history of the Negro in Chicago begins with the first man to build a home and become a permanent settler in the territory then called Checagou —Jean Baptiste Point du Sable. On his father's side he was a descendant of an ancient French family variously known as Du Sable, De Sable, or Point de Sable. His mother was Negro, probably a slave. Young Jean Baptiste Point du Sable was a well educated, French-speaking trader who came down from New France to Checagou in the winter of 1782 or 1783. The house he built, brought his wife to and raised his family, in later years became the legendary John Kinzie home, the one Kinzie's daughter-in-law described as a "mansion," on the north bank of the river directly facing Fort Dearborn. You see it in any of the early prints of Chicago, though not all the outbuildings Point du Sable erected —two barns, a horsemill, a bakehouse, a hen house, a workshop, a dairy and a smokehouse—are visible.

Long before the Civil War there was a small Negro community in the town, with roots as deep as any other settlement. But the group remained small until the two world wars created vast job opportunities and blacks began their vast migration into the city. The Negro population began doubling and sometimes tripling between one census and the next. Today it's at more than one million, and because of systematic impoverishment in the Delta, migration is again accelerating.

Chicago is a syphon for the Negroes of Mississippi. The link is the Illinois Central Railroad heading north in a direct line between New Orleans and Chicago. The points of entry in the city are the 63rd Street and 12th Street Illinois Central stations. If you want to see nightly migration of unbelievable dimensions, be at the latter at one minute to midnight when the human flood leaving the train is so great that it's channeled through a separate gate rather than directly into the station.

The problems of the illiterate or semi-literate backcountry Negro coming north and finding the only shelter available to him to be in the ghetto obviously can't be explored in this book. But the ghettos, though easily inconspicuous to the visitor, are thoroughly self-evident if you want to see them.

The ghetto solution is not merely the bulldozing of decaying buildings and the substitution of concrete block high rises. Chicago did that in a $70 million project and created a concrete ghetto even more appalling than the one it replaced. The 28 buildings of the Robert Taylor Homes on State Street between 39th and 54th are the tragic consequences of a city's insistence that its bottom-of-the-barrel poor be geographically confined—in high-rise containers that could not be "home" to anyone, but especially not to people with rural backgrounds. You don't have to go out of your way to see these—the project begins precisely where the south end of the Illinois Institute of Technology campus stops.

The phrase "Black Power" didn't originate in Chicago, but it finds tremendous expression in the West Side and South Side ghettos precisely because it offers the one thing the ghettos haven't—hope. **The Wall of Respect,** at 43rd and Langley, in a ghetto slum filled with Soul Brother signs, is a remarkable expression of that hope—a huge mural of paintings and photographs on the long side of an old building. It was created in the summer of 1967 by artists in a black nationalist group called the Organization of Black American Culture. Some of the paintings are crude, and some are in the tradition of the great Mexican muralists; one section, which contains the finest painting of all, is "Guernica" all over again. An upraised arm with a clenched fist, used as a greeting between Black Power advocates who see each other across the street (but also the symbol of revolution or communism or both the world over), dominates one part of the mural; a sign nearby states, "This wall was created to honor our Black Heroes and Beautify Our Community." But, in a way, the wall is self-defeating. It's a protest and a protest needs to be witnessed. Yet it's in a neighborhood that resents white and nonmilitant blacks alike and is capable of being hostile to both. So most people stay away and it doesn't get seen. If you want to see it, go by cab or car in midday, preferably a Saturday, when the area is busy with its own affairs and police cars cruise through regularly.

Forty-third Street looks no more menacing than any other Chicago street. If anything, it's just another commercial street cutting across a low-income Negro neighborhood. On a Saturday, especially, it's teeming with people—a noisy, garrulous neighborhood shopping center in the truest sense of the word. In any Negro neighborhood, the sense of community affinity is strong and the streets are filled with life.

The beat is loud, unconfined, comes from transistor radios and the radios of passing cars and amplification from the record shops; from bursts of laughter, shouts, joshing and horseplay. The atmosphere is free and easy, and an inordinate amount of socializing takes place on the street against a background of barbershops, chicken and rib shacks, beauty shops, recreation parlors, secondhand furniture and appliance stores, bars, storefront tabernacles and markets advertising chitlings, pigs' knuckles, pigs' feet, fresh crabs, buffalofish, collards. No group of whites as economically depressed or as systematically excluded from the mainstream of city life copes with its ghetto environment the way Negroes do. The people on the crowded, narrow-sidewalked ghetto business streets may have little or nothing, but they've found ways to make having nothing a kind of inside joke. Seen from the outside by someone who's not a part of it and who never can be, the mystique of Negro life creates a strange kind of envy for the richness of a neighborhood that laughs though it has every right to cry, and affirms life with every breath.

On entirely different levels of Negro life in this city, the following are open to visitors. Phone first in each case for a specific appointment.

Supreme Life Insurance Co. of America, 3501 South King Drive, KE 8-5100. The largest Negro business in the North and the largest company in the country writing Negro life insurance; always on every official State Department tour.

Chicago Daily Defender, 2400 South Michigan Avenue, CA 5-2400. The largest Negro newspaper in the city and the only guaranteed-circulation Negro daily in the nation. Founded in 1905.

Johnson Publishing Co., Inc., 1820 South Michigan, CA 5-1000. The editorial offices of *Ebony, Jet, Negro Digest, Tan* magazines.

Tuesday Publications, Inc., 180 North Michigan, 726-0497. The editorial offices of *Tuesday,* a monthly newspaper magazine.

Radio Station WVON (Voice of the Negro), 3350 South Kedzie, 847-2600. Its combination of rhythm-and-blues plus editorials boosting civil rights give it one of the highest ratings in the city's hotly competitive 31-station market.

Muhammad's Mosque of Islam, No. 2, 5335 South Greenwood, MU 4-4486. Tours of the school may also be arranged by calling Minister James, MU 4-8823.

First Church of Deliverance, 4315 South Wabash, DR 3-7700. Superb gospel singing and the eminent Reverend Clarence H. Cobb, who has been its minister for some 30 years. Friday evening candle lighting at 9 PM; Sunday services at 11 AM and 8 PM; broadcast service (WCFL) at 11 PM.

Third Baptist Church of Chicago, 938 West 69th Street, 224-2838. Known for its Dorie Miller Memorial Foundation, established to perpetuate the memory of the first Negro to receive the Navy Cross for gallantry in World War II; the Dorie Miller Library, specializing in out-of-print books on Negro life in America and Africa; the annual (first Sunday in October) Dorie Miller Foundation Awards to, among others, Archbishop John P. Cody in 1966, Senator Charles

Percy (R., Ill.) in 1967. The church has an excellent choir, offers the chance to hear hymns, spirituals, gospel singing at Sunday 11 AM services and a 7:30 PM Sunday evening choir recital. Minister is the Reverend Elmer L. Fowler.

Mahalia Jackson still sings occasionally at the **Greater Salem Baptist Church,** 215 West 71st Street, TR 4-2325. You can hear some of the Arthur Logan singers in the Goodwill Spiritual Choir, of which Mr. Logan is director, at the **Monumental Baptist Church,** 729 East Oakwood, Sundays at 11 AM. Be on time because they sing early.

Chicago Urban League headquarters are at 4500 South Michigan, AT 5-5800. Chicago **NAACP** headquarters are at 431 South Dearborn, 939-5365.

ETHNIC AND GOURMET FOOD SHOPS

Long after an ethnic group seems totally assimilated, it continues to recreate its heritage through its cooking. So the neighborhood grocery store turns out to be, after all, the best way to discover Chicago's foreign flavors, to browse and buy items native to a community but epicure to you.

The proprietor of the neighborhood grocery is usually a rare character. Though he superficially may have adopted some supermarket methods of merchandising, he basically resists the whole notion of prepackaging. No matter how loudly he yells at the customer who squeezes, feels, and pinches the produce, down in his heart he knows that's the only way to buy it. The idea of selling two tomatoes plastic-wrapped in a purple cardboard basket outrages him. A customer should be able to pick up his produce and smell its freshness, just as she should be able to break off a small stalk of oregano and crumble it between her fingers and delight in its bouquet. So he continues to sell his herbs and spices in bulk from huge open burlap sacks; he hangs his garlicky sausages on hooks above the meat counter, he sells his olives from open trays and he keeps open for looking and sniffing as many other food-stuffs as he can. In short, the ethnic grocery store greets you with glorious redolence, and restraint is impossible—you buy this for yourself and that for a friend and something else for a neighbor and cart everything home in innumerable little brown paper bags and white cardboard cartons.

Conte-di-Savoia, 555 West Roosevelt, 666-3471

An Italian import shop of impressive dimensions that also accommodates foodstuffs from the entire Mediterranean area. Sensory pleasures here are innumerable; in fact, they border on gluttony, since you're confronted by provolones the size of watermelons, great black-waxed wheels of romano with a wedge removed to reveal the whiteness within, huge slabs of *fintano,* creamy *stracchio,* Italian salamis three feet long. On a marble counter in the front of the store, trays of fresh, salted capers and fresh snails. Nearby, casks of olives, sacks of herbs, of dried beans and coffee beans; barrels of crushed wheats and cornmeal, ropes of purple Italian onions and dried red peppers; bags of pignoli and pistachio nuts; fresh poppy seed; feathery bulbs of finnochio, stalks of pale fennel. Enough pasta, as somebody once said, to build a bridge of it across the Atlantic—and enough kinds of olive oil to float it when built. One concession to the present, destarched Italian rice, 22 calories per ounce. Fine Italian kitchen utensils: wood mortars and pestles, graters, whisks, espresso pots, coffee grinders, meat grinders. Some of the greatest restaurant-size utensils going, such as ladles and forks a yard long. The proprietor holds his head in horror as he recounts the time he inadvertently bought what amounts to a lifetime supply of these, looks at you hopefully as though you just might rescue him by miraculously wanting the entire lot.

Deligiannis Bros., Inc., 766 West Jackson, 782-9855

The grocery store with the good little restaurant behind traps you upon entry with a long glass counter displaying tray after tray of honey-drenched and powder-sugared pastries—*baklava, rallatourboriki, floryian, trigona, kadaife* and the like. When you can tear yourself away find sacks and barrels of pilafs, of fresh herbs and dried herbs, of Greek dill. Elsewhere, elegant white bulbed leeks, creamy young cheeses, such as feta, *kasseri, kefalotiri* and, to accompany them, Greek wines and beers. Oddly, the fish counter is possibly the only one in the city to offer all the hard-to-find classic ingredients for bouillabaisse, and though the white-aproned young clerks may never have heard of the dish by that name, they will happily volunteer a recipe that produces a less complicated Grecian version of same.

Mayoreo Supermercado La Casa del Pueblo, 1810 Blue Island, 421-4640

"Productos Importados de Mexico" a huge sign over the door proclaims, and so they are—once you work your way past the first two aisles of American breakfast cereals and canned fruit juices. This *supermercado* is run by two jolly Italians, Signori Consola and Lombardi, proprietors who take a proprietary interest in their customers far beyond mere moneymaking. They know, for instance, that every Mexican housewife will use six pounds of tomatoes daily and that at least three pounds will be peeled, seeded and chopped. So, along with fresh tomatoes in all sizes and at all prices and ripe green Mexican-grown tomatoes for *salsa verde,* you'll find small, wrinkle-skinned red versions at 10¢ per pound, a year-round bargain since peeled they're as good as any others. In contrast, the biggest Spanish onions this side of Spain. Avocados, melons, tamarinds, mangoes, bundles of the lemon-scented weed the Mexicans use for lemon tea; *calentro* (Mexican parsley); a dozen kinds of chili peppers; great open jars of black sage, oregano, coriander; little bundles of stick cinnamon; a mild, heavenly chili powder. Elsewhere, aisle after aisle of imported chili sauces, mole sauces, taco sauces; every bean that grows south of the border; cornmeals; canned cactus husks for homemade tamales; stacks of tortillas. At the meat counter, chorizos in all shapes and sizes, and plastic sacks of still-warm tamales made fresh daily by an old lady in the neighborhood. One somehow has visions of her delivering these under a blanket in a baby carriage; whatever her method, they arrive hot.

If you want Mexican cookware, such as bean pots, look on the shelves over the produce counters; there's all kinds of stuff, inexpensive and authentic. The small area set aside as a lunchroom serves good and inexpensive Mexican food. Ignore the steam table, which is filled with trays of sad-looking gringo dishes, and order from the small menus thumbtacked to the wall. Open daily to 10 PM.

Mikolajczyk Sausage Shop, 1737 West Division, HU 6-8870

Behind a perfectly ordinary storefront, in the window of which hang a few racks of smoked lean ribs and a few smoked sausages, find a grocery store catering to much of the Polish community in Chicago, even the part that's moved to the suburbs but returns weekends to shop here.

Mr. Chester Mikolajczyk, son of the original owners, and his aunt run the place. Chester cures and smokes 90 percent of the meats on the premises; his aunt makes the contents of the trays of takeout foods. Chester's sausages are all pure meat without fillings; American palates will probably best like the liver sausage, the Warsaw, Krakow, Bolshevik and ham sausages and, among meats, the smoked spareribs and meat loaf.

The hunter's stew the Poles call *bigos* is available three times weekly, not to be found anywhere else except in Polish homes. It's a marvelous cold-weather dish of sauerkraut, sausage, ham, fresh pork, mushrooms and seasonings of caraway and bay leaf, and could well be the star of any *apres* Bears' game buffet. Fresh-filled blintzes daily, extra large, extra thin, like oversized French crepes. On the shelves, fat glass jars and crocks of stuffed cabbage and haricot beans with pork; prune and raspberry jellies; dark Polish honey; the famous dried mushrooms of Poland at $16 per pound and a big-grained barley at 25¢ for a like amount. Two delicacies not to be overlooked by Chicagoans: the country cheese and the butter, which surely is the smoothest sweet butter in the city (Mr. Mikolajczyk insists it's whipped and will bubble up too fast for good cooking).

Sampolski Alliance Bakery, 1736 West Division

Few Polish pastries can compete with first rate French or Italian pastries, but Sampolski has three exceptions: form cake; a chocolate-frosted rum torte with raspberry-filled layers; and a Christmas and Easter specialty, four to five feet high, that's called a bankuch (the cake Germans call Baumkuchen).

Kuhn's Delicatessen and Liquors, 3053 North Lincoln, LA 5-4595

Kuhn's is so thoroughly German that it helps if you speak or at least read the language. The front doors are marked *Eingang* and *Ausgang,* and the signs over the shelves, counters, wines and meat market are even less helpful (since a door at least indicates which direction it will go). The place is an institution, never more so than between Thanksgiving and Christmas, when the old-fashioned imported German Christmas items of one's childhood are available —the gingerbread figures of St. Nicholas decorated with paper pictures of the saint; the shaped chocolates and candies wrapped in printed foil—tree ornaments, birds, snow madchen, bowling pins, tannenbaum; pfeffernusse and Christmas yeast dough cakes.

But Christmas or anytime, this is the place to come for Westphalian hams; German cheeses; German wines and beers and Schinkenhager (the crystal-clear, dry gin bottled in brown stoneware crocks); packaged mixes of *kartoffel-puffer* (potato pancake mix) and *knodel* (potato dumpling mix); tinned herrings entirely different from those sold in Scandinavian shops; lamprey in aspic, smoked conger eel, the livers of Baltic cods; rye and pumpernickel breads; salads and German hot dishes to take home for supper. And . . . but no. Go and discover Kuhn's for yourself. Go and stand in line behind the gentleman in the lederhosen who carries a great wicker basket on each arm and grandiosely relegates to his wife the baking and cooking ingredients while he proceeds with the far more important business of choosing the meats and cheese. Open daily to 10 PM.

Toscana Bakery, 2130 North Sheffield, 348-5576

This is the bakery that makes the superb French loaves served at the Red Carpet, Champs-Elysées, La Chaumiere, La Brasserie de Strasbourg, and the pan loaves served at The Bakery. The dough is a basic old-fashioned dough of just four ingredients; the loaves are shaped by hand and baked on a great old-fashioned brick hearth.

The hospitality in the small retail shop in front of the bakery is charming. Let Mrs. Franco Chiappa know you're interested in her baking and, if she's not too busy, you may be invited to tour the large baking room and possibly even to enter a small side kitchen for fresh coffee and hot bread served with curls of sweet butter from a stoneware crock. Over conversation you learn that the shop was opened by her parents some 35 years ago; that they sent her back to the University of San Marco in Florence to study, but that she actually graduated from Barat College in Lake Forest as a language major; that she is scandalized when people say they never know what to do with leftover French bread so they throw it out; that she has a dozen ways to use it and this is what they are; and you leave with a headful of recipes, including a way to make cookies from breadcrumbs.

From Thanksgiving through Christmas Mrs. Chiappa's mother bakes Italian specialties for the store: *panetone,* extra high, stuffed with raisins and citron; anise ring; *biscotti* cookies with almonds or raisins, lovely evocative delicacies baked by a fine Italian hand. Open Monday through Saturday, 7 AM to 7 PM.

Irish Imports, 1447 West Devon, 465-6113

Seamus McWilliams, proprietor, hails from Galway, and anyone who longs for that rolling brogue surely must drop in for a visit. "It's only this morning I was thinking of you," and he smiles that warm smile and you learn indeed he had you in his mind because a new shipment of something or other you'd once asked about has just arrived.

His small, unpretentious shop is full of Irish imports that you might find elsewhere if you worked at it long enough. But the one thing that is his alone and that brings in the Irish from as far as northern Wisconsin is his pure pork sausage. There's none like that, so lean it has to be started in butter in the pan. It comes in three sizes: American breakfast, cocktail and the rolly-plump that is standard Irish breakfast sausage.

The other items that crowd his shop are a curious hodgepodge of everything that's caught his fancy and that he could order in. The wares are arranged neatly, but you're liable to find a display of teas and oatmeals backing up to lengths of Donegal tweeds and tins of Irish relishes; marrowfat peas and gooseberries snuggling next to hand-knit fishermen's sweaters of unbleached oiled wool. Dolls dressed in Irish national costumes or as leprechauns or nuns sit on a shelf next to teapots from Tipperary; and bottled squashes, ginger beer and lime barleys hide pure damask table linens. English and Irish cigarettes are nicely displayed next to mincemeat from Scotland and Carrajeen moss, which, in some mysterious Irish fashion, is good for ulcers or a cold. Mr. McWilliams keeps exhausting hours: 10 AM to 10 PM Monday through Thursday, to midnight Friday, Saturday to 3 AM because "They get to drinking in the tavern next door and then they want sausage sandwiches." (Seamus is in Ireland as of this printing and his shop temporarily closed.)

Litberg Bakery, 1519 West Devon, RO 4-5441

One block west of Mr. McWilliams, you can plunge into the entirely different world of a bagel factory. Until an envious competitor called the Health Department, half the city of Chicago used to march into the bakery on Saturday night, scoop the kind and amount of hot bagels it wanted from a large dump cart, and pay for them on the way out. Now, a conventional retail store has been added so that the only hands touching the bagels are the bagel bakers' and those of the little old ladies behind the high glass sales counter. Formally, the Health Department has also barred visitors to the bakery, but there are occasions when you just might be told very conspiratorially that you can go in back just long enough to look at the team of 14 bagel makers who work on an assembly line system, with the two stars of the enterprise creating five dozen each in less than five minutes, because they're paid on a piecework basis. The kitchen has a lovely, warm, wet smell, and the bagels are triumphs of variety—plain, egg, onion, pumpernickel, poppyseed and sesame seed. It's open 24 hours a day.

Scandia Fish & Delicatessen, 1033 West Belmont, BI 8-1770

The last of the fine old Scandinavian food shops in an area that was once Swedish-German-Italian and now is just about everything else. The proprietors see no reason for moving—all their old customers come back on weekends, and the shop is then a good place for anyone studying Swedish. Here you buy the great Swedish cheeses and imported fish specialties; choose from 50 different kinds of herring; buy a pound of kalvsylta, the jellied veal loaf used as hors d'oeuvres, and another of smoked buckling, which is a good cocktail fish spread; and a third of fresh, homemade Swedish meatballs; and prinskorv, a cocktail sausage made of pork and veal. Or you buy one of the Swedish cookbooks and some of the imported utensils and ingredients for fruit soup; and, if it's early in the week and the shop isn't crowded, you may be offered so many slivers of this and samplings of that in return for your interest that you won't be able to eat for hours after. The shop also does catering. Open 8 AM to 6 PM Monday through Saturday.

Vollendorf's Scandia Foods, 3944 West North Avenue, BE 5-0024, is a fascinating old general store catering to other Scandinavians, Germans and Poles and offering a fine mix of the staples of each group's national cuisine. The place is a landmark, having been there since 1903, and is reputed to be the largest importer of Scandinavian goods in the country. If you study the stock you'll never dispute the claim. Open to 6:30 nightly, Thursday to 8 PM.

S. P. Rasmussen, once next door to Vollendorf's, carries fine Scandinavian imports of all kinds. The most appealing are unquestionably a line of Danish pinafores and bibs for toddlers. For new address see page 240.

Black Forest Finer Foods and Restaurant, the Austrian delicatessen attached to Schwarzwaldhaus, 8840 North Waukegan Road in Morton Grove, stocks more than 30 kinds of cheese and 80 kinds of sausage, of which some 40 are made on the premises. The shop deserves lyrical praise, especially for the items it makes, such as the three kinds of bratwurst—German (whitish, fully cooked), German-Hungarian (with paprika and onions) and Sheboygan (a raw type that's at its best cooked over charcoal). It's a madhouse on weekends when chattering North Germans, Bavarians and Austrians pour in to buy fresh geese and rendered goose fat, potato salads and herring salads, fleischsalat, strings of sausages, pastries and more. In winter, young Herr Tschurtz smokes goose breasts and legs, turkeys and whole chickens and carries fresh game. Year-round he roasts young suckling pigs and caters hot or cold trays and hors d'oeuvres. For Chicagoans, he is absolutely worth the drive out from town. Open 9 AM to 9 PM daily; Sunday from 11:30 AM. Closed Monday.

For soul food shopping go to the nameless open-air market on South State Street between 71st and 73rd streets. It's three blocks of one-story shops open to the street all summer, with produce and house and garden plants in boxes, crates, baskets, and pots all set out on most of the available side-walk—thus slowing your normal stride so the Italians who run the shops can really plead and shout for your attention. Each purveyor insists that his radishes, onion sets, collard greens, mustard greens, turnip greens, fresh okra, strawberries and tomatoes are better than his neighbor's, and each mimes pain and deep sorrow when you decide not to buy. A fish-and-meat market offers porgy, buffalo fish, butterfish, Florida mullet, turtles, white bass, silver bass, hard-shell crabs, three kinds of catfish—channel, bullhead and spoon-bill—coons, rabbits, possum, and bottled oddments, such as Louisiana hot sauce and Louisiana country syrup. The proprietor here is a majestically slow-moving man, and though his shellfish is always fresh, his fish sometimes looks as if too much time had elapsed between netting and selling. If the eyes are filmed, don't buy.

Not too far away is a meat market that specializes in exotica: bear, buf-falo, whale, wild turkey, hippopotamus, reindeer, jaguar, alligator, plus stand-ard kinds of wild game. Everything is frozen, of course, and is selected only after suitable discussion as to cuts and cooking. The place also specializes in skinning, cutting and packaging hunters' fresh game. It's **Czimer Foods,** 953 West 63rd Street, WA 5-7800, and no matter how expensive your order, it won't take a check in lieu of real cash.

A few blocks northwest from the Museum of Science and Industry find one of the largest and most cosmopolitan supermarkets in the city, the **Hyde Park Co-op.** If you're from a country where supermarkets are just being in-troduced, this one is worth seeing. It's a cooperative, serves the University of Chicago community, hence stocks produce and products from around the world. For Chicagoans, it's one of the best places in the city to buy Japanese foods and is located in the Hyde Park Shopping Center, 55th Street at Lake Park Avenue, 667-1444. The other contender is **Treasure Island,** 3460 North Broadway, EA 7-3880. It's also open on Sunday.

Back in the Loop, head for **Stop & Shop,** 16 West Washington, Chicago's oldest gourmet food shop, opened shortly after the Fire as the joint venture of two young men who'd met during the Civil War. It very quickly achieved a position it's never relinquished—*the* gourmet shop of the city, so that very early in its history, a young food salesman brash enough to walk in saying "I have something new for your store" was instantly booted out.

It's a dazzling place that greets you with the sweetness of fresh fruits, the yeasty fragrance of bakery goods, the pungency of freshly roasted coffee beans being ground to order; the fragrance of teas from India, Formosa, Ceylon, the irresistible aromas of several dozen different kinds of cheese, fresh salted nuts, beautifully prepared carry-out foods. At the meat counter, famous because all its meats are aged, hams from every part of this country—the long lean

shanks of smoked Virginia hogs, smoky Tennessee and backcountry hams—
Westphalian hams and Italian prosciuttos, lean hams from Denmark and
Poland. Smoked turkey year-round, game birds in season. Down the aisles,
80 kinds of honey from almost as many places in the world; every cocktail
tidbit that has ever been tinned, jarred, bottled or put into metal squeeze
tubes; shelves of imported cookies, cakes, biscuits. At Christmas, the gift
hampers go around the world packed with fine liquors or fruits and cheese
or any combination of anything you name. Never make the mistake of thinking you can just dash in to pick up a fancy French mustard and then be on your
way. You can't—nobody can. There are just too many temptations. Open
9 AM to 6 PM Monday through Saturday. The phone is RA 6-8500.

Note: **Field's** and **Carson's** have excellent gourmet shops, and **Le Petit Pavillon**
in the Drake Hotel specializes in elegant gift baskets of fine liquors, imported
pâtés in handsome little crocks, cheeses and cocktail tidbits. Almost everything in the shop is tinned, boxed or bottled and can travel.

C. M. Langill, 1135 North State, SU 7-3860

The last of its kind, an emporium where you know the owner and every
one of the butchers and clerks by name and they in turn know you. A shop
where you can phone in your order, ask Joe how the lettuce is today and get
an honest answer; where the meats are prime and cut to order only. A deluxe
store that sends a key employee to the wholesale market each morning to
pick the freshest, the finest and bring it into the shop. A shop that will offer
to get for you anything it may not have in stock and does, and delivers it in
time for dinner.

Langill customers are the most catered-to customers in the city. The roast
arrives with an elegant design of larding, the chops arrive Frenched, dressed
in paper frills; plump white chickens come with parsley tucked under their
wings; squab boned if that's the way you want it. Game birds in season,
splendidly dressed. Fowl and fish are fresh, not frozen, and deliveries are
made in refrigerated trucks. If you walk in and see no one but the white-
aproned staff, don't be surprised—there are days when 90 percent of the
business is done by phone.

Dinkel's Bakery, 3329 North Lincoln, BU 1-7300

A German bakery with superb chocolate cakes, cheesecakes and coffee-
cakes and fine sweet rolls. At Christmas, elaborately decorated Black Forest
cake, very rich and gooey; two kinds of stollen; marzipan, lebkuchen, and
Hansel and Gretel gingerbread children decorated with colored icings.

Guidarelli Nut Co. 732 North Wells, WH 4-7778

A wholesaler that also sells retail at lower than usual prices. Twenty kinds
of nuts for baking and eating, one of the few places where you can find

natural pistachios. Also packaged nuts for executive gifts and mail-order service.

Burhop's, 545 North State, 644-7818

The ne plus ultra of fish markets, with some 150 varieties of fish and shellfish at any given time. Also lobster-clam steamers with the contents packed in seaweed. Monday and Tuesday 9 AM to 4 PM; other days to 5 PM; Saturday to noon.

Sara Lee Resale Shop, 8007 North Milwaukee (Oakton), Niles, 282-3205

All the Sara Lee products, plus items you won't find elsewhere—frozen beef and shrimp dinners, institutional-size whipped cream cakes and cheese cakes that will serve 20, parfait-type things like strawberry or chocolate mousse in quart containers for less than $1. To give you an idea of other prices, three packages of croissants for $1. Monday through Friday 10 AM to 6 PM. Saturday to 5 PM. Expect to wait in line on weekends.

Pepperidge Farm Resale Shops are located at 7656 North Milwaukee, Niles; 139 South Oak Park Avenue, Oak Park; 738 Ogden Avenue, Downers Grove. Save about one-third on bread, rolls and a few non-Pepperidge items like pretzels.

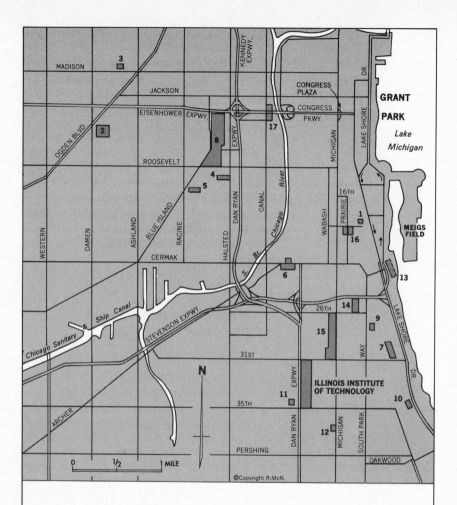

Near West and
Near South Sides

1. Site of Fort Dearborn massacre
2. West Side Medical Center, Univ. of Illinois
3. Chicago Stadium
4. Maxwell St. Market
5. South Water Street Market
6. Chinatown
7. Michael Reese Hospital
8. University of Illinois, Circle Campus
9. Lake Meadows and Prairie Shores
10. Stephen Douglas Tomb
11. White Sox Ball Park
12. Museum of African-American History
13. McCormick Place Site
14. Mercy Hospital
15. South Commons
16. Glessner House, Kimball House
17. Post Office

SIGHTSEEING: MEMORABLE MISCELLANY

17

Sunday in Chicago
Three Sunday Strolls
Chicago's Incredible Cemetery
Natural History—Outdoors
Tours—Self and Guided
Radio and Television Broadcasts
Oddments
Beyond the City Limits: North Shore and Fox River Valley

CHAPTER 17

SIGHTSEEING: MEMORABLE MISCELLANY

No city reveals itself instantly. If it's a young city with some early history that doesn't conform to the image it now wishes to project, it does its best to conceal the aberrations and eccentricities. No city is going to inform you straightaway that if you visit one of its cemeteries you'll find that its leading citizens—the personages the city is proudest of—were often so obsessed with the idea they were going to disappear that they built monuments and mausoleums approaching the grandeur that was Rome. The cemetery is Graceland and it has to be seen to be believed, but you'll find a short description of it on page 386.

All cities neglect to tell you the little things that in themselves may not be especially significant but add up to the reasons why their citizens can tolerate the constant noise and pressure and overcrowding and why they don't pick up their belongings and flee. Chicago has miraculously retained enough of the elements that elsewhere spell if not a pastoral existence a sense of openness and a closeness to nature. Rabbits still live free in the heart of the city (in the little park just east of Michigan Avenue and the Chicago Avenue Fire Station), and night people come across them busily munching roots in the small flower bed and bulbs in the little garden the firemen have planted on their side lawn.

Chicagoans also know that off season along almost any beach you can find crinoids, fossils of sea lilies that grew at the time the lake was saltwater, and that coral still comes up from the lake bottom looking like honeycomb. Adults may walk along the edge of the lake for miles without seeing more than tossed up shell refuse; but children, closer to the ground and more observant, even discover brachiopods, clam-type things, as well as the fossils. In the suburbs along the North Shore you can walk on any of the beaches during winter and make fine discoveries; and you can cut across beaches that obviously belong to the shoreline homes because riparian rights do not disallow walking.

Fossils can be found wherever there are pebbles, and the beaches in the Lincoln Park area also yield tiny Indiana snail fossils which come from the great blocks of Bedford limestone imported years ago to form part of Chicago's breakwaters.

From mid-October to Thanksgiving, and later, thousands of migrating ducks feed in the sheltered waters within the breakwater off Chicago Avenue and can be seen by anyone who loves the loneliness of a deserted lakefront—just himself and the migrants. In mid-May, Chicago is host to at least 175 species of songbirds in passage to nesting grounds in Canada, and year-round is home to another 125 species that nest regularly in the area. But unless you get up early to stroll through the parks or find the always quiet places in the city that offer sanctuary to noncity birds, as at the Stephen Douglas Memorial Park (page 444), all you're likely to see are scruffy English sparrows, grackles, bedraggled pigeons and, at night, along still-elegant old residential streets such as Bellevue or Cedar, rats.*

SUNDAY IN CHICAGO

For churches with notable choirs, page 174. For Sunday brunch, page 69.

The rule of thumb is that most Loop restaurants and bars are closed on Sunday. This is because the Loop is deserted, not because of blue laws. Shops are closed except in Old Town (page 89), where they open at noon. Legitimate theatres are dark, but community theatres aren't. Art galleries are closed, but the art museums have capacity crowds. The Field Museum is mobbed in the afternoon but gloriously empty in the morning except for Chicago fathers making discoveries with their offspring. All museums are open on Sunday. Sports events are scheduled; so are concerts and recitals. For in-city sightseeing, try one or more of these:

Maxwell Street, 1300 South at Halsted Street

In the 1920's, Maxwell Street did $1 million worth of business each week. Customers came from all parts of the city, tourists from all over the world. It was worth your life to browse without buying because the merchants were out to sell. They shouted at you from behind their pushcarts, always wheel-to-wheel along Maxwell and Jefferson streets. They grabbed your arm and harangued you into buying their wares. They hired brawny "pullers" who yanked you from the crowd, plunked you in front of the merchandise, intimi-

---

* A by-product of Rush Street restaurant garbage cans.

dated you into buying. More than one tourist filed assault and battery charges, but nothing changed.

The old Maxwell Street had a single ethnic flavor, one part screaming Yiddish, one part barter-and-haggle, one part malevolent cooking odors with cabbage predominating. Today, it's a Berlitz of dialects, languages, accents, amplified music, and the cooking odors indicate the new groups in the neighborhood—Negroes, Puerto Ricans, Mexicans, Italians, Greeks, Gypsies. The territory is greatly expanded now, running west from Halsted to the intersection of Blue Island and Racine.

Merchandise is piled on sidewalks, card tables, carts, tailgates. It's hung on racks, heaped on rickety display stands. It's used and it's new, and at least half of the latter is suspect—auto tires, electric appliances, power tools, transistor radios, phonographs, shoes, toys, cosmetics, birdseed, hamster feed, canned goods, wrenches, screwdrivers, prepackaged pairs of socks, junk jewelry, paints in unopened cans and in open-for-inspection ten-gallon drums of expensive decorator colors. Used merchandise runs heavily to old plumbing fixtures, doorknobs, clothing, boxes containing thousands of dismembered watches, worn bedspreads, exhausted hair brushes, bulky old TV sets, typewriters, dreadfully thumbed comic books at 2 for 5¢ and grease-spotted old girlie magazines at 5¢ each.

People cook and sell food on every street. For 50¢ you can buy succulent Southern fried chicken; for 25¢, a spicy Italian sausage, grilled and stuffed into a small loaf of Italian bread. Elsewhere, hamburgers, frankfurters, baloney grilled and served on slabs of rye; people push through the streets stuffing their mouths.

Browsing's no longer a sin, bargains still exist: power tools at $15 that would be twice the price anywhere else; luxurious house plants at $4 and $5 —the kind that go for $12 in a florist shop. Fruits and vegetables by the crateful, sold at prices so low you can't resist. Still, caveat emptor. Nobody's above quoting prices at higher than retail if he thinks he can get away with it.

By custom, Maxwell Street is a place you visit in the morning or about noon. This gives you enough time to get to nearby Chiam Restaurant, in Chinatown, for Sunday brunch or to come back up to the Near North Side for the same. Chiam serves brunch until 2 PM; the Near North restaurants until 3 PM. Or, you may have eaten enough on the street to simply want to continue sightseeing. You're just a few blocks south of the University of Illinois Circle Campus and Jane Addams' Hull House. Check map (page 374) and text (page 333). Also within walking distance east on Roosevelt Road: Fishman's, on page 277; Chernin's, page 277; Conte-di-Savoia, page 365. Incidentally, you can't drive into Maxwell Street for the crowds; the nearest parking is north of Roosevelt Road (12th Street) in one of the U. of I. parking lots. CTA Sunday schedules frequently change, so call MO 4-7220 and ask for fastest Sunday bus or elevated train route.

Sightseeing cruises on the lake. Depending on the arrival of spring, all of the following run from mid-April or early May through September.

Shoreline Marine Sightseeing, docks at the John G. Shedd Aquarium, 1200 South Lake Shore Drive, WE 9-4681; cruises from 11 AM to 6 PM; docks evenings in the harbor opposite Buckingham Fountain. Takes you north along the shoreline for half an hour. Adults, $1. Children, 50¢.

Skyline Sightseeing Boats, docks at the riverfront at North State and the lower level of Wacker Drive, 236-9717. One- and two-hour cruises down the river to Congress Street and back, north on the lake to Diversey, south to McCormick Place, the convention hall that went up in the winter of 1967, one of Chicago's disastrous fires. Boats sell soft drinks and have toilets.

Wendella Sightseeing Boats, on the lowel level of the north side of the Michigan Avenue Bridge (400 north), DE 7-1446. Two-hour cruises, at 10 AM, 1:15 PM, 7:30 PM; also 3:15 PM weekends. Saturday night cruises at 10 PM and 12:05 AM. Adults, $2. Children under ten, $1.

Mercury Sightseeing Boat Excursions, at the Michigan Avenue Bridge and Wacker Drive, DE 2-1353. One- and two-hour cruises similar to Wendella.

THREE SUNDAY STROLLS

To Navy Pier, Grand Avenue and Lake Michigan

The Michigan Avenue Bridge is as good a starting point as any. The bronze markers in the sidewalk at the southwest corner of Michigan and Wacker outline part of the site of **Fort Dearborn.** Since old prints and maps show the fort on the north bank of the river, the marker is thoroughly confusing until you remember that when the fort was erected in 1803 the mouth of the river was down at Madison Street. The bridge is a bascule and opens from the center. All the bridges across the river split at their center seams, and it's great watching unless you're trapped in a cab with the meter ticking away mercilessly.

The two plazas just north of the bridge are flower-filled in summer. The marble memorial at the **Equitable Building Plaza** commemorates the site of the **Point du Sable-John Kinzie** house, the first private home to be erected in what was then Indian real estate. The plaza across the street, between the Wrigley Building and 430 North Michigan Building, flying flags of the Pan-American countries, is the **Plaza of the Americas.** North half a block take the stairway leading down to the lower level of Michigan Avenue and to Grand Avenue which intersects it. Turn east on Grand, walk past several long uninspired blocks to **Navy Pier.** Use the stairway to the right of the pier building to get onto the viewing promenade that runs the length of the docks below and is enlivened with little signs telling you how many miles to Glasgow,

Rotterdam and other seaports around the world. Generally, at least four foreign merchant ships are in port, and since the stevedores work on Sunday, you can watch the wares of the world being unloaded. When the St. Lawrence Seaway closes, usually early in December, the ships disappear; but even without them, the promenade is enjoyable for it gives you a good view of the lakefront and of the locks that control the river and help it run backwards in what was one of the more enterprising engineering feats this city brought about to suit its own needs.

Just north of Navy Pier you'll find **Olive Memorial Park** and the **Ohio Street Filtration Plant** (page 160), a bit of a beach and a retaining wall that's a combination promenade-sunbathing strip-bicycle path-fishing area. The wall is weathered and crumbling but it's a great esplanade, and if you amble north you'll shortly come to the city's picture-postcard beach—the **Oak Street Beach.** If you continue on, you'll come across scuba divers in summer, and chess players hunched all year long over the inlaid boards in the **North Avenue Chess Pavilion,** a small, poetic design in reinforced concrete by architect Morris Webster. Take your choice then of a walk that becomes a curving arm of breakwater leading to a lighthouse and a dramatic view of the city, or the walk that dips west to an underpass and emerges in Lincoln Park. If you don't feel like walking this far, turn off at the Division Street underpass, which brings you up on the west side of Lake Shore Drive, a block east of Astor Street.

The Last of the Gold Coast

Astor Street, one block west of Lake Shore Drive, between Division and North Avenue, was named for John Jacob Astor, and if there's a reason for that choice it's lost in history. But this much is true—the street has been identified with Chicago society from its beginning.

Astor is a street that begs you to stroll its length, not just because some of its houses are socially important and others are architecturally significant, but because the street has a way of recreating its unhurried turn-of-the-century past. Almost all of the old homes and town houses that still remain are embellished with little Victorian surprises that you discover in the ironwork, the stonework, under the eaves. Some of the architectural details are quaint and meaningless; one, across the street and seven doors south of Madlener House (North State Parkway and Burton Place), is hilarious—the house hasn't a surface without something going on it, like a lot of typewriters all clacking away at once. Others, as at Charnley House and Madlener House, are counted among Chicago's famous buildings.

The Social Register of 1896 listed 32 Astor Street families; the 1926 edition listed 86; the 1966 edition dropped down to 39. Present residents are typical of young families who like to live in a suburban manner in town. They take pride in keeping up their homes, send their children to the best private schools, the wives do most of their own housework plus great amounts of volunteer work; but also as *city* couples they help support enough charities and civic enterprises to leave you wondering how they find time for all the social activities that also crowd their calendars.

In recent years, despite neighborhood efforts to keep Astor intact, a sad number of the old single-family homes have been replaced by high rises. The 1200 block on Astor is almost entirely apartments now, and so is much of the 1300 block. The buildings at **1260** and **1301,** designed by Philip B. Maher, are early 1930's co-ops, very slick and smooth, heavy on the chrome, built for people such as the Potter Palmers, who could if they wished (and did) take three floors at the top of 1301 and and treat them like a three-story town house. **Astor Tower Hotel** at Goethe and Astor is the plush, relatively new hotel that houses Maxim's. It was designed by Bertrand Goldberg, the Marina City architect. **1355 Astor** is still known as the Goodman House (Goodman Theatre Goodmans), although it and two adjacent buildings were long ago converted into a complex of 17 apartments with the address 1349-59 North Astor. The bronze door on the entrance at 1355 and the courtyard behind it are very much in the Goodman tradition of classical architecture; the Goodman House was inspired by a Renaissance house in Sienna. You're welcome to poke your nose into the courtyard.

The town house at **1365 Astor,** Charnley House, was built by Frank Lloyd Wright in 1892 while he was a draftsman for Adler and Sullivan. Its stained-wood balcony may be the work of Louis Sullivan; the now green copper cornice has the same leafy motif that Sullivan used at Carson Pirie Scott. Charnley House is a landmark, and its present owner has maintained it as originally built—an 11-room, three-story single-family residence. The south porch was added later to get the kitchen out of the basement and to put an end to service by dumbwaiter.

In terms of social gossip, **1406 Astor** was the Ryerson House (architect, David Adler). **1416** and **1430** are the Blair and the Bowen houses respectively. The William McCormick Blairs moved in in 1912 and are now Astor Street's longest residents. Before her marriage, Mrs. Blair lived in the house next door with her parents, the Joseph T. Bowens. The house at **1434 Astor** was an old house bought and remodeled 28 years ago by an architect who literally changed everything. What you see now looks innocent enough, but the remodeling shocked people in 1940—it seemed so out of character with the rest of the street. **1421** is headquarters of the Maryknoll Fathers; **1431** was the home of another Ryerson, Edward L., former chairman of Inland Steel. **1447** houses the Chicago Junior League. The mansion with green shutters on the northeast corner of Burton Place and Astor contains the office of the Greek Orthodox Archdiocese.

The mansion on the northwest corner was built in 1900 for Mrs. Robert W. Patterson, daughter of Joseph Medill, a one-time mayor of Chicago and publisher of the *Chicago Tribune*. Depending on how the word "room" is defined, this town house has between 42 and 90 rooms, including one on the fourth floor where the walls were lined with some 50 lockboxes which served as storage vaults for birthday, Christmas and anniversary gifts the Pattersons intended to give to members of the family and friends. Bateman School, a private elementary and high school, occupies the premises now, but the original decor has been kept intact.

1525 is the headquarters of the Polish Consulate General. The huge, improbable red brick house with 19 chimneys facing Lincoln Park has, since 1885, been headquarters of the Roman Catholic Archdiocese of Chicago and the Cardinal's residence. The construction at **1524**—the lot just south of the Cardinal's edifice—is the first private home to be constructed on Astor Street in more than half a century. Walk west one block to North State Parkway and head south. The most important piece of architecture on the street is the house architect Richard E. Schmidt designed for the Madlener family in 1902, a severe but noble town house in the tradition of a Florentine palazzo. Its address is actually **4 West Burton Place,** and it now houses the Graham Foundation for Advanced Studies in the Fine Arts. At **1340 North State Parkway** the immense old four-story residence of Dr. George Isham is now known as the Playboy Mansion. Everything you've heard about it is true.

Landmark Park

Lincoln Park, North Avenue (west of Lake Shore Drive) to Hollywood. (See the map on page 385.)

Lincoln Park is a marvelous old city park, a little seedy from overuse, but a strolling park of the best kind. Like Central Park, which it resembles,* it's a long ribbon of land. In this century it's been extended north several times on landfill, but the great strolling section shared by visitors and Chicagoans alike is the original park that begins at North Avenue. This old Lincoln Park is one of curved walks, lagoon and ponds, footbridges with lovely old wrought iron railings, underpasses, gardens, statues, two museums (Chicago Historical Society, page 140, and Academy of Sciences, page 136), zoo, children's zoo, carousel, pony rides, Viking ship, bird sanctuary, balloon men, Victorian refreshment stands with fanciful, curlicue pagoda roofs, squirrels and pigeons and monuments everywhere and one private mausoleum.

---

*Designed by Frederick Law Olmsted; Lincoln Park by nameless ingenious copyists.

The mausoleum is a leftover from the days when the park was the municipal cemetery.* It belonged to a family named Couch who fought against its removal in the courts and won on the grounds that it was on consecrated land, which was true. It's small and gray and half-hidden by shrubbery, and people who stop to admire Augustus Saint-Gaudens' magnificent standing Lincoln at North Avenue and Stockton Drive are always hopefully mistaking it for a park facility. The exedra behind Mr. Lincoln was designed by architect Stanford White.

Lincoln Park's statues date almost entirely from the era when it was popular to commemorate noted persons with heroic bronze likenesses and to symbolize ideas with sculptured personages. Thus, the huge nude Goethe in the park near Diversey represents mental power, according to the description given by the Park District, though its inscription reads "Goethe, the Master Mind of the German people." The patriotism of the era also led individuals and various groups of citizens of foreign descent into demonstrations of civic goodwill via the donations of sculptures and monuments. So Lincoln Park has at least 28 major bronzes, mostly of a size impossible to miss. The one exception is the life-size statue of Garibaldi near the South Pond; when the park is green, Giuseppe is almost buried in foliage. It's always been a wonder that Chicago's Italian-Americans don't protest. As to the Grant statue, it's an old Chicago joke that Grant canters in Lincoln Park while the most noted of all Saint-Gaudens' Lincolns (the seated Lincoln) is in Grant Park. Nobody knows why.

There's one other grave in Lincoln Park that frequently startles visiting Easterners who don't expect to find the burial plot of a Revolutionary soldier in a city that wasn't incorporated as such until 1837. It belongs to David Kennison, last survivor of the Boston Tea Party, who died in 1852, age 115. A half-century later, the Sons and Daughters of the American Revolution inscribed a granite boulder to him and rolled it into the park in the immediate vicinity of his grave. It's just off the sidewalk on the east side of Clark Street near the Academy of Sciences.

The **Viking Ship** is a piece of large-scale memorabilia left from the Columbian Exposition of 1893. Norway built a replica of a 10th-Century vessel, and it was sailed across the Atlantic by a 12-man crew, arriving at the opening of the exposition with a scroll of good wishes for the citizens of Chicago from the country whose ancestors first discovered the North American continent. So

---

* By the time of the Great Fire, the city was getting out of the cemetery business, the graves were being opened and the coffins removed to private cemeteries. When the Fire roared north, people fled and, when they reached the empty graves, took fox-hole shelter there to escape its heat and the sparks overhead. A macabre steel engraving shows families racing along a path among fallen tombstones, and mothers with children cowering behind the monuments and coffins in disarray by the open graves.

much for the 1965 Italian-Norwegian furor over the discovery at Yale University of the Vinland map. The Norwegians have been convinced all along.

The **Zoo** is exactly what a zoo about to celebrate its centennial should be—a bit scrubby but filled with the right kind of animals, the ones you remember from your childhood: bison, lions, tigers, great apes, seals, polar bears. From time to time, the zoo has tried kangaroos, but they always cause problems; either they leap over the enclosures and go bounding along the paths or they get rheumatism in cold weather. The zoo got its start when two pairs of swans arrived from Central Park as a donation. The first bear cub was purchased for $10. It was also the first animal purchased, and it lived in a wooden cage, as did all subsequent bears, until the small outdoor enclosures were built. Zoo feeding schedule is: Monkey house, 1:00 PM (11:00 AM in summer); Sea lions, 1:15 PM; Bird house, 1:30 PM; Bears, wolves, foxes, 2:00 PM; Small mammal house, 2:30 PM; Lion house (except Monday), 4:00 PM.

Children's Zoo houses all the baby animals born each winter and spring. At feeding time baby cubs get bottles; young chimps are seated in high chairs and outfitted with bibs and spoons. The animals may be patted and petted. Hours are 10 AM to 5 PM daily.

Farm-in-the-Zoo recreates the typical farm architecture that is so very familiar in the old storybooks—all bright and shiny and red. Farm machines are around to add authenticity, but no child can take off in the two-ton grain harvester. Interestingly, children from rural areas tend to enjoy the animals more than city youngsters.

West of the bear pits lie splendid formal flower gardens, water lily ponds, **Grandmother's Garden,** filled with old-fashioned blooms, and the **Conservatory.** Some of its five show houses date to 1891; as a result, the late-Victorian passion for potted palms gives this generation a chance to see some of the oldest and tallest species in captivity, along with a fernery and a tropical forest glade that includes propagating banana, orange and lemon trees. A meticulous Japanese garden nestles in another show house; if you're in luck, one or two of the Conservatory's 18 propagating houses will also be open to view.

The Conservatory has four special exhibits annually: azaleas in February and March; lilies and spring plants in April; chrysanthemums in November; poinsettias and Star of Bethlehem in December and January.

Perhaps the best time of all to visit the Conservatory is after you've mushed across the deserted park on a cold, snow-swept afternoon. Then to enter the old-fashioned building, with its warm, moist climate and the fragrance of wet earth and green things growing, is to escape winter with the ease of opening a door.

For the stroke and trailing-hand crowd, **rowboat rental** in Lincoln Park is $1.00 per hour, at Cafe Brauer at the edge of the lagoon.

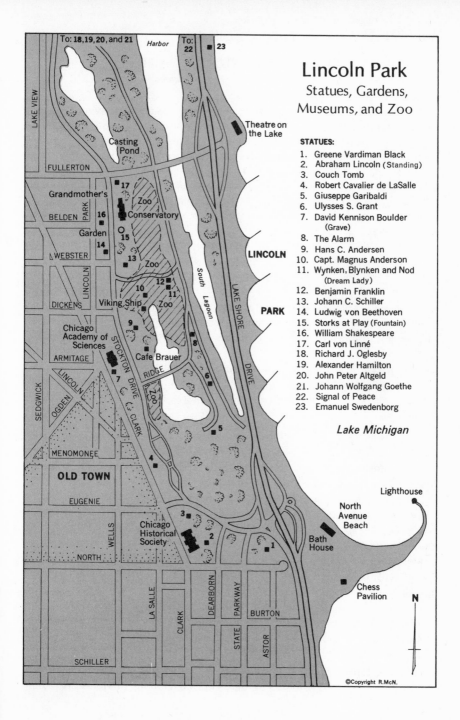

Lincoln Park
Statues, Gardens, Museums, and Zoo

To: 18,19,20, and 21
Harbor
To: 22
23

LAKE VIEW

Theatre on the Lake

Casting Pond

FULLERTON

Grandmother's
Zoo
Conservatory
BELDEN
Garden
WEBSTER

LINCOLN

Zoo

South Lagoon

LAKE SHORE DRIVE

LINCOLN

PARK

DICKENS
Viking Ship
Zoo

Chicago Academy of Sciences
ARMITAGE
Cafe Brauer
STOCKTON DRIVE
RIDGE
Zoo

SEDGWICK
LINCOLN
OGDEN
CLARK

MENOMONEE

OLD TOWN

EUGENIE

WELLS

Chicago Historical Society

NORTH

LA SALLE
CLARK
DEARBORN
PARKWAY
STATE
ASTOR
BURTON

SCHILLER

STATUES:

1. Greene Vardiman Black
2. Abraham Lincoln (Standing)
3. Couch Tomb
4. Robert Cavalier de LaSalle
5. Giuseppe Garibaldi
6. Ulysses S. Grant
7. David Kennison Boulder (Grave)
8. The Alarm
9. Hans C. Andersen
10. Capt. Magnus Anderson
11. Wynken, Blynken and Nod (Dream Lady)
12. Benjamin Franklin
13. Johann C. Schiller
14. Ludwig von Beethoven
15. Storks at Play (Fountain)
16. William Shakespeare
17. Carl von Linné
18. Richard J. Oglesby
19. Alexander Hamilton
20. John Peter Altgeld
21. Johann Wolfgang Goethe
22. Signal of Peace
23. Emanuel Swedenborg

Lake Michigan

Lighthouse

North Avenue Beach

Bath House

Chess Pavilion

N

THE UNDISCOVERED CITY

CHICAGO'S INCREDIBLE CEMETERY

Graceland Cemetery, Irving Park and Clark

Graceland, established in 1860, contains the remains of some of Chicago's and the nation's famous people. One reason for visiting it is historical interest, but another, surely, is to see what may well be the most monumental cemetery in the nation. Graceland is overwhelmingly Victorian Grandiose, right down to the swans on Lake Willowmere. Though you can find other burial grounds of the same era with obelisks and mausoleums and weeping angels and draped sarcophagi, it's unlikely you'll come across one in this country in which so much has been built by private citizens on a scale usually reserved for kings and emperors.

Stop at the main building and ask for a map and a location guide to the most famous graves. Even with these you'll have to work at finding exact locations: sites aren't marked on the map in order to discourage vandals. The monuments you really want to see are:

Section S, Lorado Taft's "Death," a much-bigger-than-life shrouded figure, a bronze long turned green, standing over a black marble slab, the skull totally submerged in the shroud. On a rainy day it's terrifying. It decorates the sites of the **Graves** family.

At A-367, directly across from "Death," you'll find the remains of some 30 or 40 members of the **John Kinzie** clan, including the founder, whose coffin was moved from cemetery to cemetery in the early days until its permanent haven here.

At Edgewood 104 find Lorado Taft's statue of a Crusader distinguishing the grave of **Victor Lawson,** who founded the *Chicago Daily News.*

The **Potter Palmer** monument is startling for its size, a series of towering Greek columns set in an exedra (6 Willowmere Lake).

Louis Sullivan designed **Martin Ryerson's** black marble mausoleum at Lakeside 6. **Sullivan's** own grave marker is 105, a little to the left and behind the Ryerson mausoleum. It appears to be of his own design, and a long, eloquent message is carved across the back face. It was erected by friends and professional associates years after his death. The actual grave is behind the monument; its marker states only "Louis Henry Sullivan 1856-1928."

Kenneth Sawyer Goodman, in whose memory the Goodman Theatre was built, is buried in a mausoleum very similar in its classic design to that theatre, on a bluff at the very edge of the lake. Lord knows how they ever got the caskets in —only a narrow footpath up a steep slope leads to the entrance, and the doors face the water (24 Willowmere).

Allan Pinkerton's monument (C-554) begins with the following statement: "A friend to honesty and a foe to crime." Four generations of **Fields** are buried

386

in Ridgeland 5, where a great bronze woman sorrows in front of a pool, but only two words were needed as inscription: *Equality* and *Integrity*. The **Daniel Burnhams** are buried on the island in Lake Willowmere, and **George Pullman** (14 Fairlawn) had himself meticulously preserved against both elements and invaders. His coffin was wrapped in tar paper and bolted with steel bolts, then embedded in a room-size chamber filled with concrete and topped with bolted steel rails. A shaft rises high above the grave. Don't miss **Andre Hamilton Honore's** French Gothic cathedral, complete with cherubs and every other medieval symbol he could find. It's at 11 Lakeside.

But the great architectural prize—the one that up till now has put Graceland on the map—is the **Getty** tomb, designed by Louis Sullivan, erected in 1890 and designated a Chicago architectural landmark in 1960. It's covered with Sullivan's beautiful tracery, and its gates are exquisite. You'll find it on the west side of the lake in the northeast section of the cemetery.

NATURAL HISTORY—OUTDOORS

Brookfield Zoo, 8400 West 31st Street, Brookfield, BI 2-2630

Brookfield Zoo (formally, the Chicago Zoological Park) is a natural habitat zoo where bears, mountain sheep, goats, lions, monkeys live outdoors in season on their own man-made craggy islands encircled by protective moats; where zebras, antelopes, wild cattle, camels, rhinoceroses have their own outdoor ranges; where only the athletes—leopards, pumas, jaguars—have to be displayed in caged or barred quarters.

The zoo is a year-round attraction since most of the animals, even the camels, are outdoors winter and summer. Don't bypass a winter visit: polar bears in snow look their most polar bearish then, and animals that normally blend into the landscape can be seen as distinctly as on Japanese scroll paintings. Furthermore, if you get cold, there are enough indoor animal houses to provide shelter and several hours of viewing.

The zoo landscaping and buildings are designed in a formal 15th-Century Italianate style except for the Seven Seas Panorama, a big bubble that houses porpoises and dolphins. (Porpoise performances daily from noon on.) The Perching Bird House is an open-flight room; the Aquatic Bird House is dominated by an incredibly big, indoor flying cage. King penguins live indoors in refrigerated cases; pelicans and swans grace an outdoor formal pool; emus and ostriches parade in their ungainly fashion across an outdoor habitat. A Wildfowl Pond at Salt Creek, which runs through the western end of the park, is a place to view winged migrants in May and September.

Zoos always hope their animals will reproduce successfully, and Brookfield's animals are generally very obliging. February, March and April are usually the best months to see the new zoo babies. In summer, the Children's Zoo is filled with them and at least some may be played with.

You'll need the better part of a day here; there are 26 separate exhibition areas and 196 acres to cover. Some of this can be accomplished by riding a narrow gauge railway around the outer boundaries of the zoo past the Wildfowl Pond and behind Wolf Woods. Or you can ride one of the trackless Safari Trains which provide guided tours. Fees for both trains: adults 50¢; children 35¢. Buggies and wheelchairs can be rented at gates. Zoo guidebook (almost a necessity, 50¢) and maps available at souvenir stands. Try to come on a weekday when crowds are thin and it's much easier to see everything.

> Zoo hours: 10 AM to 6 PM from the last Sunday in April to the last Sunday in September; to 5 PM the balance of the year. Plenty of parking (50¢) outside north and south gates and inside the grounds; refreshment stands throughout the park. Free admission on Tuesday; otherwise it's 50¢ for anyone over 15. By car, Eisenhower Expressway to First Avenue exit, then south to the zoo gates. By elevated train take Douglas Park El to 22nd and Cicero; take westbound West Town bus (leaving every half hour) to the zoo. Burlington Railroad sends trains at frequent intervals from Union Station to Hollywood Station. Walk four blocks north to the zoo. Afternoon feeding hours in summer: monkeys, 3 PM; bears, 3:30 PM; lions, tigers, penguins, 4 PM; sea lions, 4:30 PM. From November through April one-half hour earlier.

Two good nearby restaurants are **Czech Lodge,** 2519 Des Plaines, North Riverside, and **Harvey's Countryside Inn,** Plainfield and La Grange Road, La-Grange. Harvey's, an everyday spot that serves half-pound hamburgers, is great with children and has a bar for adults. **Czech Lodge** serves bountiful portions in hunting lodge surroundings.

Morton Arboretum, Route 53, Lisle, WO 8-0074

Chicagoans who've discovered Morton Arboretum are convinced there's nothing comparable in the country, and they're right. Arboretums, rare at best, are mainly collections of woods and plants arranged taxonomically. But Morton Arboretum grew under a director who was a landscape architect, and he happily, carefully, pridefully arranged its plants in landscape groupings.

Morton Arboretum offers 30 miles of walking trails; 5,000 identified trees and shrubs; formal gardens; sunny hills on which plants grow in seeming random; 25 acres of native prairie plants (the 140 kinds that grew on the Illinois prairie at the time the pioneers came west); and wildlife. The entire arboretum is a natural conservatory since it offers birds the three things they need in winter—trees for shelter, water and food. The lake is kept free of ice by bubbling air through the water, and the arboretum's plants sprinkle the seed. You can see more birds here than anywhere else in the Chicago area, and you can see waterfowl every day under ideal conditions—mallards, Canadian geese, grosbeaks, crossbills, all of which stay the winter. So do snow geese, which sometimes remain for years to become the arboretum's own snow geese and to raise their young on the premises. You can see wild turkeys that the staff has practically domesticated; prairie birds; deer that yearly arrive on their own by following the rivers into the sanctuary of the grounds.

After a snowfall the arboretum is white, silent, so undisturbed that you can easily follow the snow tracks of fox, raccoons, opossum, skunk. You can drive through the arboretum rather than walk its trails but don't—you'll miss too much.

The way to understand this remarkable place is to take in a slide lecture in the main building and buy the trail guides before you set out. See the little things along the trail the way your camera would in close shots—the insects, the butterflies, the little clumps of wild flowers at the base of trees.

Chicagoans interested in nature study might investigate its year-round program of activities—courses in nature study, field trips, home landscaping, nature photography, a nature workshop for teenagers and so forth. Ask to be put on the mailing list. Teenagers seriously interested in becoming botanists may apply for part-time work. There are always far more applications than openings, but about 60 to 80 students are taken on each year.

The arboretum's Gingko Tea Shop is a charming place to lunch. The gift shop is a gem, stocks items relating to plants and animals, including sculptures, paintings, prints, books. The Thornhill Building has many of the original Audubons that made up the Elephant Folio. When you're through looking at them and at the rare books on display, cross the lounge, open the French doors, and walk out on a terrace that offers a spectacular view. It's like looking across a sweep of Virginia to the Blue Ridge Mountains, and it's breathtaking. It's the view the Morton family had before they turned their estate into this loveliest of public treasures.

Open free every day of the year from 8 AM to sunset. In December, January and February the buildings are closed Saturday afternoon and Sunday. The arboretum is so natural that it looks its worst in June because the great expanses of open fields aren't mowed until after the birds have finished nesting; any time after mid-August it's magnificent. Take Eisenhower Expy to East-West Tollway, west to marked arboretum turnoff. You can't picnic there but Herrick Forest Preserve nearby offers picnic tables on the banks of a lake where boats may be rented at $1.25 per hour; fishing is permitted. The area is all weeping willows plus spruce and hawthorn trees and is rarely overcrowded. Willowbrook Wildlife Haven near the arboretum is run by Mr. and Mrs. Richard Hogan, experts in handling injured and orphaned creatures which are brought to them by the score. It's open to visitors.

Illinois Prairie Path

A get-away-from-it-all walking, hiking, bicycling, horseback riding trail. It cuts east-west across Du Page County, beginning at Elmhurst and branching at Wheaton to both Elgin and Aurora. The path was suggested by a retired Morton Arboretum naturalist, and the route is through a close-to-natural setting that includes prairie, bird marshes, woods, ponds and streams. The project is fostered by the Open Lands Project of Metropolitan Chicago, uses land on the defunct Chicago Aurora and Elgin right-of-way, adds "demonstration blocks" complete with old street lamps, benches and special plantings. The trail has Illinois Prairie Path markers, crosses Du Page River at the canoe landing in Warrenville, and goes through the Valparaiso glacial moraine, a distinctive geological feature of this area. Direct inquiries to Open Lands Project, 53 West Jackson, Chicago 60604, or phone 427-4256.

Botanic Garden, between Dundee and Lake-Cook roads just east of Edens Expy.

Driving north from Chicago, you can see the construction of the 300-acre Botanic Garden being created on islands in one of the larger Skokie lagoons and on the perimeter shore. When complete, the garden will include a wildlife preserve, a bog garden, spring and fall gardens, summer flowers, trees and shrubs native to Illinois. It's a joint venture of the Chicago Horticultural Society and Cook County Forest Preserves, aspires to the quality of Kew Gardens near London and the Jardin des Plantes in Paris, and if it follows its blueprints it should have every chance of achieving its goal.

TOURS—SELF AND GUIDED

Merchandise Mart, north bank of Chicago River between Wells and Orleans, 527-4141

In typical Chicago style, the Merchandise Mart bills itself as the "world's greatest wholesale buying center." If by the phrase management means "largest under one roof" the claim is accurate. The Mart, whose site was old Wolf Point, covers two entire city blocks and lists in its 700-page directory of tenants the manufacturers or their representatives of 430 lines of furniture, 950 lines of china, glassware and gifts, 480 lines of housewares and appliances— and that's only the beginning.

Tour without advance arrangements between 9:30 AM and 3:30 PM; tours start approximately every half hour. Areas visited are furniture, floor coverings, giftwares and accessories, about 70 showrooms in all. Children under 12 free if with an adult; everyone over 12, 50¢.

Marina City, north bank of the Chicago River between Dearborn and State, 222-1111

Architect Bertrand Goldberg's concrete corncobs* are probably the first apartments in the world to be built over a boathouse. For 50¢ you can tour

---

* Where the windows are is where the kernels are missing.

demonstration units from 10 AM to 6 PM Monday through Saturday and noon to 6 PM on Sunday. Another 50¢ lets you view the city from the observation tower, open from late March to October. The apartments are pie-shaped, of course, and the maddening decorating problems that ensue have been spoofed so often they need no further comment here. Sports for visitors include skating, watching the skaters on the outdoor rink in winter and wandering about the office building and lower level floors of the two towers—a maze of shops, snack bars and restaurants. In summer, the ice rink becomes the site of an annual outdoor sculpture exhibit of the year's best by Illinois artists.

Board of Trade, 141 West Jackson (LaSalle), WA 2-2800

From the balcony of the world's biggest commodity market (grain) the action in the trading pit seems manic. On a floor littered with scraps of paper and discarded orders, some 500 men jump up and down, shriek at each other, wave their arms in violent gestures and jab the air with their fingers in a buy-sell and for-how-much signaling system that's a complicated version of scissors-paper-rock. The wonder is that hysteria is routine in one of the most basic industries in America, and that the daily brouhaha performs a necessary economic function. The traders are buying and selling futures on grains that may not yet have been harvested or even planted, that most certainly will not be delivered for months to come and will never be delivered to them personally. Trading, therefore, is largely speculative; but the futures market makes it possible for farmers, processors and wholesale buyers to protect themselves against damaging price fluctuations and to plan their operations in advance.

The yowling and arm waving starts promptly at 9:30 each morning, Monday through Friday, proceeds with almost unabated fury until 1:15 PM. Take your questions to the information desk outside the visitor's gallery; a free film, *The Speculators,* is shown five times during trading hours. If it's a clear day, go up to the roof of the observation tower for a high viewing spot of the city, the lake and the Indiana shore across the lake. If your camera doesn't have a telephoto lens you can shoot through the tower's high-power binoculars.

Mercantile Exchange, 130 North Franklin (Washington), RA 6-6490

The old butter and eggs and produce crowd trades here, but the Mercantile has come up in the world and now also trades cattle, frozen pork bellies,* hogs, turkeys and skinned hams. As at the Board of Trade, you can watch proceedings from a gallery from 9:05 AM to 1 PM Monday through Friday. But what you really want to catch is the 9:25 AM belly opening because it brings out the most vociferous trading. A lot of the cattle trading is done on the boards in a setting of brass spittoons strategically located for old members who

---

* Bacon in its raw state.

were part of the Mercantile when it opened in 1919. It's a much smaller futures market than the Board of Trade, only 75 to 100 traders at most, but the bartering can be just as fierce and the din just as loud.

Peoples Gas, Light & Coke Co., 122 South Michigan, 431-4824

On the main floor, in a specially designed kitchen, continuous baking demonstrations are held from 10 AM to 4 PM, plus free recipes to all comers. In April, special auditorium cooking demonstrations two afternoons and two evenings each week. Tickets are free. Chicago women often order them as early as February, but a single visitor can usually be squeezed in at the last minute if she doesn't mind standing. For four weeks during July and August, teens are invited to cooking demonstrations with emphasis on party ideas. Phone to reserve free tickets as far in advance as possible.

Chicago Post Office, 433 West Van Buren, 353-2590

This Post Office may well have one of the richest post office interiors in the world—14-carat gold (imported from France) on the niches above the customer service windows, plus marble from Italy and Belgium. To view the splendor plus the complete postal processes, phone a few hours in advance and arrive prepared to walk on a two-hour tour. Highlights include the "bridge of the battleship," the huge board that controls the sorting of parcel post. Tours from 9 AM to 11 AM and from 1 PM to 3:30 PM Monday through Friday, except during the hectic Christmas season. Starting point is the information booth in the lobby.

Chicago Civic Center, Washington to Randolph, Dearborn to Clark, 321-5500, offers group tours which a family could join but you're free to wander around on your own. Good observation facilities on the 29th floor; good restaurants in the lower level (page 65).

Marshall Field & Company, 111 North State, offers tours of one to two hours Monday through Friday at 10:30 AM and 2:30 PM, by reservation. Call ST 1-1000 and ask for the third floor information desk.

Meigs Field is a small airfield on a spit of land jutting into the lake off Achsah Bond Drive, just to the right of Adler Planetarium. It's fun to take children to the observation deck because Meigs is small and you're so close to the landing and takeoff ramp. Furthermore, the observation deck is never crowded like O'Hare. The administration-passenger building is a gem of small-scale airport architecture. (See map, page 159.)

Playboy Building, 919 North Michigan, MI 2-1000

The famous old Palmolive Building has become the Playboy Building, and you can tour the Playboy editorial offices, noted for sculptured walls and stark black and white decor. The Walton Street doorman is not a Playboy invention—he has been with the Palmolive for years, the only office doorman in the country so far as anyone knows. To arrange for a tour, phone in advance and ask for the Press Information Officer.

Sears, Roebuck & Co., 925 South Homan, 265-2500

Sears offers a plant tour which shows the routing of an order received through the mail or over the phone. Sears' public relations people say it's not an exciting tour, that you don't get to see warehouses stacked with merchandise but the minutiae of mail-order paper work. If this seems interesting, phone and tell the Sears operator you wish to make arrangements for the catalog tour that's offered from 9 AM to 3 PM Monday through Friday.

Polk City, North, 2850 North Central, NA 2-5600

One of the biggest and most successful discount retailing centers in the country, conceived by the man who's been called a combination of carnival shill and evangelist as well as "king" of American discounters. Sol Polk's showmanship is demonstrated in his promotions—he's constantly offering giveaways with purchases: a case of free oranges or pineapples or an armload of fresh roses. And he talks like an advertisement: "Here's positive proof. . . ." His evangelistic side is the more fascinating, however. He passionately desires every Chicagoan to have the things he calls "the jewels of mass production," like color TV and *all* major appliances. On a TV interview, evangelism led him to say, "We're in the business of delivering happiness. The one hundred trucks we have delivering merchandise deliver *happiness*." He's also credited as one of the originators of aluminum Christmas trees.

Union Stock Yard, Halsted at 47th, YA 7-5580

The gruesome slaughterhouses are gone, for it's now more efficient to ship meat than livestock; hence, the dispersal of the packinghouses after almost 100 years of kingpin activity.* However, the yards are still a leading stock market where basic prices are established, and a visit is worthwhile if your youngsters have never seen livestock sales. Monday is the largest cattle trading day of the week—an average of 13,000 head bought and sold. Wednesday is second choice; Friday, third. Sheep and hogs are traded daily in pens at the south end of the yards. Any touring is do-it-yourself, and the place to begin is in Room 118 of the Exchange Building, where the Public Information Office will give you a folder explaining the yards and trading procedures, send you up to the roof for a panoramic view of the entire area, then urge you to

---

* The yards came into being as Chicago developed from village to town. Little slaughterhouses had sprung up near taverns; by the Civil War there were nine of them, and each conducted its own bargaining and price setting. The result, of course, was economic chaos, and in 1865 the merits of pooled buying-and-selling facilities became obvious. The nine slaughterhouse owners joined in a union (this is where the name comes from) and what ultimately became the world's greatest stockyards in its day was born.

roam freely around cattle pens, sheep pens, hog pens. Bargaining between buyers and sellers is intelligible; eavesdropping entirely permissible. You can tell the sellers because they generally wear Stetsons and carry whips to prod cattle or to show off the animals' good points. The men zipping around in electric golf carts are buyers and sellers who converted from horses a couple of years ago; there's even a buyer who races about on a Honda, the latest in quarter horses.

Lunch at the **Sirloin Room** in the Stock Yard Inn, 4178 South Halsted, or drive to the nearby **Glass Dome Hickory Pit** (page 68).

Chicago has two wholesale produce markets. The chaotic **South Water Market** of some 800 wholesalers is centered at 14th Street and Blue Island; the best day to visit is Thursday. It opens at 2 AM. Buyers from the big grocery chains, such as National Tea, come in about 4 AM. Starting at 6 AM buyers from the best restaurants and the fine independent Chicago grocery stores show up. Delivery of meats and produce into the open warehouses of the market starts about noon and goes on until midnight. At any time the pace and congestion are frightful: trucks jammed in for blocks; produce in barrels and boxes and cartons and bushel baskets wheeled, dollied, trundled between loading platforms and trucks, and all business conducted with oaths and expletives. The vendors are still primarily Italian and Jewish, but the language of order is more cursing than anything else. In winter, though you don't see the produce outdoors, you can walk into all of the wholesale houses and view proceedings in relative warmth.

The wholesalers at South Water call those at the **Randolph Street Market** (at Halsted) scalpers because they buy somewhat inferior produce at South Water, cart it back to Randolph Street, and sell it to owners of grocery stores in poorer neighborhoods, hash houses and sometimes to individuals. On any Saturday from about 11 AM you can get produce bargains here because the sellers want to get rid of everything before they close for the weekend. The area also has a number of wholesale floral suppliers, fake and real, and you can wander in and out and buy to your heart's content. It's also a good area in which to buy Christmas trees at prices lower than those in the neighborhoods.

Amling's Flowerland, 8900 West North Avenue, ES 8-7200, has free group tours from 9:30 AM to 3:30 PM Monday through Friday. Families are welcome to attach themselves to any group. If you come alone the tour director will try to spend as much time as he can with you. The place is fascinating—a display refrigerator, for instance, holding 100 to 200 floral arrangements at all times. Tours include the grading room, where cut flowers are sorted for shipping to retailers; demonstrations of flower arranging; the rose house, where Amling grows two and a half million roses each year; other greenhouses of carnations, mums, Amazon lilies. After the tour you're invited to browse through a pet department, an area of house plants, the nursery and landscape department. A tour takes slightly more than an hour.

Hausermann's Orchids, Inc., 2N 134 Addison (Addison Road at Villa Park, North Avenue), KI 3-6855

Guided tours of greenhouses in which 300 varieties of orchids and some 125,000 plants from all over the world are grown. Tours include explanation and viewing of seeding, propagation, hybridization, cutting, packing, a free pamphlet on orchid growing and care, and the chance to ask all the questions you wish if you visit during the quieter, early part of the week. The week prior to Easter and prior to Mother's Day are probably the times to see a maximum display of beauty, but unless you can distinguish between 125,000 and 150,000 plants, stay away; nobody has time for visitors then. Hours are 7 AM to 3 PM Monday through Friday and to 5 PM Saturday, though that's not a good day to show up because the place is too busy. Instructional books on orchid growing available for purchase, but not orchids—Hausermann's is a wholesaler. Special two-day open house for hobbyists in February. The rest of the year you'll likely find agricultural groups from Europe and this country touring the premises.

> North Avenue west through Elmhurst to Addison Road (1½ miles west of Rt. 83). Or Eisenhower Expy to Elmhurst exit, north to North Ave. Make 360° turn and go west through Elmhurst as above.

Kitchens of Sara Lee, 500 Waukegan Road, Deerfield, 945-2525

Morning tours, followed by cake and coffee, of a modern, mechanized bakery at 9:30 and 10:15 AM, Monday through Friday, December through February; a third tour starts at 1 PM all other months. Tours are often booked weeks ahead, so don't just show up looking hopeful. Write or phone in advance. No children under 12 allowed. Resale bake shop on premises. Edens Expy to Deerfield turnoff.

NOTE: It's getting much more difficult for large manufacturing companies to offer tours of their facilities, mainly because when they do they're inundated by eager groups. As an individual or a family you stand a chance of visiting almost any plant you wish to see if you have legitimate reason, such as a son who's studying or planning to enter the manufacturer's field. Pick the plant you wish to visit and phone its Public Relations Office. Try to speak to the director; nine times out of ten he'll be able to meet your request, particularly if made in advance.

International visitors who wish to see manufacturing or distribution plants in fields of special interest can get a list of those operating in this area through the Chicago Association of Commerce and Industry, 30 West Monroe, Chicago, or the Illinois State Chamber of Commerce, 20 North Wacker Drive, Chicago. U.S. industry almost invariably extends a special welcome to visitors from overseas. Again, contact the Director of Public Information.

All of Chicago's daily newspapers offer guided tours that really do show you how the day's newspapers are created. For hours phone: *Chicago Sun-Times,* 321-3000; *Chicago Today,* 222-4321; *Chicago Daily News,* 321-2000; *Chicago Tribune,* 222-3232; *Chicago Daily Defender,* CA 5-2400.

Chicago Inland Waterways Tours are conducted on Sundays April through June and September through October by Chicago Travel Club, 30 West Washington, AN 3-2743. These are seven-hour, 65-mile lake and river tours, invaluable for a firsthand impression of Chicago's industrial muscle and the chance to see how Chicago modified its surrounding water resources to gain entrance to the Gulf of Mexico and, via the St. Lawrence River, the Atlantic Ocean. The creation of the St. Lawrence Seaway made Chicago the world's biggest inland port—a phrase that doesn't mean much until you realize it's 1,000 miles from the Atlantic.

Tours begin at the Michigan Avenue Bridge where you board a large sightseeing boat that steams through the locks into Lake Michigan, south to Lake Calumet, through the Calumet-Sag* channel, into the Sanitary and Ship Canal, and returns to the city via the south branch of the Chicago River. Reeled off in this fashion, the places are probably meaningless, but the size of the industrial Port of Chicago won't be. You get a sense of history en route, not only of what it means to build a city out of swamp and marsh—and you see a lot of both—but what the land must have looked like when water was the only rapid means of transportation for Indians, fur traders, pioneers.

The first industrial complex you pass is the south works of the United States Steel Company. From then on the trip is a sequence of grain elevators, bridges, iron ore boats, coal boats, dump scows, stockpiles of salt, limestone, iron ore, tank farms, the Republic Steel plant and docks, foreign tankers from around the world, Allied Chemical, a Ford plant, petroleum terminals, fireboats, warehouses, floating cranes with a lifting capacity of 110 tons.

Along the Calumet River the riverbank is low, scrubby and oddly beautiful. The names on the power boats in a little marina furnish clues to the people who own them—"Mama's Mink," "My Son," "Jolly Rajah." Beyond the marina you enter the old Cal-Sag channel, nothing but scenery, and the tour guide (a member of the U.S. Army Corps of Engineers) stops hurtling statistics at you, turns on Muzak, and the tour takes on the carefree aspects of a cruise.

The boat has enough glassed-in, heated seating space to be thoroughly comfortable if the weather should change. One wishes the guide would talk more about the history of the waterways and far less about the costs of each facility and installation and bridge; alas, his total orientation is in terms of tonnage, lengths, heights, stresses and construction costs, so you are well

---

* A calumet is a peace pipe, and sag literally meant a depression; there were two sags in the river.

advised to bone up on a little history in advance. Bring your camera, a thermos of drinking water and some packets of Wash 'n Dry towels. Though the tour provides coffee all day, breakfast sweet rolls when you board, an ample box lunch and soft drinks, and the boat has washrooms, it does not have drinking or washing water. Wear warm clothes that can be shed. On Lake Michigan it's cold, but the canals and rivers can be hot. Bring a map of the city so that you can trace the journey. The maps provided are furnished by the Army Corps of Engineers and cover only the water route. Tour fee is $12.50. Not recommended for children under 12 simply because it lasts too long.

Professor Harold Mayer of the University of Chicago also conducts several tours along the same route on Saturdays (more port activity) in early June and October. Reservations are taken by the University of Chicago, Downtown Center, Department of Geography, 65 East South Water, FI 6-8300. Fee and facilities are identical but the tour emphasis is on the geographic and economic importance of the area.

RADIO AND TELEVISION BROADCASTS

Jim Conway Show on WGN-TV is a conversation program in which Mr. Conway plays host to various guests who are experts in a variety of fields, later lets them answer questions from the audience. Tickets are free but reservations must be made one week in advance. Phone 528-2311, ext. 207, or write: Jim Conway Show, WGN-TV Guest Relations Dept., 2501 Bradley Place, Chicago 60618.

WLS, an ABC-owned and operated station, currently the top-rated pop music station in Chicago, welcomes visitors on Saturdays from 11 AM to 3 PM; you'll see deejays on the air and meet others. Write two weeks in advance to Station Manager, Station WLS, 360 North Michigan, Chicago.

Mulqueen's Kiddie A Go Go show is broadcast from 4 PM to 5 PM Monday through Friday. Write for tickets in advance to, Kiddie A Go Go, Channel 26, 141 West Jackson, Chicago.

Jack Eigen Show (interview) is broadcast from 10:20 PM to 1:00 AM. Free tickets available at WMAQ offices in the Merchandise Mart from 9 AM to midnight.

WMAQ, an NBC affiliate, offers tours Tuesday and Thursday at 9:30 AM, 10 AM and 10:30 AM. You'll see radio and TV studios and control booths but no audience shows. Write to Guest Relations one month in advance for tickets. The address is WMAQ, Merchandise Mart Plaza, Chicago.

For free tickets to the **WGN Barn Dance,** write to WGN, 2501 West Bradley, Chicago 60618. Station WGN-TV (the initials stand for "World's Greatest

Newspaper," and the *Chicago Tribune* owns the station) may be toured at 9:30 AM and 2:30 PM Monday through Friday. The 45-minute tour includes a studio, the newsroom, projection room, scene shop, radio studio, TV control room and, with luck, a glimpse of Studio #1, from which "Bozo's Circus" is broadcast. There's a three and a half-year wait for tickets to Bozo, but if you want to write that far in advance, do so, and your request will be honored.

WAIT, 3N 261 Church, Elmhurst, WH 4-6100. About 20 miles from the Loop, but you're welcome to see actual broadcasting, engineers and broadcasters. Call Mr. Lacina one week in advance for information.

Deejay radio station **WCFL** offers brief studio tours from 9 AM to 5 PM, whips you through production area, newsroom, record library, and gives you a 1-2-3 of how radio works. 300 North State, 222-1000.

Other radio-TV possibilities occasionally open up. Check with the Tourist Information Bureau on the main floor of the Civic Center. There's sometimes a chance to see the 10 PM to midnight Saturday broadcast of the **Marty Faye Show,** currently the only live variety show in Chicago. It's built on interviews with every available celebrity in town. For tickets, write four to six weeks in advance to WCIU-TV, 141 West Jackson, Chicago, or phone the Program Director, 664-7175.

ODDMENTS

Leaning Tower of Pisa, 6300 Touhy, Niles, 647-8222

Robert A. Ilg, a Chicago industrialist and inventor, built his 96-foot half-scale replica in 1933. It took a year, and it drove his architect and contractors crazy because they couldn't work with levels or normal equipment. Nevertheless, they all felt it was a miracle that Mr. Ilg didn't try to produce the exact cant of the original. The angle here is about seven feet off the perpendicular, and more than 12,000 tons of concrete, including a 35- x 40-foot base ten feet below grade, were needed to keep the tower from clunking to the ground. Mr. Ilg dedicated it to the memory of Galileo and used it as a water tower for several swimming pools on his estate. What made the original famous was Galileo's use of it to prove a theory of gravity and its functions. What eventually made Mr. Ilg's tower important beyond mere whim was its use by the Cook Electric Company, which held a government contract to design a rocket reentry system involving parachutes for manned capsules. Cook engineers used the Ilg tower in the same way Galileo used Pisa's—to drop things, parachutes in this instance, from the top.

The Ilg estate and its tower now belong to the YMCA. The first floor of the tower is a gift shop; additional shops are planned for the upper floors. If you don't mind shopping on the bias, you can have a fine time here. Open Tuesday through Friday 11 AM to 5:30 PM; Saturday, 10 AM to 5:30 PM.

If you should get into a slum neighborhood and discover a batch of ladies poking around in debris, they're not scavengers but the city's Mice Maidens examining piled-up junk which they suspect harbors rodents. They're hired and paid by the Department of Buildings.

There is one farm still within the Chicago city limits; 20 acres of truck farm with vegetables for sale in late summer and early fall. It's at 3837 West 111th Street.

At 9331 South Ewing, in an industrial area, you can find the grave of the only Chicagoan to fight against Napoleon. His tomb bears this inscription, in German:

"Andreas von Zirnigibl, born March 30, 1797. Died August 21, 1855. A veteran of 1815, the Battle of Waterloo. Here rest his ashes. Amen."

At Grand Avenue and County Line Road, Elmhurst, find an authentic Dutch windmill in Mt. Emblem Cemetery. The Dutch settled the area in the 1840's, and the rich farmland was dotted with windmills grinding wheat into flour and other grains into feed. This is the last of the mills built in the 1840's; it was used steadily until 1917 and is floodlit at night, attracting considerable attention from the tollway. The cemetery welcomes curious visitors and lets them enter and climb about the thing. In May, Mt. Emblem also welcomes thousands of visitors who come to see the 12,000 lilac bushes that are planted over 145 acres of land. Mt. Emblem officials cheerfully admit the display doesn't compete with Lombard on variety, but point out that they offer unlimited parking and free lilac sightseeing, which Lilacia Park doesn't do. The cemetery is a Mason-Eastern Star cemetery, with all headstones set flush in the lawn so it looks more like a park than otherwise.

BEYOND THE CITY LIMITS:
THE NORTH SHORE AND FOX RIVER VALLEY

With justified pride, Chicagoans always want to drive visitors through the North Shore, or west to the hills of the Fox River Valley. Generally, such expeditions are reserved for summer but a gray November day has its own advantages: leafless trees allow you to see estates otherwise camouflaged by heavy foliage. (Map, page 323.)

Two favored excursions follow. For the first one, a tour of the North Shore, simply head north along Sheridan Road, Route 42, and follow it through one suburb after the next to Lake Bluff, making little side forays whenever curiosity beckons you. The city limits on Sheridan Road are at Calvary Cemetery, a grand Roman Catholic burial place where the Cuneos have put down Oriental rugs in the family mausoleum. The suburb you enter is:

Evanston

When you think that a group of little old tea drinkers in Evanston were responsible for the rise of the Syndicate and the wealth of the Mafia, you have to marvel. Tea drinkers met at Miss Frances Willard's home and, by championing passage of the Volstead Act, created Prohibition, which in turn drove the liquor industry underground. Miss Willard's home is now national headquarters of the WCTU, which she founded in 1874, and is also a museum. It's a huge old wood frame home with gingerbread and wood lace trim and two front porches at 1730 Chicago Avenue, Evanston.

Evanston is beautiful and spacious, especially the open area bounded by Chicago Avenue, Hinman Avenue, Lake and Grove streets, known informally as Holy Ghost Square because of the four churches flanking it. It's also old and until quite recently was intensely rivalrous with Oak Park. The two suburbs were about the same size; both bordered on Chicago, were both founded by excessively conservative upper-middle-class Protestants. Their rivalry is best epitomized by the following: an Evanston matron boarded the Evanston elevated train and asked the conductor how to get to Oak Park. Something kept him from answering her immediately, and he had to look for her after she was seated. When he found her, he said, "You're the lady that wants to get to Oak Park?" She drew herself up in her best pouter-pigeon style and replied, "I don't *want* to go to Oak Park. I *have* to go there." But Evanston is gradually changing its own image of conservatism. In the fall of 1967 it successfully integrated its elementary school system, thus possesses the first integrated public school system in the entire Chicago area.

Drivers wish it would integrate its street signs as effectively. They're stacked four, five and six on top of each other and include conflicting and baffling parking regulations. Pay attention to the speed regulations. Evanston is enormously proud of its low accident record, and its speed limits are rigorously enforced.

The **Evanston Historical Society,** 225 Greenwood, is housed in the 34-room mansion of General Charles G. Dawes, Vice-President of the United States under Coolidge and author of the Dawes Plan for European Aid. It has some North Shore history and gleanings from the furnishings of old North Shore homes but is somewhat parochial in scope. The phone is GR 5-3410.

For Northwestern University, page 331.

Garrett Theological Seminary, on the east side of Sheridan Road at 2121, is known as a rather liberal Methodist seminary. Stop long enough to admire the Gothic buildings and to visit tiny Howes Chapel, which has six little stained-glass windows and one large altar window, seats 40 and is in great demand for small weddings. The Shakespeare Gardens to the north of the chapel have all the flowers Shakespeare mentioned in his plays, plus some very busy bees. The big seminary directly across the street is **Seabury Western,** an Episcopal seminary. Due to the proximity of a Northwestern technological building, Garrett is known locally as East Jesus Tech and Seabury Western as West Jesus Tech.

The federally owned and operated **Gross Point Lighthouse** and garden, located on the lakefront at Central Street and Sheridan Road, is a charmer. The lighthouse is a reasonably high location from which to take pictures and the garden is thick with wild flowers, all nicely identified. The garden also is noted for a sign which injuncts, "This is a garden. Do not step in it." Tours on Friday at 3:30 PM, 4 PM, 5 PM; Saturday and Sunday from 2:30 to 5 PM.

On the grounds just north of the lighthouse find a plaque honoring the Archange Ouilmette family, for whom Wilmette, the next suburb north, is named. Archange was a Potawatomi, and the tract of land was given to her in thanks for her father's help in arranging with Alexander Robinson* the treaty between the United States and the Chippewa and Ottawa tribes made at Prairie du Chien in 1829. The marker reads, "This tract to have and to hold for Archange and children, never to be leased or conveyed unless by Permission of the President of the United States."

The **Evanston Art Center,** 2603 Sheridan, is housed in banker Philip Clarke's stately old mansion; it has turned his garden room into a sculpture court. Open 10 AM to 4 PM, Tuesday through Saturday; Sunday 2 PM to 5 PM.

The **Brass Eagle Antiques** shop, 2644 Green Bay, specializes in Early American and 18th-Century antiques. UN 9-6660.

The **4 Arts Gallery,** 1629 Oak, hangs the work of young artists, also carries the shaped sterling silver jewelry of Roger Siegrist. His work is beautiful and priced far below its true worth.

Fanny's, at 1601 Simpson, GR 5-8686, is an outstanding example of what publicity can do for a restaurant. Fanny is a character, but one with real character and strength, all of which is explained in framed news stories about her hung along the stairway walls between the two floors of her place. Her fortes are spaghetti, fried chicken and a salad dressing for which she's long offered a cash prize to anyone guessing its ingredients. In the 15 or so years since the offer was made no one has yet been able to claim the reward. Reservations

---

* A Potawatomi chief, son of an Indian woman and a British officer who extended himself on behalf of survivors of the Ft. Dearborn Massacre. His Indian name was Chee-chee-bing-way, and he and his family are buried in solitary grandeur on land now owned and protected by the Cook County Forest Preserves. The site is just north of Lawrence Avenue, set back a little from the edge of Robinson Woods, across the road from a house numbered 4849 North Deer Road (probably marked on your map as East River Road). It's a lovely, alone kind of place to visit if you're in the vicinity of O'Hare Airport.

essential if you wish to eat downstairs, where there are checked tablecloths and a fresh flower on each table. Service at Fanny's is excellent; in fact, you're constantly being asked if everything's all right. Seconds on spaghetti are taken for granted. Bring your own bottle; Evanston is dry. Children's menus available.

Wilmette

Wilmette is an old-fashioned, ultraconservative community filled with withdrawn types; you can drive from one end to the other without ever seeing anyone on the streets. **Plaza del Lago Shopping Center,** with its insistent Spanish decor, is not indigenous to the suburb but was annexed from an area known officially as No-Man's-Land. The annexation was recent, and most Chicagoans still call it No-Man's-Land. The shop in the plaza with the sign that says **Hanna's** is known to everyone as Miss Hanna's; Miss Hanna is the lady who outfits North Shore debutantes and later does their weddings. For a fine boutique located in Plaza del Lago see La Colonna, page 228.

Wilmette began as an overnight stop on the old Green Bay Trail, and if you had time to poke about you could find Indian trail trees and houses that date back to 1849. The oldest house in the village is the **Gage House** at 1128 Greenwood; its horse barn is still intact. Present owner is Mr. Lewis W. Berghoff, Sr., of the Berghoff restaurants. There's also one working farm right in the middle of the village, twelve acres spread between Crawford Avenue, Wilmette Avenue and Old Glenview Road where farmer Michael Lautsch, 83, raises hogs, ducks, geese, vegetable crops and some flowers.

Baha'i House of Worship, Linden and Sheridan Road at Wilmette Harbor and Lake Michigan, AL 6-4400. An enigmatic nine-sided, stone lacework temple which defies precise architectural description but is admired equally by modernists and traditionalists. Much of its grace lies in the harmony of its proportions coupled with an inspired blending of architectural forms. The Baha'i faith is an independent world religion with followers in almost every country, has its own scriptures, its own laws, and revolves around three basic principles—the oneness of God, the oneness of religion, and the oneness of mankind. In a way it amounts to a blend of all the major religions, and you'll find services intriguing for their simplicity. Baha'i national headquarters adjacent to the temple, at 112 Linden Avenue, overwhelm you with explanatory literature, also provide guided tours from 9 AM through 9 PM May through October, and from 10 AM through 5 PM the balance of the year. Services are at 3:30 PM Sunday, followed by a public lecture at 4:15 PM.

Kenilworth

Kenilworth is well-heeled and superficially pretty—and also shockingly provincial in the way that any restricted community is these days. Joseph Sears, its founder, built it in pure Sir Walter Scott (the pattern was Warwickshire) and gave most of its streets the names of Scott characters and places. Despite romancing, Kenilworth has never had Scott-type action, so the Historical Society meets only once every two years. Eugene Field and his wife are buried at the **Church of the Holy Comforter** on 222 Kenilworth, and the nearby **Kenilworth Club,** 410 Kenilworth, was built around a beautiful old elm tree that shoots through its roof.

Winnetka

The phrase O.C.D.* and its corollary N.O.C.D.** may have originated here, but even if they didn't, this is where the terms seem to be used most often by Old Family parents teaching their children how to differentiate. If you're Society and live in Winnetka, you know that all other suburbs along the North Shore are secondary to yours. Lake Foresters, of course, feel the same way about Lake Forest; in the eyes of both, no other suburbs count. For visitors, the most interesting parts of the beautiful old suburb (founded 1869) are its spacious homes, especially those around the Indian Hill Country Club grounds, and its shops. Among the latter, the **Winnetka Portobello Galleries,** at the corner of Chestnut Street at Chestnut Court; it's an English antiques shop that also specializes in fine reproductions, carries some French prints from the 1750's and some small, good Chinese sculptures. Hours are 9:30 AM to 5 PM Monday through Saturday. Free delivery within 50-mile radius.

Trooping the Colour, 896 Linden, is an exceptionally attractive shop, specializing in sophisticated casuals and what are generally called Deep Country clothes for men and women. The store has a great many East Coast lines plus Murray of Hyannisport leather accessories; also, unusual items, such as women's watchbands in rep stripes and madras, and oatmeal soap. Downstairs, a sample room where you try on models of garments, select fabrics, and order imported Dorard tweed suits and coats from Scotland ($90 to $100). It's also where you find the prettiest tennis dresses going.

The house known as **"Wayside,"** at 830 Sheridan, is designated a registered national landmark. Henry Demarest Lloyd lived there, an attorney and critic of last-century monopolies.

Pick Galleries, 886 Linden, are antique dealers emphasizing fine 17th- and 18th-Century English, Spanish and French pieces. The owners also conduct excellent auctions of estates they've purchased. **Caledonian Market,** 562 Linden, is a shop that will make reproductions of antiques, also imports silver, china and furniture. **Northern Lights,** 894 Linden, Hubbard Woods (a sliver of

---

* Our class, dear.
** Not our class, dear.

a Winnetka suburb), has the best lamps and shades in Illinois and takes orders for custom shades.

Glencoe

In Glencoe, a suburb of ravines and winding roads on the North Shore, stop at architect Minoru Yamasaki's creamy **North Shore Congregation Israel**—a modern temple, which you'll find in among trees on a bluff on the east side of Sheridan Road. The outward impression of the temple in no way prepares you for its soaring interior serenity, somewhat like being inside a tulip that is just opening to greet the sun. Visiting hours are 10 AM to 4 PM Monday through Thursday; Sunday 10:30 AM to 5 PM. Services Friday evenings at 8:30 PM; Saturday at 11 AM. Family worship first Friday of each month at 8 PM.

Highland Park

Mainly, it's just a big suburb. People who have homes in the vicinity of Ravinia Park usually attend the concerts in their own gardens. **Old Elm,** 800 Old Elm, is the top men-only golf club in the entire Chicago suburban area, and the blue book of Chicago area businessmen use it. The course is never crowded and that's the way members want it. In fact, they complain if anyone else plays within three holes of their own game.

Highwood

Highwood is an anomaly among North Shore suburbs because it was settled by nonstylish Italian and Swedish laborers. But it's also the oasis of the dry North Shore, and owning a bar in Highwood is a good way to become a rich man. The town also has a clutch of good Italian restaurants: **My Favorite Inn** at 11 Highwood (Waukegan Road), has become almost too successful, won't take reservations, pays no attention to you until seats become available, but makes up for any discourtesy when they do. Steaks and Italian specialties, such as a Tenderloin in Marsala or a Tenderloin Steak Sandwich (three inches thick) and Torteloni Soup and Lasagna all too good to be ignored. If you're worried about calories, order half portions.

Del Rio, 228 Green Bay, is excellent Italian food without the steaks. It also has a bartender who makes fantastically good daiquiris which he serves in brandy snifters—mainly because his regulars never order them and he hasn't the proper stemware. You get enormous drinks as a result. Ravioli, spaghetti and other pastas are all homemade, and the bread the best in any of the suburbs. Very modest. **Nightingale Tavern,** 246 Green Bay, is the place to go for pizza and beer and, on weekends, for a good, noisy little band. **Scornavacco's Washington Gardens,** 550 Green Bay, has no gardens, Washington or otherwise, but serves enormous portions of pastas and anything else you order. It's informal—every place in Highwood is.

Lake Forest

Lake Forest is the Midwest's leading status symbol suburb—estate and large-house living on generous acreage concealed by magnificent old trees and shrubs carefully planted to assure maximum privacy. No home is demeaned by sidewalk, and a gaslight near the driveway is usually the only marker. Lake Forest is old money, old names, such as Armour, Swift, Farwell, and old ways. It's beautiful but it's also inbred and insular and wants to remain so. A member of Onwentsia, which is *the* club, insists that "in Lake Forest the world is flat and that when you get to Old Elm Road on the south or Waukegan Road on the west, or Lake Bluff to the north you fall off, and east is the lake, so you drown." Or, put another way, "You can come out of nowhere with just a little bit going for you and be accepted. But make the smallest mistake and you might as well be a child molester."

Lake Forest College is woods, ravines, vine-covered buildings and a liberal tradition. Its founding created the suburb in the same way that Northwestern University created Evanston, the sole difference being denominational—Presbyterian in this case. Head for the Admissions Office if you'd like a student guide. The campus extends along Sheridan Road a few blocks east of the center of Lake Forest, which is **Market Square,** an old, tastefully contrived shopping area just west of the railroad tracks and the commuters' station on Western Avenue; you'll probably want to park and browse. The **Country House** and **Cat & Fiddle** on Deerpath offer fine antiques. The **Trading Post Gift Shop,** 259 East Market Square, is a gift shop that helps support the Lake Forest Hospital Association by its sale of Leron linens and one-of-a-kind gift items and small furnishings. **Robertson's Men's Shop,** 240 East Deerpath, carries sophisticated country clothes similar to Winnetka's Trooping the Colour. **Deerpath Inn,** a short distance from Market Square (255 East Illinois Street) is the place to go for lunch, cocktails or dinner. It's really an inn with living quarters for permanent guests and transients, and when a Lake Forest divorce is brewing, the inn is where the one who leaves the house goes to live pending the outcome of the decree. In summer, meals are served on an outdoor porch overlooking the English garden; in winter, try the Hunt Room, which always has a blazing hearth.

As noted, Onwentsia is *the* club, but Shoreacres Golf Club, on Sheridan Road in Lake Bluff, the next suburb north, is considered a Lake Forest club second only to it.

Lake Bluff

Lake Bluff, a kind of Lake Forest suburb, was a religious and resort town in the early 1900's, with a cable car running down to the beach, two or three rambling hotels and, by way of summer events, Methodist-run churchy-preachy chautauqua-type meetings. The rest of the year it was simply the place where non-live-in Lake Forest domestics dwelt. Today, it's a bedroom suburb with a heavy commuting population of people in advertising, television and the law, and a ghetto for Great Lakes officers and Abbott Laboratories employees. The main reason for driving into it is to get to Route 176, which will provide a different, faster route back to town. Turn left, follow the signs to the Tri-State Tollway (US 94). Just before you reach the tollway entrance you'll see a sign inviting you to stop at *The Lambs*. By all means do. The combination farm, fresh vegetable stand, and Shepherds' Inn is the outgrowth of the first project in the country designed to give mentally retarded young people a chance to become productive citizens in daily contact with society. It's a not-for-profit establishment with a gift shop that has delightful items, including things like a really good chutney the young people make. Tearoom open to groups daily; a very pleasant Sunday buffet from noon to 4 PM. The nearby barn is a well-run pet shop. EM 2-4636. The tollway will bring you back directly into Chicago.

The Fox River Valley. One other expedition if you have the time—to the Fox River Valley, an hour's drive west via Northwest Tollway 90. The valley is wooded, rolling, dotted with old towns of history and charm. Route 25 on this side of the green-with-pollution Fox River meanders south from Elgin through St. Charles; Route 31 on the far side of the river winds and dips in a nicely rural way and links towns like Batavia and **Geneva,** the latter looking for all the world like the setting for an "Andy Hardy" film of the early 1940's. The shops on Franklin Street are all built to look like private homes painted cream, buff, white. On 404 South Third Street find the **Little Traveler,** a rambling old house converted into an enchanting gift shop and restaurant that's always crowded because women drive miles just to shop and lunch in its sunny, tearoom-with-style atmosphere.

Continue north to **South Elgin** where you'll find an outdoor **Trolley Museum,** with 1913 cars, a Jewett with stained-glass windows, an old Aurora-Elgin car, a 1926 dining car and more. Trolley expeditions on Sunday with stops and flag stops along the way. Cross the river into **Elgin** proper at the junction of US 20. Its **Audubon Museum** contains the Leopold Ornithological Collection, though, alas, now minus some of the best specimens, recently stolen. The **Laura Davidson Sears Academy of Fine Arts,** 210 Academy, is selling its superb collection of portraits by Gilbert Stuart, Peele, Copley, Benjamin West, Remington and Whistler to the Chicago Art Institute in exchange for traveling exhibits but may still have part of the collection intact. Elgin seems to be as much a town of dispersements as anything else. The famous Elgin Watch Company is no more; neither is the town itself any longer the world's butter market setting the world's butter prices, though the cow that served as a public monument to its position survives. **Lee Ward's Handicraft Center,** 840 North State, is the size of a warehouse, and people come from all over to shop in it. Just north of Elgin, on Route 25, find the **Milk Pail** at Fin 'n Feather Farms, an outstanding place for lunch or supper. The restaurant nestles in the romanticized rural grounds of a complex that includes butcher shop, smokehouse, bakery, gift shops and acres of lush covert where ring-necked pheasants, ducks, turkeys grow to slaughter-size. In summer, you can lunch outdoors. Phone ahead for reservations, 742-5040; the place is mobbed at noon. During good weather months it takes reservations weekdays only. Closed between Christmas and New Year and all Mondays.

Continue north a few more miles to **Dundee.** The **Haeger Potteries** at 7 Maiden Lane, East Dundee, offers six daily tours Monday through Friday and keep their display and salesrooms open weekends and holidays. The Santa's Village you'll pass is a fairly spectacular example of the type but isn't worth the hours you have to stand in line waiting to get your children onto the rides. Far more interesting, the **Frontier Museum,** page 314. Route 72 (Higgins Road) will bring you to the return journey through still-open countryside to Northwest Tollway and Chicago.

None of the above does justice to the Fox River Valley, which deserves a tour-and-history book of its own. Alas, there isn't one to refer you to, but if you're curious about this valley's history and its really splendid collection of individuals who built castles all over the place and created estates in the grand manner, stop at the libraries in the towns you visit and seek out the head librarian at each. These people are virtual gold mines of fascinating information and can direct you further.

GUIDED TOURS

Circus Club of North America conducts extensive tours to places of interest within several hundred miles of Chicago: to the annual Old Milwaukee Day weekend; Kraut 'n Wiener Day at Waterloo, Wisconsin; Our Lady of Snows National Shrine at Belleville, Illinois. To get on its mailing list, write Circus Club of North America, P.O. Box 5923, Chicago 60680, or phone Downtown Travel Center, AN 3-4032.

Loop Center YWCA offers one-day excursions and outings to such places as Honeybear Farm; the Abbey at Lake Geneva, Wisconsin; a day at Arlington Park; a day at Lake Lawn Lodge; nightclub tours that take in the Playboy Club, etc. For further information, call FR 2-6600 and ask for the Director of Trips and Tours.

ANNUAL EVENTS

18

CHAPTER 18

ANNUAL EVENTS

JANUARY

Except for private recuperative parties and the gathering of 60 or more hardy souls who cheerfully line up outside the County Building and shiver through the night to get the first picnic permits of the year, the city is exhausted and silent on New Year's. Dullsville? Maybe. But the natives are grateful.

Twelfth-Night Bonfire, Boltwood Park, Dodge Avenue at Main Street, Evanston. A dual-purpose civic celebration to commemorate the Epiphany while destroying Evanston's seasonal accumulation of Christmas trees. Ceremonies begin about 7:15 PM with a mayoral address, choral group singing, Epiphany interpretation by a local minister, high jinks by Evanston students dressed as court jesters, and as many as 10,000 trees ablaze.

The remainder of the month is eventless unless you're in some way connected with the annual Furniture Market or Housewares Show. Otherwise, the big event is getting a hotel room for visiting friends who are.

FEBRUARY

Celebration of the Chinese New Year, in Chinatown, sometime during the month. Exact date varies but is given to the next three years on page 356.

Chicago Sportsmen's Vacation and Trailer Show, early in the month at the Amphitheatre (except in 1969 when it will open the last week in January). A commercial promotion staged by resort owners and manufacturers to whet appetites for vacations and vacation equipment. Features include a stage and water show, trout-fishing pool and a "Sportsman's Paradise," where you may try your hand at archery, golf, skeet. Great bounty for brochure collectors at all booths. Admission: children, 50¢; adults, $1.75.

Note: Most commercial shows are being held at the International Amphitheatre (47th and Halsted) until McCormick Place reopens in 1970. Dates of some events will shift slightly when both spots are open. Contact the Chicago Convention Bureau, the Tourism Council of Greater Chicago or the Press Room of the Amphitheatre for exact dates.

Chicago Automobile Show, largest public show presented in the city, displays current car models plus dream cars of the future from all over the world. You're allowed to kick the tires and turn steering wheels. Admission: children, 75¢; adults, $1.50. Late February or early March.

February 17-March 10, spring arrives at the Garfield and Lincoln Park Conservatories, with the annual **Azalea and Camellia Shows.**

MARCH

The **Doll Festival,** Sunday closest to March 3. A centuries-old Japanese tradition begun in the Imperial Household, continued by Japanese-Americans of Chicago. Hundreds of Japanese dolls representing characters of legend and folk tales, courtesans and ladies-in-waiting delight visitors at the Midwest Buddhist Church, 1763 North North Park (Old Town). The dolls have delicate porcelain or silk faces, are entirely handmade by members of the church's doll-making club under the supervision of a woman whose zeal for perfection takes her back to Japan periodically to refresh her research. The festival is a noon-to-7 PM affair, with refreshments available. Some of the dolls may be purchased. Doll-making classes are open to the public; phone MI 2-4381 for information.

Greater Chicago All-Breed Cat Show. Three hundred cats, kittens, and their owners claw for top honors, usually at the Amphitheatre in mid-month. Admission: children, 50¢; adults, $1.25.

Chicago National Boat, Travel and Outdoor Show heaves to about mid-March with almost everything that floats. Hundreds of factory representatives of boat and equipment manufacturers man booths, dispense free advice on sailing, stinkpotting, travel resorts, camping, fishing, and try to make sales. Brochure collectors have a heyday. Admission: children, 75¢; adults, $1.75. At the Amphitheatre from mid-morning to 10:30 PM for eight days.

St. Patrick's Day. On March 17 the Chicago River turns green for the day. A great green stripe bisects the length of State Street. Pubs serve green beer. Bakeries color their bagels. A janitor in an uptown insurance company sweeps the floor with green sawdust. Fully half the city wears the green, and about

350,000 persons line State Street to watch the annual parade. Mayor Daley leads the troops, starting at Wacker Drive and State Street about 1:15 PM; about 70,000 marchers, including a Legion of Honor of civic leaders, labor officials, and clergy wearing green sashes and swinging shillelaghs; the Post Office Marching Society; 50 bands and drum and bugle corps; war veteran groups; Moose, Elks, Masons; Indians from the American Indian Center in full feather; the Puerto Rican Congress; the Joint Civic Committee of various German-American societies. Even the Polish are in line—the Slotkowski Sausage Company yearly sponsors one of 50 floats depicting Irish contributions to the city. If you've ever wondered about the clout of the Irish pols in Chicago, now is when you learn.

St. Joseph's Table, Sunday closest to March 19, at St. Callistus Hall, 2167 West Bowler (900 South Leavitt), 829-5225. Sicilian tradition honoring St. Joseph, celebrated with typical Latin spirit that sees nothing sacrilegious in combining pietistic and secular motives—fund raising included. Originally a home *festa* to which householders invited neighbors and the poor, it's now a parish event to which all households bring elaborate food contributions, first to be displayed on a satin-covered garlanded table that dominates the parish-hall gym, and then to be demolished in a great buffet. Culinary competition is keen; the table groans under more than 100 different festive Sicilian dishes.

The afternoon is spent walking around the table admiring the dishes and decorations: cucumbers shaped into pale green frogs with olive eyes; breads baked in unheard-of shapes; sequin-decorated pineapples; calla lilies made of cheese; eggs turned into fruits; incredible pastries; and a four-foot-high confection centerpiece which may be a church one year, a bible the next. The admiring is accompanied by innumerable thimble-size paper cups of wine, followed by heaped plates of spaghetti. Hold back—about six o'clock the buffet gets under way.

St. Joseph, removed from the church for the occasion, beams down on the proceedings, and well he should, since money donations are pinned all over his robes. As a family event, his *festa* is hard to beat, and when you leave, carrying the blessed bread you received earlier, the fact that the Loop is but 15 minutes away seems far less real than the wholly Sicilian afternoon these friendly people have just shared with you. No admission, no racial or religious restrictions, nor are donations imperative, though of course you make one. Hours are 2 PM to 10 PM, but the contents of the table will have vanished by 7:30. The parish's golden jubilee is in 1969.

Chicago World Flower and Garden Show. A pre-spring *tour de force* in which 100,000 flowers, trees and shrubs are miraculously in full bloom in woodland glades, flower-lined walks, formal and informal garden settings on opening day of the country's largest indoor floral show. Generally, the first Sunday morning following the opening is set aside for amateur photographers who have a field day shooting the various exhibits set up by the University of Illinois Horticultural Department, the 200-member clubs of the Garden Club of Illinois, the Chicago Horticultural Society and Mrs. Albert D. Farwell of Lake Forest, whose herb garden has become a show tradition. To see every plant in its full glory, buck the early-week crowds; otherwise, you'll find too many drooping and wilting displays and become irritated by the excessive number of commercial exhibitors peddling an awful lot of stuff not related to flowers or gardens in any way whatsoever. Admission: children, $1; adults, $2. Hours: 11 AM to 10 PM. Phone the Chicago Horticultural Society, 332-2868, for exact dates.

APRIL

Easter. Despite what you may read on the society pages of some of the local newspapers, Easter in Chicago does not consist solely of fashionable hotel brunches and a curiously provincial custom of Easter Bonnet and Men's Necktie contests.* Far more appealing are the flower displays in the lobbies of the Drake Hotel and the traditional Ukrainian and Polish Blessing of Easter Baskets.

On Holy Saturday take children to the Cathedral of St. Nicholas, 2243 West Rice (corner of Oakley), 276-4537, to discover the origin of Easter baskets. All afternoon the families of the parish flow into the church, bearing cloth-covered wicker baskets of foods abstained from during Lent but part of the morrow's Easter feast—ham, sausage, red horseradish, salt, pepper, a pascal lamb molded of butter with a red ribbon tied jauntily around its neck, the high *Pasca* bread Ukrainian housewives bake for the holiday, the decorated eggs.

Go to the basement where candles are lit, a priest offers a brief service, the congregation sings, holy water is sprinkled, a prayer said over each basket, the devout go back upstairs to pray in the cathedral and another group makes its way in. The entire event lasts no more than 20 minutes, but children who've never seen it before are awed.

Afterwards walk south one block to Chicago Avenue, to a Ukrainian shop where you can purchase elaborately decorated eggs (page 354), and to a bakery where you can buy your own *Pasca* bread.

At St. Hyacinth's Church, 3636 West Wolfram, DI 2-3636, you'll see a less elaborate Polish version of the blessing of the baskets in the open courtyard of the church, usually from about 2 PM to 3:30 PM.

Eastern Orthodox Easter. To witness a beautiful Easter Eve service, check dates of the Eastern Orthodox Easter, page 353, and plan to attend midnight services

---

* The *Chicago Sun-Times* society editor nobly refuses to cover them.

at Holy Trinity Russian Orthodox Cathedral, 1121 North Leavitt (Haddon). It's the exquisite cathedral, designed by Louis Sullivan in the traditional manner, without pews; it's almost as famous among church art buffs for its gem-framed Miraculous Icon of the Holy Mother of Tikhvin, which legend says was painted by St. Luke.*

Services start at 8 PM, but 11 PM is early enough to arrive for an hour of unaccompanied dirges sung by the choir while the congregation mourns to midnight. Work your way upstairs into the balcony if you can. It affords both a better view and some folding chairs. Shortly before midnight, the bishop, priests, altar boys bearing church banners and incense and holy bread, head a procession followed by the congregation and depart the cathedral to sing their way around it thrice. Their candles flicker in the wind, a few street lights cast a pale glow on the chanting, swaying group. The night air is cold, and the crowd that gathers to watch the ancient ceremony shivers. When the bishop knocks on the closed cathedral doors he is rolling back the stone and opening the tomb. Though the liturgy is in Slavonic, the phrase heard time and again, "Hristós Voskrése" (phonetically, Christos vos cres), is as familiar as the congregational answer, "Vo Istinnu Voskrése."

At 1 AM, when a priest and half the congregation leave, follow along to the church school next door and squeeze in for the Eastern Orthodox version of the Blessing of the Easter Baskets—baskets that are the most elaborate yet. Romany Gypsies turn out in force for this event—the young men handsome in a flashy way, the women glittering in spangled fashions, long rhinestone earrings, clanking bracelets.

Spring Flower Show, at the conservatories in Garfield and Lincoln parks, is a 15-day exuberance of tulips, narcissi, hyacinths, hydrangeas and Easter lilies. Dates coincide with Easter.

Annual International Kennel Club All-Breed Dog Show, usually the first or second weekend in April. Some 3,500 dogs, as many handlers and owners, and all the city's dog fanciers turn out for the nation's largest dog show of the American Kennel Club and its second most elite. Here, ring after ring of simultaneous judging, obedience trials, indoor field trials with water retrieving, whippet and afghan racing, police dog trials, sheep dog herding demonstrations and, of course, the chance to see every known registered breed of dog

* The icon's first known location was Antioch. It next appeared in Jerusalem, and still later in Constantinople, where it disappeared in 1383 before the city fell. It reappeared in Russia at an unknown date in the village of Tikhvin, where it was "seen" by fishermen on the nearby lake of Ladoga between Finland and Russia. It then graced a monastery near the village until after the Bolshevik Revolution, when it was taken to a cathedral in Riga, Latvia. Archbishop John of the Riga Cathedral brought it to America at the end of World War II. In Russia it was venerated for its miraculous healing powers.

from affenpinschers to Bouvier des Flandres to otterhounds, Scottish deer-hounds and Irish wolfhounds.

Like horse people and serious sailors, show dog owners speak a language of their own. Male dogs are dogs and females are bitches and nobody's talking dirty. If the judging seems mysterious, it is, but it's also fair. The comments you hear flying around the rings, such as "Judge Mercurial is looking for ears today," or, referring to a lady judge, "She's so fond of coats she should be examining minks," are standard. Admission: children, 75¢; adults, $2. Saturday, 9 AM to 10 PM; Sunday to 7 PM, with a glorious competitive, hushed-breath finale in the judging for Best of Show.

April also brings the four-part programs of the annual **Jewish Cultural Arts Series** that bring international musicians, actors, dancers, singers in solo programs, to the Heller Auditorium of the Bernard Horwich Jewish Community Center, 3003 West Touhy. Howard da Silva, for instance, in "An Evening with Sholem Aleichem," Martha Schlamme and the like. Series price for nonmembers, $12. Individual performances, $3.50 each. For exact dates, RO 1-9100.

Goodwill Industries Antique Sale. Last Thursday and Friday of the month. Chicagoans form a line sometimes two blocks long at this semiannual event that offers everything from antique dolls to Russian cut crystal, paintings, old silver. Antique dealers and decorators haunt it because the prices set by the Ladies' Auxiliary are bargain. $1 gets you into the premises at 120 South Ashland.

Also on the last Friday of the month, enthusiastic supporters of the **Chicago Beautiful** program attend Arbor Day tree-planting ceremonies. For those less inclined to watch Mayor Daley and other city officials shovel dirt to the musical accompaniment of such groups as the Firemen's Band or the Bell Telephone Company Chorus, the day has more tangible benefits. The Chicago Park District gives away 1,000 saplings to spectators. The kind of tree varies, but your chances are good for getting a honey locust, hackberry or maple, neatly bagged with enough soil for transplanting.

The ceremony takes place in Grant Park opposite Madison Street at Michigan Avenue about 11 AM. If you're a Chicagoan who wants to watch a tree-planting ceremony without going downtown, head for your nearest park. About 150 trees will be planted in each the same day, leaving just enough undone for neighborhood dignitaries to polish off with suitable speeches.

Zion Passion Play in Waukegan, April through June, at 3 PM each Sunday, West Campus Auditorium, 2325 Brookside Avenue. Admission: children under 16, $1; adults, $2. For tickets, Zion Passion Play Business Office, Dowie Memorial Drive, Zion, Illinois.

You can drive to Zion in a little more than an hour via Interstate 94 (tollway). Exit right on Route 173, east to Zion.

MAY

Lake Forest First Presbyterian Church Rummage Sale, first Thursday in May, is one annual everyone waits for, since what Lake Forest calls "rummage" is at least nine cuts above other varieties. Furthermore, there's Lake Forest prestige attached to every household item, every designer gown, china, furniture, silver, especially in the case of things that allow one to say, "Yes, it *is* a treasure; it came from an old Lake Forest home." Doors open promptly at 7 AM, and people are lined up waiting to pounce. Proceeds support various Presbyterian charities. The church is located at the corner of Sheridan and Deerpath roads, Lake Forest.

Edens Expy to US 41 to Deerpath exit. East to Sheridan Road.

Lilac Festival, Lombard, May 2-19. The suburb is planted in lilac, but the most spectacular display is in Lilacia Park, an extension of the considerable estate of one Colonel William R. Plum, a Civil War veteran, lawyer, horticulturist and world traveler who brought the first hybrid lilac, a double white and a double purple, from the famous Lemoine Gardens of Nancy, France. Subsequent trips provided most of the 275 varieties now growing, as well as Lombard's grand old tree, a silver aspen that's achieved a 60-foot spread. On 260 estate acres, largely landscaped by Jens Jensen, you can wander under 1,200 hybrid lilacs and among formal beds of tulips and pansies, all the while ooohing and ahhhhing and inhaling and photographing. Open 9 AM to 10 PM, floodlit at night. Admission: 50¢. On opening day, a one-hour parade with floats, a Lilac Queen, marching units, color guards, bands, the famed Medinah Black Horse Troop. For time and date, phone Lombard Village Hall, MA 7-5000. Best to avoid Mother's Day—every family with a grandmother shows up.

Eisenhower Expy to St. Charles Road, continue west to Lombard.

Brandeis Used Book Sale, in mid-May. For six hectic days under a big top in the parking lot of Edens Plaza Shopping Center, something akin to a three-ring circus takes place. The event is sponsored by the North Shore chapter of the Brandeis University Women's Committee to raise funds for the university's library. Opening night (the only time admission is charged) is insanity, what with collectors and dealers from all over the state converging on the tent in search of rare volumes that may have slipped unnoticed through the hands of the amateur bibliophiles who do the sorting. The sale has become such big business (in 1969, 100,000 books sold) that the ladies now have a year round collection depot in Wilmette and a 24-hour telephone service (AL 6-4300) for book pick-up. Books are arranged in 30 categories; those deemed pornographic by the committee are thrown away; those questionable but not conclusively "dirty" are to be found on the art tables. There is no category for "obscene." Prices: 25¢ for paperbacks to $1 for hard-covers. First editions, signed editions and leather-bound volumes higher, of course. From 10 AM to 10 PM.

Inurbia Tour of six or seven in-town private showcase homes is a scholarship fund-raiser for Francis W. Parker School. It's an every-other-year affair (the odd numbered years, '69, '71, etc.), and possibly because it always includes a chance to enter and see at least the main floor of Bunny Baron Hugh Hefner's mansion, it boosts the scholarship fund nicely. Other homes visited are not repeats, but usually include a millionaire's digs, a penthouse, the home of a well-known private art collector, and sometimes a nonresidence like the Baroque mansion on Wrightwood that houses the Swedish Engineer's Society. Tickets are $5 and maps are provided at the start of the tour. To avoid endless waiting in line at home after home, begin at the last address on the list after getting your tickets and tour in reverse. Usually the third Saturday in May. Check with Inurbia Tour Council at Francis W. Parker School, LI 9-0172.

Armed Forces Day, third Saturday in May. Open house at Glenview Naval Air Station (page 322), Great Lakes (page 321) and Fort Sheridan (page 321). Also events all over the city, including a parade of huge dimensions—bands, military units and military equipment up to howitzers—starting at State and Wacker about 2 PM, proceeding down State Street to a reviewing stand where the Mayor and a visiting dignitary make speeches.

Evanston Antique Show, see page 248.

Gymanfa Ganu. On the last Sunday in May, join Chicago's Welsh colony at its annual Festival of Song, a happy event with its origins in the hymns coal miners sang going forth and back to the mines. The festival takes place at the Hebron Welsh United Presbyterian Church, 5916 West Rice, one block north of Chicago Avenue. You'll get a song book and an invitation to join the congregation for supper. The church is a simple whitewashed structure and has a look you rarely see in a city church—scrubbed, and sunlight usually blesses the songsters by pouring through its stained-glass windows. Hymnals are printed in English and Welsh so if you can't read "O Iesu mawr! rho' th anian bur," you can sing along in English, "Come, gracious Lord, descend and dwell." The director, a man who speaks English in characteristic Welsh sing-song, leads the congregation, accompanied by piano and organ. Almost all of the music is in haunting minor key. Group songs are interspersed with solo performances. It's at 3:00 PM and again at 6:30 PM, with supper served in between at a nominal price. If you can't make this event but want to attend a Welsh language church service, the church conducts them occasionally. Phone CO 1-8234 for schedule.

Des Plaines Canoe Marathon, Sunday prior to Memorial Day. A 25-mile course from Oak Spring Road in Libertyville to Dam #2 Forest Preserve near Des Plaines. Some 300 canoes start at eight in the morning in relays of 15 or 20. Watch the start at the Libertyville site or take a picnic lunch and go to Dam #1 Forest Preserve near Wheeling. There, from a little before noon until midafternoon, watch canoeists shooting the rapids or portaging around them. Sponsors are the Illinois Paddling Council and the Cook County Forest Preserve District; would-be participants should contact Ralph Frese, council chairman, SP 7-1489.

Memorial Day (Decoration Day), May 30, starts with a small parade at Dearborn and Walton about 11:30 AM that proceeds to a memorial service at the Water Tower on Michigan Avenue. A much larger parade begins at 2 PM at Michigan and South Water and marches south on Michigan Avenue.

Out at Oak Woods Cemetery, 1035 East 67th Street (Greenwood), where some 6,000 Confederate soldiers are buried in concentric trench graves under a huge mound topped with a 40-foot monument, all the southern societies that for one obscure reason or another are located in Chicago hold services in honor of the dead. For children who've discovered and become enamored of the Civil War, this could be almost as meaningful as a visit to Arlington or Gettysburg. The Confederate Mound is decorated with Civil War field guns, and the entrance to the cemetery is flanked by a series of tall, granite, cartridge-shaped pillars to symbolize the fact that Oak Woods is a military burial ground. It's a very old cemetery divided into sections named Remembrance, Serenity Terrace, Lake of Reverence, Sacred Rest and the like; but it also contains quite a lot of Chicago history. There are graves of Union soldiers. There are graves of prominent Chicagoans, among them Enrico Fermi. There's a pathetic, old, neglected Jewish section with many tombstones decorated in the European custom of small framed photographs of the dead. There is also the grave of a Negro woman buried in 1862.*

The Confederate dead were prisoners at Camp Douglas and were first buried at the camp. In 1867 they were removed to Oak Woods. Eventually the mound was dedicated by President Grover Cleveland and his entire Cabinet, General Grant, Admiral David Farragut, some 80 top-ranking officials, plus, according to the newspapers of the time, 100,000 spectators. An abolitionist erected the monument; from its text you can see how intense feelings were about the Civil War even as late as 1895. It begins:

> To those unknown heroic men,
> Once resident in the Southern States,
> Martyrs for human freedom,
> Who at the breaking out of the Civil War
> Refused to be traitors to the Union. . . .

and goes on and on. The inscription seems to have been dedicated to the wrong people.

---

* To which a funny bit of cemetery history attaches: Oak Woods was "restricted" until quite recently, when a graduate student working on a thesis involving the early history of Negroes in Chicago discovered her grave, thus overturning a tradition of six decades in favor of an earlier and saner one.

Student Architectural Exhibit of Illinois Institute of Technology, last week in May or early in June in Crown Hall on the campus. The projects on display—drawings and models by graduate and undergraduate students—are experimental and daring. They range from plans for private homes and civic buildings to mass transportation systems and—a favorite of foreign students—urbanization plans for underdeveloped countries. Some of the projects are exceedingly extensive (and expensive), requiring monetary grants for their completion. Weekdays, 9 AM to 5 PM.

JUNE

With the arrival of the first month of predictably good weather, art fairs break out all over the city and its suburbs. The best are the juried shows, the worst run heavily to the works of Sunday painters. But nobody really minds because the fairs are a reason to be outdoors, and Chicagoans, starved for sunshine and balmy weather, flock to them. Nobody, incidentally, dresses up for art fairs.

57th Street Art Fair, first weekend in June. A juried exhibition on the South Side at 57th Street and Kimbark Avenue from noon to dusk. The oldest fair in the city, very big on crafts, pottery and weaving. Some 300 artists show at it.

Park West Community Association Alley Antique Fair, in "Antiques Alley" at Geneva Terrace (600 west and Fullerton). Victorian objects mainly and some feeling of caveat emptor since nothing from the Queen's reign falls into the classic definition of antique, pre-1833. Pleasant browsing, though, and the Bakery Booth is filled with edible rewards. Two area churches serve lunch and supper. $1 admission supports a youth center. For information, call 525-7209.

Lake Forest Antique Show, see page 247.

Old Town Art Fair, second weekend in June. It's *the* outdoor art show of the Midwest, and it's also as much spectator sport as art, a huge juried show hung from every tree, fence and wall in Old Town. Private gardens are open for tour; private parties spill out onto balconies and fire escapes. Stands sell cola, pizza and hamburgers. The garden of the Midwest Buddhist Church becomes a small outdoor restaurant where chicken teriyaki dinners are served. Twenty or 30 local celebrities run a continuous art auction of donated work from each exhibitor (proceeds go to the Menomonee Club for Boys and Girls, as does your admission fee), and the mob never thins. Don't try to drive up to it; there's no parking space for miles around. Hours are noon to 10 PM Saturday and Sunday. In case of disaster, i.e., a deluge, the fair is postponed until the following weekend. Ordinary showers are ignored.

Evanston Art Fair, on the third weekend, on the grounds of the Evanston Historical Society. Artists pray they'll be invited to show at this one because it's under the huge shade trees of the old Charles Gates Dawes estate. Demonstrations of arts and crafts on the terraces, and a fine view of the lake. From 10 AM to dusk. Sheridan Road north leads right to it.

Edens Plaza Arts and Crafts Fair, on the fourth weekend, at Edens Plaza, Wilmette, from noon to dusk. Simultaneously, the **Geneva Outdoor Art Exhibit** at the Kane County Courthouse, often coinciding with Geneva's **Swedish Festival,** generally held the weekend closest to June 21. The festival is a three-day affair, with a gala on Saturday: parade, fishing contest, games for children, local talent in the evening and, along the flag-hung, birch-bough-decorated Main Street, merchants in Swedish costume selling Swedish imports. Geneva was settled by Swedes and is one of the most historic and prettiest towns in the entire Fox River Valley. Take Eisenhower Expy to Route 31, then north to Geneva. Also see page 406.

From late June through August, the suburb of Wilmette hosts free band concerts, barbershop quartets, men's choirs and Christian Science meetings in the outdoor amphitheatre in **Gillson Park** on the lakefront. Swim on the adjacent beach (see page 201), picnic in the grove between beach and park, drop a line off a pier without a license and take your chances on the entertainment. Thursday nights are almost always musical, however. For additional information, AL 6-0442.

Last three weekends, **The Song of Hiawatha Indian Pageant,** a first-rate outdoor pageant in the woods at Camp Big Timber, five and one-half miles northwest of Elgin on Big Timber Road. For time, tickets and other information, Hiawatha Productions, Inc., 3 South Geneva, Elgin, 312-741-7412.

JULY

The Fourth is celebrated all over the city and suburbs, and if you make the rounds, just in the city you'll have quite a day, beginning at 10:30 AM at the east entrance of the Chicago Historical Society, North Avenue and Lincoln Park, with an old-fashioned celebration—band concert, oratory, demonstration of the loading and firing of Kentucky rifles, and more.

On the North Side at the **Buddhist Temple of Chicago,** 1151 West Leland (4700 north), Chicago Buddhists celebrate by serving teriyaki and watermelon and by demonstrating flower arranging and karate.

At **Soldier Field** there's an evening of massive entertainment, with marching bands, political speeches, tightwire acts, performing bears, clowns, auto demolition derby, a water fight between divisions of the Chicago Fire Department and fireworks—above all, smashing fireworks. The show starts at 7:30, runs about three hours.

Note: Check newspaper for other events, including Evanston's parade and fireworks, one of the best suburban displays.

July 6 to August 6, the **Free Fair,** 4700 Damen (Back of the Yards). A rousing fair that lives up to its name. Free parking, free admission and a number of free children's rides, free services at a health center (chest X-ray, hearing and eye examinations, vaccinations and tetanus shots), and free chances on the binightly door prize—a new car. The fair also offers free rides on some spectacular equipment, such as a portable roller coaster billed as the world's biggest, certainly the steepest; a huge space wheel; an oversize Dodgem, perhaps two dozen rides in all. Carnival food everywhere, including specialties you've never encountered at a fair—Polish *pierogi,* for instance, or tamales. Nightly, a different 3-act stage show with performances by celebrities, the city's different nationality goups, contests of every conceivable kind and rarities, such as a cancan revue on roller skates by the Grandmothers' Club of Chicago.

The money you spend is well spent; the purpose behind the fair is fundraising for improvement of a neighborhood once so old, so dilapidated, so crime-and-bigotry ridden, so filled with disease, unemployment and endless Old World rivalries between its various nationality groups as to be considered hopeless. The famous Back of the Yards (stockyards) district went steadily downhill for more than 50 years until a Roman Catholic bishop, a Jew and an Irishman began to guide the neighborhood into helping itself. Saul Alinsky made his name here as one of the organizers. It's still an old area and it still has terrible unemployment, but some of its other burdens no longer exist.

If you didn't get enough to eat on the Fairgrounds, drive to nearby **Leno's,** a sliver of a counter shop next to 1811 West 47th Street for "all the spaghetti you can eat, 88¢—children half price." Open 5 AM to midnight on weekdays, to 2 AM weekends. Closed Monday.

Antique Airplane Association Airshow, Saturday and Sunday the second weekend of the month, Du Page County Airport. The gates open at 9 AM for viewing of antique, homebuilt and experimental planes, a U.S. Air Force display of jets, classic and antique autos. The show starts at 1:30 PM, features a 1912 Curtiss Pusher, the oldest authentic American airplane still flyable; accuracy sky-diving; balloon ascensions; aerobatics; precision flying; spot landings; comedy flying; midget racers flying a tight course. Spectators can ride in a 1928 Ford Tri-Motor, a model used by Admiral Byrd. Pilots of small craft are allowed to land at the airport until show time. Free parking for everyone who arrives by car. It's a wild weekend—70,000 spectators plus all the overhead doings. Admission: adults, $2; children, $1. Cosponsor is radio station WIND but proceeds go to the not-for-profit association.

Take Eisenhower Expy to East-West Tollway to Route 59. North on 59 to Route 64. West to airport.

Obon Dance Festival, held the Saturday closest to July 15, North Park between Menomonee and Willow Streets in Old Town. An impressive Japanese festival that honors the dead with classic Japanese dances. The Midwest Buddhist Church sponsors it, strings lanterns along the tree-lined street, floats a single, beautiful kite at the entrance, and invites spectators to participate in the single-file ritual dances performed by costumed Japanese members of the church. The slow beat is set by the only authentic *taiko* drummer in the United States; Japanese instrumental music is provided by recordings on a miked-up turntable. Arrive no later than 7:30 for it's over all too soon. On Sunday, special Obon worship services at 10:30 AM and again at noon. The Obon dates alternate between mid and third Sundays of the month. Check by calling DE 7-8704.

Dearborn Street Garden Walk, Sunday closest to July 15. Twenty-five private gardens on display. The gardens, including Glen Hjort's 50-year-old formal garden of Christmas roses and lemon lilies, stretch from North Avenue to Division Street, a part of the old Gold Coast area of restored post-Fire homes, hidden coach houses and patios. St. Chrysostom's Church in the center of it all displays art in its lovely courtyard, serves refreshments and offers a carillon recital. The Three Arts Club, a residence for young women in the arts, also opens its courtyard for art and a chamber music recital. The Graham Foundation's private garden and *the* mansion itself (Madlener House, page 380) are open for the day. A private playground maintained by the sponsoring North Dearborn Association invites you to leave your small-fry while you wander; the Christian Community Center, 1409 North Dearborn, puts on a puppet show for them in midafternoon. Admission: $1 (includes self-tour sheets). Proceeds maintain and improve the area, which has battled its way back from a near slum created by the World War II rooming house conversion of many of the finest homes.

Festa of Our Lady of Mount Carmel, Melrose Park, Sunday closest to July 16. A nine-day affair that culminates in another triumphant Italian mixture of religion and carnival. In the Sunday procession everyone marches along the streets following the elaborate statue of Mary—some are singing, some are praying, some have their heads covered (and some don't), some are very dressed up and some are in housedresses, and a few of the younger girls look as if they'd just come from the beach. Some carry candles and others carry cans of Cokes, some have tears in their eyes, others beam and josh, some are profoundly moved, others show deep veneration.* Priests beam, altar boys sway under heavy banners; honor guards and church societies bear smallish floats.

---

* Prayer counts heavily out here: the big prayer up to the day of the procession is for good weather. In only one year out of 74 were there so much as scattered showers.

The procession weaves its way with police escort through much of the residential section of Melrose Park, where picnic chairs and tables for a family *festa* are set on the side lawn and the household shrine is brought out for the occasion. The young bloods of each household wait impatiently to light the firecrackers that celebrate the statue's passing of the house.

Find a curb near the return route about 2 PM and wait for the procession to arrive. It's a slow one, stopped every few feet by someone thanking Mary for her intercession during the year; a member of the honor guard does nothing but take in money.

Italians do their *festas* better than anyone else. For one thing, the air is rich with the combined odors of beer and of pungent Italian sausage broiling over charcoal grills. For another, there are enough food booths to accommodate everyone without waiting, and a staggering variety of edibles. None of the anemic hot dogs of an American fair but big sizzling Italian beef sandwiches, a dozen varieties of fat Italian sausage, every conceivable kind of pizza, clams on the half shell, stands of *cannoli,* of nuts and salted edible seeds, of Italian lemonade which is really an ice. The streets and gutters are a clutter of refuse—otherwise it wouldn't be a South Italian *festa*. Disorder is as essential to the sense of celebration as the games of chance are essential to the church coffers—the small bets placed on a live mouse game run by the Holy Name Society, a "dice" game involving colors, not numbers, with the payoff in packs of cigarettes. Which, by the way, is easy to beat: ignore the shill's offers to play your winning cigarettes and work with dimes instead.

> Eisenhower Expy to Bellwood cutoff; north on 25th Street to Melrose Park. The Church of Our Lady is located at 1101 North 23rd Street, and a mile of streets immediately surrounding the church are roped off for the festivities.

Monday Jazz Concerts, mid-July to mid-August, in the bandstand in the Old Orchard Shopping Center, by such performers as Stan Getz, Peter Nero, the Village Stompers. Free.

> Just east of Edens Expy at Skokie Hwy (Cicero) and Golf Road in Skokie. Southeast parking lot. Old Orchard is open for shopping until 9 PM.

Blessing of the Motorcycles, Sunday closest to July 22, part of the annual St. Christopher Fiesta in Midlothian, 147th Street South and Keeler. Some 3,000 cyclists and nearly as many photographers show up for the event, believed to be the only one in the country. The church sponsors a photo contest that anyone can enter; judges are usually three photo editors from Chicago newspapers, and the competition is for trophies. The cyclists also parade, starting at 144th and Halsted in Riverdale, ending at the St. Christopher shrine in Midlothian for the rituals, carnival rides, booth games and dollar dinners.

> Dan Ryan Expy to Route 83 turnoff, south to Midlothian; or, to watch the parade assemble, continue on Expy to Halsted turnoff and drive north to Riverdale.

423

Du Page County Fair, last weekend of July in Wheaton. An industrial as well as an agricultural fair, but with major emphasis on youth projects. If you're under 21, you're urged to exhibit your livestock, cooking, sewing and so forth; winners go to the state fair in Springfield two weeks later. The county fair includes a horse show, a professional rodeo, a commercial exhibit (Bell Laboratory generally has a display of some kind); political booths. Rides and concessions are handled by local groups instead of the usual carny types. Admission: free if you're under 12; otherwise, $1. From 8 AM to 11 PM.

On the Du Page County Fairgrounds. US Alt. 30 goes direct to Wheaton. Eisenhower Expy to East-West Tollway to Warrenville exit is much faster. For additional information, MO 8-6636.

AUGUST

College All-Stars vs NFL Champions Football Game, first Friday. Ceremonies, 8:30 PM; kickoff, 9 PM at Soldier Field. Tickets $1.25 to $10 (more at page 191).

Gold Coast Art Fair, Rush Street between Chicago Avenue and Cedar, first weekend in August. A nonjuried show that allows any would-be artist to exhibit, since quantity, not quality, is the sponsoring neighborhood newspaper's goal. The result is sport—finding art above the level of amateur along the narrow Rush Street sidewalks and amid the welter of canvases, sculpture on card tables, strollers, yippies, young swingers, dog walkers, neighborhood children and the just-plain-curious. From noon to 10 PM, Friday through Sunday.

Annual Steam Show and Threshing Bee at Sycamore, Thursday through Sunday, second weekend of August. The sponsors are the members of a club with a grand-sounding name, the Northern Illinois Steam Power Club. It's an organization which yearly seeks out a sentimental farmer in the Sycamore area and persuades him to plant extra acreage in oats so that vintage steam engines (c. 1880 to 1920) can thresh his fields. The threshers are even more nostalgic than the donating farmer; the affair gives them the chance to stoke up the seven- to nine-ton forerunners of the modern tractor and chuff away. Tents near the threshing fields offer shelter, home-cooked farm meals and film for camera buffs. At 1:30 daily the engines and antique gas tractors are paraded through the grounds. The $1 admission goes for the coal and wood they use, fees to the farmer and the owners of the horse teams that haul the wagons. The *Chicago Tribune* Public Information Service or the Illinois State Chamber of Commerce, FR 2-7373, should know which farm to send you to; Sycamore is approximately 20 miles west of St. Charles. Rain merely postpones the event for a week.

Bud Billiken Day Parade, on a Saturday in August (the date shifts), on South King Drive from 39th to 51st Street and then to Washington Park where the formalities dissolve into picnics and cookouts. Bud Billiken was invented by the founder of the *Chicago Daily Defender* as a patron saint of Chicago's Negro children; he stands for things as they should be. His parade has four hours of marching bands, floats filled with celebrities and personages, every South Side politician and office holder, church and business groups, high school drill units and baton twirlers, Elks and units from Navy, Air Force and National Guard. Free soft drinks are dispersed in Washington Park, and swimming shows are staged in its three Olympic-size pools. For children especially, it's an overwhelming, wonderful day. For exact date, CA 5-2400.

Ginza Festival, weekend closest to August 15. The Midwest Buddhist Church is at it again with a three-day outdoor event on the streets in front of the church to introduce Caucasians to Japanese culture via professional exhibitions of dancing, mime, brush painting, music, flower arranging, karate, judo, *kendo* and always something that's never been presented in other years. Shopping booths line the streets and demons appear at intervals. Japanese meals available from noon on. Postponed to the following weekend in case of rain.

Seminary Day Festival, on the third weekend in August. Another Italian festival in which the participants, being Italian, see no inconsistency in mixing beer and religion—and their church sees none in the blend of blessings and games of chance. Location is Sacred Heart Seminary at 3800 Division Street in Stone Park, and the event is a bilingual mixture of an outdoor noon Mass atop a man-made Calvary Hill, the blessing of automobiles, Stations of the Cross, ascension on knees of Holy Stairs (plenary indulgence), tents in which vendors hawk beer, wine, clams on the half shell, sausage, Italian beef sandwiches. The parish house serves an Italian dinner which you eat in a picnic grove under maple trees strung with colored lights. An unseen gentleman spends the day at a microphone hooked up to a PA system, exhorts all to buy chances on this or that, participate in raffles for booze, or play the mouse game. His real talent, however, is not his untaxable lungs but his ability to alliterate and romance a subject he's already covered an infinite number of times: "There's joy and joo-bi-la-a-tion at the Mouse Wheel . . . the bet-tors at Booth Three are bea-ming. . . ." The day climaxes at 9 PM with the annual Passion Play, performed against a backdrop of Calvary Hill and its encircling moat. The play is a thoroughly professional tableau, the costumes exemplary, and the cast of 100 or more gives the various Jerusalem crowd scenes total authenticity.

Mendota Sweet Corn Festival, Mendota, the first Monday and Tuesday in August when the corn is ready. A festival that begins with a mile-long parade at 10:30 AM, followed by 20 tons of free buttered sweet corn steamed in a 12,000-pound vat that once tanked a 1924 Port Huron steam engine. Also a corn-eating contest, a midway, celebrities, professional acts, and the California Packing Corporation's (Del Monte Foods) plant to tour. Cal-Pac supplies the corn for the festival and sets the dates according to its own canning schedule; be sure to check whether parade and corn serving are on the same day. For other sightseeing in the vicinity, Wild Bill Hickok's birthplace is marked with a monument and park at Troy, seven miles from Mendota.

De Kalb Corn Boil is held about August 21. So is a similar festival in Rochelle. For exact dates of all three phone Illinois State Chamber of Commerce, FR 2-7373.

Lake Shore Park Free Air and Water Thrill Show, third Sunday in August. More show than thrills, but it's a good excuse to stroll down to the lakefront at Chicago Avenue and spend the afternoon outdoors. The event has a pleasantly unprofessional quality—the much-heralded speedboat races turn out to be a small (though noisy) competition between three or four little racers; the water landings of the U.S. Army parachute team after free-fall acrobatics can't really be distinguished from the landings for accuracy; the lifeguard races consist of perhaps four guards in as many yellow rowboats, though they do pull mightily around the laps of their course; a cruiser bearing beauty contest finalists from various Chicago beaches passes back and forth in front of the reviewing stand and finally delivers the girls for the selection of a queen; the PA system always sounds as if it's strangling—and the whole affair proceeds by fits and starts. But nobody minds because it's always a somnolent August afternoon, and if intensive demands were made of the spectators it would be too much.

Venetian Night, third or fourth Friday in August, mainly in Burnham Harbor, on the lakefront just east of Buckingham Fountain (Grant Park). A waterfront spectacle that grows larger each year as more and more owners of cruisers and yachts get into the act. Decorated boats and costumed owners circle the harbor and pass before a reviewing stand amid offshore fireworks and onshore cheering. It's the climax of a week of lakefront festivities, of which the 1967 unplanned highlight was a race between two dragon boats presented to the city by the mayor of Taipei, Formosa. Each was manned by a local Chinese crew: twenty-two rowing, one man steering, one keeping upstroke time on a kettle drum and another timing the downstroke with a gong. Things got wildly out of hand aboard one dragon boat, which ultimately rammed into moored cruisers, buoys, harbor walls and the other dragon boat. Photographers and reporters on the scene had a field day—and so did the spectators.

SEPTEMBER

Zion Jubilee Days, Labor Day, the climax of a six-day celebration at Zion, Illinois. By 11 AM on Labor Day members of the Zion Exchange Club, who have been roasting steers over open pits in Shiloh Park, begin carving and serving the meat as part of a $1.50 meal of fresh corn, tomatoes and fixin's that annually attracts several thousand hungry people. Serving continues until early evening—or until the steer supply is exhausted. At 1 PM there's a parade of about 100 units, followed by a showing of antique cars in Shiloh Park. In the early evening, entertainment at the park lagoon. Between events, drive to the south limits of the town and swim at the Illinois Beach State Park. It has a handsome lodge on the premises and that rarity among state park facilities—a bar. For those who spend the last official days of summer at the lodge, the Jubilee Days include an old-fashioned ice cream social conducted by the Zion Police and Fire Belles, a water ballet, etc. Winthrop Harbor, five miles north, has an almost unused public beach but no bathhouse facilities.

Route 42 north along the lakefront or Tri-State Tollway US 94 to Route 173, east to Zion.

Armed Forces Benefit Football Game, first Friday in September at Soldier Field. Sponsored and played by the Chicago Bears, usually against the St. Louis Cardinals.

Art Fairs break forth again on the second weekend of the month—in Batavia in front of the public library; in Des Plaines at the Des Plaines National Bank's parking lot; in Brookfield at Broadway Circle; in Oak Park near Lake and Marion streets; at Oak Brook in the shopping center at Route 83 and Cermak Road; and at the Old Orchard Shopping Center in Skokie. This last is one of the best—a juried show that attracts leading Chicago area artists.

Parades occur frequently in September and October. Second Sunday in September is Bataan Day in Maywood a community that lost more men in the battle for Bataan than any other municipality in the country. Memorial parade at 1 PM, but the main activity is at 6:30 PM, when more than 100 bands, drum and bugle corps and floats enter in competition for cash prizes and trophies in the Pageant of Drums at Proviso East High School Stadium. Admission: children, $1; adults, $1.50.

Mexican Independence Day, the Saturday following September 15, is celebrated by a huge Mexican parade that gets under way at 1 PM. It's big on floats depicting various Mexican historical highlights, mariachi bands, mounted caballeros and pretty senoritas.

German-Americans take over the following Saturday to honor General Friedrich Wilhelm Ludolf Gerhard Augustin von Steuben, the German drillmaster who pulled George Washington's troops together at Valley Forge, whipped them into shape and later helped lead the campaign against Cornwallis at Yorktown. The floats run to Revolutionary War scenes featuring the general and tableaux showing the contributions of other famous German-Americans to science, politics, business and the arts. The Germans also borrow representative U.S. military units, drum and bugle corps and baton and drill teams. Starting time is 1 PM. The best vantage for both parades is anywhere on State Street between Wacker Drive and Congress.

427

Lyric Opera Opening Night, late September. Old Names and New Money turn out in mink, sable and jewels matched by a like number of people-watchers. The ogling is so much a part of the scene that society editors have suggested installing spectator stands inside the lobby of the Civic Opera House and charging admission. The idea has merit—it would clear the sidewalks and help wipe out Lyric's annual deficit. Opening night tickets to the opera itself are the devil to get.

Presbyterian-St. Luke's Fashion Show, last Wednesday in September, at Medinah Temple, 600 North Wabash, WH 4-4266. A smashing social and financial success, with almost all of the 4,072 available tickets unavailable weeks in advance. The affair is a prestigious one in which socially prominent Chicagoans model before other socially prominent Chicagoans—couturier fashions and enough jewels to require ten Pinkerton men backstage. The requirement for mannequins is that they must be tall, sufficiently slender to wear sizes 6-8 or 10, but above all that they come from "representative families." Three generations of Armour, Chappell, Wirtz and Woods women have modeled and four generations of Swift women. The affair is lavishly produced, uses 128 mannequins, most of the Elizabeth Arden hairdressing and makeup staff, cases of aspirin and everybody's patience. Proceeds go to Presbyterian-St. Luke's Hospital. If you want to see almost all of Chicago society women at one crack, write to Medinah Temple for tickets at least five weeks in advance.

OCTOBER

Puppetry Fair, first weekend. Juvenile classics presented for youngsters in afternoon programs and a Saturday night "For Adults Only" show. The Fair includes workshops, exhibits (ranging from antique to surrealistic use of puppets and marionettes) and an auction on Sunday afternoon. In the auditorium of Francis W. Parker school, 330 West Webster. Admission: children, 75¢; adults, $1.50. Proceeds further the work of the Lincoln Park Conservation Association. Tickets available at LPCA offices, 741 West Fullerton, and at the school. For hours and oher information, phone LPCA, 477-5100, or the school, LI 9-0172.

Hinsdale Antiques Show and Sale, see page 248.

Chicago Antiques Exposition and Hobby Fair, see page 248.

Fire Prevention Week, always the week that includes October 8, the anniversary of the Great Fire of 1871. It kicks off with a parade on Monday of Fire Department personnel, new equipment and the Fire Department Marching Band, and since this is the city that developed the snorkel, the equipment you're likely to see may be very experimental. The parade starts at noon at Wacker Drive and State; the reviewing stand is at State and Madison. Tuesday is Hero's Day—awards given in open City Council chambers in City Hall to policemen and firemen for distinguished service above the call of duty. Wednesday there's a demonstration evacuation drill of a hospital. Thursday, in conjunction with the Association of Commerce and Industry, an industrial building is selected for evacuation demonstration, plus lessons in putting out a fire ignited for the purpose in a wooden shack in front of the building. Saturday is open house at fire stations, from 10 AM to 6 PM—the chance to see how firemen on duty live, how alarms come in. For place and time of evacuation demonstrations, phone 744-4752 and ask for Special Services.

Chinese Independence Day (also known as Double Ten Day since it's the anniversary of the tenth day of the tenth month of the 1911 revolution that ended the Manchu Dynasty and created the Republic of China). The October tenth procession that celebrates the event is colorful, with children and ladies in classic costumes and silk brocade gowns, dignitaries of the Chinese community, the Wah Mei Drum and Bugle Corps, fireworks, banners floating everywhere. In Chinatown, starting from the Chinese Community Center at 250 West 22nd Place. For exact time, phone CA 5-0234.

CLEW Week, October 10-16, at Chicago Police Department Headquarters. CLEW is the acronym for Chicago Law Enforcement Week, and Police headquarters celebrates the week with an open house and special demonstrations and tours. The Canine Corps is put through its paces as often as every half hour in the main lobby, and there are guided tours of headquarters operations. 1121 South State Street, WA 2-4747, Ext. 531 for details.

The Arts and Riverwoods Show, the last and the prettiest of the season's outdoor art exhibitions on Saturday and Sunday, second weekend of the month. The show is in deeply wooded Riverwoods, a village that consists only of houses, winding gravel roads and occasional glimpses of the Des Plaines River in a community that is determinedly suburban. The works of the 30 or so artists invited to show are displayed on terraces and lawns and in the living and dining rooms of a half-dozen homes (different each year). The art is good and the outdoor settings especially beautiful. Wear flats; you're going to be cutting across private lawns. Tickets ordered in advance, $1.50 each from The Arts and Riverwoods, Deerfield, Illinois 60015; or $1.75 admission at the gates.

> Tri-State Tollway to Deerfield Road exit, or west on Deerfield Road from Edens Expy. Route 21 back to town (Milwaukee Avenue) is dotted with good restaurants along the way.

Columbus Day Parade, October 12. State Street pounds for two hours to the beat of 175 marching units and 62 bands of various Italian fraternal, civic and religious groups, Italian women's organizations, and Italian celebrities waving from open cars. At least several of the 60 or more floats show the intrepid explorer at the helm. The mayor leads off at 1 PM from Wacker Drive down State Street to Van Buren.

International Holiday Folk Fair, Saturday and Sunday in mid-October, at Navy Pier. Forty ethnic groups representing 30 countries set up a four-part fair with worthy exhibitions. First, displays of the native arts and crafts of a group's country of origin, often with demonstrations of their creation. Second, items for sale—imports from country of origin, such as Irish oiled-wool sweaters, Korean brass, Swedish Christmas decorations, llama rugs from Peru, Mexican silver, American Indian turquoise and silver, Manx cats from the Isle of Man at the British-American booth. Next, the foods of the participating nations. About 200 kinds of food: booth after booth offering native specialties, either individual items or entire dinners. Curries, for instance, at the East Indian booth; duck and sauerkraut dinners at the Polish booth; Lebanese exotica—doughwrapped and baked finger foods, and a Lebanese version of pizza; stuffed cabbage at the Hungarian booth; and, everywhere, the pastries of the world. If the St. Martin's Guild is exhibiting, wait and buy your coffee there since it's the only group offering coffee at a reasonable 10¢ per cup.

Finally, entertainment—native dances, folk music, songs and so forth, in a continuous program well costumed, very lively. The audience throughout is fascinating. At least 50 percent is non-American-born, come out of nostalgia as well as loyalty, gratefully and happily reverting to the use of native language for the day, reliving for a few hours the way it was in one's childhood. It's a revelation to see in a single afternoon or evening thousands of peoples of different countries who are now an integral part of this polyglot city.

Note: The cultural exhibits change yearly and are graded by a committee from the Mayor's Office to make certain they conform to a number of standards. All profits are used by the sponsoring groups for charities their organizations support. From 11 AM to 9 PM. Admission free.

Christ Church Rummage Sale, second Thursday of month, Christ Church Parish House and grounds, Winnetka. The grande dame of all rummage sales, biggest in the Midwest and possibly in the country. People on the mailing list drive in from a dozen surrounding states, sleep in their cars overnight or put cots on the lawns in order to be among the first entrants when the doors open at 7 AM. The sale is so popular that people are admitted in batches, and since approximately 12,000 show up during the day, you may have to wait awhile no matter what time you arrive.

Inside, beautifully controlled bedlam and the result of a year's accumulation of expensive suburban goods assembled by kind and meticulously displayed in various rooms—London Room for men's finer clothing; a Kris Kringle Shop; a Treasures Shop of antiques; French Room for women's designer clothing and fur coats; a special area just for women's gloves and handbags; the auditorium for toys; the parish house basement for books, kitchen and housewares, sporting goods, hot and cold food. Outside, a tent for furniture and luggage and another for garden furniture and equipment.

All told, items in 35 categories and bargain hunters in as many—rare-book dealers, antique dealers, suburbanites, Chicagoans, often a group from a university to buy men's dinner clothing for its choral group, well-dressed women and poorly dressed women, elderly gentlemen shopping on retirement incomes, and always somebody like the large lady who pounced on a single brocade mule and insisted on buying it despite protests from the acting saleslady who kept saying, "But you can't want just *one*." Her answer, "Yes, I can. I'll have it at the end of my bed and when my friends come over they'll just think the other is underneath."

Toward the end of the day, there's a sudden announcement of a dollar sale on all items in the French Room. The regular customers instinctively know when it's about to be announced, so you can watch for clues from them; from then on it's mill-push-shove to such a degree that a policeman with big booming voice takes over for the ladies of the church. All funds go outside the parish, to the Episcopal Charities of Chicago, inner-city settlement houses, the American Indian Center and the like.

> Continuous, free bus service to the church from the Linden Avenue El terminal in Wilmette. By car, Edens Expy to Winnetka. The parish house is at 470 Maple Street. To confirm date call the Guild Office, 446-4484.

Chicago International Color Slide Exhibition, third and fourth Sundays of the month. About 800 transparencies selected in a competition that yearly produces 4,000 entries from around the world. Projected in the auditorium of the Museum of Science and Industry at 2:30 PM.

Wilmette Antiques Show, see page 248.

Annual Feeder Cattle Show, last Thursday and Friday in October, in the stockyards just south of the Amphitheatre. A competition of calves from western breeders to judge their potential as steers. Prizes are ribbons, never more sought after than here since winners are enormously salable. Some 4,500 animals are displayed on Thursday and auctioned on Friday, and they're quite a show, beginning at 9 AM both mornings. Free.

Pumpkin Festival. On the Sunday before Halloween 20,000 pumpkin art lovers descend on Sycamore, Illinois. High spot of the festival are hundreds of pumpkins carved and decorated by youngsters displayed on the Sycamore courthouse lawn, there to stay in competition for about a week, until awarding of prizes. Last year's entries include whole pumpkin patches of gremlins, grandmothers, yippies and famous personages. If you drive to Sycamore via North Avenue, stop at Amling's Flowerland, 8900 West North, and let your kids go through the annual "Haunted House," filled with ghosts, goblins, skeletons, witches and spooky sound effects.

Goodwill Industries Fall Antique Sale. Last Thursday and Friday of the month. Again, go early (see page 415).

NOVEMBER

Chrysanthemum Show, November 5-26, at Garfield and Lincoln Park conservatories. Every conceivable variety, from the largest blooms to tiny daisy mums in a glorious color range.

Miracle of Books Fair, first Saturday in November through Sunday of the following week at the Museum of Science and Industry. A joyful fair that encourages children to look at, pick up and get involved in some of the 4,000 books displayed. To this end the fair presents booths of authors, illustrators, storytellers, magicians and puppeteers, while a cast of come-to-life fairy-tale characters, such as Mother Goose, the Old Woman in a Shoe and the Book Witch, wander about making friends with all. Films and plays are performed in the Museum's Little Theatre; elsewhere, a display of original art commissioned for children's books and special display of books by Chicago authors and illustrators. Of special interest to parents: the basic home library, set up by the Chicago Public Library, with helpful librarians to answer questions. Free.

American Indian Center Powwow, second weekend of November at the Chicago Avenue Armory, 234 East Chicago. There's nothing commercial about this powwow. It's an intense, genuine Indian affair, and the Indians, though willing to have spectators, won't cater to them. Indians from tribes across the country, Canada, and Alaska make the long journey to Chicago to participate in ceremonial dances and rituals, filling the neighborhood with the beat of drums and the tinkle of bells, thereby baffling guests at the nearby Pearson Hotel and Carriage House. Open-to-the-public dance performances at 8 PM Friday and Saturday, 2 PM matinee Saturday and 3 PM Sunday. Arts and crafts display open 1 PM to 9 PM Friday, Saturday, to 7 PM Sunday. Admission: children, 50¢; adults, $1. Proceeds go to the American Indian Center (see page 435).

Ebony Fashion Fair, second Friday in November. A sophisticated Negro fashion show produced and directed by Mrs. John H. Johnson, wife of the publisher of *Ebony* magazine, and sponsored by leading black and white Chicagoans and business concerns. The show is enormous, features almost 200 ensembles from European and American couture designers modeled by *Ebony* models. Tickets at all prices. Proceeds further the United Negro College Fund. Usually at 8 PM at Medinah Temple, 600 North Wabash; Box Office phone, WH 4-4266.

North Shore Antique Show and Sale, see page 248.

International Ski and Sports Show, second weekend in November, a three-day hubbub at the Amphitheatre which, perhaps because of the large numbers that attend and the absence of any discernible traffic flow pattern, seems almost unbearably harried. Travel booths loaded with giveaway material provide information on the world's ski lodges, resorts, equipment and the latest slope and apres-ski wear. Many have the added attraction of Olympic champions, such as Stein Eriksen and Toni Sailer; or they may present short movies, demonstrations, offer chances on ski prizes of considerable value—a weekend in Aspen, for example. There's also a professional show on various aspects of skiing, including lessons. For some reason many spectators show up wearing ski clothes. Don't—you'll ruin them with perspiration. Friday and Saturday from 1 PM to midnight; Sunday to 9 PM. Admission: children, 50¢; adults, $2.00. Amphitheatre parking, $1.

Veterans' Day Parade (Armistice Day), November 11. A short hike starting at 9:45 AM from the Goodman Theatre, proceeding across Adams to State and Madison for an hour-long ceremony of band music, appropriate remarks from leaders of civic and veterans' organizations, a Marine Corps salute and Army taps.

International Live Stock Exhibition and Rodeo Show, third weekend. A ten-day show in a setting authentically and incontroversibly animal—sights, sounds, smells. Most entries are recent winners in regional or state fairs; ribbons won here count in both points and dollars. Exhibitors compete for $135,000 in prizes, plus bid fees when their winners go up for auction. Some 36 breeds and 8,000 animals are exhibited, and at least one seems to cooperate each season by producing calf, colt, lamb or piglet to the wonderment of young spectators. Competitive riding events are part of an outstanding showing of jumpers and hunters, and the rodeo is a championship affair with points counting toward national cowboy ratings. 8 AM to 11 PM. Admission: children, 75¢; adults, $1.50.

Chicago International Film Festival, third week, Carnegie or Playboy Theatre. The only international film festival in the country offers the chance to see films from other countries that may never get booked into U.S. theatres. There's a smash opening night with guest speaker, such as Otto Preminger; from then on it's three or four shows daily plus a midnight screening. Each day brings films in a variety of categories: features, student experimentals, undergrounds, documentaries, industrials, educational films, TV commercials. Admission to films in the last four categories is generally free; otherwise, $2.50 to $3.75; opening night, $5. For schedule and tickets in advance, MI 2-3111. Otherwise, at the box office.

St. Chrysostom's Christmas Bazaar, November 15 or thereabouts, St. Chrysostom's Church, 1424 North Dearborn. A one-day bazaar conducted by the women of one of the wealthiest and most aristocratic churches in the city (Episcopal) with merchandise to suit. Handmade gifts for children; sophisticated accessories for travelers; a flea market of donated items; an apron booth; unusual Christmas decorations; a gourmet counter; a coffee shop; a children's corner where you can leave tots while you browse. Luncheon and dinner by reservations. From 10 AM to 9 PM. To confirm date, WH 4-1083.

Anti-Cruelty Society Christmas Bazaar, about November 17, at the animal shelter, 157 West Grand. It features one-of-a-kind stuffed animals, clothes for pets, homemade baked goods and, in the kennels, pets to take home at minimal prices (page 280). From 10 AM to 10 PM. To confirm date, call 644-8338.

Jazz on a Sunday Afternoon, third Sunday in November, St. James Catholic Church, 2942 South Wabash (Huron). An annual benefit for the Rush Street Night Pastor (page 288) by some of the city's best jazz ensembles.

Collectors' Auction, by the Chicago Public School Art Society, see page 249.

All-University Thanksgiving Turkey Shoot, Tuesday before Thanksgiving, Swift Armory, Northwestern University, Evanston. A shooting match where luck and not skill may win you one of 30 Thanksgiving turkeys weighing 15 pounds or more. No, you don't pepper away at an armory full of birds on the wing but at match targets using 22-caliber rifles supplied by the university's Naval Reserve Officers Training Corps. You get ten rounds for 50¢; the trick is to accumulate as many of 100 points as you can by spreading your shots across marked target templets. Sixty points usually brings home a bird. Because it's a gamble, women can and do win as easily as men. The crowd usually averages about 400, so your chances are good. From 9 AM to 5 PM; the armory address is 2000 Sheridan, and it's behind the Lunt Building on the east side of Sheridan. Phone 492-3324.

Thanksgiving. Most churches have special services but an appropriately moving one is the Rockefeller Memorial Chapel Community Service of Repentance and Thanksgiving at 11 AM, when Christian and Jewish clergymen from the Hyde Park-Kenwood community conduct services and a 200-voice combined children's choir sings. Approximately 2,000 persons attend, so arrive early. It's at 1156 East 59th Street (Woodlawn).

Choral Service, Sunday after Thanksgiving, at Fourth Presbyterian Church, 126 East Chestnut. The 65 singers of the morning and evening choirs, along with soloists and musicians, are generally in fine voice in a program that includes antiphonal singing of the Pilgrim Psalms. At 8 PM.

Renaissance Society Museum Art Sale, from Thanksgiving to Christmas. Fine art at astonishingly low prices. The range is from ancient hand-illuminated Persian manuscript pages ($3) to works by major contemporary painters and sculptors here and abroad, many matted and framed. See also page 157.

State Street Santa Claus Parade, Sunday after Thanksgiving. A cast of thousands, floats, bands, celebrities—the works. The parade starts at 1 PM at

Wacker and State, winds up at the Congress Street Plaza on Michigan Avenue. If it's raining, turn on your television set—WGN-TV broadcasts proceedings.

DECEMBER

Christmas in Chicago starts the day before Thanksgiving when the famous tiny white Italian lights strung in the trees of North Michigan Avenue are lighted in a little ceremony. From then on the entire city sparkles, the lions in front of the Art Institute don their annual wreaths and red ribbons, State Street store windows vie with each other in animated displays, and the stores themselves are open every night.

Annual events always include the following:

Dedication of Chicago's Official Christmas Tree, second Saturday, at the Civic Center Plaza. It's a 90-foot high "tree" constructed from 65 Canadian balsams, anchored to joined telephone poles, glittering with 10,000 lights, 2,000 ornaments and a three-foot-high Star of Bethlehem. Crews from the Bureau of Forestry are required for the decorating; the results are spectacular, especially at night. Two choirs sing Christmas carols at the early evening dedication ceremony, and the Mayor officially turns on the lights. For exact time, phone the Civic Center, ST 2-8400.

Annual Star of Bethlehem Show at the Adler Planetarium and Astronomical Museum. The identity of the star as described in the Gospel of St. Matthew, the skies of the Holy Land as they appeared at Christ's birth, the creation of our Anno Domini calendar and the Journey of the Magi as they followed the star are explained. Daily at 11 AM and 3 PM throughout the month, and 7:30 PM on Tuesday and Friday evenings. Weekends, special children's show at 11 AM, 12:30 PM, 2 PM and 3:30 PM.

Christmas Gift Fair at the American Indian Center, 1630 West Wilson, features Christmas cards designed and painted by Indians, plus gift items made by tribes all over the country. First week in December to the 25th. Proceeds benefit the center. Phone is 275-5871.

Peoples Gas Building, 122 South Michigan, has a daily mouth-watering display of holiday foods and free recipe booklets of new ideas. Home economists distribute sample cookies and demonstrate packing for mail techniques. Through December 22, 8:15 AM to 5 PM.

Christmas Scholarship Benefit of the Pan American Council, second Saturday, Thorne Hall, 710 North Lake Shore Drive. The program usually includes a film, such as *The Royal Palaces of Madrid,* a lecture by the Consul-General of Spain, traditional eggnog and *Dulces de Navidad,* served to the accompaniment of Spanish Christmas carols. Door prizes are gifts from Spain and the Pan

American countries. Admission: members, 75¢; nonmembers, $1.25. Generally at 2:30 PM.

Christmas Around the World, at the Museum of Science and Industry, displays tall Christmas trees and crèches, each decorated according to the traditions of the ethnic group that installed it. Simultaneously, the museum's main auditorium becomes the scene of a daily series of pageants showing how Christmas is observed in different parts of the world. The performers are schoolchildren, and their performances are on exactly the right level for your own youngsters. At 2 PM and 8 PM daily and 2 PM, 3:30 PM, 5 PM, 7 PM, 8:30 PM on weekends. The dining room and cafeteria are open for dinner and feature one or two national dishes of the "country of the day"; but their authenticity is unreliable. For individual country of celebration days check newspapers or phone the museum. Admission free. From December 3 to Sunday before Christmas.

Carols and Breakfast with Santa at Carson's on nine different days during the month. Tickets $1 each. Phone the store, 744-2000, for dates and reservations.

Also with children, **Breakfast** or **Lunch Under the Tree,** a phrase that in Chicago means just one place and just one tree—the towering three-story evergreen in the Walnut Room at Field's. Use Randolph Street entrances for breakfast entry before the store opens—as early as 8:30 weekdays, 8 AM on Saturday. Santa's headquarters are elsewhere in the store.

Performances of *The Messiah* are as profuse as Christmas tree ornaments. For dates, check newspapers and page 175.

In Cicero, three bakeries sell the gingerbread hobby horses used traditionally to decorate Czechoslovakian Christmas trees. They are: Charles Fingerhut's, 5537 West Cermak; Stetina's, 6516 West Cermak, Berwyn; and Vales, 6034 West Cermak, Cicero.

For traditional German Christmas specialties, **Kuhn's Delicatessen,** page 367; **Black Forest Finer Foods,** page 370; **Dinkel's Bakery,** page 372.

For Swedish Christmas specialties, **Scandia Fish & Delicatessen,** page 370.

For Italian Christmas cookies and *panetone,* **Toscana Bakery,** page 368.

The **Town Shop** in Old Town, 1516 North Wells, specializes in small waxed angels for Christmas tree decorations, made from 600-year-old molds. At $1 and $1.50 they're snapped up fast. DE 7-3844.

At **Villa di Silvestri,** 1147 West Ohio, find import decorations of all kinds chosen by the firm known across the country for its extraordinary Christmas department store displays. Open October-December annually; a madhouse just before Christmas. Phone 666-5498 for hours and official opening.

The **Whitehall Hotel Christmas Tree,** 105 East Delaware, is a labor of love on the part of the assistant manager, who yearly creates additional miniature papier-mâché cartoon characters to hang from the branches—Mickey Mouse,

Donald Duck, Charlie Brown and the entire Peanuts crowd, Little Orphan Annie, Jiggs, Dagwood—all in perfect 3½- to 6-inch detail.

Take children to the **22nd and Canal Streets** loading docks of the M. Walter Christmas Tree Company and watch the unloading of hundreds of boxcars of evergreens.

To cut your own Christmas tree: C. M. Burlingham, 2 South 341 Finley Road, Lombard, Ill., MA 7-4123; M. G. Van Buskirk, Vanlore Acres, Barkdoll Road near 79th Street, Naperville, Ill., EL 5-4643; Howard A. Hassert, Hassert Tree Farm, US Alt. 66, ½ mile south of its junction with US 66, Lemont, Ill., 739-7949; Charles K. Ide, 1500-83rd St., Downers Grove, Ill., WO 8-5786. For other locations, write *Chicago Tribune* Public Service Office, 33 West Madison.

Federico Camacho's Posada, Monday before Christmas. A Mexican tradition in which a couple of hundred people led by a costumed group representing Mary (on burro), Joseph, the Three Kings and various shepherds, carol their way through Old Town singing Mexican carols. You're welcome to join; someone will give you a candle and sheet music. Among traditional caroling stops —St. Michael's Convent in Old Town, where the nuns gather on the front steps to carol the carolers. The group wends its way for about an hour, then repairs to Mr. Camacho's Cafe Azteca (page 61) for free tamales in the garden. The restaurant is closed to all but participants this night. Starting time is 7 PM.

Chicago Historical Society offers the heart-warming sight of an old-fashioned, traditional Christmas tree.

Drake Hotel Lobby welcomes you with its blazing fire and festoons of greens and holly.

Nutcracker Ballet, December 15 to January 2 at the Civic Opera House, 20 North Wacker Drive. Box Office phone: 346-0270.

Great Lakes Dredge and Philharmonic Society (Friends of Music). The august gentlemen of the society—long mufflers wrapped around their necks, tall beaver hats on their heads, kerosene lanterns and song books in hand—sing before homes in the old Gold Coast on December 22 between 4:30 PM and 6:30 PM. By tradition, they stop only at houses with lighted candles (electric candles don't qualify), and host and hostess at each house invite them in for cups of cheer—which may account in no small measure for the increased vigor of their singing as they proceed up Astor, North State Parkway and along the side streets in between.

A GLOSSARY FOR THE CURIOUS

19

CHAPTER 19

A GLOSSARY FOR THE CURIOUS

Bathhouse John, 1860-1938

Otherwise known as John "The Bath" Coughlin, not because he had any great predilection for bathing but because he was once a rubber in a Turkish bath. With Michael "Hinky Dink" Kenna, the other First Ward (Levee district) alderman, he built an empire in the Levee, invented new ways to be corrupt and left a blueprint for political corruption in the ward that is still in use. Bathhouse John and Hinky Dink yearly sponsored the notorious First Ward Ball, profited by at least $50,000 yearly from the wildest public party in the city. Top guests were eminent politicians, eminent gamblers, eminent saloonkeepers, eminent pimps, eminent brothel owners and the hoi polloi. For the whole incredible story, read *Lords of the Levee* by Herman Kogan and Lloyd Wendt.

Booze

Booze runs through all of Chicago's history, beginning with John Kinzie, who sold it illegally to the Indians and defended his position on the grounds that everyone did, and furthermore, his at least didn't blind or kill the customers. Though moralists changed city references to alcohol—Whiskey Point Road became Grand Avenue, for instance—and fought for years to get adoption of Sunday saloon-closing laws, Chicagoans regularly battled the Spirit of Carrie Nation, and won. During Prohibition, Chicago had 12,000 speakeasies, beer flats and bordellos selling liquor, and Johnny Torrio, the second man to run Chicago's crime dynasty, grossed $4 million from beer peddling in a single year.

Brothels

At the time of the Chicago Fire, the city's red-light district was impressive —350 houses in an area commonly called the Tenderloin. By the 1880's, the brothels were elegantly appointed bordellos that vied for the trade of Chi-

440

cago's wealthy gentlemen and transcontinental travelers. A reform movement shuttered them in 1911.

Chicago Fire of 1871

It started at De Koven and Jefferson, roared east across the business district and north to Fullerton. Chicagoans fled to the lakefront and to Lincoln Park. It wasn't the first major fire in Chicago's history, but it was the largest, destroying more than 17,000 homes, one-third of the city's wealth, killing

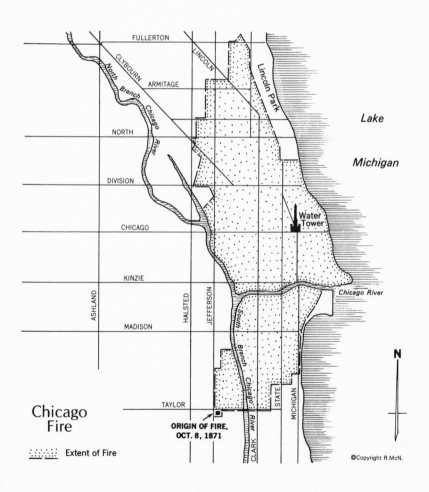

Chicago
Fire

:::::::: Extent of Fire

©Copyright R.McN.

about 300 people and leaving 90,000 homeless. Yet, within four years, the city was entirely rebuilt. The story about the O'Leary cow has never been authenticated.

Buildings That Survived the Fire

There weren't many. The only building in the Loop that survived and is still standing is the narrow 20' x 20' frame structure now known as the 22 East (Jackson) Restaurant (page 44). On the Near North Side, part of the Cathedral of St. James, the walls and tower of the Scottish Rite Cathedral at 915 Dearborn Street and the Water Tower survived. Policeman Henry Bellinger's little one-story frame house at 2121 North Hudson still stands. Bellinger is supposed to have saved it by dousing the roof with his casks of homemade wine.

Al Capone

Alfonso Caponi swore he would be buried in consecrated ground, and he was, though nobody knows how he managed it. His grave is now in Mt. Carmel Cemetery, marked only by a large gray family headstone; the whole family is buried in the same plot. Actually, the cemetery is far more interesting for its overall exuberant Italian tone and for its sentimental monuments.

Chicago Cottage

A type of frame house with a peaked roof and a flight of stairs leading to the main entrance on the second floor. It was built as a result of an ordinance of the 1850's, which required that the grade level of streets be raised four to seven feet in order to create space for sewers and drainage, neither of which existed at the time. Contractors, not knowing just where streets would finally lie, developed the Chicago Cottage in anticipation, and you can find hundreds of examples of it on side streets off such main thoroughfares as Chicago Avenue or North Avenue, and in Old Town on Eugenie Street. The 1900 block of Maud Street is almost solidly filled with Chicago Cottages, plus one pre-Fire wood cottage.

Big Jim Colosimo

White slaver and founding father of the crime dynasty that ruled Chicago from about 1915 on. By marrying the owner of a string of Levee brothels, he gained instant money and instant power, and in typical Chicago fashion, the Wabash Avenue cafe he subsequently opened became one of the fashionable places to dine. Big Jim was gunned down by a hired New York murderer, and his huge funeral, drenched in bathos and publicity, openly flaunted the relationship between crime and politics in the city. Honorary pallbearers included three judges, an assistant state's attorney, two congressmen, a state representative who later became a federal judge and a great many aldermen.

442

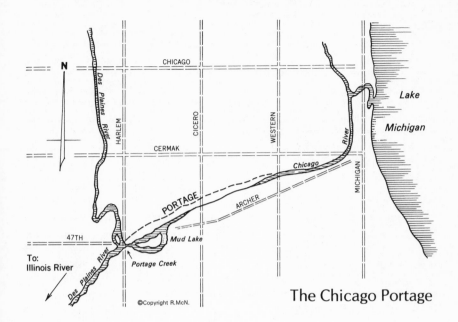

The Chicago Portage

Chicago Portage

The portage linked the Des Plaines and Chicago rivers, a distance of nine miles, ending at what is now 47th Street and Harlem. Actually it was part of a mud lake channel that could be navigated in spring but almost always dried up by mid-summer, thus had to be portaged in order to continue the trip south to the Mississippi. There may still be a stone wall at 49th and Harlem with a plaque saying, "Chicago Portage 1673," and on a boulder a few hundred feet west a Chicago Historical Society plaque marking, "The west end of the carrying or connecting place uniting the waters of the St. Lawrence and the Great Lakes with those of the Mississippi River, its tributaries and the Gulf of Mexico." The area of the original mud lake extended from nearby Portage Creek to what is now Kedzie Avenue and ran north and south from what is now Ogden Avenue to Archer.

Chicago River

By dredging the riverbed, the flow was reversed in 1900 to stream from the lake rather than into it; gravity did the rest. The reason for the undertaking was that Chicago could no longer afford to pollute its lake, its source of fresh water. (The strange looking "castle" structures you see at intervals in the lake are cribs still working as part of the city's water intake system.)

443

Clout

The word originated in Chicago years ago and as late as the 1950's intrigued newsmen transferred to the city who had never heard it elsewhere. It has since spread to the East—New York and Philadelphia at least. The most formal definition: influence or leverage through acquaintanceship that allows Chicagoans who have clout to do whatever they want regardless of custom, ordinances, or law. Clout in Chicago is political and interracial, and just about everyone but the city's bottom-of-the-barrel poor has it to some degree. In a small town, the equivalent would be the illegal favor someone like a judge does for you, say, pardoning your son from a speeding offense because you're a friend.

John Dillinger

Famed bank robber of the 1930's, shot at the Biograph Theatre, 2433 North Lincoln. He fell by a wooden telephone pole in the alley at the back of the theatre, riddled by a fusillade of bullets. The bar next door, one of those neighborhood places called Hank's or Stanley's, cashed in immediately. Dillinger, a habitué of the place, always ordered his whiskey served in a pilsner shell. According to the bartender-owner's immediately released story, Dillinger had stopped in for a drink before going to the movie the night he was mowed down. He hadn't finished his whiskey. The bartender-owner, who cheerfully admitted he was a slob, had shoved all the used glasses to one side, figuring he'd wash them at one crack at the end of evening. After the shooting he realized he still had Dillinger's last glass of whiskey sitting on the sink; he retrieved it and made a display of it. He also chained down the stool that he claimed Dillinger had been sitting on, papered the walls with newspaper extras and headline editions, and changed the name of the place to Dillinger's Last Stop. For years the rubberneck tours made a stop of it so people could see the enshrined relics.

Stephen A. Douglas

Stephen A. Douglas, always referred to as either Judge Douglas or the Little Giant, was Illinois' first national figure. With other senators he introduced the Kansas-Nebraska bill, which opened the slavery question, split the Democratic party, led to the formation of the Republican party and the subsequent, famous Lincoln-Douglas debates. But when Lincoln defeated him in 1860, the Little Giant rallied country-wide Democratic support for the new President of the Union. He died in 1861 and was buried on land he had purchased in 1849, about 53 acres at the then south edge of Chicago (now 33rd Street) just west of the Illinois Central tracks. Part of his Oakenwald estate still exists as an Illinois park, and the tall pillar topped by his statue and floodlit at night, which you see from Lake Shore Drive at 31st Street, is the monument that caps his tomb.

Long ago, one Herman Williams was appointed custodian. He really should be called the proprietor. He starts his planting in mid-May; by July the grounds are a riot of flowers under oaks, lindens, catalpas, and a sweeping horse-chestnut tree. He's proud of his flowers, his trees and the birds that have found a sanctuary here. He moved the flagpole from the back of the property to the front so people could see it from Lake Shore Drive, and he raises two flags daily, the "state's and the federal government's." If you come at a time when there are no school tours, you'll find yourself in the most remote garden in the city and will be given his point-by-point tour, including every detail of the tomb, which is distinguished by four bronze maidens. "This one is Justice . . . that one is Eloquence . . . that one is Illinois; she carries the ear of corn because Illinois was the corn state in those days . . ."

Camp Douglas

A Civil War camp for Confederate prisoners erected during the winter of 1863-64. Bounded by 31st and 33rd streets it extended west from Cottage Grove to now Forest Avenue. The custodian of Douglas Park can give you all the details.

Eastland Disaster

The Eastland, an excursion steamer, turned over in the Chicago River at the Clark Street Bridge, taking more than 800 people to their deaths. The date was July 24, 1915.

Mickey Finn

An ex-pickpocket who became the proprietor of the Lone Star Saloon and Palm Garden at the south end of Whiskey Row, a vice district section that flourished during the 1880's and 1890's. The drink that immortalized his name was his concoction of raw alcohol, snuff-saturated water, and something white that he wouldn't name but had gotten from a voodoo doctor. The three ingredients produced the famous Mickey Finn Special and could knock a man cold for as long as three days.

Fort Dearborn Massacre

If you dig into all available history of the massacre you just may become convinced that it need never have occurred in the first place, and that the commanding officer of the fort was in no small way responsible for the slaughter. The massacre took place on the morning of August 15, 1812, at what is now approximately 18th Street and Calumet Avenue but was then a low sand dune along the lake. The fort was being evacuated; of the 95 evacuees, only 43 survived.

Gang Wars

A big thing during the 1920's, especially the years 1926-27 when some 300 hoodlums murdered each other in Al Capone's battle for control of Chicago's bootleg liquor traffic. It contributed greatly to the Great Chicago Tally—1000-plus slayings.

Texas Guinan

She ran a kind of prototype Chicago nightclub where patrons went to be fleeced.

Haymarket Riot

From the mid-1870's on, Chicago was a center of labor-capital strife. The Haymarket Riot climaxed events during mounting unemployment between 1884-86. A strike at the McCormick Harvester works brought on a May 3 clash between strikers and Pinkerton police. August Spies, editor of the *Arbeiter Zeitung,* a German laborers' paper, got out a circular calling for a mass meeting of armed workers the following night. About 2,000 arrived and were entirely orderly until a police officer commanded the crowd to disperse. Just as the speaker answered, "We are peaceful," somebody threw a bomb into the police ranks, disintegrating seven cops and an unknown number of workers. Arrests followed in retaliation; four "radicals" were hanged, and three sentenced to lengthy or life imprisonment. Governor John Peter Altgeld, one of the liberal young Germans who had immigrated to Illinois, wrecked his promising political career by pardoning the three, an action worthy of any profile in courage. There's a statue of Governor Altgeld in Lincoln Park. Haymarket Square was at Randolph Street between Des Plaines and Halsted. The actual site is now part of the Kennedy Expressway, but a memorial statue to the policemen who were killed stands to the right of the expressway on Randolph and has been designated a Chicago Historical Landmark.

Iroquois Theatre Fire

On December 30, 1903, 571 fatalities in less than half an hour during a gala Christmas holiday matinee performance.

I Will

Never an official city slogan, it originated in an era when slogans were good for patriotism. In 1891 a local newspaper suggested that Chicago have a device—a figure typical of its character in the same way that Uncle Sam represented the U.S. and Father Knickerbocker Manhattan. A Chicago artist designed an "I Will" statue—a heavily muscled lady who looked far more like a laborer made up to look like a female than anything else. One description of "Miss I Will" only enhanced the impression:

> The expression of the features, the forehead and the far seeing eye is a token of the plan and mentality behind the intellectual and material development of the city. The leathern strap about the wrist is symbolic of a device frequently used by athletes for reinforcement of the muscles. . . .

To locate a painting of I Will, see page 10. To understand its true 20th-Century reference, see Mike Royko's definition in "The Way It Is. . . ."

Landfill

In the early days Michigan Avenue ran directly along the beach. Everything east of it, all of Lake Shore Drive in fact, has been created as landfill. Much of Grant Park was built on a combination of refuse of the Fire and the earth dug from under the streets of the Loop when the 62-mile underground tunnel system was constructed there. That Grant Park exists today as a park is mainly due to the efforts of A. Montgomery Ward, the mail-order baron, who fought time and again to preserve an ordinance barring buildings from the area. The park really ought to be renamed Ward Park; Grant never did a thing for this city.

Father Marquette

The cabin in which he spent a winter here was at Damen Avenue and the south branch of the Chicago River.

Pols

Two guys with cigar ashes down their vests who enter an elevator at City Hall in the morning and the one says to the other, "Good morning, Councilor"—and they start talking about judges. To see pols in action, visit Council Chambers at City Hall during any open session, usually about a month apart. In times of crises (scandal that can no longer be ignored) sessions may be held as often as every two weeks. The most important pols in the hierarchy have lunch at the Walnut Room in the Bismarck Hotel and the next echelon lunches at the Celtic Lounge in the Sherman House. Both groups return to the same places when the drinking hours begin.

Population

This book and every other on Chicago is filled with references to the city's phenomenal population growth. Here's what the figures mean in terms of people. Note the leaps every decade until 1940.

1833	350	1890	1,100,000
1834	1,800	1900	1,700,000
1837	census when Chicago	1910	2,185,000
	incorporated as city, 4,170	1920	2,700,000
1840	4,470	1930	3,376,438
1850	29,963	1940	3,396,808
1860	109,260	1950	3,620,962
1870	300,000	1960	3,550,404
1880	503,185		

St. Valentine's Day Massacre

What columnist Virginia Kay called "the spot of spots"—the garage—is gone and has been replaced by a highrise. Some smarthead saved the bullet-riddled brick wall, numbered the bricks, stored them in the back room of an antique shop. A Canadian food company executive recently made the highest of 50 or more bids and will reassemble the wall in the den of his home. Miss Kay's description of the massacre is as follows: "The spot of spots . . . where seven Bugs Moran henchmen were tidily wiped out on Feb. 14, 1929. Frank Gusenberg, one of the dying victims, was asked who shot him. 'Nobody shot me,' the noble man snarled."

Second City Syndrome

Chicago's inferiority complex vis-a-vis New York City. It stems from the passionate native conviction that Chicago is a *great* city, and it manifests itself on those occasions when New York turns out to be greater. The symptoms are easy to spot—bragging followed by defensiveness. The phrase "Second City" was coined by New York writer A. J. Liebling for a three-part profile on Chicago, which he wrote for *The New Yorker* magazine in 1951 and which appeared in January, 1952.

Society

Chicago society was founded on money, not bloodlines. The three most impressive family dynasties were created by Cyrus Hall McCormick, Marshall Field and Potter Palmer. Families sired by meat packing became society (Swift, Armour, Cudahy, for example) and by steel (Ryerson) and by railroads (Pullman) and by more retailing (Pirie) and by the great mail-order houses (most notably Ward, Thorne, and Gen. Robert E. Wood). You can round out the list of original society in this city by looking at the names of leading citizens who undertook the launching of the Columbian Exposition of 1893, and when you've done that, you know who the First Families were.

Most of them wound up in Lake Forest as commuters.* But the McCormicks and the Ryersons built their mansions in town, along present Rush Street and Astor Street. At one time there were so many McCormick residences on Rush that, had they wished to do so, they could literally have commanded the street.

Private Clubs

If you're invited to any of the following, you're far ahead of most Chicagoans. Clubs listed in the Social Register are indicated with an asterisk; invited to any of these, dress conservatively. For women, the understated look

---

* Interestingly, in all the cities that front Lake Michigan from Chicago north through Wisconsin, social migration has always been north of the city, never south or west.

is the right look; good country clothes are acceptable at noon and so, of course, is the North Shore Uniform (page 218).

*The Casino, 195 East Delaware, SU 7-2100

Considered Chicago's most exclusive club, a fact that neither the name nor the building conveys. The building is squat, boxy and painted charcoal gray. The design was intentional—to conceal from public eye the treasures within. Inside one finds a magnificent oval ballroom, complete with slender pillars and mirrored walls. The room regularly holds the full-piece orchestras of such noted band leaders as Meyer Davis and Lester Lanin. The club also contains various dining rooms, one with its own fountain called, naturally, the Fountain Room. Although mainly a ladies' luncheon club, The Casino (and it's *always* referred to as *The* Casino) is frequently used for large wedding receptions and the debuts of First Family daughters. Due to its location (page 115) it has in the last couple of years been mistaken, by those who don't know it, as facilities for the John Hancock construction crew. Members couldn't care less.

*The Racquet Club of Chicago, 1363 North Dearborn, SU 7-3200

The closest thing to the Leather Armchair School of clubs you can get and still have women and children running through the premises. The Racquet Club is primarily athletic, with a swimming pool, racquets, squash and tennis courts. The Men's Grill is filled at lunchtime with executives who take an hour for two drinks, lunch and a quick backgammon game. The main dining room at noon might be filled with Cousin Marthas and Aunt Harriets in town for a niece's wedding, but usually, it's the quietest place in Chicago for an intimate lunch since it's just you, the four walls and the waiter. Evenings are something else—cocktail parties, smallish dinners and, in the main dining room on Thursday (cook's night out), social Chicago being marvelously social at the weekly buffet. The club has facilities for overnight guests and out-of-town members, and on busy weekends the house is, so to speak, full.

*The Chicago Club, 81 East Van Buren, HA 7-1825

If you're in business in Chicago but not a member—forget it. It is the most exclusive men's club in the city. Members are the upper echelon of commerce and industry, and the atmosphere is Imperishable Deep Leather Armchair. Luncheon rooms are scattered on various floors; visiting presidents and chairmen of boards are often entertained in them at night. As in many clubs, this one has a community table at which members without lunch dates may sit to eat with their peers. The *Chicago Tribune* once observed, "The Chicago (club), being roughly twice as splendid as any other spot in town, has TWO community tables, a senior and a junior." There are also several famous clubs within the club—the 100 on the fifth floor is THE club in the city (founded 1869). The total club makes absolutely no allowances for women. Nor does it tolerate stand-up drinking in the barroom. New Year's Day buffet luncheon is famous.

If you're invited to the Chicago, you might want to follow the advice of one young, irreverent member, to "be sure to wear your hat and carry your briefcase when you enter the front door, as you might otherwise be mistaken for a crasher."

*The Woman's Athletic Club, 626 North Michigan, WH 4-6123

Venerable and nonathletic except for swimming, bridge and vigorous luncheon chatter. Don't joke about it, however—the members won't be amused. The food is wonderful, even the hamburgers on the protein lunch, so the place is teeming at noon though dead after five, unless the private dances for the younger set are in full swing, and then the lights shine until midnight.

*The Arts Club (see page 156).

*Saddle and Cycle, 900 West Foster, LO 1-5220

The only town club with the atmosphere of a country club (South Shore and Bryn Mawr are country clubs now encircled by the city). The Saddle has large expanses of green lawns and carefully tended gardens. A pool, miniature golf course, tennis courts and hockey rink used in winter for curling keep members occupied. Like so many other clubs, the athletics give way at night to large private parties. In summer, the club offers its city-bound members a cool, open-air place to lunch, meet friends and get the children out of the house; in winter, a cozy fireplace atmosphere.

The Mid America Club, Prudential Plaza, 130 East Randolph, WH 4-6430

Handsomest newish club in the city. Primarily, a luncheon club, with an outstanding wine cellar which is in full view as you enter. So is the city: the club has a spectacular 39th-floor view of the lakefront and skyline. No prices are listed on the menu; a bottle of Burgundy can run as high as $40. Still, you needn't worry too much about your host's tab—in all likelihood he's on a company expense account. Cuisine is Continental. Women have their own dining room for luncheon and a pink powder room.

The Attic, 135 South LaSalle, ST 2-6240

A distinguished luncheon club for brokers, bankers, lawyers and investment men who are said to do more important business in it than in their offices.

The Mid-Day Club, 33 South Clark, CE 6-3100

Men only, mainly bankers, industrialists and business leaders. Primarily a luncheon club in which $3.25 for an entree is tops and liquid diets and dairy lunches are also available. A staff of 60 serves an average of 300 members and guests at noon.

*University Club of Chicago, 76 East Monroe, RA 6-2840

Much like University Clubs elsewhere, with floor after floor of athletic facilities and guest rooms. Separate small entrance for women just west of the main entrance.

Tavern Club, 333 North Michigan, 263-1166

A luncheon and dinner club with very good food and a fine view of the surrounding towers. Its glass-enclosed terrace is one of the most delightful places to dine. Members include a considerable number of men in advertising and graphic design. (Also see page 112).

The Standard Club, 320 South Plymouth, HA 7-9100

Founded but a few months after the Chicago Club (1869), it has a membership of the oldest and proudest Jewish families in the city and a reputation for unexcelled club food.

*The Union League Club, 65 West Jackson, HA 7-7800

Like the University Club, Standard Club, Illinois Athletic, Lake Shore and Chicago Athletic clubs, a club with full club facilities. The food is good.

Chicago Yacht Club, Monroe Street and the Yacht Basin, WH 4-7575

Outdoor drinking, indoor dining; the terrace on the harbor is always a summer joy. Best to politely refuse invitations to club parties during the sailing season unless you sail, too, as conversation will center exclusively on a rehash of the day's race.

Cliff Dwellers, 220 South Michigan, WH 2-8080

Membership composed of men in the arts, interested laymen and about half of Chicago's consular corps chiefs. The dining room is known for its communal tables and communal conversation.

Squatters

Chicago was to a considerable degree settled by squatters. The two most famous built their own lakefront empire. They were Cap'n Wellington Streeter and his wife Maria, and their story began in 1886. While testing a boat that ran on a secondhand boiler, Streeter, an aberrant mariner, went aground on a sandbar in Lake Michigan about 400 yards east of the beach at approximately Chicago Avenue. The boat sank so low the bulwarks stood only two feet above water, and it was obvious he would never dislodge it to take off on the expedition he had in mind, which was running guns to a South American rebellion.

That act of God turned him into a water squatter, and he signed an agreement with garbage haulers to dump their refuse into the lake in front of his boat. The refuse, combined with shifting sands and hauled-in planks and bricks, rather quickly gave him 186 acres of Chicago lakefront which he named "the District of Lake Michigan" claiming allegiance only to the federal government. His first few years of squatting were peaceful enough, but as he began to build a shanty town on his landfill and as the sandbar that had trapped his ship grew in size and merged with the former shoreline, eminent Chicagoans whose lakefront mansions faced directly onto the miserable acreage called in the cops. Cap Streeter couldn't have cared less. He blithely rowed Columbian Exposition sightseers about the District of Lake Michigan and sold lots and house sites, using legal-looking documents as deeds. For the next few years there was constant warfare on the Near North Side, with Streeter behind a gun, Maria variously wielding an axe or pots of boiling water, and the entire squatter colony armed to the hilt with brickbats and other weapons.

In 1902 a policeman was killed during one of the bloody battles, and Streeter was arrested and convicted of manslaughter. Howling that he'd been railroaded, he was dragged to the Joliet Penitentiary, only to be paroled nine months later. Maria had died, but he returned to the district; his squatters had held on, and about 40 people still claimed title to the lots he'd sold them. He opened a district saloon and laughed at Sunday closing laws. Finally, in 1918, the police got him on the charge of selling liquor on Sunday and burned the shanties to the ground. Streeter repaired to a nearby pier to sell hot dogs and coffee until his death in 1921; because he was a Civil War veteran, the GAR arranged for his burial.

Houseboat colonies formed the next best-known squatters. They regularly moored along the north branch of the Chicago River from Fullerton to Montrose Avenue up to the 1950's. Intermittently, because of complaints of shore residents and the action of Sanitary Department Police, they were ordered away but always returned, a colorful if unsanitary addition to the city. Yearly somebody claims they're back, but the numbers are so few they can no longer be called colonies.

The Syndicate

The businesslike venture of Al Capone which began with just four commodities—booze, babes, pols, drugs—now also includes linen supplies, bar supplies, diaper services, car parking services, jukeboxes and all other coin-operated machines, ownership of hotels, motels, highrises, nightclubs, restaurants—a never-ending list of vendable goods.

Tunnels

Chicago built tunnels under its river to keep the city from coming to a dead halt every time the water was full of boats, which was constantly. The first tunnel was 1,605 feet long and was used from 1859 to about 1929. The second tunnel, at LaSalle Street, was completed shortly before the Fire. As you approach the LaSalle Street Bridge from the North Side you can see the now-blocked entrance in the center of the street. In all, there were six tunnels under the river, plus a remarkable tunnel system under the Loop for underground deliveries to stores and office buildings. These were eventually abandoned because of seepage, constant possibility of flooding, and bankruptcy of the tunnel company.

Underground Drive

From Grand Avenue, directly under Michigan Avenue, and Wacker Drive to the Congress Street expressway (Eisenhower) there's a lower level expressway for automotive traffic. Chicagoans who use it to avoid the stops and starts of surface traffic refer to it as the underground. You can enter it from the east at Grand Avenue, and from the west via a turnoff from the Eisenhower (just after you drive through the main post office—it was designed to accommodate an expressway), or from several entries along West Wacker Drive.

SOME RECOMMENDED HOTELS

(P) = Prestige Hotels (may be semi-residential)
(C) = Commercial Hotels (run primarily for businessmen and conventions)
(R) = Mainly Residential

Downtown	Single Rooms	Double Rooms	One-Bedroom Suites	Two-Bedroom Suites
Bismarck (C), 171 West Randolph, CE 6-0123	$18 - $23	$22 - $30	$45 - $65	From $90
Comfortable downtown hotel with a loyal following, somewhat Germanic atmosphere.				
Conrad Hilton (C), 720 South Michigan, WA 2-4400	$17 - $22	$27 - $33	$44 - $70	$103 - $124
The epitome of the commercial convention hotel. Big, busy, noisy.				
Executive House (C), 71 East Wacker Drive, FI 6-7100	$18 - $24	$23 - $29	$40 - $55	
Strictly for the expense account trade. Very modern, with balcony rooms and suites.				
LaSalle (C), Madison and LaSalle, FR 2-0700	$12 - $20	$18 - $25	From $50	From $85
A businessman's hotel in the old style.				
Palmer House (C), State and Monroe, RA 6-7500	$21	$29	$70 - $103	$103 - $145
Its in-section is The Towers, offering concierge service, direct red plush elevators and an honor system bar.	Special student rates on single and double rooms			

454

	Single Rooms	Double Rooms	One-Bedroom Suites	Two-Bedroom Suites
Pick-Congress (C), 520 South Michigan, HA 7-3800 Grand old masonry exterior, modernized interior.	$13 - $23	$19 - $30	$30 - $70	$56 - $100
Sheraton-Blackstone (P), 636 South Michigan, HA 7-4300 The only downtown luxury hotel.	$13.50 - $22.50	Twin and Double Beds: $18.50 - $27.50	$35 - $65	$61.50 - $87.50 Deluxe Suites: $100 - $125
Sherman House (C), Clark and Randolph, FR 2-2100 A cloak and suit salesman's hotel.	$10 and up	$15 and up	$35 - $70	$85 and up

Near North Side

	Single Rooms	Double Rooms	One-Bedroom Suites	Two-Bedroom Suites
Astor Tower (P), 1300 North Astor, WH 3-1111 Very posh, with a decidedly French flavor.		$25 and up	$38 - $43	$75 and up
Allerton (C,R), 701 North Michigan, SU 7-4200 The lobbies have the loudest piped-in music in the city, but rates are the lowest you'll find on North Michigan Avenue.	$11 - $12.50	$15 - $16	$26.50 - $31.50	From $38

Continued

SOME RECOMMENDED HOTELS—continued

	Single Rooms	Double Rooms	One-Bedroom Suites	Two-Bedroom Suites
Near North Side—continued				
Ambassador Hotels (P), 1300 North State, SU 7-7200	$22 - $29	$26 - $35	From $40	From $75
Two chairs in the exquisitely decorated lobby of the Ambassador East sport markers: "Her Majesty Queen Elizabeth II sat here July 6, 1957," "His Royal Highness, the Prince Philip sat here July 6, 1957."				
Carriage House (P), 215 East Chicago, WH 3-5000	From $20.50	From $24.50	From $50	From $60
Half-residential. All transient rooms have complete kitchen and dressing rooms. Outdoor pool.				
Continental Plaza (P,C), 909 North Michigan, 943-7200	$22 - $34	$28 - $36	$80	$130
Celebrities often choose it because management offers them privacy. Rooftop pool.				
Delaware Apt. Hotel (R), 211 East Delaware, WH 4-4450	$9.50 - $12	$12 - $16		
Older Near North Side apartment hotel run as such. No glamour, few services, but the rates are outstanding for the neighborhood.				

	Single Rooms	Double Rooms	One-Bedroom Suites	Two-Bedroom Suites
Drake Hotel (P), 140 East Walton, SU 7-2200 Luxury in the style of old grand manner hotels. Really outstanding.	$15 - $25	$20 - $29	$38 - $90	$64 - $125
Forty East Oak (R), 40 East Oak, WH 4-6040 Big time show biz people and a sporty crowd.	Apartments only, daily $20 - $35			
Holiday Inn-Lake Shore Drive (C), 644 North Lake Shore Drive, 943-9200 The tallest Holiday Inn in the world.	$16.50 - $19	$21.50 - $24	$42	$62
Knickerbocker (C), 163 East Walton, WH 3-2000 A commercial hotel on a smaller scale than in the Loop, so none of the disadvantages.	$18	$20 - $24	$40	$60 - $75
Lake Shore Drive (P), 181 East Lake Shore Drive, SU 7-8500 Semiresidential, tasteful, comfortable. Top floors offer a magnificent view of the lake.	$14	$18	From $25	From $65
Lake Tower Inn (C), 600 North Lake Shore Drive, SU 7-4700 A towering motel facing the lake.	$14 - $20	$19 - $24	$37 - $45	$65
Park Dearborn (R), 1260 North Dearborn, WH 4-5620 Primarily residential. A good value for the neighborhood.	$9.50 - $14	$12.50 - $17	From $16	From $28

Continued

SOME RECOMMENDED HOTELS—*continued*

	Single Rooms	Double Rooms	One-Bedroom Suites	Two-Bedroom Suites
Near North Side—*continued*				
Pearson (*P*), 190 East Pearson, SU 7-8200	$12 - $16	$14 - $20	From $29	From $46
Personalized, dignified, semi-residential; very much like the Dorset in New York.				
Sheraton-Chicago (*C*), 505 North Michigan, WH 4-4100	From $15	From $21.50	$25 - $53	$68 - $100
A bustling Sheraton with an excellent location. Splendid indoor Olympic-size pool.				
Water Tower Hyatt House (*C*), 800 North Michigan, WH 3-5600	$20 - $28	$26 - $34	$28 - $34	$75 - $100
Facing Chicago's famous Water Tower, a new hotel, newly remodeled to turn studios into bedrooms.				
Whitehall (*P*), 105 East Delaware, WH 4-6300	From $16.75	From $26.50	From $43	
Probably the only hotel in the U.S. where you can walk in and meet the proprietor. Dignified and exclusive. As much residential as transient.				
Mid-North Side				
Belden-Stratford (*P*), 2300 North Lincoln Park, DI 8-6610	$14 - $16	$17 - $19	$25 (when available)	
Fine older hotel facing Lincoln Park. Semi-residential; only 15 minutes from Loop via CTA buses.				

	Single Rooms	Double Rooms	One-Bedroom Suites	Two-Bedroom Suites
Park Lane (R), 2842 North Sheridan, BI 8-3800. Quiet place catering to elderly people; 90 percent residential. Transients mainly business people.	From $12	From $16	$16 - $25 (when available)	
North Side				
Holiday Inn (C), 4800 North Marine Drive, BR 5-3000. Convenient if you want to stay on the Far North Side.	From $11.50	$14 - $18		
South Side				
Del Prado (R), 5307 South Hyde Park, HY 3-9600. Sturdy older hotel. Very convenient to Loop via Illinois Central local trains.	$9 - $12	$11 - $16	$25 - $45	
Shoreland Hotel (R), 5454 South South Shore Drive, PL 2-1000. Older hotel with a very grand exterior. Top floors offer lake view.	$10 - $14	$12 - $18	$25 - $40	$35 - $60

Continued

SOME RECOMMENDED HOTELS—*continued*

	Single Rooms	Double Rooms	One-Bedroom Suites	Two-Bedroom Suites
South Side—*continued*				
Windermere (R), 1642 East 56th Street, FA 4-6000	From $10.50	From $14	$20	
Handsome older hotel with gracious ways. Overlooks Jackson Park, Museum of Science and Industry.				
Far South Side				
Country Club (R), 6930 South South Shore Drive, PL 2-2200	$10 - $12	$12 - $15	$15 - $40	
Overlooks South Shore Country Club. Convenient to Loop via Illinois Central local trains.				
Outlying Motels				
Howard Johnson's Motor Lodge (C), 8201 West Higgins, 823-1122 Near Kennedy Expy.	$15.50 - $18.50	$18 - $24		
Hyatt House (C), 4500 Touhy, Lincolnwood, 677-5400	$16 - $21	$19 - $27	One at $32 Others are $55 - $80	$20 for additional bedroom
Just off Edens Expy. Slightly off the beaten path; very comfortable; pool.				
Marriott Motor Hotel (C), 8535 West Higgins, Chicago, 693-4444	$17 - $24	$22 - $28	$30 - $50	$58 - $125
New, very well run, very plush.				

CHURCHES, TEMPLES, AND OTHER HOUSES OF WORSHIP

The list below is by no means representative of the variety of religious edifices in Chicago. What it does represent are those places that have architectural or historic significance or are places where outstanding choral or other music may be heard. See also entries by name in Index.

Alice Millar Chapel (Protestant-Christian), Northwestern University, 1870 Sheridan, Evanston
Baha'i House of Worship, 112 Linden, Wilmette
Bond Chapel (Interdenominational), University of Chicago, 1025 East 58th Street
Buddhist Temple of Chicago, 1151 West Leland
Cathedral of the Holy Name (Roman Catholic), Chicago and State
Cathedral of St. James (Episcopal), Wabash and Huron
Cathedral of St. Nicholas (Roman Catholic), 2243 West Rice
Christ Church (Episcopal), 784 Sheridan, Winnetka
Church of the Ascension (Episcopal), 1133 North LaSalle
Church of the Holy Comforter (Episcopal), 222 Kenilworth, Kenilworth
Congregational Church (Japanese), 701 Buckingham
First Church of the Deliverance (Spiritualist), 4315 South Wabash
Fourth Presbyterian Church, Michigan and Delaware
Greater Salem Baptist Church, 215 West 71st Street
Hebron Welsh United Presbyterian Church, 5916 West Rice
Holy Trinity Church (Roman Catholic), 1118 North Noble
Holy Trinity Russian Orthodox Cathedral, 1121 North Leavitt
Howes Chapel (Methodist), Garrett Theological Seminary, 2121 Sheridan, Evanston
Methodist Church (Japanese), 900 West Sheridan
Monumental Baptist Church, 729 East Oakwood
Muhammad's Mosque of Islam, No. 2, 5335 South Greenwood
North Shore Congregation Israel (Reformed), 840 Vernon, Glencoe
Northminster Presbyterian Church, 2515 Central Park, Evanston
Park Synagogue Shaare Sholom, 505 North Michigan (Sheraton-Chicago Hotel)
Presbyterian Church (Japanese), 3500 North Sheffield
Rockefeller Memorial Chapel (Interdenominational), University of Chicago, 59th Street and Woodlawn
St. Chrysostom's Church (Episcopal), 1424 North Dearborn
St. Hyacinth Church (Roman Catholic), 3636 West Wolfram
St. Saviour Chapel (Interdenominational), Illinois Institute of Technology, 3200 South Wabash
St. Stanislaus Kostka Church (Roman Catholic), 1351 West Evergreen
Temple Sholom (Reformed), 3480 North Lake Shore
Third Baptist Church of Chicago, 938 West 69th Street
Unitarian-Universalist Church, 875 Lake, Oak Park

INDEX

Index

Index

Index

Index

Index

Index

Index

Index

Index

formal wear
men's, 230-31
rental, men's and wom-
en's, 231, 299-300
Fort Dearborn Massacre,
445, 121, 401
exhibit, 140
Fort Dearborn site, 379
Fort Sheridan, tours, 321
Forty East Oak Hotel, 457
Foucault pendulum, Mu-
seum of Science and
Industry, 138
4 Arts Gallery, 401
400 Theatre, 88
Fourth of July celebration,
420-21
Fourth Presbyterian Church
& Parish House
architecture, 117
Thanksgiving service, 434
Fowler, Rev. Elmer L., 365
Fox, Dan, 276
Fox Millinery Supply, 276
Fox River Valley, 406-7
Fox Trails, skiing, 210
Franchini, Barbara, 228-9
Franchini, Marcello, 228-9
Francis W. Parker School,
417
Frank & Co. See Charles
Frank & Co.
Frank's Drum Shop, 275
Franklin, John Hope, 362
Franklin, Malcolm, 241
Franklin, Paul, 241
Franklin Bayer, linens, 271
Fred A. Block, fashions, 276
Fred Glaser Fashion Cen-
ter, 262

Fredman, Bea, 181
Free Fair, 421
Freedom Hall, Institute of
Human Relations, 145-6
freighter lines, 293
French Cultural Service, 295
French Impressionist art
collection, Art Institute,
153
gallery, 166
French post-Impressionist
art, gallery, 166
French restaurants
Champs-Elysées, 29

French restaurants—cont.
French Room, Hartford
Plaza, 30
La Brasserie de Stras-
bourg, 31
La Chaumiere, 31
Maxim's de Paris, 25-6
Whitehall Club, 37
French Room, Hartford
Plaza, 30
Frese, Ralph, 205, 418
Friday Jazz at Noon Club,
82
Fritz Reuter & Sons, 274-5
Fritzel's, 20-21
Sunday brunch, 70
Fromm Music Foundation,
173
Frontier Museum, 314-15,
407
Frost & Granger
Northern Trust Bldg., 110-
11
Frumkin Gallery, Allan, 162
Fullersburg Forest Preserve
canoe concession, 205
rowboat rental, 206
Fullerton Tennis Club, 203
Function Junction Five, 82
fur rugs, 306
furniture, 272-3
antique, 241-2
repairs, 303-4
salvage, 279
thrift shops, 280-81
furriers, 237
furs. See also resale shops
for, dogs, 280-81
rental, 300
Furst, Mark, 243

G

G. D. Searle & Co., 340
G. Fishman's Sons, Inc.,
277
Gabby Hartnett Recreation
Inc., sporting goods,
214
Gaelic Imports, 355
Gage Bldg., 103-4
Gage House, 402
galleries. See art galleries
Gallery Book & Magazine
Shop, 301
game meat, 371

game menu, 25, 42
Game Theatre, 76
Gamma Photo Labs, Inc.,
299
Gander Mountain, skiing,
210
gang wars, Chicago and,
445-6
Gannon, Sr. M. Ann Ida,
336
Gaper's Caterers, 296
Garden, Mary, 175-6
garden awnings, rental, 302
garden cafes. See sidewalk
and garden cafes
Garden Club of Illinois, 413
garden show, 422
garden supplies and sculp-
ture, 253-4
Garden Tavern, 92
Garden Theatre (North-
western Univ.), 183
Garfield Park, fishing, 207
garment repair, 304-5
Garrett Theological Sem-
inary, 400-401, 332
Garrison, John, 262
gas station, 24-hour, 305
Gaslight Club, 75
Gaston, Lucy Page, 72
Gavel Room (Civic Center),
65
Geja's Wine & Cheese
Cafe, 92
gem collection, Lizzadro
Museum, 141-2
gem-cutting demonstra-
tions, 142
Gene & Georgetti's Res-
taurant, 23
general hospitals, 286-7
Geneva, 406
Outdoor Art Exhibit, 420
Swedish Festival, 420
Gennaro's Tavern, 52-3
George Hessberger's. See
Heidelberger Fass
George Mashbitz, Inc., 233
George Wienhoeber, flo-
rist, 256
bargain flowers, 277
Gerhard's Red Plush. See
Maestro Gerhard's
German Expressionist art,
gallery, 162

476

Index

Index

Index

Index

Ivanhoe Children's Theatre, 315
Ivanhoe Dinner Playhouse, 183
Ivanhoe Restaurant, 179, 67
Ivanhoe Theatre, 179
Iwan Ries & Co., 256

J

Jack Eigen Show, 397
Jack Mooney's, 82
Jack Schwartz, tobacconist, 255
Jackson, Mahalia, 365, 361
Jackson Park
  fishing, 207
  golf course, 202
  harbor, 197
  horseback riding, 206
Jacobson, Joe, 21
Jacques
  bar, 5
  restaurant, 32
Jacques Baruch Gallery, 166
jade collection, Field Museum, 133
Jade House, 236
Jane Addams Center, Hull House, theatre, 180
Jane Estabrooks Household Registry, 300
Janek, Jim, 42
Japanese art supplies, 273
Japanese neighborhood, 359-60. See also celebrations
  grocery store, 371
Japanese restaurants, 63-4
  Azuma House, 36
  Naka-No-Ya, 36
  Senba, 36-7
Jax, 226
jazz, 80-84, 87, 423, 275
Jazz, Ltd., 81
Jazz Record Mart, 275, 87
Jazz on a Sunday Afternoon, 434
Jean, Mrs. Helen Wong, 356
Jeanette, artificial flowers, 254
Jegen Florist, 257
Jenney, William Le Baron, 99, 104
  Leiter Bldg. I, 111
  Leiter Bldg. II, 105
  Manhattan Bldg., 105

Jensen, Jens, 416
Jensen Slides, sledding and tobogganing, 210
Jerrems, 321
jewel collection, Lizzadro Museum of Lapidary Arts, 141-2
jewelry, 233-36, 224, 225, 401. See also antiques
  African and Middle East, 269
  custom design, 235, 236
  enameled, 236
  one-of-a-kind, 236
  Oriental, 226, 236
jewelry making, instruction, 142
Jewish archives, 345
Jewish Book Mart of Chicago, 265
Jewish Community Center children's matinees, 317
Jewish Cultural Arts Series, 415
Jewish history, museums, 144-45
Jewish restaurants, 64
Jim Conway Show, 397
Joe Berlin's Peoples Food Mart, 354
Joe Lala Barber Shop, 260
Joe's Cigarstand
  tickets: theatre, opera, sports, 179-80
Joe's La Siesta, 62
John A. Colby, furniture, 272
John Barleycorn Pub, 10-11
John Crerar Library, 342-4
  architecture, 122
John E. Maloney Co., funeral home, surplus flowers, 277
John G. Shedd Aquarium. See Shedd Aquarium
John Garrison, beauty salon, 262
John Hancock Center, architecture, 115
John M. Smyth, furniture, 272
Johnnie Held's Brown Bear. See Brown Bear
Johnny Coulon Physical Training Club, 212
Johnson, E. Gustav, 358

Johnson, John H., 362
Johnson, Mrs. John H., 432
Johnson, Mrs. S. C., 164
Johnson & Harwood, Inc., 223
Johnson Publishing Co., Inc., 364
Jonas Karvelis Gifts, 357
Jones, T. See T. Jones
Joseph E. Dimery Coach House Antiques, 242
Joseph Salon Shoes, 227
Judaica. See also Maurice Spertus Museum of Judaica; Morton B. Weiss Museum of Judaica
  bookstore, 265
  library, 345
  museums, 144-5
judo demonstration, 425
Juergens & Andersen Co., 235
Julian, Dr. Percy, 362
Junior Academy, Chicago Academy of Sciences, 137
Junior Curator Program, Chicago Academy of Sciences, 137
junk, 270

K

K. Schlanger Co. See Schlanger Co.
Kalo Shop, 236
Kankuro Matsumoto, china repair, 303
Kansas City Red's, 86
Kaplan, Myrtle, 318-19
Kaplan, Ronnie, 304
Kaplan, Terry, 228
karate demonstrations, 420, 425
Karpuszko, Kazimir, 163
Karvelis Gifts, 357
Katos, Pete, 10
Kay, Virginia, 77, 448
kayak rental, 205
Kaye-Pierre Salon, 262-3
Kazimir Gallery, 163
Keller, Sidney, 22
Keller, William, 22
Kemys lions, Art Institute, 158

Index

Index

Index

Index

Index

Index

Index

Index

Index

Index

Index

Index

Printed in U.S.A.

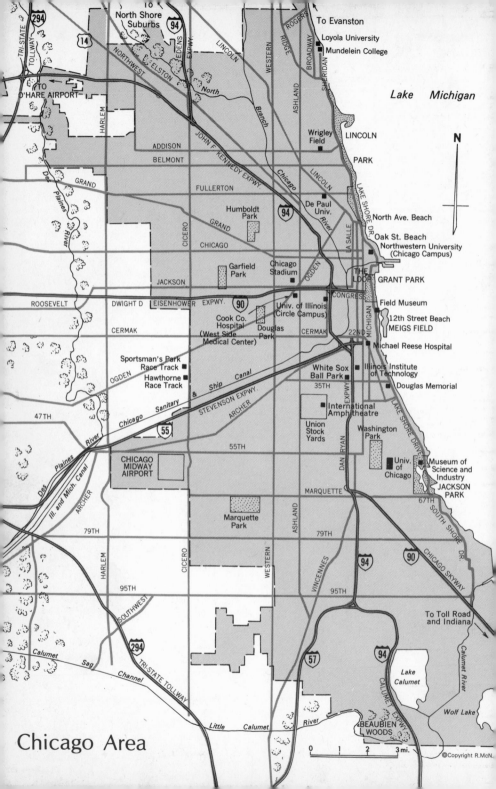

Chicago Area